Organizing Business Knowledge

Organizing Business Knowledge
The MIT Process Handbook

Thomas W. Malone, Kevin Crowston, and George A. Herman, editors

The MIT Press
Cambridge, Massachusetts
London, England

This book was set in Times New Roman on 3B2 by Asco Typesetters, Hong Kong, and was printed and bound in the United States of America.

Library of Congress Cataloging-in-Publication Data

Organizing business knowledge : the MIT process handbook / Thomas W. Malone, Kevin Crowston, and George A. Herman, editors.
    p. cm.
Includes bibliographical references and index.
ISBN 0-262-13429-2 (hc. : alk. paper)
ISBN-13 978-0-262-13429-3 (hc. : alk. paper)
  1. Knowledge management. 2. Organizational behavior. I. Title: MIT process handbook. II. Malone, Thomas W. III. Crowston, Kevin. IV. Herman, George A. (George Arthur), 1953–
HD30.2.T67   2003
658.4′038—dc21   2002045174

10 9 8 7 6 5 4 3 2

In memory of Charles S. Osborn

Contents

Contributors

Abraham Bernstein
University of Zürich

Nicholas G. Carr
Harvard Business Review

Kevin Crowston
Syracuse University

Chrysanthos Dellarocas
University of Maryland

Michael Grunninger
University of Toronto

George A. Herman
Massachusetts Institute of Technology

Yan Jin
Stanford University

Mark Klein
Massachusetts Institute of Technology

Jintae Lee
University of Colorado, Boulder

Thomas W. Malone
Massachusetts Institute of Technology

Elisa O'Donnell
A. T. Kearney

Wanda Orlikowski
Massachusetts Institute of Technology

Charles S. Osborn
late of Babson College

John Quimby
Massachusetts Institute of Technology

Brian T. Pentland
Michigan State University

Austin Tate
University of Edinburgh

George M. Wyner
Boston University

JoAnne Yates
Massachusetts Institute of Technology

Takeshi Yoshioka
Fuji-Xerox Co., Ltd.

Gregg Yost
Digital Equipment Corporation

Acknowledgments

This book is dedicated to Charley Osborn, a key member of the Process Handbook research team starting when he was a graduate student at Harvard Business School and continuing throughout his time as a professor at Babson College. Charley died in December 2001, after a long illness with amyotrophic lateral sclerosis (ALS), and he will be sorely missed by those of us who knew and worked with him. The royalties from this book will be donated, in his memory, to the Osborn Family Fund.

The work described in this book was supported, in part, by the National Science Foundation (Grant Nos. IRI-8903034, IRI-9224093, DMI-9628949, and IIS-0085725), the US Defense Advanced Research Projects Agency (DARPA), and the US Defense Logistics Agency. It was also supported by the following corporate sponsors: Boeing, British Telecom, Daimler Benz, Digital Equipment Corporation, Electronic Data Systems (EDS), Fuji Xerox, Intel Corporation, Matsushita, National Westminster Bank, Statoil, Telia, Union Bank of Switzerland, Unilever, and other sponsors of the MIT Center for Coordination Science and the MIT Initiative on "Inventing the Organizations of the 21st Century."

The people who made significant contributions to different aspects of this work are listed as authors of the chapters in this volume, and in the acknowledgments sections of those chapters. It is worth mentioning separately here, however, the following people who played continuing roles throughout large parts of the project:

Co-Principal Investigators for the project: Thomas W. Malone (Project director), Kevin Crowston, Jintae Lee, and Brian Pentland

Full-time project research staff: John Quimby (Software Development Manager) and George Herman (Managing Editor)

Other major contributors: Chrysanthos Dellarocas, Mark Klein, George Wyner, the late Charley Osborne, Abraham Bernstein, and Elisa O'Donnell

Project advisors: Marc Gerstein, Fred Luconi, Gilad Zlotkin, and John Gerhart

Project management: Martha Broad, Bob Halperin, Ed Heresniak, and Roanne Neuwirth

Process Handbook Advisory Board: Michael Cohen, John McDermott, and the late Gerald Salancik.

The software described in this volume is the subject of the following patents: US Patent Nos. 5,819,270; 6,070,163; 6,349,298; European Patent No. 0692113; and other pending patent applications by MIT.

I INTRODUCTION

If you are an organizational researcher or business educator, imagine that you had a systematic and powerful way of organizing vast numbers of things we know about business: basic principles, key scientific results, and useful case examples. Imagine that you could easily create and share this knowledge electronically with researchers, educators, and students all over the world. And imagine that all this knowledge was structured in a way that helped you quickly find the things you needed and even helped you come up with new organizational ideas that no one had ever thought of before.

If you are a computer scientist, information technologist, or software developer, imagine that different versions of this same kind of knowledge base could help you systematically organize and share many of the basic patterns and components that are used in a wide variety of computer programs. And imagine that computational tools that use this knowledge base could significantly reduce the effort required to develop new software programs from existing components and tailor them for use in specific organizations.

Finally, if you are a manager or consultant, imagine that you could use all this general knowledge about "best practices," case examples, and software from all over the world. And imagine further that you could also create your own specific versions of these knowledge bases to share detailed information about the key activities in your own company or your clients' companies: what needs to be done, who is responsible for doing it, and what resources are available to help.

That is the vision that has guided the MIT Process Handbook project since its beginning over a decade ago, and that is the vision that continues to guide our work. There is still much to be done to achieve the full promise of this vision, but we believe that the work we have done so far demonstrates that the vision is both feasible and desirable. This book is the story of what we have done, what we have learned, and what is left to do. It is also an invitation to others to join in the quest to help make this vision a reality.

What Have We Actually Done?

Our goal in the Process Handbook project has been to lay the foundations for the vision we have just described. To do this, we have developed an extensive, publicly available on-line knowledge base,[1] including over 5,000 activities, and a set of software tools to maintain and access this knowledge base.

1. See *ccs.mit.edu/ph*.

More specifically, the Process Handbook today is a combination of four things:

1. A set of fundamental *concepts* that can help organize and analyze knowledge about any kinds of activities and processes. The two key concepts we use involve the notions of "specialization" and "coordination."

2. A specific *classification framework* for organizing very large amounts of knowledge using these concepts. Even though parts of this framework can be used to classify activities of any kind, we have put a special emphasis on developing categories for business activities.

3. A representative set of generic *business templates* and specific *case examples* to illustrate how the concepts and framework can be used. This knowledge base includes, for example, generic templates for activities like buying and selling, and case examples of companies doing these things in innovative ways.

4. A set of *software tools* to organize and manipulate large amounts of knowledge (e.g., these templates and examples) using the concepts and framework.

In principle, one could use any subset of these things without the others. But the combination of all four elements provides a uniquely powerful set of capabilities.

As the examples throughout this volume illustrate, this on-line Process Handbook can be used to help people: (1) redesign existing business processes, (2) invent new processes, especially those that take advantage of information technology, (3) organize and share knowledge about organizational practices, and (4) automatically, or semiautomatically, generate software to support or analyze business processes.

What Other Things Are Like the Process Handbook?

One of the best ways to convey an intuitive understanding of the Process Handbook is to describe other, more familiar, things that are like it.

For example, one key element of the Process Handbook is a classification system for business activities. Classification systems are ubiquitous in scientific fields. They provide a way to divide up the world and name the pieces. In this way classifications provide a language for scientific communication and a filing system to organize knowledge about the world. The best go deeper, and provide a conceptual basis for generalization and new discovery.

Periodic Table of the Elements
Perhaps the most widely known and unequivocally successful such system is the Periodic Table of the Elements, whose design is usually credited to Mendeleev in 1869. Though numerous other researchers made proposals to bring order to the ele-

ments, Mendeleev got credit because he used his Periodic Table to predict the existence and even the basic properties of as yet undiscovered elements and to rule out the existence of others.

Of course, the success of the Periodic Table is due, in part, to the nature of the elements themselves. Elements are unarguably distinguishable from each other based on chemical tests and have properties that do not change. The ordering of elements in the Table is based on an essential property, atomic number, and the arrangement of elements into groupings is based on other essential properties, such as the valence electron configuration (though these properties were in fact only fully understood after the discovery of the Periodic Table). In other words, the Periodic Table is a success because its order reflects a deeper order within the elements.

While we doubt that it will ever be possible to describe business processes with the same degree of precision as is possible for chemical elements, we do believe that a classification system like ours can significantly help organizational researchers and others to represent the deeper order within organizational activities.

Biological Classification

Another classification system with strong analogies to the Process Handbook is the system biologists use to classify living organisms. In fact the search for a way to organize the chemical elements was inspired by the hierarchical classification of living organisms first proposed by Linnaeus in 1758. Biological classification serves many of the functions we envision for the Process Handbook: it provides a standard nomenclature for describing species (so scientists can be sure they are talking about the same animals); it organizes information about different species; and it serves as a basis for generalization in comparative studies (a fact about one species is more likely to apply to other closely related species).

However, classifying living organisms is more problematic than classifying chemical elements for several reasons. First, scientists study individual specimens (a "holotype," or representative individual), but the basic unit of the classification system is a species, that is, the population of similar individuals. Unfortunately, the definition of a species is not unequivocal, and scientists may disagree about whether two individuals are members of the same or different species. Second, the properties of species can and do change over time. Both of these properties also hold for the processes in the Handbook.

Finally, species (and processes) are much more complex than elements. As a result it is not obvious which properties should be used to organize a collection. A classification will ideally group species that share more than a surface similarity so that the groups serve as a basis for theoretically grounded comparisons. Linnaeus's original system formed families of species on the basis of common characteristics. More recently some biologists have proposed classifying species on the basis of their hypothesized common ancestors (e.g., Wiley et al. 1991).

Though the biological classification system is intended to be objective, it also has a strong social component. The classification system is supported by a well-developed social structure, including codified rules for naming, a bureaucracy for registering names, and conferences for vetting and accepting changes to the hierarchy. Development of some kind of similar support structure will be necessary for the full potential of our vision to be fulfilled.

Human Genome Project

Perhaps one of the closest analogies to the Process Handbook project is the Human Genome Project (HGP). The first five goals of the HGP are to:

1. "identify all the approximately 30,000 genes in human DNA,

2. determine the sequences of the three billion chemical base pairs that make up human DNA,

3. store this information in databases,

4. improve tools for data analysis,

5. transfer related technologies to the private sector"

(*http://www.ornl.gov/hgmis/project/about.html*).

The goals of the Process Handbook are broadly similar, though more modest. In our version of goals 1 and 2, we aim to identify a large number of processes and to develop a comprehensive classification for organizing them. Because of the diversity and detail of organizational processes, it would be impossible to completely describe all processes in all organizations, but the HGP will probably not sequence every variation on every gene either. Goals 3, 4, and 5 can be adopted with little change, the most significant difference being that we will organize processes in a hierarchy, implying a different set of tools for storing and analyzing them.

Engineering Handbooks

A final parallel can be drawn to engineering handbooks. Handbooks of various kinds are common in engineering disciplines to present and organize information to support designers. For example, the *Multi-media Handbook for Engineering Design*, created by the Design Information Group of the University of Bristol offers:

... a concise source of ... elementary engineering design principles, design details of machine elements and specific component information. It provides:

• design guides for a variety of design situations including the design, selection and application of components and systems

• catalogue information from component manufacturers to provide standard sizes and dimensions, ratings and capacities

• good practice guides to the proper design of components and systems in terms of increased strength, reduced cost, more efficient manufacture and assembly

• materials data for common engineering materials including properties, standard forms of supply, special treatments and typical applications.

Similar handbooks exist for chemical engineering (Perry, Green, and Maloney 1997), civil engineering (Merritt, Loftin, and Ricketts 1995), electrical engineering (Fink, Beaty, and Beaty 1999), industrial engineering (Maynard and Zandin 2001), mechanical engineering (Avallone and Baumeister 1996), and so on. Most of these handbooks include sections on basic science as well as specific applications. The Process Handbook is intended to provide at least the application-type information to support the design of business processes. Such information is represented as semi-structured information associated with various process descriptions.

The Process Handbook is not quite like any one of these other examples from various branches of science and engineering, but each of these other examples illustrates important aspects of our vision for the Process Handbook.

History of the Project

Even though we had been working on its intellectual precursors for years, the first work specifically on the Process Handbook project began in 1991. Since that time, over forty university researchers, students, and industrial sponsors have worked on developing the software and knowledge bases that today constitute the Process Handbook. For all that time this project has been one of the primary projects in the MIT Center for Coordination Science.

Even though we have refined our ideas over the years, the key conceptual ideas of specialization and coordination were present in the first full proposal we wrote for this project in 1992. For the first few years of the project's life, our main focus was on developing software tools to manipulate knowledge about processes using these theoretical concepts. Over the course of the project there have been at least four complete re-implementations of the software tools and uncounted variations and improvements along the way.

Starting in about 1995, we also began to devote significant efforts to developing business content for this framework. At first we had very ad hoc classification structures and a few more-or-less randomly chosen business examples. Over time we added many more examples and developed much more comprehensive and systematic classification structures.

In part because of our belief that the potential for this vision would never be realized without commercial-scale efforts, several members of our project team helped start an MIT spin-off company, called Phios Corporation (*www.phios.com*), in 1996. Under a license from MIT, Phios developed commercial versions of the Process Handbook software tools and extended the knowledge base. For example, one of the two main versions of the Process Handbook we use at MIT today uses the commercial version of the software tools.

Over all these years, we have also used the basic knowledge base and software tools in classes, presentations to business audiences, and other research projects. In the last few years, our primary focus has shifted to demonstrating the utility of the tools and knowledge base in different applications. Today, for example, we are working on projects that integrate the Process Handbook with other tools for visualizing supply chain processes (Goncalves et al. 2002) analyzing organizational change (Brynjolfsson, Renshaw, and van Alstyne 1997), and classifying company's business models (Herman, Malone, and Weill 2003).

Structure of the Book

This book includes a number of articles previously published in a variety of different publications, as well as several chapters published here for the first time. Together, this collection of readings presents a comprehensive view of the work we have done in our first decade of work on this project.

Introduction

This initial section of the book gives an overview of the whole project. It contains a chapter by Malone and colleagues that gives a comprehensive summary of all the key concepts and major results of the project as of 1999. This chapter is both a summary of, and a foundation for, the rest of the book.

The main body of the book contains three more detailed subsections on theoretical foundations, current contents, and uses of the Process Handbook.

Theoretical Foundations of the Process Handbook

The first main section (section II) focuses on the theoretical foundations of the Process Handbook. Subsection IIA presents in three chapters the basic ideas of *coordination theory*, the source of some of the key concepts embodied in the Process Handbook. The basic premise behind coordination theory is that many activities in a process can be viewed as coordination activities whose purpose is to manage the relationships among other activities. A key insight of the theory is that many of these coordination activities are very similar across many different kinds of processes. Furthermore, for any given coordination activity (e.g., assigning resources to a task), there are several plausible alternative approaches (e.g., first come–first served, managerial decision, auction). This means that one coordination mechanism can often be substituted for another to generate many different possibilities for how the same basic process can be performed.

Subsection IIB is comprised of a single chapter that discusses the concept of *specialization of processes* in detail. Processes in the Handbook are organized in an extensive hierarchical network, somewhat similar to the organizing principle used in biological classification. In the Process Handbook, however, we also take advantage of the concept of *inheritance* from computer science. We apply that concept here in such a way that the specialized versions of a process automatically "inherit" characteristics from more general processes.

Subsection IIC presents two discussions of what is meant by a process in the first place. One chapter uses concepts from linguistics to describe processes as grammars; the other shows how process descriptions themselves can constitute an important kind of theory for organizations.

Current Contents of the Process Handbook
Section III describes the current contents of the Handbook. Subsection IIIA begins with a summary of all the knowledge currently represented in the Handbook. This chapter shows how the basic concepts described in section II lead to a comprehensive, intuitive, and theoretically based classification framework for a wide range of business knowledge, and how this framework can be used to classify a number of specific business templates and case examples.

Subsection IIIB provides in two chapters examples of two very different kinds of knowledge included in the Handbook: organizational methodologies for business process redesign and coordination methods used in computer programs.

Subsection IIIC shows how more content can be added to the Process Handbook. It describes an approach to using the basic concepts of the Process Handbook to analyze business processes from real organizations in order to include them in the on-line Handbook.

Uses of the Process Handbook
Section IV gives examples of how the Handbook has been used in research and in practice. Subsection IVA includes three examples that demonstrate the Process

Handbook's usefulness in redesigning business processes. For some of these cases the Process Handbook serves as a well-organized but essentially passive knowledge base; for others, it is used to actively generate new organizational possibilities for people to consider.

Subsection IVB contains three chapters that show how the Process Handbook can be used for knowledge management. The first discusses managing knowledge about operational business processes, the second potential problems in product design, and the third communication genres used in organizations.

Subsection IVC focuses, in three chapters, on using the Process Handbook concepts and infrastructure to help generate and customize software systems. The first deals with the fundamental problems in specifying the architecture of any software system; the second more specifically with customizing software-based production processes, and the third with systems to support cooperative work by people in dynamically changing situations.

Conclusion

Section V concludes by a brief survey of what has been accomplished so far in the Process Handbook project. It then discusses the major challenges ahead in fulfilling the vision that has guided the project since its beginning.

A Guide for Readers from Various Disciplines

We believe one of the strengths of this project is the way it draws upon and makes deep connections among different academic disciplines. One consequence of this, however, is that not all parts of the book will be of equal interest to all readers.

To help you find the parts of the book that are likely to be of most interest to you, we therefore wish to offer a small bit of guidance about how to navigate through this book. First, we recommend that all readers start with the overview paper in this introductory section. Most readers might also want to look at chapter 8 which gives an overview of the contents of the Process Handbook.

Most of the other chapters in the book were written with readers from one of two disciplinary backgrounds as the intended audience (see table I). The two primary disciplines are computer science (including related disciplines like information technology, artificial intelligence, and software engineering), and organizational studies (including related disciplines like sociology, political science, and many parts of management).

Table I.1
Primary disciplinary perspectives of different chapters in this volume

		Primary discipline	
		Computer science	Organization theory
I	**Introduction**		
1	Malone et al.	*	*
II	**How can we represent processes?**		
IIA	*Coordination as management of dependencies*		
2	Malone and Crowston	*	*
3	Crowston	*	*
4	Dellarocas	*	
IIB	*Specialization of processes*		
5	Wyner and Lee	*	
IIC	*Different views of processes*		
6	Crowston		*
7	Pentland		*
III	**Contents of the process repository**		
IIIA	*Overview of the contents*		
8	Herman and Malone		*
IIIB	*Examples*		
9	Wyner		*
10	Dellarocas	*	
IIIC	*Creating process descriptions*		
11	Crowston and Osborn		*
IV	**Process repository uses**		
IVA	*Business process redesign*		
12	Klein et al.		*
13	Bernstein, Klein, and Malone	*	*
14	Klein and Dellarocas		*
IVB	*Knowledge management*		
15	Carr		*
16	Klein	*	
17	Yoshioka et al.		*
IVC	*Software design and generation*		
18	Dellarocas	*	
19	Bernstein	*	
20	Bernstein	*	
V	**Conclusion**		
	Appendix		
	Lee et al.	*	

Here are some suggestions for readers with these (and other) backgrounds:

Computer scientists, software developers, and information technologists may find the theoretical perspectives on coordination (section IIA) and specialization of processes (section IIB) of special interest. They may also be interested in a number of the applications of our framework from the perspective of software engineering (chapters 10, 18, and 19), cooperative work (chapter 20), knowledge management (chapters 15 and 16), and process redesign (chapters 12, 13, and 14). Readers with an interest in artificial intelligence may find it interesting to compare our efforts to develop a comprehensive knowledge base about business intended for use primarily by human readers with Lenat's (1995) even more ambitious efforts to develop a comprehensive knowledge base about "common sense" intended for use by automated reasoning programs.

Researchers in organization studies, management science, and related disciplines may find it interesting to contemplate the possibility of a comprehensive classification system in these disciplines analogous to those in biology and chemistry. The concepts of coordination (subsection IIA), and process as theory (chapter 6) may be of special help in this goal. In addition these readers may be interested in a number of the applications of our approach to research questions in process design (chapters 9 and 12), analytical methodologies (chapter 11), and communication genres (chapter 17).

Business educators may find it interesting to consider the possible uses of approaches like this (especially chapters 8 and 9) in organizing and retrieving business school cases and other course material.

Researchers in cognitive science may find it interesting to think about the theoretical approach to studying organizations described here (especially in section II) as being, in some ways, analogous to the computational approach to studying intelligence in cognitive science.

Researchers in library science and related disciplines may be especially interested in the activity-oriented approach to classification described in chapter 8.

Managers, consultants, and others in business should find the uses of our approach described in section IV to be of special interest.

We hope also that readers from all these different backgrounds will find it interesting to look at some of the chapters outside their immediate field of interest in order to understand better how all these different disciplinary perspectives can contribute to the overall vision.

1 Tools for Inventing Organizations: Toward a Handbook of Organizational Processes

Thomas W. Malone
Kevin Crowston
Jintae Lee
Brian T. Pentland
Chrysanthos Dellarocas
George M. Wyner

John Quimby
Abraham Bernstein
George A. Herman
Mark Klein
Charles S. Osborn
Elisa O'Donnell

1.1 Introduction

In recent years we have seen striking examples of process innovations that have transformed the way organizations work. Although initially uncommon and perceived as radical, ideas like 'just-in-time' inventory control and concurrent engineering have become accepted as so-called best practice (Carter and Baker 1991). These innovative practices have clearly been beneficial, but most organizations remain in need of improvement, as suggested by the on-going popularity of 'total quality management', 'business process redesign', and 'the learning organization'. These slogans summarize ideas with real value, but they provide too little guidance about what the improved organization might look like in particular situations. They hold out the promise of innovation but lack the details needed to accomplish it.

The gap between the need to innovate and the tools for doing so leaves us with a problem: How can we move beyond the practices of today to invent the best practices of tomorrow? And where will we keep getting new ideas for organizational processes to adapt to a continually changing world? For instance, how can we understand and exploit the new organizational possibilities enabled by the continuing, dramatic improvements in information technology? In time managers and employees of companies will certainly develop new ways of working that take advantage of these new opportunities. For quicker progress on these problems, however, our best hope is to develop a more systematic theoretical and empirical foundation for understanding organizational processes. If we are to understand successful organizational practices, we must be able to recognize and represent the organizational practices we see. And to improve organizational practice in a particular situation, we must also be able to imagine alternative ways of accomplishing the

An earlier version of this chapter appeared as T. W. Malone, K. G. Crowston, J. Lee, B. Pentland, C. Dellarocas, G. Wyner, J. Quimby, C. S. Osborn, A. Bernstein, G. Herman, M. Klein, and E. O'Donnell (1999), Tools for inventing organizations: Toward a handbook of organizational processes, *Management Science* 45 (March): 425–43. © 1999 The Institute for Operations Research and the Management Sciences (INFORMS), 901 Elkridge Landing Road, Suite 400, Linthicum, MD 21090-2909 USA. Reprinted by permission.

same things. Finally, we need some way of judging which alternatives are likely to be useful or desirable in which situations.

This chapter reports on the first five years of work in a project to address these problems by (1) developing methodologies and software tools for representing and codifying organizational processes at varying levels of abstraction and (2) collecting, organizing, and analyzing numerous examples of how different groups and companies perform similar functions. The result of this work is an on-line "process handbook" that can be used to help people: (1) redesign existing business processes, (2) invent new processes (especially those that take advantage of information technology), and (3) organize and share knowledge about organizational practices. We also expect this Process Handbook to be useful in automatically (or semi-automatically) generating software to support or analyze business processes, but that is not the focus of this chapter (see Dellarocas 1996, 1997a, b).

The goal of compiling a complete handbook of business processes is, of course, a never-ending task. Our goal in this research project is more modest: to provide a "proof of concept" that limited versions of such a handbook are both technically feasible and managerially useful. Even though this project is not yet complete, the initial goal of demonstrating the basic technical feasibility of this approach has been achieved, and that is the primary focus of this chapter. We have also conducted field tests that demonstrate the potential managerial usefulness of such handbooks and we include a description of one such test.

1.2 The Key Intellectual Challenge: How to Represent Organizational Processes?

In order to develop a system that could be used in the ways listed above, the key theoretical challenge is to develop techniques for representing processes. Fortunately, the last several decades of research in computer science and other disciplines have resulted in a number of well-developed approaches to representing processes, such as flowcharts and data-flow diagrams (e.g., Yourdon 1989), state transition diagrams (e.g., Lewis and Papadimitriou 1981; Winograd and Flores 1986), Petri nets (e.g., Peterson 1977; Holt 1988; Singh and Rein 1992), and goal-based models (e.g., Yu 1992). These approaches have been used by many organizations to map their own specific processes, and some have used them to represent widely used generic processes (e.g., Scheer 1994; Maull et al. 1995; Winograd and Flores 1986; Carlson 1979). For example, a number of consulting firms and other organizations have already developed best practice databases that include verbal descriptions, key concepts, and sometimes detailed process maps for a variety of generic processes such as logistics, marketing, and manufacturing (e.g., Peters 1992, pp. 387–90; *CIO Magazine*, 1992). It is clear therefore that it is technically feasible to assemble a large set of process descriptions collected from many different organizations. It is also clear that such libraries of process descriptions can be useful to managers and consultants. The research question, then, is not whether it is possible to have a useful repository of knowledge about business processes. These databases already demonstrate that it is. Instead, the question is, 'How can we do better than these early databases?'

To answer this question, we have developed a new approach to analyzing and representing organizational processes that explicitly represents the similarities (and the differences) among a collection of related processes. Our representation exploits two sources of intellectual leverage: (1) notions of *specialization of processes* based on ideas about inheritance from object-oriented programming, and (2) concepts about *managing dependencies* from coordination theory.

1.2.1 Specialization of Processes

Most process mapping techniques analyze business processes using only one primary dimension: breaking a process into its different *parts*. Our representation adds a second dimension: differentiating a process into its different *types*. Figure 1.1 illustrates the difference between these two dimensions. In this figure, the generic activity called 'Sell product' is broken apart into parts (or *subactivities*) like 'Identify potential customers' and 'Inform potential customers'. The generic activity is also differentiated into types (or *specializations*) like 'Sell by mail order' and 'Sell in retail store'.

As in object-oriented programming (e.g., Stefik and Bobrow 1986; Wegner 1987; Brachman and Levesque 1985), the specialized processes automatically inherit properties of their more generic "parents," except where they explicitly add or change a property. For instance, in 'Sell by mail order', the subactivities of 'Delivering a product' and 'Receiving payment' are inherited without modification, but 'Identifying prospects' is replaced by the more specialized activity of "Obtaining mailing lists."

Using this approach, any number of activities can be arranged in a richly interconnected two-dimensional network. Each of the subactivities shown in figure 1.1, for instance, can be further broken down into more detailed subactivities (e.g., 'Type mailing list name into computer') or more specialized types (e.g., 'Sell hamburgers at McDonald's retail restaurant #493') to any level desired. In general, we use the term "activity" for all business processes, including all their subparts and subtypes at all levels.

We have found the "process compass" shown in figure 1.2 to be a useful way of summarizing the two dimensions. The vertical dimension represents the conventional

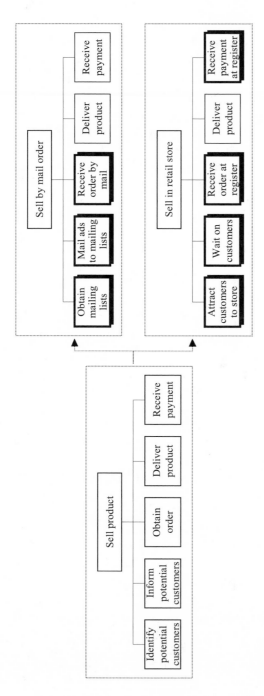

Figure 1.1

Sample representations of three different sales processes. 'Sell by mail order' and 'Sell by retail store', are specializations of the generic sales process 'Sell something'. Subactivities that are changes are shadowed.

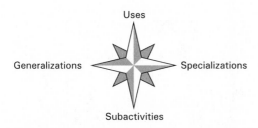

Figure 1.2
The 'Process compass' illustrates two dimensions for analyzing business processes. The vertical dimension distinguishes different *parts* of a process; the horizontal dimension distinguishes different *types* of a process.

way of analyzing processes: according to their different *parts*. The horizontal dimension is the novel one: analyzing processes according to their different *types*. From any activity in the Process Handbook, you can go in four different directions: (1) *down* to the different parts of the activity (its "subactivities"), (2) *up* to the larger activities of which this one is a part (its "uses"), (3) *right* to the different types of this activity (its "specializations"), and (4) *left* to the different activities of which this one is a type (its "generalizations").

Comparison with Object-Oriented Programming To readers familiar with conventional object-oriented programming techniques, it is worth commenting on the difference between our approach and conventional object-oriented programming. The difference is a subtle, but important, shift of perspective from specializing *objects* to specializing *processes* (see Stefik 1981; Friedland 1979; Thomsen 1987; Madsen, Moller-Pedersen, and Nygard 1993; Wyner and Lee 1995; and other references in the section below on related work in computer science).

In a sense this approach is a kind of "dual" of the traditional object-oriented approach. Traditional object-oriented programming includes a hierarchy of increasingly specialized *objects*, which may have associated with them *actions* (or "methods"). Our approach, by contrast, includes a hierarchy of increasingly specialized *actions* (or "processes") that may have associated with them *objects*. Loosely speaking, then, traditional object-oriented programming involves inheriting down a hierarchy of *nouns*; our approach involves inheriting down a hierarchy of *verbs*.

In a sense, of course, these two approaches are formally equivalent: anything that can be done in one could be done in the other. The two approaches can also, quite usefully, coexist in the same system. The process-oriented approach we are describing, however, appears to be particularly appropriate for the analysis and design of business processes.

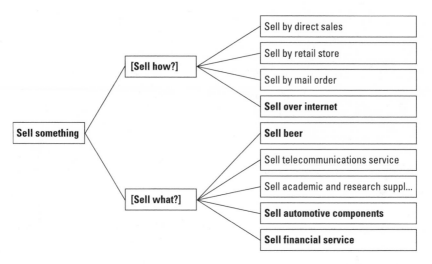

Figure 1.3
Summary display showing specializations of the activity 'Sell something'. Items in brackets (e.g., '[Sell how?]') are "bundles" that group together sets of related specializations. Items in bold have further specializations. (Note: The screen images used in this and subsequent figures were created with the software tools described below.)

Bundles and Trade-off Tables   In developing tools to support specialization, we have found it useful to combine specializations into what we call "bundles" of related alternatives. These bundles do not have a direct parallel in traditional object-oriented languages; however, they are comparable to "facets" in information science (Rowley 1992). For instance, figure 1.3 shows part of the specialization hierarchy for sales processes. In this example one bundle of specializations for 'Sell something' is related to *how* the sale is made: direct mail, retail storefront, or direct sales force. Another bundle of specializations has to do with *what* is being sold: beer, automotive components, financial services, and so on.

Comparing alternative specializations is usually meaningful only *within* a bundle of related alternatives. For example, comparing "retail store front sales" to "direct mail sales" is sensible, but comparing "retail store front sales" to "selling automotive components" is not. Where there are related alternative specializations in a bundle, our handbook can include comparisons of the alternatives on multiple dimensions, thus making explicit the tradeoff between these dimensions. For example, figure 1.4 shows a "trade-off matrix" that compares alternatives in terms of their ratings on various criteria; different specializations are the rows and different characteristics are the columns. As in the Sibyl system (Lee and Lai 1991), items in the cells of this

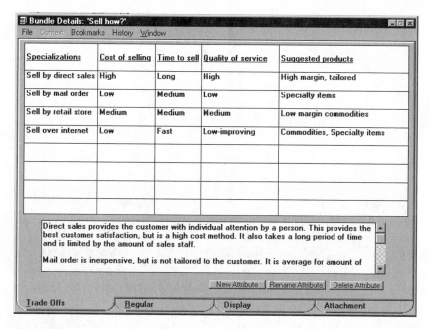

Figure 1.4
A trade-off matrix showing typical advantages and disadvantages of different specializations for the generic sales process. (Note that the values in this version of the matrix are not intended to be definitive, merely suggestive.)

matrix can be associated with detailed justifications for the various ratings. For very generic processes such as those shown here, the cells would usually contain rough qualitative comparisons (e.g., "high," "medium," and "low"); for specific process examples, they may contain detailed quantitative performance metrics for time, cost, job satisfaction, or other factors. In some cases, these comparisons may be the result of systematic studies; in others, they may be simply rough guesses by knowledgeable managers or consultants (with appropriate indications of their preliminary nature), and, of course, in some cases, there may not be enough information to include any comparisons at all.

1.2.2   Dependencies and Coordination

The second key concept we are using is the notion from coordination theory (e.g., Malone and Crowston 1994) that *coordination* can be defined as *managing dependencies among activities*. From this perspective we can characterize different kinds of *dependencies* and the alternative *coordination processes* that can manage them. Such

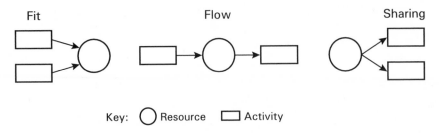

Figure 1.5
Three basic types of dependencies among activities (adapted from Zlotkin 1995)

coordination processes are both ubiquitous (i.e., the same mechanisms are found in many different processes) and variable (i.e., there are many different mechanisms that can be used to manage a particular dependency). Therefore, identifying dependencies and coordination mechanisms offers special leverage for redesigning processes. The power of analyzing processes in terms of dependencies and coordination mechanisms is greatly increased by access to a rich library of alternative coordination mechanisms for different kinds of dependencies. A critical component of the Process Handbook is a library of generic coordination mechanisms.

Figure 1.5 suggests the beginnings of such an analysis (see Crowston 1991; Zlotkin 1995). The figure shows three basic kinds of dependencies: *flow*, *sharing*, and *fit*. These three types of dependencies arise from resources that are related to multiple activities. *Flow dependencies* arise whenever one activity produces a resource that is used by another activity. This kind of dependency occurs all the time in almost all processes and is the focus of most existing process mapping techniques (e.g., flow-charts). *Sharing dependencies* occur whenever multiple activities all use the same resource. For example, this kind of dependency arises when two activities need to be done by the same person, when they need to use the same machine on a factory floor, or when they both use money from the same budget. Even though this kind of dependency between activities is usually omitted from flowcharts, allocating shared resources is clearly a critical aspect of many management activities. Finally, *fit dependencies* arise when multiple activities collectively produce a single resource. For example, when several different engineers are designing different parts of a car (e.g., the engine, the transmission, and the body) there is a dependency between their activities that results from the fact that the pieces they are each designing need to fit together in the completed car.

Table 1.1 extends this analysis by showing how the different kinds of dependencies can be associated with a set of alternative coordination processes for managing

Table 1.1
Examples of elementary dependencies between activities and alternative coordination mechanisms for managing them

Dependency	Examples of coordination mechanisms for managing dependency
Flow	
Prerequisite ('right time')	Make to order vs. make to inventory ('pull' vs. 'push').
	Place orders using 'economic order quantity', 'just in time' (kanban system), or detailed advanced planning.
Accessibility ('right place')	Ship by various transportation modes or make at point of use
Usability ('right thing')	Use standards or ask individual users (e.g., by having customer agree to purchase and/or by using participatory design)
Sharing	'First come–first serve', priority order, budgets, managerial decision, marketlike bidding
Fit	Boeing's total simulation vs. Microsoft's daily build

them. For example, the table shows that "sharing" dependencies (shared resource constraints) can be managed by a variety of coordination mechanisms such as 'first-come–first-serve', priority order, budgets, managerial decision, and marketlike bidding. If three job shop workers need to use the same machine, for instance, they could use a simple 'first-come–first-serve' mechanism. Alternatively, they could use a form of budgeting with each worker having pre-assigned time slots, or a manager could explicitly decide what to do whenever two workers wanted to use the machine at the same time. In some cases the owner might even want to sell time on the machine and the person willing to pay the most would get it. In this way new processes can be generated by considering alternative coordination mechanisms for a given dependency.

While the dependencies shown in table 1.1 are certainly not the only ones possible, our current working hypothesis is that all other dependencies can be usefully analyzed as specializations or combinations of those shown in the table. Similarly, even though there are many other possible coordination processes, the table illustrates how a library of generic coordination processes can be organized according to the dependencies they manage.

Specialization and Decomposition of Dependencies Some dependencies can be viewed as specializations of others. For instance, *task assignment* can be seen as a special case of sharing, where the "resource" being shared is the time of people who can do the tasks. This implies that the coordination mechanisms for sharing in general can be specialized to apply to task assignment. In other cases some dependencies can be seen as being composed of others. For instance, *flow dependencies* can be viewed as a combination of three other kinds of dependencies: *prerequisite* constraints (an item must be produced before it can be used), *accessibility* constraints (an item that is produced must be made available for use), and *usability* constraints, (an item that is produced should be "usable" by the activity that uses it). Loosely speaking, managing these three dependencies amounts to having the *right thing* (usability), in the right place (accessibility), at the right time (prerequisite). Each of these different kinds of dependencies, in turn, may have different processes for managing it; for example, the prerequisite dependency might be managed by keeping an inventory of the resource or by making it to order when it is needed, while usability may be managed through a product design process.

1.2.3   Related Work in Organization Theory and Design

In some respects this work represents another step on what Sanchez (1993, p. 73) calls "the long and thorny way to an organizational taxonomy." Because our work draws heavily on the concept of specialization (and therefore classification), it is related to other taxonomies of organizations (e.g., Woodward 1965; Thompson 1967; Pugh, Hickson, and Hinings 1968; Mintzberg 1979; Ulrich and McKelvey 1990; Salancik and Leblebici 1988). The main difference is that except for Salancik and Leblebici (1988), most work in this area has classified whole organizations (or parts of organizations). Instead, we classify processes. McKelvey (1982) argues that the study of organizations is at a "pre-Linnaean" stage, awaiting a more systematic taxonomy to enable further scientific progress. By focusing on processes, the perspective introduced here extends previous work and provides a significant new alternative in this important problem area.

For example, our work not only provides a framework for classification but also a framework for identifying possible alternatives and improvements. Previously Salancik and Leblebici (1988) introduced a grammatical approach to analyzing specific organizational processes that enabled the generation of new processes by the constrained rearrangement of component activities. Our representation extends this approach, adding specialization and inheritance of activities as well as explicit representation of various kinds of dependencies. Specialization enables us to generate new processes by using alternative sets of more primitive actions. Explicit representation of dependencies allows us to generate many possible coordination processes for managing these dependencies. For example, Salancik and Leblebici's alternative orderings can all be generated as alternative ways of coordinating the basic flow and other dependencies among the activities.

Our framework also emphasizes the importance of coordination in organizational design. Our concept of dependencies, for instance, elaborates on and refines the traditional concept of interdependence from organization theory (Thompson 1967). As

Thompson (1967) makes clear, interdependence between organizational subunits is a result of the way work flows are organized between them. Thompson identified three kinds of interdependence: pooled, sequential, and reciprocal. For each of these, he identified typical coordination strategies, such as standardization, planning, and mutual adjustment. As these concepts have been applied over the years, however, the concept of interdependence has come to describe relationships between organizational subunits. In a sense, therefore, our approach reasserts Thompson's (1967) original insight by emphasizing that dependencies arise between activities in a process, not between departments per se. We extend Thompson's (1967) work by identifying a much finer grained set of dependencies and a much richer set of coordination mechanisms for managing them.

We are able to explicitly relate dependencies and coordination mechanisms in this manner because our typology of dependencies is based on the pattern of use of common resources that creates the dependency, rather than on the topology of the relationship between the actors, as in Thompson's three categories. This approach makes it clearer which coordination mechanisms should be considered as alternatives, namely those that address the same kinds and uses of resources.

In representing processes computationally, our work is also similar to other computational organizational models (e.g., Cohen, March, and Olsen 1972; Carley et al. 1992; Levitt et al. 1994; Gasser and Majchrzak 1994; Baligh, Burton, and Obel 1990; Masuch and LaPotin 1989). One major difference from most of this work, however, is that we focus on *organizing knowledge*, and not on *simulating performance*. We can, of course, include simulation models and their results in the knowledge we organize, but our focus is on useful ways of organizing this knowledge, and not on generating it.

For instance, Carley et al. (1992) developed Plural Soar, a simulation of a team of actors retrieving items from a warehouse. They used this simulation to study the effect of communications between actors and of individual memory on the performance of the group. In our system the basic processes followed by the group could be stored and specialized to include or omit communication and memory. We could also include the performance of each variation as found from the simulation.

The Process Interchange Format (PIF), described below, is intended to simplify the task of translating process descriptions between a wide variety of such systems.

1.2.4   Related Work in Computer Science

The idea of generic processes (or "scripts" or "plans") has a long history in the field of artificial intelligence (e.g., Schank and Abelson 1977; Schank 1982; Chandrasekaran 1983; Clancey 1983; Tenenberg 1986; Bhandaru and Croft 1990;

Lefkowitz and Croft 1990; Chandrasekaran et al. 1992; Marques et al. 1992). Of particular relevance to our work is the work on "skeletal plans" (Stefik 1981; Friedland 1979; Friedland and Iwakasi 1985), where an abstract plan is successively elaborated (and "specialized") for a given task. The Process Handbook can also be viewed as a case-based reasoner (Kolodner 1993) since many of the processes represented in the Handbook are case examples from specific organizations.

Unlike these AI systems, however, the Process Handbook uses both process specialization and dependencies with coordination mechanisms to generate and organize a large number of examples and generalizations about them. For example, unlike a conventional case-based reasoner with only a library of previous cases, the Process Handbook can also contain an extensive (human-generated) network of generic processes that summarize and organize the existing cases and that also help generate and evaluate new possibilities.

Outside the area of artificial intelligence, the notion of specializing processes has also been used occasionally in other parts of computer science. For example, a few programming languages (e.g., Thomsen 1987; Madsen, Moller-Pedersen, and Nygard 1993) include mechanisms for defining specialization hierarchies of processes and combining actions from different levels in various ways at run-time. However, even in the parts of computer science where this work has been done, the potential power of systematically inheriting patterns of activities, dependencies, and other properties though networks of increasingly specialized processes does not seem to be widely appreciated.

In recent years the idea of explicitly representing the processes associated with connections between activities has begun to receive some attention (e.g., Stovsky and Weide 1988). For example, several recent Architecture Description Languages (ADLs) are used to describe software systems in terms of components and connectors, where both components and connectors are first-class entities (Allen and Garlan 1994; Shaw et al. 1995; Shaw and Garlan 1996). Components are analogous to our activities, while connectors correspond to our coordination processes. However, in these ADLs connectors are implementation-level abstractions (e.g., a pipe, or a client/server protocol). In contrast, the process handbook notion of dependencies also supports hierarchies of specification-level abstractions for interconnection relationships.

A key difference between our work and most previous work in all these areas of computer science comes from the difference in goals. The previous work in artificial intelligence and programming languages was primarily focused on building computer systems that, themselves, design or carry out processes. Our primary goal, on the other hand, is to build computer systems that help people design or carry out processes.

Because we have focused on *supporting* human decision-makers—not replacing them—there is no requirement that all our process descriptions be detailed or formalized enough to be executable by automated systems. Instead, it is up to the users of the Handbook to describe different processes at different levels of detail depending on their needs and the costs and benefits of going to more detailed levels. Therefore, unlike some of the well-known attempts to create comprehensive ontologies of actions (e.g., Lenat 1995; Schank and Abelson 1977), users of the Process Handbook do not have to wait for the resolution of difficult knowledge representation issues nor invest a large amount of effort in formalizing knowledge that is not immediately useful.

For domains in which the processes are formalized in enough detail, however, the Handbook can greatly facilitate the re-use of previously defined models such as simulations, workflow systems, transaction processing systems, or other software modules (e.g., Dellarocas 1996, 1997a, b).

1.3 Results

The combination of approaches described above should make it practical to store large numbers of processes, and, more importantly, enable users to generate a rich set of possible alternative processes. To test the feasibility of our approaches, we developed a series of prototype versions of a Process Handbook. The primary results of this work have been a set of *software tools* for viewing and manipulating process descriptions and a body of *information content* about business processes. In addition to these primary results, this section also includes brief descriptions of our *methodologies* for analyzing and organizing process descriptions and a *field test* of our approach.

1.3.1 Software Tools: The Process Handbook System

To date, the most visible product of our project is a set of software tools for storing and manipulating process descriptions. The core system manages the database of process descriptions and displays and edits selected entries. Our current system is implemented under the Microsoft Windows operating system using Microsoft's Visual Basic programming language and numerous third-party modules for that environment (i.e., VBXs). The process descriptions are stored in a relational database (currently Microsoft Access) with an interface layer above the database that represents processes using the concepts described above (Ahmed 1995; Bernstein et al. 1995). This interface allows users to retrieve, view, and edit process descriptions, including adding new subactivities and specializations.

The user interface includes (1) *templates for describing activities*, including standard fields (like name, description, and author) and custom fields for specialized information about particular kinds of activities, (2) *links between activities*, including standard links (like generalizations, specializations, and subactivities), as well as arbitrary "navigational links" with which users can group activities in any way they want; and (3) *summary views of specializations and decompositions*, which allow direct manipulation of the database, including operations such as adding, changing, deleting, or moving entries.

The system also provides (4) *automated support for inheritance*, so that changes in an activity are automatically made in all its specializations that have not over-ridden them, and (5) *automated support for dependencies*, so that users can specify the kind of dependency that exists between two or more activities and then search the space of possible coordination mechanisms for that dependency to identify a coordination mechanism (Elly 1996).

With this last feature users can easily switch back and forth between viewing the dependency or the coordination mechanism that manages the dependency (see figure 1.6). By successively replacing dependencies with coordination mechanisms and activities with their specializations, users can easily see many different views of the same process, from the most abstract to the most detailed.

Web Interface   We have also developed a World Wide Web interface to the system that allows users to view (but not to change) the contents of the Process Handbook from anywhere on the Internet. Using a standard Web browser, users can see information structured with templates, links, and inheritance, and they can contribute to on-line discussions about each of the activities.

Process Interchange Format   While we believe the tool described above has several unique advantages, there are many other process tools available for tasks such as flowcharting, simulation, work flow, and Computer-Aided Software Engineering (CASE). To increase the potential sources and uses for process descriptions in the Handbook, we wanted to be able to move processes back and forth between these different tools. To help make this possibility more likely, we organized a working group, including people from our project and from several other university research groups and companies sponsoring our research. This group has developed a Process Interchange Format (PIF) for moving process descriptions between systems that use diverse representations (Lee et al. 1994, 1996). Via PIF, a process in one system (e.g., a process modeler) can be used by another (e.g., a simulator), whose result in turn can be used by yet another system. Each system uses as much as possible of the pro-

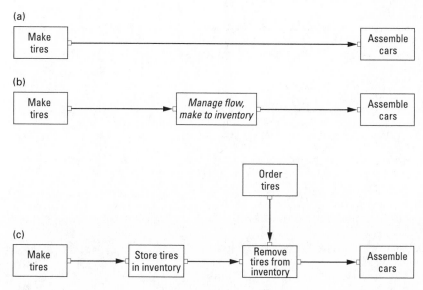

Figure 1.6
Alternative views of the same sample process. The first view (a) shows a "flow" dependency between two activities. The second view (b) shows the flow dependency replaced by the coordination process that manages it. The third view (c) shows the subactivities of the coordination process and the respective dependencies among them. Users can easily switch back and forth among these different views of the same process.

cess descriptions and passes on information it cannot "understand" to other systems (Lee and Malone 1990; Chan 1995).

1.3.2 Information Content: The Process Handbook Database

To test the feasibility of our approach it was critical to enter a significant number of process descriptions into the system. As table 1.2 summarizes, the handbook currently contains over 3,400 activities, some from specific organizations and some generic processes. This information content is the second major result of our work to date.

Examples from Specific Organizations In addition to using secondary sources of data (such as published descriptions of innovative business practices), we have focused our primary data collection on the domain of "supply chain management"— the process by which an organization (or group of organizations) manages the acquisition of inputs, the successive transformations of these inputs into products, and the distribution of these products to customers. For example, the handbook

Table 1.2
Summary of current contents of the Process Handbook database

Kind of activity	Approximate number of specific organizations represented	Approximate number of activities	Maximum number of levels of specialization	Maximum number of levels of decomposition	Sample activity names
Examples from specific organizations					
Manufacturing	3	325	2	6	Brew beer
Other 'supply chain' processes	4	235	4	5	Build walls
Others	143	240	4	2	Select human resources
Generic processes					
Generic business processes	NA	200	3	4	Sell something
Generic coordination processes	NA	200	7	2	Manage accessibility by collocation
Other generic activities	NA	2,200	20	10	Acquire human resources
Total	150	3,400	20	10	

includes results from several MIT master's thesis studies of supply chain processes ranging from a Mexican beer factory to a university purchasing process (Geisler 1995; Leavitt 1995; Lyon 1995; Ruelas Gossi 1995). The entries also include a number of examples drawn from the "Interesting Organizations Database" collected from published sources and student projects as part of an MIT research initiative on "Inventing the Organizations of the 21st Century."

Generic Business Processes   To take advantage of inheritance and to help find useful process analogies, we need to integrate specific process examples into a more general framework. To develop such a framework of generic processes, we first reviewed generic business process models from a variety of published sources (e.g., Davenport 1993). Based on this work, we defined the broadest *organizational* process in the Process Handbook as "Produce something." This term is intended to include both manufacturing organizations (which produce products) and service organizations (which produce services). We intend that every activity that occurs in an organization should fit somewhere in one of the five subactivities of this all-encompassing process: (1) design, (2) purchasing and inbound logistics, (3) production, (4) sales and outbound logistics, and (5) general management and administrative functions. Drawing on our general knowledge of business and a variety of published sources, including textbooks in marketing (Kotler 1997) and product design (Ulrich and Eppinger 1995), we have developed several levels of more detailed subactivities for these generic business activities.

However, the Process Handbook does not force a single perspective on these activities. For example, several of the generic business process models we reviewed are now included in the handbook as alternative specializations of 'Produce something'. These different models provide different *views* of how a business can be decomposed into subactivities. When several different specializations of an activity all include the same lower level subactivities, but group them in different ways we define the different specializations as alternative "views." Many such views are possible, and they are all functionally equivalent, so it would not make sense to claim that any particular set of generic business processes is definitive or intrinsically superior. Instead, users can pick the views they find most useful or appealing.

Other Generic Activities   In addition to the high-level generic business processes and generic coordination mechanisms described above, many other kinds of activities occur as basic building blocks of business processes. For example, activities like making a decision or approving an application are parts of many organizational processes. In order to take advantage of process inheritance and maximize the generativity of our framework, all activities need to be placed somewhere in the specialization hierarchy.

We have explored several alternatives for how to organize the specialization hierarchy that makes this possible. The most promising approach we have found so far (which we currently use in the handbook) is illustrated in figure 1.7. The basic idea is to create a high-level framework of a small number of very generic activities, and then to classify all other activities as specializations of these high-level activities.

In the current version of this taxonomy, the top level consists of very general activities like Create, Destroy, Modify, and Preserve. These most general processes can occur for any kind of object. As the table illustrates, these generic processes are further specialized down to the lowest level of activity in the handbook. We have found it useful in many cases to group specializations into bundles based on questions about who, what, where, why, when, and how. For example, the bundles under the generic 'Get' activity, include 'Get what?' and 'Get how?' As with the other areas of the Process Handbook, the further development of this part of the process taxonomy is an active part of our ongoing research. The taxonomy we have developed so far demonstrates the basic feasibility of organizing large numbers of activities in a unified specialization hierarchy.

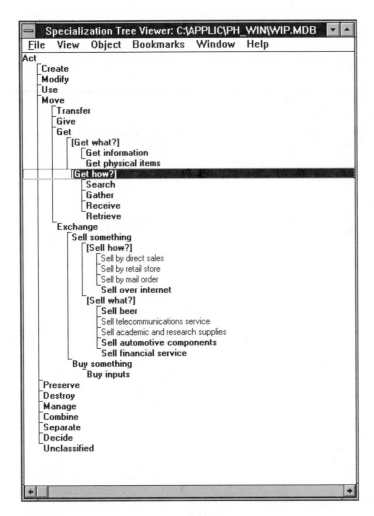

Figure 1.7
An outline view of the first two levels of the specialization hierarchy and selected further specializations of
the generic activity 'Move'

1.3.3 Methodologies

For this approach to be feasible for large-scale use, we need to be able to systematically analyze processes and integrate them into the Process Handbook. In addition to developing methods for analyzing processes (with or without the Process Handbook repository), we are also refining methods for editing and integrating information about processes into the handbook database. For instance, a top-down approach to analyzing a new process for the handbook is to start with similar examples already in the handbook, create a new specialization, and then modify the specialization as needed to describe the new process. An alternative bottom-up approach is to start by entering a description of the new process and then connecting it to existing processes in the handbook that are generalizations of the whole process or its subactivities. In the course of adding these new specializations to existing processes, the existing processes may be modified to include generalizations of elements in the new processes.

In many cases we believe the best approach is a combination of both these approaches: working both top-down and bottom-up to successively refine both old and new process descriptions and maximizing the insights along the way. Our experiences with these methodologies are now being formalized (e.g., Crowston and Osborn 1996; Pentland et al. 1994) and integrated into teaching materials.

1.3.4 Field-Testing the Process Handbook: A Case Study

In a sense each new process description entered into the handbook is a field test of the framework because it raises the question: Can this process be adequately represented? But the more important question is: What can we get back from the handbook? What kinds of activities can this representation support? To answer this question, we have begun to field test the handbook in real organizations that are engaged in process improvement efforts. While not in any sense controlled experiments, these field studies provide concrete illustrations of the potential managerial usefulness of the Process Handbook concepts. One such study is summarized here (for additional details, see chapter 12, Roth 1997). This study was done in collaboration with one of our corporate research sponsors, the AT Kearney consulting firm, and one of their clients which we call Firm A to preserve the client's anonymity.

Firm A was experiencing increasing problems with their hiring process. They were growing rapidly in a tightening labor market, and they had a culture of independent, competitive business units. Together, these factors led to increases in the time and cost to hire people and to increasingly frequent instances of business units "hoarding" candidates or bidding against each other for the same candidate.

In an effort to improve their hiring process, the organization had invested a great deal of time and energy into "as is" process analysis using conventional techniques such as flowcharting. But they also wanted some way to come up with highly innovative ideas about how to improve their process. In this spirit they agreed to participate in a field test of the Process Handbook system and concepts. A study team of about eight people was formed consisting of members from MIT, AT Kearney, and Firm A.

The team's first step was simply to see how the hiring process was represented in the Process Handbook. Several of the steps in the Handbook activity called "Hire human resources" were similar to those already identified by the "as is" analysis (e.g., identify need, determine source, select, and make offer). One immediate insight, however, resulted from the fact that the Process Handbook representation of hiring included a step of "pay employee" which had not been included in the "as is" analysis. Even though they hadn't previously thought of it in this way, the team members from Firm A found it surprising and useful to realize that the employee receiving a first paycheck is, in a sense, the logical culmination of the hiring process. Receiving a (correct) paycheck, for instance, confirms that the hiring information has been entered correctly in the relevant administrative systems.

Using the Concepts of Specialization   To generate further insights and alternatives, the team looked in the Process Handbook at specializations of the overall hiring process and then at the specializations of each of its subactivities. In terms of the process compass mentioned above, the team looked first to the right, and then down and to the right. In doing so, they came across examples such as Marriott Hotels, where an automated telephone system asks job candidates a series of questions about their qualifications and salary requirements. At the end of the call, callers are immediately told if they're qualified for the position and invited to schedule an interview through the system's automated scheduling feature. Although most appropriate for lower-level personnel, this example was very thought provoking for the project team.

The team found numerous other similarly intriguing examples in the Handbook. For example, they found descriptions of (1) BMW using a simulated assembly line to help select assembly line workers, (2) Whirlpool having a corporatewide "human capital war room" with databases of projected skill needs and capacities, and (3) Doubletree which seeks to systematically identify dimensions of employee success in their organization and then hire candidates with similar traits.

This use of the Process Handbook is similar to the traditional "benchmarking" or best-practice approach of learning from other examples of the same process. Even here, however, the use of specialization in the Handbook allows much richer ways of indexing large numbers of examples than any other best-practices database of which we are aware.

In an effort to expand their horizons even further, the team's next step was to look in the handbook for more distant analogies (or "cousins") of the hiring process. That is, they looked first at generalizations ("ancestors") of the hiring process and then at other specializations ("descendants") of these generalizations. (In terms of the process compass, they moved left and then right again.)

For example, 'hiring' is classified in the handbook as a specialization of 'buying', so a handbook user who looks at the generalizations of 'hiring' will encounter 'buying'. In retrospect, this connection may seem obvious (hiring is a form of buying someone's time), but this analogy had not been obvious to the project team, and it proved to be a very stimulating source of insights. In exploring other specializations of buying, for instance, the team encountered examples like (1) Motorola's extensive quality audits and rating systems for their suppliers, (2) Acer's different sourcing strategies for different kinds of materials, and (3) General Electric's Internet-based system through which purchasing agents can find and compare suppliers. Each of these examples stimulated specific ideas about possible improvements in the hiring process for Firm A: (1) quality ratings for recruiters, (2) creating different hiring processes for different kinds of positions, and (3) identifying candidates using the Internet, respectively.

Using the Concepts of Coordination After exploring a number of such distant analogies, the team then began to systematically explore and compare many different possible combinations of specializations and coordination processes for hiring. One of the most interesting insights from this part of the process came from focusing on the shared resource dependency for recruiter time. Firm A used a variety of internal and external recruiters, and the time of these recruiters had to be somehow shared across all the positions being filled at any given time. The coordination process Firm A currently used for managing this dependency was to have recruiting managers for each business unit assign each new search to a specific recruiter.

When analyzing this process from a coordination point of view, the team quickly identified a variety of other possible ways to manage this dependency, including all the coordination processes listed for sharing dependencies in table 1.1. The team was particularly intrigued by the idea of using marketlike bidding systems for this purpose. In one scenario the team developed, for instance, recruiters would "bid" on the opportunity to fill a new position by specifying how long they estimated it would take them to fill the position. Later, when the position had actually been filled, the recruiter's fee would be adjusted for significant over- or underperformance relative to the original bid.

One compelling advantage of this scheme is that it could more easily exploit information that is often ignored completely in the current system. For instance, a recruiter who had just filled one position for a C++ programmer, but who knew that three other highly qualified candidates identified in the same search were still available, could take this information into account in making a low bid on a new search for a C++ programmer in another business unit.

Our project ended before Firm A had implemented any of the ideas generated in this phase of the project, and no quantitative evaluation of the idea-generating phase of the project was done. However, in the meeting where the final project results were presented, the executive vice president of human resources in Firm A eloquently articulated our aspirations in the project by saying that he felt he had "passed through a doorway where all sorts of things he had never imagined before now seemed possible."

1.4   Discussion

This case illustrates a number of advantages of using a specialization hierarchy in combination with the explicit representation of coordination and dependencies. First, this field test showed that specialization can substantially reduce the amount of work necessary to analyze a new process. By simply identifying a process as a "hiring process," for example, a great deal of information can be automatically inherited. Then, only the changes that matter for the purpose at hand need to be explicitly entered. This helps support a rapid assessment of the basic features of a process, rather than laborious detailing (what Hammer and Champy 1993 refer to as "analysis paralysis"). For example in the field test, the team chose to ignore nearly all of the "as is" analysis that had previously been done by Firm A and focus on a very simple, abstract view of the hiring process and its first-level subactivities. This level of detail, alone, was sufficient to generate all the insights described above.

Second, the specialization hierarchy provided a powerful framework for generating new process ideas. For example, some of today's "best practice" databases support cross-fertilization across industries within the same business function, but we do not know of any others that would support the kind of cross-fertilization across business functions (from purchasing to human resources) described above.

Since coordination processes are often those most susceptible to being changed by information technology, a particularly important use of this approach is to use generic knowledge about alternative coordination mechanisms to generate new process ideas. For instance, the ideas about using bidding to allocate recruiter time were stimulated by very generic knowledge about coordination, and would presumably be more feasible because of the cheaper communication made possible by information technologies (see Crowston 1997 for other similar examples).

Another feature of our approach that makes it particularly useful for generating new process ideas is that we focus attention on processes as distinct entities that can be described independently of organizational structures or the roles of particular people or groups. This process-oriented approach to business seems particularly useful, in (1) identifying new ways of doing old tasks, even if the new ways involve very different actors, and (2) managing connected processes that span organizational boundaries: either across groups in a single firm or across firms in "networked" and "virtual" organizations.

In addition to these advantages, our process-oriented approach has limitations too. For instance, any static process representation can give the impression that the process is more stable and routine than most business processes actually are. In contrast to most other process representations, however, our approach helps us explicitly deal with this issue by representing the stable—or typical—aspects of a process at the generic level and then also representing as many specialized variations as is useful.

Another risk of having libraries of explicit process representations like ours is that people will interpret them too rigidly. While it is sometimes appropriate to collect prescriptive rules or procedures in a Handbook like ours, we think that in most situations a process handbook will be most useful as a *resource* to help people figure out what to do, rather than as a *prescription* of what they should do.

The Editorial Challenge One of the most important ways in which our approach differs from many other computational approaches to similar problems is that we do not rely primarily on intelligent computer systems to analyze, reason about, or simulate business processes. Instead, we place substantial importance on the role of intelligent human "editors" to select, refine, and structure the knowledge represented in the Handbook. This approach has both strengths and weaknesses.

On the one hand, it allows us to take advantage of human abilities to analyze, organize, and communicate knowledge in ways that go far beyond the capabilities of today's computers. For example, the task of developing good generic models for the marketing and sales process is similar, in many ways, to writing a good textbook or developing comprehensive theories about marketing and sales. Human abilities to do tasks like these will almost certainly exceed those of computers for the foreseeable future.

On the other hand, relying on human effort in this way means that the success of our approach depends significantly on the quality and amount of human intelligence applied to the problem of generating and organizing knowledge in the system. For example, a complex and confusing network of poorly organized process categories may be even worse than no categories at all.

In general, as process descriptions are added to the handbook, we will face a problem that is analogous to that faced by researchers in many fields: how to ensure that results cumulate in a meaningful way. Since we foresee a wide variety of potential users and contributors, it would be unrealistic to expect equal rigor from all of them. Rather than attempting to enforce uniform standards, we plan to allow a wide variety of data from diverse sources, but to require that the specific sources, methods, and significance of that data be described in enough detail to allow users of the Handbook to judge whether it is valid and reliable enough for their own purposes. In this respect the Handbook has an advantage over more formal approaches because it allows many alternatives to co-exist in the system. At the same time this openness contributes to the editorial problem of insuring that the entries are consistently and usefully classified. We believe that adopting solutions analogous to those that have already been found successful in other domains is a promising approach. For example, we have found it useful to think about roles like authors, editors, and reviewers for groups of entries in the Process Handbook.

It is also encouraging to note that the specialization structure of the Handbook provides a potentially powerful advantage that has not been widely available to any knowledge generating communities before: Well-organized and accurate process knowledge at the "left" of the specialization network is automatically inherited throughout the other parts of the network where it applies. In this sense, then, the system amplifies the effort of intelligent humans by automatically linking their work to a variety of contexts where it may be useful.

1.5 Conclusion

There is, of course, much more work to be done to develop and test the ideas described here. For example, better tools for process analysis and editing need to be created, more information content needs to be added to the Process Handbook, and systematic tests of how the ideas can be applied in different kinds of situations need to be performed. However, we believe that our work so far has demonstrated the basic feasibility and contribution of the approach and its potential for significant further progress. We hope, for example, that this research will provide a set of intellectual tools and an extensive database to help people learn about organizations, invent new kinds of organizations, and improve existing processes. Perhaps most importantly, we hope this research will help us understand the possibilities for creating new kinds of organizations that are not only more effective but also more fulfilling for their members.

Acknowledgments

Parts of this chapter appeared previously in Malone, Crowston, Lee, and Pentland (1993). The work was supported, in part, by the National Science Foundation (Grant Nos. IRI-8903034, IRI-9224093, and DMI-9628949) and the Defense Advanced Research Projects Agency (DARPA). It was also supported by the following corporate sponsors: British Telecom, Daimler Benz, Digital Equipment Corporation, Electronic Data Systems (EDS), Fuji Xerox, Matsushita, National Westminster Bank, Statoil, Telia, Union Bank of Switzerland, Unilever, and other sponsors of the MIT Center for Coordination Science and the MIT Initiative on "Inventing the Organizations of the 21st Century." The software described in this paper is the subject of pending patent applications by MIT.

We would like to thank Marc Gerstein, Fred Luconi, and Gilad Zlotkin for their long-term contributions to many aspects of this project. We would like to thank John Gerhart for his significant early contributions to the content of the database and Martha Broad, Bob Halperin, Ed Heresniak, and Roanne Neuwirth for their contributions to the management of the project. We would also like to specifically thank the following students for their contributions to the development of the software tools described here: Erfan Ahmed, Frank Chan, Yassir Elley, Umar Farooq, Phil Grabner, Naved Khan, Vuong Nguyen, Greg Pal, Narasimha Rao, and Calvin Yuen. In addition we would like to thank the dozens of students and others who contributed content to the database or who used the concepts developed in this project to analyze business processes. In particular, we would like to thank the following students whose work is specifically included in the current database: Gary Cheng, Martha Geisler, Paul Gutwald, Clarissa Hidalgo, Jeff Huang, Wilder Leavitt, William Lyon, Alejandro Ruelas Gossi, and Jin Xia. Finally, we would like to thank the members of the Process Handbook advisory board: Michael Cohen, John McDermott, and the late Gerald Salancik.

II HOW CAN WE REPRESENT PROCESSES? TOWARD A THEORY OF PROCESS REPRESENTATION

In this section we include papers on the three main theoretical foundations for the Process Handbook: coordination theory, specialization, and processes.

Coordination

The first set of papers introduces and elaborates on coordination theory. Coordination theory suggests that *dependencies* among activities and resources create *coordination problems* that constrain how the activities can be performed. To avoid or overcome these constraints, additional work must be performed in the form of *coordination mechanisms* that manage the dependencies.

Coordination theory has two important benefits for the Process Handbook. First, as with any common pattern, it can help represent a large collection of business activities more "economically" because the common elements don't need to be repeated in each case. Second, and more important in the work we have done, identifying the type of dependency involved in a process makes it easier to think of alternative ways of doing the process using alternative coordination mechanisms. For example, we can often find alternative ways of coordinating a process that are enabled or improved by information technologies without changing the fundamental goals of the process. On the other hand, replacing noncoordination activities may fundamentally change the outcome of the process.

Chapter 2, by Malone and Crowston, is the basic reference for coordination theory. The chapter presents examples of similar coordination problems encountered in a variety of disciplines and shows how they can all be analyzed as arising from dependencies among activities. For example, approaches to sharing resources have been analyzed in economics, organization theory and computer science, among others. In addition to sharing resources, the coordination problems analyzed in this chapter include producer–consumer dependencies, simultaneity constraints and task–subtask relations.

Central to the application of coordination theory is a typology of different types of dependencies and their associated coordination mechanisms. The list of coordination problems in the first chapter of this section was an early version of our thinking about what such a typology might include. Chapter 3 by Crowston, presents a much more extensive theoretical derivation of a typology of dependencies based on an analysis of the possible configurations of activities that use and create resources.

The current version of the Handbook uses a simplified version of this typology (summarized in chapter 1) that focuses attention on the common case of two activities and one resource. This typology includes the three elementary dependency types shown in the first row of figure 1.2. The first possibility, which we call *flow*, occurs when one activity creates a resource that is used by another. The second possibility, which we call *sharing*, occurs when one resource is used by two activities. And the third possibility, which we call *fit*, occurs when a single resource is jointly created by two activities. The flow dependency is further analyzed into three subdependencies, namely the dependencies that make sure the *right thing* (resource) is available at the *right time*, in the *right place*.

Chapter 4 on coordination theory, by Dellarocas, shows how the perspective of coordination can be applied to designing computer software. In particular, it shows that the management of dependencies among software components can be viewed as a distinct design problem itself, orthogonal to the problem of implementing the core functional pieces of an application. This chapter gives an overview of how the different dependency types we have already identified arise in computer programs. For instance, many different kinds of programming techniques (e.g., pipes, procedure calls, and semaphores) can be viewed as alternative ways of managing different kinds of flow dependencies. A much more detailed view of this typology of software dependencies is included below in chapter 10.

Specialization

The second, and in many ways even more important, conceptual tool in the Process Handbook is specialization of processes. This concept allows us to represent both the commonalities and differences in large "families" of related processes in a very precise way. It also lets us take advantage of these relationships to let our software tools simplify the task of maintaining these large databases. For instance, when you make a change in one activity, the system can automatically make the same change in all the other related activities where it should apply.

Most readers with a background in computer science will already be familiar with the concepts of specialization and inheritance as used, for instance, in object-oriented programming systems. Our use of specialization and inheritance is very similar to this traditional use, but with one very important difference. Traditional object-oriented programming systems apply these concepts to objects ("nouns"); we apply them to activities ("verbs"). Furthermore processes are composed of activities, so specialization of a process may change the decomposition as well as properties of the processes. Chapter 5, by Wyner and Lee, analyzes what this means in more precise terms.

Process

Chapters 6 and 7 examine processes from a research perspective. Chapter 6, by Crowston, was originally presented at a conference on information systems research, but its key message—that process descriptions themselves can constitute an important kind of theory about organizations—applies to organization theory in general. The chapter analyzes alternative perspectives on processes, building up to a view of processes as assemblies of activities. This analysis includes the coordination theory view that dependencies between activities impose constraints on the ways the activities can be assembled. The theoretical perspectives in this chapter are illustrated with brief case examples of different variations in restaurant service processes.

Chapter 7, by Pentland, presents an alternative theoretical perspective for analyzing organizational processes—the perspective of formal grammars from linguistics. A grammar provides a way to represent a potentially infinite set of patterns (in this case, the set of possible processes) in a concise way. Using a lexicon of elementary actions and rules for how the actions can be combined, grammatical models provide a natural way of describing the kinds of layering and nesting of actions that typify organizational processes.

IIA *Coordination as the Management of Dependencies*

2 The Interdisciplinary Study of Coordination

Thomas W. Malone
Kevin Crowston

2.1 Introduction

In recent years there has been a growing interest in questions about how the activities of complex systems can be coordinated (e.g., Huberman 1988b; Johansen 1988; Rumelhart et al. 1986; Winograd and Flores 1986; NSF-IRIS 1989; NSF 1991; Bond and Gasser 1988; Huhns and Gasser 1989). In some cases this work has focused on coordination in parallel and distributed computer systems; in others, on coordination in human systems; and in many cases, on complex systems that include both people and computers.

Our goal in this chapter is to summarize and stimulate development of theories that can help with this work. This new research area—the interdisciplinary study of coordination—draws upon a variety of different disciplines including computer science, organization theory, management science, economics, linguistics, and psychology. Many of the researchers whose efforts can contribute to and benefit from this new area are not yet aware of each other's work. Therefore, by summarizing this diverse body of work in a way that emphasizes its common themes, we hope to help define a community of interest and to suggest useful directions for future progress.

There is still no widely accepted name for this area, so we will use the term coordination theory to refer to theories about how coordination can occur in diverse kinds of systems. We use the term "theory" with some hesitation because it connotes to some people a degree of rigor and coherence that is not yet present in this field. Instead, the field today is a collection of intriguing analogies, scattered results, and partial frameworks. We use the term "theory," however, in part to signify a provocative goal for this interdisciplinary enterprise, and we hope that the various studies reviewed in this chapter will serve as steps along the path toward an emerging theory of coordination.

2.1.1 A Motivating Question

We begin with one of the questions that coordination theory may help answer: How will the widespread use of information technology change the ways people work together? This is not the only possible focus of coordination theory, but it is a particularly timely question today for two reasons:

An earlier version of this chapter appeared as T. W. Malone and K. Crowston (1994), The interdisciplinary study of coordination, *ACM Computing Surveys* 26 (March): 87–119. © 1994 ACM. Reprinted by permission.

1. In recent years large numbers of people have acquired direct access to computers, primarily for individual tasks like spreadsheet analysis and word processing. These computers are now beginning to be connected to each other. Therefore we now have, for the first time, an opportunity for vastly larger numbers of people to use computing and communications capabilities to help coordinate their work. For example, specialized new software has been developed to (a) support multiple authors working together on the same document, (b) help people display and manipulate information more effectively in face-to-face meetings, and (c) help people intelligently route and process electronic messages (see detailed references in section 2.3.3).

It now appears likely that there will be a number of commercially successful products of this new type (often called 'computer-supported cooperative work' or 'groupware'), and to some observers these applications herald a paradigm shift in computer usage as significant as the earlier shifts to time-sharing and personal computing. It is less clear whether the continuing development of new computer applications in this area will depend solely on trial and error and intuition, or whether it will also be guided by a coherent underlying theory of how people coordinate their activities now and how they might do so differently with computer support.

2. In the long run the dramatic improvements in the costs and capabilities of information technologies are changing—by orders of magnitude—the constraints on how certain kinds of communication and coordination can occur. At the same time there is a pervasive feeling in businesses today that global interdependencies are becoming more critical, that the pace of change is accelerating, and that we need to create more flexible and adaptive organizations. Together, these changes may soon lead us across a threshold where entirely new ways of organizing human activities become desirable.

For example, new capabilities for communicating information faster, less expensively, and more selectively may help create what some observers (e.g., Toffler 1970) have called "adhocracies"—rapidly changing organizations with highly decentralized networks of shifting project teams. As another example, lowering the costs of coordination between firms may encourage more market transactions (i.e., more 'buying' rather than 'making') and, at the same time, closer coordination across firm boundaries (e.g., 'just-in-time' inventory management).

2.1.2 How Can We Proceed?

If we believe that new forms of organizing are likely to become more common, how can we understand the possibilities better? What other new kinds of coordination structures will emerge in the electronically connected world of the near future? When are these new structures desirable? What is necessary for them to work well?

To some extent, we can answer these questions by observing innovative organizations as they experiment with new technologies. But to understand the experiences of these organizations, we may need to look more deeply into the fundamental constraints on how coordination can occur. And to imagine new kinds of organizational processes that no organizations have tried yet, we may need to look even further afield for ideas.

One way to do both these things—to understand fundamental constraints and to imagine new possibilities—is to look for analogies in how coordination occurs in very different kinds of systems. For example, could we learn something about trade-offs between computing and communicating in distributed computer systems that would illuminate possibilities for coordination in human organizations? Might coordination structures analogous to those used in bee hives or ant colonies be useful for certain aspects of human organizations? And could lessons learned about coordination in human systems help understand computational or biological systems, as well?

For these possibilities to be realized, a great deal of crossdisciplinary interaction is needed. It is not enough just to believe that different systems are similar; we also need an intellectual framework for "transporting" concepts and results back and forth between the different kinds of systems.

In the remainder of this chapter, we attempt to provide the beginnings of such a framework. We first define coordination in a way that emphasizes its interdisciplinary nature and then suggest an approach for studying it further. Next, we describe examples of how a coordination perspective can be applied in three domains: (1) understanding the effects of information technology on human organizations and markets, (2) designing cooperative work tools, and (3) designing distributed and parallel processing computer systems. Finally, we briefly suggest elements of a research agenda for this new area.

2.2 A Framework for Studying Coordination

2.2.1 What Is Coordination?

We all have an intuitive sense of what the word "coordination" means. When we attend a well-run conference, when we watch a winning basketball team, or when we see a smoothly functioning assembly line we may notice how well coordinated the actions of a group of people seem to be. Often, however, good coordination is nearly invisible, and we sometimes notice coordination most clearly when it is lacking. When we spend hours waiting on an airport runway because the airline can't find a gate for our plane, when the hotel where we thought we had a reservation is fully booked, or when our favorite word processing program stops working in a new version of the operating system, we may become very aware of the effects of poor coordination.

For many purposes, this intuitive meaning is sufficient. However, in trying to characterize a new interdisciplinary area, it is also helpful to have a more precise idea of what we mean by "coordination." Appendix A lists a number of definitions that have been suggested for this term. The diversity of these definitions illustrates the difficulty of defining coordination, and also the variety of possible starting points for studying the concept. For our purposes here, however, it is useful to begin with the following simple definition:

Coordination is managing dependencies among activities.[1]

This definition is consistent with the simple intuition that, if there is no interdependence, there is nothing to coordinate. It is also consistent with a long history in organization theory of emphasizing the importance of interdependence (e.g., Thompson 1967; Galbraith 1973; Lawrence and Lorsch 1967; Pfeffer 1978; Rockart and Short 1989; Hart and Estrin 1990; Roberts and Gargano 1989).

As the definition suggests, we believe it is helpful to use the word "coordination" in a fairly inclusive sense. For instance, it is clear that actors performing interdependent activities may have conflicting interests and that what might be called "political processes" are ways of managing them (e.g., Ciborra 1987; Williamson 1985; Schelling 1960; Kling 1980). Similarly, even though words like "cooperation," "collaboration," and "competition" each have their own connotations, an important part of each of them involves managing dependencies between activities.[2]

It should also be clear that coordination, as we have defined it, can occur in many kinds of systems: human, computational, biological, and others. For instance, questions about how people manage dependencies among their activities are central to parts of organization theory, economics, management science, sociology, social psychology, anthropology, linguistics, law, and political science. In computer systems, dependencies between different computational processes must certainly be managed, and, as numerous observers have pointed out, certain kinds of interactions among computational processes resemble interactions among people (e.g., Fox 1981; Hewitt

1. This definition was particularly influenced by Rockart and Short (1989) and Curtis (1989). The importance of coordination in this very general sense was perhaps first recognized by Holt (1980, 1983).

2. These terms also, of course, have broader meanings. For instance, cooperation usually implies shared goals among different actors, competition usually implies that one actor's gains are another's losses, and collaboration often connotes peers working together on an intellectual endeavor. However, it is sometimes useful to consider all these terms as describing different approaches to managing dependencies among activities, that is, as different forms of coordination.

1986; Huberman 1988a, b; Miller and Drexler 1988; Smith and Davis 1981). To give a sense of the approaches different fields have taken to studying coordination, we summarize in appendix B examples of results about coordination from computer science, organization theory, economics, and biology.

Even though we believe there are more similarities among these different kinds of systems than most people appreciate, there are obviously many differences as well. One of the most important differences is that issues of incentives, motivations, and emotions are usually of much more concern in human systems than in other kinds of systems. In computer programs, for example, the "incentives" of a program module are usually easy to describe and completely controlled by a programmer. In human systems, on the other hand, the motivations, incentives, and emotions of people are often extremely complex, and understanding them is usually an important part of coordination. Even in human systems, however, analogies with other kinds of systems may help us understand fundamental constraints on coordination and imagine new kinds of organizations that might be especially motivational for people.

2.2.2 Basic Coordination Processes

A primary vehicle for facilitating transfer among these different disciplines is identifying and studying the basic processes involved in coordination: Are there fundamental coordination processes that occur in all coordinated systems? If so, how can we represent and analyze these processes? Is it possible to characterize situations in a way that helps generate and choose appropriate coordination mechanisms for them?

One of the advantages of the definition we have used for coordination is that it suggests a direction for addressing these questions. If coordination is defined as managing dependencies, then further progress should be possible by characterizing different kinds of dependencies and identifying the coordination processes that can be used to manage them.

Table 2.1 suggests the beginnings of such an analysis (for more details, see Malone et al. 1993). For example, one possible kind of dependency between different activities is that they require the same (limited) resources. The table shows that shared resource constraints can be managed by a variety of coordination processes such as 'first-come–first-serve', priority order, budgets, managerial decision, and marketlike bidding. If three job shop workers need to use the same machine, for instance, they could use a simple 'first-come–first-serve' mechanism. Alternatively, they could use a form of budgeting with each worker having pre-assigned time slots, or a manager could explicitly decide what to do whenever two workers wanted to use the machine at the same time. In some cases they might even want to "bid" for use of the machine and the person willing to pay the most would get it.

Table 2.1
Examples of common dependencies between activities and alternative coordination processes for managing them

Dependency	Examples of coordination processes for managing dependency
Shared resources	'First come–first serve', priority order, budgets, managerial decision, marketlike bidding
Task assignments	(same as for 'shared resources')
Producer/consumer relationships	
Prerequisite constraints	Notification, sequencing, tracking
Transfer	Inventory management (e.g., 'just in time', 'economic order quantity')
Usability	Standardization, ask users, participatory design
Design for manufacturability	Concurrent engineering
Simultaneity constraints	Scheduling, synchronization
Task/subtask	Goal Selection, task decomposition

Note: Indentations in the left column indicate more specialized versions of general dependency types.

The lists of dependencies and coordination processes in table 2.1 are by no means intended to be exhaustive. It is important to note, however, that many specific processes that arise in particular kinds of systems (e.g., design for manufacturability) can be seen as instances of more generic processes (e.g., managing "usability" constraints between adjacent steps in a process).

In fact we believe that one of the most intriguing possibilities for coordination theory is to identify and systematically analyze a wide variety of dependencies and their associated coordination processes. Such a Handbook of coordination processes could not only facilitate interdisciplinary transfer of knowledge about coordination, it could also provide a guide for analyzing the coordination needs in particular situations and generating alternative ways of fulfilling them (see Malone et al. 1993).

One question that arises immediately is how to categorize these dependencies and coordination processes. Table 2.1 provides a start in this direction. Crowston (1991) suggests a more structured taxonomy based on all the possible relationships between "tasks" and "resources."

To illustrate the possibilities for analyzing coordination processes, we will discuss in the remainder of this section the coordination processes listed in table 2.1 and how they have been analyzed in different disciplines.

Managing Shared Resources   Whenever multiple activities share some limited resource (e.g., money, storage space, or an actor's time), a resource allocation process is needed to manage the interdependencies among these activities. Resource allocation is perhaps the most widely studied of all coordination processes. For example, it has received significant attention in economics, organization theory, and computer science.

ECONOMICS   Much of economics is devoted to studying resource allocation processes, especially those involving marketlike pricing and bidding mechanisms. As economists have observed, for instance, markets have a number of interesting properties as resource allocation mechanisms (Simon 1981). For one thing, they can be very decentralized: many independent decision makers interacting with each other locally can produce a globally coherent allocation of resources without any centralized controller (e.g., Smith 1776). For another thing, markets have a built-in set of incentives: when all participants in a perfect market try to maximize their own individual benefits, the overall allocation of resources is (in a certain sense) globally "optimal" (e.g., Debreu 1959).

ORGANIZATION THEORY   Organization theory has also paid great attention to resource allocation issues. For instance, control of resources is intimately connected with personal and organizational power: those who control resources have power, and vice versa (e.g., Pfeffer and Salancik 1978). In general, organization theorists emphasize hierarchical resource allocation methods where managers at each level decide how the resources they control will be allocated among the people who report to them (e.g., Burton and Obel 1980a, b). In practice, however, resource allocation in organizations is much more complex than a simple hierarchical model suggests. For instance, managers may try to increase their own power by attracting resources (e.g., employees and money) away from other possible activities (Barnard 1964) or by using their resources in a way that is very suboptimal from the point of view of the whole organization.

How can we choose between different resource allocation methods? Recent work in transaction cost theory addresses part of this question by analyzing the conditions under which a hierarchy is a better way of coordinating multiple actors than a market (e.g., Williamson 1975, 1985). For example, if there are extra costs associated with a market transaction (e.g., extensive legal and accounting work), then the costs of internal transactions within a hierarchical firm may be lower and therefore preferable. A related question involves the conditions under which it is desirable to use marketlike resource allocation mechanisms (such as transfer pricing) within a hierarchical organization (Eccles 1985).

COMPUTER SCIENCE   Resource allocation issues also arise in computer systems and much work has been done on these topics (e.g., Cytron 1987; Halstead 1985). For instance, operating systems require algorithms for allocating resources—such as processors and memory—to different processes and for scheduling accesses to input/ output devices, such as disks (e.g., Deitel 1983). As we will see below, there have also already been examples of cross-fertilization of ideas about resource allocation between computer science and other fields. For example, in section 2.2.3, we will see how ideas about distributed computer systems helped understand the evolution of human organizations, and in section 2.3.4, we will see how analogies with human markets have generated novel resource allocation schemes for computer systems.

TASK ASSIGNMENT   One very important special case of resource allocation is task assignment, that is, allocating the scarce time of actors to the tasks they will perform. An insight of the approach we are taking here, therefore, is that all the resource allocation methods listed in table 2.1 are potentially applicable for task assignment too.

For instance, in trying to imagine new coordination processes in a human organization, one might consider whether any given situation requiring task assignment could be better managed by managerial decision, by prior assignment according to task type, or by a pricing mechanism. To illustrate the surprising ideas this might lead to, consider Turoff's (1983) suggestion that employees within a large organization should be able to "bid" for the internal projects on which they wish to work, and that teams could be selected using these bids. There are obviously many factors to consider in determining whether such an arrangement would be desirable in a particular situation, but it is interesting to note that one potential disadvantage—the significantly greater communication required—would be much less important in a world with extensive computer networks.

Managing Producer–Consumer Relationships   Another extremely common kind of relationship between activities is a "producer–consumer" relationship, that is, a situation where one activity produces something that is used by another activity. This relationship clearly occurs in all physical manufacturing processes, for instance, where the output of one step on an assembly line is the input to the next. It also occurs with information whenever one person in an organization uses information from another or when one part of a computer program uses information produced by another.

Producer–consumer relationships often lead to several kinds of dependencies:

1. Prerequisite constraints. A very common dependency between a "producer" activity and a "consumer" activity is that the producer activity must be completed before the consumer activity can begin. When this dependency exists, there must at least be some notification process to indicate to the consumer activity that it can

begin. For instance, when an automobile designer delivers a completed drawing of a part to the engineer who will design the manufacturing process for that part, the arrival of the drawing in the engineer's in-box "notifies" the engineer that her activity can begin.

Managing prerequisite dependencies also often involves explicit sequencing and tracking processes to be sure that producer activities have been completed before their results are needed. For instance, techniques from operations research, such as PERT charts and critical path methods, are often used in human organizations to help schedule large projects with multiple activities and complex prerequisite structures. These and other project tracking systems are also often used by managers to identify activities that are late and then use their authority to "motivate" the people responsible for the late tasks.

What alternatives can we imagine for managing this dependency? One possibility would be computer-based tracking systems that make it easy for everyone in the project to see status information about all other activities and their dependencies. In this case late tasks would be visible to everyone throughout the project, and "authoritarian" motivation by managers would become less important.

Sequencing problems arise frequently in computer systems, as well. For instance, one of the key issues in taking advantage of parallel processing computers is determining which activities can be done in parallel and which ones must wait for the completion of others (Arvind and Culler 1986; Holt 1988; Peterson 1977, 1981). Some of these ideas from computer science have also been used to help streamline processes in human organizations by taking advantage of their latent parallelism (e.g., Ellis et al. 1979).

2. Transfer. When one activity produces something that is used by another activity, the thing produced must be transferred from the "producer" activity to the "consumer" activity. Managing this dependency usually involves physical transportation. In this sense physical transportation can be considered a coordination activity, since it involves managing a dependency between a "producer" activity and a "consumer" activity. When the thing transferred is information, we usually call the transfer "communication," rather than transportation.

In addition to simply transporting things, managing the transfer dependency also often involves storing things being transferred from one activity to another. For instance, one way of managing this aspect of the transfer dependency is to carefully control the timing of both activities so that items are delivered 'just in time' to be used, and no storage is needed. This technique, for example, is becoming increasingly common in manufacturing environments (Schonberger 1982, 1986). A more common approach is maintain an inventory of finished items, ready for the second activity to use, as a buffer between the two activities. Operations researchers, for instance, have developed techniques for determining at what stock levels and by how much to replenish an inventory in order to minimize costs (e.g., the "economic order quantity"; McClain et al. 1992).

Managing this dependency is also important in certain parts of computer science. For example in parallel processing systems, the rate of execution of processes must sometimes be regulated to ensure that the producer does not overwhelm the consumer, and vice versa (e.g., Arvind et al. 1986). As our framework would suggest, a common approach to this problem is to place a buffer between the two processes and allocate space in the buffer to one process or the other. Network protocols manage similar problems between communicating processes that do not share any memory (Tannenbaum 1981).

3. Usability. Another, somewhat less obvious, dependency that must often be managed in a producer–consumer relationship is that whatever is produced should be usable by the activity that receives it. One common way of managing this dependency is by standardization, creating uniformly interchangeable outputs in a form that users already expect. This is the approach on assembly lines, for example. Another approach is to ask users what characteristics they want. For instance, in human organizations this might be done by market research techniques such as surveys and focus groups (Kinnear and Taylor 1991).

A third, related, alternative is participatory design, that is, having the users of a product actively participate in its design (Schuler and Namioka 1993). This is a widely advocated approach to designing computer systems, for example, and it is interesting to note that the increasingly common practice of "concurrent engineering" (Carter and Baker 1991) can also be viewed as a kind of "participatory design." In concurrent engineering, people who design a product do not simply hand the design "over the transom" to those who design its manufacturing process. Instead, they work together concurrently to create designs that can be manufactured more easily.

In computer systems the usability dependency occurs whenever one part of a system must use information produced by another. In general, this dependency is managed by designing various kinds of interchange languages and other standards.

Managing Simultaneity Constraints   Another common kind of dependency between activities is that they need to occur at the same time (or cannot occur at the same time). Whenever people schedule meetings, for instance, they must satisfy this constraint.

Another example of this constraint occurs in the design of computer systems in which multiple processes (i.e., instruction streams) can be executed simultaneously. (These systems may have multiple processors or a single processor which is shared between the processes.) In general, the instructions of the different processes can be executed in any order. Permitting this indeterminacy improves the performance of the system (e.g., one process can be executed while another waits for data to be input) but can cause problems when the processes must share data or resources. System designers must therefore provide mechanisms that restrict the possible orderings of the instructions by synchronizing the processes (i.e., ensuring that particular instructions from different streams are executed at the same time; Dubois et al. 1988).

Synchronization primitives can be used to control sharing of data between a producer and consumer process to ensure that all data is used exactly once (the producer–consumer problem) or to prevent simultaneous writes to a shared data item (the mutual exclusion problem). For example, if two processes simultaneously read and then update the same data (e.g., adding a deposit to an account balance), one process might overwrite the value stored by the other.

One example of interdisciplinary transfer involving this concept is the work of Singh and colleagues in using computer science concepts about synchronized interactions to model process in human organizations (Singh and Rein 1992).

Managing Task–Subtask Dependencies

TOP-DOWN GOAL DECOMPOSITION   A common kind of dependency among activities is that a group of activities are all "subtasks" for achieving some overall goal. As we discuss in more detail below, there is a sense in which some overall evaluation criteria or "goals" are necessarily implied by the definition of coordination. The most commonly analyzed case of managing this dependency occurs when an individual or group decides to pursue a goal, and then decomposes this goal into activities (or subgoals) that together will achieve the original goal. In this case we call the process of choosing the goal selection, and the process of choosing the activities goal decomposition.

For example, the strategic planning process in human organizations is often viewed as involving this kind of goal selection and goal decomposition process. Furthermore an important role for all managers in a traditionally conceived hierarchy is to decompose the goals they are given into tasks that they can, in turn, delegate to people who work for them. There are, in general, many ways a given goal can be broken into pieces, and a long-standing topic in organization theory involves analyzing different possible decompositions such as by function, by product, by customer, and by geographical region (Mintzberg 1979). Some of these different goal decompositions for human organizations are analogous to ways computer systems can be structured (e.g., Malone and Smith 1988).

In computer systems we usually think of the goals as being predetermined, but an important problem involves how to break these goals into activities that can be performed separately. In a sense, for example, the essence of all computer programming is decomposing goals into elementary activities. For instance, programming techniques such as subroutine calls, modular programming, object-oriented programming, and so forth can all be thought of as techniques for structuring the process of goal decomposition (Liskov and Guttag 1986). In these cases the goal decomposition is performed by a human programmer. Another example of goal decomposition in computer systems is provided by work on planning in artificial intelligence (e.g., Chapman 1987; Fikes and Nilsson 1971; Allen et al. 1990). In this case goals are decomposed by a planning program into a sequence of elementary activities, based on knowledge of the elementary activities available, their prerequisites, and their effects.

In some cases techniques for goal decomposition used in computer systems may suggest new ways of structuring human organizations. For example, Moses (1990) suggests that human organizations might sometimes be better off not as strict hierarchies but as multilayered structures in which any actor at one level could direct the activities of any actor at the next level down. This multilayered structure is analogous to successive layers of languages or "virtual machines" in a computer system (see Malone 1990).

Bottom-up Goal Identification   Even though the most commonly analyzed cases of coordination involve a sequential process of goal selection and then goal decomposition, the steps do not necessarily happen in this order. Another possibility, for instance, is that several actors realize that the things they are already doing (with small additions) could work together to achieve a new goal. For example, the creation of a new interdisciplinary research group may have this character. In human systems this bottom-up process of goal selection can often engender more commitment from the actors involved than a top-down assignment of responsibility.

Managing Other Dependencies   As noted above, the dependencies discussed so far are only a suggestive list of common dependencies. We believe there are many more dependencies to be identified and analyzed. For instance, when two divisions of a company both deal with the same customer, there is a shared reputation dependency between their activities: what one division does affects the customer's perception of the company as a whole, including the other division. As another example, when several people in the same office want to buy a new rug, a key problem is not how to allocate the rug, but what color or other characteristics it should have. We might call this, therefore, a shared characteristics dependency.

More generally, there are many types of dependencies between objects in the world that are managed by coordination processes. For instance, an important part of managing the design of complex manufactured products involves managing the dependencies between different subcomponents. At first glance our definition of coordination (as managing dependencies between activities) might appear to omit dependencies between objects that are not activities. We believe, however, that this focus has the advantage of greatly simplifying the analysis of a coordinated situation. In fact it appears that all dependencies that require coordination can be treated this way. For example, dependencies between components matter because they, explicitly or implicitly, affect the performance of some activities (e.g., designing or redesigning the components), and they can therefore be viewed as a source of dependencies between those activities.

In general, as these examples illustrate, there may be many ways of describing different dependencies, coordination processes, and their relationships to each other (e.g., Crowston 1991). We believe that there are many opportunities for further work along these lines.

Summary of Basic Coordination Processes   Table 2.2 loosely summarizes our discussion so far by listing examples of how common coordination processes have been analyzed in different disciplines. The key point of this table, and indeed of much of our discussion, is that the concepts of coordination theory can help identify similarities among concepts and results in different disciplines. These similarities, in turn, suggest how ideas can be transported back and forth across disciplinary boundaries and where opportunities exist to develop even deeper analyses.

2.2.3 Example: Analyzing the Task Assignment Process

So far, the examples we have described have mostly involved a single field or analogies that have been transported from one discipline to another. To illustrate the possibilities for developing abstract theories of coordination that can apply simultaneously to many different kinds of systems, let us consider the task assignment process as analyzed by Malone and Smith (Malone 1987; Malone and Smith 1988; see also related work by Baligh and Richartz 1967; Burton and Obel 1980a). As we have described in more detail elsewhere (Malone 1992), these analyses illustrate the kind of interdisciplinary interaction that our search for coordination theory encourages: the models grew originally out of designing distributed computer systems, they drew upon results from operations research, and they led eventually to new insights about the evolution of human organizations.

Table 2.2
Examples of how different disciplines have analyzed coordination processes

Coordination process	Computer science	Economics and operations research	Organization theory
Managing shared resources (including task assignments)	Techniques for processor memory allocation	Analyses of markets and other resource allocation mechanisms; scheduling algorithms and other optimization techniques	Analyses of different organizational structures; budgeting processes, organizational power, and resource dependence
Managing producer/consumer relationships including prerequisites and usability constraints)	Data flow and Petri net analyses	PERT charts, critical path methods; scheduling techniques	Participatory design; market research
Managing simultaneity constraints	Synchronization techniques, mutual exclusion	Scheduling techniques	Meeting scheduling; certain kinds of process modeling
Managing task/subtask relationship	Modularization techniques in programming; planning in artificial intelligence	Economies of scale and scope	Strategic planning; management by objectives; methods of grouping people into units

A Generic Task Assignment Problem   Consider the following task assignment problem: A system is producing a set of "products," each of which requires a set of "tasks" to be performed. The tasks are of various types, and each type of task can only be performed by "server" actors specialized for that kind of task. Furthermore the specific tasks to be performed cannot be predicted in advance; they only become known during the course of the process and then only to actors we will call "clients." This description of the task assignment problem is certainly not universally applicable, but it is an abstract description that can be applied to many common task assignment situations. For instance, the tasks might be (1) designing, manufacturing, and marketing different kinds of automobiles, or (2) processing steps in different jobs on a computer network.

Possible Coordination Mechanisms   One (highly centralized) possibility for solving this task assignment problem is for all the clients and servers to send all their information to a central decision maker who decides which servers will perform which tasks and then notifies them accordingly. Another (highly decentralized) possibility is suggested by the competitive bidding scheme for computer networks formalized by Smith and Davis (1981). In this scheme a client first broadcasts an announcement message to all potential servers. This message includes a description of the activity to be performed and the qualifications required. The potential servers then use this information to decide whether to submit a bid on the action. If they decide to bid, their bid message includes a description of their qualifications and their availability for performing the action. The client uses these bid messages to decide which server should perform the activity and then sends an award message to notify the server that is selected.

Malone and Smith (Malone 1987; Malone and Smith 1988) analyzed several alternative coordination mechanisms like these, each of which is analogous to a mechanism used in human organizations. In particular, they developed formal models to represent various forms of markets (centralized and decentralized) and various forms of hierarchies (based on products or functions). Then they used techniques from queueing theory and probability theory to analyze trade-offs among these structures in terms of production costs, coordination costs, and vulnerability costs. For instance, they showed that the centralized schemes had lower coordination costs but were more vulnerable to processor failures. Decentralized markets, on the other hand, were much less vulnerable to processor failures but had high coordination costs. And decentralized hierarchies ("product hierarchies") had low coordination costs, but they had unused processor capacity that led to high production costs.

Applying These Models to Various Kinds of Systems   Even though these models omit many important aspects of human organizations and computer systems, they help illuminate a surprisingly wide range of phenomena. For instance, as Malone and Smith (1988) show, the models are consistent with a number of previous theories about human organizational design (e.g., March and Simon 1958; Galbraith 1973; Williamson 1985) and with major historical changes in the organizational forms of both human organizations (Chandler 1962, 1977) and computer systems. These models also help analyze design alternatives for distributed scheduling mechanisms in computer systems, and they suggest ways of analyzing the structural changes associated with introducing new information technology into organizations (section 2.3.2; Crowston et al. 1987; Malone and Smith 1988).

2.2.4   Other Processes Needed for Coordination

In addition to the processes described above for managing specific dependencies, two other processes deserve specific attention: group decision-making and communication. It is sometimes possible to analyze these processes as ways of managing specific dependencies. For instance, communication can be viewed as a way of managing producer–consumer relationships for information. However, because of the importance of these two processes in almost all instances of coordination, we describe them separately here.

Group Decision-Making   Many coordination processes require making decisions that affect the activities of a group. For instance, in sharing resources, a group must somehow "decide" how to allocate the resources; in managing task–subtask dependencies, a group must "decide" how to segment tasks. In all these cases the alternative ways of making group decisions give rise to alternative coordination processes. For example, any group decision can, in principle, be made by authority (e.g., a "manager" decides), by voting, or by consensus (resulting from negotiation).

Because of the importance of group decision-making in coordination, answers to questions about group decision making (e.g., Simon 1976; Arrow 1951) will be important for developing coordination theory. For instance, what are the decision-making biases in groups (e.g., Janis and Mann 1977) as opposed to individuals (Kahneman and Tversky 1973)? How do computer-based group decision-making tools affect these processes (e.g., Kraemer and King 1988; Dennis et al. 1988; Kiesler et al. 1984)? Can we determine optimal ways of allocating tasks and sharing information for making group decisions (Miao et al. 1992)? How do (or should) decision-making processes change in situations where both rapid response and high reliability are required (Roberts et al. 1994).

Communication   As with decision-making, there is a already a great deal of theory about communication, both from a technical point of view (e.g., Shannon and Weaver 1949) and from an organizational point of view (e.g., Allen 1977; Rogers and Agarwala-Rogers 1976; Weick 1969). One obvious way of generating new coordination processes, for example, is by considering alternative forms of communication (synchronous vs. asynchronous, paper vs. electronic) for all the places in a process where information needs to be transferred.

A coordination framework also highlights new aspects of these problems. For example, when we view communication as a way of managing producer–consumer relationships for information, we may be concerned about how to make the information "usable." How, for instance, can actors establish common languages that allow them to communicate in the first place? This question of developing standards for communication is of crucial concern in designing computer networks in general (Dertouzos 1991) and cooperative work tools in particular (e.g., Lee and Malone 1990). The process by which standards are developed is also of concern to economists, philosophers, and others (e.g., Farrell and Saloner 1985; Hirsch 1987).

A related set of questions arises when we are concerned about how a group of actors can come to have "common knowledge," that is, they all know something, and they also all know that they all know it. There is a growing literature about this and related questions in fields as diverse as computer science, economics, and linguistics (Halpern 1987; Aumann 1976; Milgrom 1981; Gray 1978; Cohen and Levesque 1991; Shoham 1993).

2.3 Applying a Coordination Perspective

2.3.1 Approaches to Analyzing Coordination in Different Kinds of Systems

Any scientific theory (indeed, any statement about the world) must neglect some things, in order to focus on others. For example, Kling (1980) describes how different perspectives (e.g., rational, structural, and political) on the use of information systems in organizations each illuminate aspects of reality neglected by the others. In some situations, one or another of these perspectives may be most important, and all of them are involved to some degree in any real situation. In applying coordination theory to any particular system, it may therefore be necessary to consider many other factors as well.

For instance, in designing a new computer system to help people coordinate their work, "details" about screen layout and response time may sometimes be as important as the basic functionality of the system, and the reputation of the manager who introduces the system in a particular organization may have more effect on the motivation of people to use it in that organization than any incentive structures designed into the system. Similarly, in designing a distributed processing computer system, the failure rates for different kinds of communications media and processors may be the primary design consideration, overwhelming any other considerations about how tasks are allocated among processors.

Parametric Analysis versus Baseline Analysis There are at least two ways an interdisciplinary theory can help deal with differences like these among systems: (1) parametric analysis and (2) baseline analysis.

PARAMETRIC ANALYSIS In parametric analysis the abstract theories include parameters which may be different for different kinds of systems. For instance, the principles of aerodynamics apply to both birds and airplanes, even though parameters such as size, weight, and energy expenditure are very different in the two kinds of systems. Similarly abstract models of coordination may include parameters for things like incentives, cognitive capacities, and communication costs which are very different in human, computational, and biological systems. Examples of models that have been applied to more than one kind of system in this way are summarized later in this section.

BASELINE ANALYSIS   In baseline analysis one theory is used as a baseline for comparison to the actual behavior of a system, and deviations from the baseline are then explained with other theories. For example, in behavioral decision theory (e.g., Kahneman and Tversky 1973), mathematical decision theory is used to analyze the ways people actually make decisions. In the cases where people depart from the prescriptions of the normative mathematical theory, new theories are developed to explain the differences. Even though the original mathematical theory does not completely explain people's actual behavior, the anomalies explained by the new theories could not even have been recognized without a baseline theory for comparison. This suggests that an important part of coordination theory will be behavioral coordination theory in which careful observations of actual coordination in human systems are used to develop, test, and augment abstract models of coordination.

Identifying the Components of Coordination in a Situation   In order to analyze a situation in terms of coordination, it is sometimes important to explicitly identify the components of coordination in that situation. According to our definition of coordination above, coordination means "managing dependencies between activities." Therefore, since activities must, in some sense, be performed by actors," the definition implies that all instances of coordination include actors performing activities that are interdependent.[3] It is also often useful to identify evaluation criteria for judging how well the dependencies are being "managed." For example, we can often identify some overall "goals" of the activity (e.g., producing automobiles or printing a report) and other dimensions for evaluating how well those goals are being met (e.g., minimizing time or costs). Some coordination processes may be faster or more accurate than others, for instance, and the costs of more coordination are by no means always worthwhile.

It is important to realize that there is no single right way to identify these components of coordination in a situation. For instance, we may sometimes analyze everything that happens in a manufacturing division as one activity, while at other times, we may want to analyze each station on an assembly line as a separate activity. As another example, when we talk about muscular coordination, we implicitly regard different parts of the same person's body as separate actors performing separate activities.

CONFLICTING GOALS   One important case of identifying evaluation criteria occurs when there are conflicting goals in a situation. In analyzing coordination in human

---

3. See Baligh and Burton (1981), Baligh (1986), Barnard (1964), Malone (1987), Malone and Smith (1988), McGrath (1984), and Mintzberg (1979) for related decompositions of coordination.

organizations, it is often useful to simply ask people what their goals are and evaluate their behavior in terms of these criteria. However, some amount of goal conflict is nearly always present (e.g., Ciborra 1987; Williamson 1985; Schelling 1960), and people may be unable or unwilling to accurately report their goals, anyway. To understand these situations, it is often useful to both try to identify the conflicting goals and also to analyze the behavior of the system in terms of some overall evaluation criteria. For instance, different groups in a company may compete for resources and people, but this very competition may contribute to the company's overall ability to produce useful products (e.g., Kidder 1981).

Another important example of conflicting goals occurs in market transactions: as we saw above, all participants in a market might have the goal of maximizing their own individual benefits, but we, as observers, can evaluate the market as a coordination mechanism in terms of how well it satisfies overall criteria such as maximizing consumer utilities (e.g., Debreu 1959) or "fairly" distributing economic resources.

Preview of Examples   In the remainder of this section we describe examples of how concepts about coordination have been applied in three different areas: (1) understanding the new possibilities for human organizations and markets provided by information technology, (2) designing cooperative work tools, and (3) designing distributed and parallel computer systems. The early examples use very general notions of coordination; the later ones are more explicit in their identification of specific components of coordination.

This list is not intended to be a comprehensive list of all ways that theories of coordination could be applied. In fact most of the work we describe here did not explicitly use the term "coordination theory." We have chosen examples, however, to illustrate the wide range of applications for interdisciplinary theories about coordination.

2.3.2   Understanding the Effects of Information Technology on Organizations and Markets

Managers, organization theorists, and others have long been interested in how the widespread use of information technology (IT) may change the ways human organizations and markets will be structured (e.g., Leavitt and Whisler 1958; Simon 1976). One of the most important contributions of coordination theory may be to help understand these possibilities better.

To illustrate how the explicit study of coordination might help with this endeavor, we begin with a very general argument that does not depend on any of the detailed analyses of coordination we have seen so far in this chapter.[4] Instead, this argument starts with the simple observation that coordination is itself an activity that has costs. Even though there are many other forces that may affect the way coordination is performed in organizations and markets (e.g., global competition, national culture, government regulation, and interest rates), one important factor is clearly its cost, and that is the focus of this argument. In particular, it seems quite plausible to assume that information technology is likely to significantly reduce the costs of certain kinds of coordination (e.g., Crawford 1982).

Now, using some elementary ideas from microeconomics about substitution and elasticity of demand, we can make some simple predictions about the possible effects of reducing coordination costs. It is useful to illustrate these effects by analogy with similar changes in the costs of transportation induced by the introduction of trains and automobiles:

1. A first-order effect of reducing transportation costs with trains and automobiles was simply some substitution of the new transportation technologies for the old: people began to ride on trains more and in horse-drawn carriages less.

2. A second-order effect of reducing transportation costs was to increase the amount of transportation used: people began to travel more when this could be done more cheaply and conveniently in trains than on foot.

3. Finally, a third-order effect was to allow the creation of more "transportation-intensive" structures: people eventually began to live in distant suburbs and use shopping malls—both examples of new structures that depended on the widespread availability of cheap and convenient transportation.

Similarly we can expect several effects from using new information technologies to reduce the costs of coordination:

1. A first-order effect of reducing coordination costs with information technology may be to substitute information technology for some human coordination. For instance, many banks and insurance companies have substituted automated systems for large numbers of human clerks in their back offices. It has also long been commonplace to predict that computers will lead to the demise of middle management because the communication tasks performed by middle managers could be performed less expensively by computers (e.g., Leavitt and Whisler 1958). This prediction was not fulfilled for several decades after it was made, but many people believe

---

4. See Malone (1992) and Malone and Rockart (1991) for more detailed versions of the argument in this section.

that it finally began to happen with large numbers of middle management layoffs in the 1980s and 1990s.

2. A second-order effect of reducing coordination costs may be to increase the overall amount of coordination used. In some cases this may overwhelm the first order effect. For instance, in one case we studied, a computer conferencing system was used to help remove a layer of middle managers (see Crowston, Malone, and Lin 1987). Several years later, however, almost the same number of new positions (for different people at the same grade level) had been created for staff specialists in the corporate staff group, many of whom were helping to develop new computer systems. One interpretation of this outcome is that the managerial resources no longer needed for simple communication tasks could now be applied to more complex analysis tasks that would not previously have been undertaken.

3. A third-order effect of reducing coordination costs may be to encourage a shift toward the use of more "coordination-intensive" structures. In other words, coordination structures that were previously too "expensive" will now become more feasible and desirable. For example, as noted above, information technology can facilitate what some observers (e.g., Mintzberg 1979; Toffler 1970) have called adhocracies. Adhocracies are very flexible organizations, including many shifting project teams and highly decentralized networks of communication among relatively autonomous entrepreneurial groups. One of the disadvantages of adhocracies is that they require large amounts of unplanned communication and coordination throughout an organization. However, technologies such as electronic mail and computer conferencing can help reduce the costs of this communication, and advanced information sharing tools (e.g., Malone et al. 1987; Lotus 1989) may help make this communication more effective at much larger scales.

What might these new coordination-intensive structure be like? Let us consider recent work on two specific questions about the effects of information technology on organizations and markets: (1) How will IT affect the size of organizations? and (2) How will IT affect the degree of centralization of decision-making in organizations? This work does not focus explicitly on any specific dependencies. Instead, it compares two pairs of general coordination mechanisms that can manage many such dependencies: (1) market transactions versus internal decision-making with firms and (2) centralized versus decentralized managerial decisions.

Firm Size   Malone, Yates, and Benjamin (1987) have used ideas from transaction cost theory to systematically analyze how information technology will affect firm size and, more generally, the use of markets as a coordination structure. They conclude that by reducing the costs of coordination, information technology may lead to an overall shift toward smaller firms and proportionately more use of markets—rather than internal decisions within firms—to coordinate economic activity.

This argument has two parts. First, since market transactions often have higher coordination costs than internal coordination (Williamson 1985; Malone, Yates, and Benjamin 1987), an overall reduction in the "unit costs" of coordination should lead to markets becoming more desirable in situations where internal transactions were previously favored. This, in turn, should lead to less vertical integration and smaller firms.

For example, after the introduction of computerized airline reservation systems, the proportion of reservations made through travel agents (rather than by calling the airline directly) went from 35 to 70 percent. Thus the function of selling reservations was "disintegrated" from the airlines and moved to a separate firm—the travel agents. Econometric analyses of the overall US economy in the period 1975 to 1985 are also consistent with these predictions: the use of information technology appears to be correlated with decreases in both firm size and vertical integration (Brynjolfsson et al. 1994).

If we extrapolate this trend to a possible long-run extreme, it leads us to speculate that we might see increasing use of "firms" containing only one person. For instance, Malone and Rockart (1991) suggest that there may someday be electronic marketplaces of "intellectual mercenaries" in which it is possible to electronically assemble "overnight armies" of thousands of people who work for a few hours or days to solve a particular problem and then disband. Flexible arrangements like this might appeal especially to people who had a strong desire for autonomy—the freedom to choose their own hours and working situations.

Centralization of Decision-Making Gurbaxani and Whang (1991) have used ideas from agency theory to systematically analyze the effects on centralization of the reductions in coordination costs enabled by IT. They conclude that IT can lead to either centralization or decentralization, depending on how it is used. While this conclusion may not be surprising, the structure of their analysis helps us understand the factors involved more clearly: (1) When IT primarily reduces decision information costs, it leads to more centralization. For instance, the Otis elevator company used IT to centralize the reporting and dispatching functions of their customer service system, instead of having these functions distributed to numerous remote field offices (Stoddard 1986). (2) On the other hand, when IT primarily reduces agency costs, it leads to more decentralization. As used here, agency costs are the costs of employees not acting in the interests of the firm. For instance, when one insurance company developed a system that more effectively monitored their salespeople's overall performance, they were able to decentralize to the salespeople many of the decisions that had previously been made centrally (Bruns and McFarlan 1987). Overall, this bidirectional trend for IT and centralization is consistent with empirical studies of this question (Attewell and Rule 1984).

An alternative approach to this question is provided by (Danziger et al. 1982). In a sense this work can be considered a kind of "behavioral coordination theory." In studies of computerization decisions in forty-two local governments in the United States, they found that changes in centralization of power were not best explained any of the formal factors one might have expected. Instead, they found that since people who already have power influence computerization decisions, the new uses of computers tend to reinforce the existing power structure, increasing the power of those who already have it.

2.3.3 Designing Cooperative Work Tools

There has recently been a great deal of interest in designing computer tools to help people work together more effectively (e.g., Greif 1988; Johansen 1988; Ellis et al. 1991; Peterson 1986; Tatar 1988, 1990; additional references in table 2.3). Using terms such as "computer-supported cooperative work" and "groupware" these systems perform functions such as helping people collaborate on writing the same document, managing projects, keeping track of tasks, and finding, sorting, and prioritizing electronic messages. Other systems in this category help people display and manipulate information more effectively in face-to-face meetings and represent and share the rationales for group decisions.

In this section we will describe how ideas about coordination have been helpful in suggesting new systems, classifying systems, and analyzing how these systems are used.

Using Coordination Concepts from Other Disciplines to Suggest Design Ideas   One way of generating new design ideas for cooperative work tools is to look to other disciplines that deal with coordination. For instance, even though the following authors did not explicitly use the term "coordination theory," they each used ideas about coordination from other disciplines to help develop cooperative work tools.

Using ideas from linguistics and philosophy about speech acts. Winograd and Flores (Flores et al. 1988; Winograd 1987; Winograd and Flores 1986) have developed a theoretical perspective for analyzing group action based heavily on ideas from linguistics (e.g., Searle 1975). This perspective emphasizes different kinds of speech acts, such as requests and commitments. For example, Winograd and Flores analyzed a generic "conversation for action" in terms of the possible states and transitions involved when one actor performs a task at the request of another. An actor may respond to a request, for instance, by (1) promising to fulfill the request, (2) declining the request, (3) reporting that the request has already been completed, or (4) simply acknowledging that the request has been received. The analysis of this conversation type (and several others) provided a primary basis for designing the Coordinator, a computer-based cooperative work tool. For example, the Coordinator helps people make and keep track of requests and commitments to each other. It thus supports what we might call the "mutual agreeing" part of the task assignment process.

Using ideas from artificial intelligence and organization theory about blackboards and adhocracies. Malone (1990) describes how ideas from artificial intelligence and organization theory combined to suggest a new tool for routing information within organizations. In the "blackboard architecture," program modules interact by searching a global blackboard for their inputs and posting their outputs on the same blackboard (Nii 1986; Erman et al. 1980). This provides very flexible patterns of communication between different program modules: any module can communicate with any other module, even when this interaction is not explicitly anticipated by the program designer. In adhocracies, as we saw above, just this kind of unplanned, highly decentralized communication is essential for rapidly responding to new situations (Mintzberg 1979; Toffler 1970). Stimulated, in part, by this need for an "organizational blackboard," Malone and colleagues designed the Information Lens system (Malone et al. 1987). A central component of this system is an "anyone server" that lets people specify rules about what kinds of electronic messages they are interested in seeing. The system then uses these rules to route all nonprivate electronic messages to everyone in the organization who might want to see them. (To help people deal with large numbers of messages, another part of the system uses a different set of rules to sort and prioritize the messages people receive.)

Using ideas from philosophy and rhetoric about decision-making. Two cooperative work tools, gIBIS (Conklin and Begeman 1988) and Sibyl (Lee 1990), are designed to help groups of people make decisions more effectively. To do this, they explicitly represent the arguments (and counterarguments) for different alternatives a group might choose. Both these systems are based on ideas from philosophy and rhetoric about the logical structure of decision-making. For example, the basic elements in the gIBIS system (issues, positions, and arguments) are taken from a philosophical analysis of argumentation by Rittel (1970). The constructs for representing arguments in Sibyl are based on the work of philosophers like Toulmin (1958) and Rescher (1977).

Using ideas from computer science about parallel processes. Holt (1988) describes a theoretical language used for designing coordination tools that is based, in part, on ideas about Petri nets, a formalism used in computer science to represent process flows in distributed or parallel systems (Peterson 1981, 1977). This language is part of a larger theoretical framework called "coordination mechanics" and has been used to design a "coordination environment" to help people work together on computer networks.

SUMMARY OF EXAMPLES   Clearly, ideas about coordination from other disciplines do not guarantee our developing useful cooperative work tools. However, we feel that considering these examples within the common framework of coordination theory provides two benefits: (1) it suggests that no one of these perspectives is the complete story, and (2) it suggests that we should look to previous work in various disciplines for more insights about coordination that could lead to new cooperative work tools.

A Taxonomy of Cooperative Work Tools   As shown in table 2.3, the framework we have suggested for coordination provides a natural way of classifying existing cooperative work systems according to the coordination processes they support. Some of these systems primarily emphasize a single coordination-related process. For instance, electronic mail systems primarily support the message transport part of communication, and meeting scheduling tools primarily support the synchronization process (i.e., arranging for several people to attend a meeting at the same time). There is a sense, of course, in which each of these systems also support other processes (e.g., a simple electronic mail system can be used to assign tasks), but we have categorized the systems here according to the processes they explicitly emphasize.

Some of the systems also explicitly support several processes. For example, the Information Lens system supports both the communication routing process (by rules that distribute messages to interested people) and a form of resource allocation process (by helping people prioritize their own activities using rules that sort messages they receive). And the Polymer system helps people decompose goals into tasks and sequence the tasks (e.g., to prepare a monthly report, first gather the project reports and then write a summary paragraph).

One possibility raised by this framework is that it might help identify new opportunities for cooperative work tools. For instance, the Coordinator focuses on supporting one part of the task assignment process (mutual agreement on commitments). However, it does not provide much help for the earlier part of the process involving selecting an actor to perform the task in the first place (see section 2.3). New tools, such as an "electronic yellow pages" or bidding schemes like those suggested by Turoff (1983) and Malone (1987) might be useful for this purpose.

Table 2.3
Taxonomy of cooperative work tools based on the processes they support

Process	Example systems
Managing shared resources (task assignment and prioritization)	Coordinator (Winograd and Flores 1986)
	Information lens (Malone et al. 1987)
Managing producer/consumer relationships (sequencing prerequisites)	Polymer (Croft and Lefkowitz 1988)
Managing simultaneity constraints (synchronizing)	Meeting scheduling tools (e.g., Beard et al. 1990)
Managing task/subtask relationship (goal decomposition)	Polymer (Croft and Lefkowitz 1988)
Group decision-making	gIBIS (Conklin and Begeman 1988) Sibyl (Lee 1990) electronic meeting rooms (e.g., Stefik et al. 1987; Dennis et al. 1988; DeSanctis and Gallupe 1987)
Communication	Electronic mail, Computer conferencing (e.g., Lotus 1989) Electronic meeting rooms (e.g., Stefik et al. 1987; Dennis et al. 1988; DeSanctis and Gallupe 1987) Information lens (Malone et al. 1987) Collaborative authoring tools (e.g., Fish et al. 1988; Ellis et al. 1990; Neuwirth et al. 1990)

Another intriguing possibility suggested by this framework is that it might be possible to implement "primitives" for a number of different coordination-related processes in the same environment, and then let people combine these primitives in various ways to help solve particular coordination problems. This is one of the goals of the Oval system (Malone et al. 1992; Lai et al. 1988).

Analyzing Incentives for Using Cooperative Work Tools Another use for coordination theory in designing cooperative work tools can be to help systematically evaluate proposed or actual systems. For example, Markus and Connolly (1990) systematically analyze how the payoffs to individual users of a cooperative work system depend on how many other people are using the system. They do this by using an economic model from Schelling (1978) to extend Grudin's (1988) insights about the incentives to use cooperative work systems. For instance, on-line calendars and many other cooperative work applications involve "discretionary databases" which users can view or update as they see fit. For each individual user, however, the benefits of viewing the database can be obtained without contributing anything. Thus it is often in the interests of each individual user to use the database without making the effort required to contribute to it. Unfortunately, the equilibrium state of a system like this is for no one to ever contribute anything!

An interesting empirical illustration of this phenomenon occurred in a study of how one large consulting firm used the Lotus Notes group conferencing system. In this study Orlikowski (1992) found that there were surprising inconsistencies between the intended uses of the system and the actual incentives in the organization. For instance, Orlikowski observed that this organization (like many others) was one in which people were rewarded for being the "expert" on something—for knowing things that others did not. Should we be surprised, therefore, that many people were reluctant to spend much effort putting the things they knew into a database where everyone else could easily see them?

These observations do not, of course, mean that conferencing systems like this one cannot be useful in organizations. What they do mean, however, is that we must sometimes be sensitive to very subtle issues about things like incentives and organizational culture in order to obtain the full benefits of such systems. For instance, it might be desirable in this organization to include, as part of an employee's performance appraisal, a record of how often their contributions to the Notes database were used by other people in the organization.

2.3.4 Designing Distributed and Parallel Processing Computer Systems

Much recent activity in computer science has involved exploring a variety of distributed and parallel processing computer architectures. In many ways physically connecting the processors to each other is easy compared to the difficulty of coordinating the activities of many different processors working on different aspects of the same problem.

In this section we describe examples of work that has addressed these issues in an explicitly interdisciplinary way, drawing on insights from other disciplines or kinds of systems to design or analyze distributed or parallel computer systems. In particular, we consider examples of (1) analogies with social and biological systems as a source of design ideas and (2) quantitative tools for analyzing alternative designs.

Analogies with Social and Biological Systems as a Source of Design Ideas   Competitive bidding markets for resource allocation. One of the basic problems in designing distributed or parallel computer systems is how to assign tasks to processors, and several distributed computer systems have addressed this problem with competitive bidding mechanisms based on analogies with human markets. For example, the Contract Nets protocol (Smith and Davis 1981; Davis and Smith 1983) formalizes a sequence of messages to be exchanged by computer processors sharing tasks in a network. The "contracts" are arbitrary computational tasks that can potentially be performed by any of a number of processors on the network, the "clients" are machines at which these tasks originate, and the "contractors" are machines that might process the tasks (i.e., the servers). The sequence of announcement, bid, and award messages used by this protocol was described above in our analysis of the task assignment process (section 2.3). One of the desirable features of this system is its great degree of decentralization and the flexibility it provides for how both clients and contractors can make their decisions. For instance, clients may select contractors on the basis of estimated completion time or the presence of specialized data; contractors may select tasks to bid on based on the size of the task or how long the task has been waiting.

Using these or similar ideas, a number of other bidding systems have been developed (e.g., Stankovic 1985; Kurose and Simha 1989). For instance, several bidding systems have been developed to allow personal workstations connected by a local area network to share tasks (Malone et al. 1988; Waldspurger et al. 1988). In this way users can take advantage of the unused processing capacity at idle workstations elsewhere on the network. Furthermore the local bidding "negotiations" can result in globally coherent processor scheduling according to various priorities (e.g., Malone et al. 1988). (For a review of several related systems and an analysis of a variety of bidding algorithms, see Drexler and Miller 1988; Miller and Drexler 1988.)

The notion of competitive bidding markets has also been suggested as a technique for storage management by Miller and Drexler (Miller and Drexler 1988; Drexler and Miller 1988). In their proposal, when object A wishes to maintain a pointer to object B, object A pays "rent" to the "landlord" of the space in which object B is stored. These rents are determined by competitive bidding, and when an object fails to pay rent, it is "evicted" (i.e., garbage collected). Their proposal includes various schemes for how to determine rents, how to pass rents along a chain of references, and how to keep track of the various costs and payments without excessive overhead. They conclude that this proposal is not likely to be practical for small-scale storage management (e.g., garbage collection of individual Lisp cells), but that it may well be useful for sharing large objects in complex networks that cross "trust boundaries" (e.g., interorganizational networks). The scheme also appears useful for managing local caching and the migration of objects between different forms of short-term and long-term storage.

"Scientific Communities" for Information Routing and Resource Allocation   Another central problem that arises in distributed and parallel processing systems is how and when to route information between processors. For instance, one interesting example of this problem arises in artificial intelligence programs that search a large space of possibilities, whose nature is not well known in advance. It is particularly useful, in this case, for processors to exchange information about intermediate results in such a way that each processor can avoid performing work that is rendered unnecessary by work already done elsewhere.

One solution to this problem is suggested by the Scientific Community Metaphor embodied in the Ether system (Kornfeld and Hewitt 1981; Kornfeld 1982). In this system, there are a number of "sprites," each analogous to an individual scientist, that operate in parallel and interact through a global database. Each sprite requires certain conditions to be true in the global database before it is "triggered." When a sprite is triggered, it may (1) compute new results that are added to the global database, (2) create new sprites that await conditions that will trigger them, or (3) stifle a collection of sprites whose work is now known to be unnecessary. In one example use of this system, Kornfeld (1982) shows how sharing intermediate results in this way can dramatically improve the time performance of an algorithm (even if it is executed by time-sharing a single processor). He calls this effect "combinatorial implosion."

This system also uses the scientific community metaphor to suggest a solution to the resource allocation problem for processors. Each sprite is "supported" by a "sponsor," and without a sponsor, a sprite will not receive any processing time to do its work. For instance, a sponsor may sometimes support both work directed toward proving some proposition and also work directed toward proving the negation of the proposition. Whenever one of these lines of work is successful, support is withdrawn from the other.

Analyzing Stability Properties of Resource Allocation Algorithms   Another way of applying coordination concepts is to help evaluate alternative designs of distributed and parallel processing computer systems. For instance, Huberman and his colleagues (Huberman and Hogg 1988; Lumer and Huberman 1990) have applied mathematical techniques like those used in chaos theory to analyze the dynamic behavior of distributed computer networks. In one case they analyze, for example, heavily loaded processors in a network transfer tasks to more lightly loaded processors according to a probabilistic process. When any processor in such a system can exchange tasks with any other processor, the behavior of the system is unstable for large numbers of processors (e.g., more than twenty-one processors in a typical example). However, when the processors are grouped hierarchically into clusters that exchange tasks frequently among themselves and only occasionally with other clusters, the system remains stable for arbitrarily large numbers of processors. This hierarchical arrangement has the disadvantage that it takes a long time to reach stability. In an intriguing analogy with human organizations, however, Huberman and his colleagues find that this disadvantage can be eliminated by having a few "lateral links" between different clusters in the hierarchy (Lumer and Huberman 1990).

Table 2.4
Sample applications of a coordination perspective

Application area	Examples of analyzing alternative designs	Examples of generating new design ideas
Organizational structures and information technology	Analyzing the effects of decreasing coordination costs on firm size, centralization, and internal structure	Creating temporary 'intellectual marketplaces' to solve specific problems.
Cooperative work tools	Analyzing how the payoffs to individual users of a system depend on the number of other users	Designing new tools for task assignment, information routing, and group decision-making
Distributed and parallel computer systems	Analyzing stability properties of load sharing algorithms in computer networks	Using competitive bidding mechanisms to allocate processors and memory in computer systems. Using a scientific community metaphor to organize parallel problem-solving.

2.3.5 Summary of Applications

As summarized in table 2.4, the examples we have described show how a coordination perspective can help (1) analyze alternative designs and (2) suggest new design ideas. In each case these applications depended upon interdisciplinary use of theories or concepts about coordination.

2.4 Research Agenda

We have seen how a number of different disciplines can contribute to answering the questions about coordination, and how theories of coordination can, in turn, be applied to the concerns of several different disciplines. What is needed to further develop this interdisciplinary study of coordination?

As we suggested above, a central concern of coordination theory should be identifying and analyzing specific coordination processes and structures. Therefore a critical item on the agenda for coordination research should be developing these analyses. A number of questions arise, as will be explored next.

2.4.1 Representing and Classifying Coordination Processes

How can we represent coordination processes? When should we use flowcharts, Petri nets, or state transition diagrams? Are there other notations that are even more perspicuous for analyzing coordination? How can we classify different coordination processes? For instance, can we usefully regard some coordination processes as "special cases" of others? How are different coordination processes combined when activities are actually performed?

Characterizing Dependencies   What kinds of dependencies are there? Are there ways to organize them that highlight common possibilities for managing them? Are some special cases of others? What causes dependencies? As we modify or alter a process, what techniques will be useful for keeping track of existing dependencies or identifying new ones? What techniques are useful for identifying dependencies in a field study of a particular process?

How General Are Coordination Processes?   Another set of questions has to do with how generic coordination processes really are: How far can we get by analyzing very general coordination processes, and when will we find that most of the important factors are specific to coordinating a particular kind of task? For example, are there general heuristics for coordination that are analogous to the general problem-solving heuristics studied in cognitive science and artificial intelligence?

2.4.2   Analyzing Specific Processes

At least as important as these general questions are analyses of specific processes. For example, how far can we go in analyzing alternative coordination processes for problems such as resource allocation? Can we characterize an entire "design space" for solutions to this problem and analyze the major factors that would favor one solution over another in specific situations? Could we do the same thing for other processes such as goal selection or managing timing dependencies? Are there other processes (e.g., managing other kinds of dependencies) that could be analyzed systematically in ways that have not yet been done?

In analyzing alternatives processes for specific problems, we might consider various kinds of properties: Which processes are least "expensive" in terms of production costs and coordination costs? Which processes are fastest? Which processes are most stable in the face of failures of actors or delays of information? Which processes are most susceptible to incentive problems? For instance, how does the presence of significant conflicts of interest among actors affect the desirability of different resource allocation methods? How do information processing limitations of actors affect the desirability of different methods? For example, are some methods appropriate for coordinating people that would not be appropriate for coordinating computer processors, and vice versa? What new methods for coordinating people become desirable when human information processing capacities are augmented by computers?

2.4.3   Applications and Methodologies

A critical part of the research agenda for this area is developing coordination theory in the context of various different kinds of systems. For instance, in the preceding section, we suggested numerous examples of these possibilities for human organizations and computer systems.

In some cases this work may involve applying previously developed theories to these application areas. In many cases, however, we expect that new systems or new observations of these systems will stimulate the development of new theories. For example, all of the following methodologies appear likely to be useful in developing coordination theory: (1) empirically studying coordination in human or other biological systems (e.g., field studies, laboratory studies, or econometric studies), (2) designing new technologies for supporting human coordination, (3) designing and experimenting with new methods for coordinating distributed and parallel processing computer systems, and (4) formal modeling of coordination processes (e.g., mathematical modeling or computer simulation).

2.5   Conclusions

Clearly, the questions we have just listed are only the beginning of a set of research issues in the interdisciplinary study of coordination. However, we believe they illustrate how the notion of "coordination" provides a set of abstractions that help unify questions previously considered separately in a variety of different disciplines and suggests avenues for further exploration.

While much work remains to be done, it appears that this approach can build upon much previous work in these different disciplines to help solve a variety of immediate practical needs, including (1) designing computer and communication tools that enable people to work together more effectively, (2) harnessing the power of multiple computer processors working simultaneously on related problems, and (3) creating more flexible and more satisfying ways of organizing collective human activity.

Appendix A: Previous Definitions of Coordination

"The operation of complex systems made up of components." (NSF-IRIS 1989)

"The emergent behavior of collections of individuals whose actions are based on complex decision processes." (NSF-IRIS 1989)

"Information processing within a system of communicating entities with distinct information states." (NSF-IRIS 1989)

"The joint efforts of independent communicating actors towards mutually defined goals." (NSF-IRIS 1989)

"Networks of human action and commitments that are enabled by computer and communications technologies." (NSF-IRIS 1989)

"Composing purposeful actions into larger purposeful wholes." (A. Holt, personal communication, 1989)

"Activities required to maintain consistency within a work product or to manage dependencies within the workflow." (Curtis 1989)

"The integration and harmonious adjustment of individual work efforts towards the accomplishment of a larger goal." (Singh 1992)

"The additional information processing performed when multiple, connected actors pursue goals that a single actor pursuing the same goals would not perform." (Malone 1988)

"The act of working together." (Malone and Crowston 1991)

Appendix B: Results about Coordination from Selected Fields

Even though use of the term "coordination theory" is quite recent, a great deal of previous work in various fields can contribute to the interdisciplinary understanding of coordination. In this appendix we briefly describe examples of such work from several different disciplines. These examples focus on cases where coordination has been analyzed in ways that appear to be generalizable beyond a single discipline or type of actor. We have not, of course, attempted to list all such cases; we have merely tried to pick illustrative examples from several disciplines.

Computer Science

Sharing Resources   Much research in computer science focuses on how to manage activities that share resources, such as processors, memory, and access to input–output devices (e.g., Deitel 1983). Other mechanisms have been developed to enforce resource allocations. For example, semaphores, monitors, and critical regions for mutual exclusion are programming constructs that can be used to grant a process exclusive access to a resource (e.g., Hoare 1975; Dijkstra 1968). Researchers in database systems have developed numerous other mechanisms, such as locking or timestamping, to allow multiple processes to concurrently access shared data without interference (e.g., Bernstein and Goodman 1981).

Managing Unreliable Actors   In addition protocols have been developed to ensure the reliability of transactions comprising multiple reads or writes on different processors (e.g., Kohler 1981). In particular, these protocols ensure that either all a transaction's operations are performed or none are, even if some of the processors fail.

Segmenting and Assigning Tasks   One of the important problems in allocating work to processors is how to divide up the tasks. For example, Gelernter and Carrerio (1989) discuss three alternative ways of dividing parallel programs into units: according to the type of work to be done, according to the subparts of the final output, or simply according to which processor is available.

Managing Information Flows   Another important set of issues involves managing the flow of information. For instance, researchers in artificial intelligence and particularly in distributed artificial intelligence (DAI; e.g., Bond and Gasser 1988; Huhns and Gasser 1989) have used "blackboard architectures" to allow processes to share information without having to know precisely which other processes need it (Nii 1986; Erman et al. 1980), and "partial global plans" to allow actors to recognize when they need to exchange more information (Durfee and Lesser 1987).

Economics and Operations Research

In a sense, almost all of economics involves the study of coordination, with a special focus on how incentives and information flows affect the allocation of resources among actors. For example, classical microeconomics analyzes how different sources of supply and demand can interact locally in a market in ways that result in a globally coherent allocation of resources. Among the major results of this theory are formal proofs that (under appropriate mathematical conditions) if consumers each maximize their individual "utilities" and firms each maximize their individual profits, then the resulting allocation of resources will be globally "optimal" in the sense that no one's utilities can be increased without decreasing someone else's (e.g., Debreu 1959).

   Some more recent work in economics has focused on the limitations of markets and contracts for allocating resources. For instance, transaction cost theory analyzes the conditions under which a hierarchy is a better way of coordinating multiple actors than a market (e.g., Williamson 1975). Agency theory focuses on how to create incentives for some actors ("agents") to act in a way that advances the interests of other actors ("principals") even when the principals cannot observe everything their agents are doing (Ross 1973). One result of this theory is that there are some situations where no incentives can motivate an agent to perform optimally from the principal's point of view (Jensen and Meckling 1976).

Finally, some parts of economics focus explicitly on information flows. For example, team theory and its descendants analyze how information should be exchanged when multiple actors need to make interdependent decisions but when all agents have the same ultimate goals (e.g., Marschak and Radner 1972; Hurwicz 1973; Reiter 1986). Mechanism design theory also analyzes how to provide incentives for actors to reveal information they possess, even when they have conflicting goals. For example, this theory has been applied to designing and analyzing various forms of auctions. In a "second price auction," for instance, each participant submits a sealed bid, and the highest bidder is only required to pay the amount of the second highest bid. It can be shown that this mechanism motivates the bidders to each reveal the true value they place on the item being sold, rather than trying to "game the system" by bidding only enough to surpass what they expect to be the next highest bid (Myerson 1981).

Operations research analyzes the properties of various coordination mechanisms, but operations research also includes a special focus on developing optimal techniques for coordination decisions. For instance, operations research includes analyses of various scheduling and queueing policies and techniques such as linear programming and dynamic programming for making resource allocation decisions optimally (e.g., Dantzig 1963).

Organization Theory

Research in organization theory, drawing on disciplines such as sociology and psychology, focuses on how people coordinate their activities in formal organizations. A central theme in this work has involved analyzing general issues about coordination (e.g., Simon 1976; March and Simon 1958; Thompson 1967; Galbraith 1977; Lawrence and Lorsch 1967; summarized by Mintzberg 1979; and Malone 1990). We can loosely paraphrase the key ideas of this work as follows:

All activities that involve more than one actor require (1) some way of dividing activities among the different actors and (2) some way of managing the interdependencies between the different activities (March and Simon 1958; Lawrence and Lorsch 1967). Interdependencies between activities can be of (at least) three kinds: (a) pooled, where the activities share or produce common resources but are otherwise independent, (b) sequential, where some activities depend on the completion of others before beginning, and (c) reciprocal, where each activity requires inputs from the other (Thompson 1967). These different kinds of interdependencies can be managed by a variety of coordination mechanisms, such as standardization, where predetermined rules govern the performance of each activity; direct supervision, where one actor manages interdependencies on a case-by-case basis, and mutual adjustment, where each actor makes ongoing adjustments to manage the interdependencies (March and Simon 1958; Galbraith 1973; Mintzberg 1979).

These coordination mechanisms can be used to manage interdependencies, not only between individual activities, but also between groups of activities. One criterion for grouping activities into units is to minimize the difficulties of managing these intergroup interdependencies. For example, activities with the strongest interdependencies are often grouped into the smallest units, then these units are grouped into larger units with other units with which they have weaker interdependencies. Various combinations of the coordination mechanisms, together with different kinds of grouping, give rise to the different organizational structures common in human organizations, including functional hierarchies, product hierarchies, and matrix organizations. For instance, sometimes all activities of the same type (e.g., manufacturing) might be grouped together in order to take advantage of economies of scale; at other times, all activities for the same product (e.g., marketing, manufacturing, and engineering) might be grouped together to simplify managing the interdependencies between the activities.

Biology

Many parts of biology involve studying how different parts of living entities interact. For instance, human physiology can be viewed as a study of how the activities of different parts of a human body are coordinated in order to keep a person alive and healthy. Other parts of biology involve studying how different living things interact with each other. For instance, ecology can be viewed as the study of how the activities of different plants and animals are coordinated to maintain a "healthy" environment.

Some of the most intriguing studies of biological coordination involve coordination between different animals in a group. For example, Mangel (1988) discusses the optimal hunting pack size for lions, who trade the benefit of an increased chance of catching something against the cost of having to share what they catch. Deneubourg (1989) point out that the interaction between simple rules—such as "do what my neighbor is doing"—and the environment may lead to a variety of collective behaviors.

The most striking examples of such group behaviors are in social insects, such as honey bees or army ants, where the group displays often quite complex behavior, despite the simplicity of the individuals (e.g., Franks 1989; Seeley 1989). Using a variety of simple rules, these insects "allocate" individual workers at economically efficient levels to a variety of tasks-including searching for new food sources, gathering nectar or pollen from particular sources (bees), carrying individual food items back to the bivouac (ants), guarding the hive (bees) and regulating the group temperature. For example, in honey bees, the interaction of two simple local rules controls the global allocation of food collectors to particular food sources. First, nectar storing bees unload nectar from foraging bees returning to the hive at a rate that depends on the richness of the nectar. Second, if bees are unloaded rapidly, they recruit other bees to their food source. The result of these two rules is that more bees collect food from better sources. Seeley (1989) speculates that this decentralized control may occur because it provides faster responses to local stresses (Miller 1978), or it may be simply because bees have not evolved any more global means of communication.

Acknowledgments

Parts of this chapter were included in three previous papers: Malone (1988), Malone and Crowston (1990), and Malone and Crowston (1991). The work was supported, in part, by Digital Equipment Corporation, the National Science Foundation (Grant Nos. IRI-8805798 and IRI-8903034), and other sponsors of the MIT Center for Coordination Science.

We are especially grateful to Deborah Ancona, John Carroll, Michael Cohen, Randall Davis, Rob Kling, John Little, and Wanda Orlikowski for comments on earlier versions of the chapter, and to participants in numerous seminars and workshops at which these ideas have been presented.

3 A Taxonomy of Organizational Dependencies and Coordination Mechanisms

Kevin Crowston

Although you will perform with different ingredients for different dishes, the same general processes are repeated over and over again. As you enlarge your repertoire, you will find that the seemingly endless babble of recipes begins to fall rather neatly into groups of theme and variations . . .
—*Child, Bertholle, and Beck* (1981)

3.1 Introduction

Interdependency and coordination have been perennial topics in organization studies. The two are related because coordination is seen as a response to problems caused by dependencies. For example, Thompson (1967) hypothesized three coordination mechanisms—standardization, plan, and mutual adjustment—used in response to three different patterns of dependencies—pooled, sequential, or reciprocal (pp. 54–55). Most studies, however, describe dependencies and coordination mechanisms only in general terms, without characterizing in detail differences between dependencies, the problems dependencies create or how the proposed coordination mechanisms address those problems (Grant 1996; Medema 1996). This vagueness makes it difficult or impossible to determine what alternative coordination mechanisms might be useful in a given circumstance. Similarly it is hard to translate from dependencies to specifications of individual activities or to uses of information and communication technologies (ICT) to support a process (e.g., as part of a business process redesign effort; Davenport and Short 1990; Hammer 1990; Harrington 1991; Harrison and Pratt 1993).

For example, consider the process of fixing bugs in a software product, a process that Crowston (1997) analyzed in a search for alternative coordination mechanisms. Using Thompson's theory, we might note that programmers all contribute code to a final product, and thus share a pooled dependency, and that they occasionally rely on each other's work, thus creating a sequential or sometimes reciprocal dependency. Furthermore, we might find, as predicted, that standardization, plans and mutual adjustment are all used. This analysis leaves many questions unanswered however. For example, how else might we organize this process? What dependencies would be left (or created) if instead of dividing the work among specialists, it were performed by generalists? Can we design a process that would reduce or eliminate the sequential dependencies between programmers? If not, what information do sequentially dependent programmers need to exchange and when? Would electronic mail or computer conferencing be useful to support this information exchange?

Although past conceptions of dependency do not directly address these questions, newer perspectives in artificial intelligence offer a more precise notion of dependency that do. In this chapter I draw on both literatures to develop a taxonomy of organizational dependencies and associated coordination mechanisms. The taxonomy suggests that there are four basic dependencies—task-resource, sharing, flow, and common output—each managed by a set of coordination mechanisms. The typology also suggests possible coordination problems caused by the fact that activities and objects in the world can be divided into subcomponents. The central section of this chapter is devoted to explaining these dependencies, their derivation, and the details of each.

3.2 Dependencies and Coordination

In this section I briefly review work on dependencies and coordination from the organizational and artificial intelligence literatures as a basis for formulating a new framework relating the two.

3.2.1 Organizational Research

Organizational researchers have long studied dependencies and coordination. Indeed, concern for this topic can be found among the earliest works. For example, Gulick and Urwick (1937) started with the need to divide work among multiple individuals, either because of the scope and scale of the work to be done or because of differences in individual capabilities. Division of labor in turn lead to the problem of coordinating interdependent work that is to be performed separately. Gulick and Urwick (1937) noted that without coordination, "a great deal of time may be lost, workers may get in each other's way, material may not be on hand when needed, things may be done in the wrong order, and there may even be a difference of opinion as to where the various doors and windows are to go" (p. 90).

Most organizational researchers have conceptualized dependencies as arising between actors (individuals, groups or organizations). For example, Litwak and Hylton (1962) defined interdependency as when two or more organizations must take each other into account if they are to accomplish their goals. Victor and Blackburn (1987) made this view of interdependency more precise by casting it in a game-theoretic framework. Dependency is defined by "extent to which a unit's outcomes are controlled directly by or are contingent upon the actions of another unit" (p. 490). McCann and Ferry (1979) similarly defined interdependency as, "when actions taken by one referent system affect the actions or outcomes of another referent system" (p. 113). They operationalized the degree of dependency in terms of the amount of resources exchanged, the frequency of transactions and the value of the resources to the recipient. Salancik (1986) proposed a technique for measuring dependency that accounts for transitive dependencies and allows for dependencies of different importance.

While dependencies are usually assumed to cause problems for the actors, these problems are rarely spelled out in detail. Instead, most authors suggest that as dependency increases, increasingly powerful coordination mechanisms be used, without specifying precisely what problems these mechanisms address. Alternately, actors might engage in actions to reduce the degree of dependency (McCann and Ferry 1979).

Rather than explicating the effects of a dependency on what actors can or should do, many researchers have focused on describing patterns of dependencies. Thompson (1967) hypothesized three patterns of dependency—pooled, sequential, and reciprocal—with corresponding coordination mechanisms, which he arranged in order of increasing strength. He further suggested that organizational hierarchies will tend to cluster groups with reciprocal interdependencies most closely, then those with sequential interdependencies, and finally those with pooled interdependencies. Van de Ven, Delbecq, and Koenig (1976) identified three modes of coordinating work activities—impersonal (plans and rules), personal (vertical supervision), and group (formal and informal meetings)—and discuss situational factors, including interdependency, that might determine which are used. They built upon Thompson's (1967) view of dependency, adding a fourth, team arrangements, in which tasks are worked on jointly and simultaneous (rather than being passed back and forth). They hypothesized that "increases in work flow interdependency from independent to sequential to reciprocal to team will be associated with ... large increases in the use of group coordination mechanisms" (p. 325), which they supported with data from sixteen offices and the headquarters of a state agency. Mintzberg (1979) described a similar set of coordination mechanisms: mutual adjustment, direct supervision and four kinds of standardization: of work processes, outputs, norms and skills.

Finally, much of this work hypothesized a one-to-one relationship between levels of patterns of dependencies and coordination mechanisms. One exception is McCann and Galbraith (1981), who discussed the possibility of alternative mechanisms. They suggested that coordination strategies vary along three dimensions—formality, cooperativeness, and localization—and that as dependency increases, the amount of coordination necessary increases and as conflict increases, coordination strategies chosen become increasingly formal, controlling and centralized. They therefore proposed a two-by-two matrix showing conditions under which organizations will choose to coordinate by rules, mutual adjustment, hierarchy or a matrix structure.

To summarize, most organizational conceptions of dependencies view them as arising between actors and describe patterns of actor-to-actor dependencies. Furthermore most researchers have viewed the dependency as given and sought to identify the mechanisms used to manage dependencies, although some have suggested assigning tasks in order to create desired dependencies or minimize undesired ones (e.g., as in "administrative management theory"; Simon 1976).

3.2.2 Research in Artificial Intelligence and Other Fields

I will attempt to develop a richer conception of organizational dependencies by using concepts drawn from work in artificial intelligence (AI). These researchers, particularly those in the field of distributed AI, have also considered dependencies and coordination in an effort to develop systems. Because of the need to program system behaviors, these researchers have considered the nature of tasks in considerable detail. In contrast to most organizational researchers, researchers in the field of artificial intelligence have analyzed dependency as arising between tasks. This approach has the advantage that it permits consideration of the implications of different patterns of task assignment. Once an assignment is determined, however, we can still determine implications of a dependency for a particular actor.

Researchers in artificial intelligence have categorized the various types of dependencies that can arise between pairs of goals or activities (e.g., Decker and Lesser 1989; Stuart 1985; von Martial 1989; Wilensky 1983). Von Martial (1989) developed a taxonomy of relationships, both positive, such as synergies or equality, and negative, such as conflicting use of resources or logical incompatibility. He suggested several dimensions for this taxonomy, including explicit versus implicit and resource versus non–resource-based interactions. Alexander (1964) suggested expressing the dependency between design variables (essentially goals of a design task) as a correlation coefficient. This view allows for both conflicting (negative) and facilitative (positive) dependencies. He noted further that some dependencies may be logically necessary or a product of physical laws, while others may simply be true in all designs in the sample considered. He therefore recommended that two variables be considered as interacting only if, "the designer can find some reason (or conceptual model) which makes sense to him and tells him why they should do so" (p. 109). A fully specified design space forms a network of linked goals; this space can then be partitioned into weakly interacting subcomponents to be worked on independently.

However, while these researchers have catalogued dependencies, few have discussed in detail what coordination methods might be used in response to these problems. Yu and Mylopoulos (1993) did suggest specific actions that can be taken to manage different kinds of dependencies. For example, they suggested mechanisms that might be appropriate if one actor depends on another to achieve a goal, perform a task or provide a resource (p. 35).

3.2.3 A Framework for Studying Dependencies and Coordination Mechanisms

To clarify the relationship between dependencies and coordination, I use the framework presented by Malone and Crowston (1994), who define coordination as "managing dependencies." They analyzed group action in terms of *actors* performing *interdependent activities* to achieve *goals*. These activities might also require or create *resources* of various types. For example, in the case of software bug fixing mentioned above, the *actors* are the customers and various employees of the software company. In some cases a group of individuals may be represented as a single collective actor (Abell 1987). For example, to simplify the analysis of a particular subunit, the other subunits with which it interacts might all be represented as collective actors. *Activities* in the software example include reporting a problem, diagnosing the problem, developing a fix, and delivering the fix to the customer. The *goal* of the process in this case appears to be eliminating problems in the system, but alternative goals—such as appearing responsive to customer requests—could also be analyzed. Finally, *resources* include the bug reports, information about known bugs, computer time, bug fixes, and so on.

Coordination Problems and Mechanisms In Malone and Crowston's (1994) view, actors in organizations face *coordination problems* arising from dependencies, which constrain how the tasks can be performed. For example, a software engineer planning to change one module in a computer system must check that the changes will not affect other modules or arrange for any necessary changes to modules that will be affected. Two engineers working on the same module must each be careful not to overwrite the other's changes. Alternately, the problem might be that we want to be sure that a particular dependency exists; for example, we want actors to choose tasks to perform that will accomplish particular goals. In other cases, the dependency provides an opportunity; for example, if two different customers have reported the same bug, then the company can save time by diagnosing and fixing the bug once and sharing the solution. The first goal of this chapter is to present a taxonomy to organize dependencies and thus coordination problems.

Having identified a coordination problem, it is necessary to address it through some coordination mechanism. Coordination mechanisms may be quite specific, such as different kinds of code management systems to control changes to software, or quite general, such as hierarchies or markets to manage assignment of activities to actors. Malone and Crowston (1994), for example, identified several common dependencies and analyze coordination mechanisms to manage them including *goal decomposition*, *resource allocation*, and *synchronization*. In general, there may be many different coordination mechanisms that could be used to address the same coordination problem. Therefore a taxonomy of dependencies—the product of this discussion—would also serve as a way to organize coordination mechanisms. As I present the taxonomy, I will explain the possible coordination mechanisms along with the different kinds of dependency they address.

To distinguish different kinds of dependencies, I consider what the dependencies might exist between. For simplicity, I group the elements of Malone and Crowston's (1994) framework—goals, activities, actors, and resources—into two categories:

• *Tasks* that include goals to be achieved or activities to be performed.

• *Objects* that make up the world, in particular, those resources needed to perform activities and the actors themselves.

In any situation there may be multiple instances of each of these elements, possibly interdependent. These two elements will be discussed in more detail below.

Tasks   By tasks I mean both achieving goals and performing activities. Goals (desired states of the world) and activities (actions performed to achieve a particular state) are clearly different. However, analyzing activities and goals together makes clear the parallel between decomposing a goal into subgoals to be achieved and decomposing it into primitive activities to be performed. In this way both goals and activities are descriptions of the task to be undertaken. A second advantage of this unification is that it eliminates the need to analyze all situations to the level of primitive activities performed by individuals. Treating higher-level goals as activities to be performed by a subunit allows us to analyze assignment of goals to a subunit in the same way that we consider assigning activities to individuals. For example, an outsider (or an analyst interested in other parts of a company) might think of the purchasing department as performing a "purchase materials" activity. To the members of the purchasing department, however, this is a high-level goal to be achieved by performing numerous activities, such as qualifying suppliers, soliciting bids, and awarding contracts.

More powerful conceptualizations of tasks may help suggest the different ways tasks may be interdependent. A frequently used model of action from AI includes *preconditions* (states of the world that must hold before the activity can be performed) and *effects* (states of the world that become true or false as a result of the activity); see Fikes and Nilsson (1971). For example, before engineers can diagnose problems, they must know the symptoms of the problems; afterward they also know the diagnosis. (Of course, it is possible that they will be unable to diagnose the problem or that their diagnoses will be incorrect. Additional refinements could be made to this model to handle such events. Since such refinements do not change the basic analysis presented here, I will omit them for the purposes of this discussion.) From such a model it is clear that tasks may be dependent on each other in several different ways, with different implications. These dependencies will be discussed in detail later in this chapter.

Resources   I include everything used or affected by activities together in the category of resources. Resources in this broad conception include both material goods and the effort of actors. For example, in the case of the software company, resources include computers, source code, bug reports, and bug fixes, as well as the effort of the employees of the company. Note that actors are viewed simply as a particularly important kind of resource. I group actors and other kinds of resources together in this way despite their significant differences because many of the steps necessary in assigning tasks to actors parallel those involved in assigning other kinds of resources to tasks, as will be made clear below. Clearly, there are important differences among all these various resources. The implications of some of these distinctions for the choice of coordination mechanisms are discussed in the following sections.

3.3   Managing Task-Resource Dependencies

The implications of the possible dependencies between a task and one or multiple resources can be represented graphically as in figure 3.1. In the two-component framework discussed in the previous section, a task can depend on a resource either as a precondition or as an effect. For example, the preconditions for fixing a bug include knowing what the bug is, having access to the source code, and having the

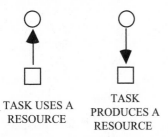

TASK USES A RESOURCE

TASK PRODUCES A RESOURCE

Figure 3.1
Tasks use or produce resources

capability of fixing bugs. The effect of patching a bug is having a patch that fixes the code. Of these two dependencies involving one task and one resource, only the first, a task using a resource, seems to create a coordination problem, in that it requires additional work to manage.

3.3.1   Task Uses One Resource

Consider a task that requires or consumes some resource. The coordination problem implied by this dependency is acquiring the necessary resource. If there is just one appropriate resource available, then that resource must be the one to be used. This simple case includes an actor deciding that it should perform a task itself or knowing only one other actor that could perform it. For example, when customers have problems with a piece of software, typically their only choice is to report the problem to the manufacturer's help desk and ask them to fix the bug. More commonly, however, there are many possibly appropriate resources, requiring a more elaborate coordination mechanism. The mechanism can be decomposed into the following steps:

1. Identifying what resources are required by the task.
2. Identifying what resources are available.
3. Gathering information about the resources.
4. Choosing a particular resource.
5. Assigning the resource (e.g., getting an actor to work on the task).

The steps in this mechanism are derived from the steps in a decision process—intelligence, design, and choice—where the first step is divided into intelligence about the needs of the task and about the available resources and a final step is added to execute the decision.

   In principle, these steps can be performed in any order. For example, tasks can be chosen that can be performed with resources available (and that achieve higher level goals). For example, in software development, a manager might divide a system into modules based on the abilities of the programmers who will work on them, rather than on some a priori division of the problem. A garbage can model might suggest that all steps go on simultaneously and occasionally connect more or less by chance (Cohen, March, and Olsen 1972). For convenience, however, I will discuss the steps in the order listed.

Identifying Necessary Resources   First the resources needed by a task must be identified. For example, determining the module of the system in which a bug appears identifies the resources needed by that task (i.e., an engineer with expertise in that module). In some cases the assigner may need to know what kind of resources are available to be able to characterize the task requirements along the same dimension. For example, if actors are specialists and only one actor can perform any given task, then the needs of the task must be identified in terms of these actors' specializations. If actors are generalists, then any actor can perform the task, so the assignment can be based on other factors.

Identifying Available Resources   Second, a set of appropriate resources must be identified. In the simplest case there is only one potential resource, for example, only one actor, who can perform the task. In the general case there may be several resources that could be used for the task, making it necessary to choose one. The available resources may be known a priori to the assigner; the assigner may know a larger set of resources, some of which may be appropriate; or the assigner may have to spend some effort identifying what resources might be appropriate (e.g., by investigating the background of each possible actor or by asking someone else for a recommendation).

Gathering Information about the Resources   Third, information about the resources must be gathered to evaluate how good a fit a particular resource will be for the task. Obviously there are many possible bases for such a decision, such as speed, quality, availability, and motivation. The necessary information might be gathered by asking potential resources to identify themselves, for example, by submitting bids, in which case this step and the previous one are essentially merged.

Choosing a Resource   Fourth, the most appropriate resource must be chosen based on the information collected and whatever criteria are important for the task.

Assigning Resources   Finally, the assignment of the resource must be communicated to the actor performing the task. As well, for nonshareable resources, the resource must be marked as "in use" or other assigners warned to avoid conflicting assignments, as discussed below. When the resource is the effort of an actor, the actor must be asked or convinced to perform the task. Where the personal goals of the individual actors differ significantly (e.g., when the interaction is nonroutine or when the actors are whole firms rather than individuals), the assigner may have to convince the performer to do the task by designing appropriate incentives schemes or monitoring performance. Kraus (1993) discusses techniques for obtaining cooperation in noncooperative distributed problem solving systems. In other cases, effort to influence the performer will be unnecessary. For example, if employees are asked by a legitimate requester to do a task that fits their definition of their job, they are likely to agree to do it.

Once the resources have been acquired, additional work may be necessary to manage the flow dependency between acquiring and using the resources, as will be discussed below. For example, it may be necessary move the resources to the task that will use them and to ensure that they are available at the appropriate time.

Example Resource Allocation Mechanisms   Different coordination mechanisms for resource assignment can be analyzed as particular choices for these five steps. For example, to assign a task to an employee, a manager must:

1. Determine what skills are necessary to perform the task.

2. Identify which employees are available (which might be done from memory).

3. Collect information about which employees have the necessary skills (again, possibly from memory).

4. Decide which employee is the most appropriate, based on skills, workload, and so on.

5. Ask the employee to work on the task.

Buying a product has equivalent steps:

1. Determining needs.

2. Identifying possibly appropriate products.

3. Collecting brochures, reviews, and other sources of information about the products.

4. Picking the most appropriate products.

5. Arranging payment for and delivery of the product.

More generally, these steps can be used to distinguish broad classes of organizational form. Take, for example, the market-hierarchy dichotomy. In a hierarchy the available resources are those owned by the organization. If the resources are specialized, there may be only one appropriate for a given task. If the resources are generalized, the choice between them may be made based on factors known to the assigner, such as workload, or be delegated to the group. In a market the available resources are those competing in the market place. Appropriate resources are identified through advertising or requesting bids and the choice between them made based on the bids submitted by the interested resources. In a network organization (Ching, Holsapple, and Whinston 1992; Nohria and Eccles 1992) the resources are those that belong to the network; typically each member has a particular specialization it brings

Table 3.1
Decompositions of different mechanisms for resource allocation

Step	Market	Hierarchy	Network
Identify needs	Based on specializations in market	Based on specializations in firm	Based on specializations in network
Identify resources	Broadcast a RFB and wait for replies; check advertising	Use known set of resources in firm	Use known set of resources belonging to network
Choose resource	Evaluate bids	Specialization; workload	Specialization
Assign resource	Contract	Employment relation	Network membership

to the network. The basis for assignment is reciprocal relations, rather than contracts or hierarchy. These alternatives are summarized table 3.1.

3.3.2 Task Uses Multiple Resources

I will next consider cases where a single task uses multiple resources. There are three cases where a task is dependent on multiple resources—using multiple resources, producing multiple resources, or using one resource and producing another, as shown in figure 3.2. Of the three, only the first, a task using multiple resources, seems to pose unique coordination problems, namely constraints on the performance of the task and thus the need for a coordination mechanism. In this case there is a need to synchronize the availability of multiple resources.

One way to manage this dependency is to simplify it by permanently assigning all resources, or all resources but one, to the task. For example, a particular production task might always be performed on a particular machine, which is always operated by a particular operator. Such pre-assignments reduce this dependency to a task using a single resource, as discussed above.

More generally, the dependency can be managed by scheduling the use of all of the needed resources. However, the need to use multiple resources creates additional potential problems, such as deadlock (where one task waits for a resource held by the another, which in turn is waiting for a resource held by the first) and starvation (where a task waits forever for all the resources it needs to become available). For instance, a meeting convener may not be able to find a time at which everyone is available, resulting in the meeting being repeatedly postponed. For computer systems a variety of algorithms have been developed for assigning resources to avoid these problems. For example, deadlocks can be avoided by requiring that all needed resources be assigned at once (preventing a task holding a resource while waiting for another) or by always assigning resources in a specified order (preventing a loop). Alternately, deadlocks can be periodically searched for and one task canceled if a

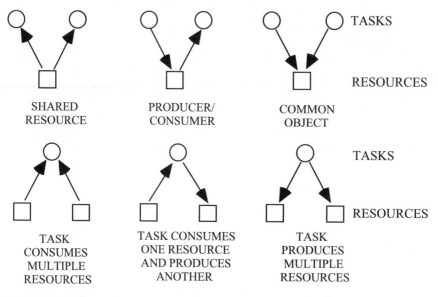

Figure 3.2
Dependencies between multiple tasks and resources.

deadlock is detected. Some of these approaches have analogues in human systems (e.g., if nothing has happened with your resource request for a while, call again to check on the status).

3.4 Managing Dependencies among Multiple Tasks and Resources

In the previous section we considered the dependency between a single task and one or more resources. In general, however, there are multiple tasks and resources to be considered. In our analysis, the primary way two tasks can be dependent is via some kind of common resource. Figure 3.2 shows the set of possible dependencies between two tasks (the circles) and one resource (the boxes); the arrows indicate flows of a resource that are either produced or used. In this framework there are three ways two tasks might have a resource in common and therefore three major kinds of dependencies: two tasks use the same resource as input (a "sharing" dependency), two tasks create the same resource as output (a "common output" dependency), and one task creates a resource used by another (a "flow" dependency). Similarly a single task might use several resources, use one resource and create another or create multiple resources. Each of these cases will be considered in turn below.

Table 3.2
Examples of resources classified by shareability and reusability

	Shareable	Nonshareable
Reusable	Information: designs, problem reports, fixes	Tools: test systems, meeting rooms
Consumable		Raw materials: components, assemblies

3.4.1 Sharing

The first case I will consider is when two tasks are interdependent because both have the same resource as a precondition (a "sharing" dependency). One approach to this situation is to eliminate the dependency, such as by giving each task a dedicated resource or by redesigning one of the tasks to not need the resource. These approaches correspond to Galbraith's (1974) suggestion to create slack resources or self-contained tasks (pp. 30–31). For example, office workers are usually given their own staplers, desks, and even computers to eliminate the need to coordinate stapling, writing, or computing.

In general, though, additional work is required to share the resource. Clearly, the nature of the resource will determine what additional work is necessary. I consider in particular two dimensions along which resources differ: *shareablity* and *reusability*, as shown in table 3.2.

• *Shareablity* describes how many tasks can use the resource simultaneously. Most resources—raw material, tools, or effort—are nonshareable. Note that an actor may be assigned to multiple tasks but works on only one at any instant. Information and other states of the world are important exceptions, since multiple tasks can use the same resource if it is not changed by the tasks.

• *Reusability* describes how many tasks can use the resource over time (von Martial 1989). Some resources, such as tools or information, can be used and reused, at least until they wear out; others, such as raw materials, can only be used once.

We will now consider the implications of these resource types for the nature of the resulting coordination problem and mechanisms.

Shareable Resources If the common resource is shareable, then it is not a conflict for two tasks to use it at the same time. For example, two engineers can use the same piece of information without any problem (although there may be conflicts for the physical media on which the information is stored, a nonshareable resource). Instead, shareable resources create the problem of ensuring that tasks use the same version of the resource. For example, two designers working on detailed component design should work from the same version of the overall design. Solutions include destroy-ing obsolete copies to ensure that there is only one resource, making a new copy of the resource from or checking the versions against a master prior to each use, or even tolerating a certain level of disagreement and repairing problems after the fact. Likewise, when the resource is changed, it must be treated as nonshareable to ensure that other tasks do not use the resource in an inconsistent state.

Nonshareable Resources   If the resource is not shareable, then the two tasks cannot be performed simultaneously with the available resources. Note, in particular, that this applies to an actor performing multiple tasks: the actor needs to pick an order in which to do the tasks (e.g., by prioritizing them and doing the most important or urgent ones first).

One solution is to plan the use of the resource ahead of time and perform both tasks accordingly, corresponding to Van de Ven, Delbecq, and Koenig's (1976) impersonal mode of coordination. If the resource is reusable, then the conflict can be resolved simply by performing the tasks at different times. Numerous techniques have been developed to schedule resources. For example, conference rooms and other facilities are frequently allocated with a sign-up list. Ripps (1991) presents a taxonomy of mechanisms for task synchronization in a real-time programming sys-tem that includes numerous mechanisms for transferring information between tasks or avoiding conflicts over resources. Sen (1993) discusses coordination mechanisms that might be applied to distributed resource scheduling, including contract-nets (Smith and Davis 1981), distributed search and multi-agent planning. On the other hand, if the resource is consumable, then rescheduling will not suffice; instead, the resource must be divided among tasks, additional resources acquired, or only one of the tasks selected to be performed.

A second solution to resource sharing is to resolve the conflicts as the tasks are performed (rather than ahead of time). For consumable resources, this approach reduces to 'first-come–first-served' allocation of the resource. For shareable re-sources, this approach is similar to the "mutual exclusion" problem in computer science, so many of the solutions developed for that problem may be applicable. There are two steps to the solution. First, conflicts must be made visible, typically by marking the resource as being in use. For many physical resources, the act of using it may be sufficient (e.g., sitting in front of a computer terminal or in a conference room will signal to anyone else that it is in use). For less tangible resources, such as information, more elaborate schemes are necessary. For example, a code checkout system prevents two engineers from modifying the same source code module at the same time; most databases provide some kind of locking mechanism to prevent concurrent updates to a piece of information. Second, if the resource is not marked as being used, the performer of the task can so mark it and then use it. If it is marked as being used, then a flow dependency exists between the current and potential user of the resource, which must be managed as discussed below.

3.4.2 Flow

The second case I will consider is when a resource is the effect of one task and a precondition of another. This situation creates what is known in computer science as a producer–consumer dependency, or more simply a "flow" dependency. Such a dependency requires that the tasks be performed in the correct order and the flow of the resource between the two be managed. This relationship frequently holds between steps in a process, as well as between sequential uses of a resource. For example, in software changes, fixing the bug has the effect of creating a patch that is a precondition for integrating the complete system. Malone and Crowston (1994) and Dellarocas (1996) point out that flow dependencies imply additional constraints on how tasks are performed; three such constraints—usability, precedence, and accessibility—will be discussed in turn.

USABILITY   Additional work may be necessary to ensure that the resource in question must be usable by the second task (data in the correct format, parts of the proper shape and material, etc.). Usability constraints can be managed by a designer who creates standards for the resource, by giving the creator additional information about the needs of the user or by negotiation between the user and creator. For example, in an engineering context, design and manufacturing engineers might work together to develop products that are easy to manufacture or designers might be trained in the requirements of manufacturing processes ("design for manufacturability"). Quality control tasks can be seen as a way of ensuring that an output of one task is in fact the correct input for the next. Many other kinds of approval processes also appear to serve this function, explicitly or implicitly.

PREREQUISITE   The second aspect of a flow dependency is prerequisite, meaning that the production of the resource must occur before its consumption. There are two aspects to this constraint: (1) the producer knows that the production is required and (2) the consumer knows that the production is done.

On the producer's side, the producer might produce continually, according to a pre-arranged plan or triggered by the consumer, either by monitoring the consumer's use of the resource to determine when to produce or waiting for notification of need from the consumer. Likewise, the rate of production may have to be matched to the rate of consumption. Dellarocas (1996, p. 93) lists several types of prerequisites for different types of resources, such as persistent prerequisites (the producing task has to be performed only once before any number of consuming tasks) to lockstep prerequisites (the producing task has to be performed exactly once before each performance of the consuming task). The matching can be managed also by adding buffers between the two processes to smooth the flow of material or tying the rate of production to the rate of use, as with the "producer–consumer" problem in computer science.

On the consumer's side, additional work may be necessary to ensure that the producing task is performed before the consuming task. For physical resources, such a step may be unnecessary, as it will probably be physically impossible to perform the consuming task without the results of the producing task. Even here, however, effort may be wasted before the lack is noticed. For information resources, or states of the world more generally, ensuring that things are ready is necessary. Precedence can be managed either by monitoring the state of the previous task to determine when it completes and the resource is available or by having the performer of the prior task notify the next when the resource is ready. Crowston (chapter 6 in this volume) discusses the implications of this difference for the operations of a restaurant.

ACCESSIBILITY   Finally, accessibility (i.e., right place) means that additional work may have to be performed to ensure that the consuming task can access the resource, for example, to move the resource from where it is created to where it is used. Physical goods might be moved in a truck, on an assembly line, and so on; information can be moved on paper, verbally, by computer, and so on.

EXAMPLE FLOW MANAGEMENT MECHANISMS   Flow management mechanisms have been extensively studied in operations management. Different inventory management techniques can be seen as variations along the dimensions explored above. These techniques differ primarily in management of the prerequisite dependency, as these techniques do not manage usability or accessibility. In almost all cases the consumer notifies the producer of its need.

In a traditional inventory system, the consumer keeps an inventory of the resource on hand to meet its needs. When the level of the inventory drops below a reorder point (calculated from the delay in filling an order and the expected rate of use), an order is placed for a new supply (the order quantity being calculated to balance the cost of ordering and the cost of holding inventory). In other words, the producer is informed by the consumer when resources are needed, while the consumer draws from inventory, only waiting if the reserve inventory is depleted. By contrast, in a 'just-in-time' system, no inventory is kept; resources arrive 'just-in-time' to be consumed. Making such a system work requires careful planning and communication of needs (and in practice, a small level of inventory at the consumer and perhaps a larger level at the producer). Finally, in many grocery stores, suppliers take responsibility for periodically checking the level of inventory on the shelves and restocking as necessary. The stores thus outsource both communicating the need for and monitoring the arrival of new resources.

Analogous processes are used in computer systems to manage flow dependencies. For example, network protocols must coordinate receivers (consumers) and senders (producers) to ensure that the sender does not send faster than the receiver can receive. One approach is for the receiver to periodically inform the sender of how much data it can handle; the sender can then send up to that amount before waiting for further permission. In other words, as above, the consumer periodically notifies the producer of its needs, and takes resources (in this case data) from a buffer or waits for more to arrive.

3.4.3 Common Output

The third and final case I will consider is when the effects of two tasks are the same resource, resulting in a "common output" dependency (note that this type of dependency is called "fit" by Malone et al., chapter 1 in this volume). This dependency can have either positive or negative effects, which requires additional effort to exploit or avoid. There are three cases.

First, if both tasks do the same thing, meaning create the same resource, then it may be desirable to merge the two tasks, reusing a resource or taking advantage of economies of scale in production. To exploit these possible synergies requires additional coordination mechanisms, such as checking for duplication before one or both of the tasks have been performed and distributing the output. For example, the same problem may be reported to a software company multiple times. Rather than fixing and refixing the same problem, the customer service centre and marketing engineers check if a reported problem is in a database of known problems. If it is, then the already known solution to the problem can simply be reused, thus eliminating a task that would create a duplicate resource (the bug fix).

Second, if two tasks specify different aspects of a common resource, then each may be constrained to ensure that their results fit together. For example, engineers developing interacting software modules negotiate the modules' interface—a common object created jointly by the design of the modules. This dependency can also be viewed as usability dependencies between the two (or more) resource-creating tasks and some using task (e.g., integration), allowing us to apply the coordination mechanisms discussed above. For example, the fit can be assured by performing each task according to a common plan or design (as when a composer creates the score that guides the musicians in a group), through negotiation between the performers and users, or on the fly, as in a jazz ensemble. Explicitly noting the using task and considering the dependencies as between it and the producing tasks also brings into question the other components of the flow dependencies.

Finally, if the effects conflict, for example, both doing a task and not doing it, then it may be impossible to perform both tasks. Possible resolutions of this dependency are similar to the case where two tasks both require the same nonshareable resource, discussed in more detail above: either abandoning one task or scheduling them so the effects do not have to be achieved at the same time.

3.4.4   Multiple Modes of Use

A resource may appear as both a precondition and effect of some task. For example, modification or consumption of a resource can be modeled this way. The resulting dependencies are the combination of the dependencies from the individual operations. For example, if two engineers both want to modify a single software module (a shareable/reusable resource), they must manage both shared resource and common output dependencies. From the previous discussion we can see that the shared resource dependency causes no conflict (they both can read the module freely), but the common output dependency might. If they are both making the identical change, then one of the tasks can be eliminated; otherwise, they will have to negotiate to ensure the resulting module is acceptable to both (i.e., that both bugs are fixed). Alternately, the module could be viewed as a nonshareable/reusable resource. In this case, the shared resource dependency must also be managed, such as by scheduling the engineers' use of the module so one makes changes and then the other.

3.5   Dependencies among Tasks or among Resources

So far I have considered only dependencies between tasks and resources. Of course, it is possible to consider dependencies that arise among tasks or among resources.

3.5.1   Simultaneity

One dependency that might be considered among tasks is simultaneity: one task might require the concurrent execution of another task, or several tasks might have to be performed all at the same time. For example, all attendees of a meeting must attend at the same time, which might be modeled as several "attend meeting" tasks joined with a simultaneity constraint. However, this situation might instead be modeled as a "hold meeting" task that requires multiple resources simultaneously, as discussed earlier. Similarly two people lifting a piano must lift their ends simultaneously, but again this task is probably best modeled as a lifting task that requires multiple people to perform. Uniform application of this approach eliminates the need for simultaneity dependencies, but for some cases might require the conceptual creation of an unnatural aggregate task.

Other analyses of task dependencies (e.g., von Martial 1989) include additional relationships, such as a requirement that the two tasks not be performed at the same time. In our typology such relationships would be analyzed by looking for shared resources that create the restriction. For example, it might be that two tasks cannot be performed at the same time because they require the same tool. Again, this strategy eliminates the need for additional dependencies but, for some, might require the conceptual creation of a new shared resource.

3.5.2 Composition

A second possible dependency is a composition dependency: both tasks and resources can be thought of as forming decomposition hierarchies: higher-level tasks can be decomposed into subtasks, and an object into components.

Given such a model of a task, planning might be viewed as a way to manage the relationship between tasks and subtasks, that is, a way to choose a set of tasks that accomplish a desired task. In the AI literature, many methods have been investigated for planning (e.g., see Allen, Hendler, and Tate 1990). For example, an engineer with a large change to implement might decompose the work into smaller changes made to several different parts, such as to different modules of the system, and then work on each of those changes independently. Similarly process engineers decompose a design into specific operations that the assembly workers can perform to assemble the cars. Alternately, an actor might proceed one step at a time, choosing a task that appears to move closer to the desired goal, performing it and then reassessing the situation.

Similarly resources might be interdependent by being connected together in some kind of assembly, such as the parts of a car or of a computer system. These interdependencies are clearly important: an essential part of change management, for example, is managing the interfaces between parts to ensure that changes to one part do not interfere with the function of another. If two tasks use different resources that are interdependent in this way, then the two tasks can be analyzed as both depending on a larger common resource. Conversely, two tasks may appear to be using a common resource because they are each dependent on components of a more complex resource. To manage these dependencies though, actors must first identify that they exist, which requires a coordination mechanism. For example, for engineering change management, engineers must spend some effort to identify which other engineers need to be informed of a proposed change to a part.

3.5.3 Integration

Finally, if multiple subtasks are performed to accomplish some effect, it may be necessary to integrate their results. This integration step is frequently viewed as a kind of coordination task. Another view is that integration is simply another part of performing the task, that is, a task is decomposed into multiple subtasks, one of which is to integrate the results. For example, an engineer who decomposes a task and requests changes from other engineers may be responsible for compiling the changes together to be submitted. In any case it is necessary to manage the producer–consumer dependencies between each of the subtasks and the integration task.

3.6 Conclusion

In this chapter I presented a taxonomy of dependencies and associated coordination mechanisms. This taxonomy is based on a simple ontology that includes resources (actors or other objects) and tasks (activities or goals to be accomplished). For simple task-resource dependencies, I present the steps in a resource assignment mechanism. Other dependencies are analyzed by considering how a common resource is used by the two tasks (in contrast to prior organizational conceptions of dependencies that view them as arising between actors) or how one task can use multiple resources. Finally, the typology includes possible dependencies between tasks and between resources, although some of these situations can be analyzed more simply in terms of other dependencies. Only composition of tasks and of resources seems to pose particular coordination problems. The resulting dependencies and coordination mechanisms are summarized in table 3.3.

The framework presented here makes a theoretical claim about the design of organizations: given a coordination problem caused by a dependency, some coordination mechanism is necessary to manage it. This claim has implications for the analysis and design of organizations.

To analyze an organizational process, it is important to identify the dependencies that arise and the coordination mechanisms that are used to manage those dependencies. Fortunately, as Simon (1981) points out, in practice "most things are only weakly connected with most other things; for a tolerable description of reality only a tiny fraction of all possible interactions needs to be taken into account" (p. 221), what he calls the "empty world hypothesis." Applied to organizational analysis, the

Table 3.3
Summary of dependencies and coordination mechanisms

Task uses resource
1. Determine needs
2. Identify resources
   - ads
   - prepared list
   - only one resource
3. Collect information on resources
   - by bidding
   - manager knows
4. Pick best
5. Do assignment
   - mark resource in use
6. Manage flow dependencies from acquiring resource to using resource

Task requires multiple resources simultaneously
1. Pre-assign resources to simplify coordination problem
2. Manage dependency on the fly
   - avoid or detect and resolve deadlock
   - detect and resolve starvation

Sharing: Multiple tasks use the same resource
- Ensure same version of sharable resources
  - destroy obsolete versions
  - copy master prior to use
  - check versions prior to use
  - detect and fix problems after the fact
- Schedule use of nonshareable but reusable resources
  1. check for conflict before using and then mark the resource as in-use
  2. manage flow of resource from one task to another
- Allocate nonreusable resources
  - divide the resource among the tasks
  - abandon one task
  - get more resources

Flow: One task uses a resource created by another
1. Usability (i.e., the right thing)
   - user adapts to resource as created
   - creator gets information from user to tailor resource
   - third party sets standard, followed by both producer and consumer
2. Prerequisite (i.e., at the right time)
   - producer produces first
     - follow plan
     - monitor usage
     - wait to be asked
       - standard reorder points
       - when out
       - just-in-time

Table 3.3
(continued)

     • consumer waits until produced
       • monitor
       • be notified
  3. Accessibility (i.e., in the right place)
     • physical goods
       • truck
     • information
       • on paper
       • verbally
       • by computer

Common output: Multiple tasks create the same output
  1. Detect common output
     • database of known problems
  2. Manage common outputs
     • effects overlap or are the same
       • eliminate one task (manage shared resource)
       • merge tasks take advantage of synergy
     • effects are incompatible
       • abandon one
       • don't try to achieve them at the same time

Composition of tasks
     • choose tasks to achieve a given goal (a planning problem)

Composition of resources
     • trace dependencies of between resources to determine if a coordination problem exists

---

Note: Dependencies are shown in bold. Numbered items are components of the coordination mechanism for managing the given dependency. Bulletted items are alternative mechanisms or components of the mechanism for the given dependency.

implication is that any given task likely uses only a small set of resources and will thus likely be interdependent with only a few other tasks.

To design a new process, it will be useful to consider alternative coordination mechanisms that could be used to manage those dependencies (see Crowston and Osborn, chapter 11 in this volume). One question I posed at the beginning of this chapter was, in what ways can a given organization be arranged differently while achieving the same goals? Understanding the coordination problems addressed by an organization suggests alternative coordination mechanisms that could be used, thus creating a space of possible forms.

3.6.1 Assessment of the Typology
The primary focus of this work has been the theoretical constructs included in this taxonomy, namely dependencies, the coordination problems created by dependencies

and the coordination mechanisms actors use to manage these problems. Since a taxonomy per se is not a theory (Bacharach 1989), the primary evaluation of this work should be on the quality of these constructs: their *comprehensiveness* and *parsimony* (Whetten 1989) and their *validity* (Bacharach 1989). Likewise we ask if the typology is *useful*.

• The taxonomy attempts to be *comprehensive*, in the sense that all dependencies fit into one of the four categories. On the other hand, I do not claim that the typology is comprehensive in the sense that I have described all possible dependencies and coordination mechanisms. The description of specific dependencies could be further refined and additional coordination mechanisms added. Further refinement of the dependencies and mechanisms is an important topic for future research.

• The taxonomy probably errs on the side of *parsimony* since it characterizes coordination methods on the basis of a small number of factors, while obviously there are many reasons to choose a mechanism.

• The constructs are *valid*, in the sense of being distinct from one another and actually found in practice, as indicated by the examples.

• Finally, another way to assess the value of the taxonomy is to ask if it has been useful in any research projects. The answer to this question appears to be yes: earlier versions of the typology (e.g., Malone and Crowston 1994) have been used in several papers (e.g., Bailetti, Callahan, and DiPietro 1994; Bailetti, Callahan, and McCluskey 1998; Sikora 1998; Cohen and Regan 1996; Crowston 1997; Crowston and Kammerer 1998).

3.6.2   Future Research

Much remains to be done. The focus on processes suggests that it is important to collect many examples of processes to compare the coordination problems that arise (e.g., Malone et al., chapter 1 in this volume) and identify the coordination mechanisms used. Other kinds of organizations may have somewhat different kinds of problems, although there is likely to be substantial overlap. For example, do Web design companies or open source software development teams use a different set of mechanisms to manage software changes than traditional software companies? Do Japanese companies use a different set to manage engineering, more generally?

It is important to identify limitations of this work. The overall framework is focused on managing dependencies between tasks. While this focus is generally useful, it is by no means universal. Some tasks (e.g., software requirements analysis for complex computer systems) seem to be more about developing a shared understanding of the tasks and dependencies as opposed to performing specific tasks (Crowston and Kammerer 1998). In other words, an analysis of dependencies provides a useful but partial view of organizations.

Even with these limitations the initial results show this work to be useful in several ways. A better understanding of what is necessary for coordination may provide a more principled approach for designing new computer applications, for analyzing the way organizations are currently coordinated, and for explaining perceived problems with existing approaches to coordination. By systematically exploring the space of possible coordination strategies, we may even be able to discover entirely new organizational forms, forms that are more efficient, flexible, or satisfying to their members.

Acknowledgment

This research was supported by the Center for Coordination Science at the Massachusetts Institute of Technology and by a fellowship from the Ameritech Foundation through the Information and Organizations Program of the University of Michigan Institute for Public Policy Studies. The author thanks Brian Pentland, Michael Prietula, and Thomas W. Malone for their comments on earlier drafts of this chapter. This work has also benefited from discussions and suggestions from members of the Process Handbook Project, in particular, George Wyner, Gilad Zlotkin, George Herman, and Martha Broad.

4 Toward a Design Handbook for Integrating Software Components

Chrysanthos Dellarocas

4.1 Motivation

As the size and complexity of software systems grows, the identification and proper management of interconnection dependencies among various pieces of a system has become responsible for an increasingly important part of the development effort. In today's large systems, the variety of encountered interconnection dependencies (e.g., communication, data translation, resource sharing, and synchronization dependencies) is very large, while the complexity of protocols for managing them can be very high.

Dependencies among software components are especially important in component-based software development. In this case, the core functional elements of an application are implemented using off-the-shelf components. The focus of the design effort then lies in integrating these components by identifying and properly managing their interdependencies and mismatches. The practical difficulty of achieving widespread software reuse is a manifestation of the fact that component integration is not a trivial problem. Nevertheless, most current programming languages and tools have so far failed to recognize component interconnection as a distinct design problem that should be separated from the specification and implementation of the underlying components.

The distinct nature and equal importance of components and dependencies is captured relatively well in high-level, architectural descriptions of systems. In such descriptions components are typically depicted using boxes and dependencies using arrows. However, at that level of description dependencies are usually informal artifacts and their exact translation into implementation-level concepts is not obvious.

As design moves closer to implementation, current design and programming tools increasingly focus on components, leaving the description of interdependencies among components implicit, and the implementation of protocols for managing them fragmented and distributed in various parts of the system. At the implementation level, software systems are sets of modules in one or more programming languages. Although modules come under a variety of names (procedures, packages, objects, clusters, etc.), they are all essentially abstractions for components.

Most programming languages directly support a small set of primitive interconnection mechanisms, such as procedure calls, method invocations, and shared

An earlier version of this chapter appeared as C. Dellarocas (1997), Towards a design handbook for integrating software components, *Proceedings of the 5th International Symposium on Assessment of Software Tools* (SAST'97), Pittsburgh, PA, June 2–5, 1997, pages 3–13. © 1994 IEEE. Reprinted by permission.

variables. Such mechanisms are not sufficient for managing more complex dependencies that are commonplace in today's software systems. Complex dependencies require the introduction of more complex managing protocols, typically comprising several lines of code. By failing to support separate abstractions for representing such complex protocols, current programming languages force programmers to distribute and embed them inside the interacting components (Shaw et al. 1995). Furthermore the lack of means for representing dependencies and protocols for managing them has resulted in a corresponding lack of theories and systematic taxonomies of interconnection relationships and ways of managing them.

This expressive shortcoming of current languages and tools is directly connected to a number of practical problems in software design:

• *Discontinuity between architectural and implementation models.* There is currently a gap between architectural representations of software systems (sets of activities explicitly connected through rich vocabularies of informal relationships) and implementation-level descriptions of the same systems (sets of modules implicitly connected through defines/uses relationships).

• *Difficulties in application maintenance.* By not providing abstractions for localizing information about dependencies, current languages force programmers to distribute managing protocols in a number of different places inside a program. Therefore, in order to understand a protocol, programmers have to look at many places in the program. Likewise, in order to replace a protocol, modifications must be made in many different modules.

• *Difficulties in component reuse.* Components written in today's programming languages inevitably contain some fragments of coordination protocols from their original development environments. Such fragments act as (often undocumented) assumptions about the structure of the application where such components will be used. When attempting to reuse such a component in a new environment, such assumptions might not match the interdependency patterns of the target application. In order to ensure interoperability, the original assumptions then have to be identified, and subsequently replaced or bridged with the valid assumptions for the target application (Garlan et al. 1994). In many cases this requires extensive code modifications or the introduction of additional code around the component. In most cases such modifications are designed and implemented in an ad hoc manner.

Based on the previous observations this chapter claims that if we are to achieve large-scale component-based software development, we need new methodologies and tools that treat the interconnection of software components into new applications as a distinct design problem, entitled to its own representations and design frameworks. Such methodologies will be based on theories of component interconnection that organize and systematize the existing knowledge in the field of component integration, as well as facilitate the creation of new knowledge in the field.

To this end, section 4.2 proposes a framework for studying software component interconnection. The framework is based on software system representations that provide distinct abstractions for components and their interdependencies. Such representations allow the systematic classification of different kinds of dependencies and associated coordination protocols into design handbooks of component integration, similar to the well-established handbooks that assist design in more mature engineering disciplines. Section 4.3 briefly reports on SYNTHESIS, a component-based software development environment based on our framework. Section 4.4 discusses related work. Finally, section 4.5 sums up the conclusions and presents some directions for future research.

4.2   A Framework for Studying Software Component Interconnection

4.2.1   A Coordination Perspective for Representing Software Systems

One of the reasons behind the failure of today's programming languages and methodologies to recognize component interconnection as a distinct design problem is the lack of expressive means for representing interdependencies and their associated coordination protocols as distinct and separate entities from the interacting components. Therefore the first ingredient of our framework is a representation that achieves this distinction. The representation is based on the principles of coordination theory.

Coordination theory (Malone and Crowston 1994) is an emerging research area that focuses on the interdisciplinary study of coordination. One of the intended applications of coordination theory is the design and modeling of complex systems, ranging from computer systems to real-life organizations. Coordination theory views such systems as collections of interdependent processes performed by machine and/or human actors. Processes are sets of activities. Coordination theory defines coordination as the management of dependencies among activities. It makes a distinction between two orthogonal kinds of activities:

• *Production (or core) activities.*   Activities directly related to the stated goals of a system. For example, the SQL engine of a database system would qualify as a production activity in that system.

• *Coordination activities.*   Activities which do not directly relate to the stated goals of a process, but are necessary in order to manage interdependencies among production activities. Algorithms that control concurrent access in multi-user databases would be considered coordination activities under this framework.

The definitions above suggest representations in which software systems are depicted as sets of interdependent software activities. At the specification level, activities represent the core functional elements of the system while dependencies represent their interconnection relationships and constraints. At the implementation level, activities are mapped to software components that provide the intended functionality, while dependencies are mapped to coordination protocols that manage them. Figure 4.1 depicts an example of a software system specification and implementation using such a representation.

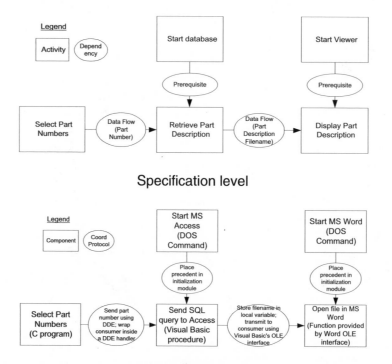

Figure 4.1
Representing a software application as a set of activities interconnected through dependencies

4.2.2   A Design Handbook for Integrating Software Components

The existence of representations that treat dependencies and coordination processes as distinct entities enable the construction of taxonomies of software interconnection problems and solutions. This section presents the beginnings of such a taxonomy. The taxonomy contains the following elements:

• A catalog of the most common kinds of interconnection dependencies encountered in software systems

• For each kind of dependency, a catalog of sets of alternative coordination protocols for managing it

Our taxonomy uses multidimensional design spaces to classify both dependencies and coordination protocols. It begins by identifying a small number of generic dependencies. For each generic dependency, it defines a number of design dimensions that can be used to further specialize the relationship. These dimensions form a design space that contains different specializations of the given dependency. Each point in the design space defines a different specialized dependency type.

Furthermore, for each dependency, our taxonomy identifies a few generic coordination processes that manage it. It also defines a design space that contains several related specialized versions of these coordination protocols. The dimensions of the design space are the questions the designer will have to answer in order to select one of the available coordination processes for managing a given dependency.

Overview of the Dependencies Space   An important decision in making a taxonomy of software interconnection problems is the choice of the generic dependency types. If we are to treat software interconnection as an orthogonal problem to that of designing the core functional components of an application, dependencies among components should represent relationships which are also orthogonal to the functional domain of an application. Fortunately this requirement is consistent with the nature of most interconnection problems: whether our application is controlling inventory or driving a nuclear submarine, most problems related to connecting its components together are related to a relatively narrow set of concepts, such as resource flows, resource sharing, and timing dependencies. The design of associated coordination protocols involves a similarly narrow set of mechanisms such as shared events, invocation mechanisms, and communication protocols.

After making a survey of existing systems, and building on earlier results of coordination theory (Malone and Crowston 1993, 1994), we can base our taxonomy of dependencies on the assumption that component interdependencies are explicitly or implicitly related to patterns of resource production and usage. *In other words, activities need to interconnect with other activities, either because they use resources produced by other activities, or because they share resources with other activities.*

Based on this assumption, we include the most generic dependency families in our taxonomy:

• *Flow dependencies.*   Flow dependencies represent relationships between producers and consumers of resources. They are specialized according to the kind of resource, the number of producers, the number of consumers, and so on. Coordination protocols for managing flows decompose into protocols which ensure accessibility of the resource by the consumers, usability of the resource, as well as synchronization between producers and consumers.

• *Sharing dependencies.*   Sharing dependencies encode relationships among consumers who use the same resource or producers who produce for the same consumers. These are specialized according to the sharing properties of the resource in use (divisibility, consumability, concurrency). Coordination protocols for sharing dependencies ensure proper enforcement of the sharing properties, usually by dividing a resource among competing users, or by enforcing mutual exclusion protocols.

• *Timing dependencies.*   Timing dependencies express constraints on the relative flow of control among a set of activities. Examples include *prerequisite dependencies* and *mutual exclusion dependencies*. Timing dependencies are used to specify application-specific cooperation patterns among activities which share the same resources. They are also used in the decomposition of coordination protocols for flow and sharing dependencies.

It is not possible to complete describe the taxonomy in the limited space of this chapter. Instead, the following sections will present a small subset of the taxonomy of flow dependencies, as well as an example of how it can be used to guide the design of software interconnection protocols. A full description of the taxonomy is contained in (Dellarocas 1996).

A Taxonomy of Flow Dependencies   Flow dependencies encode relationships among producers and consumers of resources. This section presents a generic model for classifying flow dependencies and a framework for designing coordination protocols for such dependencies. The framework is based on some results of coordination theory, extended and adapted for the field of software components.

Malone and Crowston (1994) have observed that whenever flows occur, one or more of the following subdependencies are present:

• *Usability.* Users of a resource must be able to effectively use the resource.

• *Accessibility.* In order for a resource to be used by an activity, it must be accessible to that activity.

• *Prerequisite.* A resource can only be used after it has been produced.

The following paragraphs will introduce dependency and coordination process design spaces for each of the lower-level dependencies. The design space for generalized flow dependencies is defined by the product of the design spaces of the component dependencies.

USABILITY DEPENDENCIES Usability dependencies state the fact that resource users should be able to properly use produced resources. This is a very general requirement that encompasses some compatibility issues:

• Data type compatibility

• Format compatibility

• Database schema compatibility

• Device driver compatibility

The exact meaning and range of usability considerations varies with each kind of resource. One interesting observation resulting from this work is that regardless of the particular usability issue being managed, coordination alternatives for managing usability dependencies can be classified using the design dimensions listed in table 4.1.

ACCESSIBILITY DEPENDENCIES Accessibility dependencies specify that a resource must be accessible to a user before it can be used. Since users are software activities, accessibility specifies more accurately that a resource must be accessible to the pro-

Table 4.1
Design dimensions of usability coordination protocols

Design dimension	Design alternatives
Who is responsible for ensuring usability?	Designer (standardization) Producers Consumers Both producers and consumers (use intermediate format) Third party
When are usability requirements fixed?	At design-time At run-time (format negotiation might take place)

Table 4.2
Design dimensions of accessibility coordination protocols

Principal design alternatives	First level of specialization	Second level of specialization
Place producers and consumers "close together"	Place at design-time	Package in same sequential module Package in same executable Assign to same processor Assign to nearby processors
Transport resource	Place at run-time	Code is accessible to all processors Physical code transportation required
		Actual protocols depend on resource kind (see table 4.3)

Table 4.3
Examples of transport protocols for data resources

Producers-consumers	Generic mechanism	Examples
One–one	Point-to-point channels	OCCAM channels (Inmos 1984) UNIX sockets
	Pipes	UNIX pipes
One–many	Broadcast calls	ISIS Multicast (Birman et al. 1991)
Many–one	Asynchronous calls Synchronous calls	Asynchronous message passing Procedure calls RPC MS Windows DDE
Many–many	Broadcast calls	ISIS Multicast (Birman et al. 1991)

cess that executes a user activity before it can be used. Important parameters in specifying accessibility dependencies are the number of producers, the number of users, and the resource kind.

There are two broad alternatives for making resources accessible to their users (tables 4.2 and 4.3):

· Place producers and users "close together."

· Transport resources from producers to users.

Depending on the type of resource being transferred, either or both alternatives might be needed. Placing producer and user activities "close" to one another generally decreases the cost of transporting the resource. Combinations of placing activities and transporting resources should be considered in situations where the cost of placing the activities is lower than the corresponding gain in the cost of transporting the resource.

Table 4.4
Generic processes for managing prerequisite dependencies

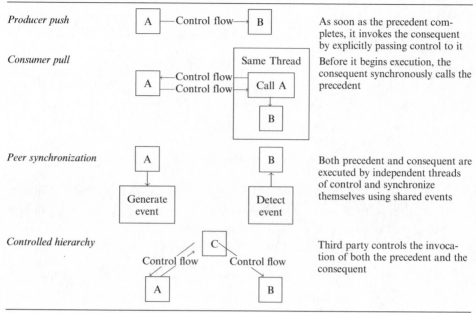

Producer push	A —Control flow→ B	As soon as the precedent completes, it invokes the consequent by explicitly passing control to it
Consumer pull	Same Thread; A ←Control flow—, ←Control flow— Call A, B	Before it begins execution, the consequent synchronously calls the precedent
Peer synchronization	A → Generate event; B ↑ Detect event	Both precedent and consequent are executed by independent threads of control and synchronize themselves using shared events
Controlled hierarchy	C; Control flow ↙ ↘ Control flow; A B	Third party controls the invocation of both the precedent and the consequent

PREREQUISITE DEPENDENCIES   A fundamental requirement in every resource flow is that a resource must be produced before it can be used. This is captured by including a prerequisite dependency in the decomposition of every flow dependency.

Prerequisite dependencies can be further classified according to:

- Number of precedent activities
- Number of consequent activities
- Relationship (and/or) among the precedent activities

In *And-prerequisites,* all activities in the precedent set must occur before activities in the consequent set can begin execution. By contrast, in *Or-prerequisites,* occurrence of at least one activity in the precedent set satisfies the prerequisite requirement.

Table 4.4 shows four generic processes for managing prerequisite dependencies. Each generic process can be further specialized according to a number of design dimensions specific to the process. For example, peer synchronization can be specialized according to the type of event used for synchronization. Table 4.5 contains a partial list of events. For each event, different execution environments provide

Table 4.5
Examples of synchronizing events

Event type	Generate	Detect	Reset
Semaphore	Signal semaphore (V)	Wait on semaphore (P)	Reset semaphore
File creation	Create file	Test file existence	Delete file
File modification	Write file	Compare file modification time with stored modification time	Set stored modification time to file modification time
Process creation	Create process	Test process existence	Kill process

Figure 4.2
A simple software system

different sets of corresponding system calls, providing yet another level of protocol specialization.

Designing Interconnection Protocols   This section will provide an example of how the framework can be used to guide the design of interconnection protocols among software components. Because only a small subset of the taxonomy is presented in this chapter, the example will also, by necessity, be very simple.

Suppose that we need to connect two existing pieces of code: a C program providing a graphical interface that repeatedly asks the user for part numbers, and a Visual Basic program that queries a database and displays descriptions of the corresponding parts. The C program returns integer part numbers while the Visual Basic program expects strings. Figure 4.2 shows the components and their interconnection relationship, in this case a simple data flow.

According to our framework, in order to interconnect the two components, we need to design a coordination protocol for the data flow dependency. Following our generic model for flows, this means that we have to design protocols for managing usability, accessibility, and prerequisite dependencies.

To manage usability, we elect that the producer will be responsible for making the data usable to the consumer (see table 4.1). In this example this will require the addition of code at the C component for converting data from integers to strings.

To manage accessibility, we first preclude the possibility of integrating the two components in the same executable, because they are written in different languages.

We therefore have to transport the data from producer to consumer. Our framework provides a set of possibilities for doing this.

One possibility would be to use an RPC protocol to transmit the data from producer to consumer. DDE (dynamic data exchange) is one such protocol supported by Microsoft Windows. The advantage of such a protocol is that it explicitly passes control from producer to consumer, thus managing the prerequisite dependency as well. The resulting protocol is depicted in figure 4.3. In this protocol, the C component acts as a client, while the Visual Basic component is wrapped inside a handler for a DDE call and acts as a server.

Another possibility would be to use a shared memory location or a shared file, whose filename is fixed in advance and known to both parties. This solution would require us to address the prerequisite relationship separately: Make sure that the Visual Basic program only reads the next part number after it has been written by the C program. We select a peer synchronization mechanism specialized to use semaphores as the synchronization event. Finally, as shared memory locations are best for storing numbers, conversion from integers to strings is done at the consumer side. Our choices result in the protocol depicted in figure 4.4. Notice that, in this protocol, the two components are eventually wrapped in two executables that run independently and synchronize implicitly.[1]

In conclusion, our framework not only can guide the design of interconnection protocols in a systematic way but also point out the range of alternatives available to the designer at each step.

4.3 The SYNTHESIS Application Development Environment

4.3.1 Overview

The coordination perspective on software design introduced in the previous section has been reduced to practice by building SYNTHESIS, an application development environment based on its principles. SYNTHESIS is particularly well suited for component-based software development. This section is devoted to a very brief description of the SYNTHESIS system. A detailed description can be found in (Dellarocas 1996).

---

1. The protocol for managing prerequisite dependencies shown in figure 4.3 allows more than one part numbers to be generated before one of them is displayed. In this application such behavior would most likely not be acceptable. Dellarocas (1996) contains a taxonomy of different variations of prerequisite dependencies and corresponding coordination protocols that would give a fully satisfactory solution to this problem.

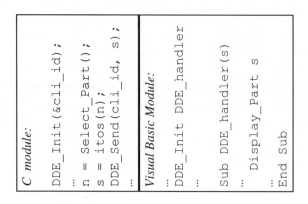

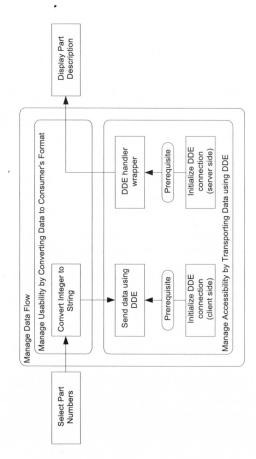

Figure 4.3
One protocol for managing the data flow dependency of figure 4.2

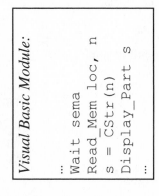

C module:

```
Reset(sema);

...
n = Select_Part();
Write_Mem(loc, n);
Signal(sema);
...
```

Visual Basic Module:

```
...
Wait sema
Read_Mem loc, n
s = CStr(n)
Display_Part s
...
```

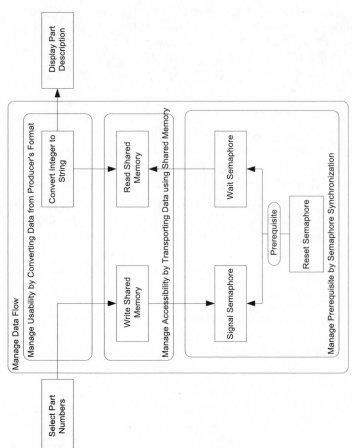

Figure 4.4
An alternative protocol for managing the data flow dependency of figure 4.2

SYNTHESIS consists of three elements:

• SYNOPSIS, a software architecture description language.

• An on-line design handbook of dependencies and associated coordination protocols.

• A design assistant that generates executable applications by successive specializations of their SYNOPSIS description.

SYNOPSIS: An Architecture Description Language SYNOPSIS supports graphical descriptions of software application architectures at both the specification and the implementation level. The language provides separate language entities for representing software *activities* and *dependencies*. It also supports the mechanism of *entity specialization*. Specialization allows new entities (activities and dependencies) to be defined as variations of other existing entities. Specialized entities inherit the decomposition and attributes of their parents and can differentiate themselves by modifying any of those elements. Specialization enables the incremental generation of new designs from existing ones, as well as the organization of related designs in concise hierarchies. Finally, it enables the representation of reusable software architectures at various levels of abstraction (from very generic to very specific).

A Design Handbook of Software Interconnection A prototype version of a handbook of common software interdependencies and coordination protocols has been developed. The handbook is an on-line version of our taxonomy of dependencies and coordination processes. The design spaces of our framework have been implemented by hierarchies of increasingly specialized SYNOPSIS entities. For example, figure 4.5 shows a partial hierarchy of increasingly specialized processes for managing prerequisite dependencies. Each process contained in the handbook contains attributes that enable the system to automatically determine whether it is a compatible candidate for managing a dependency between a given set of components.

A Design Process for Generating Executable Applications SYNTHESIS supports a process for generating executable systems by successive specialization of their SYNOPSIS descriptions. The process automates the reasoning we used in section 4.2.2 to design a coordination protocol for the flow dependency and integrate our two components into a complete system. It can be summarized as follows:

• Users describe their application using SYNOPSIS, as a pattern of activities connected through dependencies.

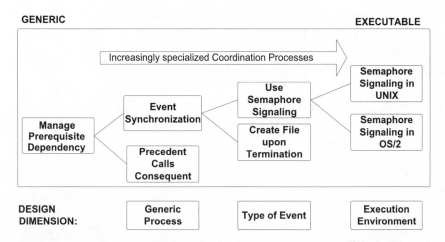

Figure 4.5
A hierarchy of increasing specialized coordination protocols for managing prerequisite dependencies

· The design assistant of SYNTHESIS scans the application description and iteratively does the following for each application element which is still not specific enough for code generation to take place (e.g., a dependency for which no coordination protocol has been specified):

1. It searches the on-line design handbook for compatible specializations.

2. It selects one of the compatible specializations found, either automatically, or by asking the user. If no compatible specialization can be found, it asks the user to provide one.

3. It replaces the generic application element with the selected specialization (e.g., it replaces the above dependency with a compatible coordination protocol for managing it) and recursively applies the same process to all elements in the decomposition of this element.

· After all application elements have been replaced by implementable specializations, the design assistant integrates them into a set of modules in one or more languages and generates an executable application out of the collection.

The design process above minimizes the manual effort required to integrate software components into new systems. Users only need to participate in the specialization process by making the final selection when more than one compatible specializations have been found. In the rare cases when no compatible specialization can be found, users need to provide the code for such a specialization. Specializations thus provided become a permanent part of the repository.

4.3.2 Using SYNTHESIS to Facilitate Component-Based Software Development
We tested the capabilities of SYNTHESIS by using it to build a set of applications by integrating independently written pieces of software. Each experiment consisted of four phases:

• Describing a test application as a SYNOPSIS diagram of activities and dependencies.

• Selecting a set of preexisting components exhibiting various mismatches to implement activities.

• Using the design process outlined above to semi-automatically manage dependencies and integrate the selected components into an executable system.

• Exploring alternative executable implementations based on the same set of components.

The results of our experiments were very encouraging. Overall, I used SYNTHESIS to build 4 test applications. Each application was integrated in at least two different ways. For example, for one application I built one implementation where components were organized around client/server interactions, and a second where the same components were organized around peer-to-peer interactions. This resulted in a total of 14 different implementations. SYNTHESIS was able to build all 14 implementations, typically generating between 30 and 200 lines of additional glue code in each case in order to manage interdependencies and integrate the components. In only 2 cases, users had to manually write 16 lines of code (each time), to implement two data conversion routines that were missing from the design handbook. Dellarocas (1996) contains a detailed description of these experiments.

4.4   Related Work

4.4.1   The Process Handbook Project
The work reported in this chapter grew out of the Process Handbook project at MIT's Center for Coordination Science (Dellarocas et al. 1994; Malone et al. 1993). The Process Handbook project applies the ideas of coordination theory to the representation and design of business processes. The goal of the Process Handbook project is to provide a firmer theoretical and empirical foundation for such tasks as enterprise modeling, enterprise integration, and process re-engineering. The project includes (1) collecting examples of how different organizations perform similar pro-

cesses and (2) representing these examples in an on-line Process Handbook that includes the relative advantages of the alternatives. SYNOPSIS has borrowed the ideas of separating activities from dependencies and the notion of entity specialization from the Process Handbook. It is especially concerned with (1) refining the process representation so that it can describe software applications at a level precise enough for code generation to take place and (2) populating repositories of dependencies and coordination protocols for the specialized domain of software systems.

4.4.2 Architecture Description Languages

Architecture Description Languages (ADLs) provide support for representing the high-level structure of software systems in terms of their components and their interconnections (Kogut and Clements 1994; Shaw and Garlan 1994). They are an evolution of Module Interconnection Languages (MIL), first proposed in the 1970s (DeRemer and Kron 1976). Most ADLs provide separate abstractions for representing components and their interconnections. SYNOPSIS shares many of the goals and principles of ADLs. However, whereas previously proposed architectural languages only provide support for implementation-level connector abstractions (e.g., a pipe, or a client/server protocol), SYNOPSIS is the first language that also supports specification-level abstractions for encoding interconnection relationships (dependencies). Furthermore, apart from introducing a new architectural language, this work proposes a more general perspective on designing systems which also includes the development of design handbooks for activities and dependencies as well as a design process for generating executable systems by successive specializations of their architectural descriptions. The project that comes closest to our work is UniCon (Shaw et al. 1995).

4.4.3 CASE Tools and Software Design Assistants

A number of research tools attempt to facilitate the design and development of software systems by providing graphical, architectural views of systems and automated assistants which guide users through the design process. STILE (Stovsky and Weide 1998) provides good support for graphical component-based design but does not provide particular support for distribution or for managing component mismatches. The Software Architect's Assistant (Kramer et al. 1993) is a visual environment for constructing distributed applications. Aesop (Garlan et al. 1994) exploits the notion of architectural style to assist users in constraining their design alternatives and verifying the correctness of their designs.

Broadly speaking, SYNTHESIS also provides a graphical architecture description language and a design assistant for generating executable applications. However, the specific models (activities, dependencies, and coordination processes), relationships (decomposition, specialization), and design operations (replace dependencies with compatible coordination processes) supported by SYNTHESIS are different from the systems above and specifically geared to facilitate the integration of heterogeneous, multilanguage, and possibly incompatible software components. It will be interesting to see how good ideas from various software design assistants can be constructively combined.

4.4.4 Component Frameworks

Component frameworks such as OLE, CORBA, and OpenDoc (Adler 1995) and our coordination perspective were both motivated by the complexity of managing component interdependencies. However, the two approaches represent very different philosophies. Component frameworks enable the interoperation of independently developed components by limiting the kinds of allowed relationships and by providing a standardized infrastructure for managing them. Only components explicitly written for a framework can interoperate with one another.

Our coordination perspective, in contrast, is based on the belief that the identification and management of software dependencies should be elevated to a design problem in its own right. Therefore dependencies should not only be explicitly represented as distinct entities, but furthermore, when deciding on a managing protocol, the full range of possibilities should be considered with the help of design handbooks. Components in SYNOPSIS architectures need not adhere to any standard and can have arbitrary interfaces. Provided that the right coordination protocol exists in its repository, SYNTHESIS will be able to interconnect them. Furthermore SYNTHESIS is able to suggest several alternative ways of managing an interconnection relationship and thus possibly generate more efficient implementations. Finally, open interconnection protocols defined in specific component frameworks can be incorporated into SYNTHESIS repositories as one, out of many, alternative ways of managing the underlying dependency relationships.

4.5 Conclusions and Future Directions

This work was motivated by the increasing variety and complexity of interdependencies among components of large software systems. It has observed that most current programming languages and tools do not provide adequate support for identifying and representing such dependencies, while the knowledge of managing them has not yet been systematically codified.

The initial results of this research provide positive evidence for supporting the claim that software interconnection can usefully be treated as a design problem in its own right, orthogonal to the specification and implementation of the core functional pieces of an application. More specifically, software interconnection relationships and coordination protocols for managing them can be usefully represented as independent entities, separate from the interdependent components. Furthermore they can be systematically organized in a design handbook. Such a handbook can assist, or even automate, the process of integrating a set of independently developed components into a new application.

Our experience with SYNTHESIS, a prototype application development environment based on these principles has demonstrated both the feasibility and the practical usefulness of this approach. Nevertheless, we view the work reported in this chapter as only the beginning of an ongoing effort to develop better methodologies and tools for supporting component-based software development. Some tasks remain that we plan to address in the immediate future:

• *Classify composite dependency patterns.*   Our current taxonomy includes relatively low-level dependency types, such as flows and prerequisites. In a sense, our taxonomy defines a vocabulary of software interconnection relationships. A particularly promising path of research seems to be the classification of more complex dependency types as patterns of more elementary dependencies.

• *Develop coordination process design rules.*   It will be interesting to develop design rules that help automate the selection step by ranking candidate processes according to various evaluation criteria such as their response time, their reliability, and their overall fit with the rest of the application. For example, when managing a data flow dependency, one possible design heuristic would be to use direct transfer of control (e.g., remote procedure calls) when the size of the data that flows is small, and to use a separate carrier resource, such as a file, when the size of the data is large.

• *Develop guidelines for better reusable components.*   The idea of separating the design of component functionality from the design of interconnection protocols has interesting implications about the way reusable components should be designed in the future. At best, components should contain minimal assumptions about their interconnection patterns with other components embedded in them. More research is needed to translate this abstract requirement to concrete design guidelines.

IIB Specialization of Processes: Organizing Collections of Related Processes

5 Defining Specialization for Process Models

George M. Wyner
Jintae Lee

5.1 Introduction

As the literature on object-oriented analysis and design attests, specialization of objects is a powerful source of advantage for the design as well as the implementation of information systems (Booch 1991; Coad and Yourdon 1990; De Champeaux 1991; De Champeaux et al. 1990; Maksay and Pigneur 1991; Rogers 1991; Rumbaugh et al. 1991; Taivalsaari 1996; Takagaki and Wand 1991). For example, the specialization hierarchy, in which each object inherits the features of its parent and modifies them incrementally, promotes comprehensibility, maintainability, and reusability.

When modeling system behavior, however, systems analysts continue to rely on traditional tools such as state diagrams and dataflow diagrams. While such diagrams capture important aspects of the processes they model, they offer limited guidance as to the ways in which a process can be improved.

Malone et al. (1999) have argued that this limitation of the current approach to information systems design can be addressed by employing a specialization hierarchy of *processes*. In addition to the benefits of comprehensibility and reusability, a process specialization hierarchy offers two major advantages from the organizational design perspective. First, it supports systematic generation of design alternatives. Variants of an existing process can be generated systematically and then evaluated along the dimensions of specialization. This *generativity*[1] is especially important in the absence of tools that support the design generation stage (Alexander 1979). Second, it offers an organizational framework in which to index and search for relevant processes (Malone et al. 1999). This support for locating relevant processes is especially important in the context of a large database of reusable process models, such as the Process Handbook, designed to support component-based process modeling and design.

The potential value of such an approach is especially promising in light of dramatic changes introduced into organizations by the rise of new information technologies, most recently Web computing and the resulting development of electronic commerce. In this chapter we focus on the specialization of *processes*. We argue that

---

1. There is recent precedent for employing the term "generativity" to refer to the capacity of a system to generate novel expressions, combinations, ideas, or productions. See, for example, Alexander (1979) and Malone et al. (1999).

a clear understanding of when one process is a special case of another and a mastery of the means by which specialized processes can be generated systematically will offer significant support for a more effective exploration of the new design territory opened up by these technologies, since it is arguably processes which must be transformed if business is to tap the potential of these technologies. Once generated by specialization, process variants can be explored and tested for their fit to the new environment (Malone et al. 1999).

Implementing such a process hierarchy, however, will require a clear definition of what it means for one process to be a specialization of another, and some guidelines as to how to go about specializing a process in practice.

One obvious approach to this problem is to treat the process as a class with a set of attributes and then to specialize processes in the same way that objects are specialized: by subtyping attributes and adding new attributes. It is not obvious, however, how this approach applies to process descriptions, which are typically complex aggregates of nodes and arcs. Consider, for example, the two state diagrams in figure 5.1. Diagram A contains two states R and S. Diagram B is identical except that a third state T has been added. Following the usual approach to specialization, we might argue that the diagram with the additional feature, diagram B, is a specialization of diagram A. However, one might also maintain that diagram A is the specialization, since diagram B includes all the behaviors of diagram A, but not vice versa, and thus diagram A is a special case of diagram B. Any approach to specializing

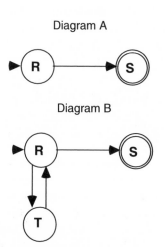

Figure 5.1
Which diagram is the specialization?

process representations must yield an operationalization that can explain such a puzzle.

In this chapter we propose a definition of process specialization that resolves this puzzle and supports organizational design by enabling the systematic generation and location of design alternatives. We do not claim at this point that our results generalize beyond the two representations discussed (state diagrams and dataflow diagrams), although we believe that such general results will be possible. Nor do we claim to be defining a new paradigm in the sense that object-oriented analysis and design is one. Rather, the major goal of this chapter is to define *process* specialization so that process representations as well as object representations can be subjected to existing object-oriented methods especially in the context of organizational design.

The rest of the chapter proceeds as follows: Section 5.2 develops a general framework for process specialization. Section 5.3 applies this approach to state diagrams, deriving a set of transformations which, when applied to any state machine, result in a specialization. Section 5.4 illustrates the potential benefits of this approach by means of a restaurant information system example. Section 5.5 extends the analysis to dataflow diagrams, and section 5.6 provides an example of how a simple dataflow diagram can be specialized. Section 5.7 compares this approach to related work. Section 5.8 identifies and resolves a number of apparent inconsistencies between this approach to process specialization and the approach taken in the object-oriented paradigm. Finally, section 5.9 summarizes the results and suggests directions for future research.

5.2   Process Specialization

Consider a system consisting of one or more objects of interest. This may be an existing system that is to be modeled or a new system which is to be designed. Such a system has characteristics that may evolve over time. These changes in the system constitute its *behavior*. We define the *execution set* of a system as the set of all possible behaviors associated with that system. A *process class* describes a set of such systems in terms of their execution sets. A system whose execution set is consistent with a process class is an *instance* of that process class and may be said to *realize* that process. The set of all instances of a process class is referred to as the *extension* of that process class.

Then a process class P' is said to be a *specialization* of a class P if every instance of P' is also an instance of P, but not necessarily vice versa.

5.2.1 Extension Semantics

There are many methods by which a process class can describe the execution sets of its instances. For example, a class might be defined as including all systems whose execution sets are supersets of some "minimal execution set"—that is, whose execution sets must include at least all the behaviors specified by the minimal execution set. In contrast, one might define a process class as including all systems whose execution sets are subsets of some "maximal execution set"—that is, whose execution sets can include at most the behaviors specified by the maximal execution set.

For example, in figure 5.1 the process class represented by diagram B is a specialization of the class represented by diagram A under minimal execution set semantics, because B refers to all systems whose execution sets include at least all the behaviors specified in the diagram, and this is clearly a subset of the collection of all systems whose execution sets need include only the behaviors specified in diagram A. In other words, under minimal execution set semantics, each transition represents a constraint, and the more constraints, the *smaller* the extension.

Conversely, under maximal execution set semantics, the process class represented by diagram A is a specialization of that represented by B because A refers to all systems that exhibit a subset of the behaviors in the diagram while B refers to the larger collection of systems that may include any of the additional executions described in diagram B. In other words, in the maximal interpretation, each transition represents an option, and the more options, the *larger* the extension.[2]

We will refer to this relationship between a process class and its extension as the *extension semantics* of the particular process representation. The key point here is that what counts as a specialization of a given process model depends critically on what extension semantics have been assigned to that model. From this perspective we can see that this matter is not dealt with explicitly in the semantics of most process representations.[3]

This lack of extension semantics introduces an ambiguity into attempts to specialize and classify processes, an ambiguity with important consequences for attempts to redesign and reuse process models, as discussed in section 5.5.

It follows then, that in carrying out our analysis of state diagrams and dataflow diagrams, we will need to adopt some kind of extension semantics. In the interest of

2. One can also imagine approaches that are more elaborate than either of these methods, but these suffice for the current analysis.

3. As will become apparent when we contrast our approach with that of Nierstrasz (1993), there is room for interpretation in this regard even in the apparently straightforward case of state diagrams.

simplicity, we will use the "maximal execution set" approach described above. While this choice may not be optimal for many practical situations, it is ideal for our purposes, in that it highlights the potential difficulties that must be addressed in a consistent approach to process specialization.

5.2.2   Maximal Execution Set Semantics

Under maximal execution set semantics, each process model is understood as defining the universe of behaviors from which any process instance is to be constructed. This semantics seems especially well suited to circumstances in which it is more important to prevent undesirable consequences than to allow for creative elaboration because the system is not allowed to have any behavior outside the specified set (e.g., consider the case of modeling the operations of a nuclear reactor or intensive care unit). This movement from an all inclusive general case to more restricted special cases may also provide valuable support to the system designer by offering an explicit set of variations to choose from rather than an open-ended space of unspecified possible extensions (as would be the case with minimal execution set semantics).

Given this choice of extension semantics, we can describe specialization in terms of the maximal execution sets themselves:

PROPOSITION   Given processes P and P' defined under maximal execution set semantics, with S_P the maximal execution set for P and $S_{P'}$ the maximal execution set for P', then P' is a specialization of P if and only if $S_{P'}$ is a subset of S_P.

Proof   See appendix A.[4]

Having specified an execution set semantics and derived its implications for specialization, we now address the frame of reference used to describe a process and develop criteria for comparing processes with different frames of reference. This is critical to our treatment of activity decomposition which is an important feature of many process representations. Having completed this analysis, we then introduce the notion of *specializing transformation*.

5.2.3   Frame of Reference

A process is among other things a set of possible behaviors, which we have been referring to as the *execution set* of a process. Note that any description of an execution set is made with respect to some *frame of reference* for the system: the frame of

---

4. For briefer exposition, all the proofs are presented in the appendices.

reference corresponding to the collection of attributes used to describe the set of possible behaviors that constitute that process. As we will see, it is possible to develop equivalent descriptions of a process (and its execution set) in a number of different frames of reference. In particular, we will introduce the notion of refinement, which denotes a change to a finer-grained frame of reference.[5]

For example, if the system of interest is an object moving in space, one might begin with a frame of reference with attributes for the position, mass, and velocity of the object, and then refine the frame of reference either by adding a new attribute such as the temperature of the object, or refining an existing attribute such as measuring position to the nearest meter as opposed to the nearest kilometer.[6] To fully develop our approach to specializing transformations, we will need to integrate this notion of refinement into our view of specialization:

We have shown that specialization can be viewed as a restriction on the maximal execution set of a process: a process p_1 is a *specialization* of a process p_0 if its maximal execution set is a subset of the maximal execution set of p_0. This result must now be restated to take into account frame of reference. There are two cases to consider:

1. *Both processes are described using the same frame of reference.*   In this case the maximal execution sets of the processes are described in the same terms and can be compared directly. Thus p_1 is a specialization of p_0 if and only if the maximal execution set of p_1 as described using the given frame of reference is a subset of the maximal execution set of p_0 as similarly described.

2. *The processes are described using different frames of reference, but there exists a "common" frame of reference (which is a refinement of both of these).*[7]   In this case p_1 is a specialization of p_0 if and only if the refinement of p_1 is a specialization of the refinement of p_0 under the common frame of reference. Thus this second case is reduced to the first by means of refinement.

5.2.4 Specializing Transformations

We propose one useful way to operationalize this notion of specialization. This is in terms of a set of transformations for any particular process representation, which,

---

5. The discussion that follows is in the spirit of the treatment of refinement and abstraction given by Horning and Randell (1973), who provide a lucid and wide-ranging exploration of this topic.

6. A more formal definition of refinement is given in appendix B and is employed in deriving further results below.

7. Note that the common frame of reference may be identical to one of the given frames.

when applied to a process description, produces a description of a specialization of that process. The two-part definition of specialization given above suggests that two sorts of transformations will be needed:

1. A *specializing transformation* is an operation that, when applied to a process described using a given representation and a given frame of reference, results in a new process description under that representation and frame of reference corresponding to a specialization of the original process. Specializing transformations change the extension of a process while preserving the frame of reference.

2. A *refining transformation*, in contrast, is an operation that changes the frame of reference of a process while preserving its extension, producing a process description of the same process under a different frame of reference.

For each type of transformation there is a related inverse type: a *generalizing transformation* acts on a process description to produce a generalization of the original process and is thus the inverse of a specializing transformation. Similarly an *abstracting transformation* is the inverse of the refining transformation, producing a new description of the same process under a frame of reference for which the original frame is a refinement.

Given that the refining/abstracting transformations preserve the extension of a process, it follows from our definition of process specialization that a specializing transformation composed with refining/abstracting transformations in any sequence produces a specialization. The analogous statement holds for generalizing transformations.

A set of refining/abstracting transformations is said to be *complete* if for any process p described under a frame of reference, the description of that process under any other frame of reference can be obtained by applying to p a finite number of transformations drawn from the set.

A set of specializing transformations is said to be *locally complete* if for any frame of reference and any process p described using that frame of reference, any specialization of p described under that frame of reference can be obtained by applying to p a finite number of transformations drawn from the set. Local completeness corresponds to the first part of the definition of process specialization given above.

There is also a notion of completeness corresponding to the second part of the definition. A set of specializing transformations and refining/abstracting transformations is said to be *globally complete* if for any process p, any specialization of p for which a common frame of reference exists can be obtained by applying to p a finite number of transformations drawn from the set.

PROPOSITION   Let A be a complete set of refining/abstracting transformations and S be a locally complete set of specializing transformations. Then $A \cup S$ is globally complete.

Proof   See appendix C.

5.3   State Diagrams

The first example of process representation that we will consider is the finite state machine or state diagram. State diagrams are often used to represent the dynamic behavior of systems. The circles in a state diagram correspond to states of the system being modeled, and the arcs connecting those circles correspond to the events that result in transitions between those states. The state diagram thus defines a set of possible sequences of events and states. Each state diagram must include at least one initial state (identified by a wedge, known as an "initial state marker") and one final state (identified by a double circle, known as a "final state marker"). All sequences must begin with an initial state and continue until they terminate with a final state. The set of states included in a state diagram can be thought of as a one-dimensional attribute space where the single attribute has values that correspond to the possible states. A system behavior corresponds to a sequence of these states, and each state diagram defines a set of such behaviors, which we interpret here as a maximal execution set. Under maximal execution set semantics, the process class described by this state diagram is taken to include all systems whose execution set is some subset of this maximal execution set. For example, the state diagram in figure 5.2 permits the event sequences *ac*, *abac*, *ababac*, *abababac*, and so on. This entire set of sequences can be described by the regular expression $a(ba) * c$.

Using the approach developed in section 5.2, we can then define a state diagram D' to be a specialization of state diagram D if and only if either:

1. The set of sequences permitted by D' is a subset of the set of sequences permitted by D.

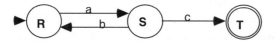

Figure 5.2
State diagram as a class of possible event sequences

2. Either D or D' can be refined such that condition 1 holds. (This essentially amounts to resolving differences in the granularity of the two process descriptions by decomposing states into substates.)

We will first identify a complete set of refining/abstracting transformations. Then we will identify a set of specializing transformations which is locally complete. Global completeness of the union of these transformation sets then follows from the proposition given at the end of section 5.2.

5.3.1 Refining/Abstracting Transformations for State Diagrams

PROPOSITION   The following constitutes a complete set of refining/abstracting transformations for state diagrams:

Refinement by exhaustive decomposition.   Replace a state by a mutually exclusive collectively exhaustive set of substates. Add events corresponding to all possible transitions between substates. For each event associated with the original state, add a corresponding event for each of the substates.

Abstraction by total aggregation.   If a set of states is completely interconnected by events and an identical set of "external" events is associated with each state in the set (i.e., if this set of states has the properties of an exhaustive decomposition as described above), replace that set of states by a single state that represents their aggregation. Associate with this state the same set of events that was associated with each of the substates.

Proof   The proof is found in appendix D.

5.3.2 Specializing Transformations for State Diagrams

PROPOSITION   The following constitutes a locally complete set of specializing transformations for state diagrams:

Delete an individual event.   This removes a possible transition between events, and thus the new diagram is specialized to exclude all behaviors that involve such a transition.

Delete a state and its associated events.   The new diagram is specialized to exclude all behaviors that involve the deleted state.

Delete an initial state marker.   This transformation is subject to the condition that at least one initial state marker remains. The new diagram is specialized to exclude all behaviors that begin with the affected state.

Delete a final state marker.   This transformation is subject to the condition that at least one final state marker remains. The new diagram is specialized to exclude all behaviors that end with the affected state.

Proof   The proof is found in appendix E.

It follows directly from the propositions proved so far that the union of the sets of transformations given above is globally complete.

Finally, while the preceding set of transformations is thus complete it may sometimes be convenient to employ other specializing transformations. In particular we will make use of the following transformation:

Specialize a state.   Replace a state in the original state diagram by one of its substates. This transformation can be expressed in terms of the set above by first exhaustively decomposing a state into substates and then deleting all but one of them.

5.4   Example: Restaurant Information System

To better understand how the approach we have developed might be of practical value, we present the following stylized example involving a restaurant information system based loosely on the work of Salancik and Leblebici (1988). This example is chosen because of its relative simplicity, and because of the familiarity of the restaurant domain.

Imagine that you are a systems analyst charged with developing an information system to support the operational side of a large restaurant or chain of restaurants. You might include as part of your analysis a state diagram representing the flow of events involved in a "meal transaction" in a restaurant. This would be the flow of events involved in the delivery of meals to customers and the collection of payment.

We will assume that based on interviews and observations, you have determined that any meal transaction will be composed of the following set of five activities: ordering a meal, cooking, serving, eating, and paying. Furthermore your interviews suggest that in the restaurants in question these steps always occur in a single sequence, leading to the simple state machine depicted in figure 5.3.[8]

---

8. While we have labeled the events in figure 5.3, in general, we will leave them unlabeled because the specific nature of the events is usually obvious, and in any case of limited relevance to the present analysis.

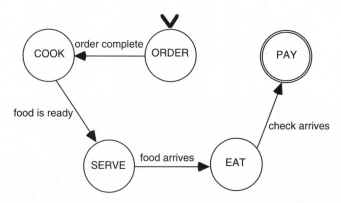

Figure 5.3
State diagram for full service restaurant

5.4.1 Building a Specialization Hierarchy

Having successfully developed software to support the operations of this first group of restaurants, you are called upon to modify the software to work in three other food service environments: a fast food restaurant, a buffet, and a church supper. Based on further interviews and analysis you develop the state diagrams shown in figure 5.4 to describe each of these processes.

Having observed that none of the four state diagrams developed so far is a specialization of any other, you apply the generalizing transformations to generate a generic restaurant process for which each of the above state diagrams is a specialization. As the diagrams differ only in the events they include, generalizing is simply a matter of adding each of the events from the other diagrams to the original diagram. The resulting diagram is shown in figure 5.5

You have thus generated the specialization hierarchy depicted in figure 5.6. Such hierarchies can contribute to software (and design) reuse by providing a taxonomy of previous designs that can be searched easily.

5.4.2 Generating New Processes

Of special interest is the fact that design knowledge propagates up this hierarchy to the most generic diagram, which contains accumulated knowledge about all variants of the restaurant process. This generic diagram can then be used to generate additional diagrams.

For example, imagine that you are now called upon to develop a specification to support a restaurant with both table service and a buffet. You can obtain a state

fast food restaurant

all you can eat buffet

church supper

Figure 5.4
Additional restaurant state diagrams

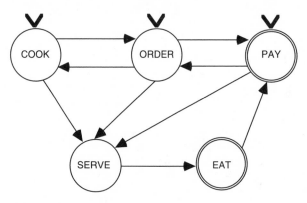

Figure 5.5
Generalized restaurant transaction

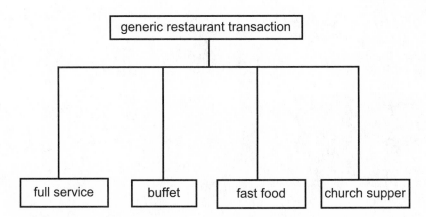

Figure 5.6
Initial specialization hierarchy for restaurant information system

diagram for such a hybrid by applying a series of specializing transformations to the generic diagram (see figure 5.7).

To the extent that one is choosing among a set of preexisting functions resident in the most generic diagram, a story about the great artist Michaelangelo would seem to be relevant. Michaelangelo was asked how it was that he was able to produce the extraordinary sculpture of David for which he is famous. He replied that he began with a block of marble and simply removed all the pieces that were not David, until only David remained. So with the most generic state diagram in a hierarchy, many diagrams can be generated simply by removing states and events that do not apply.[9]

5.5   Dataflow Diagrams

Having explored specialization of state diagrams in some detail, we now turn to dataflow diagrams. Dataflow diagrams are intended to show the *functionality* of a system: the various processes, and the flows of information and material that link them to each other, to inventories (data stores), and to various agents external to the system. A dataflow diagram (DFD) consists of a collection of processes, stores, and terminators linked by flows. A simple example taken from Yourdon (1989, p. 141) is given in figure 5.8. This discussion follows the approach taken by Yourdon (1989, ch. 9), to which the interested reader is directed for a more detailed exposition.

9. One hesitates to draw such a presumptuous comparison, but we can all aspire to produce systems with the grace, beauty, and intrinsic value exemplified by Michaelangelo's work!

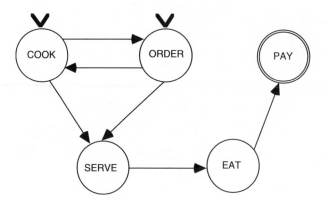

Figure 5.7
Full service restaurant with buffet

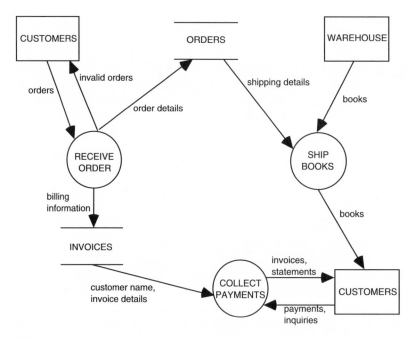

Figure 5.8
Example of a dataflow diagram: Order processing

Processes, shown as circles in the DFD, are the component actions or subprocesses which together constitute the overall process or system being represented in the diagram. *Stores*, represented by pairs of parallel lines in the DFD, are repositories of the data or material carried in the flows. *Terminators*, shown as rectangles in the DFD, represent the actors, external to the system being modeled, that interact with the various system processes. *Flows*, shown as arrows in the DFD, represent the movement of information or material between processes, terminators, and stores.

5.5.1   Specialization of Dataflow Diagrams

Before discussing specialization of dataflow diagrams, we must be more precise about the set of behaviors described by a dataflow diagram. While the DFD approach as usually presented does not specify what such a "DFD behavior" would look like, it seems reasonable to describe it as a sequence of processes and flows.[10] An immediate consequence of this approach under maximal execution set semantics is that executions of a particular DFD may only include processes and flows contained in that DFD. Note that terminators and stores are implicitly included in executions as the endpoints of flows.

A dataflow diagram does more, however, than simply list what processes and flows may occur in an instance. It also says something about the relationship between those flows and processes. For example, for each segment of a process that occurs in a DFD instance, one would expect some and possibly all of the flows into and out of that process to also occur.

In attempting to state these constraints precisely, one must take a position on certain questions about how a DFD is to be interpreted. For example, in the present discussion we will assume that in general, all flows into or out of a store or terminator may occur independently of each other.[11] We will also assume that each process instance must be accompanied by *at least* one inflow and one outflow, but that (without extending the dataflow representation) one cannot, in general, say more about which flows accompany a process execution without appealing to the semantics of the domain being modeled. For example, in figure 5.8, any instance of Ship

---

10. This discussion omits many aspects of DFDs that are worthy of attention, such as duration and sequencing of processes and flows.

11. For example, one might have a store of customer information that is updated by one process and queried by another, with the two processes and their flows occurring asynchronously. One can, of course, easily imagine dataflow diagrams in which the semantics require synchronization of flows into and out of a data store, and in these situations the approach we are taking is somewhat lax, permitting sequences that should be prohibited. While addressing this issue is beyond the scope of the present chapter, it is worth noting that this problem might be resolved by introducing additional constructs to indicate the presence of such synchronous flows.

books must involve all three flows: an incoming shipping memo and books, which are transformed into an outgoing shipment to the customer. However, in the same diagram the flow of an order into Receive order may result in a flow of order details into the Orders store or the flow of an invalid order back to the customer, but (presumably) not both. This latter issue appears to represent a fundamental ambiguity in the dataflow representation: it would seem that there is no domain independent interpretation of a DFD that permits a consistent definition of its class membership.

Since we have no domain independent interpretation of a DFD as defining a class, specialization cannot be extended to DFDs in a domain independent fashion. That is, in general, one cannot determine whether one DFD is a valid specialization of another without explicating which flows are mandatory and which are optional, and under what circumstances, information that is not captured in the DFD itself.

These ambiguities in the dataflow diagramming technique are well known and resolutions have been proposed (France 1992). We can proceed without such extensions, however, by limiting ourselves to transformations that neither add flows to nor delete flows from a process component. These transformations will then be specializing under any interpretation of process flows, because such flows are left intact under the transformation. Interestingly, even under this constraint we obtain a set of transformations that is rich enough to be useful, as will be illustrated in section 5.6.

We are now in a position to specify what executions are in the maximal execution set of a dataflow diagram. We can then identify transformations which result in a restriction on the maximal execution set and thus (as argued in section 5.2) result in a specialization. The maximal execution set of a dataflow diagram includes all sequences of processes and flows that satisfy the following constraints:

All processes and flows in the sequence appear as components of the dataflow diagram.

Each input flow or output flow to a process that appears in the sequence must be associated with at least one instance of that process in the sequence.

Each process that appears in the sequence must have at least one associated input flow and one associated output flow.

We can now give a definition of specialization for dataflow diagrams that follows directly from section 5.2. We can define a dataflow diagram D' to be a specialization of dataflow diagram D if and only if either:

1. The set of sequences permitted by D' is a subset of the set of sequences permitted by D.

2. Either D or D' can be refined such that condition 1 holds. (This essentially amounts to resolving differences in the granularity of the two process descriptions by decomposing process components.)

Having defined the relationship between a dataflow diagram and its execution set in terms of the constraints above, we are now in a position to identify a set of specializing transformations which operationalize the above definition. For this it will be useful to first introduce a set of refining/abstracting transformations, and this in turn requires a formal definition of the dataflow diagram and its attribute space. The formal definitions and analysis are given in appendixes F and G. In the discussion that follows we will summarize and briefly motivate the results.

5.5.2   Specializing and Refining Transformations for Dataflow Diagrams

For purposes of the current analysis of dataflow diagrams, we need only consider a single refinement—*exhaustive process decomposition*—and its corresponding abstraction—*total process aggregation*. Intuitively we achieve exhaustive process decomposition by replacing a component process with a set of subprocesses (including a generic process so that the decomposition is exhaustive) interconnected by all possible generic flows and with a copy of each "external" input and output flow linked in turn to each of the subprocesses. The presence of all possible flows and the generic process insures that the decomposed process represents a true refinement (i.e., does not restrict the extension of the original dataflow diagram in any way). In practice, of course, decomposition of processes in dataflow diagrams does not include all possible flows and subprocesses, for such decomposition involves both a refinement and a specialization (restriction of extension) of the original dataflow diagram (which is also consistent with other decompositions). The exhaustive process decomposition is thus of primarily theoretical interest: a kind of refinement benchmark against which specializations that involve decomposition can be analyzed.

As noted above, in developing a set of specializing transformations we will limit ourselves to transformations which preserve flows in and out of processes. Note that any such transformation must be specializing, because any executions in the maximal execution set of the resulting dataflow diagram must satisfy the MES conditions for the original dataflow diagram as well, since these only involve the relationship between flows and their associated processes, and these are not affected if we preserve

flows in and out of processes. We can identify several useful specializing transformations which are consistent with this constraint:

Deletion[12] *of a connected collection of components whose bordering components in
the original diagram are all either terminators or stores.* To get the sense of this
transformation, imagine the original DFD as a physical structure constructed by
bonding the various components together, and further imagine that these bonds are
unbreakable with the exception of any bond between a flow and either a terminator
or store. By breaking these latter bonds, one may in some cases be able to separate
the diagram into several pieces. This transformation consists of removing a single
one of these pieces while leaving the rest of the diagram and all its bonds intact (e.g.,
figures 5.11, 5.12, and 5.13 in section 5.6). Note that this transformation preserves
the constraint on flows since all remaining processes have all their flows intact (the
only components with deleted flows are terminators and stores). The intuitive justification for this transformation is that we take stores and terminators to be asynchronous and thus an execution may be restricted to one side or the other of a boundary
defined by these components.

Decomposition of a Process Any process in a DFD can be decomposed into a
lower-level DFD as long as the flows into and out of the decomposition are consistent with the flows in the top-level diagram. Note that this kind of decomposition is
not exhaustive in the sense of exhaustive process decomposition (which we argued
above is a refinement). This "nonexhaustive" decomposition can be thought of as
a refinement (exhaustive process decomposition) composed with a specialization
(deleting some subprocesses and decomposed flows). Note that our constraint that
flows associated with a process are preserved is satisfied by the "flow consistency"
aspect of this form of decomposition. That is, we require that for each flow into or
out of the decomposed process, there be at least one identical flow into or out of one
of the resulting subprocesses.

Specialization of a Component If one specializes any component (terminator, store,
process, or flow) of a dataflow diagram, the resulting diagram will be a specialization
of the original diagram. Note that here again we preserve flows associated with each
process. In particular, a specialized process can be thought of as a kind of subset of

---

12. The notion that a diagram can be specialized by deleting (rather than adding) a component may seem
at odds with our common understanding that an object is specialized by adding (or subtyping) an attribute.
This apparent contradiction can, however, be resolved. The short version of the argument is that deletion
of a process component is in this case analogous to the subtyping of an attribute rather than the deletion of
an attribute. (See section 5.8 for fuller discussion of this issue.)

the original process, which is to say, we replace the original process with a sub-process, and this means that specialization of a process is nothing more than a kind of process decomposition. A similar argument might be made for the specialization of flows. Finally, under the semantics we are employing for dataflow diagrams, terminators and stores figure into the maximal execution set of a dataflow diagram only as endpoints of a flow, which is to say, they are essentially attributes of some flow, and this means that specialization of terminators and stores is a kind of flow specialization. As we have just noted, this flow specialization can be understood as a kind of flow decomposition.

5.6   Example: Generating Order Processing Alternatives for E-Business

Having established a method for systematically generating process specializations, how might we use this method to support process redesign? We illustrate the possibility here with an e-business design scenario.

Consider a manager exploring possible changes to an order fulfillment process occasioned by a shift from a traditional brick and mortar enterprise to an e-business. For such a manager a generic account of this process (e.g., that taken from Yourdon (1989) and depicted in figure 5.10) is of potential value in that it identifies the key activities and flows to be addressed. However, the role played by these elements may change, up to and including the possibility that some of them may simply go away when order fulfillment moves onto the internet.

What we propose here is a procedure, based on the notion of process specialization, that this manager might employ to generate a set of process variants that call into question assumptions implicit in the generic order fulfillment process and that therefore support a systematic exploration of design possibilities for the new process. This procedure is illustrated in figure 5.9 which can be read from top to bottom as a sequence of steps.

1. First, a suitably generic representation of order processing must be obtained. For purposes of our example, we begin with the Yourdon diagram and generalize it in a manner consistent with how we have defined specialization for dataflow diagrams: the process 'Ship books' is generalized to 'Ship product', and the flows labeled "books" are generalized to product flows. The resulting generalization is depicted in figure 5.10.

2. Having established a starting point for her analysis, the manager then systematically applies one or more specializing transformations to the generalization in

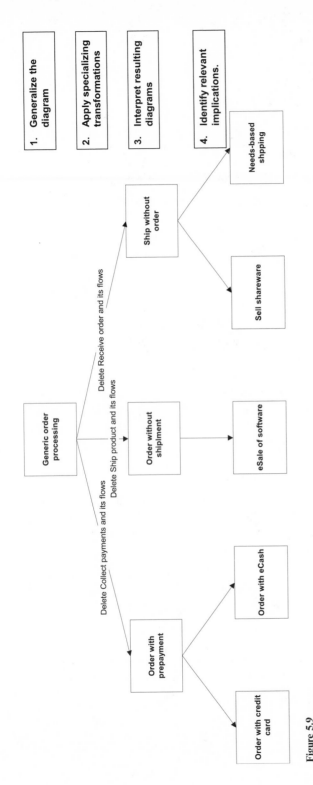

1. **Generalize the diagram**

2. **Apply specializing transformations**

3. **Interpret resulting diagrams**

4. **Identify relevant implications.**

Generic order processing

Delete Collect payments and its flows

Delete Ship product and its flows

Delete Receive order and its flows

Order with prepayment

Order without shiplment

Ship without order

Order with credit card

Order with eCash

eSale of software

Sell shareware

Needs-based shpping

Figure 5.9
Taxonomy of order processes

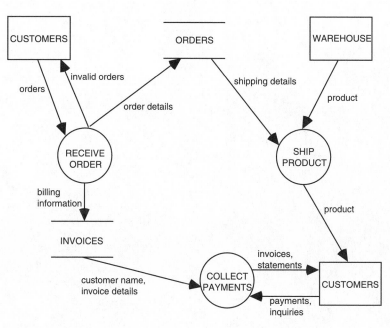

Figure 5.10
Order processing abstracted from books to products

order to generate a set of alternatives. In this example we focus on the set of dataflow diagrams which are generated by deleting connected portions of the DFD that border on stores and terminators.[13]

3. Once these specializations are obtained, the next step is to find a meaningful interpretation for the resulting diagrams: How do assumptions need to change so that one can make sense of each specialization as some kind of order fulfillment process? Note that it is possible that several interpretations will arise (in which case they should all be included), or that no plausible specialization arises. In this latter case one might then consider whether the proposed specialization violates some implicit constraint (a realization that is, no doubt, useful in itself). In the absence of such an "impossibility argument," one might want to retain the specialization

13. Note that the original DFD consists of three connected groups of components joined by the two stores' Orders and Invoices, and the terminator Customers. There are thus six possible specializations that result from deleting one or more of these groups from the diagram: three specializations in which two of the groups are deleted, and three specializations in which one of the groups is deleted. In this example we will restrict ourselves to the "less radical" transformations in which only one of the groups is deleted.

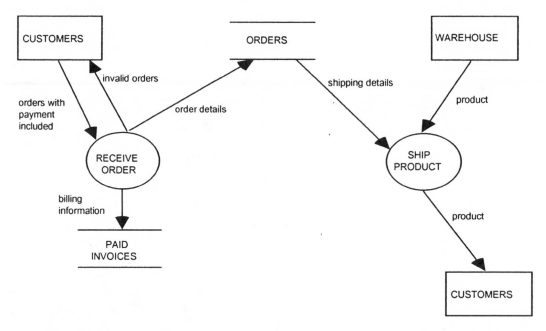

Figure 5.11
Order processing with pre-payment

against the future possibility of a plausible interpretation. For example, this may provide a framework for identifying new organizational forms as they emerge in the future (by understanding them as instances of a previously hypothetical specialization).

4. Finally one must consider the relevance of each specialization to the problem at hand, in this case the transition to electronic commerce.

What follows is a brief discussion of the specializations that result from this procedure.

5.6.1 Order Processing with Prepayment

Figure 5.11 depicts a specialization of the original DFD in which the 'Collect payments' process and its associated flows have been deleted. Note that the flow of orders has been specialized as well to indicate that cash must accompany each order. In this specialization any order without accompanying payment is returned to the customer as invalid, otherwise the order is forwarded to the 'Ship product' process and the invoice information is stored in the Paid invoices store (a specialization of the original Invoices store that reflects the lack of unpaid invoices in this system). One example of this alternative is the common form of order processing for e-business companies whereby payment with credit card accompanies the order. Other examples include the uses of e-cash or gift certificates, which may require simple accounting adjustments for the payment. These examples constitute further specializations of this alternative.

5.6.2   Order Processing without Shipment

Figure 5.12 depicts a diagram that was derived from the original DFD by deleting the 'Ship product' process and specializing its associated flows and the various stores and flows appropriately. This specialization would be possible to implement when there is a way for customers to obtain products without the company shipping them. For example, software products can be made available over the net for the customers to download, as with the company software.net, while the payment can follow later.

5.6.3   Order Processing without Order

Figure 5.13 depicts a specialization of the original DFD in which the 'Receive order' process and its associated flows have been deleted. This diagram might be interpreted as depicting a process in which products are shipped, unasked for, to prospects who are then billed for the products. Although this practice sounds unscrupulous, there do appear to be acceptable instances of this process as, for example, when "shareware" is shipped with a computer system or book, along with an electronic invoice that the recipient has no obligation to pay but can pay if he or she likes the product. Another example is when a company can detect your need and automatically ships the products to fulfill the need. Although it sounds somewhat futuristic, some companies come close to implementing this alternative. For example, the e-company, streamline.com, manages your household food inventory for you and delivers what you need without you having to ask for it.

This analysis of specialization in dataflow diagrams can be summarized by the specialization/generalization hierarchy given at the outset of this section (figure 5.9). Such a hierarchy provides both a process taxonomy and a structure that facilitates the systematic consideration and reuse of alternative designs. Thus one can enter the hierarchy with a particular process, "move up" to a more abstract process, and then consider not only plausible alternative process designs, but also identify other processes which might serve as sources of inspiration (Malone et al. 1999). The analysis above demonstrates that the use of specializing transformations, even when they are applied to a commonly understood business process such as order processing, can help us explore organizational alternatives.

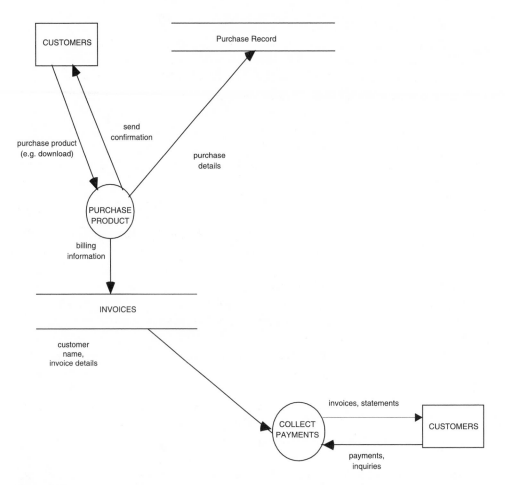

Figure 5.12
Order processing without shipment

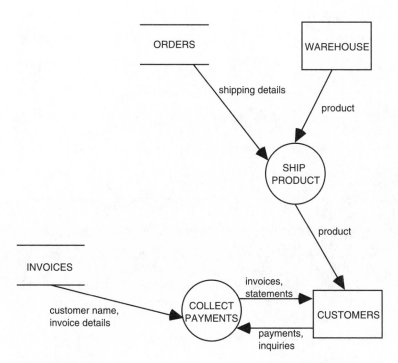

Figure 5.13
Order processing without order

5.7 Related Work

The notion that processes can be specialized is not new. An informal notion of process specialization can be found in a number of organizational design approaches. Checkland (1981) builds the design process on an idealized abstract model (referred to as a "root definition") that is then adapted and interpreted to the situation at hand. Senge (1990) introduces the notion of systems archetypes, which provide a generalized vocabulary that can be adapted to particular organizational situations. The practice of benchmarking can also be viewed as constructing idealized models of best practice, which are to be adapted to specific organizations. Our approach can be viewed as formalizing the intuitions behind these studies.

More formal notions of process specialization can be found in the studies of AI planning (Friedland and Iwasaki 1985; Stefik 1981), conceptual modeling (Borgida et al. 1993), object-oriented design (Nierstraz 1993),[14] and work flow (van der Aalst and Basten 1999). In all of these studies, however, process specialization is defined for the specific representation being proposed and none of these studies are concerned with process design.

Keller and Teufel (1998), in their approach to SAP customization, propose a series of transformations (e.g., selection of relevant modules, deletion of extraneous functionality, and setting of parameters) to be applied to the SAP code base. These transformations, when formalized, can be viewed as a precursor to our notion of specializing transformation. However, this work makes no attempt to extend the notion of process specialization beyond the SAP context.

There are other studies of process representation that take approaches similar to the one we propose. For example, the process formalism in this chapter and the definition of refinement, in particular, are somewhat similar to the approach taken by Horning and Randell (1973). Horning and Randell also develop a notion of one process *containing* another, which is equivalent to our definition of process specialization. This concept, however, plays a secondary role in their analysis. The F-ORM method, a method for specifying applications, discusses "transformation operations" among process representations (De Antonellis et al. 1991). In this method, however, these transformations pertain to the decomposition relation, and not specialization.

What is unique in our approach, then, is the notion that process specialization can be defined in a way that permits it to be incorporated into existing process representations by means of a set of specializing transformations. These transformations, when applied to a process in a given representation, result in a specialization of the original process. It is this transformational aspect of our approach that we claim provides a kind of generativity, and this will prove invaluable to process redesign. By supporting specialization for existing process representations, we hope to make this approach available as an extension to existing systems analysis and design methods.

As mentioned at the outset, the suggestion by Malone et al. (1999) that specialization can be applied to processes has been the foundation for this research effort. In their Process Handbook, Malone et al. arrange business processes in a specialization hierarchy. Entries in this Handbook can be viewed at various levels of decomposition. One can also traverse the specialization hierarchy to identify interesting variants

---

14. Interestingly Nierstrasz operationalizes specialization for state machines in a manner almost diametrically opposed to our own. As we discuss in section 5.8, however, this apparent inconsistency can be resolved as a difference in how the state machines are interpreted as objects—what we refer to in section 5.2.1 as the distinction between *maximal* and *minimal execution semantics*.

of a given process, including specializations, generalizations, and "siblings" (alternative specializations of the process's parent in the hierarchy).

Some modeling languages such as TAXIS (Borgida et al. 1993) define a kind of specialization specific to their process representation. Our goal, on the other hand, is to define a general method for specializing processes under any process representation (even one that does not build the notion of specialization into its semantics, e.g., the state diagram or dataflow diagram).

As we have emphasized throughout this chapter, the most obvious point of comparison for our work is the specialization of objects. Indeed, the research most closely related to our own would appear to be Nierstrasz's work on defining a subtyping relationship for active objects (Nierstrasz 1993). Nierstrasz treats an object as a finite state machine that defines the communications protocol supported by that object: the messages it accepts and the services it provides. He then defines a subtyping relationship on these state machines. This would appear to be quite similar to our own efforts to define a specialization relationship for state machines.

In comparing our work with Nierstrasz, four differences are evident:

1. Nierstrasz is concerned with state machines as defining the interactions between individual objects, whereas we are concerned with state machines as describing the internal behavior of entire systems.

2. Nierstrasz provides an algorithm for *determining* whether the subtype relationship holds between any two state machines. We provide a set of transformations for *generating* specializations and generalizations from a state machine. These two operationalizations would appear to be complementary; one could imagine situations in which it would be desirable to have the capability both to analyze and generate specializations.

3. Nierstrasz is concerned exclusively with state machines, whereas we are interested in applying our approach to a number of process representations.

4. Probably most intriguing is that our definition of specialization is almost exactly the opposite of Nierstrasz's definition of subtyping. For Nierstrasz, a state machine that is a subtype must accept a *superset* of the sequences accepted by the supertype; otherwise, it cannot be substituted safely for that supertype (Nierstrasz 1993). For us, a state machine that is a specialization must accept a *subset* of the sequences accepted by its generalization; otherwise, it will not represent a restriction in extension.

This apparent contradiction is easily resolved by observing that Nierstrasz implicitly employs a minimal execution set semantics instead of the maximal execution set approach taken here. Given the minimal execution set semantics, clearly a specialization must support a superset of the original minimal execution set, and thus a state diagram is specialized by *adding* states and events. As shown above, our choice of semantics leads to exactly the opposite result.

While this dramatic divergence can thus be explained by a difference in semantics, the question remains whether an approach that involves specialization by deletion can be reconciled with the standard object-oriented framework. In section 5.8 we argue that despite surface differences our approach is entirely consistent with the object-oriented approach to specialization: what appear to be significant inconsistencies between the two types of specialization disappear when one looks more fully into the matter.

5.8   Are There Two Kinds of Specialization?

In reconciling our approach with object specialization, there are two salient issues to be addressed. The first, raised in the Nierstrasz comparison above, is whether it is proper to specialize a process by deleting components, given that objects are specialized by doing what appears to be exactly the opposite: adding attributes.

The second issue follows as an implication of the first: if we specialize by deletion, then adding an attribute to a process requires adding the same attribute to its parents in the specialization hierarchy. Thus process modifications may propagate upwards, again in apparent contradiction of the object-oriented approach, where changes propagate downwards in the specialization hierarchy.

We deal with these two issues in turn.

5.8.1   Issue: Specialization by Deletion
Deleting attributes when specializing is generally not permitted because, among other things, it violates the principle of substitution, in that the specialized object cannot be universally substituted for the original because references to the missing attribute may result in error. Under maximal execution set semantics, however, process specialization appears to make extensive use of this forbidden "specialization by deletion." For example, many of the specializing transformations for state diagrams described above involve deleting parts of the diagram. A closer examination reveals that this is not a case of deleting attributes: when deleting parts of a state diagram one is altering a representation of the process, but the things deleted are not themselves attributes of the process. In other words, one should not confuse the *maximal execution set* of a process *description* with the *execution set* of a process *instance*.

One way to see this is to note that object specialization involves subtyping one or more attributes, and subtyping is in a sense a kind of deletion: one makes the type of the attribute more restrictive and thus makes the set of permissible values smaller (which is kind of like deleting from a list of permissible values). If one represents the type of an attribute graphically, this subtyping may be manifested as deleting elements from the graphical representation.

To take a simple example, consider a numeric attribute with type: INTEGER IN 1–10. One might choose to represent this type as a list of allowable numbers. Thus the type would be represented as

1   2   3   4   5   6   7   8   9   10

If one specializes by subtyping to INTEGER IN 4–7, one must delete elements from the representation to obtain

4   5   6   7

This may appear to be "specialization by deletion" if one focuses on the representation, but clearly it is simply specialization by subtyping.

While this example may appear to be contrived, it is exactly analogous to the state diagram example. Deleting transitions in a state diagram corresponds to subtyping an attribute of the corresponding process. More specifically, the execution set of a process instance can be viewed as the value of an "executions" attribute. The maximal execution set of the process class is then the type of this attribute. As it turns out, one can represent this type as a collection of ordered pairs of states that are equivalent to the state machine depicted in the state diagram. One can then show that subtyping this attribute corresponds to deleting events or states from the state diagram as follows:

Observe that under maximal execution set semantics, an instance of the process described by a state diagram is a system that realizes some subset of that diagram's maximal execution set. Then the *actual* execution set of this instance is an attribute of the process. The value of this *ExecutionSet* attribute is then a set whose elements are of type *execution*. An element e of type execution is in turn defined as an ordered tuple of length $n > 1$, such that for any i, $1 \leq i \leq n$, if a and b are the ith and $(i + 1)$th components of e respectively, then $\langle a, b \rangle \in E$, where E is the set of all events in the state diagram, represented as ordered pairs of states. Note, then that we can subtype execution by restricting the scope of E to some proper subset. Note that this restriction involves removing ordered pairs from E which is equivalent to deleting these events from the state diagram. Thus the state diagram is a graphical representation of the execution type of the ExecutionSet attribute of a process, and deleting events is a form of subtyping.

Thus "specialization by deletion" can be seen to actually be specialization by subtyping.

5.8.2 Issue: Upward Propagation or Downward Propagation

In object specialization hierarchies, the inheritance of attributes flows downward but changes at the leaves of a *process* hierarchy seem to propagate upward. In fact we will argue that this upward propagation can occur in any specialization hierarchy, and that this phenomenon is of potential interest to the systems designer.

Consider what happens to an object in a specialization hierarchy when one changes the attributes of one of its specializations (i.e., one of its children). Clearly, adding attributes or further subtyping of attributes simply further specializes the child object and has no effect on the parent object. However, say for some reason one needs to "supertype" an attribute of the specialization (e.g., one is validating the object model and discovers that the type of an attribute of some object is overly restrictive). Then a conflict may be introduced into the specialization hierarchy if the new type of this attribute is no longer a subtype of the corresponding attribute in the parent process, and the child process is no longer a specialization.

If one is to be strict about specialization and it turns out that the new change in type is unavoidable, then one would have to resolve the situation by modifying the type of the parent object in a similar fashion. This would follow logically given that the child is a specialization of the parent and the type of the child is now correct. Thus, by definition of specialization, the type of the parent must be at least as inclusive. Now one has modified an attribute in the parent by supertyping, and the same issue may arise with *its* parent with the result that a change in a leaf may necessitate changes in one or more ancestors, possibly all the way to the root of the tree.

Thus we can see that upward propagation is at least a theoretical possibility in any specialization hierarchy. It is important to note that such upward propagation is not normally supported in implementations of object oriented languages and would have to be carried out manually by a series of edits to the class definitions.

It is also important to note that upward propagation occurs only when one takes a strict approach to specialization, that is, requiring that the attributes of a specialization always be identical to or subtypes of the original attributes. If this strict approach is not enforced, then in the scenario above one would be free to add an inconsistent specialization without changing the attributes of the parent, and upward propagation would not occur. One would, of course, still be free to choose to modify the parent to reflect insights gained from developing the specialization, but there would be no requirement that such modifications be made.

The benefits of downward propagation (inheritance) are well known, and include the ability to define a new object incrementally by specifying only those aspects of the object that have changed, thus inheriting all the design knowledge associated with the parent node in the specialization hierarchy.

The benefits of upward propagation are those advanced by Malone et al. (1999) when they suggest that a specialization hierarchy of processes will allow one to systematically identify a wide range of design alternatives. Upward propagation makes this possible by forcing all design knowledge upward from the leaves to the highest level of abstraction at which it is relevant. Thus each process or object in the hierarchy reflects all the possibilities inherent in its descendants as illustrated with the restaurant and the order processing examples. This gathering of all possibilities can in turn lead to the other benefit mentioned by Malone et al.: generativity. For example, upward propagation may bring together a set of features originally present in distinct processes, which can then be recombined in unique ways by specialization, as for example, the different ways of providing a meal service or processing orders were generated from the respective generalized diagrams in the examples above.

5.9 Conclusions

We have explored how specialization can be applied to processes to take full advantage of the generative power of a specialization hierarchy. We have shown how specialization can be defined for state diagrams and dataflow diagrams in the form of a set of transformations that results in process specialization when applied to a particular diagram. Furthermore this method can be used to generate a taxonomy of processes to facilitate the exploration of design alternatives and the reuse of existing designs.

We have demonstrated that the rules by which a process diagram can be manipulated in order to produce a specialization (or a generalization) depend heavily on the semantics of the particular process representation. Thus the rules for specializing the state diagram differ in significant ways from those consistent with specialization of dataflow diagrams. Choose a different diagramming technique, and you create a new hierarchy of diagrams that may offer additional insights.

The work presented is only a preliminary exploration of how the generative power of specialization hierarchies can be harnessed in support of organizational design. One natural extension of this work is to explore additional process representations such as Petrie Nets and UML. One might also explore how the notion of specializing and generalizing transformations can be useful in other contexts, for example, the specializing of composite objects.

In summary, this chapter has suggested that specialization, currently applied to great advantage in the modeling of objects, the nouns of the world, can be fruitfully applied to processes, the verbs of the world, as well. Together, specialization and abstraction give rise to a method of process analysis that shows promise as a means both for identifying new and interesting process possibilities and for gathering the multitude of alternatives so generated into process taxonomies, which can then serve as reservoirs of process knowledge (Malone et al. 1999).

Appendix A   Maximal Execution Set Semantics

PROPOSITION   Given processes P and P' defined under maximal execution set semantics, with S_P the maximal execution set for P and $S_{P'}$ the maximal execution set for P', then P' is a specialization of P if and only if $S_{P'}$ is a subset of S_P.

Proof   If P' is a specialization of process class P, then for each behavior $b \in S_{P'}$, by definition of maximal execution set semantics, there is a process instance whose execution set contains b. This instance must also be in the extension of the more general class P and hence $b \in S_P$. It follows that $S_{P'} \subseteq S_P$. Conversely, let $S_{P'} \subseteq S_P$. Then consider any instance of P' with execution set e. By definition of maximal execution set semantics, $e \subseteq S_{P'}$; hence $e \subseteq S_P$ and therefore p is an instance of P as well. It follows that all instances of P' are instances of P, and thus P' is a specialization of P. $\square$

Appendix B   Refinement

The state of the system at any time is characterized in terms of some set of attributes that are ascribed to the system by an observer. The exact set of attributes may vary considerably from observer to observer and will reflect the abilities and interests of the observer, available technology, environmental conditions, and so forth. The set of attributes employed in observing a system may be thought of as a frame of reference for that system, one of many possible such frames.

We assume that the set of attributes employed is fixed and finite and that each attribute can take on some set of possible values. We refer to this set of possible values as the range of that attribute.

We define an attribute space as the cartesian product of the attribute ranges of all the attributes in a frame of reference. It follows that whenever the system is observed under that frame of reference, its state will correspond to some point in the corresponding attribute space. Furthermore each point in the attribute space corresponds to what may be a possible state of the system, although some of these points may refer to states that are not realizable.

By behavior of a system we mean the evolution of that system's state over time, which is to say the path the system traces out in some attribute space. Thus any description of a system's behavior is made with respect to some frame of reference for that system.

Definition An attribute space A' is a *refinement* of attribute space A if there is a surjective mapping M from A' onto A (i.e., the range of M includes every point in A; note that M maps the refinement into the original space rather than vice versa), with the property that a point a' in A' describes the state of the system if and only if $M(a')$ also applies. The intuition here is that if you refine your description of the system, there are more possible state points. So for each point in the original attribute space there is at least one point in the refined attribute space that is a description of the same state.

An attribute space A' is said to be a *strict refinement* if M is as above and is not also injective. That is, the inverse of M is not a function, or in other words, A is not also a refinement of A'. (This eliminates the trivial sense of refinement in which A and A' are essentially isomorphic.)

Given A', a refinement of A, then a behavior b' in A' is said to be a *refinement of a behavior b* in A if the following conditions hold: (1) for every x' in b', $M(x')$ is in b; (2) for every pair of points $x_{1'}$, $x_{2'}$ in b', if $x_{1'}$ precedes $x_{2'}$ in the path, then $M(x_{1'})$ precedes $M(x_{2'})$ or is identical to it. This last condition has to do with the fact that a path is a directed curve in attribute space, and we need to make sure that the points are traced out in the same order in both curves. The idea here is that the refined version of the behavior maps point by point onto the original behavior. Note that given the finer grained view of a process which results from refinement, we must allow for the possibility that $M(x_{1'})$ and $M(x_{2'})$ are identical, and hence that several points in one curve may correspond to a single point in the other. Note too that it follows from this definition that every behavior in A will have at least one (and possibly more) refinements in A'.

Similarly a process class p' in A' is said to be a *refinement of a process class p* in A, if for every behavior in the maximal execution set of p, all A' refinements of that behavior are included in the maximal execution set of p', and conversely, all behaviors in the maximal execution set of p' are A' refinements of some behavior in the maximal execution set of p. Then it follows that every process represented as a maximal execution set in A will have exactly one refinement in A', and that this refinement is equivalent to the original process description in that both process descriptions lead to the same classification of behaviors.

Appendix C   Completeness of Specializing Transformations

PROPOSITION   Let A be a complete set of refining/abstracting transformations and S be a locally complete set of specializing transformations. Then $A \cup S$ is globally complete.

Proof   Consider a process p_0 and a specialization p_1 for which a common frame of reference exists. Since A is complete, one can apply a finite sequence of transformations from A to p_0 to produce its refinement in the common frame of reference. By local completeness, one can then apply specializing transformations to produce the refinement of p_1 (since it is a specialization of the refinement of p_0 by assumption). Finally, by the completeness of A, one can transform the refinement of p_1 into p_1. Thus there is a finite set of transformations from $A \cup S$ which produces p_1 from p_0. $\square$

Appendix D   State Diagrams: Refining Transformations

PROPOSITION   The following constitutes a complete set of refining/abstracting transformations for state diagrams:

Refinement by exhaustive decomposition.   Replace a state by a mutually exclusive collectively exhaustive set of substates. Add events corresponding to all possible transitions between substates. For each event associated with the original state, add a corresponding event for each of the substates.

Abstraction by total aggregation.   If a set of states is completely interconnected by events and an identical set of "external" events is associated with each state in the set (i.e., if this set of states has the properties of an exhaustive decomposition as described above), replace that set of states by a single state that represents their aggregation. Associate with this state the same set of events that was associated with each of the substates.

Proof   As noted above, the attribute space of any state diagram consists of a single attribute corresponding to the current state of the system. It follows that the only permissible refinement of this attribute space (consistent with the definition of state diagram) is a finer grained representation of states. That is, refinement must consist of decomposing one or more states into substates.

Consider first the case of refinements where a single state is so decomposed. It follows immediately that such a refinement must consist precisely of the "exhaustive decomposition" transformation described above: if one omits any of the possible transitions involving the newly introduced substates, one excludes behaviors that constitute refinements of the original behaviors under this decomposition, and by definition of refinement the refined state diagram must include all such behaviors.

In the most general case, a refinement may involve decomposition of several states. Clearly such a refinement can always be obtained by exhaustive decomposition of the individual states, that is, by a sequence of exhaustive decompositions. Therefore the exhaustive decomposition transformation is sufficient to generate all possible refinements of a state diagram.

Now observe that the total aggregation transformation is the inverse of exhaustive decomposition. It then follows, by arguments analogous to those just given, that total aggregation is sufficient to generate all possible abstractions of a state diagram.

So far we have demonstrated that exhaustive decomposition suffices to generate all refinements of a given state diagram and total aggregation suffices to generate all abstractions. It remains to show that these transformations suffice to relate state diagrams represented under any two frames of reference (even those not related directly by a direct chain of refinements or a direct chain of abstractions).

Consider a state diagram described under two frames of reference. As observed above, these frames of reference are defined entirely by the set of states involved in each. Let the states for the first frame of reference be $S_A = \{A_1, A_2, \ldots, A_m\}$ and the corresponding state diagram be denoted by SD_A. Let the states for the second frame of reference be $S_B = \{B_1, B_2, \ldots, B_n\}$ and the state diagram be denoted by SD_B.

We can assume without loss of generality that there is some S such that $S = \bigcup A_i = \bigcup B_i$ so that the A_i and B_i are alternative partitions of S.[15] Then define $C_{ij} = A_i \cap B_j$.

CLAIM $S_C = \{C_{ij} \mid i = 1, \ldots, m, j = 1, \ldots, n\}$ is a refinement of S_A and S_B.

Proof of Claim   For all $A_i \in S_A$, $A_i \subseteq S = \bigcup B_j$; hence $A_i = A_i \cap S = A_i \cap \bigcup B_j = \bigcup_{j=1}^{j=n} (A_i \cap B_j) = \bigcup_{j=1}^{j=n} C_{ij}$. Then $C_{ij} \subseteq A_i$ for $j = 1$ to n. As a result the mapping $M(C_{ij}) = A_i$ preserves the state and is surjective and not bijective (assuming $n > 1$). Thus, by definition, S_C is a refinement of S_A, and by analogous reasoning, S_C is a refinement of S_B.

Then we can apply a set of exhaustive decompositions to SD_A to obtain the refinement SD_C (the state diagram refined under the frame of reference S_C). Then since S_C is a refinement of S_B, SD_B is an abstraction of SD_C, and there is a sequence of total aggregations that when applied to SD_C results in SD_B. Then combining these

---

15. To see that this assumption is warranted, let $S = \bigcup A_i \cup \bigcup B_i$ so $\bigcup A_i \subseteq S$ and $\bigcup B_i \subseteq S$. If $\bigcup \{A_i\} \neq S$, then define an additional state $A_{m+1} = \bigcup (S - \bigcup A_i)$ and similarly for B.

results, we have a sequence of exhaustive decompositions and total aggregations that when applied to SD_A results in SD_B. Since the choice of S_A and S_B was arbitrary, we conclude that the set of exhaustive decompositions and total aggregations together form a complete set of refining/abstracting transformations for state diagrams. □

Appendix E   State Diagrams: Specializing Transformations

PROPOSITION   The following constitutes a locally complete set of specializing transformations for state diagrams:

Delete an individual event.   This removes a possible transition between events, and thus the new diagram is specialized to exclude all behaviors that involve such a transition.

Delete a state and its associated events.   The new diagram is specialized to exclude all behaviors that involve the deleted state.

Delete an initial state marker.   This transformation is subject to the condition that at least one initial state marker remains. The new diagram is specialized to exclude all behaviors that begin with the affected state.

Delete a final state marker.   This transformation is subject to the condition that at least one final state marker remains. The new diagram is specialized to exclude all behaviors that end with the affected state.

Proof   For any frame of reference and any processes p_0 and p_1 described under that frame of reference, if p_1 is a specialization of p_0, then every sequence permitted in the maximal execution set of p_1 must be permitted in the maximal execution set of p_0 as well. Then all initial states of p_1 must also be initial states of p_0, and similarly for final states. Furthermore any state or event in p_1 must be a state or event in p_0 as well; otherwise, p_1 will permit a sequence involving a state or transition that cannot appear in a sequence of p_0. Thus p_0 includes all elements of p_1, and one can obtain p_1 by deleting some set of events, states, initial state markers, and final state markers. Since p_0 is itself finite, there can be only a finite number of such deletions. Thus p_1 can be obtained from p_0 by applying a finite number of transformations from the given set. □

Appendix F   Formal Definition of Dataflow Diagram and Its Attribute Space

Unlike state diagrams, where a single state in an execution sequence captures the entire state of the system at that point in the sequence, a single flow or process in a dataflow diagram does not capture the state of the dataflow, which depends on the state of multiple flows and processes. In a sense the issue here is the parallelism supported by the dataflow diagram representation, where several component processes may execute simultaneously.

As it turns out, this parallelism can be captured by a single state attribute, but that attribute must take into account whether each process or flow in a dataflow diagram is currently active or inactive. A process is said to be active when it is executing (i.e., transforming inputs into outputs) and inactive otherwise. A flow is said to be active when it is available to the downstream process as an input. When a process is active it has access to those flows which are simultaneously active, and only those flows.

More formally, we define a dataflow diagram as the tuple $\langle P, F, T, R, I, O \rangle$, where:

P is a finite set of component processes.

F is a finite set of component flows.

T is a finite set of component terminators.

R is a finite set of component stores.

P, F, T, and R must be disjoint.

$I : F \rightarrow (P \cup T \cup R)$ is a function defined so that $I(f)$ is the component that consumes flow f.

$O : F \rightarrow (P \cup T \cup R)$ is a function defined so that $O(f)$ is the component that produces flow f.

We require that all flows be either inputs to or outputs from a process. That is, for all flows f, $I(f) \in (T \cup R) \rightarrow O(f) \in P$ and $O(f) \in (T \cup R) \rightarrow I(f) \in P$.

To define a suitable attribute space, let S denote the power set $2^{P \cup F}$, that is, the set of all subsets of $P \cup F$. Then each $s \in S$ corresponds to a possible state of the dataflow diagram in which the flows and processes in s (which, recall, is a subset of $P \cup F$) are active and all other flows and processes are not active. This list of active processes and flows is clearly an attribute of the dataflow diagram, and hence S is an attribute space.

Having formalized the dataflow diagram and its attribute space, we are now in a position to formally define the maximal execution set of a dataflow diagram. First, however, we must introduce additional notation concerning dataflow diagram behavior:

Recall that a dataflow diagram behavior b is a sequence of states in S. Such a sequence can be denoted by the n-tuple $\langle s_1, s_2, \ldots, s_n \rangle$. Then we define $\varphi(b, i)$ as the ith item in the n-tuple associated with b.

Then for any dataflow diagram $D = \langle P, F, T, R, I, O \rangle$, the maximal execution set of D, henceforth denoted $\text{MES}(D)$ is defined (consistent with our informal discussion above) as $\{b \mid b$ is a sequence of states and the two conditions defined below hold for $b\}$, where the two conditions are:

1. We have informally asserted above that each input flow or output flow to a process which appears in b must be associated with at least one instance of that process in b. In order to formalize this condition, we must elaborate it further: any flow f active in b must be active in a consecutive subsequence S_f of b such that if f is produced by a process p_1, then p_1 is active in the first state of S_f, and if f is consumed by a process p_2, then p_2 is active in the last state of S_f.[16] Formally this condition becomes: for all s in b and for all flows $f \in F$, $f \in s \rightarrow (\exists m, n, p$ integers $0 < m \le n \le p)$ such that $\varphi(b, n) = s$ and $f \in \varphi(b, i)$ for $m \le I \le p$ and $O(f) \in P \rightarrow O(f) \in \varphi(b, m)$ and $I(f) \in P \rightarrow I(f) \in \varphi(b, p)$.

2. We asserted informally above that each process in the sequence must have at least one associated input flow and one associated output flow. In formalizing this statement, we restate it in slightly different form: whenever a process is active in a state s in b, then at least one input flow and output flow must also be active. Stated formally this becomes: for all $p \in P$ and for all $s \in b$, $p \in s \rightarrow (\exists f_1, f_2 \in F) f_1 \in s \land f_2 \in s \land I(f_1) = O(f_2) = p$.

Henceforth we will refer to these two conditions as the *MES conditions*.

Appendix G   Refining/Abstracting Transformations for Dataflow Diagrams

We proceed by first formally defining exhaustive process decomposition and then proving that it is a refinement. Let $D = \langle P, F, T, R, I, O \rangle$ and $D' = \langle P', F', T', R', I', O' \rangle$ be two dataflow diagrams. Then we define exhaustive process decomposition as a binary relation R_P on dataflow diagrams, with $R_P(D, D')$ if and only if:

1. P' replaces the process to be decomposed with its subprocesses:

$$P' = (P - P^-) \cup P^+$$

where P^- is the set containing the single process component to be decomposed and

---

16. Note that in the event f is produced (or consumed) by a terminator or store, the corresponding condition does not apply since terminators and stores are not directly included in the attribute space.

P^+ is the set containing the subprocesses in the decomposition. Since P^+ must contain a generic process and at least one specific subprocess, we have

$$|P^-| = 1 \quad \text{and} \quad |P^+| > 1.$$

2. F' removes all flows involving the decomposed process and add all possible flows to, from, and among the subprocesses:

$$F' = F - (F_I^- \cup F_O^-) \cup F_I^+ \cup F_O^+ \cup F_+^+$$

where F, F_I^+, F_O^+, and F_+^+ are all disjoint

$$F_I^- = I^{-1}[P^-]$$

$$F_O^- = O^{-1}[P^-]$$

$|F_I^+| = |F_I^-||P^+|$ (one new input flow per subprocess and original input)

$|F_O^+| = |F_O^-||P^+|$ (one new output flow per subprocess and original output)

$|F_+^+| = |P^+|(|P^+| - 1)$ (all possible flows among subprocesses)

and we require that none of the new flows share both input and output (i.e., no duplicate flows): $f_1, f_2 \in (F' - F) \wedge I'(f_1) = I'(f_2) \wedge O'(f_1) = O'(f_2) \to f_1 = f_2$.

3. $I' : F' \to P'$ is a function with the following properties:

$f \in F - F_I^- - F_O^- \to I'(f) = I(f)$ (remaining original flows have same consumer)

$I'[F_+^+] = P^+$ (internal flows have subprocesses as consumers)

$I'[F_I^+] = P^+$ (new input flows have subprocesses as consumers)

$I'[F_O^+] = I[F_O^-]$ (new output flows have same consumers as originals)

4. $O' : F' \to P'$ is a function with the following properties:

$f \in F - F_I^- - F_O^- \to O'(f) = O(f)$ (remaining original flows have same producer)

$O'[F_+^+] = P^+$ (internal flows have subprocesses as producers)

$O'[F_O^+] = P^+$ (new output flows have subprocesses as producers)

$O'[F_I^+] = O[F_I^-]$ (new input flows have same producers as originals)

5. S' is defined as the powerset $2^{F' \cup P'}$, corresponding to an attribute space for D' as described above.

Having defined exhaustive process decomposition, it remains to be proved that it is a refinement:

CLAIM $R_P(D, D') \to D'$ is a refinement of D.

Proof Recall that to prove that one process representation is a refinement of another, we must prove the following three assertions:

Assertion 1. S' is a refinement of S (one attribute space is a refinement of the other).

Assertion 2. For every behavior $b' \in \text{MES}(D')$ there is a behavior $b \in \text{MES}(D)$ such that b' is a refinement of b.

Assertion 3. For every behavior $b \in \text{MES}(D)$ and every behavior b' in S', if b' is a refinement of b, then $b' \in \text{MES}(D')$.

Proof of Assertion 1 By definition of refinement, it suffices to show that there is a map $M : S' \to S$ such that M is surjective, noninjective and $M(s')$ and s describe the same state of the world. Intuitively such an M must map the subprocesses and flows in D' to the original process and flows from which they were decomposed. More formally, we first define maps Φ and θ that take the flows in F_I^+ and F_O^+ to the original flows from which they were derived:

$$\Phi : F_I^+ \to F_I^- \quad \text{and} \quad \Phi(f) = O^{-1}[O'(f)] \wedge I^{-1}[P^+]$$

$$\theta : F_O^+ \to F_O^- \quad \text{and} \quad \theta(f) = I^{-1}[I'(f)] \wedge I^{-1}[P^+]$$

Φ and θ yields the set of all original flows with the same producer and consumer as a given f. Typically this would be a single flow (assuming no "duplicate" flows in the original dataflow diagram):

$$\text{Define} \quad \Gamma : (P^+ \cup F_+^+ \cup \varnothing) \to P^- \cup \varnothing \quad \text{with} \quad \Gamma(x) = \begin{cases} \varnothing, & x = \varnothing \\ P^-, & x \in (P^+ \cup F_+^+) \end{cases}$$

We will use Φ, θ, and Γ to map active flows and processes in the decomposition to active flows and processes in the original dataflow diagram and this will be the underlying basis for the map M. Recall that a state in the attribute space of a dataflow diagram is a set of flows and processes that is active. Then what M needs to do is to take such a set for D' and by adding and deleting flows and processes, convert it to the corresponding set in D. We define M as follows:

$$M(s') = s' - F_I^+ \cup \Phi[s' \cap F_I^+] - F_O^+ \cup \theta[s' \cap F_O^+] - (P^+ \cup F_+^+) \cup \Gamma(s' \cap (P^+ \cup F_+^+))$$

Note that the domain of M is contained in S, since we create $M(s')$ by removing all elements of $S - S'$ (subtracting out the elements of F_I^+, F_O^+, F_+^+, and P^+). Further all elements added to s' are from S (since the domains of Φ, θ, and Γ are all subsets of S). It remains to show that M is surjective and not injective.

To show that M is surjective, for any $s_0 \in S$, let

$$s_1 = s_0 - P^- \cup \Gamma^{-1}[P^- \cap s_0] - F_I^- \cup \Phi^{-1}[s_0 \cap F_I^-] - F_O^- \cup \theta^{-1}[s_0 \cap F_O^-]$$

Since we have subtracted out all elements of $S - S'$ and added only elements from S', $s_1 \in S'$. Thus we can apply M to s_1. We have carefully constructed s_1 so that $M(s_1) = s_0$, which we now prove. Note that once we have established this fact we have shown that M is surjective, since the choice of s_0 was arbitrary.

By definition of M above, we have

$$M(s_1) = s_1 - F_I^+ \cup \Phi[s_1 \cap F_I^+] - F_O^+ \cup \theta[s_1 \cap F_O^+] - (P^+ \cup F_+^+) \cup \Gamma(s_1 \cap (P^+ \cup F_+^+))$$

We now evaluate several terms of $M(s_1)$ as follows:

$$\Phi[s_1 \cap F_I^+] = \Phi[\Phi^{-1}[s_0 \cap F_I^-] \cap F_I^+]$$

(since all other terms in s_1 are disjoint with respect to F_I^+)

$$= \Phi[\Phi^{-1}[s_0 \cap F_I^-]] \quad (\text{since } \Phi^{-1}[s_0 \cap F_I^-] \subseteq F_I^+)$$

$$= s_0 \cap F_I^-$$

By similar arguments, we have

$$\theta[s_1 \cap F_O^+] = s_0 \cap F_O^- \quad \text{and} \quad \Gamma(s_1 \cap (P^+ \cup F_+^+)) = P^- \cap s_0$$

Substituting these results and expanding the remaining s_1 term, we have

$$M(s_1) = s_0 - P^- \cup \Gamma^{-1}[P^- \cap s_0] - F_I^- \cup \Phi^{-1}[s_0 \cap F_I^-] - F_O^- \cup \theta^{-1}[s_0 \cap F_O^-]$$
$$- F_I^+ \cup (s_0 \cap F_I^-) - F_O^+ \cup (s_0 \cap F_O^-) - (P^+ \cup F_+^+) \cup (P^- \cap s_0)$$

Noting that disjoint terms in this expression can be freely rearranged, we can reorder the terms as follows:

$$M(s_1) = s_0 - P^- \cup (P^- \cap s_0) - F_I^- \cup (s_0 \cap F_I^-) - F_O^- \cup (s_0 \cap F_O^-) \cup \Gamma^{-1}[P^- \cap s_0]$$
$$\cup \Phi^{-1}[s_0 \cap F_I^-] \cup \theta^{-1}[s_0 \cap F_O^-] - F_I^+ - F_O^+ - (P^+ \cup F_+^+)$$

Now since $s_0 - P^- \cup (P^- \cap s_0) = s_0$, we have

$$M(s_1) = s_0 - F_I^- \cup (s_0 \cap F_I^-) - F_O^- \cup (s_0 \cap F_O^-) \cup \Gamma^{-1}[P^- \cap s_0] \cup \Phi^{-1}[s_0 \cap F_I^-]$$
$$\cup \theta^{-1}[s_0 \cap F_O^-] - F_I^+ - F_O^+ - (P^+ \cup F_+^+)$$

Simplifying further, we have $s_0 - F_I^- \cup (s_0 \cap F_I^-) = s_0$, yielding

$$M(s_1) = s_0 - F_O^- \cup (s_0 \cap F_O^-) \cup \Gamma^{-1}[P^- \cap s_0] \cup \Phi^{-1}[s_0 \cap F_I^-] \cup \theta^{-1}[s_0 \cap F_O^-]$$
$$- F_I^+ - F_O^+ - (P^+ \cup F_+^+)$$

Substituting $s_0 - F_O^- \cup (s_0 \cap F_O^-) = s_0$, we obtain

$$M(s_1) = s_0 \cup \Gamma^{-1}[P^- \cap s_0] \cup \Phi^{-1}[s_0 \cap F_I^-] \cup \theta^{-1}[s_0 \cap F_O^-] - F_I^+ - F_O^+ - (P^+ \cup F_+^+)$$

Since s_0 is disjoint with respect to all the other terms, we can regroup the terms so that

$$M(s_1) = s_0 \cup (\Gamma^{-1}[P^- \cap s_0] \cup \Phi^{-1}[s_0 \cap F_I^-] \cup \theta^{-1}[s_0 \cap F_O^-] - F_I^+ - F_O^+ - (P^+ \cup F_+^+))$$

Given disjoint terms, we can further rearrange to obtain

$$M(s_1) = s_0 \cup (\Gamma^{-1}[P^- \cap s_0] - (P^+ \cup F_+^+) \cup \Phi^{-1}[s_0 \cap F_I^-] - F_I^+ \cup \theta^{-1}[s_0 \cap F_O^-] - F_O^+).$$

Now given the domain of Γ, Φ, and θ, we have

$$\Gamma^{-1}[P^- \cap s_0] \subseteq (P^+ \cup F_+^+)$$

$$\Phi^{-1}[s_0 \cap F_I^-] \subseteq F_I^+$$

$$\theta^{-1}[s_0 \cap F_O^-] \subseteq F_O^+$$

Hence

$$\Gamma^{-1}[P^- \cap s_0] - (P^+ \cup F_+^+) = \varnothing$$

$$\Phi^{-1}[s_0 \cap F_I^-] - F_I^+ = \varnothing$$

$$\theta^{-1}[s_0 \cap F_O^-] - F_O^+ = \varnothing$$

Substituting into $M(s_1)$, we obtain $M(s_1) = s_0$. Thus M is surjective. M cannot be bijective since M maps a finite domain S' onto a finite range S and $|S'| > |S|$. To see this, note that $|S| = 2^{|P \cup F|} = 2^{(|P|+|F|)}$ and $|S'| = 2^{|P' \cup F'|} = 2^{(|P'|+|F'|)}$.

Now from the definition of R_P above, we have $|P'| = |(P - P^-) \cup P^+|$, but since P^- and P^+ are disjoint and $P^- \subseteq P$, this simplifies to $|P'| = |P| - |P^-| + |P^+|$. Recall that $|P^-| = 1$ and $|P^+| > 1$. Hence $|P^-| < |P^+|$ from which it follows that $|P'| > |P|$.

Furthermore, again from the definition of R_P, we have $|F'| = |F - (F_I^- \cup F_O^-) \cup F_I^+ \cup F_O^+ \cup F_+^+| = |F| - |F_I^-| - |F_O^-| + |F_I^+| + |F_O^+| + |F_+^+|$. Since $|P^+| > 1$ and $|F_I^+| = |F_I^-||P^+|$, we have $|F_I^+| > |F_I^-|$, and similarly we have $|F_O^+| > |F_O^-|$. Hence it follows that $|F'| > |F|$.

Now since $|P'| > |P|$ and $|F'| > |F|$, we have $|S'| = 2^{(|P'|+|F'|)} > 2^{(|P|+|F|)} = |S|$, and thus M is not injective.

Finally, it follows directly from the definition of M that for any $s' \in S'$, $M(s')$ differs from s' only in that any active subprocesses and their associated flows are removed from s' and replaced with the corresponding process and flows in S and thus $M(s')$ and s' describe the same state of the world.

Thus S' is a refinement of S. □

Proof of Assertion 2   Recall that we must show that $b' \in \text{MES}(D') \rightarrow \exists b \in \text{MES}(D)$ such that b' is a refinement of b. Let $M[b']$ denote the sequence obtained by applying M to each element of b' and consolidating any repeated elements in the resulting sequence. It clearly follows that b' is a refinement of $M[b']$, and it only remains to show that for each $b' \in \text{MES}(D')$, $M[b'] \in \text{MES}(D)$. By definition of maximal execution set above, it suffices to show that $M[b']$ satisfies the two MES conditions which together define the relationship between active flows and active processes in the maximal execution set. That $M[b']$ satisfies both these conditions follows immediately from the property of refinement, which ensures that $M(s)$ and s describe the same state of the world in different frames of reference. Since each process or flow in D' has a corresponding process or flow in D (albeit the mapping is many to one), and the input and output relations are preserved under the refinement associated with M, then both MES conditions must be preserved by M as well. □

Proof of Assertion 3   Recall that we must show that for every behavior $b \in \text{MES}(D)$ and every behavior b' in S', if b' is a refinement of b, then $b' \in \text{MES}(D')$. It suffices to show that $b \in \text{MES}(D) \wedge M[b'] = b \rightarrow b'$ satisfies the MES conditions. Since, as we noted in the proof of assertion 2, the MES conditions are preserved by M, this must be so, for if one of the MES conditions failed to hold for b', it would also fail to hold for $M[b']$, which would contradict the assumption that $b \in \text{MES}(D)$. Hence b' must satisfy both MES conditions. □

Having proved all three assertions, the overall claim is proved: exhaustive process decomposition is a refinement. □

Acknowledgments

The authors would like to thank Paul Resnick for suggesting this topic and providing detailed comments, as well as Tom Malone for his feedback and encouragement. In writing this chapter, we have benefited greatly from discussions with Brian Pentland,

Kevin Crowston, Chris Dellarocas, Fred Luconi, and Charley Osborn. Bob Halperin, Lorin Hitt, Kazuo Okamura, John Quimby, Ignascio Silva-Lepe, Tor Syvertsen, Marshall Van Alstyne, and the late Cheng Hian Goh also provided helpful comments. This research was sponsored by the Center for Coordination Science at the Massachusetts Institute of Technology and by the National Science Foundation (No. IRI-9224093).

IIC *Different Views of Processes*

6 Process as Theory in Information Systems Research

Kevin Crowston

6.1 Introduction

Many researchers have searched for evidence of organizational productivity improvements from investments in information and communication technologies (ICT). Unfortunately, evidence for such payback is spotty at best (e.g., Meyer and Gupta 1994; Brynjolfsson and Hitt 1998). On the other hand, at the individual level, ICT are increasingly merging into work in ways that make it impossible to separate the two (e.g., Gasser 1986; Zuboff 1988; Bridges 1995). The contrast between the apparently substantial impact of ICT use at the individual level and the apparently diffuse impact at the organizational level is but one example of the problem of linking phenomena and theories from different levels of analysis.

The intent of this chapter is to show how individual-level research on ICT use might be linked to organization-level research by detailed consideration of the organizational process in which the use is situated. The term "process" is considered here as an interrelated sequence of events that occur over time leading to an organizational outcome of interest (Boudreau and Robey 1999). Understanding this linkage is useful for those who study ICT, and especially useful for those who design them (Kaplan 1991).

In section 6.2, I briefly present the problem of cross-level analysis. In section 6.3, I discuss the concept of a process to explain how processes link to individual work and ICT use, on the one hand, and to organizational and industrial structures and outcomes, on the other. As well, I briefly discuss the potential use of process theories as a milieu for interplay between research paradigms. In sections 6.4 and 6.5, I illustrate the application of this framework in a study of the use of an information system in a restaurant. In section 6.6, I conclude by sketching implications of my process perspective for future research.

6.2 The Problem of Multi-level Research

Information systems research (I/S) has in recent years shifted its attention to organizational issues (Benbasat et al. 1987). Organizational research in turn has historically

An earlier version of this chapter appeared as K. Crowston (2000), Process as theory in information systems research, in R. Baskerville, J. Stage, and J. I. DeGross, eds., *Proceedings of Conference on the Social and Organizational Perspective on Research and Practice in Information Technology*, Kluwer Academic Publishers, Dordrecht, 2000, pp. 149–64. © 2000 Kluwer Academic Publishers. Reprinted by permission.

been divided between micro- and macro-level perspectives. Unfortunately, many organizational issues are multi-level and thus incompletely captured by single-level theories. ICT impact is clearly multi-level, as the same ICT has discernable impacts on individuals, groups and organizations. For such topics, multi-level theories are preferable because they provide a "deeper, richer portrait of organizational life—one that acknowledges the influence of the organizational context on individuals' actions and perceptions *and* the influence of individuals' actions and perceptions on the organizational context" (Klein et al. 1999, p. 243). However, multi-level research is difficult, so theorizing at different levels is often disconnected, leading to misleading theoretical conclusions.

Klein et al. (1994, p. 196) stress the primacy of theory in dealing with levels issues. However, multi-level work to date has been restricted to a few domains, such as climate or leadership (Klein et al. 1994, p. 197). The lack of focus on information issues suggests that there is an opportunity and a need for multi-level research and theorizing on ICT use.

6.3 Processes as Theory

Most theories in organizational and I/S research are variance theories. Variance theories comprise constructs or variables, and propositions or hypotheses linking them. Such theories predict the levels of dependent or outcome variables from the levels of independent or predictor variables, where the predictors are seen as necessary and sufficient for the outcomes. A multi-level variance theory is one that includes constructs and variables from different levels of analysis. The link between levels takes the form of a series of bridging or linking propositions involving constructs or variables defined at different levels of analysis.

An alternative to a variance theory is a process theory (Markus and Robey 1988). Rather than relating levels of variables, process theories explain how outcomes of interest develop through a sequence of events (Mohr 1982). Typically process theories are of some transient process leading to exceptional outcomes, such as events leading up to an organizational change or to acceptance of a system. However, I will focus instead on what might be called "everyday" processes: those performed regularly to create an organization's products or services.

A description of a process has a very different form from the boxes and arrows of a variance theory, but it is still a theory, in that it summarize a set of observations and predictions about the world. In a process theory the observations and predictions are about the performance of events leading up to organizational outcomes of interest. Such a theory might be very specific, that is, descriptive of only a single performance in a specific organization. More desirably the theory might describe a general class of performances or even performances in multiple organizations. As Orlikowski (1993) puts it, "Yin (1984) refers to this technique as 'analytic generalization' to distinguish it from the more typical statistical generalization that generalizes from a sample to a population. Here the generalization is of theoretical concepts and patterns."

Kaplan (1991, p. 593) states that process theories can be "valuable aids in understanding issues pertaining to designing and implementing information systems, assessing their impacts, and anticipating and managing the processes of change associated with them." The main advantage of process theories is that they can deal with more complex causal relationships than variance theories, and provide an explanation of how the inputs and outputs are related, rather than simply noting the relationship. Likewise I argue that process theories provide a link between individual and organizational phenomena and a milieu for interplay between research paradigms. However, to make this point, I will first describe the components of a process theory, in contrast to the variables and hypotheses of a variance theory.

6.3.1 Components of a Process

In this section, I develop a series of increasingly elaborate process conceptualizations. I begin by discussing processes as wholes, and then as compositions of activities with constraints on assembly. The goal of this discussion is to understand the connection between processes and individual work, on the one hand, and processes and organizational outcomes on the other.

Processes as Wholes A simple view is that processes are ways organizations accomplish desired goals. In fact, as Malone et al. (1999) point out, processes are often named by the goals they accomplish (e.g., product development or order fulfillment). The goal identifies the desired result or output of the process, or the set of constraints the process satisfies (Cyert and March 1963; Simon 1964), that is necessary to link to organizational outcomes (i.e., how quickly or efficiently different process options meet the constraints and produce the output). By focusing at the level of a process, I seek to avoid the problems outlined by March and Sutton (1997) who noted the instability of organizational performance.

A related view is that a process is a transformation of an input to an output. This view focuses on the resources that flow through the process. The business process concept has strong roots in industrial engineering (IE) and its subfield of process engineering (Sakamoto 1989). Other process concepts borrow heavily from operations research (OR) and operations management (OM), in particular, the design and control of manufacturing and product-producing processes of the firm. This view of a process is also similar to the root definition (RD) from soft systems methodology (SSM) (Checkland and Scholes 1990).

A key point in SSM, to which I also adhere, is that there is not a single correct RD for a process. Instead, there can be many RDs reflecting different view of the process. For example, one RD might focus on the official rationale for the process and the concrete items created. Another might focus on the way the organization allocates resources to different processes. Instead of arguing that whichever model chosen is a true representation of the work, I view the description as a discursive product, that is, as an artifact, with an author, intended to accomplish some goal. Checkland (1981) similarly describes models as "opening up debate about change" rather than "what ought now to be done" (p. 178).

Describing a process as a way to accomplish a goal or as a transformation of an input to an output establishes the link between processes and organizational outcomes. For example, at this level of detail the efficiency of a process can be stated as the process outputs divided by the inputs. However, at this level of detail, the link to individual work or ICT use is not yet apparent.

6.3.2 Processes as Activities and Interdependencies

To progress further, we need a more detailed view of processes that will allow us to say more about differences in how individuals contribute to processes and especially how the use of ICT might make a difference to these contributions. To do so, I start with the definition of a process as a sequence of events, focusing specifically on events as activities performed by individual or groups. Such a description will be a theory of the process in the sense that it summarizes a set of observations about what activities happened when the process was performed in the past and a set of predictions about what will happen when the process is performed in the future.

Representing a process as a sequence of activities provides insight into the linkage between individual work and processes, since individuals perform the various activities that comprise the process. As individuals change what they do, they change how they perform these activities and thus their participation in the process. Conversely, process changes demand different performances from individuals. ICT use might simply make individuals more efficient or effective at the activities they have always performed. However, an interesting class of impacts involves changing which individuals perform which activities. Buyers might search real estate listings themselves, performing activities that the agent used to perform. ICT might be used to automate the performance of certain activities, thus changing the activities that comprise the process. Analysis of these possibilities requires an even more detailed view of the process, which I present next.

To understand how changes in individual work might affect the process, it is necessary to examine the constraints on assembling activities that limit the possible arrangements and rearrangements of activities into processes. To identify these constraints, I focus in particular on the implications of dependencies for process assembly. In focusing on dependencies, I both follow and diverge from a long tradition in organization theory. Thompson (1967) viewed subunit interdependency as the basic building block of organizational structure and behavior. Following Thompson, two basic conceptualizations of organizational interdependency have evolved: resource interdependency, generated through exchanges between organizational members (e.g., people); and work flow interdependency, generated between organizational units located in the division of labor (Victor and Blackburn 1987).

In both cases dependencies were seen as arising between individuals or groups. In contrast to these earlier views, I believe that conceptualizing dependencies as arising between *activities* provides more insight into processes. This view makes it easier to consider the implications of reassigning work to different actors. In my view, the limits on the orders of activities arise from the flow of resources between them, that is, on resource interdependencies.

Malone and Crowston (1994) proposed two major classes of dependencies: *flow* or *producer/consumer* dependencies and *shared resource* dependencies. *Producer/ consumer* dependencies arise when one activity creates a resource that is then used by another activity. *Shared resource* dependencies arise when two or more activities require the same resources (because of space limitations, this class of dependency will not be discussed further in this chapter).

Both kinds of dependencies have implications for changes to processes. Since the activities can not be performed without the necessary resources, the existence of the dependencies constrains how the process can be assembled. In particular, *producer/ consumer* dependencies restrict the order in which activities can be performed. On the other hand, activities that are not involved in a dependency can be freely rearranged. Therefore we can limit possible arrangements of the activities in analyzing existing processes or in designing new ones.

As well as constraining the order of activities, interdependencies often require additional activities to manage them. According to Malone and Crowston (1994), the *producer/consumer* interdependency described above not only constrains the order of the activities (a *precedence* dependency) but may also require additional activities to manage the *transfer* of the resource between or to ensure the *usability* of the resource. *Precedence* requires that the producer activity be performed before the consumer activity. This dependency can be managed in one of two ways: either the person performing the first activity can notify the person performing the second that a resource is ready, or the second can monitor the performance of the first. ICT may have an effect by providing a mechanism for cheap monitoring. *Transfer* dependencies are managed by a range of mechanisms for physically moving resources to the actors performing the consuming activities, and vice versa. For example, inventory management systems can be classified here. *Usability* can be managed by having the consumer specify the nature of the resources required or by having the producer create standardized resources expected by the user, among other mechanisms.

In general, there may be numerous different coordination mechanisms that could be used to address a given dependency. Different organizations may use different mechanisms to address similar problems, resulting in a different organizational form. Because these coordination mechanisms are primarily information processing, they may be particular affected by the use of ICT.

Processes as a Milieu for the Interplay of Research Paradigms   As should be clear from the preceding discussion, developing a model of a process raises numerous problems, such as how activities are identified and determined to be relevant to the process or choosing an appropriate level of decomposition for the process description. These choices can be problematic because processes involve numerous individuals with possibly different interpretations of the process. Resolution of these choices raises questions about the theoretical assumptions underlying the theory.

As a framework for discussing these underlying assumptions, Burrell and Morgan (1979) suggest a 2 by 2 categorization of social theories: order-conflict and subjective-objective (assumptions about ontology, epistemology, human nature, and methodology). The combination of these two dimensions results in four distinct paradigms for research. Burrell and Morgan (1979) present their four paradigms as incommensurable approaches to research. However, Schultz and Hatch (1996) suggest a research project can draw on and contrast multiple paradigms. They identify several ways research might cross paradigms, including sequential (e.g., Lee 1991), parallel, bridging, and interplay. Schultz and Hatch argue that interplay "allows the findings of one paradigm to be recontextualized and reinterpreted in such a way that they inform the research conducted within a different paradigm."

In Burrell and Morgan's (1979) framework, theories of processes clearly focus on the ordering of society—stability, integration, functional co-ordination, and consensus—rather than on conflict. However, they could provide a milieu for interplay between subjective and objective perspectives. A process study might contrast realist and nominalist ontologies to achieve a richer description. Activities performed might be viewed as real (e.g., stamping metal) or nominal (e.g., many information processes). Flows of physical goods have a physical reality, though many interesting processes are largely information processing for which a nominalist position is more appropriate.

A study might contrast positivist and antipositivist epistemologies. On the one hand, viewing a process as a way to accomplish organizational goals implies a positivist conception of the process. On the other, focusing on individuals and their conceptions of their work implies an antipositivist view of activities. A possible result of this contrast is to explicitly problematize the question of how individuals come to contribute to the higher-order goals. For example, although individuals make sense of the world themselves, there must still be some degree of agreement among members of a group, such as about the meaning and nature of a shared process, meaning that individual perceptions are subjective but not completely arbitrary. Numerous researchers have investigated the nature of such shared cognitions and the social processes by which they are built (Walsh 1995). For example, Weick and Roberts (1993) show how aircraft carrier flight deck operations are made reliable by the "heedful interrelating" of flight deck personnel.

A study might contrast deterministic and voluntaristic assumptions about human nature. Individuals working in a group do not have total freedom in what they do if they are to contribute to the group, but are not totally constrained either. Again, consideration of interplay between these positions is possible. For example, Simon (1991) raises the question of why individuals adopt organizational goals in the first place.

To summarize, the objective-subjective debate is often presented as a dichotomy and a matter of prior assumption. However, as Schultz and Hatch (1996) say, "the assumption of impermeable paradigm boundaries reinforces and is reinforced by 'either–or' thinking. We believe that paradigm boundaries are permeable and claim that when paradigm contrasts are combined with paradigm connections, interplay becomes possible." Process theories provide a milieu for such interplay.

6.3.3 A Process-Centered Research Framework

Crowston and Treacy (1986) noted that linking the use of ICT to any kind of organizational-level impact requires some theory about the inner workings of organizations. Processes provide a possible bridge between individual, organizational- (and even industrial) level outcomes of the use of ICT. This framework is shown pictorially in figure 6.1. The framework acknowledges that ICT, by themselves, do not change organizations, nor are they merely tools of managerial intent. Rather, ICT

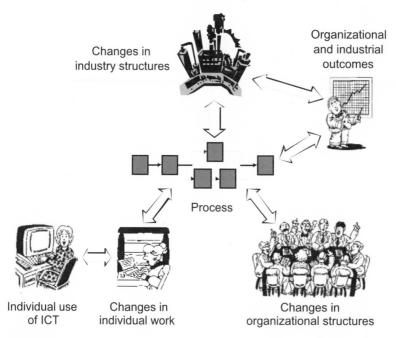

Figure 6.1
Relationship between ICT-induced changes in individual work and changes in organizational and industrial structures and outcomes

use opens up new possibilities for individual work, and these changes in work in turn have implications for the processes and thus the organizations in which these individuals participate.

These work and process changes, in turn, may involve changes in organizational structures and outcomes, and vice versa. In other words, as individual workers incorporate various forms of ICT in their work, they alter both how they conduct their work and how they participate in the organization's structure, and thus indirectly how their organizations participate in the industrywide value chain. Conversely, there are organizational and industrywide forces shaping how work is done. These forces also affect how individuals do their work. The interaction of these forces is what shapes the uses of ICT, new forms of work and new ways of organizing.

In the next section, I use this framework in the study of the use of an information system in a restaurant to show how processes can provide a link between individual- and organizational-level phenomena.

6.4 Illustrative Example: Service Processes in Two Restaurants

To illustrate the use of a process-centered framework, I will compare the service processes in two restaurants, one with and one without a seating information system (Crowston 1994). This example demonstrates how consideration of the process helps to link phenomena observed at the individual and organizational levels. Restaurants have long been studied as important forums for coordination. The essential characteristics of restaurants—many customers, many orders, frequent deliveries, continuous monitoring of customers and of personnel in accomplishing work, and perishable products—makes them particularly illuminating for studies of logistical flows, information flows, and resultant needs for coordination.

6.4.1 The Research Setting

The two restaurants I compare—one in Lake Buena Vista, Florida and the other in Southfield, Michigan—belong to the same national chain. They differ significantly, however, in their use of information technology. My analysis is based on observations of lunch and dinner service at the two restaurants, discussions with staff, and analysis of documentation describing the IT system provided by the software services company that developed and sold the system to the restaurant chain (Karp 1994; Rock Systems 1994).

The Southfield restaurant is a conventional sit-down restaurant, organized for high-volume operations. Seats are allocated by assigning tables on a conventional grease pencil-and-acetate record used by the hostess. Communications were face to face. By contrast, the Lake Buena Vista restaurant uses an information system to track table status and to automate some communications with restaurant staff.

When I arrived at the Lake Buena Vista restaurant, the hostess consulted a computerized display of tables in the restaurant to select a table for me and my guests. The system can balance customers across wait staff or maintain a waiting list if the restaurant is full. As we were seated, my hostess pointed out a button under the table. Pressing the button updated the status of the table in the information system, such as from free, to occupied, to waiting-to-be-bused, and finally back to free. The system also included pagers carried by the wait staff. When the table button was pressed indicating that we had been seated, the system paged the waitress responsible for the table, indicating there were new customers. When our meals were ready, the kitchen used the pagers to inform the waitress that our order was ready to be picked up and served. When the waitress collected the bill after we had left, she could page a buser to clean that table. Similarly, when the buser had finished, he or she could inform the hostess (and the system) that the table is available and the next customer could be seated.

This system apparently had a significant practical impact: it is reported, for example, that "diners spend 15 to 30 minutes less time in the restaurant [after the installation of the system] because of swifter service" (Karp 1994). The question I wish to answer is, Why does the system have such a profound impact on organizational performance? This question cannot be answered by a single-level theory. On the one hand, focusing only on individual use of the system cannot explain how the system has an effect on the overall performance of the organization, especially considering that the system does not seem to dramatically affect how any individual works. On the other hand, considering only the organization as a whole (e.g., by comparing a number of organizations with and without systems), quantifies but does not illuminate how the system provides benefit.

6.4.2 Analysis

In this section, I show how the process of seating and serving customers in the two restaurants changes individual work and thus the organizational outcomes. The changes in individual work as described above involved the use of an information system to track table status and to communicate with individual employees. The organizational outcomes were also described: reduced waiting time and increased table turns and profitability. I am interested here in how consideration of the process can clarify the links among these phenomena.

The first step in this analysis is to describe the activities involved in the process. A simple description is provided in figure 6.2. In the figure the actors are on the left and activities they each perform are shown across the page in time order. Activities performed jointly are connected by dotted lines. While there may be some disagreements about details, I believe that most people will recognize the sequence of activities as representative of a restaurant. I argued above that process descriptions should be viewed as resources for action rather than as necessarily valid descriptions of reality. In that spirit and in deference to a limited page count, I will bracket discussion of the validity of this model and instead focus on the insights possible from the analysis.

In these restaurants a particularly important type of dependency is the producer/consumer dependency among activities. These dependencies can be easily identified by noting where one activity produces something that is required by another. These resource flows and the dependencies of activities are shown in figure 6.3. For example, the activity of cooking creates food that can then be served and eaten, customers' departure produces a table ready for busing, and busing and resetting a table produces a table ready for another customer.

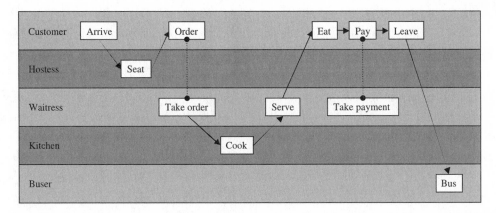

Figure 6.2
Restaurant service process. Actors are shown down the left side, activities performed by each are shown in order across the page. Activities performed jointly are connected with dotted lines.

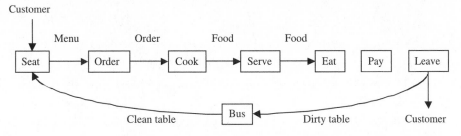

Figure 6.3
Flow of resources between activities and resulting dependencies in the restaurant service process

This distinction clarifies the role of the information system used. Recall that in Crowston's analysis (chapter 3 in this volume), such a dependency can be managed in one of two ways: either the person performing the first activity can notify the person performing the second that a resource is ready, or the second can monitor the performance of the first. Employees in Southfield can not be easily notified that they can now perform an activity. They must instead spend time monitoring the status of the previous activity. For example, a bused table, ready for a customer, waits until the host or hostess notices it. In Lake Buena Vista, by contrast, the buser can use the system to notify the host or hostess that a table has been bused and is ready. Similarly the wait staff can monitor the kitchen to notice when an order is ready or, using the system, the kitchen can page the wait staff to notify them that it is. Such changes can be made throughout the process. The appropriate waiters or waitresses can be paged when customers arrive at their tables; a buser can be paged when the table has been vacated and is waiting to be bused.

The effect of this change in coordination mechanism is to slightly reduce the interval between successive activities. The change likely comes from increasing the pace at which the restaurant employees work. Since there are many such intervals, the result of the system can be a noticeable decrease in the interval between successive customers or, alternately, a higher number of table turns and increased utilization of the restaurant's tables. (Of course, this analysis assumes that there are a large number of customers waiting to be seated and that these customers are not seeking a leisurely dining experience, both factors that were true of the restaurants I studied.)

6.4.3 Summary

This example demonstrates how examination of the process helps to link phenomena observed at the individual and organizational levels. The changes in individual work include use of an information system to track table status and to communicate between individual employees. The organizational outcomes include reduced waiting time and increased table turns and profitability. My analysis of the process suggests that the system allows individuals to change how they manage precedence dependencies, from noticing to notifying, thus decreasing the interval between activities, and overall, increasing table turns and profitability for a certain class of restaurant.

6.5 Recommendations for Process Research and Practice

As I have argued above, in the study of ICT use and organizations, it seems reasonable to adopt a process perspective. When investigating the many organizational problems that have an ICT component, I have five recommendations to offer as are outlined below for incorporating processes in ICT research and practice.

6.5.1 Develop Richer Process Analysis and Design Techniques

Researchers need to develop richer process analysis and design techniques. Analyses of processes must include the flow of resources, the dependencies created by these flows, and how these dependencies are managed (Crowston and Osborn 1998), and not just focus on the sequence of activities. Researchers in these areas might consider how their instruments can be adapted for broader use.

A difficult challenge is developing a meta-theory for processes comparable to the well-defined and well-understood set of terms and concepts for variance theories (e.g., 'construct', 'variable', 'proposition', 'hypothesis', 'variance', and 'error') and statistical tools for expressing and testing hypotheses. The framework developed in this chapter is but a small first step toward such a meta-theory.

6.5.2   Use Processes as a Unit of Analysis

Organizational theorists have found it problematic to develop generalizations that hold for entire organizations, reflecting the diversity of activities and micro-climates found in most modern organizations. Mohr (1982) describes organizational structure as "multi-dimensional—too inclusive to have constant meaning and therefore to serve as a good theoretical construct." Processes provide a useful level of analyses to narrow the study of organizational form (Mohr 1982; Abbott 1992). As Crowston (1997) states, "to understand how General Motors and Ford are alike or different, researchers might compare their automobile design processes or even more specific subprocesses" (p. 158). Within this finer focus, it may be possible to reach more meaningful conclusions about a range of theoretical concerns (Price and Mueller 1986).

For example, March and Sutton (1997) note the difficulties in studying antecedents of organizational performance due to the instability of this construct. However, it may be meaningful to consider performance at the level of a process. Similarly it is probably not meaningful to measure the level of centralization or decentralization of an entire organization (Price and Mueller 1986), but such measures may be appropriate and meaningful within the context of a single process.

6.5.3   Develop the Theory of Organizational Processes

More research is necessary to properly establish processes and the various constraints on process assembly as valid theoretical constructs. For example, research methods need to be developed or adapted to operationalize activities, resource flows, and dependencies and to validate models built around these constructs. Likewise research is needed to characterize the range of possible dependencies and the variety of coordination mechanisms possible and, in general, to document the assembly rules used in organizations. Work already done on work design and agency needs to be adapted to the general process perspective. Most important, research is needed to characterize the trade-offs between different mechanisms. Ultimately such work may allow some degree of prediction of the performance of a selected configuration of activities.

6.5.4   Expand to Richer Contexts

Consideration of organizational processes has been used primarily in an applied fashion, and as a result its use has mostly been restricted to processes in companies, often with the intent of designing a more efficient process, employing fewer workers.

Certainly this is not the only or even most interesting application of these ideas. The use of organizational process analysis should be expanded to more complex contexts.

6.5.5 Use Multiple Theories

Cannella and Paetzold (1994) argued that use of multiple theories is a strength of organizational science. Following their argument, I recommend the use of a process perspective with complementary theories, resulting in a multi-level and multi-paradigm understanding of the organization. One example of this approach is an ongoing study of the use of ICT in the real estate industry (Crowston et al. 1999; Crowston and Wigand 1999; Sawyer et al. 1999). To accomplish the objectives of this research, researchers have synthesized several theoretic perspectives to integrate findings from multiple levels of data collection. Specifically, at the individual level, they have drawn on theories of work redesign and social capital. At the organizational and industrial levels, they have applied transaction cost and coordination theory.

6.6 Conclusion

In this chapter, I argued that individual-level research on ICT use can be linked to organization-level research by detailed consideration of the organizational process in which the use is situated. Viewing a process as the way organizations accomplish desired goals and transform inputs into outputs makes the link to organizational outcomes. Viewing processes as ordered collections of activities makes the link to individual work, since individual actors perform these activities. Likewise process theories can be a useful milieu for theoretical interplay between interpretive and positivist research paradigms (Schultz and Hatch 1996). An analysis of the process of seating and serving customers in the two restaurants illustrates how changes in individual work affect the process and thus the organizational outcomes.

Acknowledgments

Sections of this chapter are derived from work done jointly with Jim Short, Steve Sawyer, and Rolf Wigand. The chapter was greatly improved by comments from the track chair, associate editor, and two anonymous reviewers. The work has been partially funded by the National Science Foundation, Grant IIS 97-32799 and by a grant from the Office of the Dean of the School of Information Studies, Syracuse University. This version of the chapter was edited to fit the page restrictions of the conference. A complete version is available from the author.

7 Grammatical Models of Organizational Processes

Brian T. Pentland

7.1   Introduction

Process thinking has been attracting more interest lately from both theorists and practitioners. Some sociologists are beginning to adopt the view that "social reality happens in sequences of actions located within constraining and enabling structures" (Abbott 1992, p. 428). Organization theorists argue that process models provide a unique perspective on innovation (Van de Ven and Poole 1990), strategic change (Van de Ven 1992), and organizational behavior in general (Mohr 1982). Practitioners believe that a process-centered view of organizational design can yield dramatic improvements in organizational performance (Hammer 1990; Davenport 1993). Whether one regards this wave of interest in processes as a case of theory leading practice, or practice leading theory (Barley, Meyer, and Gash 1988), it seems clear that there is a need for more understanding of this domain.

Recent studies of innovation (Pelz 1985; Van de Ven, Angle, and Poole 1989), group processes (Gersick 1989; Poole and Roth 1989; Olson, Herbsleb, and Rueter 1994), software development (Sabherwal and Robey 1993), and careers (Abbott and Hrycak 1990) have begun to introduce sequential concepts and methods to a wider audience of organizational scholars. But more than ten years after Mohr's (1982) rallying cry for research that takes process seriously, organizational theorists are still generally content to study the variable properties of static objects using traditional variance models (Van de Ven 1992). Processes, if mentioned at all, are often used as "just-so stories" that describe the causal chain that relates independent and dependent variables (Abbott 1992, p. 429). Empirical studies of actual sequences of events (e.g., Van de Ven, Angle, and Poole 1989; Sabherwal and Robey 1993) are still quite rare. We are accumulating an increasingly powerful set of tools for describing and comparing sequences of events (Hewes 1980; Holmes and Poole 1991; Abbott 1990), but these methods lack the capability to express the nested, layered quality that characterizes many kinds of organizational processes. As interest in process research grows, we will need increasingly sophisticated ways of representing and reasoning about complex sequences of events.

An earlier version of this chapter appeared as B. T. Pentland (1995), Grammatical models of organizational processes, *Organization Science* 6(5): 541–56. © 1995 The Institute for Operations Research and the Management Sciences (INFORMS), 901 Elkridge Landing Road, Suite 400, Linthicum, MD 21090-2909 USA. Reprinted by permission.

In this chapter, I argue that a special class of process models based on the metaphor of grammar can provide unique insights into the sequential structure of organizational processes. In recent years, the metaphor of grammar has been used more frequently in connection with organizational processes. One of the first instances was Weick (1979, p. 3) who defined "organizing" as a "consensually validated grammar for reducing equivocality by means of sensible interlocked behaviors," and went on to argue that "organizing resembles a grammar, a code, or a set of recipes." More recently Drazin and Sandelands (1992, p. 230) argue that the "deep structure" of organizing consists of a "generative grammar." By describing organizations and interactions in grammatical terms, these scholars and a host of others (Skvoretz and Farraro 1980; Barley 1986; Abell 1987; Sandelands 1987; Salancik and Leblebici 1988; Coulter 1989; White 1992) are implicitly suggesting that, like human language, human *organization* has syntax. A syntax of organizational processes is an exciting possibility because it provides a new paradigm for organizational science. In the same way that ecological concepts (e.g., population, niche, and density) provide new ways to theorize about organizational forms, grammatical concepts (e.g., lexicon and syntactic structure) provide new ways to theorize about organizational processes. The most convenient starting point in this effort would be simple "business processes" (Davenport 1993): goal-oriented sequences of actions that repeat over time, such as customer service (Ventola 1987). Eventually it may be possible to create grammatical models for other kinds of processes that embody change over time, such as organizational life cycles, innovation (Van de Ven and Poole 1990), and strategy formation (Van de Ven 1992).

In this chapter, I define the basic terms of grammatical models of organizational processes, and attempt to clarify the limits and possibilities of a research agenda based on such models. The question is, What might we learn if we took Weick's (1979) metaphor seriously and applied it in empirical research? To answer this question, we need a method for rigorously mapping concepts from the domain of grammar to the domain of organizing. Organization theory is filled with metaphors (Morgan 1986), but with the notable exception of the ecological metaphor, very few of them have been systematically developed. Tsoukas (1991) describes a way to develop metaphorical language into rigorous theoretical language by progressively mapping ideas from one domain to another until one arrives at a language that is isomorphic between domains. Another way of framing this line of inquiry would be to ask: What can we learn about organizational processes by thinking of them as products of a language? The argument here is that the grammatical metaphor opens up new ways of modeling and analyzing process. These models are not substitutes for variance models, or other kinds of sequential models. Rather, they add to the stock of analytical tools that organization theorists can bring to bear on this important class of phenomena.

In typical metaphors the source domain is quite familiar to the audience, so it helps them form interpretations or insights about the less familiar target domain (Tsoukas 1991). For this Process Handbook audience, the source domain (grammar) is less familiar than the target (organizations). Therefore I begin by defining the concept of grammar and explaining some of its key features. Given this introduction, I will examine some ways that these concepts can be exploited to construct grammatical models of organizational processes. The analysis indicates that basic grammatical concepts can be used to create rigorous, disconfirmable models of organizational processes. In the final sections of the chapter, I discuss some methodological aspects of developing and testing such models, and suggest what we might learn from a grammatical research agenda.

7.2   What Is a Grammar?

Before we can begin mapping concepts of grammar and organization, we need to familiarize ourselves with the critical features of the source domain. I will start with a basic definition of grammar:[1]

A grammar describes a (potentially infinite) set of patterns in terms of a finite lexicon and a finite set of rules or constraints that specify allowable combinations of the elements in the lexicon.

In English, for example, the "patterns" are sentences, the "lexicon" consists of words, and the "constraints" are the rules of English syntax. By specifying how words can be combined to create sentences, a grammar provides a concise way of describing a language (i.e., the set of all correct sentences and only these). A grammar embodies hypotheses about what patterns are possible, but it is not intended to predict individual patterns. English grammar offers no insight at all into what my next sentence will be, yet it describes the form of every correct English sentence. Likewise Salancik and Leblebici's (1988) grammar of food service transactions describes the set of all possible restaurants but cannot predict whether a particular

---

1. There are a large number of different kinds of formalisms that can be used to represent a grammar. A more general definition is offered by Chomsky (1956, p. 114): "By a grammar of the language L we mean a device of some sort that produces all of the strings that are sentences of L and only these."

restaurant will offer cafeteria style or sit-down service. Like discrete, stochastic process models (Hewes 1980), grammars describe a set of possible outcomes, and not an individual outcome. Given that grammar is perhaps the purest form of structuralism, it should not be surprising to find that, like any structuralist perspective, grammar emphasizes patterns over individual cases (Mayhew 1980).

In addition to describing a set of patterns, grammars can also embody a set of testable hypotheses that provide the basis for a theoretical explanation of the observed patterns. The explanatory power of grammatical models lies in the way in which they embody structural constraints on the set of possible patterns. As Simon (1992, p. 154) notes, a description becomes an explanation when it refers to "structural characteristics of the system." For example, when linguists observe a sentence construction that seems valid, yet violates some hypothesized grammatical constraint, it forces them to revise the hypothesis to account for the new observation. Similarly, in other domains where grammars have been used, the process of fitting the grammar to the data progressively improves one's understanding of the structure of the data (Olson, Herbsleb, and Rueter 1994). In this way grammar provides a logical framework for testable theories about the constraints that account for any given set of observations.

Grammars also provide a framework for generating new instances of a set. In linguistics, grammars are called "generative" because they possess the mathematical capability of generating an infinite set of sentences from a finite lexicon and a finite set of rules. Generativity is an interesting property for organization theorists as well, because it suggests the possibility of predicting new organizational processes and forms based on a given set of constraints, or changes in a set of constraints (Salancik and Leblebici 1988). From a practical point of view, the generative properties of grammatical models may provide new ways to design processes (Malone et al. 1993).

Grammars are similar to scripts, but there are two important differences. First, as used in the organizational literature, the concept of a script (or event schema) is general treated as an individual level cognitive structure (Abelson 1981; Gioia and Poole 1984). By contrast, the grammatical concepts I will describe below are tied to a more general set of structures that enable and constrain the flow of events, including physical and organizational structures. Second, grammars are a more powerful representational device than scripts. Schank and Abelson's (1977, pp. 11–17) original formulation of plans and scripts was built upon a lexicon of eleven primitive actions or "meaning units." These units could then be combined or recombined to form any particular plan or script, such as the restaurant script. To the extent that the restaurant script is a combination of this lexicon of meaning units, it is the product of an implicit "restaurant grammar" of the kind proposed by Salancik and Leblebici

(1988). From the perspective of formal representation, generative grammars form a complete superset of scripts; there is no script that cannot also be expressed by a grammar. This is an important observation because it suggests that a grammatical approach to representing routines is not an alternative to a script based approach. Rather, it is a more powerful generalization of the same basic idea.

Since we are attempting to apply grammatical concepts to a domain other than language, it is important to realize that linguists do not hold a monopoly on the concept of grammar. Grammars can be constructed for any phenomenon that can be given a sequential representation. There are grammars for DNA, polygons, curves, Korean characters, computer programs, electrical circuits, and more (see Gonzalez and Thomason 1978; Miclet 1986). Grammatical models have also been applied extensively to the study of stories and narratives (Prince 1973; Ryan 1979; Lenhert 1981; Colby, Kennedy, and Milanesi 1991). In many respects story grammars provide the most readily applicable set of grammatical tools for the analysis of organizational processes because they have been applied to the kinds of events that comprise organizational life (e.g., situated actions by individuals). To the extent that we conceive of organizational life as a kind of living narrative, story grammars are an obvious analytical tool. The utility of grammatical techniques to domains other than linguistics also helps to underscore the distinction between the general concept of grammar and the highly specific (and controversial) hypotheses of Chomskian generative grammar which are discussed in more detail below. This distinction helps define the limits and possibilities of grammatical models of organizational processes.

7.3   Grammar and Organizational Process

For some, the idea of a "social grammar" of any kind is troublesome because the word "grammar" carries some very powerful philosophical connotations: essentialism, deep structure, and universality. Because of these connotations, the notion that social life of any kind can be represented by grammatical formalisms has been disputed by social theorists such as Bourdieu (1977, 1990), Brint (1992), de Certeau (1984), Fabian (1979, 1990), and Heritage (1984), among others. As typically conceived, grammars depend on rules of syntax that determine what is grammatical and what is not. But as Heritage (1984, p. 126) argues, "social action cannot be analyzed as 'governed' or 'determined' by rules in any straightforward sense." Heritage (1984, p. 216) points out that flaunting a well-known rule (e.g., "greet only acquaintances") can be actively used to reconstitute the meaning of a situation. In

Table 7.1
Mapping between grammar and organizational processes

Grammar	Organizational processes
Core concepts	
Lexicon	Moves (Goffman 1981; Pentland 1992)
Syntactic constituents	Performance programs (March and Simon 1958)
	Routines (Ashforth and Fried 1988)
	Molecular actions (Abell 1987)
Constraints (rules)	Institutional structures (Jepperson 1991)
	Culture (Schein 1985)
	Technology (Barley 1986)
	Coordination (Malone et al. 1993)
Sentences	Processes (Weick 1979)
	Transactions (Salancik and Leblebici 1988)
Chomskian concepts	
Universality	*No analogy*
Competence versus performance	*Limited analogy*
Deep structure	*No analogy*

this way participants may strategically use a rule without following it at all. Fabian (1979, pp. 11–12) notes that a complete grammar would need to contain "rules for the proper violation of its rules, or rules for the change of rules," which would lead logically to a *regress ad infinitum*. The objectification of rules and rule-following is only one problem. The grammatical metaphor has also been criticized for being ahistorical (Fabian 1990, p. 14) and for relying on objectivist assumptions that have been long discredited by philosophers and empirical psychologists alike (Lakoff 1987, pp. 8–10). These objections raise serious questions about the extent to which the grammatical metaphor can be applied to organizations.

To address these concerns, it is critical that we not import grammatical concepts without careful consideration of their connotations and implications. We must restrict ourselves to clear mappings between the source domain and the target domain and discard those features of the source domain that do not fit (Tsoukas 1991). The proposed mapping between grammar and organizational processes is summarized in table 7.1, and each of the rows is explained in the text that follows. To help make the mapping concrete, I will use a simple example to illustrate each part of the overall metaphor: a trip to a supermarket in the United States. We will examine this process from the shopper's perspective, since this is the perspective that will be most familiar. One could just as easily consider the processes of stocking the shelves, taking inventory, or other aspects of supermarket operations. The purpose, of course, is not to make a contribution to a substantive theory of shopping but simply to illustrate the use of the terminology.

7.3.1 Moves Are Like Words

The basic elements of a language are usually called an "alphabet" or a "lexicon" (Miclet 1986). Like atoms in chemistry these are the basic building blocks that can be combined to create more complex structures. The definition of these basic elements depends on the kind of sequences being studied. In story grammars the basic units are sometimes called "plot units" (Lenhert 1981) or "meaning units" (Colby, Kennedy, and Milanesi 1991). In studies of human interaction, the term "lexicon" is more common (Hymes 1972; Fabian 1979), so this term is used here. Note that the definition of these units is always somewhat arbitrary; lexemes can be decomposed into phonemes, plot units into actions, atoms into particles, and so on. The point is that they are treated analytically as the most detailed level of description necessary for the problem at hand.

In organization theory, moves can be used to define a lexicon of organizational action (Pentland 1992). Goffman (1981, p. 24) defined moves as "any full stretch of talk or of its substitutes which has a distinctive unitary bearing on some set or other of the circumstances in which participants find themselves." Using this definition, Pentland (1992) identified a set of basic moves in the lexicon of a software support organization (e.g., *assign, transfer, refer, escalate*, and so on). Moves have some conceptual and practical advantages over other possible lexical elements, such as speech acts (Searle 1969; Winograd and Flores 1986). First, unlike speech acts and other purely linguistic concepts, the concept of a move encompasses nonlinguistic behavior (Goffman 1981). As an interaction unit, a move might consist of a combination of several different utterances and actions, the combined effect of "has a distinctive, unitary bearing" on the situation. Furthermore moves are connected to structural features of the situation; they are constrained and enabled by the physical, ritual, and competence structure of the situation (Pentland 1992). Given Abbott's (1992, p. 428) definition of processes as "sequences of actions located within constraining or enabling structures," moves are an obvious choice for the elements of a lexicon.

Example Consider a trip to a typical suburban supermarket in the United States. Because of the organization of the physical space and the general expectations of the shoppers and the store management, there are certain kinds of moves that are likely to be observed: a shopper might park a car, get a shopping cart, select items, and so on. In some stores, shoppers may also request special assistance (e.g., in a meat department or at a deli counter). The shopper usually empties his or her cart onto a checkout counter of some sort (often a conveyer belt), where a cashier "rings up" the items and the shopper pays. In some supermarkets, there may be a "bagger" who places the purchased items in bags; in other supermarkets, shoppers do this for themselves. Finally, the shopper removes the items from the store, loads them into his or her car, and drives away. Note that this level of description is quite abstract; it does not specify the number or kind of items selected, or how payment was made. Without further specifying some constraints on the sequence, these moves could be used to construct descriptions of impossible or nonsensical processes (e.g., ringing up items that have not been selected). All we have at this point is a lexicon.

7.3.2 Performance Programs Are Like Syntactic Constituents

In addition to a lexicon, grammars often include a more abstract notion of "syntactic constituents" (Newmeyer 1983; Cook 1988). Linguists identify categories of words or phrases that serve a particular function in the syntax of a sentence, such as noun phrases (e.g., "the official," "the document") or verb phrases (e.g., "is shredding"). These constituents can be combined according to grammatical rules to create sentences (e.g., "The official is shredding the document"). Syntactic constituents provide a way of describing the structural features of a pattern without elaborating it all the way down to the specifics of the lexicon. Syntactic constituents also provide a way of categorizing interchangeable chunks of a sequence that are functionally similar. In the example just given, one can substitute a wide variety of different noun phrases as the subject of the sentence: "the copier," "the dog," and so on. The meaning of the sentence changes, of course, but these forms are structurally equivalent. Another powerful feature of syntactic constituents is the way they can be nested together. To return to the example of the official, we can substitute a different, compound noun phrase at the end of the sentence: "The official is shredding *the document that contains the incriminating evidence.*" The ability to substitute equivalent constituents and nest them together is an important part of grammar.

In organization theory, "performance programs" (March and Simon 1958) provide an analogy to syntactic constituents. In their discussion of performance programs, March and Simon (1958, pp. 140–44) describe the way in which programs can be nested together and recombined to create larger programs. These "programs" embody chunks of behavior that have been routinized and possibly even automated in some way. More recently Ashforth and Fried (1988) build on the concept of scripts (Schank and Abelson 1977) to describe "mindless" routines that can be initiated by a very limited stimulus and run through until completion, unless interrupted. Abell (1987) uses the term "molecular actions" to describe a similar concept: actions that are so tightly bound together that we usually think of them as a unified whole. These routinized chunks of behavior would seem to make excellent candidates for the syntactic constituents of organizational processes.

Example   In our description of the supermarket, there are several candidates for syntactic constituents. For example, "ringing up" a set of items involves a highly routinized set of discrete steps. Once started, it tends to go through to completion. Further, ringing up can be accomplished in several ways (e.g., manually or with a universal product code scanner). "Making payment" also involves a set of routinized actions that can be accomplished in several different, interchangeable ways (Ventola 1987). While particular ways of ringing up or making payment may only be possible in a supermarket (e.g., coupons and food stamps are usually not accepted at restaurants), these generic activities are syntactic constituents of every kind of retail transaction.

7.3.3   Processes Are Like Sentences

Sentences are the basic unit of analysis in grammatical theories of language. In other domains, it would be individual children's stories, electric circuits, polygons, or whatever. This is perhaps the most critical aspect of the mapping because it fixes the unit of analysis—thereby determining the kinds of methodological tools that are required and the kinds of theoretical statements that are possible. In linguistics, grammar defines the set of valid sentences in a language, thereby defining the language itself.

In organization theory, the appropriate unit for grammatical analysis is a process. This seems to be the intuition that Weick (1979) was building on when he suggested that organizations construct processes from a set of "cycles" or "double interacts" using a set of "assembly rules." The grammatical metaphor applies most readily to "stationary" processes (Hewes 1980). These are processes that involve sequences of discrete events (or states) that may repeat over time but do not change over time. Grammars, by their very nature, are synchronic, not diachronic (de Saussure 1959; Barley 1990). Grammars describe sequences of actions that are situated in time, but the time scale for any given occurrence of a sequence could be relatively short. For example, in Salancik and Leblebici (1988), the unit of analysis was a food service transaction; depending on the kind of restaurant, the entire sequence might be completed in a few minutes or a few hours, at most. For any given food service establishment, the basic sequence identified in their grammar would stay relatively constant over time. These sequences are what Van de Ven (1992) calls a "unitary" progression of events, where only one event occurs at a time. This is the most intuitive mapping, because it compares directly to words in a sentence, or plot units in a story. However, other kinds of progressions identified by Van de Ven (1992) (parallel, divergent, and convergent) are well within the representational capacity of more advanced grammatical models (e.g., Miclet 1986 describes grammars for tree structures of various kinds).

Example In our supermarket example one can imagine recording the sequence of events in one shopper's trip to a particular store. This sequence is like a "sentence" that could be represented and analyzed grammatically. Note that even in a single supermarket there are an enormous number of possible sequences (think of all the available items, and every possible sequence in which you could select them and pay for them). One could also collect data from multiple markets, or other kinds of retail sales interactions. If one were using a typical variance-based approach, one would summarize these sequences using a set of variables (total time, total cost, number of items, item placement, item price, etc.) that could be used to answer a variety of questions concerning consumer behavior and marketing. There is, of course, a great deal more information in the data if we retain its sequential structure. Like other sequential analysis techniques, grammatical models allow us to make use of this information by analyzing the sequences themselves, as sequences. Grammatical models allow us to ask a very different set of questions: What sequences are possible? Why do we observe these sequences and not others? What would happen if some aspect of the context were changed? These questions depend on the hypothesized nature of the structures that constrain and enable the observed processes, so let us turn our attention to this topic.

7.3.4 Organizational and Institutional Structures Provide Constraints and Affordances

Grammatical constraints are often expressed as rules for combining the elements of a lexicon. Without constraints, words in any order could be a sentence, any set of line segments could be a polygon, and any sequence of nucleic acids could be DNA. In each field where grammatical models have been applied, there is a clear set of constraints on what is and is not a proper instance of the set. Furthermore the hypothesized origin and nature of these constraints forms the basis of explanations of why certain patterns exist and others do not. Constraints form the basis for disconfirmable theory: if one observes patterns that violate a hypothesized constraint, that hypothesis can be disconfirmed. These hypotheses are often expressed as *phrase structure* rules (Black and Wilensky 1979; Gazdar et al. 1985) that specify the allowable combinations of syntactic constituents and other lexical items.

In organization theory, constraints on action are often thought of as rules (e.g., Drazin and Sandelands 1992). While the arguments against rule-following mentioned above would seem to preclude any rule-based grammar of organizing, that would be a hasty and incorrect conclusion. This is because grammars do not predict particular patterns or actions; the rules in a grammar do not "determine" anything. Rather, they generate the set of possibilities for the agents in the situation. As a result it is helpful to think in terms of constraints and affordances (Gibson 1982; Norman 1988; Pentland 1992), rather than thinking of rules. This implies a shift away from deterministic, rule-like statements, toward an articulation of what is feasible in a given situation. This shift is logically equivalent to that suggested by Mohr (1982) in his distinction between variance models and process models. In Mohr's terms, a variance model implies a necessary and sufficient relationship between an antecedent and a consequent condition. In a process model, the antecedent condition is necessary but is generally not sufficient; in other words, it creates the possibility of the consequent but does not guarantee it. For this reason grammatical models are an example of the kind of process models described by Mohr (1982). As long as one keeps this distinction in mind, one can still express constraints and affordances in terms of rules, as in Salancik and Leblebici (1988). One of their rules for food service transactions states that a meal must be cooked before it is eaten. Note that this rule does not obligate anyone to eat a meal just because it has been cooked; it merely points out that reversing the sequence is impossible.

Because of the importance of structure in organization theory, we have an extensive vocabulary about constraints and affordances, as suggested in the following examples. Like any set of idealized analytical categories, they may combine in practice.

Institutional Structures   The general idea of identifying constraints and affordances on action is a familiar aspect of institutional theory (Commons 1950; Jepperson 1991). It is also a central part of Giddens's (1984) concept of structure, where rules are conceptualized as resources for action. One can explore the implications of various institutional arrangements for the configuration of various kinds of transactions (Leblebici et al. 1991). Under different institutional regimes, one should observe different sequences. In some sense the whole idea of "a trip to the supermarket" is a reflection of the institutional structures surrounding agriculture, food distribution, and the social division of labor in an industrialized economy. On a more concrete level, the range of acceptable means of payment (credit cards, food stamps, etc.) reflects specific institutional arrangements that may vary from setting to setting.

Technological Structures   Norman (1988) offers an analysis of how the physical properties of technical artifacts affect the actions of users. In organization theory, technology is an important source of structure (Orlikowski 1992). Of course, technological constraint does not imply technological determinism. As Barley (1986) showed, the same technical system can result in different patterns of social interaction. Technology accounts for one of the most visible changes in American supermarkets in recent years: the introduction of universal product code scanners. This new technology eliminates the need for cashiers to type in the prices of most items. Note that if we were studying the inventory process, or the marketing process, the implications of this technological innovation would be even more significant.

Coordination Structures   There are also a wide variety of constraints that emerge because of different kinds of interdependencies between actions (Malone et al. 1993). In addition to sequential constraints (e.g., step *A* must be completed before step *B*), there may be usability or simultaneity constraints on the steps of a process. Interdependencies are often introduced by the particular technology being applied in a situation; as technology changes, the degree of interdependence and the ability to manage it may change, as well. Because they explicitly affect the timing and sequence of steps in a process, coordination constraints may be a particularly interesting source of grammatical hypotheses. In a supermarket one finds a variety of sequential dependencies, such as needing to select items before you bring them to the checkout line.

Cultural Structures   Cultural structures operate at many levels in an organization, including the level of appropriate behavior (Schein 1985). Culturally based norms and expectations place a great many constraints on what moves are possible, and on the appropriate sequence of moves in a given situation. While these constraints are pervasive in social interactions, they are also the most subject to strategic flaunting. As Heritage (1984) suggests, one can reconstitute the meaning of a situation by explicitly violating a rule like, "greet only acquaintances." In the supermarket, cultural norms govern interactions with the cashier and other customers.

Constraints and their sources should be especially interesting to organization theorists because of our interest in problems of stability and change (Gersick 1991; Leblebici et al. 1991). Depending on how the rules of organization are grounded, one would expect very different properties in terms of persistence, volatility, and so on. For example, a rule or a lexical item that is grounded primarily in a technological feature of a process subject to very abrupt revision if that technology undergoes a major change. The disruption of organizational forms resulting from technological innovation (Tushman and Anderson 1986) could be potentially be analyzed in these terms. However, a rule that has a cultural basis may persist regardless of technological changes, or it may change only slowly.

Example   We are now ready to continue our supermarket example with a set of grammatical rules that embody the constraints and affordances on the process. Table 7.2 shows a generic phrase structure grammar for a trip to a suburban supermarket.

Table 7.2
Generic phrase structure grammar for a trip to a suburban supermarket

---

Trip → arrive, select items, check out, leave.
Arrive → park car, get cart.
Select items → [(pick item, put in cart), . . .].
Check out → unload cart, ring up items, pay, bag items.
Leave → wheel cart to car, unload cart, (return cart), start car, drive away.

This example has been deliberately simplified so that the general ideas will be as clear as possible. At this level of generality the rules embody combinations of technological, institutional, cultural, and coordination constraints; it is difficult to isolate pure examples of each category. A more detailed description of the process of payment (e.g., credit card validation or check approval) would start to reveal clear technological structures, for example.

In figure 7.2, the arrow symbol is read as "consists of." The arrows are not "condition–action" or "if–then" rules; they imply sequence but not causality. Thus the first rule states that a trip to the supermarket consists of 'arrive', 'select items', 'check out', and 'leave'. Each of these can be considered a syntactic constituent for the shopping trip, and is further decomposed in the subsequent rules. The process of selecting items, for example, consists of an indefinite number of repetitions of 'pick item' and 'put in cart'. One could further elaborate the process of picking an item to include comparison shopping, and so on. Similarly the check out process has a set of constituents that could be further elaborated to describe various forms of payment. Finally, one can indicate optional steps, such as "return cart" in the rule for leaving. By using these simple rules, one can describe a limited variety of different "trips to the supermarket" that differ mainly in the number of items selected. By adding more rules to describe alternative forms of payment, special requests at the meat counter (an alternative way to 'pick item'), one can describe a more complex set of transactions.

The grammar in figure 7.2 represents a set of hypotheses about the sequential structure of trips to the supermarket. One could test these hypotheses against actual observations of trips to various supermarkets. By coding observations in terms of the relevant lexicon, one could quite easily determine whether these rules capture the observations. In doing so, one might discover that suburban supermarkets systematically violate certain parts of the pattern. These violations would suggest revisions to the grammar, which could then be tested again. If one restricted one's attention to supermarkets, the results of this line of inquiry would be a detailed but rather boring "theory of supermarkets."

If one looked at other kinds of retail sales transactions, however, the questions one might ask start to get more interesting. For example, how can one describe and explain the differences between a traditional country store, where the clerk picks items for the customer, and the modern supermarket? What about differences between clothing stores (where items are routinely "tried on" to test their usability), and food stores, where "trying" items might be considered petty theft? One might also be interested in exploring the differences between a regular retail store and mail order. In short, there are many ways to organize the process of retail sales that depart systematically from the basic supermarket model. Grammatical models provide a way to state explicit hypotheses about these sequential processes and test them against empirical data.

So far, the concepts we have explored have been generic to any kind of grammar, whether linguistic or otherwise, and they seem to map quite well as process descriptions. In addition, there are a number more specific concepts and hypotheses that derive from Chomskian generative grammar (Newmeyer 1983; Cook 1988). They are not part of the definition of grammar per se, but given the dominance of the Chomskian perspective, concepts like deep structure have become a part of the grammatical metaphor in general and have started to emerge in the organizational literature (Gersick 1991; Drazin and Sandelands 1992). To a large extent, these additional concepts revolve around the hypothesized nature of constraints on human language: the so-called language faculty (Chomsky 1986). It is worth noting that Chomsky himself would be the last person to advocate extending these specifically linguistic ideas beyond their source domain. Despite this, these linguistic hypotheses seem to have drawn the most heated objections in the debates over the applicability of grammar to social action. Thus, for the sake of clarity and completeness, it is important to consider these additional connotations of the grammatical metaphor quite closely.

7.3.5 Organizations Have No "Language Faculty"

In Chomskian linguistics a central hypothesis is that there exists a universal grammar for all human languages that depends on a feature of the human brain called the "language faculty" (Chomsky 1986; Cook 1988). Universal grammar is essentially an hypothesis about the source of rules and constraints in human language. Chomskians argue that grammar is a feature of the human brain that enables people to learn languages the way that birds learn to fly. Given even a modest opportunity (e.g., a typical upbringing), humans cannot help learning a language. Which particular language we learn is determined by context, but our ability to learn it is innate, because the language faculty is a physical structure in the human brain.

In organization theory it is very hard to imagine anything that could sustain a rigorous, isomorphic analogy to this hypothesized structure of the human brain. This can be seen by recalling the list of structural constraints and affordances reviewed in the previous section. Each of these is historically situated, culturally embedded, and generally stands in a recursive relation to action (Giddens 1984). It is difficult to imagine an institutional, technological, cultural, or coordination constraint that does not vary with context and is not subject to revision with the passage of time. Universality is simply not a characteristic that applies to the social world. The lack of an organizational "language faculty" eliminates the possibility of a *universal* grammar for organizational processes: a single set of universal rules or principles that govern the syntactic structure of all organizing processes. Unless organizational theorists can identify a similar structure that is ahistorical and acultural (which we cannot), we will have to be content to apply grammatical methods to historically and culturally bounded domains.

7.3.6 Limited Distinction between Competence and Performance

Once we rule out the possibility of a structure analogous to the language faculty, a number of closely related concepts must also be questioned. For example, Chomskians traditionally distinguish between "competence" and "performance" (Newmeyer 1983). Competence refers to the core grammatical knowledge of an idealized speaker-hearer, while performance refers to actual utterances produced in social interaction. In Chomskian linguistics a grammar is a model of the idealized language embodied in the language faculty, not of the performances produced by speakers as they go about their daily lives. Grammar embodies the normative rules for producing correct sentences, although these rules are regularly violated in actual speech.

In organizational research we could develop this analogy by treating the idealized, normative account of how a process *should* work as competence, and observations about how it actually *does* work as performance. To the extent that normative expectations have a great deal of influence on satisfaction and a host of other outcomes, this may be a valuable analogy. One might also point to formal rules or procedures as an analogy to linguistic competence because they also express an important kind of normative expectation. We could model these kinds of expectations in the form of scripts or prototypical sequences (Schank and Abelson 1977) that provide a yardstick against which actual performance could be assessed. In the supermarket, for example, if a shopper selects items and then leaves without the intervening checkout process, it is a serious violation of the normative constraint against stealing. However, these kinds of cultural or institutional constraints are, at best, only a partial description of what generates the observed patterns in a situation

(Bourdieu 1977). For this reason it seems unreasonable to give them the special status implied by the analogy to Chomskian linguistics, where competence refers to the complete set of formal structures that specify the syntax of a language.

7.3.7 Organizations Have No Deep Structure

This lack of isomorphism has some additional consequences. First, it implies that the appealing notion of deep structure is inapplicable to organization theory. When organizational scholars use the term "deep structure" (e.g., Gersick 1991; Drazin and Sandelands 1992), they are referring to the accumulation of institutional, technological, and other kinds of structures that tend to make organizations relatively stable over time. These familiar kinds of structures have little in common with the formal, decontextualized, ahistorical "deep structure" of syntax as conceived in linguistics. Although organizational and institutional structures are obviously important, there is little to be gained by calling them "deep." Perhaps more important, the lack of deep structure implies that organization theorists will never achieve the strong, intuitive sense of a pattern being "ungrammatical" that linguists have relied on so heavily in their research. We will still be able to formulate disconfirmable hypotheses about what kinds of patterns and processes are possible, but these must be tested empirically against observations of surface structure. In the following section, I discuss a number of considerations involved in doing so.

7.4 Methodological Considerations of Grammatical Models

To apply the kind of grammatical model outlined here in empirical research on organizational processes, there are a number of methodological considerations that need to be addressed. It is worth noting that an emphasis on processes as a unit of analysis implies a significant departure from conventional methodologies. We are much more accustomed to using individuals, organizations, or networks as the unit of analysis, treating them as hypostatized objects, and formulating theories based on their variable properties (Mohr 1982; Abbott 1992). Nonetheless, the growing interest in process analysis has given rise to a variety of methodologies for analyzing sequences of events (Hewes 1979; Procter and Abell 1985; Bakeman and Gottman 1986; Gottman and Roy 1990; Abbott 1990; Abbott and Hrycak 1990; Van de Ven and Poole 1990). These methodologies are too numerous to review in detail, but they are generally designed to discover meaningful regularities in sequences of events that can be observed, coded, and compared. Grammatical models add to this growing family of tools for analyzing process data by providing a way to link what Poole, Folger, and Hewes (1987) call the "syntagmatic" structure of a process to its global sequential structure. To the extent that grammatical models rely on sequential data, they share many of the same methodological considerations as sequential techniques in general, such as reliability of coding. Grammatical models, however, provide a rather different approach to understanding the connections between sequences of events and the structural features that enable and constrain them. As a result there are several issues that deserve attention here.

7.4.1 Identifying a Lexicon and Syntactic Constituents

To perform a grammatical analysis of a class of organizational processes, the first step would be to identify the lexicon of moves and the appropriate syntactic constituents. The questions here are, What is the vocabulary of action in this process? What are the steps in the process? What are the different ways in which the steps can be accomplished? These questions bear a striking resemblance the "structural questions" described by Spradley (1979, pp. 116–17) in his primer on ethnographic interviewing. The objective of Spradley's (1979) technique is to map out the semantic domain used by the members of a particular cultural group to describe some aspect of their work or lives. In process research, the two most relevant semantic domains would be sequence ("X is a step (stage) in Y") and means-ends ("X is a way to Y") (Spradley, p. 111). In these relationships, Y is called a "cover term" and X is called an "included term." For each cover term, there is generally more than one included term, and there may be many. In terms of the grammatical metaphor outlined above, the included terms will tend to correspond to moves and the cover terms are likely to correspond to syntactic constituents. This nesting of lexical items is a distinctive feature of organizational processes that the grammatical metaphor encourages us to explore explicitly. Other process models treat data as flat, with each element having roughly equivalent status (e.g., Holmes and Poole 1991).

In practice, one may need to abstract somewhat from an informant's talk to arrive at a set of syntactic constituents that can be generalized across settings. The necessity of creating more abstract categories of action to facilitate analysis raises a familiar question: Do we impose our own, *etic* terminology for the actions we observe, or do we use the *emic* terminology of our informants (Spradley 1979)? This is essentially the same problem that we confront when we collect survey data that are presumed to mean the same thing to different respondents, so that their responses can be subjected to mathematical transformation and analysis (Cicourel 1964). The important issue here is not so much the use of member's own terminology but the semantic relationship between covering terms and included terms. The included terms must be "steps in" or "ways to" complete the action described in the covering term (e.g., paying is a step in checking out).

7.4.2 Identifying and Formulating Constraints

To formulate meaningful explanations, the critical problem is to identify the relevant sources of constraint on the lexicon and the ways in which its elements can be recombined. The most convenient way of formulating a constraint is as a rule, as in this kind of sequential coordination constraint: "A product must be designed before it can be manufactured." It is interesting to note that there may be a large number of different steps in the process that intervene between design and manufacturing (dealing with strategy, marketing, finance, etc.). A simple sequential constraint does not require adjacency (although one could formulate a more stringent constraint that would). This simple example points to one of the major advantages of this approach: syntactic models provide explicit ways of stating hypotheses about constraints on events in a process that are widely separated in the observed sequence. This is a special property of syntactic models that is not shared by statistical techniques such as Markov models (Chomsky 1956). In a supermarket, for example, you may have any number of iterations of 'select item' before you 'check out'. For this reason a Markov model would do poor job of capturing the sequential dependence between arriving at the store and checking out, though these events are structurally constrained to occur in this order in every complete transaction.

7.4.3 Comparison to Phasic Analysis and Other Sequential Techniques

Although a detailed review of sequential methods is beyond the scope of this chapter, there are some points of reference in the literature that might be helpful for some readers. For example, Holmes and Poole (1991) describe a method called phasic analysis that has some interesting similarities but also some important differences. The basic idea of phasic analysis is to code sequential data in terms of a set of events that mark a particular phase of activity. For example, in a stage model of organizational development (e.g., Greiner 1972), there might be an early stage of creativity and leadership marked by certain kinds of behavior, followed by a stage of direction and autonomy, delegation and control, and so on. Using phase analysis, one can test the observed sequence of stages against a predicted model or analyze typical sequences of stages (Pelz 1985; Holmes and Poole 1991). Poole and Roth (1989), for example, used phasic analysis to develop a typology of group decision-making processes.

There are a number of terminological similarities between phasic analysis and the grammatical models suggested here. Holmes and Poole (1991, p. 295) write about testing phase models by "parsing of a sequence of phase markers into discrete phases." Grammatical models are also tested by parsing sequences of events into syntactic constituents, but these constituents can have a much more elaborate internal structure. Furthermore a grammatical constituent is typically marked by a single event rather than a sequence of similar events. Holmes and Poole (1991, p. 293) also discuss the use of coding systems that include 'major categories' and 'subcategories,' which in some ways are like Spradley's (1979) covering terms and included terms. However, the semantic characteristics of the respective coding scheme are very different. In the coding schemes described by Holmes and Poole (1991), the sub-categories are *indicators* of the major categories, not steps used to accomplish it, and the categories are basically etic (which include things like 'denial and equivocation', 'noncommittal remarks', 'topic management'). In the grammatical approach, the included terms should be steps needed to accomplish the covering term (e.g., paying is a necessary part of checking out). In further contrast to the phasic approach, it is helpful if the coding scheme at the lowest level (moves) is basically emic. The use of emic categories is not essential, but it facilitates the collection of data by asking people to describe what they are doing. Furthermore, grounding the lexicon in ethnographically derived categories helps keep the analysis more closely connected to the phenomenon.

7.4.4 Logic of Analysis

Testing grammatical models raises some interesting problems concerning what, exactly, should count as evidence of disconfirmation. Linguists can often disconfirm a grammatical rule by pointing to a single sentence construction that intuitively seems grammatical but violates a hypothesized constraint. As mentioned above, organization theorists are not so lucky, because we do not have introspective access to a hypothesized universal structure that guides our theorizing. Rather, we must collect data in the field, a procedure that is fraught with all kinds of possibilities for error in coding, sampling, and so on. While we might want to follow a strict rule of single case disconfirmation, it would tend to lead to spurious rejections of the hypothesized model.

Alternatively, we might also follow a statistical approach, similar to that used for testing traditional variance models. Unfortunately, no rigorous statistical tests have yet been developed to test the goodness of fit of grammatical models or other rule-based models (Olson, Herbsleb, and Rueter 1994; Simon 1992). Simon (1992) notes that in cognitive science, the general heuristic for the adequacy of rule-based models of human performance is that the model must explain many more cases than the number of rules it uses. In this context Simon's (1992) usage of the term "explain" simply means that the behavior described by the model matches the observed behavior, either in functional form or in exact detail. In the case of our simple grammar of suburban shopping trips, this criterion is easily met; at the level of detail expressed in the grammar, I would expect it to fit nearly every supermarket in the United States. This seems like a reasonable basis for proceeding until the statistical properties of these models can be worked out.

7.4.5 Limits of Applicability

There are limits on the kind of processes and level of detail for which a grammatical approach may be appropriate. Levinson (1983) notes that conversation analysts have had limited success in formulating interaction grammars of the kind Hymes (1972) proposed. In essence, there are just too many possibilities and contingencies available in interaction, and too strong a tendency toward the strategic use of cultural constraints (e.g., Grice's 1975 maxims for conversational cooperation) to create irony and implicature. There is no point, as Abell (1987) points out, in attempting to unpack every little motion or inflection as a separate piece of data. The kinds of processes that seem more natural and appropriate for grammatical analysis are more deeply embedded in organizational structures, less fine grained, and hence less subject to capricious variation. This suggests that it is important to limit the level of granularity with which one describes a process to those moves that can be easily observed and reliably coded (Folger, Hewes, and Poole 1984; Van de Ven and Poole 1990). The difficulty involved here should not be underestimated. We have a natural ability to parse sentences into recognizable words and constituents, but our ability to parse organizational processes depends on artificial methods. The development of reliable coding schemes for moves and syntactic constituents that can be generalized across organizational settings will be an important research question in and of itself.

Furthermore the culturally and historically embedded quality of organizational processes implies that it is important to bound the scope of the data one is drawing upon in constructing a grammar so that it is relatively homogeneous. In their discussion of grammatical techniques in cognitive anthropology, Colby, Kennedy, and Milanesi (1991, p. 383) note that grammars of folktales can only be developed for a culturally bounded group of people.

To reiterate the condition for analyzing plot grammars, it is necessary that the sample of texts be geographically bound to a particular language using group of people and that it consist of the same genre and same general time period. With these restrictions, and if the sample is sufficiently large (numbering at least over fifty and preferably twice as much) it should be possible to eventually work out a plot grammar.

The same basic recommendations seem quite appropriate for the analysis of organizational processes. The critical issue here is one of sampling, and the scope of data that one can hope to meaningfully incorporate into a single grammar. One cannot expect processes operating within different institutional, cultural, and technological structures to fit the same grammar, unless that grammar is very abstract. While these limitations need to be taken seriously, they are not especially different in kind or severity than the limitations on traditional variance models. What is different, of course, are the kinds of phenomena that grammatical models can express, and the kinds of research questions they allow us to pursue.

7.5   A Grammatical Research Agenda

As suggested in the introduction, grammatical models create a variety of opportunities in organizational research by providing a novel way to describe the sequences of actions that make up organizational processes. More important, the grammatical metaphor has explanatory power because of the way it connects structures and possible actions. This connection suggests the possibility of several interesting kinds of research questions. Because the grammatical metaphor applies most clearly to processes that occur repetitively with relatively little change over time (i.e., synchronic rather than diachronic processes), I have chosen to emphasize those examples here.

7.5.1   Classification of Processes

Organization theorists have been concerned with the classification of organizational structures and forms (McKelvey 1982; Rich 1992). Grammars provide a conceptual framework for classification that is quite different from the typologies and taxonomies that are prevalent in organization theory. Instead of classifying organizations based on their structural features (M-form, U-form, etc.), their industry (e.g., by SIC code), their strategy (prospector, defender, etc.), or some other variable property, the grammatical metaphor suggests the possibility of classifying organizational units according to their internal processes. There are two main ways in which processes can be differentiated within the grammatical framework: differences in the lexicon and differences in the constraints.

Differences in the lexicon of a process are easy to identify, because they would show up immediately in the domain analysis as described above. For example, some customer service processes can dispatch a technician to your location (e.g., to fix your computer), while others cannot. Processes that have the "dispatch" move in their lexicon could be called "field service," whereas processes without this move might be "walk-in" or perhaps just "hot lines." Similarly, in a retail sales operation, there may be a variety of lexical differences that create whole new possibilities for interaction and service, as in the case of catalog stores that allow customers to enter their orders directly using a computer terminal. Sequential differences are also important, as Salancik and Leblebici (1988) illustrated in their restaurant grammar. In a sit-down restaurant, the sequence is *order, cook, serve, eat, pay*, but in a fast-food restaurant, it is usually *cook, order, pay, serve, eat*. The grammatical metaphor makes classification relatively easy because it isolates differences within syntactic constituents. For example, most retail stores have an overall pattern similar to a supermarket. But in a clothing store the "select item" constituent often involves a specialized sequence required to try on the clothing. This syntactic specialization provides a formal way to identify clothing stores as a kind of retail store, and to further differentiate kinds of clothing stores, and so on.

7.5.2   Explaining the Variation and Distribution of Processes
As one starts to develop a taxonomy of processes, it becomes possible to start asking questions about what explains the observed distribution of instances, a problem that parallels the classic problem of explaining the distribution of organizational forms (Singh and Lumsden 1990). Furthermore grammatical models make it is possible to predict organizational forms that have not yet been observed (Salancik and Leblebici 1988). This is a unique and potentially very interesting contribution that is not possible with existing ways of modeling organizations. Given a set of unobserved forms, one might attempt to explain their absence.

To explain the observed distribution of processes, there are several strategies that one can adopt that roughly mirror the kinds of explanations used for organizational forms. For example, economic efficiency, institutional legitimacy, or resource availability might all be used as explanatory constructs. To the extent that the processes under consideration here are core business processes that transform inputs to outputs, economic efficiency is clearly a critical consideration. One interesting feature of the grammatical metaphor is that it suggests the possibility of separating this consideration from the internal structure of the process itself. To see why this is so, recall that the theory of the firm treats organizations as black boxes, without much if any consideration for internal structure. Economic theories are largely indifferent to the possible ways of organizing, except insofar as organizing effects efficiency. Likewise pragmatics is largely indifferent to syntax, except insofar as syntax effects the force of an utterance. Excluding economic considerations from grammar does not exclude them from organization theory, but it does simplify the theoretical work to be done by each. We can begin to imagine piecing together a set of modular, interacting components that would explain the existence of observed organizational forms. Consider, again, Salancik and Leblebici's (1988) restaurant grammar. Their grammar explains the variety of possible restaurants without any reference to whether one form is more economically viable. This makes sense because these are logically separate questions. Implicitly Salancik and Leblebici (1988) are relying on the modularity of their grammar. If we were to ask questions concerning the competitiveness of the restaurants that their grammar generates, or whether the food is tasty, we would need to look elsewhere because these questions are outside the scope of the grammar.

7.5.3   Comparative Statics: Why Do Processes Differ?

The grammatical framework outlined here contains no endogenous explanation for change. Following the traditions of structural linguistics, grammars are generally treated as synchronic; they can be used as indicators of diachronic change but cannot be used to explain such changes. Within the grammatical framework one can formulate a variety of testable hypotheses concerning the effects of changing constraints on organizational processes. For example, "as constraint X changes, what new patterns or classes of action are predicted?" This is the logic underlying Malone and Rockhart's (1991) analysis of the effects of information technology on organizational processes. As the cost of this technology goes down, it reduces certain kinds of coordination constraints. As a result new organizational forms are possible.

The grammatical method suggested here is particularly well suited to the empirical comparison of "discrete structural alternatives" (Williamson 1991) as they are actually practiced. Williamson (1991) maps out the structural alternatives that economize on transaction costs under various institutional regimes. While one can gain considerable insight through the study of hypothetical or idealized contracts, Leblebici (1992) suggests that differences in transactions under various institutional regimes can be conveniently expressed by using grammatical models similar to the kind proposed here. In using these models, it may be interesting to observe the sequential structure of various kinds of transactions within markets, hierarchies, and hybrid forms, to see how they differ empirically. Does the lexicon or sequence of moves in a market transaction differ from the sequence of moves in a hierarchy or a hybrid form? What accounts for the differences or lack or differences? It would be quite interesting, for example, if we learned that institutional structures have relatively little effect on the configuration of transactions compared to technological or cultural considerations.

7.5.4   Design of Organizational Processes

On a more practical level, grammatical methods may offer insights into the design and redesign of organizational processes (Malone et al. 1993). To the extent that syntactic constituents can be identified that generalize across organizational settings, a grammar provides a framework for generating and comparing alternatives. For a given syntactic constituent (or covering term), it may be possible to substitute a functionally equivalent alternative. By studying the syntax of a wide variety of processes, it may be possible to start predicting which specific kinds of routines are more effective in various situations. Malone et al. (1993) have initiated an effort to accumulate just such a Handbook of organizational processes that would not only classify existing processes but help design new ones. A closely related practical question confronting managers is how to measure the relative performance of existing processes. While so-called benchmarking studies are widely used, there is often little systematic basis for assessing the validity of the comparison. By using the idea of syntactic constituents, persons interested in comparing parts of larger processes should be able to gain a firmer point of reference on which to base comparisons.

7.6 Conclusion

The analysis presented here suggests that it is possible to construct rigorous, disconfirmable process models using the grammatical metaphor. The particular advantage of such models is that they suggest an explicit connection between structural features of the context and the set of possible processes. In addition grammatical models make the layered quality of many organizational processes explicit through the use of syntactic constituents. As a result grammatical models provide a unique window into the relationship between institutional, technological, coordination, and cultural structures and the details of organizational actions, routines, and processes. The generative quality of grammatical models suggests the possibility of predicting or designing new processes, as well. In short, the grammatical metaphor seems to offer a great deal to organization theory.

Acknowledgments

An earlier version of this chapter was presented at the University of Michigan, Interdisciplinary Conference on Organization Studies Working Conference on Generative Theories of Organization, January 17–19, 1992. The author would like to acknowledge the support of the Ameritech Foundation, through the Information and Organizations Program of the Institute for Public Policy Studies at the University of Michigan. This chapter has benefited greatly from discussion with Michael Cohen, Kevin Crowston, Chris Dellarocas, Jintae Lee, Fred Luconi, Thomas Malone, Peter Manning, George Wyner, and feedback from Andrew Van de Ven and the anonymous *Organization Science* reviewers.

III CONTENTS OF THE PROCESS HANDBOOK

Now that we have seen the core theoretical concepts upon which the Process Handbook is based, this section gives an overview of the various types of content that presently exist in the Handbook.

Chapter 8, by Herman and Malone, provides an overview of the Process Handbook's contents. In a sense, this chapter is a "guided tour" of what is present in the Handbook as of this writing (July 2002). The chapter describes and gives examples of the three primary elements that the Handbook contains today: (1) generic models of typical business activities, (2) specific case examples of particular companies, and (3) classification frameworks.

The chapter also describes our rationales for the selection and structure of the content we have included. For example, this chapter shows how we derived the basic MIT Business Activity Model, in part, using a fundamental analysis of the basic coordination problems that must be solved by most businesses.

The next part of this section includes chapters 9 and 10 with more detailed examples of content in specific domains. Chapter 9 is excerpted from Wyner's Ph.D. thesis. It presents several well-known approaches to business process redesign (e.g., Davenport 1993; Hammer and Champy 1993). One interesting aspect of this chapter is the way it represents and compares the previous approaches based on a careful textual analysis of the documents that describe them.

Chapter 10 is an excerpt from Dellarocas' Ph.D. thesis, and it describes part of a detailed taxonomy of the different types of dependencies that arise in software programs and the different kinds of coordination mechanisms that can be used to manage them. In particular, this chapter focuses on different types of resources and different mechanisms for managing flow dependencies in software systems.

The last part of this section addresses the problem of how to create new content for the Process Handbook. One promising approach to this problem is described in chapter 11, by Crowston and Osborn. This chapter focuses on how to go into an organization and gather the kind of information that is useful in creating descriptions for the Process Handbook. These techniques are illustrated by a case example of a specific company. The example shows that the same approaches to analyzing activities for description in the Process Handbook can also give important insights about the organization that are of value in their own right.

IIIA *Overview of the Contents*

8 What Is in the Process Handbook?

George A. Herman
Thomas W. Malone

8.1 Introduction

What kinds of things are included in the Process Handbook? How are they organized? And why did we choose to organize them in this way? This chapter gives our answers to these questions.

In developing content for the Process Handbook so far, our primary goal has been to demonstrate that the long-term vision for the project is feasible. That is, we have tried to demonstrate that our basic approach can be used to develop a *comprehensive framework for organizing large amounts of useful knowledge about business*.

In order to achieve these goals, we have focused on creating three primary kinds of entries in the Handbook: (1) generic models of typical business activities (e.g., buying, making, and selling) that occur in many different businesses, (2) specific case examples of interesting things particular companies have done, and (3) frameworks for classifying all this knowledge.

The chapter begins with an overview of the kinds of things that are included, the number of entries of each type, and a description of a sample entry. Then it describes each of the major types of content in more detail: generic models of business activities, specific case examples, and frameworks for classifying activities. Finally, it briefly describes several other kinds of things (e.g., resources and exceptions) that are not themselves *activities*, but that are represented in the Process Handbook.

8.2 Overview of the Process Handbook Contents

Table 8.1 summarizes the number of entries of different types that were included in the Process Handbook at MIT as of July 2002. Of course, there is an infinite amount of knowledge about business that could, in principle, be included in a repository like ours. In a sense, we have just begun to scratch the surface of what is possible in terms of organizing business content in this way. But we believe that the work we have done so far has achieved our initial goals. That is, so far we have demonstrated the potential of this approach to comprehensively organize large amounts of useful knowledge about business in a richly interconnected, consistent, and powerful way.

Different Versions of the Process Handbook There is no reason why there cannot be multiple versions of repositories like the Process Handbook. For example, as of this writing (July 2002), we have two such versions at MIT: the "research" version of the

Table 8.1
Summary of contents of the MIT Process Handbook (July 2002)

Type of entry	Number of entries	Example entries
Activities		
Generic business activity models		
MIT Business Activity Model	381	Buy, Make, Sell
MIT Business Models Archetypes	30	Produce as a Creator, Produce as a Broker
Comprehensive business process models developed elsewhere	689	International Benchmarking Clearinghouse's Process Classification Framework
Coordination processes	300	Manage by market with bidding
Subtotal	*1400*	
Case examples		
Supply chain	100	Balance supply chain resources with requirements {Honda}
Hiring	50	Select human resources using agent software {Humana}
e-Business examples	420	Distribute books via electronic store {Amazon}
Subtotal	*570*	
Classification structure		
Generic verbs and other activity categories	*3252*	Create, Modify, Preserve, Destroy,..., Develop, Make product, Provide service
Total activities	**5232**	
Other kinds of entries		
Dependencies	73	Flow of information
Resources	163	Human agent, software agent, location
Conceptual frameworks for specific research projects		
Exceptions	260	Agent unavailable, resource shortfall
Systems dynamics elements	200	Goal-gap molecule, backlog molecule
Total nonactivity entries	**696**	
Total entries	**5928**	

Process Handbook, and the "eBusiness Process Handbook" (ePH). The numbers summarized in table 8.1 are for the research version of the Handbook. This version is where we first introduce experimental new content, and it includes some content that we expect to be of interest primarily to other researchers. This version also uses the original user interface developed in our research project at MIT.

The eBusiness Process Handbook includes a subset of the content in the research version that we expect to be of interest to a broader audience including business school students and managers. This version uses the simpler-to-understand user interface from the commercial software product developed by Phios Corporation under license from MIT. The screen images included in this chapter come from this version of the Process Handbook (except those from the research version where noted). Both of these versions are currently available to the public over the Web at *http://ccs.mit.edu/ph*.

8.3   A Sample Entry in the Process Handbook

Before describing the different types of entries in more detail, it is useful to see a specific example of what a Process Handbook entry looks like. Figure 8.1 shows an example of one such entry: the generic activity called 'Sell'.

Description   In addition to its name ('Sell') the first important part of this entry to notice is the description (labeled "Description of *Sell*"). In this case the description is

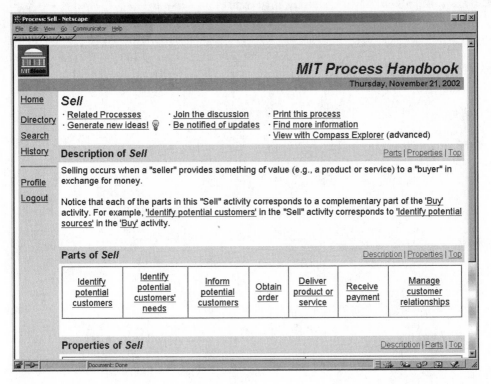

Figure 8.1
Screen image of a sample entry in the Process Handbook

very short: only a few sentences giving a very general definition of selling and some observations about how it relates to buying.

In other cases, especially in the case examples, descriptions may be many paragraphs long. In general, descriptions can include any kind of information the author of an entry thinks will be useful or interesting to readers: definitions, comments, figures, sources for further information, links to other entries, or links to other Web pages.

Parts   The second important element of the sample entry is the list of its parts ("Parts of 'Sell'"). In this case the entry shows seven parts (or subactivities) of 'Sell': 'Identify potential customers', 'Identify potential customers' needs', 'Inform potential customers', 'Obtain order', 'Deliver product or service', 'Receive payment', and 'Manage customer relationships'.

The point of view embodied in this entry is that these activities constitute one possible representation of the "deep structure" of selling. That is, almost all ways (specializations) of selling must somehow perform these basic activities. As we will see later, each of these parts can in turn include subparts that include subparts. In principle, there is no limit to the number of levels of subparts that can be included. In practice, the maximum number of levels included anywhere in the Handbook today is ten.

Properties   The third element of the 'Sell' activity shown in the figure is a list of its properties (labeled "Properties of *Sell*"). In this case the only property shown is the date this entry was last modified. However, the authors of entries can define properties to systematically store any other kind of information they want: time required to do the activity, cost of doing the activity, location of the activity, and so on.

Related Processes   One unique aspect of the Process Handbook is the way it automatically maintains an extensive network of relationships among different entries. For instance, if you were to select the link called "Related processes" near the top left of figure 8.1, you would see a list of processes that are related to 'Sell'. This list includes three parts, excerpts of which are shown in figures 8.2a, 8.2b, and 8.2c.

Specializations   Figure 8.2a shows some of the different ways 'Sell' can be done, that is, its *specializations*. For example, this list includes possibilities like 'Sell via store', 'Sell via face-to-face sales', and 'Sell via other direct marketing'. Many of these entries, in turn, have further specializations of their own representing even more specialized ways of doing things. For example, 'Sell via store' has further specializations like 'Sell via physical store' and 'Sell via electronic store'. These further specializations are not shown in this figure. To see them, you could click on 'Sell via store' and then look at its "Related processes." There is no limit, in principle, to the number of levels of specialization that can be represented in the Handbook. In some cases today, the Handbook includes up to 18 levels of increasingly specialized activities.

Bundles Notice that there are many different "kinds" of specializations shown in the list in figure 8.2a. Some of the specializations, for instance, focus on *how* something is sold; others focus on *what* is sold. Rather than just lumping all these different kinds of specializations into a single undifferentiated list, we separate them into categories (like 'Sell how?' and 'Sell what?'). We call these categories *bundles*.

A "bundle" in the Process Handbook is simply a group of related specializations.[1] In general, we have found that it is often very useful to create bundles based on the basic questions you can ask about any activity: how? what? who? when? where? and why? For most activities in the Handbook, some subset of these questions provides a systematic and logical way of grouping the different specializations that appear.

In addition we have adopted the convention of using two other kinds of bundles to group particular kinds of entries: *example bundles* and *view bundles. Example bundles* are simply groups of specific case examples. It is often useful to have a variety of different specific cases grouped together.

We use *view bundles* to group specializations that do not represent different physical activities in the real world, but simply a different way of *viewing* the same activities. Usually these different views come from different sources. For instance, there is a bundle under 'Sell' called 'Sell-views'. This bundle includes several different models of the general selling process. It includes, for example, parts of a model developed by the International Benchmarking Clearinghouse, a model developed by the Supply Chain Council, and a model from a well-known marketing textbook.

Uses Figure 8.2b shows another set of activities related to Sell. This list shows all the other activities in the Handbook where the 'Sell' activity is used as a part of another activity. For activities like 'Sell', which are used in many different places, this list can be very long.

Generalizations Figure 8.2c shows the last set of "Related processes" for 'Sell'. In this case the activities are other processes that are "like" 'Sell' because they are *generalizations* of 'Sell', or they are other specializations of these generalizations. If we say that a specialization of an activity is like its "child," then this list shows

---

1. Even though, strictly speaking, bundles are not themselves activities, they are groups of activities, and we have included them in the counts of activities in table 8.1.

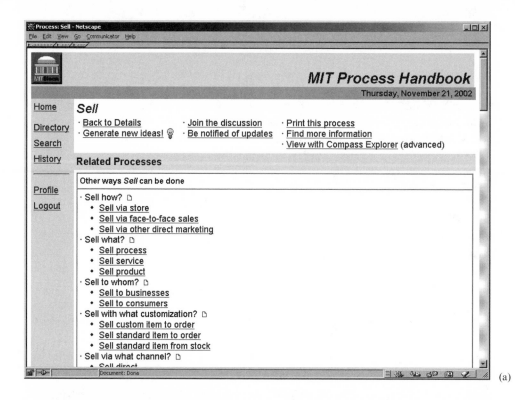

(a)

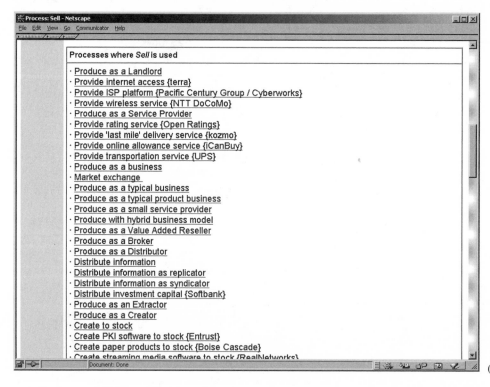

(b)

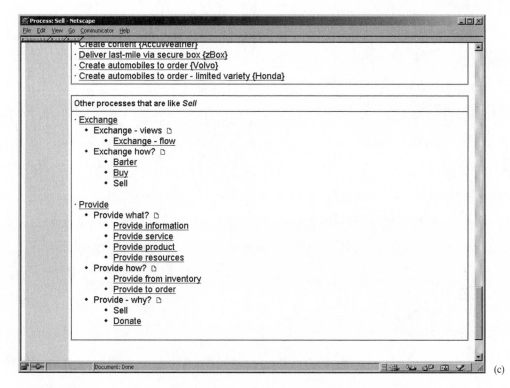

Figure 8.2a
Excerpt of the "related processes" shown for 'Sell': Other ways 'Sell' can be done
Figure 8.2b
Excerpt of the "related processes" shown for 'Sell': Processes where 'Sell' is used
Figure 8.2c
Excerpt of the "related processes" shown for 'Sell': Other processes that are like 'Sell'

part of the "family tree" of Sell: its "siblings," "ancestors," "aunts," "uncles," and "cousins."

For instance, the figure shows that 'Sell' has two generalizations. The first one is 'Exchange', and 'Sell' is included in the 'Exchange how?' bundle. This part of the figure represents the fact that selling is one way of exchanging things. Other kinds of exchange shown in the figure include bartering and buying.

The other generalization of 'Sell' is 'Provide', and 'Sell' is included in the 'Provide-why?' bundle. This part of the figure represents the fact that selling is one way of providing things. Another way, shown in the figure, is donating them, that is, giving them away for free.

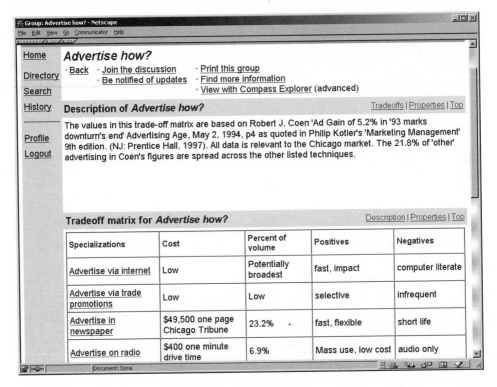

Figure 8.3
Sample trade-off matrix for the 'Advertise how?' bundle

Of course, each of the generalizations of 'Sell' shown in this figure has generalizations of its own. For instance, to see the generalizations of Exchange you could click on 'Exchange' and then look at its "Related processes."

Trade-off Tables In some cases it is useful to compare the different specializations in a bundle using what we call a *trade-off table*. For example, one of the parts of "Sell" shown in figure 8.1 is 'Inform potential customers', and one of the specializations of 'Inform potential customers' (not shown in the figure) is 'Advertise'. 'Advertise' includes a bundle called 'Advertise how?' The trade-off table associated with this bundle is shown in figure 8.3.

The rows in a trade-off table are simply the different specializations in the bundle. For example, here they are different ways of advertising, such as 'Advertise via internet', 'Advertise in newspaper', and 'Advertise on radio'. The columns of the trade-off table are selected properties of the entries being compared. For example, here they include general dimensions like costs, advantages, and disadvantages that can apply to almost any activity. They can also include more specialized dimensions (e.g., percent of volume) that apply only in specific situations.

The values shown in the cells are simply the values of the selected properties for each of the specializations. In some cases, the values shown in a trade-off table represent very general comparisons (e.g., high, medium, and low). In other cases, they may be specific values like the costs for advertising in different media shown in this figure. The sources of values represented in a trade-off table can range from informal judgments by experts to detailed systematic empirical studies. In the example shown here the data come from an article in *Advertising Age*.

Other Information for an Entry   In addition to the kinds of information already described, there are several additional kinds of information available through the Process Handbook. For example, as shown at the top of figure 8.1, any entry can be linked to an on-line "threaded" discussion, and users can be automatically notified of changes made to discussions in which they are interested. Users who click on "Generate new ideas" see an automatically generated list of potential new activities whose names are constructed by combining words from the current activity name with words from the names of other activities in the Handbook that are structurally similar to the current activity. (See chapter 13 for further information about this capability.)

Users who click on the "Find more information" link can perform automatic Web searches using the name of the activity they are currently viewing. And users who click on "View with Compass Explorer (advanced)" can explore the information in the Process Handbook with a user interface based on the compass metaphor introduced in chapter 1. For example, the different specializations shown in figure 8.2a can also be viewed with this compass-based interface as shown in figure 8.4. This user interface lets advanced users navigate more easily over long "distances" in the Process Handbook. For instance, this user interface lets you expand and contract lists in outline format. If you want to see the further specializations of a specialization, for example, you can just click on the boxes containing plus signs to expand the next level of specializations.

8.4   Generic Models of Business Activities

The 'Sell' activity shown in the previous section is an example of the first major kind of content in the Process Handbook: generic models of business activities. These generic models represent important activities that occur—in some form—in lots of businesses.

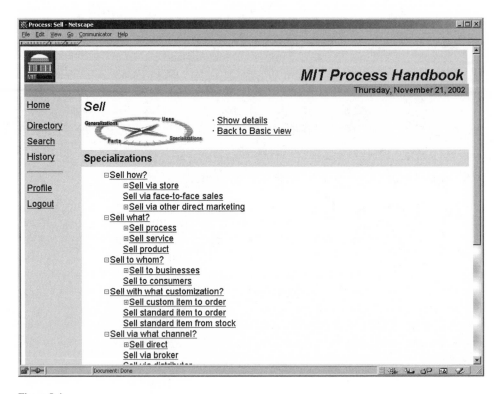

Figure 8.4
Specializations of 'Sell' shown with the compass explorer user interface

The generic models can be used in a number of important ways. First, they can be used as a framework for organizing and grouping many other kinds of business knowledge: case examples, best practices, software tools, contact information for knowledgeable experts, or on-line discussions for communities of practice (e.g., see chapters 15, 16, and 17). Second, they can provide a useful starting point for modeling the specific details of a particular company, process, or software module (e.g., see the chapters in section IV). Third, as a systematic list of process possibilities, they can be used to stimulate new ideas about what is possible that might not have occurred to you otherwise (e.g., see chapters 12 to 14).

The current version of the Process Handbook includes four primary kinds of generic models of business activities: (1) the MIT Business Activity Model, (2) the MIT Business Model Archetypes, (3) a collection of comprehensive business process models developed elsewhere, and (4) models of basic coordination processes.

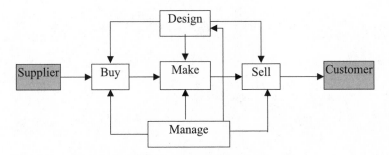

Figure 8.5
The top level of produce as a business in the MIT business activity model

8.5 The MIT Business Activity Model

One of the most important kinds of generic business knowledge included in the Process Handbook is a high-level model of everything that goes on in a business. We call this model the MIT Business Activity Model (BAM). The top level of the model is shown in figure 8.5. The overall activity is called 'Produce as a business', and it includes as parts five basic activities that occur—in some form—in most businesses: 'Buy', 'Make', 'Sell', 'Design', and 'Manage'.

As shown in table 8.2, each of these top-level activities, in turn, has subparts. For example, 'Buy' includes parts like 'Identify own needs', 'Identify potential sources', and 'Select supplier'. Notice that 'Make' does not include any subparts because the core "making" activity of a business can vary so widely in different companies and industries. For example, we were unable to find useful subparts of 'Make' that would apply in industries as diverse as manufacturing, consulting, leasing, and brokering. However, all the other activities and their subparts appear to be quite general across almost all businesses—large and small, profit and nonprofit—in all industries. To achieve this goal, we have tried to use terms and breakdowns that are generic, enduring, and fundamental, rather than purely arbitrary, current, or industry specific. In other words, we have tried to represent a view of the "deep structure" of business.

In addition to this very generic model, the MIT Business Activity Model also includes a specialization of 'Produce as a business' that is called 'Produce as a typical business'. This model is intended to represent a more detailed view of the things that go on in most large companies, but that might not occur, for instance, in a small grocery store. Our intention here is to still be quite generic, but to focus on activities that are common in, for example, typical large manufacturing companies.

Table 8.2
Lower levels of 'Produce as a business' in the MIT Business Activity Model

1. Buy
   a. Identify own needs
   b. Identify potential sources
   c. Select supplier
   d. Place order
   e. Receive
   f. Pay
   g. Manage suppliers
      i. Evaluate suppliers
      ii. Manage supplier policies
      iii. Manage supplier relationships
2. Make
3. Sell
   a. Identify potential customers
   b. Identify potential customers' needs
   c. Inform potential customers
   d. Obtain order
   e. Deliver product or service
   f. Receive payment
   g. Manage customer relationships
4. Design
   a. Identify needs or requirements
   b. Identify product capabilities
   c. Develop product and process design
      i. Develop the characteristics of a product/service
      ii. Develop the process of producing a product/service
5. Manage
   a. Develop strategy
   b. Manage resources by type of resource
      i. Manage human resources
      ii. Manage physical resources
      iii. Manage financial resources
      iv. Manage information resources
   c. Manage learning and change
   d. Manage other external relationships
      i. Manage regulatory relationships
         (1) Manage tax and duty compliance
         (2) Manage legal compliance
      ii. Manage competitor relationships
      iii. Manage societal relationships
      iv. Manage environmental relationships
      v. Manage stakeholder relationships

Table 8.3
Second level of 'Produce as a typical business' in the MIT Business Activity Model

---

1. Buy
    a. (subparts same as in table 8.2)
2. Make
3. Sell
    a. (subparts same as in table 8.2)
4. Design as a typical business
    a. Determine customer needs and wants
    b. Develop offering concept {Typical product design process}
    c. Develop design with subcomponents
    d. Modify design
5. Manage a typical business
    a. Develop business strategy and organization
    b. Manage physical resources in a business
    c. Manage human resources in a business
    d. Manage information in a business
    e. Manage financial resources in a business
    f. Manage learning and change in a business
    g. Manage other external relationships

The models of 'Buy', 'Make', and 'Sell' are identical here to those in 'Produce as a business'. But 'Design' and 'Manage' are represented by more specialized activities and a more detailed breakdown of subparts. The first level of these breakdowns is shown in table 8.3, but each of the subparts of 'Design' and 'Manage' shown in table 8.3 also has an even more detailed breakdown. In most cases, the more detailed breakdown includes one or two additional levels; in a few, it includes three.

8.5.1 Desirable Characteristics of the MIT Business Activity Model

Of course, there are many ways to categorize and organize business activities. We certainly don't believe that our approach is the only way, or even the only good way, of doing so. But our approach does have at least three desirable and important characteristics: it is *comprehensive*, it is *intuitively appealing*, and it is *theoretically based.*

Comprehensive   In developing the MIT Business Activity Model, we drew upon the informal knowledge of dozens of MIT students, faculty, researchers, and corporate sponsors. We have also repeatedly tested the model by using it to classify new case examples, student projects, and other process models. Many of these examples are no longer included in the general versions of the Process Handbook because we did not feel they were of general interest, but they contributed to our experience in refining the model.

In addition, as described later in section 8.7, we sought out, analyzed, and explicitly cross-referenced a number of other comprehensive models of business processes. Based on all this experience, we believe that all the important things that go on in business can be "naturally" classified into one of the subparts of the MIT BAM. While such judgments are necessarily somewhat subjective, we feel that all our experience taken together provides substantial evidence for the claim that the MIT BAM is a *comprehensive* model of business activities.

Intuitively Appealing   A judgment that something is "intuitively appealing" is also subjective, and we have not systematically tested people's reactions to the categories used in the MIT BAM. However, our impression after working with dozens of students, researchers, and others is that many people find the terminology and breakdown of activities in the model to be logical and understandable.

In addition to being understandable, the structure of the model has other intuitively appealing features. For instance, as shown in figure 8.6, there is a "pleasing" symmetry between the breakdown of activities in the 'Buy' activity and those in the 'Sell' activity. Each of the subactivities in buying and selling has a natural mapping to a corresponding subactivity in the opposite activity. There is a close relationship, for example, between the buyers' activity of placing an order and the sellers' activity of obtaining an order.

Many business process models are based primarily on descriptions of current processes in typical companies, and they therefore give more emphasis to activities that

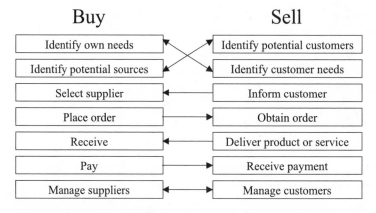

Figure 8.6
The subparts of 'Buy' and 'Sell' in the MIT business activity model have an intuitive correspondence with each other

currently require more resources or attention. In the same spirit we have tried to create breakdowns of activities that emphasize important activities. But, unlike many process models, we have also tried to create activity breakdowns that are compelling from a purely logical point of view. For instance, we believe that from a purely logical point of view, it is hard to imagine how anyone could buy or sell anything without somehow doing the activities shown in figure 8.6. This therefore gives us more confidence that we have truly captured a view of the "deep structure" of these activities.

Theoretically Based   Another appealing property of the MIT Business Activity Model is that it is based on a theoretical analysis of business from the perspective of coordination theory. In the next section we show how the top-level model (shown in figure 8.5) can be "derived" step by step from a consideration of the basic dependencies that need to be managed in a business.

8.5.2   Deriving the MIT Business Activity Model Using Coordination Theory

To "derive" the MIT Business Activity Model, we begin with one of the simplest possible views of the activities in a business (shown in figure 8.7). We start by assuming that the business consists of only one activity (called 'Make'), and that this activity involves producing whatever product or service the business sells to a Customer. We also assume that the 'Make' activity uses some inputs from another activity (which we call a Supplier). Using the terminology of coordination theory, we can say that this figure includes two dependencies: a "flow" dependency from the Supplier to the 'Make' activity, and a "flow" dependency from the 'Make' activity to the Customer.

Coordinating the Flow Dependencies: Buy and Sell   From the perspective of coordination theory, whenever there is a dependency between two activities there is an opportunity (often a need) to manage it. In this case, the two flow dependencies shown in figure 8.7 need to be managed. In the case of a business, we can call the

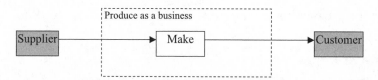

Figure 8.7
One of the simplest possible views of the activities in a business

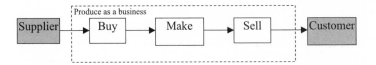

Figure 8.8
'Buy' and 'Sell' activities are needed to manage the input flows and the output flows, respectively

coordination activities that manage these two dependencies 'Buy' and 'Sell', respectively. That is, we can view the buying activity as a way of managing the flow of inputs needed to make whatever the business makes, and we can view the selling activity as a way of managing the flow to the customer of whatever the business makes. Adding these two coordination activities results in the diagram shown in figure 8.8.

It is important to realize, by the way, that the arrows shown in these figures should not necessarily be interpreted as simple one-way flows. In managing the flow dependencies from 'Make' to the Customer, for example, the 'Sell' activity may involve a very complex pattern of two-way communication and flows of products and money. All these lower-level flows, however, are summarized in the diagram by the one-directional arrows that represent the overall flow of the product from the 'Make' activity to the Customer.

Coordinating the Fit Dependency: Design   Many typical process diagrams are flowcharts that show only the flow dependencies in a process. Coordination theory identifies two other types of dependency: *fit* and *sharing*. A *fit dependency* occurs when more than one supplier produces a single resource. In this case there is a fit dependency among all the different activities involved in producing the product or service that is sold to the customer: the results of the different subparts of the 'Make' activity need to fit together, the 'Buy' activity needs to buy inputs that will work together, and the 'Sell' activity needs to be selling what is actually being made using these inputs.

A business needs to somehow manage this complex fit dependency, and we call the activity that does so 'Design'. Figure 8.9 shows the results of adding this activity to the diagram.

Coordinating the Sharing Dependencies: Manage   From a coordination perspective there is one more type of critical dependency between the activities shown in figure 8.9. That is the *sharing* dependencies among all the activities. The activities shown in figure 8.9 have to share resources like money, people, information, and physical

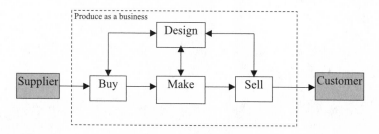

Figure 8.9
'Design' activity is needed to manage the fit dependency between the different activities that collectively produce the product a customer buys.

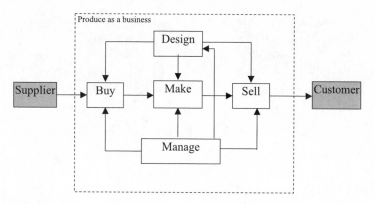

Figure 8.10
'Manage' activity is needed to manage the sharing dependencies among all the other activities.

facilities. Any business needs to somehow manage all these sharing dependencies, and we call the coordination activity that does so 'Manage'. Figure 8.10 shows the results of adding this final key activity to our basic business activity model.

Deriving the MIT Business Activity Model: Summary This, then, is the derivation of the MIT Business Activity Model from a coordination perspective: the 'Buy', 'Make', and 'Sell' activities manage the *flow* dependencies in the company's supply chain. The 'Design' activity manages the *fit* dependencies among the activities that create different parts of the company's product. And the 'Manage' activity manages the dependencies for *sharing* key resources among all the other activities in the company.

Of course, the MIT Business Activity Model is not the only way to categorize the activities in a business, but the fact that the MIT model can be theoretically derived from the principles of coordination theory provides one additional piece of evidence for its desirability.

8.6 MIT Business Model Archetypes

In addition to the MIT Business Activity Model, the Process Handbook also includes a set of six different business model archetypes that companies can use. Our hypothesis is that all the different business models companies use can be naturally classified into one of these six types or some combination of them. We call these six models the MIT Business Model Archetypes (for a more detailed description of these models and how they were derived, see Herman, Malone, and Weill 2003).

We define a *business model* as consisting of two parts: (1) what a business does and (2) how the business makes money from its activities. For example, the traditional part of General Motors' business model is to make and sell automobiles and to make money from the difference between the costs of making the cars and their sales prices. We call this business model a Creator. Walmart, by contrast, distributes products they don't make, and makes money from the difference between what they pay for the products and what they sell them for. We call this business model a Distributor.

Figure 8.11 shows the six different models classified according to the two dimensions that distinguish them: what is sold and how much the inputs are transformed. The definitions of the different models are as follows:

What is sold?	How much transformation of inputs?		
	Lot	Little	None
Ownership of asset	Creator	Distributor	Broker
Use of asset	"Landlord"		
Human effort	Contractor		
Human attention	"Attractor"		

Figure 8.11
MIT Business Models Archetypes (from Herman, Malone, and Weill 2003). "Asset" can be physical, informational, or financial. "None" means broker never takes ownership of what is sold.

1. A *Creator* buys raw materials or components from suppliers and transforms or assembles them to create a product (or service) sold to buyers. The product or service may be physical, informational or financial (e.g., an insurance policy). This business model is common in industries like manufacturing and construction.

2. A *Distributor* buys a product and resells the product to someone else. The Distributor may provide additional value by, for example, transporting or repackaging the product, or providing customer service. This business model is common in wholesale and retail trade.

3. A *Broker* facilitates sales by matching buyers and sellers. A Broker may also provide advice to either or both parties. Unlike a Distributor, a Broker does not take possession of the product being sold. The Broker receives a fee from the buyer, the seller, or both. Often this fee is in the form of a commission based on a percentage of the sale price or on volume. This business model is common in a number of industries, such as real estate brokers, stockbrokers, and insurance brokers.

4. A *Landlord* sells the right to use, but not own, an asset. The asset may be a location (e.g., a hotel room, apartment, or amusement park), an event (e.g., a concert), or equipment (e.g., a rental car or recording studio). Depending on the kind of asset, the payments by customers may be called "rent," "lease," "admission," or other similar terms. This business model is common in industries like real estate rental and leasing, accommodation, arts, entertainment, and recreation.

5. A *Contractor* sells a service provided primarily by people, such as consulting, construction, education, personal care, and healthcare. Payment is in the form of a fee for service, often (but not always) based on the amount of time the service requires. Most services involve a combination of both people and nonhuman assets, but if the service being sold involves more nonhuman assets than people, the business model is classified as a Landlord rather than a Contractor.

6. An *Attractor* attracts people's attention by providing things like television programs or web content and then "sells" that attention to advertisers. The attractor may devote significant effort to creating or distributing the things that attract attention, but their source of revenue is from the advertisers who pay to deliver a message to the audience that is attracted. This business model is common in radio and television broadcasting, some forms of publishing, and some Internet-based businesses.

Of course, many real businesses include some combination of these six business model archetypes, but our experience so far suggests that these models can be used to classify all the different combinations that exist in reality. In a related project (see Herman, Malone, and Weill 2003), we have so far classified over 500 companies (including over 450 of the Fortune 500) according to the combinations they use of these six business model archetypes. In addition the Process Handbook includes over 200 innovative ebusiness case examples classified according to these categories.

These different business models are included in the Process Handbook as specializations of 'Produce as a business' in a bundle called 'Produce with what business model?'

8.7 Comprehensive Models of Business Processes Developed Elsewhere

In addition to the MIT Business Activity Model and Business Model Archetypes, the Process Handbook also includes a number of other models of business processes developed by other organizations. We have certainly not included all such models, but we believe we have included a representative sample of some of the most comprehensive and well-known alternative models of business processes.

Each of these other models represents a different way of grouping some (or all) of the same physical activities as those included in 'Produce as a business'. Therefore most of these other models are classified as specializations of 'Produce as a business' in a "view" bundle (called 'Produce as a business-views').

In addition we have systematically and explicitly cross-referenced several of these other models to the MIT Business Activity Model (BAM) by categorizing all their subparts as specializations of some subpart of the MIT BAM. For example, the International Benchmarking Clearinghouse's Process Classification Framework includes an activity called 'Understand markets and customers'. We have classified this activity in the Process Handbook as a specialization of 'Identify potential customers' needs', one of the subparts of 'Sell' in the MIT BAM.

By this approach our framework is able to accommodate many different, even contradictory, views of the same basic activities. In contrast to our approach, most previous approaches to classifying business processes are much more rigid, requiring people to use only a single view of the activities. We believe this flexibility of our approach is another one of its advantages.

8.7.1 International Benchmarking Clearinghouse Process Classification Framework
The first, and most comprehensive, alternative model included in the Process Handbook is the Process Classification Framework (PCF) developed by the International Benchmarking Clearinghouse (IBC, part of the American Productivity and Quality Center). The IBC worked with Arthur Andersen and over 80 other organizations to develop this framework in the early 1990s.

The top level of the PCF framework includes 13 activities, such as 'Understand markets and customers', 'Develop vision and strategy', and 'Design products and services'. Most of these activities are broken down into two levels of subparts, and a few go down three levels. For instance, the lowest level under 'Understand markets and customers' includes activities like 'Conduct customer interviews', and 'Conduct focus groups'. The PCF includes a total of 271 activities in all.

8.7.2 Supply Chain Operations Reference (SCOR) Model

The Supply Chain Council, a trade association of over 400 companies interested in supply chain management (see *www.supply-chain.org*) developed a model called the Supply Chain Operations Reference (SCOR) model. The top level of this model includes four key activities to represent a company's supply chain: 'Plan', 'Source', 'Make', and 'Deliver'.[2] These activities are broken down into subparts, in most cases down to two additional levels. For instance, the 'Source' activity, includes a subpart called 'Source stocked materials', which, in turn, includes subparts called 'Schedule material deliveries', and 'Receive and verify material'. The SCOR model also includes standard process definitions, standard terminology, standard metrics, supply chain best practices, and references to enabling information technology. This model includes a total of 215 activities.

8.7.3 Lean Enterprise Manufacturing Model

The Lean Enterprise Manufacturing model was developed by the Lean Aircraft Initiative consortium led by MIT. The portion of the model included in the Process Handbook focuses on the "enabling practices" and metrics that help to promote a "lean" approach to product and process design and manufacture. For instance, it includes high-level activities like 'Identify and optimize enterprise flow' and 'Nurture a learning environment'. The Process Handbook includes a total of 72 activities from this model.

8.7.4 European Foundation for Quality Management (EFQM) Model

This model was developed by the European Federation for Quality Management to help organizations assess their progress along a path to excellence. The portion of the model included in the Process Handbook includes activities in five categories: leadership, people management, policy and strategy, resources, and processes. For

2. The MIT Process Handbook includes version 3.0 of the SCOR model. As of this writing, a later version (5.0) is now available from the Supply Chain Council and has been included in the Phios version of the Process Handbook. This later version adds another activity, 'Return', at the top level of the model.

instance, People management includes activities like 'Plan resources', 'Develop resources', and 'Review performance'. This model includes 30 activities in the Process Handbook.

8.7.5 Xerox Management Model

As part of their extensive quality improvement program Xerox Corporation developed a comprehensive model of their operational process, and this model is included in the Process Handbook. For instance, it includes a high-level activity called 'Time to market' representing the design process and another one called 'Integrated Supply Chain' representing the manufacturing and related supply chain activities. Each of these high-level activities is broken down to one more level. For example, 'Integrated Supply Chain' includes subparts like 'Acquire materials' and 'Manage inventories'. This model includes 51 activities in the Process Handbook.

8.7.6 Textbook Models

In addition to models developed by other organizations, we have also included representative models from two well-known business school textbooks in marketing and product design.

The marketing textbook we used is *Marketing Management* by Philip Kotler. We included Kotler's view of marketing as an alternative "view" (or specialization) of 'Sell'. It includes top-level activities like 'Analyze markets' and 'Implement market strategy'. 'Analyze markets', in turn, includes subparts like 'Analyze market environment' and 'Analyze industry/competitors'. A total of 17 activities are included in the Process Handbook for this activity.

The product design textbook we used was *New Product Design* by Steven Eppinger and Karl Ulrich. We used this textbook to create a new specialization of the 'Design' activity from the MIT Business Activity Model. This new specialization is called 'Design product {Ulrich/Eppinger by phase}' and is classified in a bundle called 'Design-views'. This view focuses on the design of engineered, discrete manufactured products. The five top-level activities in this model are 'Concept development', 'System level design', 'Detail design', 'Testing and refinement', and 'Production ramp-up'. Most of these activities have one to three further levels of subparts. For instance, 'Concept development' includes subparts like 'Identify customer needs' and 'Establish target product specifications'. This model includes a total of 74 activities in the Process Handbook.

Of course, there are vast numbers of other business textbooks that could, in principle, be included in a repository like this one. We selected these two examples to illustrate the possibilities, in part because they both included explicit frameworks that could be easily interpreted as activity models.

8.8   Models of Coordination Processes

The final type of generic business activity model in the Process Handbook includes models of different kinds of coordination processes. Since we define *coordination* as the "management of dependencies among activities" (see chapter 1) the "root" of all this knowledge is an activity called 'Manage dependency'.

The three basic types of dependencies (described in chapter 1) give rise to the first three specializations of the 'Manage dependency' activity: 'Manage flow', 'Manage sharing', and 'Manage fit'. In addition the three subparts of managing flow dependencies give rise to three more specializations of 'Manage dependency'. They are called 'Manage prerequisite', 'Manage accessibility', and 'Manage usability'.

Each of these six types of coordination, in turn, has a number of "bundles" which contain further specializations of these generic coordination processes. For instance, 'Manage sharing' includes bundles like 'How is sharing managed?' 'What kind of resource is being shared?' and 'When is sharing managed?' Within these bundles are various kinds of sharing mechanisms such as 'Manage by manager decision', 'Manage by market', and 'Manage by chance {lottery}'.

In some cases these generic coordination mechanisms even include further specializations that describe specific examples. For example, 'Manage by market' includes a specialization called 'Manage recruiter time by market bidding' that was added as part of our project about new ways to do hiring (described in chapters 1 and 12).

Much more information about coordination theory is included in section II and detailed descriptions of some of the specific kinds of coordination knowledge included in the handbook are provided in chapter 3.

8.9   Case Examples

One of the most important uses of repositories like the Process Handbook is to help people organize and share examples of innovative or otherwise interesting business case examples. For instance, these repositories can include "best practices," "typical practices," and even instructive examples of "bad practices." They can include cases for benchmarking, for business school classes, and for consulting firm practice development. Organizing case examples in this way can help you find relevant examples more easily than with, for example, keyword searches, and it can help you easily find and compare examples that have deep similarities, even if the words used to describe the cases are very different.

To illustrate these possibilities, the Process Handbook already includes hundreds of case examples of business activities in specific companies. These case examples were developed by students, faculty, and staff at the MIT Sloan School of Management; students at the London Business School; and staff at Phios Corporation. In most cases these examples were based on previously published descriptions from business journals, magazines, and newspapers. In a few cases the examples were based on original field research in the companies described.

Most of the case examples currently included in the Process Handbook fall into one of three main categories:

1. *Supply chain examples.* The Process Handbook currently includes over 100 case examples of interesting or innovative supply chain practices. For instance, it includes examples like Cisco's use of their corporate intranet for electronic purchasing and Toyota's use of narrowing sets of design possibilities to enhance concurrent engineering.

2. *Hiring examples.* As part of our project to develop innovative ideas for hiring (described in chapters 1, 12, and 13), we added a number of case examples of hiring practices used in different companies. For example, the Process Handbook includes descriptions of Cisco's use of focus groups of current employees to help target on-line recruiting ads, and Marriott's use of automated telephone screening of job candidates. There are approximately 50 of these case examples.

3. *Innovative eBusiness examples.* During the peak of the eBusiness boom, we entered over 400 case examples of innovative uses of eBusiness concepts. These examples include all 70 finalists in the MIT eBusiness Awards program for two years, as well as a number of other examples from other sources. For instance, the Process Handbook includes descriptions of Amazon.com's electronic book distribution and eBay's electronic auctions. To illustrate what these examples look like, an excerpt of the Amazon.com example is shown in figure 8.12.

These eBusiness examples are all organized into the business model categories above (Creator, Distributor, etc.) and thus provide some interesting comparisons across industries. For example, this organization puts Mattel and Dell close together as Creators that allow their end customers to configure their products, even though Barbie dolls and computers are in very different industries.

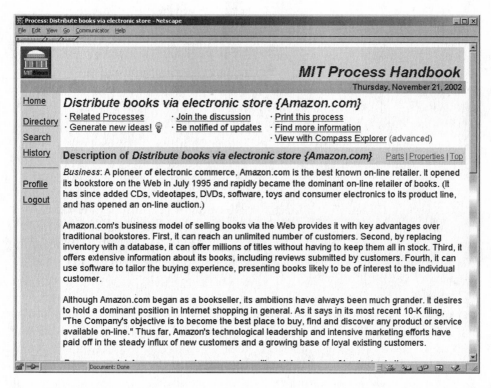

Figure 8.12
Sample case example describing the way Amazon.com distributes books via the Internet

8.9.1 Updating the Database of Case Examples

We believe that most of the current content of the Process Handbook (e.g., the generic business activity models and the classification structure) has enduring value over long periods of time. It is unlikely, for example, that significant new forms of business will be invented that do not involve some form of buying and selling.

But other parts of the Process Handbook, especially the case examples, have much shorter "half-lives" of usefulness. A number of the companies whose eBusiness case examples we entered a few years ago, for instance, have already gone out of business. In some of these companies there is still value in seeing the basic ideas and, perhaps, the lessons to be learned from their failures. But the value of a topical database of case examples depends critically on it being continually updated.

8.10 Classification Structure for Activities

It would be possible to use the generic kinds of business knowledge and the case examples we have already discussed without any further categorization. If one wants to find knowledge about a particular business function, for example, one could just find that business function in the MIT Business Activity Model and then look at its specializations. Or one could do conventional searches of the knowledge base using names, keywords, or other dimensions like date, company, industry, and so forth.

It is also useful for human editors to be able to manually group Process Handbook entries in various ways to help readers find the things they want. We call such linkages *navigation links*, and the Handbook includes a number of them. For instance, there is a group of links to "eBusiness Case Examples" that occur in various parts of the Handbook, and there are other manually created links to examples of various business functions (e.g., Procurement, Supply Chain Management, and Marketing). All these conventional ways of organizing and searching the Process Handbook are certainly useful.

But some of the most powerful and interesting capabilities of the Process Handbook require more extensive use of the specialization hierarchy. For example, finding other entries that are "like" a given entry (as shown in figure 8.2c) or finding "distant analogies" (as described in chapter 12) depends on having the entries classified in a "family tree" of increasingly general types of activities. These capabilities of the Process Handbook work only on activities that are classified in useful ways in the specialization hierarchy. Therefore, to take full advantage of these capabilities, it is desirable to have as many entries as possible classified in the specialization hierarchy.

To make this as easy as possible, the Process Handbook includes an extensive classification structure for the specialization hierarchy. This classification structure (including over 3,000 activities) provides "logical" places for you to classify any business activity whatsoever. In fact, at its most general levels, this structure can even be used to classify any activities, whether or not they involve business.

To see how this structure works, let us start with an example of the 'Sell' activity we saw in section 8.3. Figure 8.13 shows all the direct and indirect generalizations of this activity (all its "ancestors" in the specialization hierarchy). This figure uses the Compass Explorer view, which shows more information than the standard view in figure 8.2c, and shows the information in a different format.

Since 'Sell' has two generalizations ('Exchange' and 'Provide'), two complete generalization paths for 'Sell' are shown in the "Ancestors" part of the figure. The first path, for example, shows that 'Sell' is a specialization of 'Exchange' (with 'Sell' being in the bundle called 'Exchange how?'). 'Exchange', in turn, is a specialization of

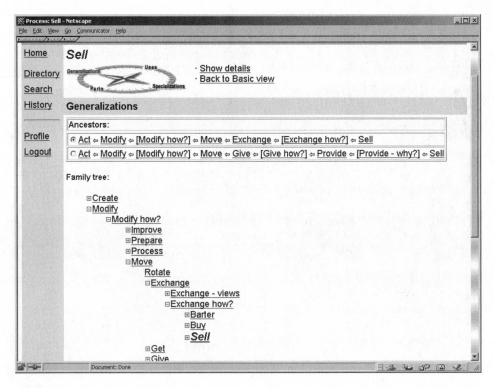

Figure 8.13
Generalizations of 'Sell' (shown in the compass explorer view). The "Ancestors" part of the figure shows the direct and indirect generalizations of 'Sell'. The "Family tree" part of the figure also shows some of the other relatives of 'Sell' in the specialization hierarchy.

'Move', and 'Move' is a specialization of 'Modify' (in the 'Modify how?' bundle). And, finally, 'Modify' is a specialization of 'Act'. 'Act' is the most general activity of all. All the activities in the entire Process Handbook are either direct or indirect specializations of 'Act'.

But if 'Act' is the "root" of all activities, what is the next level of specialization below 'Act'? Are there hundreds of different kinds of activities at the next level? We have actually organized the entire Process Handbook with only nine entries at the next level. We call all but one of these entries "generic verbs."

8.10.1   The Generic Verbs

Figure 8.14 shows the next level of specializations of 'Act'. The first eight of these entries are generic verbs: 'Create', 'Modify', 'Preserve', 'Destroy', 'Combine', 'Sepa-

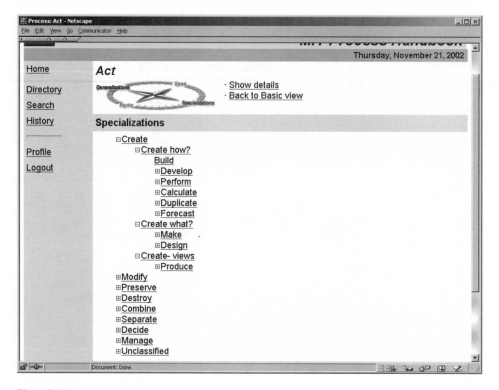

Figure 8.14
First-level specializations of 'Act' (shown in the compass explorer view). The next two levels of specialization under 'Create' are also shown here.

rate', 'Decide', and 'Manage'. The first four ('Create', 'Modify', 'Preserve', and 'Destroy') are actions that can occur for any object. The next two ('Combine' and 'Separate') are actions that can occur when multiple objects are involved. And the final two verbs ('Decide' and 'Manage') are informational actions that could have been included under the earlier verbs but that are given special emphasis here because of their importance in business. The last entry 'Unclassified' is simply a place to put entries that the author doesn't want to classify further (or which will be further classified at a later time). All these entries have many more levels of specialization. To illustrate what these further levels of specialization look like, the next two levels of specialization under the first entry, 'Create', are shown expanded in the figure.

8.10.2 Desirable Characteristics of the Generic Verbs

Where did these eight generic verbs come from? Is this the only way to organize a repository like ours? Why should things be organized this way? We don't think that this is the only possible way to organize a repository like ours, but we believe this organizational structure has the same desirable characteristics we discussed earlier in section 8.5.1: it is *comprehensive*, it is *intuitively appealing*, and it is *theoretically based.*

Perhaps the best way to see how the framework has these characteristics is to consider the process by which we developed the framework. We began by searching widely in the literature of linguistics, philosophy, library science, computer science, and elsewhere for an existing taxonomy of actions that we could use. We were unable to locate any existing taxonomy that seemed suitable for our purposes: comprehensive, parsimonious, broadly understandable, intuitively appealing, and potentially relevant to business.

We therefore embarked on the task of developing our own such taxonomy. Our first step was to find a comprehensive list of actions that would need to be encompassed by our taxonomy. To do that, Jintae Lee (a member of our project team) located and searched an extensive on-line dictionary (more precisely, a "lexical database") called Wordnet that was developed by cognitive scientist George Miller and others at Princeton University (see *http://www.cogsci.princeton.edu/~wn/*). Lee analyzed the dictionary to find all the verbs that did not have any generalizations ("hypernyms") shown. This resulted in a list of about 100 to 200 verbs.

All the other verbs in the dictionary had generalizations, so they were all—directly or indirectly—specializations of the verbs in this list. In a sense, then, this list of 100 to 200 verbs subsumed all the verbs in the English language represented in this on-line dictionary.

We next took this list and reduced it further by removing all the verbs that seemed to us to be direct specializations of other verbs already there. In other words, we removed words for which we felt a generalization had incorrectly been omitted in the on-line dictionary.

Then we continued refining the list of verbs by grouping the remaining verbs into hierarchies with more general verbs subsuming more specific ones. We did not insist, in these cases, that the general verbs be strict generalizations for all the verbs grouped under them, but we tried to make groupings for which there was at least a plausible, intuitive connection. For example, we grouped all the following verbs under 'Create': 'Build', 'Develop', 'Perform', 'Calculate', 'Duplicate', 'Forecast'. All these verbs are, in some sense, ways of creating things.

We continued in this way until we finally arrived at a hierarchical structure with the eight generic verbs shown above as the top level of our hierarchy and the more specialized verbs grouped hierarchically under them. As shown in figure 8.14, for example, the lower-level verbs ('Build', 'Develop', 'Perform', etc.) are now included in the Process Handbook at various levels of specialization below the highest-level generic verbs.

Of course, there was a substantial amount of subjective judgment in this grouping process. Other reasonable people might certainly have made different choices about the details of how to group specific verbs. Even in cases where a given action might be sensibly classified in multiple ways, however, the value of the Process Handbook is not eliminated. You just get the benefits of all the connections that *are* represented, and not of the ones that are not.

Overall, we feel that this structure provides an intuitive and logical way of grouping all possible actions that can be described in the English language. It thus, of course, includes all actions that can occur in business. We have now used this structure to classify thousands of entries developed by dozens of people, and we believe that all this experience provides substantial evidence that our theoretically based structure is comprehensive and intuitive.

8.10.3   Classifying All the Other Entries in the Process Handbook

To see how the generic verbs can be used to classify even the most detailed actions in business, consider the specializations of 'Create' shown in figure 8.15a. The figure shows how various views and case examples of negotiating contracts are all classified as ways of "discussing"—which is in turn classified as a way of "developing" which is itself classified as a way of "creating." Figure 8.15b shows how Produce as a business is also a specialization of 'Create' through the bundle called 'Create-views'.

As figure 8.15 illustrates, we have, in general, tried to maintain a branching factor of about "7 plus or minus 2" in the specialization hierarchy. This number comes from the psychological study of the limits of human short-term memory,[3] but we use it primarily as a rough guideline for editing the Process Handbook. In general, also, we have tried to create logical groupings at each level. We have tried, for example, to create groupings at each level that include alternatives that seem "comparable" to each other and that have roughly equal importance. Wherever possible, we have tried to create groupings that constitute a mutually exclusive and exhaustive partitioning of the possible specializations of that activity.

---

3. George A. Miller, The magical number seven, plus or minus two: Some limits on our capacity for processing information, *Psychological Review* 63(1956): 81–97.

To visualize how all the elements of the Process Handbook are connected, recall the metaphor of the Process Compass (as described in chapter 1). From any activity in the repository, you can think about going in any of the four directions shown on the compass: *down* to the parts of the activity, *up* to the activities of which this one is a part, *right* to the specializations of this activity, and *left* to the generalizations of this activity.

Using this metaphor, you can think of all the actions in the Process Handbook as a vast, interconnected web (see figure 8.16). The most general activity of all, 'Act', is at the far left and the next level of generic verbs is just to the right of it. Then the links spread out into a very complicated, tangled web of more and more specialized activities. This web includes, not just the classification structure, but all the business activities represented in the Process Handbook, all the way down, in principle, to even the most detailed things that go on in business.

Along the top fringe of the web are the various specializations of 'Produce as a business'. These entries are at the top because many other things are part of them, but they are not part of anything else.

8.10.4 Naming Conventions for Activities

As you may have noticed in the figures so far, almost all of the activities in the Process Handbook have names that begin with a verb. Most of the activities also include other modifiers or objects as part of their names. Usually these additional parts of the name give information about some dimension of the activity, such as how, who, when, and where.

Some of the activities also include a further description in {curly brackets} after the name. We use these bracketed suffixes for several purposes: (1) to represent the names of specific companies in case examples, (2) to give the source of models developed by other organizations (e.g., the Supply Chain Council's SCOR model), and (3) to distinguish between any other easily confused activities that would otherwise have the same name.

While we have not followed these naming conventions in every single case, we have used them in all cases where we did not see some compelling reason to do otherwise. In general, we have found that these naming conventions are useful for several reasons: First, they result in lists of activities that seem consistent and comparable. Second, they emphasize the action-oriented perspective that is embodied in a structure based on activities. Third, they usually provide enough information in the names of activities shown in a list to allow one to determine which activity to examine in detail.

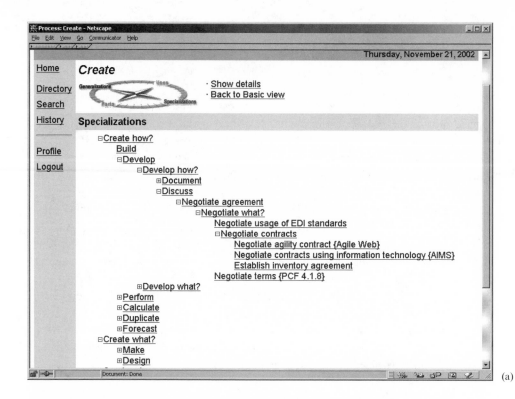

(a)

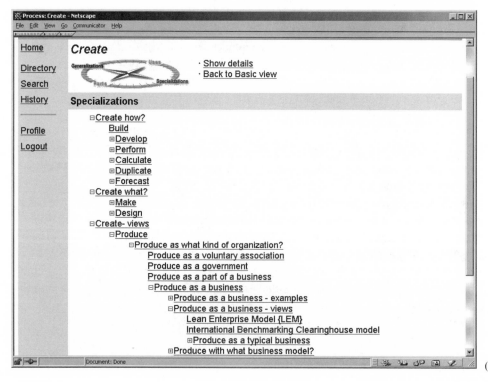

(b)

8.11 Other Kinds of Entries

While we have focused most of our effort on representing various business processes and activities in the Process Handbook, the basic structure of the repository is general enough to include any other kinds of entities authors and editors want to define. In this section we will briefly review several other types of entries included in the Handbook.

8.11.1 Dependencies

As described in chapter 2, dependencies play a central role in coordination theory, and they can be represented in the Process Handbook as shown in figure 8.17. The dependencies are classified as specializations of the three basic dependency types: flow, fit, and sharing.

8.11.2 Resources

Resources are the inputs and outputs of a process. Resources define a dependency, in that a dependency exists when a resource produced by one activity is consumed by another activity.

The Process Handbook currently distinguishes two specific types of resources:

1. *Actors*—resources that perform activities. Actors can be people, organizations, software agents, and so forth. The Process Handbook currently includes a limited taxonomy of actors, including people, organizations, and software agents.

2. *Locations*—places at which activities occurs. The current taxonomy of locations includes physical locations and virtual (cyberspace) locations.

8.11.3 Exceptions

Process models typically describe the "normal" or expected flow of events. In reality, however, there are often complications. During the enactment of a process, deviations from the ideal sequence of events often occur. We call these deviations *exceptions* (Dellarocas, Klein). As described in much more detail in chapters 14 and 16 of this volume, Dellarocas and Klein have developed a taxonomy of exception types

Figure 8.15a
Part of the specialization hierarchy below 'Create' going all the way down to specific views and case examples of negotiating contracts
Figure 8.15b
Part of the specialization hierarchy below 'Create' showing 'Produce as a business' and some of its specializations

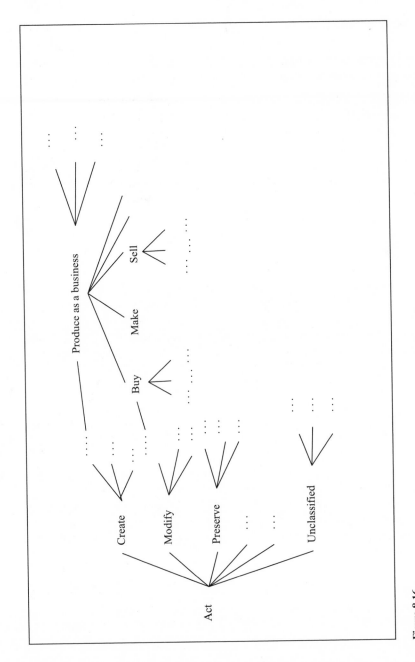

Figure 8.16
Simplified map of the entire network of activities in the Process Handbook

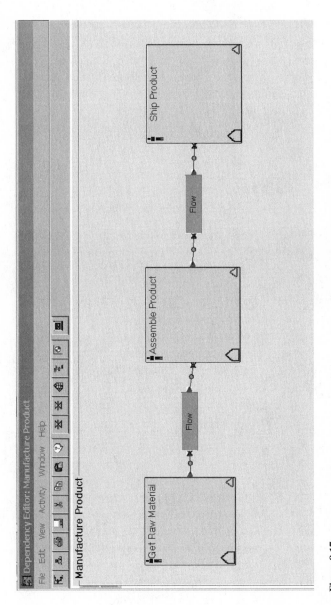

Figure 8.17
Sample dependency diagram showing two flow dependencies connecting three activities in an example of a process to manufacture a product. (This figure is from the "research" version of the Process Handbook.)

and the ways in which these exceptions can be detected, anticipated, avoided, and/or resolved.

This taxonomy and a variety of tools for using it are included in the research version of the Process Handbook. For example, the Process Handbook can represent a relationship or link between activities and the types of exceptions that are associated with it ("has exception"). In addition exceptions can be linked to the ways in which they can be addressed ("handled by"). This allows for a powerful connection between the ideal process flow, its exceptions and ways to handle those exceptions without "cluttering" up the ideal process flow representations. (See chapter 14 for a more detailed explanation of the kinds of exceptions represented and how they can be used.)

8.11.4 Systems Dynamics Elements

Many process representations tend to be developed to support a "discrete" view of the world—a sequence of activities to perform an iteration of some task. The feedback inherent in a system is not captured in this discrete view. As part of a current project on "supply chain visualization," we are expanding the Handbook to be able to support a systems dynamics view of processes too (see Hines et al. 2003).

To do this, we are creating a taxonomy of reusable systems dynamics components or "molecules." While the systems dynamics discipline had considered these, by creating a taxonomy, we have been able to highlight "missing" molecules. In this ongoing work we are exploring how this taxonomy allows for easy building of systems dynamics models using the same techniques incorporated in the handbook for building discrete models (see figure 8.18).

8.12 Conclusions

We believe that the work we have done so far on the Process Handbook has achieved our initial goal of demonstrating the potential of this framework for *comprehensively organizing large amounts of useful knowledge about business* in a richly interconnected, logical, and consistent way. We also believe that our conceptual framework for doing this was both intuitive and theoretically based. Finally, as we have shown in the other parts of this book, when business knowledge is organized in this way, powerful software tools to access and manipulate it can significantly increase its value.

We do not believe that our approach is the only useful way of organizing business knowledge. There are certainly other useful ways of organizing business knowledge

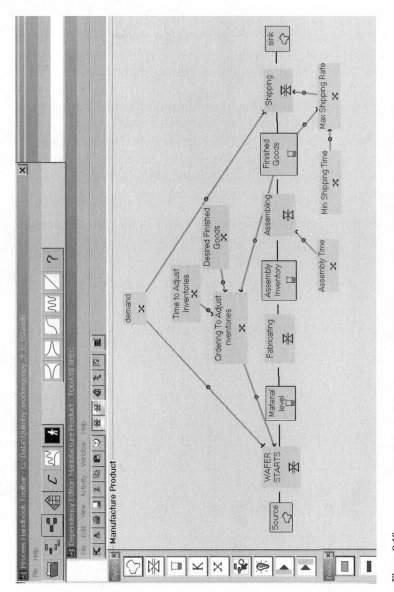

Figure 8.18
Systems dynamics diagram. (This figure is from the "research" version of the Process Handbook.)

for various purposes. But we do not know of any other approach to organizing business knowledge that is as comprehensive and powerful as ours, nor any that has been as extensively developed.

As researchers and educators, we have already devoted substantial resources to developing and updating the Process Handbook knowledge base. But we believe that the long-term potential of such a knowledge base can never be realized by the work of a single academic institution. Instead, we believe that there are many opportunities for other researchers, educators, and commercial enterprises to cooperate in the long-term, large-scale, development of a knowledge base like the Process Handbook. We hope that the publication of this volume will help stimulate such an endeavor.

IIIB *Examples of Specific Domain Content*

9 Let a Thousand Gardeners Prune: Cultivating Distributed Design in Complex Organizations

George M. Wyner

9.1 Process Models

In this chapter, I illustrate my approach to modeling design methods by providing a detailed account of three such modeling exercises: process innovation as treated by Davenport (1993), business process reengineering as described by Hammer and Champy (1993), and the design of high risk systems according to Perrow (1984). These three examples illustrate how the method can be applied both to texts in which the design method is an explicit focus, and those in which the design method is implicit and must be uncovered by the reader. The examples form a progression along this continuum:

• Davenport provides a decomposition of the activities that comprise his process innovation method.

• Hammer and Champy do not map the reengineering process but do discuss its characteristics.

• Perrow has as his primary concern the understanding and classification of complex engineered systems. He does ultimately give an account of such systems that can be construed as a design method, but this involves more detective work on the part of the reader.

By setting forth these examples in some detail, we have the opportunity to explore the strengths and limitations of my modeling method and its potential applicability to the analysis of distributed process design.

9.2 Example: *Process Innovation* (Davenport 1993)

The following analysis is based on the account of process innovation given in Davenport's *Process Innovation: Reengineering Work through Information Technology* (1993).[1] Early in his book, Davenport proposes an innovation process consisting

This chapter is adapted from chapter 3 of G. M. Wyner (2000), Let a thousand gardeners prune: Cultivating distributed design in complex organizations, Ph.D. dissertation, Sloan School of Management, MIT.
1. The process names are mostly directly quoted from Davenport. I have in some places modified the names to conform with the Process Handbook's verb-noun format. Where I depart from Davenport's terminology I will note this explicitly. Unless otherwise indicated, all references to "Davenport" refer to (Davenport 1993).

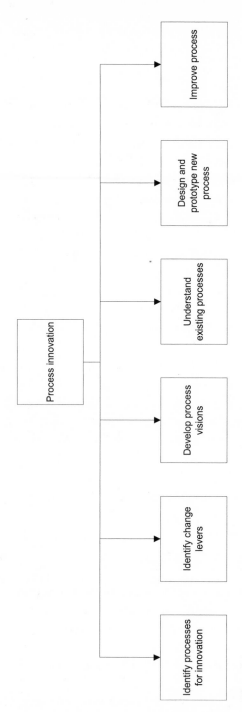

Figure 9.1
Steps in process innovation as described in Davenport (1993)

of the steps diagrammed in figure 9.1. Most of Davenport's book can be understood as a working through of the details involved in each of these substeps.[2]

9.2.1 Subactivities

Here then are the subactivities that have been identified:

Identify processes for innovation.   It can be argued that this is outside the scope of a design taxonomy, in that process design takes as a starting point a given process to be designed. However, it can also be argued that choosing a design problem can be a key element of design. I adopt the latter approach. (Source: Davenport, p. 27)

Identify change levers.   Davenport considers three potential sources for process innovation: new information technologies, better use of information as process resource, and innovations in organizational structure. (Source: Davenport, p. 48)

Develop process visions.   The process vision is the link between potential process innovation and the broader sense of business vision and strategy. (Source: Davenport, p. 121, figure 6.1)

Understand existing processes.   This refers to describing and analyzing the process as it exists. (Source: Davenport, p. 139, fig. 7.1). This step does not appear to be a focus for Davenport. He seems to mostly "outsource" this step by appealing to existing methods. "We look to [traditional process-oriented approaches] for tools and techniques ... They are most appropriately used to complement the components of the innovation approach described in this book" (Davenport 1993, pp. 150–51).

Design and prototype new process.   "Ironically, there is less to say about the design phase of process innovation than about the activities that lead up to it. The design activity is largely a matter of having a group of intelligent, creative people review the information collected in earlier phases of the initiative and synthesize it into a new process. There are techniques for facilitating the review process, but the success or failure of the effort will turn on the particular people who are gathered together" (Davenport, p. 153). Note that this approach implicitly assumes a relatively centralized process, where the key is to "gather together" the right group of people.

Improve process.   Process improvement does not play a central role in Davenport's account of process innovation. In reviewing my original analysis of this text, I can see that I have given process improvement a different role than that intended by

---

2. Davenport mentions IMPROVE PROCESS in the context of his discussion of understanding existing processes, but he does not include it in his original diagram. I include it at the outset as a potential additional activity, but as it turns out I ultimately consider it to be outside the scope of this analysis.

Davenport. Where Davenport views process improvement as a short-term complement to process innovation, I have conceived of it in the maps which follow as a
potential follow on to process innovation. That is, while it is the design team that
is charged with achieving dramatic breakthroughs in the process, such innovation
can be viewed as setting the stage for ongoing process improvement. In retrospect,
it would have been more in keeping with my intent to capture Davenport's view of
things to drop my interpretation in favor of the one he so clearly sets forth (e.g., on
pp. 140–41). However, I will allow my (questionable) view of process improvement
to stand as a record of my original reading of the text. As it turns out, this does not
prove a critical pitfall for my analysis in the end, because I ultimately restrict the
scope of my map of process innovation such that the process improvement activity is
eliminated from this analysis.

9.2.2 Resource Flow Graph

Our goal at this point is to move from the simple activity decomposition in figure 9.1
to an enumeration of the key dependencies in PROCESS INNOVATION. Given our stance
that dependencies can be viewed as resource-based, a first step in this direction is to
construct a *resource flow graph* that captures the flow of resources among the activities, as described in section 9.1.2.2, and thereby facilitates identifying dependencies
among those activities. The approach I take here is to identify inputs and outputs
associated with each activity in figure 9.1. This done, I am able to construct the
resource flow graph shown in figure 9.2, including both activities (indicated by rectangles in figure 9.2) and resources[3] (indicated by circles). This is done by adding
flows from an activity to all resources that are outputs of that activity, and a flow
from each resource to the activities where it is an input.

A first step toward a dependency diagram is to simplify the resource flow graph by
generalizing and aggregating its components, as shown in figure 9.3:

One test for a good aggregation is that one can imagine alternative decompositions
for the aggregate activity or resource:

1. The current decomposition of DEFINE PROBLEM is an example of identifying a
problem by reviewing a preexisting list of potential problems (in this case in the form
of list of existing processes). This is just one particular example of the more general
notion of DEFINE PROBLEM. Indeed, this is one possible specialization of DEFINE
PROBLEM.

---

3. Resources are not an explicit component of Davenport's process diagrams and are thus the result of my
own analysis.

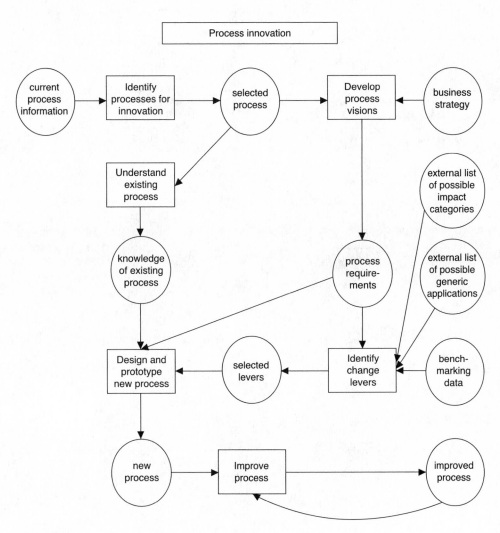

Figure 9.2
Resource flow diagram for process innovation

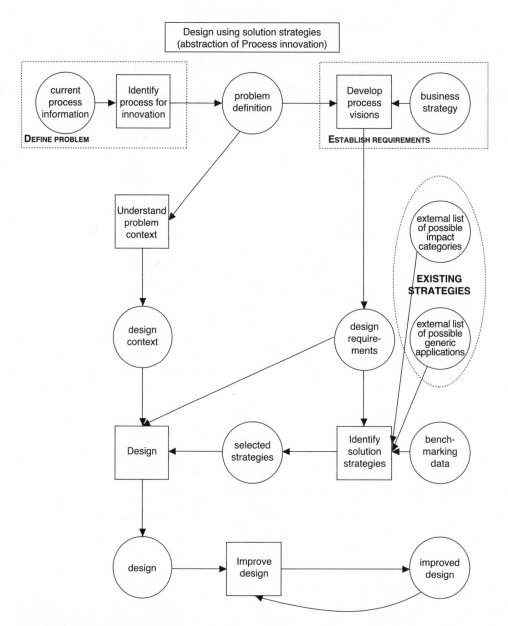

Figure 9.3
Simplification of process innovation

2. Similarly the current decomposition of ESTABLISH REQUIREMENTS is but one possible implementation of this process (i.e., develop requirements from analysis of strategic doctrine).

One technique for identifying potential resource aggregations is to look at resources that can be viewed as parts or kinds of a more general resource. Thus in figure 9.3 we have identified the list of impact categories and the list of generic applications as two strategies available in the design process and have aggregated them accordingly into *existing strategies.*

Figure 9.4 results from abstracting away the decomposition of the aggregates we introduced in figure 9.3. While this diagram highlights important features of Davenport's approach to process innovation and does so in a somewhat more general (and hence reusable) form, the diagram is still so complex that some of the key features and trade-offs of this approach are not easily seen.

9.2.3 Dependency Diagram

To address this issue, we move from a resource flow graph to a dependency diagram in which the focus shifts to just those flows that seem to be the critical dependencies. As mentioned earlier, we categorize dependencies into three types: flow, sharing, and fit. Notice that there is an isomorphism between a resource flow and a flow dependency. This suggests that one could produce a dependency diagram simply by replacing each resource flow with a flow dependency. There are, however, a few issues to deal with here:

1. Flows into a common resource may indicate a fit dependency.

2. Flows out of a common resource may indicate a sharing dependency.

3. It is not obvious what to do with flows into or out of an external resource. One might replace such a flow with a dependency involving an "external" or "boundary" activity. I would argue that one could also suppress external resources in certain cases as discussed below.

4. Unlike a resource flow graph that typically represents *all* the flows involving resources important to the activities shown, the dependency diagram represents only those *dependencies* that are important to the process; these critical dependencies correspond to a subset of the flows in the corresponding resource flow graph.

Note that in this sense a dependency diagram represents a further abstraction and hence simplification of a resource flow graph, one must bear in mind that the "importance" of a dependency is relative to the point of view and judgment of the process observer. One might imagine starting with all the flow, sharing, and fit

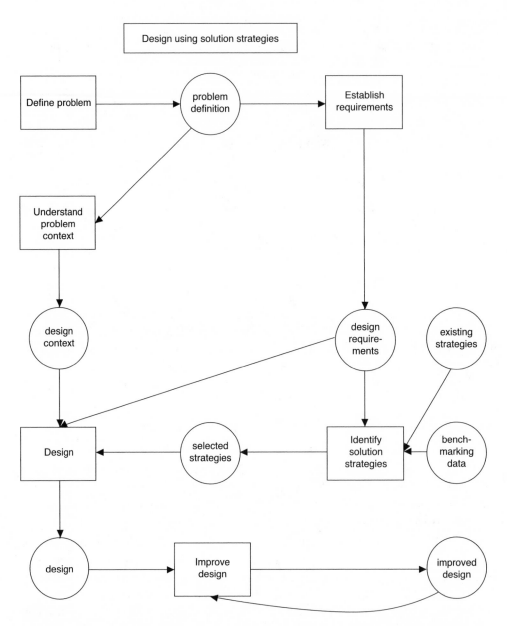

Figure 9.4
Design using solution strategies

dependencies which are implicit in the resource flow graph (see items one and two above), and then removing those dependencies that are unimportant to the observer. A dependency might be unimportant for several reasons:

• Its effect on the process outcomes of interest is insignificant.

• It has a significant effect but is easily managed.

• It has a significant effect and raises nontrivial issues, but the problem has been solved (at least to the satisfaction of the process observer) and has been excluded from analysis.

5. As suggested in item 3 above, a special case of suppressing dependencies exists when there are external resource flows. It is easy to see that when an external resource flows to just a single activity in the process, it may be due to a local coordination issue that can be considered nonproblematic at the level of the process as a whole.

Figure 9.5 is an annotated version of figure 9.4, which shows how these issues are dealt with in the current analysis to produce the dependency diagram shown in figure 9.6.

The numbered annotations in figure 9.5 identify elements of the resource flow diagram that are to be suppressed in the dependency diagram. The remaining resource flows are converted to flow dependencies, resulting in figure 9.6. Here is a brief discussion of the reasoning behind each annotation in figure 9.5:

1. Two flows in this diagram can be viewed as part of the coordination mechanisms used to manage the dependencies associated with *other* flows in the diagram: (a) the flow of *problem definition* to UNDERSTAND PROBLEM CONTEXT is employed to manage the usability (in this case, primarily relevance) of the flow of *design context* from UNDERSTAND PROBLEM CONTEXT to DESIGN. (b) the flow of *design requirements* to IDENTIFY SOLUTION STRATEGIES is similarly used to manage the usability (relevance) of the flow of *selected strategies* to DESIGN. Thus, when we move to a dependency diagram, these two flows are encompassed by the dependencies of which they are a part.

2. The two inputs to IDENTIFY SOLUTION STRATEGIES are tagged as *local resources* because they are used only by that activity in this process and the coordination of these flows is not the focus of our analysis, which centers on the design step. Thus we do not include dependencies for these resources in the dependency diagram, and they are therefore omitted in figure 9.6.

3. Note that while Davenport acknowledges the importance of process improvement, this is more or less *outside* the *scope* of his analysis. This is clear for several reasons:

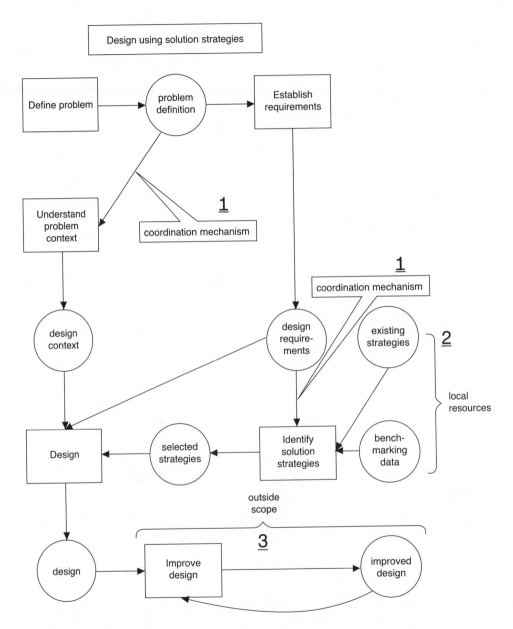

Figure 9.5
Transforming a resource flow graph into a dependency diagram

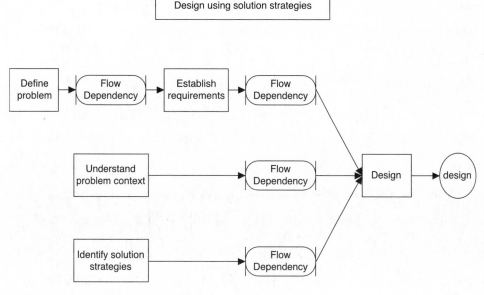

Figure 9.6
First attempt at a dependency diagram

• He does not include a process improvement step in his representation of process innovation. (Davenport, p. 25, fig. I.2)

• He identifies process improvement as an essential adjunct to process innovation (the focus of his book) and as clearly distinct from it. (Davenport, pp. 140–41)

• His discussion of process improvement mainly directs the reader to existing methods rather than presenting novel techniques in the book. (Davenport, p. 139) In contrast, Davenport's discussion of process innovation is clearly an original contribution rather than a recapitulation of existing work.

Once the elements noted above are suppressed and the remaining flows mapped as dependencies, one obtains the diagram in figure 9.6.

In reviewing figure 9.6, I make the following observations:

1. The three intersecting flow dependencies could be represented as a single fit dependency. Not only is this a simpler representation, but it is consistent with the two flows we abstracted away in figure 9.5. In retrospect, these flows can be understood as coordinating the interaction among the flow dependencies in figure 9.6, as

they flow between DEFINE PROBLEM and ESTABLISH REQUIREMENTS and the other two flows. Indeed, one implication of the fit dependency is that more such coordination may exist (although I did not surface such flows in the preliminary analysis above). Stating this as a modeling heuristic, we might say that if one has a number of flow dependencies involving the same consumer and with lots of cross-connections of a secondary nature (especially coordination flows), there is a strong implication that it will be useful to model this as a fit dependency.

2. If, for the moment, we assume that it is useful to explore the possibility of symmetry as a modeling heuristic, we can identify at least four ways to make the diagram symmetric:

• Declare DEFINE PROBLEM to be outside the scope of our analysis.

• Aggregate DEFINE PROBLEM and ESTABLISH REQUIREMENTS.

• Make the case that DEFINE PROBLEM is a fourth parallel flow in the fit dependency.

• Add two additional flows: from DEFINE PROBLEM to both UNDERSTAND PROBLEM CONTEXT and IDENTIFY SOLUTION STRATEGIES.

I adopt the second of these strategies, and argue that ESTABLISH REQUIREMENTS can be thought of as a part of a larger notion of problem definition. That is, requirements can be thought of as an extension of a problem definition and hence part of that definition. Thus we can aggregate DEFINE PROBLEM (in the narrower sense in which we have used it here) with ESTABLISH REQUIREMENTS. The resulting aggregation can be thought of as DEFINE PROBLEM USING REQUIREMENTS, which can be further generalized to DEFINE PROBLEM (in a larger sense of that term).

This aggregation illustrates an issue that frequently arises in this kind of process modeling: the same term (here "Define problem") takes on multiple meanings during our analysis. I argue that this "overloading" of terminology is inevitable and points to the confusion that can occur when a process is described using ordinary language. By keeping track of both the evolution of the process model and the context the model provides for each term, we can untangle the multiple meanings and keep them straight. Thus this model as it appears in figure 9.7 links back to the context that distinguishes this larger sense of DEFINE PROBLEM from the narrower sense employed in earlier diagrams.

Note that we could as easily have explored the other options for introducing symmetry. The issue here is not which option is correct but which options are plausible, and of these, which are most useful. Having chosen an approach, the resulting simplified dependency diagram can be seen in figure 9.7.

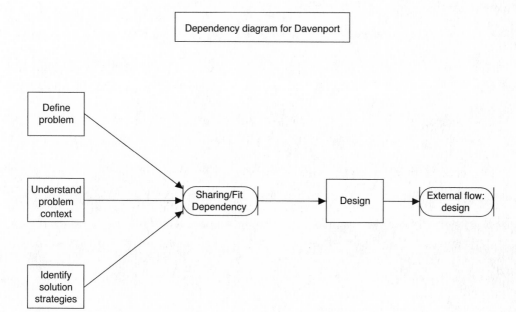

Figure 9.7
Symmetric dependency diagram

This diagram seems to argue for the virtues of the symmetry heuristic.[4] One could argue that given two diagrams that take the same point of view and express the same process, the one that is simpler (in this case more symmetric) is often likely to be the more useful diagram because it is easier to understand and easier to analyze.

9.2.4 Analysis

This dependency diagram emphasizes the inputs to the design process and the fit among them. This seems to be a key insight at the core of Davenport's account of process innovation: *To manage and cultivate the innovation process, attend to the critical inputs to the design activity.* As Davenport says in his opening paragraph in the design chapter: "Ironically, there is less to say about the design phase of process innovation than about the activities that lead up to it" (Davenport 1993, p. 153). Thus the focus here is on identifying the critical inputs to the design step and figuring out how to manage their usability and fit.

4. My thanks to Tom Malone for pointing out to me the usefulness of symmetry in this context.

One implication of the presence of this fit dependency in the innovation process is the potential importance of managing the interconnections among the inputs. For example, consider the activity UNDERSTAND PROBLEM CONTEXT. This is the activity that represents mapping the current state of the organization, including the existing process. In practice, this activity can very easily get disconnected from the design process it is embedded in and become an independent exercise that generates so much data as to become practically useless as a resource to support design. The value of context is in danger of being outweighed by the burden of sorting through the massively complex process maps.

In coordination terms, the issue here is the usability of the flow of context information. One approach that is often used to manage this kind of flow is for the receiver to filter out what is not useful. Note that this approach is doubly expensive, as we have the cost of compiling the information and then the cost of throwing extraneous or low-value information away. One solution proposed to this costly information flow is to avoid mapping the as-is process. However, as Davenport points out, this has the disadvantage of losing lots of important context.

9.3 *Example: Reengineering* (Hammer and Champy 1993)

Reengineering the Corporation (Hammer and Champy 1993) popularized the notion of business process reengineering, an approach to process redesign which underwent the boom and bust associated with many business fads.[5] This book stands as the manifesto of the reengineering "movement." The analysis that follows offers an opportunity to assess what distinguishes reengineering from other approaches and to place it more accurately between the extremes of opinion which have marked its meteoric trajectory across the business stage.

Unlike Davenport (1993), described in section 9.2, this book does not provide an explicit process description of reengineering. As a consequence the analysis involves additional steps at the outset to identify the activities and resources that comprise the reengineering design process.

9.3.1 Review of the Text
I begin by reviewing the text and flagging material that seems to indicate components of the process or otherwise seems especially important to my understanding of the

---

5. Unless otherwise noted, all references to "Hammer and Champy" refer to (Hammer and Champy 1993).

process. Having extracted these relevant chunks of text from the book, the next step is to begin to make sense of this material as a process. What follows is an analysis very similar to that employed for Davenport (1993): I will identify the resource flows involved and then create a resource flow graph and a dependency map.

9.3.2 Resource Flow Graph

Having identified both the activities and the resources from a preliminary analysis of the text, the next step is to represent all these components on a single diagram (figure 9.8). We start by just listing the resources and activities so that later we can associate them with each other.

In associating resources with particular activities, I found it useful to make certain changes in both the list of activities and the list of resources depicted in figure 9.8:

• Combine SELECT PROCESSES and PRIORITIZE PROCESSES into a single compound step. Selection is a kind of prioritization, and given finite resources at hand, prioritization is a form of selection. At this level of analysis it is useful to consider the two activities as one.

• Create a new activity IMPLEMENT REDESIGNED PROCESS. MAKE CASE FOR CHANGE would appear to be about generating support for the redesigned process and is thus a part of implementation, rather than the initial design process. The presence of MAKE CASE FOR CHANGE thus only makes sense if this implementation activity also appears in the process map.

• Add activity UNDERSTAND REENGINEERING. This is done to clarify that the resource _heuristics_ arises in part from ongoing efforts to understand reengineering, for example, as described in the Hammer and Champy text. Hammer and Champy seem to expect these generic reengineering heuristics arise from efforts such as theirs and to be primarily provided as external resources to a given reengineering effort. We include this activity in our flow graph, however, in order to tell a coherent story.

• Replace the resource _process name_ with the more generic resource _identified processes_. Naming a process can be thought of as one part of this identification activity. I have introduced some additional resources suggested by the function of activities (e.g., the output of SELECT PROCESSES is, naturally, _selected processes_).

• Note that the resource _context_ is implied by activities that employ the verbs IDENTIFY (context is the background from which the things to be identified are distinguished), UNDERSTAND (implies a rich set of inputs, i.e., context), and RETHINK (similar to UNDERSTAND).

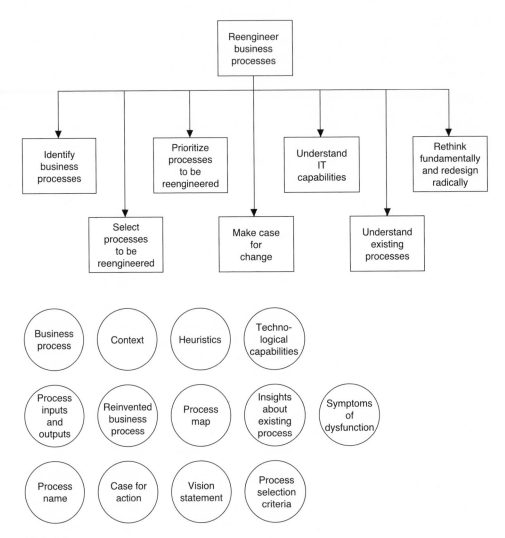

Figure 9.8
Identify activities and resources

Figure 9.9 is the resource flow graph I developed based on the analysis above. Note that I did not bother neatening up the layout, since I will be refining this diagram further momentarily.

As with Davenport above, I now create an abstraction of this process based on the following observations:

• *Process map*, which is not yet connected in figure 9.9, turns out (upon further review of the text) to be an output from IDENTIFY BUSINESS PROCESSES and an input to SELECT & PRIORITIZE. It seems reasonable to view *process map* as subsuming the *identified processes* resource, so I simply replace the latter with the former.

• As in my Davenport analysis, for purposes of coordination analysis one can absorb external resources that have only one internal consumer into the description of that subactivity. Thus I can remove the explicit representation of *technological capabilities* and *process inputs and outputs*. Note the potential loss of information concerning possible additional activities that might use these resources. In the current analysis, however, the gain in simplicity seems to outweigh this loss. Similarly I can remove the two inputs to SELECT & PRIORITIZE.

• I also propose to combine UNDERSTAND REENGINEERING with UNDERSTAND IT CAPABILITIES since both are about identifying relevant heuristics. Note that this diminishes the emphasis that Hammer and Champy place on IT and also the distinction between the heuristics that Hammer and Champy propose as a kind of universal set for reengineering and the IT heuristics that they expect a business to identify as part of its own analysis. This seems like a useful abstraction in that it emphasizes the core issue here that is obtaining a relevant set of heuristics to push the design process in the direction of radical and effective change. The abstraction also introduces the possibility of other approaches to obtaining these heuristics.

• I was concerned at one point in this analysis that the relationship between UNDERSTAND EXISTING PROCESSES and SELECT & PRIORITIZE PROCESSES TO BE REENGINEERED seems to restrict the understanding effort to the processes that are selected, which makes the diagram more complex. However, one can view this as an issue of coordination for efficiency, and apply resources to those processes that are most critical to the reengineering effort. This issue can be addressed in the dependency diagram, where it surfaces in the form of a fit dependency, thus allowing us to abstract the complexity away from the current diagram.

• I have simplified the title SELECT & PRIORITIZE PROCESSES TO BE REENGINEERED to PRIORITIZE PROCESSES TO BE REENGINEERED. As I argued above, "prioritize" can stand in here for "select" as well.

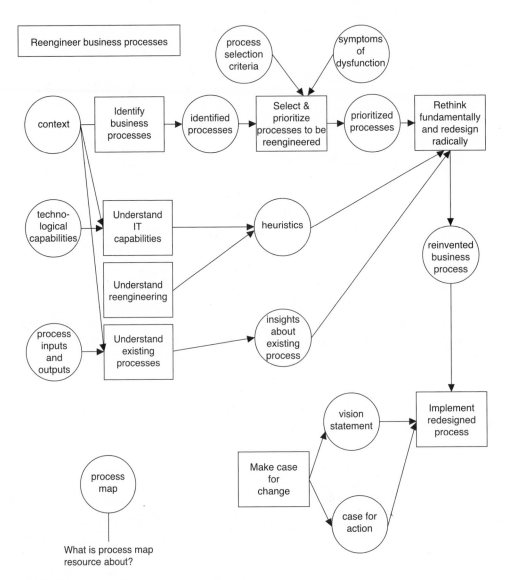

Figure 9.9
Preliminary resource flow graph

Figure 9.10 represents the implications of these changes for the resource flow graph, while figure 9.11 shows the abstracted resource flow graph that results. Note that when one abstracts away individual heuristics, what remains seems almost a generic example of heuristic design rather than something particular to reengineering. As I suggest below, this has important implications for understanding the place of reengineering in the history of organizational design.

9.3.3 Dependency Diagram

In examining this resource flow graph, we can identify the following key dependencies (among others) and some of their implications for process design:

• *Shared context.* Are all reengineering participants invoking the same context for their deliberations? How do they resolve differences in framework and perspective? Clearly, the reengineering team meetings serve as one key coordination mechanism for managing this dependency.

• *Process selection flow.* Early decisions about the process map have a huge influence on the eventual focus of reengineering. This suggests the value of thinking "out of the box" early in the reengineering effort. The process map enables but it also confines thinking. This flow dependency suggests we should look at the role that process maps might play in reengineering success and failure. It would be interesting to consider the extent to which additional reengineering opportunities can be enabled by more creative map making.

• *Fit between prioritized processes, insights, and heuristics.* This dependency suggests that problems may result when too broad or too narrow a "relevance filter" is placed on the heuristic and insight streams. It might be useful to consider the role that heuristics and insights might play in the selection of reengineering projects, as well as the role that they might play in process mapping.

The full set of dependencies implied by figure 9.11 is shown in figure 9.12.

Having thus arrived at a preliminary dependency diagram, there are several simplifications that we can make:

• Aggregate the two processes IDENTIFY BUSINESS PROCESSES and PRIORITIZE PROCESSES TO BE REENGINEERED to form the process IDENTIFY PROCESSES TO BE REENGINEERED. This latter name implies both identification and prioritization of processes. Note that the flow dependency between the two original activities is also absorbed into the aggregation.

• Restrict scope of the diagram to exclude the context sharing dependency. This restriction can be thought of as a narrowing of attention to a subset of the dependency

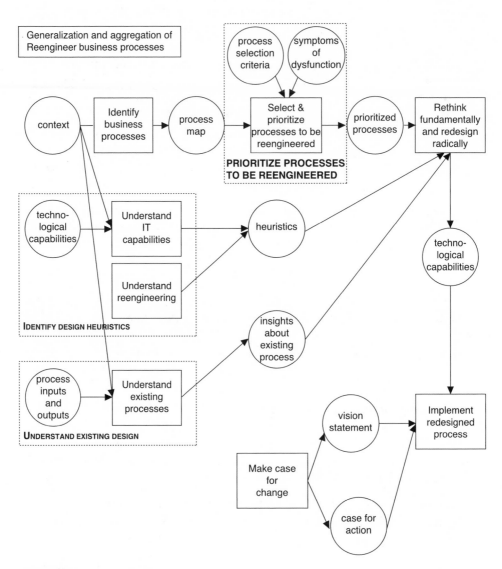

Figure 9.10
Simplifying the resource flow graph

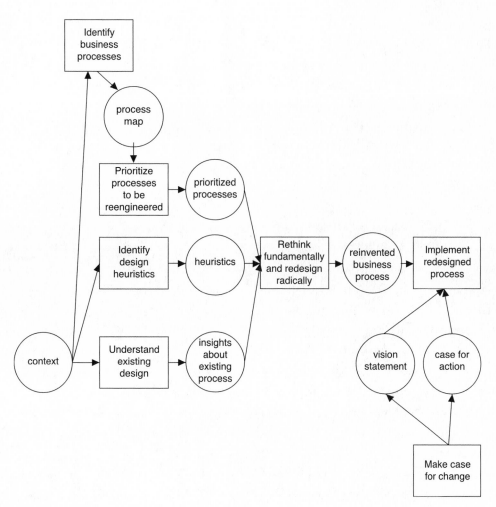

Figure 9.11
Simplification of reengineered business processes

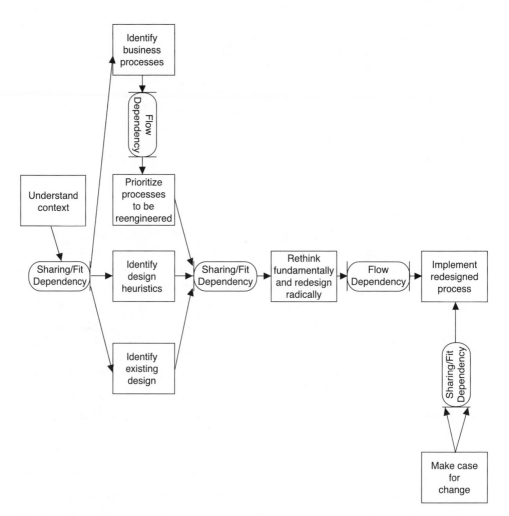

Figure 9.12
First pass at a dependency diagram

issues (we could always consider including this context dependency in a separate analysis). Note that this restriction in scope works here because UNDERSTAND CONTEXT is on the periphery of the dependency diagram.

• Absorb the activity MAKE CASE FOR CHANGE into IMPLEMENT REDESIGNED PROCESS. Justification: MAKE CASE FOR CHANGE, as described by Hammer and Champy, is not a part of the design process but rather the process by which such a design is to be implemented in the organization.

These changes result in the simplified diagram of figure 9.13.[6]

9.3.4 Discussion

While the primary purpose of these examples is to illustrate the modeling process, I will briefly explore some implications of this dependency diagram. Note that far more becomes possible when we consider a dependency diagram in the broader context of the design taxonomy, but some insight can also be gained by considering it on its own terms.

The Power of Abstraction   This dependency diagram, and the process that produced it, make a particularly nice illustration of the power of abstraction in this approach. In a sense the entire text has been reduced through a series of abstractions to two major dependencies. Note, however, that much of the value of this abstraction lies in its links back to the context established by the original text and the series of more complex maps developed during this analysis. In a sense the dependency diagram becomes not only a map of business process reengineering but a kind of index to the modeling process which produced this map.

How Are These Dependencies Coordinated?   While the authors do address various aspects of the two dependencies we have identified, they are not a central concern of the text. It is, however, possible to construct an account of how the authors address (at least implicitly) these coordination issues.

COORDINATING THE FIT DEPENDENCY   By insisting that UNDERSTAND EXISTING DESIGN should produce *insights* rather than *details*, Hammer and Champy (1993, p. 129) have provided a mechanism for managing the fit between choice of process, choice of design heuristics, and understanding of existing design. This approach partially manages the fit dependency by producing a much more manageable and reusable set

---

6. Note that I also revise dependency descriptions to incorporate more information about the nature of the dependencies (something that would otherwise be lost when moving from the resource flow graph to the dependency diagram).

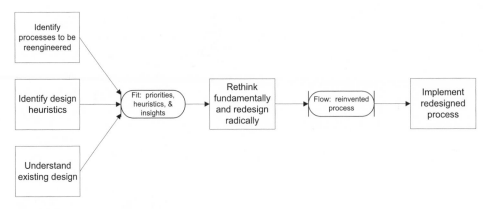

Figure 9.13
Simplified dependency diagram

of outputs from UNDERSTAND EXISTING DESIGN. While this approach is arguably inadequate by itself, the authors effectively augment this mechanism by insisting that
this be a centralized design effort. That is, the work is to be carried out by a reengineering team that, in the scenario provided in the book, sits down in a room together and works through all the issues. This kind of centralization provides a
plausible strategy for managing the fit dependency at the center of figure 9.13, by
assignment of all four activities[7] involved in that dependency to a single actor or
team of actors. Given this approach, the reengineering meeting becomes the single
crucial coordination mechanism for managing this fit dependency. This implies that
effective coordination of this dependency comes to depend heavily on the quality of
the team and the effectiveness of its meetings. This introduces a potential weak link
in the reengineering process, and a source of variability in outcomes that may be
hard to manage.

COORDINATING THE FLOW DEPENDENCY   For a method whose authors themselves
estimate a failure rate of 50 to 70 percent (Hammer and Champy, p. 200), one would
expect the flow dependency between design and implementation to be a critical one.
Coordination of this flow is further complicated by the large number of actors necessarily involved in the actual implementation of reengineering in a large organization. Interestingly the authors do not elaborate much on this issue. The aspect of this
flow that is most directly addressed is the need to make the case for change. While

7. Identify processes to be reengineered, Identify design heuristics, Understand existing design, and
Rethink fundamentally and redesign radically.

this may be important, it does not seem to be sufficient for managing the design-implementation flow.

In defense of the approach taken in the text, however, MAKING THE CASE FOR CHANGE does provide some support for coordinating this flow dependency. The more the entire organization shares the vision of the reengineering team, the more likely coordination of the design-implementation flow is going to work. The entire organization becomes in effect an extension of the team and is placed in a position to coordinate and effect the changes from within.

This implicit coordination of the design-implementation flow would presumably be more likely to succeed where a new process is closely aligned with the existing process, in that intuitions about how the existing process is implemented are more likely to be relevant to the implementation of the new process. In the case of reengineering, however, we have radical changes which may be entirely confusing, mysterious, and at odds with how things are done now, and thus in the absence of an explicit coordination mechanism one would expect implementation failure to be far more likely.

POSSIBLE COORDINATION MECHANISM: USE TOTAL QUALITY MANAGEMENT TO COORDINATE THE DESIGN-IMPLEMENTATION FLOW   Hammer and Champy identified the complementarity between total quality management (TQM) and reengineering, where TQM refers to the technique for systematic process improvement pioneered by W. Edwards Deming and brought to fruition by Japanese manufacturers (Shiba et al. 1993). Where reengineering is about radical change, TQM is about incremental improvement. The complementarity that Hammer and Champy proposed is a kind of punctuated equilibrium model (Gersick 1991) in which reengineering is followed by an extended period of continuous improvement (Hammer and Champy 1993, p. 219). Can we imagine an approach in which TQM is used to manage the flow dependency between reengineering design and reengineering implementation? In this scenario TQM would become a way to iteratively correct any problems during the implementation phase. Presumably this might happen naturally in an organization in which TQM is in place for process implementation, provided that the obvious connection is made.

9.4   *Example: Normal Accidents* (Perrow 1984)

Perrow's monograph on high-risk technologies (1984)[8] includes specific recommendations about taking action to address the risks of certain complex systems.

---

8. Unless otherwise noted, all references to "Perrow" refer to (Perrow 1984).

These recommendations for action can be construed as a kind of design text for high-risk systems.

My analysis of Perrow illustrates an interesting variant on the modeling process I have described so far: I first discovered a generalization of Perrow's design method and then moved to a more specific model via process specialization. This analysis also illustrates how one must sometimes read between the lines to construct an account of design from a text whose primary concerns are elsewhere.

Perrow's principal focus in the book is on understanding the nature and cause of the risks associated with certain complex technologies. It is in the concluding chapter, "Living with High-Risk Systems," that Perrow addresses the question of what can be done to mitigate these risks, and thus it is here that I will focus the analysis.

9.4.1   The Text

Perrow's main concern is with understanding the nature of the risks associated with complex tightly coupled systems. He offers a theoretical framework in which risks are associated with the underlying structure of the system. Much of the book is a case-by-case presentation of various systems and their risks. Along the way Perrow develops a framework in which he classifies systems according to the degree of coupling (tightly coupled systems vs. loosely coupled systems) and the nature of the interactions (linear systems vs. complex systems). The degree of coupling is largely a matter of the amount of buffering between components in a system. In a tightly coupled system a local event produces rapid effects on other components in the system and therefore requires a rapid response. The distinction between linear and complex systems seems to be mainly a question of whether the interactions are unexpected. However, Perrow also talks about feedback loops and one-to-many causal links.

In addressing the design of systems in his concluding chapter on living with high-risk systems, (pp. 304–52), Perrow's main proposal is that systems should be evaluated along two dimensions:

1. For their "catastrophic potential" (which depends both on the nature of the system and the current level of organizational effectiveness associated with such systems).

2. For the cost of alternative systems.

Perrow then groups systems into three categories, each of which requires a different intervention:

1. Systems where catastrophic potential is high relative to the cost of alternatives. These should be abandoned in favor of one of the alternatives.

2. At the other extreme, systems where the cost of alternatives is high relative to the catastrophic potential. In this case the existing system should be improved.

3. In between, systems that cannot be easily replaced but pose significant threats. Perrow proposes that these systems be restricted to situations where the risks are lowest and/or the benefits are greatest.

9.4.2 A Generalization

My first step in analyzing this process was to adopt a point of view. Point of view is especially critical in a case like this where the text is not explicitly an account of a design process.

Where Davenport provided an explicit map of the innovation process, and Hammer and Champy provided an informal description of the reengineering process, Perrow is primarily concerned with establishing a framework for classifying high-risk systems. Here we want to look more closely to identify where and how he speaks to the process of designing such systems. The outcome of this close reading must initially be a point of view which then guides the further development of the process map.

The point of view I developed follows from Perrow's proposal for living with high-risk systems (Perrow, ch. 9). At the core of this proposal is the classification of such systems into three categories each of which warrants a different intervention (Perrow, p. 349). I chose to construe this as a kind of "design using classification." This point of view then immediately suggested to me a very simple process map which I represent in figure 9.14.[9]

9.4.3 Dependency Diagram

Having developed this general scheme for framing Perrow's texts as a design story, I then developed a specialization by decomposing APPLY APPROPRIATE INTERVENTION into the three specific interventions that Perrow proposes. As a consequence the single flow from CLASSIFY to APPLY APPROPRIATE INTERVENTION must be decomposed into three flows corresponding to the three types of system that Perrow matches to the three interventions. The resulting dependency diagram is given in figure 9.15.

---

9. This process characterization is my own as are the activity names (unless otherwise noted). Note that in this analysis I show the dependency diagrams without going through the intermediate phase of resource flow graphs. This was possible because of the relative simplicity of the generalization that anchors this analysis.

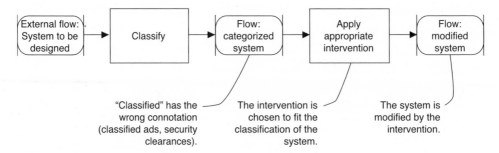

Figure 9.14
Design using classification

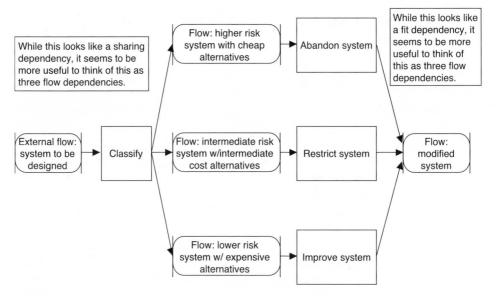

Figure 9.15
Design of high-risk systems

9.5 Summary

My purpose in presenting these three examples has been to give a sense of how my approach to process modeling actually unfolds in practice. However, even without the use of the taxonomy, it is still possible to get some insights about these processes. For example, I identified some critical coordination issues for business process reengineering:

1. The need to manage the hand off (flow dependency) between the design task and the implementation task.

2. The critical coordination role played by the centralized design team in managing the fit dependency among the various inputs to the reengineering design activity.

Even in this limited analysis, I was able to arrive at an interesting possible response to some of these issues: the use of TQM as a way to coordinate these dependencies. This gives a rather different view of the relationship between TQM and business process reengineering than the one put forward in the Hammer and Champy text itself.

I would argue that this analysis follows from two key features: a representation that focuses on the main coordination issues, and a chain of abstraction that leads from the text to a concise graphical representation of the design method it depicts. These aspects of my modeling approach work in concert to make salient aspects of a design method that might otherwise remain obscured.

10 A Coordination Perspective on Software Architecture: Toward a Design Handbook for Integrating Software Components

Chrysanthos Dellarocas

10.1 Introduction

Previously I argued for separating the core functional pieces of a software application from their interconnection relationships. Then I introduced an architectural language that enables this separation by providing separate abstractions for activities and dependencies. This chapter goes one step further: It observes that when taken out of context, many interconnection problems in software applications are related to a relatively narrow set of concepts, such as resource flows, resource sharing, and timing dependencies. These concepts are orthogonal to the problem domain of most applications, and can therefore be captured in an application-independent vocabulary of dependency types. Likewise the design of associated coordination processes involves a relatively narrow set of coordination concepts, such as shared events, invocation mechanisms, and communication protocols. Therefore it can also be captured in a design space that assists designers in designing a coordination process that manages a given dependency type, simply by selecting the value of a relatively small number of design dimensions. The proposed vocabulary of dependencies and design space of coordination processes, taken together, can form the basis for a design handbook for integrating software components. The development of such a handbook aims to reduce the specification and implementation of software component interdependencies to a routine design problem, capable of being assisted, or even automated, by computer tools.

10.2 Motivation

The purpose of this chapter is to give an answer to the following two questions:

· Why do software components interconnect with one another?
· How do software components interconnect with one another?

We would like to organize the answers to the first question in a vocabulary of *dependency types*, and the answers to the second question in a design space of *coordination processes*. Finally, we would like to connect each of the *whys*, with a set of

This chapter is adapted from chapter 4 of C. Dellarocas (1996), A coordination perspective on software architecture: Towards a Design Handbook for Integrating Software Components, Ph.D. dissertation, Sloan School of Management, MIT. Section 4.6 containing control flows, data flows, and other flows and section 4.8 on composite dependencies are omitted.

hows, that is, associate each dependency type with a set of coordination processes for managing it.

A vocabulary of interdependency patterns would greatly aid designers in constructing application architectural diagrams. Instead of always inventing a new dependency to express a given component relationship, designers would often simply choose one from the dependency vocabulary.

Furthermore the existence of a coordination process design space would reduce the step of managing dependencies with coordination processes to a routine, or even automatic, selection of an element from a coordination process repository.

Finally a vocabulary of dependency types and coordination processes would contribute to an increased understanding of the problems of software interconnection. Over time researchers have developed a vast arsenal of algorithms and techniques for process synchronization, communication, and resource allocation. What has been missing so far is a unified framework for relating those algorithms to the problems they are attempting to solve. Such a framework should encompass (and relate) synchronization, communication, and resource allocation considerations. It should relate techniques and algorithms that are currently being studied by a number of different research areas (programming languages, operating systems, concurrent and distributed systems). Therefore it could form the basis for developing *a design handbook of software component interconnection*. Such a handbook could help reduce the integration of existing software components into new applications to a routine design problem.

The approach taken in this chapter is based on coordination theory (Malone and Crowston 1994), an emerging research area that focuses on the interdisciplinary study of coordination. Coordination theory defines coordination as the process of managing dependencies among activities. One of its objectives is to characterize different kinds of dependencies and identify the coordination processes that can be used to manage them. This work extends the frameworks presented in Malone and Crowston (1994) and is the first detailed application of the theory to the understanding of software component relationships. Coordination theory is discussed in more detail in section 10.3.

It is important to emphasize that the results described in this chapter do not claim rigorous generality and completeness. Our goal was to develop a dependency vocabulary and coordination process design space that covers a *useful* subset of the component relationships and constraints encountered in practice. The SYNOPSIS machinery enables designers to incrementally enrich this vocabulary with new abstractions and processes. It is our hope that this work will provide a useful starting point that will lead in interesting extensions by future research.

10.3   Overview of the Dependencies Space

The vocabulary of dependencies presented in this chapter is based on the simple assumption that component interdependencies are explicitly or implicitly related to patterns of resource production and usage. *In other words, these activities are those that need to interact with other activities, either because they use resources produced by other activities or because they share resources with other activities.*

The definition of resources can be made broad enough to make this assumption cover most (if not all) cases of component interaction encountered in software systems. Our current definition of resources encompasses four components:

- Processor time (control)
- Data of various types
- Operating system resources (memory pools, pipes, sockets, etc.)
- Hardware resources (printers, disks, multimedia adapters, etc.)

In every resource relationship, participating activities can be distinguished by one of two roles:

- Resource producers
- Resource consumers

The existence of two different roles in resource relationships implies the existence of three different classes of dependencies:

- Dependencies between producers and consumers
- Dependencies among consumers who use the same resources
- Dependencies among producers who produce for the same consumers

Dependencies between producers and consumers are modeled using a family of dependencies called *flow dependencies*. Malone and Crowston (1994) have observed that in general, whenever flows occur, one or more other subdependencies are present. In particular, flow dependencies can be decomposed to the following set of lower-level dependencies:

- *Usability.*   Users of a resource must be able to effectively use the resource. For data resources, this dependency encompasses issues relating to format conversion, semantic equivalence, etc.
- *Accessibility.*   In order for a resource to be used by an activity, it must be accessible by that activity (more precisely, it must be accessible by the processor that

executes the activity). This requirement might require physical transportation of a resource, or conversely, relocation of an activity.

• *Prerequisite.* A resource can only be used after the producer activity has been completed. Producers must notify users, or conversely, users must be able to detect when production is complete.

• *Resource sharing.* When more than one activity requires usage of a resource, some protocol must manage how the resource will be shared among them. For example, if concurrent access of a resource is not permitted, some kind of mutual exclusion protocol must be put in place.

• *User sharing.* When more than one producers are producing for the same users, a dependency analogous to resource sharing exists among them. Users become a shared "resource" for producers and some protocol must manage how they are "shared" among multiple producers. For example, users might not be able to use more than one, out of many, resources directed to them. In such cases selection among producers might have to take place.

Sections 10.6 and 10.7 are devoted to a detailed discussion of flow dependencies.

Dependencies contained inside flows are shared on the assumption that multiple users of a resource are independent, and therefore *competing* with one another for resource access. In many applications, however, users (or producers) of a resource are *cooperating* in application-specific ways. In those cases designers must *explicitly* specify additional dependencies that describe the patterns of cooperation among users (or producers). Imagine, for example, a database resource that is generated by some activity and subsequently used by three other activities. In a particular application, one of the users of the database is using it to write values that will be read by the other users. This application-specific pattern of cooperation among users of the database requires the specification of an additional prerequisite relationship between the writer and the reader activities (figure 10.1).

Application-specific patterns of cooperation among activities that share resources are expressed using additional flows and another family of dependencies called timing dependencies. *Timing dependencies* express constraints on the relative flow of control among a set of activities. The most widely used are *prerequisite dependencies* (A must complete before control flows into B) and *mutual exclusion dependencies* (A and B cannot execute at the same time).

In addition to specifying application-specific cooperation patterns, timing dependencies are often used to specify *implicit resource relationships*. For example, mutual exclusion dependencies are often used to specify implicit resource-sharing relationships, in which support for resource accesses is embedded inside the code of each

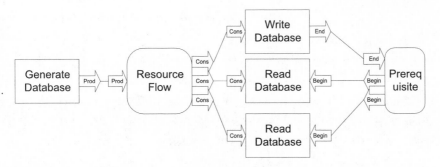

Figure 10.1
Example of cooperative resource use

activity. Also prerequisite dependencies often specify implicit flow relationships in which resource production and consumption are embedded inside the code. Section 10.8 describes a family of timing dependencies. For each dependency, its relationship with a resource dependency is illustrated.

Throughout the chapter it becomes apparent that apart from classifying and enumerating elementary dependency types, it is also useful to begin to collect and classify sets of frequently occurring *composite dependency patterns*. In many cases designers have developed specialized, more efficient *joint* coordination processes for such patterns. Section 10.9 will present a few useful composite patterns of flows and joint coordination processes for managing them.

10.4 The Concept of a Design Space

As with any complex taxonomy, it is useful to classify both dependencies and coordination processes using multidimensional *design spaces* (Bell 1972; Lane 1990). Each dimension of the design space describes variation in some design choice. Values along a dimension are called *design alternatives*. They correspond to alternative requirements or implementation choices. For example, when selecting a data transportation mechanism, the number of data readers could be one design dimension; the location of readers relative to the writer could be another. Figure 10.2 illustrates a tiny design space for selecting a data transportation mechanism. Specific designs are described by points in the design space, identified by the dimensional values that correspond to their design choices.

Successful design spaces reduce the problem of design to that of answering a simple set of questions. They also organize related design alternatives "close" to each

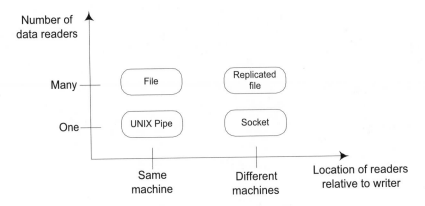

Figure 10.2
Simple design space for selecting a data transportation mechanism

other and expose correlations between various aspects of design. Finally they can be easily translated into computerized knowledge bases that can help semi-automate the design task.

Our problem requires the construction of two, related, design spaces:

• *A dependency design space.*   Dependency design dimensions represent interaction requirements that are significant for choosing a coordination processes. For example, the number of users of a resource and the degree of concurrency allowed by a resource are two dependency design dimensions.

Each point in the dependency design space defines a different *dependency type.*

• *A coordination design space.*   Coordination design dimensions represent design alternatives available to satisfy interaction requirements. For example, the protocol used to share a nonconcurrent resource is an implementation design dimension.

Each point in the coordination design space defines a different *coordination process.*

In addition, each point in the dependency design space (dependency type) must be associated to a coordination design space for managing it. Our objective in the following sections is to define related dependency and coordination design spaces for each family of dependencies.

The success of a design-space description of design alternatives clearly lies in the choice of dimensions and specific dimensional values (design alternatives). There is no obvious rigorous way of defending a particular set of choices. Neither Bell and

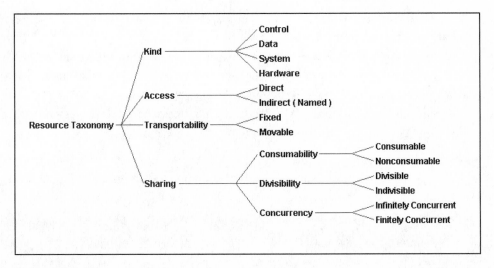

Figure 10.3
Taxonomy of resources

Newell (1972) nor Lane (1990) have offered any justification for their dimensions and alternatives, except for their own intuition and the usefulness of the resulting description. I will follow the same path, simply proposing a set of dimensions and trying to show empirically that they form a useful description of design alternatives.

10.5   A Taxonomy of Resources

Before we begin the description of resource flow dependencies, we present a taxonomy of resources occurring in software systems. This taxonomy will be useful both for distinguishing between different special cases of flow relationships and for determining the range of alternative ways of managing them. The taxonomy is summarized in figure 10.3. The next section provides a discussion of its principal dimensions.

10.5.1   Resource Kind

• *Control.*   The resource usually referred to in computer science as *control* is more accurately described as *a thread of processor attention*. In order for any software activity to begin execution, it needs to receive control *from somewhere*; that is, it needs to receive the attention of some processor. Control flow dependencies thus describe the flow of processor attention from one activity to another.

• *Data.*   Data resources include data values such as integers, strings, and arrays. They are further distinguished by their data type.

• *System.*   System resources represent various services offered by operating systems. They include *passive* resources such as shared memory pools, pipes, communication sockets, and *active* resources, such as name servers, and remote file transfer servers.

• *Hardware.*   Hardware resources correspond to hardware devices, such as printers, disk and tape drives, and multimedia adapters.

10.5.2   Resource Access

Resource access determines how producers and users access their corresponding resources.

• *Direct access resources.*   Control and simple data resources are communicated directly from producer to users. In a sense they are their own identifiers.

• *Indirect (named) access resources.*   Indirect access resources are accessed using a secondary data resource called the *resource name* or *identifier*. Flows of indirect access resources involve the communication of identifiers, rather than the resources themselves.

The use of identifiers is extremely widespread in software systems. Identifiers provide mappings that allow a wide variety of resources (system, hardware, complex data structures) to be accessed by software components that can only interface with their environment through relatively simple data resource ports.

   System and hardware resources are always accessed indirectly. Complex data resources, such as files and databases, are also typically accessed using identifiers.

10.5.3   Resource Transportability

Transportability determines whether resources can be moved around in the system.

• *Fixed* resources cannot be moved. They have a fixed location in the system, and in order to be used, software activities have to be located "close" to them. Hardware resources, such as printers, are examples of fixed resources.

• *Movable* resources can be made accessible to other activities by transporting them to other locations in the system. Transportation of a movable resource usually involves an additional auxiliary resource called the *carrier resource*. Data resources are usually movable. For example, a data structure can be moved from one process to another by converting it into a byte stream and transmitting it through a pipe. The pipe (classified as a system resource) acts as the carrier resource in this case.

Table 10.1
Divisibility of resources

Resource	Usage	Description
Divisible		
Memory heap	Read/write	Heaps can be divided into independent smaller blocks
Network channel	Connect	Physical network channels can support multiple independent connections
Indivisible		
Scalar variable	Read/write	Scalar variables can only store one value
pgp Encrypted file	Decrypt	Encrypted files can only be decrypted in their entirety

10.5.4 Resource Sharing

This section describes a framework for reasoning about shared resources that was developed by George Wyner and Gilad Zlotkin (1995a) at the MIT Center for Coordination Science.

Wyner and Zlotkin proposed a small number of important resource attributes that can help designers classify coordination requirements for shared resource dependencies. They observed that these important attributes are not merely a function of the resource type but of the intended *mode of usage* as well. That is, the same resource type used in different modes (e.g., read vs. written) might display different sharing behavior along those attributes. For that reason they refer to them as attributes of *resources-in-use*. These attributes are divisibility, consumability, and concurrency.

Divisibility Divisibility specifies whether a resource-in-use can be divided into independent subresources. Some examples of divisible and indivisible resources are shown in table 10.1.

Consumability Consumability specifies whether a resource-in-use is being destructively consumed. Consumable resources can be used a finite amount of times. Nonconsumable resources can be used an arbitrarily large amount of times. Some examples of consumable and nonconsumable resources in use are shown in table 10.2.

Concurrency Concurrency specifies whether a resource-in-use can be used by more than one users at the same time. Concurrency can be finite, setting a finite limit on the number of concurrent users, or infinite (arbitrarily large). Shown in table 10.3 are examples of finitely and infinitely concurrent resources.

Table 10.2
Consumability of resources

Resource	Usage	Description
Consumable		
Pipe channel	Read	Values "disappear" from the channel as they are being read
PROM	Write	PROMs (programmable read only memories) can only be written once
Nonconsumable		
File	Read	Files can be read an arbitrarily large amount of times
Processor	Start task	Processors can be used to start an arbitrarily large number of tasks

Table 10.3
Concurrency of resources

Resource	Usage	Description
Infinitely concurrent		
File	Read	In most systems multiple users are allowed to read files concurrently
Multitasking processor	Start task	Multitasking systems appear to execute multiple tasks concurrently
Finitely concurrent		
Ftp server	Connect	Ftp servers often limit the number of concurrent connections for performance reasons
Printer	Print file	Printers cannot interleave the printing of different files

10.6   A Generic Model of Resource Flows

This section presents a generic model for classifying flow dependencies and a generic process for managing them. Section 10.7 describes how this generic model can be specialized to manage different special cases of flow dependencies.

In the most general case, flow dependencies exist between a number of resource producers and a number of consumers (figure 10.4). Dependencies are connected to activities through resource producer and consumer ports. Producer and consumer ports are *abstract ports* (see section 10.6.3). That is, they are composite ports that contain implementation-specific groupings of low-level interface ports that logically participate in the production and consumption of a given resource.

We assume that by default, a flow dependency between a set of activities implies a *stream* of resource flows over the lifetime of an application execution. Coordination processes for managing flow dependencies are designed with this assumption in mind. Situations where resources are produced or consumed only once during the lifetime of an application execution are represented by special types of dependencies.

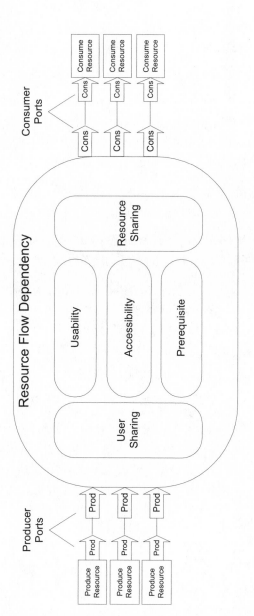

Dependency	Description
Usability	Produced resources must be in a form usable by each user
Accessibility	Produced resources must be made accessible to each user
Prerequisite	Resources must be produced before they can be used
Resource sharing	Multiple consumers share the same resources
Consumer sharing	Multiple producers produce resources for the same consumers

Figure 10.4
Generic model of resource flow dependencies

Our objectives in this section are the following:

• Introduce a set of dependency design dimensions that define a flow dependency design space. These dimensions represent the interaction requirements that are significant in choosing a coordination process. Every point in this design space defines a different special case of a flow dependency.

• Introduce a set of coordination design dimensions that define a coordination process design space. Every point in this design space will be an alternative implementation of a flow dependency managing process.

• Specify how each dependency type restricts the range of possible coordination processes for managing it.

Both design spaces are based on a generic model for decomposing flow dependencies into lower-level dependencies, shown in figure 10.4. Managing a flow dependency implies managing all lower-level dependencies. This model extends the ideas introduced in (Malone 1994) and attempts to capture the different considerations that must be addressed whenever resources are exchanged or shared among different activities.

The generic model for managing flow dependencies focuses on the relationships between producers and users of resources. It assumes that different consumers (producers) are independent from one another and compete for access to resources (consumers).

In the following sections we will first introduce dependency and coordination processes design spaces for each of the lower-level dependencies. The design space for generalized flow dependencies will then be defined by the product of the component dependencies design spaces.

10.6.1 Usability Dependencies

Types of Usability Dependencies Usability dependencies state the simple fact that resource users should be able to properly use produced resources. This is a very general requirement that encompasses compatibility issues such as:

• Data type compatibility

• Format compatibility

• Database schema compatibility

• Device driver compatibility

The exact meaning and range of usability considerations varies with each kind of resource. Section 10.7, which describes specializations of flow dependencies for a

Design Dimension	Design Alternatives
Who is responsible for ensuring usability?	- Designer (Standardization) - Producers - Consumers - Both producers and consumers - Third party
When are usability requirements fixed?	- At design-time - At run-time

Figure 10.5
Framework for managing usability dependencies

variety of different resources, also discusses in more detail the meaning of usability dependencies for each of them.

Managing Usability Dependencies   One interesting observation resulting from this work is that regardless of the particular usability issue being managed, coordination alternatives for managing usability dependencies can be classified by the following two design dimensions (figure 10.5): (1) who is responsible for ensuring usability and (2) are the usability requirements fixed?

WHO IS RESPONSIBLE FOR ENSURING USABILITY?   The following alternatives are possible:

• *Designer is responsible (no run-time coordination is necessary).*   Components are specially selected at design time so as to be compatible with one another. This is often achieved by developing applications using standardized components. Examples of standardized component families include OLE objects, OpenDoc components, Visual Basic VBXs, and so on (Adler 1995). The advantages of this approach include run-time efficiency and reliability. On the other hand, it limits the choice of components for a particular functional requirement to those explicitly designed for the particular standardized environment.

• *Producers are responsible for ensuring usability.*   This implies that the producer knows the format expected by the users, and is able to generate or convert its resources to the user format.

• *Consumers are responsible for ensuring usability.*   This requires the consumer to recognize the format of resources it receives, and to be able to convert the format to its own format, if necessary.

• *Third party ensures usability between producers and consumers.* The third party must know and be able to handle both formats.

• *Both producers and consumers convert to and from an interchange format.* The advantage of this approach is that it does not require prior knowledge of the formats produced and expected by producers and users. This is particularly desirable if producers and users are dynamically changing, and each of them is using a different native format. The disadvantage is that two conversions take place, which might be inefficient if conversions are computationally costly. Producers and users must agree on the interchange format.

ARE USABILITY REQUIREMENTS FIXED? Coordination processes can be further classified depending on whether the producer and consumer formats are fixed and known at design-time, or whether they are negotiated at run-time. In the latter case, the management of usability dependencies might introduce additional flow dependencies to the system that have to be managed in turn.

10.6.2   Accessibility Dependencies

Types of Accessibility Dependencies Accessibility dependencies specify that a resource must be accessible to a user before it can be used. Since users are software activities, accessibility specifies more accurately that a resource must be accessible to the process that executes a user activity before it can be used. Important parameters in specifying accessibility dependencies are the number of producers, the number of users, and the resource kind.

Managing Accessibility Dependencies   There are two broad alternatives for making resources accessible to their users (figure 10.6):

• Place producers and users "close together."

• Transport resources from producers to users.

Depending on the type of resource being transferred, either or both alternatives might be needed. Placing producer and user activities "close" to one another generally decreases the cost of transporting the resource. Combinations of placing activities and transporting resources should be considered in situations where the cost of placing the activities is lower than the corresponding gain in the cost of transporting the resource. A discussion of the two alternatives follows.

PLACE PRODUCERS AND USERS "CLOSE TOGETHER"   This can be done either at design-time, or at run-time:

Principal design alternatives	First level of specialization	Second level of specialization
Place producers and consumers "close together"	• Place at design-time	- Package in same sequential module - Package in same executable - Assign to same processor - Assign to nearby processors
	• Place at run-time	- Code is accessible to all processors - Physical code transportation required
Transport resource	*Actual processes depend on resource kind*	

Figure 10.6
Framework for managing accessibility dependencies

• *Place activities at design-time.*   The ways to manage this step is in decreasing order of efficiency:

1. *Package activities together in the same sequential code block.*   In this case transport of data resources becomes trivial through the use of local variables. However, such a packaging is subject to a large number of restrictions (all activities must be in source code form; they must be written in the same language and must be assigned to the same processor and executable; data resource must be transportable through local variables) and is not always possible.

2. *Package activities in the same executable.*   Transport of data resources can be done cheaply through global variables.

3. *Assign activities to the same processor.*   Transport of data resources can be done through shared memory.

4. *Assign activities to neighboring processors.*   Transport of data resources will require network communication, but this is still potentially cheaper than if producer and users were randomly assigned.

• *Move activities at run-time.*   Producers can be moved close to users, and vice versa. In the simplest case, this would imply assigning the producer to the processor where user activities are assigned. In more complicated cases, this step might require physically transferring an activity's code to the target machine.

TRANSPORT RESOURCE FROM PRODUCERS TO USERS   This step depends on the kind of resource that is flowing. It is discussed in more detail in section 10.7.

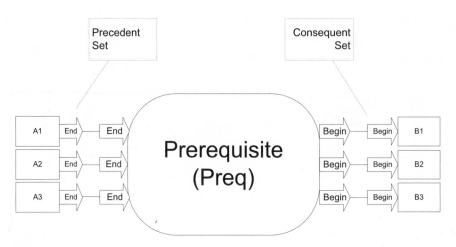

Figure 10.7
Prerequisite dependency

10.6.3 Prerequisite Dependencies

Types of Prerequisite Dependencies A fundamental requirement in every resource flow is that a resource must be produced before it can be used. This is captured by including a prerequisite dependency in the decomposition of every flow dependency.

Prerequisites are relationships between two sets of activities (figure 10.7). In the following discussion we will refer to set A as the *precedent set* and to set B as the *consequent set*. As is the case with flow dependencies, prerequisite dependencies in our vocabulary have *stream semantics*: they assume that precedent and consequent activities might execute multiple times over the lifetime of an application execution. Prerequisite dependencies thus specify constraints on the allowed execution inter-leavings of precedent and consequent activities.

Prerequisite dependencies occur very frequently in software architectures. They are the most frequently used member of the dependency family we call timing dependencies. Timing dependencies express constraints in the timing of control flow into a set of activities. They are discussed in section 10.8.

Prerequisite dependencies form a family of related sequencing constraints. The most useful members of the prerequisite family are the following:

• *Persistent prerequisites* specify that a single occurrence of activity A is an adequate prerequisite for an infinite number of occurrences of activity B. This requirement arises often in system initialization processes: an initialization activity must be executed once before any number of system use activities can take place.

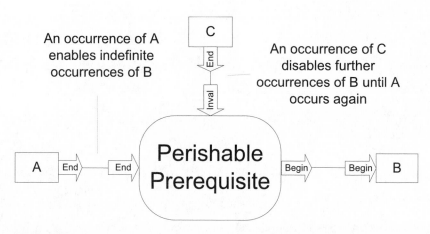

Figure 10.8
Perishable prerequisites

• *Perishable prerequisites* are a special case of permanent prerequisites. They specify that a single occurrence of activity A is an adequate prerequisite for an indefinite number of occurrences of activity B. However, occurrence of a third activity C invalidates the effect of activity A, which must then be repeated (figure 10.8). Examples of this dependency arise in situations where resources (communication channels, files) are opened and periodically closed. If no activity C is connected to their invalidation port, perishable prerequisite dependencies become identical to persistent prerequisites.

• *Cumulative prerequisites* permit occurrences of activity A and activity B to be interleaved as long as the number of occurrences of activity B is always smaller than or equal to the number of completed occurrences of activity A. This prerequisite arises in asynchronous resource flows with buffering.

• *Transient prerequisites* specify that at least one new occurrence of activity A must precede each new occurrence of activity B. Transient prerequisites satisfy the definition of cumulative prerequisites and can be thought of as a special case of that dependency type. Perishable prerequisites reduce to transient prerequisites (figure 10.8), when B and C are the same activity.

• *Lockstep prerequisites* specify that *exactly one* occurrence of activity A must precede each occurrence of activity B. They occur in resource flows without buffering, where it must be ensured that every produced element is used before the next one can be produced. Lockstep prerequisites are a special case of transient prerequisites.

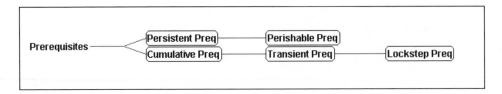

Figure 10.9
Specialization relationships among different prerequisite dependency types

The preceding variations of prerequisite relationships can be organized in a specialization hierarchy, as shown in figure 10.9. The implication of prerequisite specialization relationships is that coordination processes for managing a prerequisite relationship can also be used to manage any of its parent relationships in the specialization structure. For example, in order to manage a cumulative prerequisite, in addition to using processes specifically designed for this type of prerequisite, designers can also consider using coordination processes for transient or lockstep prerequisites.

Prerequisite dependencies can be further classified according to:

· Number of precedent activities

· Number of consequent activities

· Relationship (and/or) among the precedent activities

In *And-prerequisites*, all activities in the precedent set must occur before activities in the consequent set can begin execution. By contrast, in *Or-prerequisites*, occurrence of at least one activity in the precedent set satisfies the prerequisite requirement.

Managing Prerequisite Dependencies   There are four generic processes for managing prerequisite dependencies (figure 10.10): producer push, consumer pull, peer synchronization, and controlled hierarchy.

PRODUCER PUSH   This process decomposes into a control flow dependency (section 10.7.1). The alternatives for managing it are the same as those of managing the corresponding control flow dependency.

Producer push processes manage lockstep prerequisites. Consequents are invoked once each time the precedents complete execution.

CONSUMER PULL   This process family decomposes into a synchronous call pattern of control flow dependencies. The alternatives for managing it are the same as those of managing the corresponding pattern of control flows.

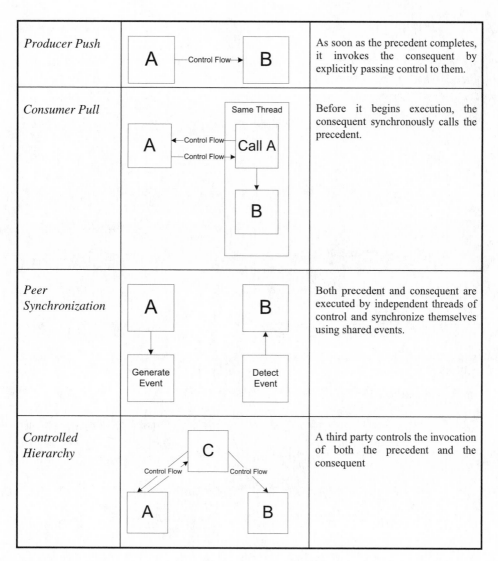

Figure 10.10
Generic processes for managing prerequisite dependencies

Consumer pull processes manage lockstep prerequisites. Precedents are invoked once before each consequent. Consumer pull organizations can also be used to manage persistent and perishable dependencies: before starting itself, each consequent checks whether the prerequisite condition is valid, and invokes the precedent activities if it is not.

PEER SYNCHRONIZATION   Peer synchronization processes can be used to manage all kinds of prerequisites. Figure 10.11 shows their generic form for each kind of one-to-one prerequisite. All processes can be generalized to handle many-to-many prerequisites.

Peer synchronization processes rely on the generation and detection of shared events in the system. Events can be classified as follows (figure 10.12):

• *Memoryless events.*   Such events are only capable of recording binary states (occurred/did not occur). They can be used for managing permanent, perishable, transient, and lockstep prerequisites. Memoryless events can be further distinguished into persistent and transient.

Persistent event protocols keep a record of whether the event has occurred or not. Therefore the detection of the event need not take place at the time of event generation. *Transient* event protocols do not keep a record of whether an event has occurred. Events are either detected at the time they are generated, or go unnoticed. This requires some extra coordination to make sure that event detection activities have been started before event generation takes place.

• *Cumulative events.*   Cumulative events are capable of remembering how many times they have occurred. They are used in the management of cumulative prerequisites. Apart from being resetted, cumulative events can be incremented and decremented.

CONTROLLED HIERARCHY   There are three variations on this process:

• Third party synchronously calls precedent, then calls consequent.

• Third party asynchronously calls precedent, then schedules consequent after sufficient delay.

• Third party schedules both precedent and consequent with sufficient relative delay.

Controlled hierarchy processes can be used to manage lockstep prerequisites. Permanent prerequisites can also be managed by this approach by placing the prerequisite code before any other code in the system (e.g., in an initialization module or at the top of the main program). Figure 10.13 summarizes the design dimensions of prerequisite dependencies and coordination processes.

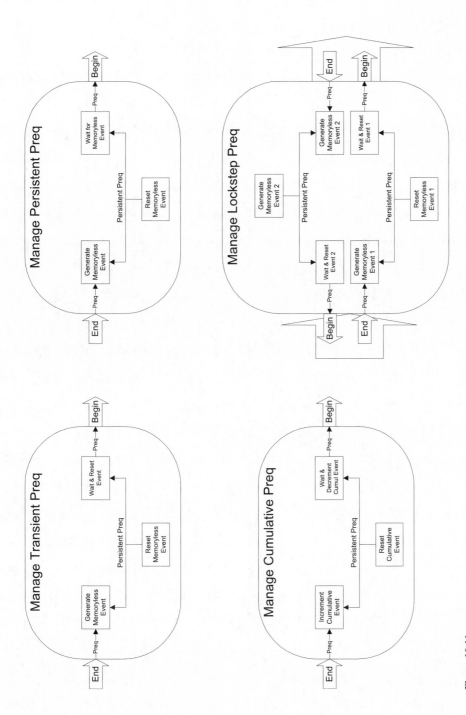

Figure 10.11
Generic processes for managing prerequisite dependencies using peer event synchronization

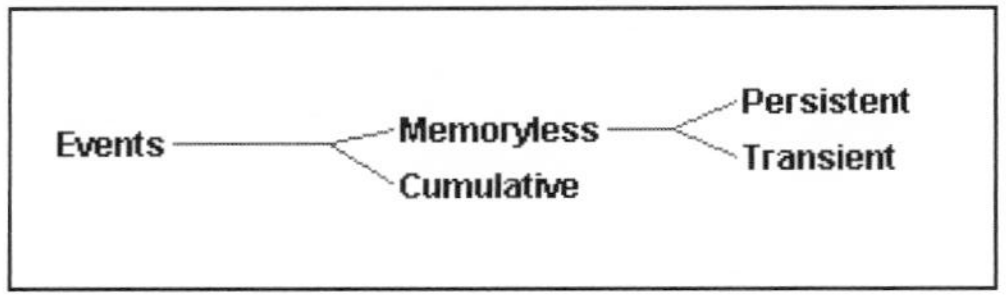

Events ── Memoryless ┬ Persistent
                     └ Transient
          Cumulative

Persistent Memoryless Events

Event type	Generate	Detect	Reset
Semaphore	Signal Semaphore (V)	Wait on Semaphore	Wait on Semaphore (P)
File Creation	Create File	Test File Existence	Delete File
File Modification	Write File	Compare file modification time with stored modification time	Set stored modification time to file modification time
Process Creation	Create Process	Test Process Existence	Kill Process

Transient Memoryless Events

Event type	Generate	Detect
UNIX Signal mechanism	signal system call	wait system call
Windows DDE mechanism	send DDE transaction	initialize DDE conversation

Cumulative Events

Event	Reset	Increment	Decrement	Detect
Counting Semaphore	Set semaphore to zero	Signal semaphore	Wait on semaphore	
List	Clear List	Add element to list	Remove element from list	Check if list is empty

Figure 10.12
Taxonomy and examples of event types

Principal Design Dimensions	Design Alternatives	Other Design Dimensions
Type of prerequisite	- Persistent - Perishable - Cumulative - Transient - Lockstep	
Organization of coordination mechanism	- Producer Push	- Synchronous vs. Asynchronous control flow
	- Consumer Pull	- Type of shared event used
	- Peer Synchronization	
	- Controlled Hierarchy	- Wait for precedent completion vs. pre-scheduling

Figure 10.13
Framework for managing prerequisite dependencies

10.6.4   Sharing Dependencies

Types of Sharing Dependencies   Sharing arises when more than one activity requires access to the same resource. Sharing dependencies can be specialized using the three dimensions of the resource-in-use framework of section 10.5.4. For each different combination of resource-in-use parameters (e.g., indivisible, consumable, concurrent), a different specialization of sharing dependency can be defined.

Sharing dependencies arise in one-to-many, many-to-one, and many-to-many flow dependencies in two distinct situations:

· Resource sharing
· User sharing

RESOURCE SHARING   Resource sharing considerations arise in one-to-many flow dependencies because more than one activity uses the same resource. Resource users are assumed to be independent. Therefore the sharing coordination requirements depend solely on the sharing properties of the resource. The different possibilities are as follows:

· *Divisible resources.*   Resources can be divided among the users.
· *Consumable resources.*   The total number of users must be restricted.
· *Nonconcurrent resources.*   The number of concurrent users must be restricted.

CONSUMER SHARING   Consumer sharing dependencies arise in many-to-one flow dependencies because more than one producers produce for the same consumer activity, viewed as a "resource." Consumer "resources" can be characterized using the resource-in-use framework. The different dimensions are as follows:

· *Divisibility.*   Consumer activities either occur or do not occur. Therefore they are considered indivisible resources.
· *Consumability.*   Consumability of a consumer activity means that it can occur a limited number of times or, equivalently, that it can accept a limited number of produced resources. This implies the need for coordination in order to select which resources will be accepted. Modeling consumer activities as consumable resources enables many-to-one flow dependencies to be used for modeling *race conditions.*
· *Concurrency.*   Concurrency determines whether multiple instances of a consumer activity can be active at the same time. Some consumer activities are nonconcurrent (e.g., non-reentrant procedures). In that case coordination should be installed to restrict simultaneous execution of more than one activity instances.

Many-to-many flow dependencies contain a combination of both resource- and consumer-sharing dependencies.

Managing Sharing Dependencies   The problem of resource sharing has been studied extensively by researchers in various areas and there exists a huge literature of related algorithms and techniques. Our purpose in this section is to take an architectural look at resource sharing techniques, showing how their interfaces can be abstracted to a small number of generic processes, and how they relate to the other components of a resource flow management process in a small, well-defined number of ways.

There are three general techniques for coordinating resource sharing requirements (figure 10.14):

· Divide resource

· Restrict access to resource

· Replicate resource

DIVIDE RESOURCE   This technique applies to divisible resources. It can be represented by a process that uses the entire resource and produces a set of new subresources (figure 10.15). Subresources are considered independent resources and can then flow to each user with no further coordination.

There are two different ways a resource divide can be combined with the rest of a flow coordination process:

· *Divide resource before transportation* (figure 10.15a).   This is the most common case. The entire resource is divided at the site of production, and the generated sub-resources are independently transported to their users.

· *Divide resource after transportation* (figure 10.15b).   The resource is first transported at each site and a new subresource is extracted locally. Examples of such resources are circulating tokens in which successive users write or reserve data areas.

RESTRICT ACCESS TO RESOURCE   This very general technique applies to both consumable and nonconcurrent resources. In both cases the function of the coordination process is to restrict the flow of control into activities accessing the resource (figure 10.16). More specifically:

· For consumable resources, the process restricts the total number of resource accesses.

· For nonconcurrent resources, the process limits the total number of concurrent resource accesses. The most common case is when only one concurrent access can be

Resource Type	Sharing Coordination Required	Specializations
Divisible Resources	Divide Resource	- Divide before transportation - Divide after transportation
Indivisible Resources		
Consumable and/or Finitely Concurrent	• Restrict access to resource • Replicate resource	- Restrict consumer activity execution - Restrict resource transportation - Restrict resource production
Nonconsumable and Infinitely Concurrent	No sharing coordination is required	

Figure 10.14
Framework for managing sharing dependencies

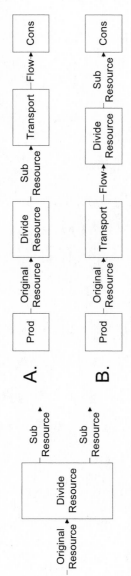

Figure 10.15
Sharing of divisible resources in a flow dependency

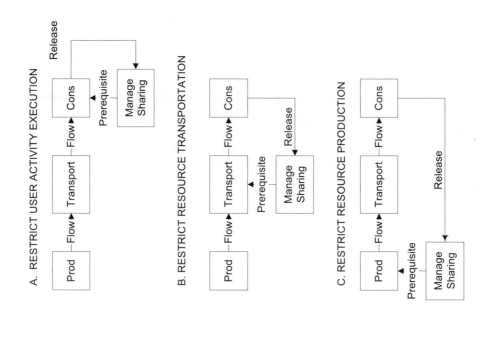

A. RESTRICT USER ACTIVITY EXECUTION

B. RESTRICT RESOURCE TRANSPORTATION

C. RESTRICT RESOURCE PRODUCTION

Figure 10.16
Sharing by restricting access to resource

allowed. Then resource sharing becomes equal to a mutual exclusion dependency (Raynal 1986).

From an architectural perspective, there are three different ways an access restriction process can be integrated with the rest of a flow coordination process:

• *Restrict consumer activity execution* (figure 10.16a).   This method is used when a resource is accessible to all consumers (e.g., a fixed hardware resource), or when each consumer is using a local protocol to restrict access.

• *Restrict resource accessibility* (figure 10.16b).   This method prevents the resource from being transported to consumers until they are allowed to use it. It has efficiency advantages in situations where resource transportation is costly (e.g., for large files), and only a subset of the candidate consumers is allowed to use the resource.

• *Restrict resource production* (figure 10.16c).   This alternative should be considered when managing user-sharing dependencies. In situations where only a subset of the produced resources is ever used, it might be more efficient to not produce unless usage has been guaranteed.

REPLICATE RESOURCE   Resource replication is a technique that jointly manages accessibility and resource sharing dependencies. Its more general architectural form is similar to that of a resource division process. However, it applies to indivisible resources.

COMBINATIONS OF DIVISION AND RESTRICTION   The previous techniques can be combined to handle more complex resource sharing requirements. For example, in order to share a resource that is nonconcurrent and finitely divisible among a potentially infinite number of users a combination of division and access restriction can be used. Whenever an access is desired, extraction of a new subresource is first attempted. If that fails, time sharing is used. This algorithm, for example, manages the sharing of finite capacity buffered input/output channels among a potentially infinite number of user processes.

10.6.5   Putting It All Together: Flow Dependencies

The design dimensions of generalized resource dependencies are the sum of the design dimensions of their component dependencies (figure 10.17). For each combination of dimension values, a different special case of resource flow can be defined. The following is a discussion of the different dimensions and the alternative flow dependencies they can be used to define.

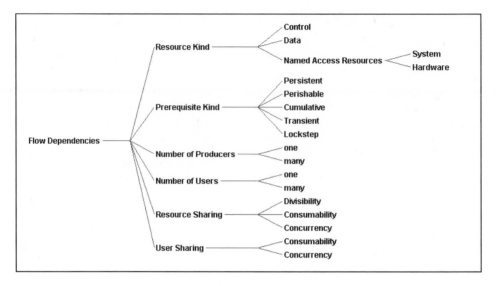

Figure 10.17
First two levels of design dimensions for flow dependencies

Resource Kind   The most important design dimension is the kind of resource. Section 10.7 will describe how resource dependencies are specialized according to this dimension.

Prerequisite Relationship   Another important dimension is the kind of prerequisite requirement. According to this dimension, resource relationships are classified as follows:

• *Persistent flows.*   In these situations one or more resources are produced once, and can then be used an infinite amount of times. In software systems, they arise often to describe the use of calculated constants, and system resources (printers, network channels, etc.) that are set up once and then used an indefinite amount of times.

• *Perishable flows.*   This more refined special case of permanent dependencies describes situations where produced resources can be used an indefinite amount of times until they become invalidated. File caching provides an example application where this type of flow describes the underlying interdependency. Cached file blocks are transferred (produced) once from disk and can then be read an arbitrary number of times until some other process modifies their corresponding disk block. Then the cached file blocks become invalidated and have to be refreshed from disk before they can be read again.

• *Cumulative flows.* In these situations every resource produced can only be used once. Producers and users can proceed asynchronously, but at no time can the number of user accesses exceed the number of produced resources. Reading and writing a pipe channel by two separate processes is an example of this type of flow.

• *Transient flows.* In these situations a stream of resources is produced, but the use of each resource is optional. Thus new resources in the stream can overwrite previous ones, possibly before they have been used. One example application where transient flows describe the underlying interdependency is a log file that is periodically being updated and can be printed by a user at will. Not all versions of the file need to be printed. Therefore new updates can overwrite the previous contents of the file without the need for additional coordination.

• *Lockstep flows.* These situations occur where there must exist tight synchronization between producers and users of resources. All resources produced must be used and no resource can be produced until all previous resources have been used by all designated users. Stream data flows using nonbuffered (indivisible) carriers are examples of lockstep flows.

MANAGING PREREQUISITE COORDINATION PROCESSES   The coordination process selected to manage a prerequisite dependency at the heart of a resource flow has a profound influence on the overall organization of the interacting activities. Corresponding to the four generic classes of prerequisite coordination processes, we have an equivalent taxonomy of flow organizations:

• *Producer push.* In push organizations, also called *eager flows*, resource users explicitly receive control from producers every time a new resource has been produced. Only lockstep flows can be implemented in this manner.

If control is transferred to users using synchronous calls, this organization reduces to what is commonly called *client/server architecture*. The resource producers act as clients and resource users act as servers.

• *Consumer pull.* In pull organizations, also called *lazy flows*, resource producers are invoked by users whenever the latter require a new resource. Only lockstep and permanent flows can be implemented in this manner.

Pull organizations of flow dependencies also reduce to *client/server architectures*. Resource users act as the clients and resource producers act as the servers. Note, however, that the direction of the client/server relationship is the *inverse* of the direction of the flow relationship.

• *Peer synchronization.*   In peer organizations producers and users are executed by separate threads of control and synchronize themselves through events. This is a more loose organization, appropriate for managing all kinds of flows. It is particularly suitable for organizing cumulative and transient flows. It might not be as efficient for managing lockstep flows, where tight synchronization is required. Examples of flow processes that are organized in this manner include pipe channel flows, shared memory flows with separate semaphore synchronization, tuple space flows, and so on. Ada's *rendezvous* interprocess communication paradigm (DoD 1983) is one well-known specialization of peer organizations. Other researchers have used the term *implicit invocation architectures* to characterize such organizations (Garlan 1988).

• *Controlled hierarchy.*   Such organizations typically result in systems with centralized control, where a main program explicitly controls the sequence of flow participants.

Number of Producers and Users—Sharing Dimensions

• *One-to-one dependencies.*   These are the simplest kinds of dependencies. The defining dimensions are the kind of resource and the kind of prerequisite relationship. There are no sharing considerations.

• *One-to-many dependencies.*   In one-to-many dependencies, resource sharing becomes an issue. Different dependency types can be defined for each combination of resource sharing dimensions of each of the users. Some interesting special cases are:

One-to-all dependencies.   Each resource flows to all users

One-to-one-of-many dependencies.   Each resource flows to one of the users. This can be managed in an application-independent way (e.g., first come–first served), or in an application-specific way. In the latter case, user consumer ports usually provide additional pieces of information, such as user priorities.

• *Many-to-one dependencies.*   In many-to-one dependencies, user sharing issues have to be addressed. Users might not be willing to receive all resources produced, or they might not be able to receive them concurrently.

Situations where users are not willing to receive all resources produced are often referred to as *race conditions*. In our framework, race conditions are modeled as many-to-one dependencies where the user activity acts as a consumable "resource." General ways of managing consumable resources can be used to manage the dependency.

• *Many-to-many dependencies.* These dependencies are the most complex family because they can specialized according to both resource- and user-sharing dimensions. Some interesting special cases include:

Each-to-all. Every resource produced flows to all users

Each-to-one. Every resource produced flows to one user only

Each-from-one. Each user receives one resource only

All-from-one. Only one of the resources produced flows to (all) users

The design alternatives for managing resource dependencies are the product of the different alternatives for managing each component dependency. In principle, each of the component dependencies can be managed by independent coordination processes. In practice, however, there often exist opportunities to increase efficiency by managing patterns of dependencies using joint coordination processes. This gives rise to additional design alternatives that designers should be aware of. We have already encountered the opportunity to use *joint* coordination processes for managing accessibility and sharing (restrict resource transportation, replicate resource). In the following sections we will encounter more opportunities for joint dependency management.

10.7 Timing Dependencies

Timing dependencies specify constraints on the relative timing of two or more activities. The most widely used members of this dependency family are *prerequisite dependencies* (A must complete before B starts) and *mutual exclusion dependencies* (A and B cannot overlap).

Timing dependencies are used in software systems for two purposes:

• To specify implicit resource relationships
• To specify cooperation relationships among activities that share some resources

Specify Implicit Resource Relationships Implicit resource relationships arise in situations where parts of a resource flow coordination protocol have been hard-coded inside a set of components. Other parts of the protocol might be missing, and explicit coordination might be needed to manage the missing parts only. One example is a set of components for accessing a database. Each of the components contains all the functionality needed in order to access the database built into its code. The name of the database is also embedded in the components and does not appear in their interface. However, none of the components contains any support for sharing the

Table 10.4
Allen's taxonomy of relationships between time intervals

Relation	Symmetric relation	Pictorial example
X before Y		XXX YYY
X equal Y		XXX
		YYY
X meets Y		XXXYYY
X overlaps Y		XXX
		YYY
X during Y	X equal Y	YYYYYY
		XXX
X starts Y	X, Y simstart	XXX
		YYYYY
X finishes Y	X, Y simend	XXX
		YYYY

database with other activities. In applications that require concurrent access of the database by all components, designers need to specify and manage an external mutual exclusion dependency among the components.

Specify Cooperation Relationships   Flow dependencies assume that different users of a resource are independent from one another. In many applications, however, users of a resource are cooperating in application-specific ways. Section 10.3 describes an example of such patterns of cooperation. In those cases designers must specify additional dependencies that describe the cooperation among the users. Some of those dependencies could be other resource dependencies. Other could be timing dependencies.

To derive a useful family of timing dependencies we have used the following approach, based on Allen's (1984) taxonomy of time interval relationships. Allen has enumerated all possible relationships between two time intervals (table 10.4). An occurrence of a software activity can be represented by a time interval: *[Begin_time, End_time]*. Timing dependencies express constraints among activity occurrences. These constraints can be expressed by equivalent constraints between time intervals. Constraints can either *require* or *forbid* that a given time interval relationship hold. By enumerating "required" and "forbidden" constraints for each of Allen's time interval relationships, we get a list of potentially interesting elementary timing dependencies (table 10.5). These dependencies can be combined to define additional, composite timing relationships. Finally, the resulting set of dependencies can be organized in a specialization hierarchy, as shown in figure 10.18.

Table 10.5
Deriving timing dependency types from Allen's time interval relationships

Allen's relation	"Relation required" dependency	"Relation forbidden" dependency	Comments
X before Y	X prerequisite Y	X prevents Y	
X equal Y			Can be expressed as a composite pattern: *X, Y simstart AND X, Y simend*
X meets Y	X meets Y		Special case of prerequisite
X overlaps Y	X overlaps Y	X, Y mutex	
X during Y	X during Y	X, Y mutex	During can be expressed as a composite pattern: *X overlaps Y AND Y finishes X*
X starts Y	X starts Y		
X, Y simstart	X, Y simstart		
X finishes Y	X finishes Y		
X, Y simend	X, Y simend		

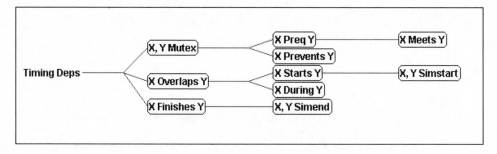

Figure 10.18
Specialization relationships among timing dependencies

The following paragraphs describe each of the dependencies shown in figure 10.18. For each dependency type, we describe:

- The timing constraint it specifies
- The dependency design dimensions
- The principal ways to manage it
- Some situations where it might be useful

10.7.1   Mutual Exclusion Dependencies (*X, Y* Mutex)

Description	Mutual exclusion dependencies among a set of activities limit the total number of activities of the set that can be executing at any one time
Design dimensions	Degree of concurrency (maximum number of concurrently executing activities)
Coordination processes	See Raynal (1986)
Typical use	Mutual exclusion dependencies typically arise among *competing* users who share resources with limited concurrency

10.7.2   Prerequisite Dependencies (*X* Prereq *Y*)

Description	Prerequisite dependencies specify that an activity *X* must complete execution before another activity *Y* begins execution
Design dimensions	See section 10.6.3
Coordination processes	See section 10.6.3
Typical use	Prerequisites arise in two general situations: • Between producers and consumers of some resource. A resource must be produced before it can be consumed. • As a special way of managing mutual exclusion dependencies. Mutual exclusion relationships can be managed by ensuring that the activities involved occur in a statically defined sequential order. The ordering can be specified by defining appropriate prerequisite relationships.

10.7.3 Prevention Dependencies (*X* Prevents *Y*)

Description	Prevention dependencies specify that the occurrence of an activity *X* prevents further occurrences of another activity *Y*
Design dimensions	• In *permanent* prevention dependencies, an occurrence of *X* prevents all further occurrences of *Y* • In *temporary* prevention dependencies, occurrence of a third activity *Z* re-enables occurrences of *Y*
Coordination processes	Prevention relationships are closely related to perishable prerequisites (see section 10.6.3). As shown in figure 10.19, every prevention dependency can be mapped to an equivalent perishable prerequisite.
Typical use	Prevention relationships often arise among competing activities that share some resource, where one of the competing activities *X* has higher priority, and thus the power to restrict access to (prevent) other competing activities *Y*

10.7.4 Meets Dependencies (*X* Meets *Y*)

Description	Meets dependencies specify that an activity *Y* should begin execution after completion of another activity *X*
Design dimensions	Minimum or maximum delay between the completion of *X* and the initiation of *Y*
Coordination processes	Most of the coordination processes for managing lockstep prerequisites can be used to manage this dependency. Delay parameters between *X* and *Y* can determine which alternatives are appropriate for each special case (e.g., if *Y* must start immediately after *X* completes, direct transfer of control is usually preferable to loose event synchronization).
Typical use	Meets dependencies are a special case of prerequisite and can also be used to describe relationships between producers and users of resources. The explicit specification of maximum delay between the two activities is useful in situations where resources produced have finite lifetimes and must be used within a specified time interval.

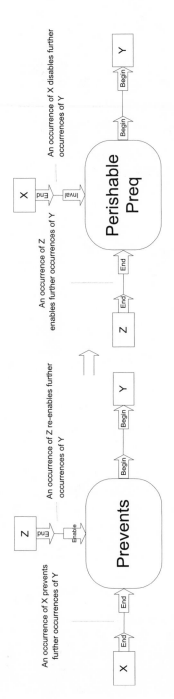

Figure 10.19
Relationships between prevention and perishable prerequisite dependencies

10.7.5 Overlap Dependencies (*X* Overlaps *Y*)

Description	Overlap dependencies specify that an activity *Y* can only begin execution if another activity *X* is already executing
Design dimensions	None
Coordination processes	This dependency can be managed in two different ways: • Proactively scheduling *Y* when *X* starts execution. This is equivalent to decomposing *X* overlaps *Y* to *Y* starts *X* with specified delay. • Waiting for *X* to begin execution before allowing *Y* to start. This is equivalent to defining a perishable prerequisite (enabled by initiation of *X*, invalidated by completion of *X*) between *Y* and *X*.
Typical use	Overlap relationships typically imply resource relationships between *Y* and *X*. In most cases, during its execution *Y* produces some resource or state required by *X*. Overlap dependencies occur most frequently as components of During dependencies.

10.7.6 During Dependencies (*X* during *Y*)

Description	During dependencies specify that an activity *X* can only execute during the execution of another activity *Y*
Design dimensions	None
Coordination processes	This dependency is a composite pattern of the following two dependencies: • *X* overlaps *Y*, so *X* can begin execution only if *Y* is already executing. • *Y* finishes *X*. Termination of *Y* also terminates *X*. It can be managed by composing processes for managing its two component dependencies.
Typical use	During dependencies imply that *X* uses some resource or state generated during *Y*'s execution. For example, a network client can only execute successfully during execution of the system's network driver.

10.7.7 Starts Dependency (*X* Starts *Y*)

Description	Starts dependencies specify that an activity *Y* must start execution whenever *X* starts execution
Design dimensions	Minimum or maximum delay between initiation of the two activities
Coordination processes	Combinations of direct control flow and scheduling can be used to manage this dependency
Typical use	This dependency is often used to describe application-specific patterns of cooperative resource usage or implicit resource dependencies. For example, when starting a word processor program, the printer driver is often initialized as well, in anticipation to the word processor's need for its services.

10.7.8 Simultaneity Dependency (*X, Y* Simstart)

Description	Simultaneity dependencies specify that all activities in a set must start execution at the same time
Design dimensions	Minimum and maximum tolerances between the actual time each activity in the specified set begins execution
Coordination processes	Simultaneity dependencies can be transformed into many-to-many prerequisite dependencies and managed as such (see figure 10.20)
Typical use	Simultaneity dependencies are most often used to describe patterns of cooperative resource or mutual resource dependencies

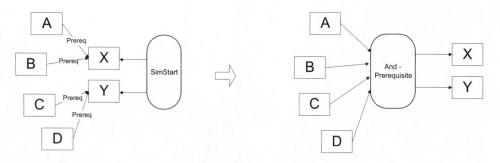

Figure 10.20
A simultaneity dependency can be transformed and managed as a composite prerequisite. Before activities *X* and *Y* can begin execution, all four prerequisite activites must occur. Then both *X* and *Y* can occur together.

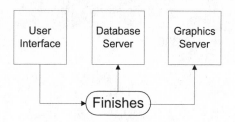

Figure 10.21.
Termination of the user-interface also requires termination of the database and graphics servers

10.7.9   Finishes Dependency (*X* Finishes *Y*)

Description	Finishes dependencies specify that completion of an activity *X* also causes activity *Y* to terminate execution
Design dimensions	Minimum or maximum delay between completion of *X* and termination of *Y*
Coordination processes	Termination of the process that executes *Y* using machine-specific system primitives
Typical use	This dependency is most often used to specify application termination relationships (figure 10.21)

10.7.10   Simultaneous End Dependency (*X, Y* Simend)

Description	Simultaneous end dependencies specify that all activities in a set must terminate if any of them completes execution
Design dimensions	Minimum or maximum tolerances between the actual time each member of the specified set terminates
Coordination processes	• *Centralized.* Each activity in the set sends a signal to a monitor process upon termination. The monitor process terminates all other activities in the set. • *Decentralized.* Terminating activities generate an event. All participant activities periodically check for that event and terminate themselves if they detect it.
Typical use	*Speculative concurrency.* Multiple worker activities are jointly or independently working on a problem. All of them terminate if at least one of them arrives at a solution.

IIIC *Creating Process Descriptions*

11 A Coordination Theory Approach to Process Description and Redesign

Kevin Crowston
Charles S. Osborn

11.1   Introduction

Most managers develop usable understandings of the work they and their colleagues do, but the scope and complexity of their work practices often makes it difficult to comprehend them fully. Understanding is particularly difficult for semistructured, knowledge-oriented work, where the flow of work is not reflected in physical production lines. Difficulties in understanding become most apparent when the way the work is done must be changed, for example, as information technologies are deployed to support or partially automate the work. Our goal is to help people understand their work as a prelude to changing and improving the way they do it or to document their process for use with the Process Handbook (chapter 21 in this volume). In this chapter we propose and demonstrate a technique to analyze and represent work based on coordination theory (chapter 2 in this volume).

We identified several potentially conflicting requirements that led to our developing a new technique, rather than applying one of many existing techniques.

First, and most important, we wanted a technique that is generative, that is, capable of not only documenting what people do now but also suggesting feasible alternatives. We are not aware of any other technique that was designed to meet this requirement.

Second, it was important that documenting a process not become an end in itself. While understanding the current process is important, documentation is not the only aspect of organizational change that managers must consider, and probably not even the most critical one. Therefore, as a general principle, we add complexity to a description only if it helps answer some question important for a redesign.

Third, we want the technique to be valid. By this we mean that the suggestions of the technique must make sense to the individuals involved in the work.

To achieve these goals, we were willing to sacrifice a degree of reliability in that two analysts studying the same process will develop exactly the same description. So we applied a looser but perhaps more practical criterion: one analyst studying a process in some context should derive descriptions that can be readily understood and debated by another. The analysts then should be able to combine their individual descriptions into a jointly acceptable representation that incorporates the characteristics identified by each. Such a representation might serve as the foundation of an explicit consensus between different analysts that recognizes a shared interpretation of the configuration and priorities of process details.

Our resulting technique draws on three conceptual tools. First, as with most process mapping techniques, we *decompose* processes into sequences of activities. Second, drawing on coordination theory (Malone 1994), we explicitly search for and represent *dependencies* within the process and *coordination mechanisms* used to manage those dependencies. Coordination theory has been used as the basis for a number of analyses (e.g., Crowston 1997), but until now, there has been no description of how to apply the techniques. Finally, we analyze the process and the activities in the process as *specializations* of more generic processes and activities, thus linking activities together into an organized inheritance hierarchy.

In the next section we review the theoretical bases for our technique, with particular attention to dependencies and coordination theory. In section 11.3 we walk through the stages in our proposed technique and present an extended example. Our overall approach draws heavily on Checkland's Soft Systems Methodology (1981, 1989, 1990). In section 11.4 we discuss how the representations developed can be used to suggest alternative processes, satisfying our first requirement of generativity. We conclude by presenting an evaluation of our technique and its implications for action.

11.2   Theoretical Basis: Processes, Dependencies, and Coordination

In this section we review the theoretical bases for our technique, briefly discussing processes, coordination theory and dependencies, and specialization.

11.2.1   Processes

In the past few years "business process" has become a potent buzzword for those interested in organizational change. Practitioners usually define "business processes" as sequences of goal-oriented actions undertaken by work units or business firms that repeat over time and are measured in performance terms, such as time, resources expended or costs (e.g., Harrington 1991; Davenport 1993). For example, Davenport and Short (1990, p. 12) define business processes as "logically related tasks performed to achieve a defined business outcome." Harrington (1991, p. 9) defines processes as "any activity or group of activities that takes an input, adds value to it, and provides an output to an internal or external customer." In both definitions, key elements are activities, actors, and resources.

In our work we build on these definitions of process. However, we acknowledge that the relationship between work and its description can be problematic. Except in the most routine processes, people do not do exactly the same things, and yet we as analysts want somehow to identify a set of "repeated activities" in the process they perform. Even identifying a particular set of things someone does as an "activity" can be difficult. It may be easy to label the one-minute cycle of an assembly line worker, for example, but finding the boundaries between coming up with an idea and writing it down, for example, is much more difficult. In general, though, we adopt a pragmatic attitude toward these issues. It is true that there are problems in representing processes, but in most cases it is possible to develop a meaningful and recognizable model. Therefore our criteria in assessing a model is not some Platonic ideal, but rather that it makes sense to the users of the models, or at least, that users are able to come to some agreement about them.

Furthermore, instead of arguing that our models are somehow true representations of work, we view descriptions as discursive products, that is, as artifacts, with authors, intended to accomplish some goal. Checkland (1981) similarly describes models as "opening up debate about change" rather than "what ought now to be done" (p. 178). In this view, process descriptions are resources for action. Someone doing the work may find them useful as a reference or justification for particular actions.[1] Particularly important for this chapter, someone may find a description useful as a basis for suggesting changes in the processes. Our goal in this chapter is to describe how we build such potentially useful process models.

11.2.2 Coordination Theory

The second conceptual basis for our method is coordination theory. A major drawback to many process representations is that they are, ironically, static: they describe the current state of a process but do little to illuminate possible changes or improvements. We use coordination theory suggest alternative ways a process could work. According to coordination theory, actors performing activities face *coordination problems* arising from dependencies that constrain how the activities can be performed. These coordination problems are managed by activities that implement *coordination methods*.

The first key claim of coordination theory is that dependencies and the mechanisms for managing them are general, that is, a given dependency and a mechanism to manage it will be found in a variety of organizational settings. For example, a common coordination problem is that certain activities require specialized skills, thus constraining which actors can work on them. This dependency between an activity and an actor arises in some form in nearly every organization. Coordination theory

---

1. Lucy Suchman suggested this formulation in a presentation at a University of Michigan CREW workshop on process modeling.

suggests identifying and studying common dependencies and their related coordination mechanisms across a wide variety of organizational settings.

The second claim is that there are often several coordination mechanisms that can be used to manage a dependency. For example, mechanisms to manage the dependency between an activity and an actor include, among others, (1) having a manager pick a subordinate to perform the task, (2) first-come–first-served, and (3) a labor market. Again, the claim of coordination theory is that these mechanisms may be useful in a wide variety of organizational settings. Organizations with similar goals achieved using more or less the same set of activities will have to manage the same dependencies, but they may choose different coordination mechanisms, resulting in different processes. Taken together, these two claims suggests that alternative processes can be created by identifying the dependencies in the process and considering what alternative coordination methods could be used. Therefore, looking for dependencies and coordination methods is a useful start to process analysis and redesign.

Many organizational researchers have studied dependencies and coordination. In this chapter, we draw on the typology presented by Crowston (chapter 3 in this volume), who categorized dependencies between activities by examining how the activities use common resources. Not surprisingly, knowledge-intensive work is often coordination intensive. Knowledge workers within an organizational hierarchy are often asked to adjudicate conflicting claims on resources in order to maintain acceptable levels of process performance. Consider a company where an account executive (AE) develops job quotations for customers and is also responsible for supervising the quality of internal work required to complete that job. In this role the AE coordinates a process that crosses the boundary between the company and its customers—managing a flow dependency that critically affects the usability of the company's output to its customer as well as the usability of the customer's input (e.g., the quote) to the company. It is not difficult to see how the success of the AE's organization depends greatly on the success with which the AE manages this dependency. In this chapter we will consider an example of such as cross-boundary dependency in some depth to illustrate our process-analysis technique.

11.2.3 Specialization

The final conceptual tool is specialization. A specialization hierarchy organizes objects from most general to most specific, with a parent object having more specific objects as children. In our technique, processes (and activities) are arranged in a specialization hierarchy. When applied to the domain of actions, the familiar "kind of" relation becomes "ways to." For any given activity there may be several more specific ways to accomplish it. For example, in the process of making coffee, there are many ways to perform the activity of infusing the coffee and the water (drip, perk, espresso machine, etc.). Similarly there are several different ways to grind beans or boil water. Likewise the specialization hierarchy includes entire processes, where each process is a complex entity that can inherit a decomposition from its parents. For example, the whole process of making coffee can be seen as a specialization of a more generic process of preparing hot beverages. The process of making coffee then inherits steps such as heating water, infusing the water and the flavoring, and serving.

11.3 A Coordination Theory Approach to Processes Description

In this section we describe our process-description technique in six stages. Our overall approach draws on Checkland's (1989) Soft Systems Methodology. For data collection, we draw on four field-based research traditions: grounded theory (Glaser 1967), ethnographic research (Spradley 1979), case study research (Yin 1984), and the clinical perspective in fieldwork (Schein 1987). We have found these perspectives useful because they focus on the categories and terms that process participants themselves use to describe the process while imposing a minimum level of external preconceptions on process representation.

The technique starts by setting the boundaries of the process to analyze. Second, sources of data on the process are identified and data collected. The heart of the analysis is the identification of activities, actors, and resources and dependencies between them (steps 3, 4, and 5). Finally the process model must be verified. Although we present the steps in this order, in practice, analysis and data collection are likely to be interleaved, as analysis reveals gaps in understanding, which motivate further data collection. For example, some data are necessary to set the process boundaries, while the process boundaries are necessary to bound the data collection. Similarly the steps in an analysis will be performed iteratively, as a greater understanding of one aspect of the process will suggest additional alternatives to consider in the others.

11.3.1 Source of Examples

We will illustrate our technique using examples drawn from a case study of a small marketing services company. We offer this case as a demonstration that our method has helped at least one organization. We chose this company because its core processes are simple enough to present in a chapter, yet sufficiently complex to permit a discussion of generative process design. To motivate our discussion, we will first briefly describe the company, which we will refer to by the pseudonym "MAG Services" or simply "MAG."

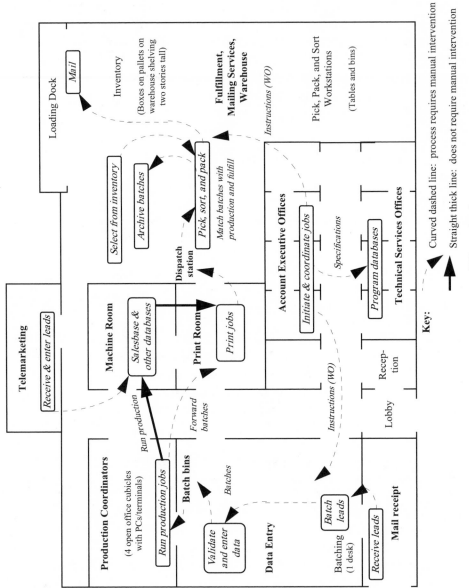

MAG Services is a wholly owned subsidiary of a direct mail company that provides mailing and inquiry fulfillment services for corporate marketing departments of Fortune 500 corporations. MAG receives requests for information about a client's product(s) from individuals and fulfills the requests by mailing out appropriate marketing materials. MAG provides two kinds of service: custom and noncustom. Figure 11.1 shows the basic workflow through MAG's facility for both kinds of job.

• In the *noncustom business*, fulfillment is similar for all clients. A typical job would work as follows. A company runs an ad in *Business Week*. The ad includes a tear-off postcard bound into it saying, "Send me more information about ..." and offering choices of products (e.g., "I want to know about blue widgets, or large widgets, or oil-resistant widgets"). On the front of the card is MAG's mailing address. A filled-out card with a return address, demographic information, and product interest arrives by mail at MAG's data-entry room. MAG mails back product brochures according to the selections made by the person who sent in the card, and collects the data from the cards to feed back to MAG's client as marketing leads. In noncustom work, jobs typically run for an extended period (usually longer than a year), mailing materials are relatively standard and supplied in bulk by the client, mailing and production tasks do not vary significantly over time, and MAG performance reporting is largely limited to tracking the number of qualified sales leads.

• *Custom business* is performed for clients on a one-time basis. An example of this nontraditional work might be a contract in which MAG provides inquiry fulfillment services following a trade show. At the show anyone passing by the booth can tear off a postcard with "Send me more information ..." on the back of it. Fulfillment of these requests is similar to the noncustom case. Based on these inquiries and other data, MAG creates a database of leads, including the addresses of people who have inquired, the inquirers' demographics, lists of prequalified leads, structured customer feedback, and the like. In contrast to noncustom jobs, these jobs run for only a limited time with a concentrated volume of work, materials may be specific to the particular job and include materials customized to the requester, and performance reporting includes both volume of contacts and measures of the quality of leads generated.

During a ten-year period in which MAG became a leader in the traditional mailing services business, the company developed a sophisticated database system that produced most of the mailings required by high-volume, standardized inquiry

Figure 11.1
Basic work flow at MAG Services

fulfillment and the reports required by long-time clients. By 1994 the company was actively engaged in applying the same database to customized services. By that year customized services accounted for more than 40 percent of revenue. However, at the same time MAG's management recognized severe operational and profitability problems with the custom business. These issues captured management's attention because custom contracts were straining the capacity of the organization and customers dissatisfied with MAG's performance on custom work were beginning to direct follow-on business to competitors. MAG managers gave high priority to custom work because they believed that it represented the area into which the company would have to grow in order to maintain its market share within the mailing services industry.

In the remainder of this section we will describe how we analyze the work done in MAG to suggest alternative processes that might be more efficient or effective, working through our technique step by step.

Step 1: Setting Process Boundaries   The first step in our analysis is setting the process boundaries. Boundary-setting involves decisions about which actors, resources, and activities are central to the analysis and which are included only as tangential links to other processes or not at all. We focus our analyses around the stated goal of the process. Activities, actors, and resources that contribute to this goal are included in the analysis; activities that are peripheral are included only abstractly or not at all. In many cases there may be multiple possibilities for the overall goal of the process. In these cases the process boundaries are particularly important because they define the "problem" and thus the scope of the solutions considered (Smith 1988).

IDENTIFYING GOALS   An obvious way to identify goals is to ask process actors why they perform process activities. However, Spradley (1979) is quite emphatic about not asking people "why" questions. He points out that intentions and motivations are subject to a great deal of rationalization as well as interviewer "demand characteristics," so much so that their reported intentions must often be handled with suspicion. Instead of asking "why," Spradley suggests asking, "Under what circumstances would you do X?" or "Describe a situation where X would be appropriate." For the top-level goals, we ask more general questions about the business purpose and overall objectives (e.g., How does this process fit into the business?). For the lower-level activities/goals, we suggest more specific questions:

1. What purpose does this activity serve? If you stopped doing it, what would happen?

2. How is (or how could) performance of this activity measured? What counts as a "good" or "bad" performance?

3. Who uses the results of this activity? What kinds of results to they find most important or helpful?

For MAG Service's custom business, these questions produced the following answers:

1. At the highest level of abstraction, MAG Services and its customers had divergent *purposes* in entering into custom business arrangements. MAG's customers wanted to find new customers through trade shows and targeted mailings, rather than waiting for customers to come to them as before. MAG wanted sales and profits to grow by generating new jobs that deliver such contacts with the promise of follow-on business. Custom-designed mailing programs were intended to satisfy both of these goals.

2. *Performance measurements* reflected the potential divergence of these goals. MAG's customers were interested in new sales based on leads generated by customized mailing services. MAG was interested in the profits from custom work and follow-on business.

3. The definition of *helpful results* differed in the same manner. Customers wanted to learn more about their markets, so as to build sales. MAG wanted to learn more about what services customers needed, but in a way that enabled the company to deliver those services at reasonable cost.

In other words, our initial study of the process suggests that at a general level this process has two divergent goals, first concerning customers' needs for specific attention to generate an explicit sets of sales leads and second concerning MAG's objectives of assembling and delivering mailings as efficiently and profitably as possible. Each of these views—customer and company—may be appropriate depending on the purpose of the analysis. The point is not whether there is a single, universal process perspective that fits all conditions, which seems unlikely; instead, the more appropriate question to ask is whether the boundary of the process chosen is appropriate for the problem the analysis is intended to address.

Furthermore, as an analysis proceeds, it may be useful to change the definition of the process boundaries under consideration. It is not a question of the definition being right or wrong as much as useful or not useful. As Checkland (1981) puts it, "the systems thinker must be able cheerfully to abandon his earlier choice of relevant systems and start again" (p. 223), perhaps shifting focus from a stated primary task to some latent issue that must continually be addressed (p. 222) or moving higher in a process decomposition hierarchy. For example, analysts considering supply chains might start with a process representation that describes one participant in the chain but might expand the analysis to include multiple flows coordinated by multiple corporate actors. For example, MAG might develop different strategic goals if it saw itself as an integral part of its customer's marketing processes rather than as a provider of standardized marketing services.

In our example, the focus of the analysis will be on the company that provides mailing services because the management problem under consideration is how to position the company for profitable growth. Other questions might lead to different boundaries (i.e., the definition of the system under study depends on the purpose of the study rather than being an inherent property of the system). For example, a study of companies that used account executives as sales coordinators might contrast MAG with several of its competitors using higher-level process maps.

Step 2: Collecting Data Building a process representation requires collecting considerable detail about many activities, goals, actors, and available resources, as described in the following sections. In this section, we describe our approach to data collection. Many data collection techniques have been proposed, which make different trade-offs among rigor, speed, cost, and accuracy. Many of the techniques focus on the question of reliability, in the sense that a second observer using these techniques should come to the same exact conclusions about the organization. Such rigor is clearly necessary for doing scientific studies where the goal is to make some generalizable assertion about how some phenomenon works in multiple settings. However, our goal here is different, as we simply want to say something about a particular site that others will find interesting or useful.

The methods we use include three central components:

1. Semistructured interviews based on understanding process decompositions, specializations, and dependencies.

2. Observation and participant observation where such approaches appear appropriate (this may include a range of participation from "stapling oneself to an order" to sitting in on meetings).

3. Iteration that encourages revisiting collected data repeatedly as process understanding grows during subsequent phases of analysis.

Likewise we examine existing data about the process, such as flowcharts of processes and process fragments, examples of documents created in the process, training manual, and even interviews with managers or narratives collected from line workers. Even if this evidence was originally collected for purposes other than process analysis, it can be used to increase understanding.

At MAG Services, we used a combination of these steps. One of the authors interviewed more than 15 members of an organization of 70 people, including all of the company's account managers, the managers comprising the top three levels of the company, and selected part-time employees (e.g., in data entry and operations). Participant observation accumulated during approximately 20 weeks over eighteen months, and was largely accomplished by a MAG Services manager whom we trained in process analysis techniques.

Step 3: Identifying Actors and Resources   As data are collected, we begin to create and fill the various categories of our description. Although we have presented this as a distinct step, in practice, data collection and analysis are likely to be interleaved (i.e., steps 2–5 overlap). In step 3, we identify the actors who execute the process and the resources used and created in the process. This step is also useful in refining the process boundaries because only activities performed by the selected actors around the selected resources will be included.

Identifying process actors who are direct human participants is relatively straightforward. Nonhuman actors are more difficult to identify. In some cases machines might be viewed as actors (e.g., "the database sorted the leads by zip code"); in others larger aggregations, such as departments, might be considered ("Sales qualified the customer"). Again, our general rule of thumb is to add detail only where necessary for the purposes of the study. For activities on or near the boundaries of the process description, aggregations may be appropriate for defining actors ("Federal Express takes the package from the loading dock . . ."), while for activities central to the process description, human and system-related actors may need to be described more specifically ("Martha reads the output from the quality testing equipment on the assembly line. She's the only one of us who knows how to interpret it, and she's almost always right"). Similarly we would tend to treat a computer system as an actor unless there was some reason to concern ourselves with the source of data or the programs embedded in the system.

To check that the set of actors is complete, we follow the work flow up and downstream, using questions like, "After you get done, to whom does this paperwork go?" or "From whom do you get your work?" The tracing can diminish (and the actors become increasingly aggregate) at the edges of a selected process boundary.

Once the set of actors is identified, we group them into classes of actors who perform similar activities in a similar fashion (i.e., who fill similar roles in the process). For example, we might chose to treat all accounting clerks or FedEx drivers as examples of a class and document how these actors work in general as opposed to in particular. A possible rule of thumb for this grouping is that any member of the group could perform a given task. At MAG Services we developed the list of actors shown in table 11.1.

Table 11.1
Actors in the MAG case

Class	Actor	Description
Customer	Customer representative	Contacts at the client company who represent client; usually staff members in a marketing department
Sales	MAG salesperson	Salesperson who initiates contact with new customers; works in a different department than the AEs
Operations	MAG account executive (AE)	Account executive who quotes, schedules, and manages traditional and customized mailing jobs; also initiates new jobs from existing customers
Data entry	Data entry supervisor	Schedules daily data entry work
	Data entry staff	Keypunchs incoming inquiries
Technical services	Database production manager	Executes data transformations to be completed on job-specific data using MAG-proprietary database
	Programmer	Provides job-specific programming for custom jobs
Mailing services	Batch dispatcher	Transfers jobs to packing/sorting tables
	Packer	Picks, packs, and sorts mailings

As the actors are being identified, we also begin to list the resources that are created by or pass between activities. Some of these may be physical objects, which are relatively easy to identify. Often, however, the key resource is information. To identify information resources, we ask what messages the actors send one another. For example, at MAG the account executives (AEs) write instructions for all the different production participants, such as data entry instructions, technical work orders (for programmers and Technical Services workers), and mailing services work orders (e.g., operations/production people in the warehouse). Resources identified in the case are shown in table 11.2.

Step 4: Identifying Activities The next stage in our analysis is to identify the activities that compose the process (i.e., what gets done in the process). Several problems must be addressed in this analysis. First, the same activities may be labeled and interpreted differently by different actors, and vice versa. Second, activities can be described at varying levels of detail. Third, the actual activities observed may vary between performances of the process, making identification of "the" process problematic. The solutions chosen for these problems have implications for understanding activities themselves and for identifying the resources that activities use.

Table 11.2
Resources used in the MAG case

Resource	Linking Actor(s)	Description
Job quote	Customer, AE	Defines scope of work approved by customer
Data entry instructions	AE, data entry	Instructs staff on data entry details
Batch(es)	Data entry, technical services, mailing services	Organizes the inquiry stream into batches that are processed by MAG's database and packed/shipped as separate units
Technical services Work order	AE, technical services	Instructs database production managers on how to sort and/or modify data
Mailing services Work order	AE, mailing services	Instructs mailing services staff how to pick, pack, and sort job
Mailing shipment	Technical services, mailing services	Physical components of mailing shipment as they are produced off bulk printers, picked, packed, and shipped

HOW TO IDENTIFY ACTIVITIES   Spradley describes an interviewing technique used by cognitive anthropologists in collecting complex information from informants (1979, esp. chs. 4–6). The basic technique comes in three parts.

1. One could ask "grand tour" or "mini-tour" questions. These are general, open-ended questions like, "Tell me about a typical day. What do you do?" A grand tour potentially covers all of the different work activities that go on in a particular task unit.

2. One could focus on more specific topics, like a particular part of the job or a particular process: "Tell me what happens when a customer comes in," and so on. One could follow up, probe, ask for elaboration, clarifications, and so on, but the basic idea is to elicit a general description of the work in the respondent's own words.

3. Having obtained a basic outline for groups of activities, it is possible to focus the contents of various "semantic domains" (Spradley 1979, p. 107). A semantic domain is like a category, which can be very high level or very low level. In understanding process decomposition, "activities" that can be decomposed into "steps in" or "parts of" the activity are important. To get at this information, one could ask a structural question: "What are all the steps in this process?" This would be followed up with various probes to check for completeness: "So far, you've mentioned the following steps: a, b, c, d, e, ..., Are there others?" At the most detailed level, all activities should be "direct," meaning something an actor can actually do (e.g., collect information or make plans), as opposed to the hoped-for outcomes of an action (e.g., lower costs) (Checkland 1981, p. 235).

The result of these investigations is a preliminary list of activities. This list will likely omit some of what the actors do. For example, two people may start each interaction by spending a few minutes discussing a previous night's game, yet not include that activity when describing the process. In general, we would follow the informants' lead in choosing whether to include such activities in the process description. It may be that these interactions are viewed by some of the individuals as necessary to the smooth running of the process, in which case they need to be included, or it may be that they are considered as secondary, in which case we would probably also leave them out.

DECOMPOSITION OF A PROCESS INTO ACTIVITIES   Given a description of an activity, a second problem is to choose the appropriate level of decomposition at which to represent it. For example, a flowchart might include one box for a particular actor's task or hundreds of boxes for the fine details of that task. Each level of detail might be appropriate for different purposes. We avoid this problem by developing process decomposition trees that show how a high-level task is decomposed into lower-level tasks, thus simultaneously representing varying levels of detail. Following our general rule of thumb, we keep decompositions at the most general possible level unless the problem to be analyzed provides a reason to decompose a process in more detail. For MAG Services, we represent 'Send mailing' as an atomic activity, but 'Run job' is broken down into at least four subactivities, including preparing quotes, setting up jobs, producing jobs, and providing status reports.

VARIATIONS ON A PROCESS   A third problem is representing variations on the process. In many processes the exact activities observed in a single instance of a process may never be repeated in all particulars. Even so, most organizational participants have little difficulty in recognizing the process as an abstract description that represents multiple instances of specific steps, both those that have happened and those that might happen in the future. This feature of organizational life can be described as inducing a generalized process from a relatively small set of observed activities by fitting observed actions into mental templates that define more abstract process steps. This translation usually forms an important part of "learning the ropes," the acculturation that orients newcomers to existing organizational characteristics and habits.

Our approach to this issue is to build a prototype sequence and then asking for variations. For example, ask the informant to describe a typical sequence of steps. Then ask: "Can you think of an example where the steps were done in a different order?" or "Under what circumstances would you do things differently?" These alternative ways of accomplishing the same activity may be "alternative specializations." A general activity (e.g., order entry) may be accomplished in several different ways, each of which is specialized for a particular purpose. One can elicit alternative specializations during an interview by asking: "Are there different ways that you accomplish this activity?" Alternatives might also be generated by identifying in the Process Handbook (Malone 1999) a more generic activity of which an identified activity is a specialization.

EXAMPLE   A decomposition of the activities in the MAG Services example is shown in figure 11.2. This figure shows a hierarchical decomposition of the process of providing MAG services, shown at the top of the page, into activities and subactivities, drawn down the page. This description shows that MAG engages in three phases of activity when handling a typical job. These phases include qualifying prospective customers, providing custom and noncustom mailing services, and billing clients.

The activity of providing mailing services is itself further decomposed in figure 11.2. The operational details of providing mailing services are normally handled by MAG account executives (AEs). The AE writes and distributes several sets of instructions inside the company so that the mailing that is produced ultimately matches the client's specifications (as approved in the quote). The AE also stays in touch with the client to ensure that MAG's services continue to be satisfactory as the job progresses. Most of the examples discussed below concern coordination managed by AEs in initiating new work on behalf of the company.

Figure 11.2 shows that MAG undertakes mailing contracts by qualifying prospective customers, providing services, and billing clients. Once prospects are qualified, the company sells its services. The sales activity ends when an AE takes an order for a job expressed within the company as a job quotation. Once the quote is approved, the AE prepares and distributes instructions that describe the job to operational departments within the company, and shows a copy of sample output from the job to the client. Finally, the operational departments execute the instructions and complete the job, which results in the collection of market information and a completed mailing. Sales and billing functions are performed in part by MAG's parent company.

Earlier we discussed an important variation in the processes that MAG Services used to deliver mailings: the difference between custom and noncustom work. Figure 11.3 suggests how this variation can be interpreted as representing variations in the Provide Services process. Figure 11.3 shows that the generic process of providing mailing services can be provided in to different ways, indicated by the two different specialized forms of the process—providing custom services and providing traditional services—drawn below on the page. Note that the specialized versions of the process have specialized versions of the subactivities as well. This comparison enables us to focus in useful ways upon the differences in producing mailings for

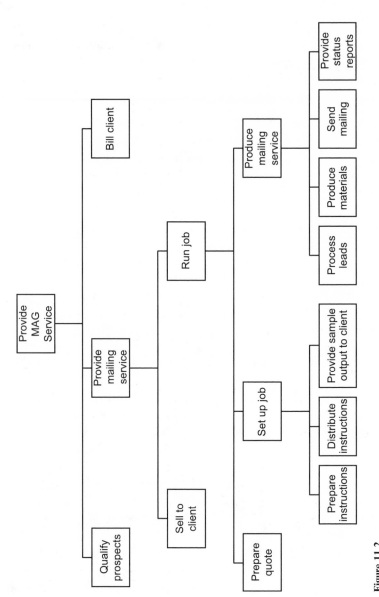

Figure 11.2
High-level process decomposition view

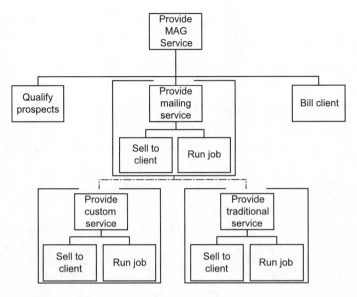

Figure 11.3
Specializations illustrate process variety

Table 11.3
Comparison of custom and noncustom work

Service	Volume	Duration	Processing	Task order	Deadlines	Contact
Custom	Potential	3–4 months	Custom	May vary	Tight	Daily
Noncustom	Certain	Year(s)	Standard	Standard	Set by MAG	Quarterly

custom and noncustom work. Table 11.3 summarizes some of these dimensions from the point of view of MAG's management.

This comparison surfaces some of the coordination challenges raised by custom jobs that a focus on production efficiency alone would not recognize. Noncustom work is long term, standardized, brings guaranteed mailing volumes, and operates against a schedule largely set by MAG. Custom work is short term, nonstandard (even with respect to the order in which specific production tasks are done), operates against tight deadlines, and requires daily contact with the customer. Custom work differs fundamentally from traditional jobs in process and coordination.

Step 5:   Identifying Dependencies   So far our technique resembles most other process mapping techniques, identifying activities, actors, and the flow of resources.

Table 11.4
Summary of initial analysis

Question	Answer
Process boundaries	Provide MAG service and its decompositions
Process goal	To generate revenue by selling company services that satisfy the needs of mailing services customers. In this sense the goal can be interpreted as providing services that convert a customer with a marketing need into a client who with a successful mailing-based marketing campaign
Process outputs	Direct mailing services on behalf of client
Process inputs	Client need for mailing services (as defined by client approval of a specific set of mailing services)
Resources	Salespeople, account executives, production staff, mailing materials, warehouse space, computer equipment, printing equipment, temporary staff, work orders, and instructions

These results for our example are summarized in table 11.4. The novel aspect of our approach is the identification of dependencies between the activities and resources and the application of coordination theory, which we discuss in this section.

Given a process description that includes goals, activities, actors, and resources, we propose two general heuristics for identifying dependencies.

1. *Dependency-focused analysis.* Identify dependencies, and then search for coordination mechanisms. In other words, look for dependencies, and then ask which activities manage those dependencies. Failure to find such activities might suggest potentially problematic unmanaged dependencies.

2. *Activity-focused analysis.* Identify coordination mechanisms, and then search for dependencies. In other words, identify activities in the process that appear to be coordination activities, and then ask what dependencies those activities manage. This approach asks directly whether all observed coordination activities are necessary.

These approaches are described and illustrated in the remainder of this section.

DEPENDENCY-FOCUSED ANALYSIS In dependency-focused analysis we examine the activities and the resources they use, determine possible dependencies by considering which resources are used by more than one activity, and then look for other activities within the process that manage these dependencies. More specifically, to identify dependencies and mechanisms, we ask questions such as the following about each activity in turn:

• What are the inputs to this activity (physical, informational and other necessary preconditions, such as permissions)? Are there flow dependencies with the activities

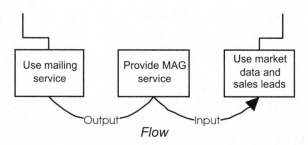

Figure 11.4
MAG Services as a step in a value chain

that create these resources? Are these resources used by other activities, creating shared resource dependencies?

• What are the outputs? Is there a flow dependency with the activities that use these resources? Do multiple activities create these resources, creating common output dependencies?

• What other resources are used, such as actors, equipment, overhead, time, and other items of importance in the process? Are there shared resource dependencies with these resources? How are these resources assigned to this activity?

• What performance problems have been reported for this process (e.g., observed divergence from stated goals)? Do these problems reflect unmanaged dependencies?

For each potential dependency identified this way, we then search for activities that manage it. The typology in Crowston (chapter 3 in this volume) is helpful, as it suggests a range of possible coordination mechanisms for each type of dependency. For example, if an activity needs a resource, then from the typology we note that the resource may be permanently assigned, taken first come–first served from a pool of resources, assigned by a manager, and so forth. A flow dependency might be managed by a single activity or the coordination mechanism might be decomposed into separate activities for managing the transfer, usability, and inventory dependencies.

To summarize, in dependency-focused analysis, we examine the use of resources in order to identify potential dependencies, and then look for activities that manage those dependencies.

Example of Dependency-Focused Analysis The analysis discussed above can be done at every level of decomposition. We will illustrate by first considering dependencies in the MAG case at a very abstract level, considering the company as a link in a value chain, as shown in figure 11.4. At this level there are several resources, such as mailings and market information, that are used by multiple activities, thus creating dependencies. The dependencies between the activities are indicated using curved lines to show the flow of resources from one activity to the next. More specifically, examining inputs and outputs suggests that MAG produces resources for the 'Using market data' activity (i.e., it provides inputs to this activity), including sales leads generated by MAG mailings and market information collected from sales inquiry forms (demographics, channel sensitivity, etc.). The 'Using market data' activity is part of some larger process, indicated schematically by the vertical lines that connect this activity to other, unshown, activities.

Taken together, these resource uses suggest two kinds of dependencies: first, a task-resource dependency between MAG's customers and MAG, shown by the fact that MAG performs certain activities on behalf of their customers, and second, a flow dependency between the activities of MAG and its customer, shown by the flow of sales that leads from MAG to the customer. We next attempt to identify the activities that manage these potential dependencies.

MAG's business starts when a customer decides to hire them to provide mailing services that leads to useful demographic data or qualified sales leads. We note that numerous activities, such as mailing marketing information, are performed by MAG on behalf of a client. Such an assignment of tasks suggests a possible task-actor dependency (a special case of a task-resource dependency). In other words, a customer needs these services but does not or cannot perform them and therefore decides to hire MAG to perform them.

The various activities needed to manage a task-actor dependency are shown in Crowston (2002). These include determining needs, identifying possible actors, collecting information, picking the best, and then assigning the task. Interestingly in this case we see the assignment from the perspective of the assigned company, as it responds to requests for information ('Sell to customer' and 'Prepare quote'), is assigned the job, and finally performs it. Likewise several other activities, such as "Qualify prospects" and "Bill client" are likely involved in managing this dependency, although, in this case, these activities were performed by MAG's parent organization. The business completes a service cycle once customers receive data in a manner that disposes them to seek more work from MAG (e.g., the 'Use market data and sales leads' process in figure 11.4). The service cycle is a process that manages a flow dependency existing between MAG's activities and those of their customers.

Coordination theory suggests that a flow dependency includes usability, prerequisite, and transfer constraints that influence process performance. Following this distinction, we can identify activities or groups of activities within the 'Provide MAG Service' process that manage such constraints (see figure 11.4). Figure 11.5 provides

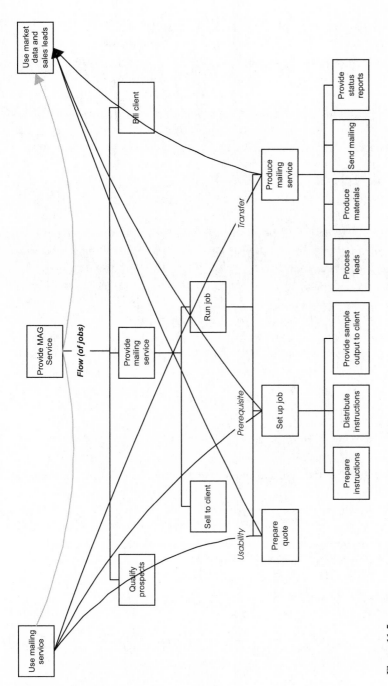

Figure 11.5
Coordinating subdependencies within the 'Run job' process

a full overview of the process representation created so far in our analysis. It includes a hierarchical process decomposition, as in figure 11.2, overlain with dependencies and coordinating activities, as in figure 11.4. In figure 11.5 we look within the 'Provide MAG Services' process to understand how subactivities manage the dependencies that act as constraints on the flow of jobs. From the customer's point of view, key variables associated with process performance appear to lie within the 'Run job' process. For example, the time dimension of MAG's performance appears to be constrained by the speed with which MAG can set up jobs and produce mailings. This implies that 'Set up job' is managing prerequisite constraints associated with the higher-level flow of jobs. The geographic nature of its work (e.g., disseminating mailings to inquirers and market data to clients) emerges clearly from the 'Produce mailing service' process. This implies that 'Produce mailing service' is managing transfer constraints associated with the flow of jobs. Preparing a quote is a critical step in ensuring that the job defined to the company is a job that will be satisfactory to the customer, which implies that 'Prepare quote' is managing usability constraints.

Figure 11.5 summarizes this analysis using a graphical notation that shows subactivities and subdependencies. The upper levels of the process representation describe MAG Services as managing a flow of resources between two of its client's processes, as discussed above. The darker arrows in the figure suggest how dependency-focused analysis moves downward within the activity hierarchy to identify coordination processes that manage subdependencies. In this case specific coordination activities manage resources associated with a subdependency that constrains the flow of jobs. 'Prepare quote' manages the *usability* of a job to a customer and to MAG. 'Set up job' ensures that the company completes the right tasks in the right sequence, thereby managing *prerequisite* constraints that affect the flow of jobs. 'Produce mailing services' generates the physical mailings that fulfill inquiries and *transfer* information back to the client. These coordination activities are summarized below in table 11.5.

Using figure 11.5 and table 11.5, we can ask how effective the chosen coordination strategies have been in practice. Table 11.6 shows the results of a coordination analysis that explicitly considers coordination strategies. It compares the effectiveness of the coordination strategies that MAG developed for noncustom business with performance observed for custom jobs. Recall that the company's existing coordination processes were designed for long-cycle, high-volume, low-variation jobs. Using our approach, it becomes possible to identify specific ways in which MAG's services are breaking down under the differing requirements of custom work. Specifically, custom business varies across dimensions such as deadlines, job complexity, and accuracy requirements in ways that MAG's existing coordination techniques are not particu-

Table 11.5
Dependency-focused analysis-coordination activities

Activity within "Run job"	Description	Purpose	Constraint managed
Prepare quote	The AE ensures that MAG is producing the exact tasks that will deliver what the customer wants	Produce the right service	Usability
Set up job	The AE prepares and distributes instructions that describe, in detail, what each functional unit with MAG must accomplish to complete the job	Produce the right service at the right time	Prerequisite
Produce mailing service	Operations completes data entry, produces the mailing, ships required materials, and distributes market data back to the client	Move the required product to the right place	Transfer

larly well prepared to handle. To illustrate, we will discuss three examples from table 11.6 in more detail. The analysis enables us to apply the notions of usability, prerequisites, and transfers to specific operations-level activities within the company. These activities represent the coordinating mechanisms that the company uses, implicitly or explicitly, to implement its services. By this means we were able to pinpoint with some accuracy how coordination breaks down within the daily work practices of the company.

QUOTES: COORDINATING USABILITY   MAG's traditional work was sufficiently standardized that AEs could successfully negotiate quotes over the telephone, taking handwritten notes that were later revised into a quotation letter signed by the customer. This approach worked well for relatively simple standard work. Custom work, however, often varies in the types of services that the customers requested, and always requires much tighter deadlines. Under such circumstances AEs did not always know how to quote jobs immediately, customers often didn't realize the cost implications of what they were asking for, and quotation letters became both delayed and increasingly controversial. In this sense, a quotation process developed for standard work proved unsuitable for coordinating quotes for custom jobs.

JOB SET UP: COORDINATING PREREQUISITES   Once a quote was complete, AEs prepared and circulated instructions for entering data and producing a job. These instructions delivered on internal forms that MAG designed for traditional work, and became increasingly dysfunctional for custom jobs. The forms were long and complex; as the custom business evolved, their options became irrelevant to the instructions that AEs needed to provide. MAG's organizational systems, in effect, were asking for the

Table 11.6
Dependency-focused analysis-coordination strategies

Dependency	Between	Managed by	Key attributes	Coordination strategy	Implications for custom jobs
Flow	Use mailing service, use market data and sales leads	Provide MAG Service	Goals: Satisfied client, profitable job Input: Job quote Output: Mailing service Resources: AEs, staff, database system, mailing system	Run job	Jobs coordinated using strategies developed for traditional, non-custom work are breaking down, leading to missed deadlines, below-target profitability, and lost business
Usability		Prepare quote, provide status reports	Key variables: Service configuration, lead times, costs	Negotiate quote with customer	Custom jobs are often so complex that the customer does not know what to ask for
Prerequisite		Set up job	Key variables: Service specification, set up time, accuracy	Prepare and distribute instructions to all operational departments	Instructions for traditional work are one-way; for custom jobs, AE does not get feedback about mistakes until it is too late
Transfer		Produce mailing service	Key variables: Delivery speed, quality, sccuracy	Process leads, pick, pack and ship mailing materials	Reporting systems were designed on a batch basis for standard work; AE cannot unravel mistakes without long delays

wrong data. Some AEs reacted to this problem by taking more time to type their own versions of instructions; others hand wrote long additions to standard company forms. Others insisted on following up all written instructions with verbal instructions. The net effect of these reactions was to slow the pace of custom work at the very time that custom jobs were requiring faster turnaround times.

MAILING SERVICES: COORDINATING TRANSFERS   MAG's internal operations were highly developed for producing standardized bulk mailings. Problems developed, however, when custom jobs required below-average batch sizes and MAG was unable to adjust. This problem surfaced when customers required AEs to report back to them on misdeliveries immediately rather than monthly or quarterly. Because MAG's reporting systems, developed for standard jobs, only traced activity by batch number, AEs had to spend hours researching potential mistakes. The net effect, again, was to slow down custom work and make MAG appear inflexible.

To summarize, in dependency-focused analysis we first identify dependencies by considering resources used or created by multiple activities. We then search for coordination mechanisms that manage those dependencies, searching through successively more detailed layers of the process until insights are gained about how process goals are implemented in practice. In a full analysis this dependency focus leads to a detailed understanding of activities that coordinate key resources associated with dependency constraints.

Activity-Focused Analysis   Our second approach to finding dependencies and related coordination mechanisms starts from the activities. Activity-focused analysis surfaces candidate coordination activities, and then looks for the dependencies that they manage. In this sense it operates inductively rather than deductively, aggregating dependencies upward through the process hierarchy to build an analysis that complements dependency-focused approaches.

In activity-focused analysis we suggest three complementary heuristics to triangulate on potentially important dependencies. These include identifying critical process tasks, identifying coordination activities, and identifying coordinators.

1. *Search for process-critical activities.* Activity-focused analysis asks which activities play a necessary role in the completion of a process; the remaining activities are likely to be coordinating these. At MAG Services, producing a mailing is a process-critical activity because it directly leads to the output desired by the customer.

2. *Search directly for coordination activities.* Activity-focused analysis examines tasks identified within a decomposition hierarchy and asks whether these activities represent coordination, namely whether they match one of the activities in table 11.1 or otherwise manage an important dependency within the process. For example, examining budget preparation cycles can identify resource allocation mechanisms; tracking the flow of chapter or other physical resources within an organization can often identify activities that manage flow dependencies.

3. *Search for actors or resources that coordinate.* Activity-focused analysis looks for actors whose work frequently suggests coordination tasks. At MAG, account executives negotiate a contract and write the instructions that define customized mailing services.

To summarize, in the activity-focused analysis, we look for activities that may implement coordination mechanisms. Candidate activities are those that are non-production, resemble coordination mechanisms, or are performed by coordinators.

Example   Figure 11.6 summarizes a search for coordinating activities at MAG Services. The illustration represents the results of the steps described above.

SEARCH FOR CRITICAL ACTIVITIES   This step asks the same question of each activity: Could the end product of the process exist without it? Of all the activities shown in figure 11.6, the only one that appears irreplaceable is 'Produce materials'. The company might use different sales processes, it can change its quoting process, it can even "send" mailings via the Internet, but jobs cannot be delivered without some production of personalized materials, be they physical, chapter, or electronic.

This focus is helpful because it offers a core from which to aggregate dependencies. If 'Produce materials' represents a key production activity in this process, the analysis can step outward from that foundation to ask what coordination other observed activities provide. From this perspective the activities related to converting client interest into instructions for producing materials (9 of the 18 activities in figure 11.6) appear to be attempts to coordinate production of mailings according to criteria that meet the performance expectations of both MAG and its customers (e.g., maximum profit with minimum time, errors, and cost).

SEARCH FOR COORDINATION   Within the 'Run job' process, the only obvious production step is 'Produce mailing service'; that is, only this step produces an output that is given to the customer. 'Prepare quote' and 'Set up job' appear to be processes that largely prepare information to ensure either that jobs meet performance criteria (e.g., 'Prepare quote') or that work will proceed error-free ('Set up job'). In other words, they appear to manage the usability of the production work found in the 'Produce mailing service' step.

Where records represent information that crosses process boundaries (i.e., they are an output that is used as input by another process), they identify potentially important flows. Thus records can form a resource within flow dependencies. By this means information-intensive activities (i.e., those that handle information used extensively by other activities) can often be understood as coordination mechanisms. Figure 11.6 shows records that cross the branches of the process tree developed for the mailing company. It describes six steps in executing a job: prospective customers produce an inquiry about mailing services, sales processes pass prospects and job proposals to MAG account executives, AEs prepare quotes in response to those proposals, quotes are converted into instructions, and instructions precede the mailings and leads gen-

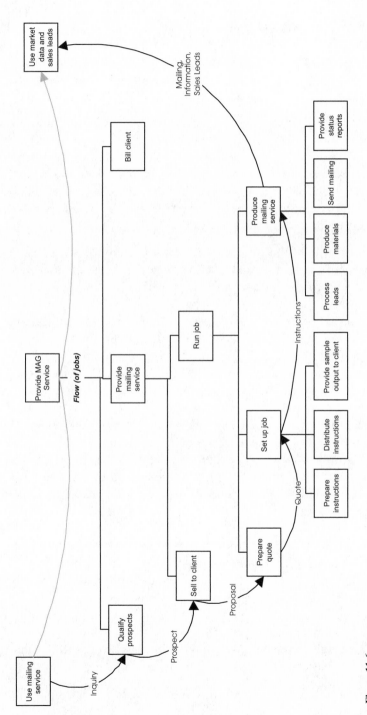

Figure 11.6
Chapter flow and resources at MAG Services

erated by a job. Each of these elements represents a resource that flows across process boundaries within MAG's operations. In figure 11.6 the 'Run job' process is shown at a lower level of decomposition because it represents internal activities over which MAG managers have greatest control (as noted above, sales and billing are performed by MAG's parent organization).

SEARCH FOR COORDINATORS   Actors perform activities that use resources. To the degree that the same actors perform multiple coordinating activities or produce resources employed by coordinating activities, they can be identified as important coordinators within a process. MAG account executives produce both quotes and instructions (resources) while performing five of the nine coordinating activities identified in the prior step. From this perspective they appear to play an important organizational role in supporting coordination.

DEPENDENCY AGGREGATION   The three steps of activity-focused analysis have so far suggested that (1) preparing quotes and instructions are at least coordination-intensive activities, (2) producing personalized mailing materials is probably a critical process step around which coordination activities cluster, and (3) AEs perform much of the coordination required to define and complete profitable jobs. These suggestions focus attention on the potential coordination provided by processes related to preparing quotes and setting up jobs.

If these coordination activities manage dependencies, it is reasonable to move one level higher in the process hierarchy and ask what coordination they perform. Doing so considers the relationship between the company and its customers as the company runs a mailing job (e.g., 'Run job'). From this perspective it appears that 'Prepare quote' manages the usability of a job to the customer and the profitability of the job to MAG; in other words, it manages usability constraints. 'Set up job' appears to manage the sequencing of activities within MAG operations (recall that three sets of instructions are prepared and distributed, one to each functional area, that direct how the functional areas are to interact during the job). In this sense 'Set up job' is managing prerequisites.

To summarize, in activity-focused analysis, we first search for activities that appear to be examples of coordination mechanisms, and then check for dependencies that are managed by these activities. This bottom-up approach offers an alternative view of the process that is complementary to the results produced by a top-down, dependency-focused perspective. Where the results overlap the two analyses offer the means for producing confirmatory evidence of coordination choices made by the organization. Either approach can confirm or disconfirm process characteristics suggested by the other. Dependency-focused analysis proceeds from the perspective of high-level goal structure, while activity-focused analysis begins with chapter flows and process artifacts that exist deep within the organization.

Step 6:   Verifying a Model   Process models may be as valuable for the insights that are developed in the process of building them as for the final process diagram. To this end verification plays a particularly important role in the techniques suggested here. We suggest two verification techniques in particular as complementary mechanisms for improving process representation and analytical accuracy.

The first of these is the negative case method (Kidder 1981). Candidate process representations are developed and discussed to discover what is missing in the representation of the process. Gaps and ambiguities identified guide further data collection. These omissions can be identified by discussing the process model as it evolves with the actors who are involved in the process—discussions that often trigger the need to go back and revisit various process representation decisions made earlier.

Triangulation provides a second opportunity to verify the faithfulness of process representations. We use the term to refer to the ways in which process models are discussed with process actors. The emphasis here complements the negative case method by assessing what process elements appear to generate broad representational agreement from groups of process participants. Representational accuracy, in this sense, can be corroborated by broad agreement among process participants.

Negative case analysis and triangulation are included here to highlight the importance of internally consistent verification of process models, context descriptions, and analyses by the individuals who participate in the process themselves. Since any organizational process is open to differing interpretations by each of its participants (Hackman 1969), and since even the problems that processes are designed to "solve" are open to definition-by-interpretation (Weick 1969), subjective verification may be the best consistency-control available to field teams.

From a research design point of view, the dangers of subjective verification, even by multiple respondents, are well known (Yin 1984). It is important to recognize, however, that managers and other professionals working within organizations face the same limitations in understanding observed behavior: for them, low-level subjective consensus represents one key mechanism whereby groups jointly interpret events. Iterative, multiple-source verification (e.g., of process descriptions) in this view represents the same level of reliability that process designers themselves must handle in actual practice. To the degree that an expanding understanding of process characteristics can add structure and consistency to process representations, the reliability of process descriptions can be improved. Absent this, however, the use of iterative, multiple-source verification seems not only an achievable means for checking descriptive fidelity but also one that very appropriately reflects real-world conditions.

11.3.2 Summary

The result of the six-step process outlined above is documentation of a process that includes activities, actors, resources, and dependencies among them, as well as identification of how the dependencies are currently managed. This process documentation can then be tested to ensure that it is reasonable, that it makes sense to people or that it can be used to communicate the process. In the next section we will see how such documentation might be useful as a basis for process improvement.

11.3.3 Using Dependency Analyses as a Basis for Process Improvement

Our main purpose in creating process representations is to support process improvements. Documenting the dependencies and coordination mechanisms of a process provides an approach to developing new processes. New activities can be proposed to manage poorly managed dependencies or alternative coordination mechanism can be considered to manage each dependency. Note that mechanisms are themselves activities, with their own set of dependencies. Replacing one mechanism may therefore eliminate some problems while creating an entirely new set to be managed.

When the custom mailing process began to break down, MAG managers responded in ways suggested by their experience with traditional, high-volume, standardized mailings. They initially fixed their attention on lowering costs by trying to make custom jobs run as smoothly as the standardized noncustom work. They focused on rearranging the company's internal production processes (e.g., the steps by which MAG sorted data and prepared mailings). Unfortunately, this perspective meant that the cures initially suggested for the custom business proved worse than the disease, as it missed the need for flexibility demanded by customized contracts.

Our analysis suggests ways in which to modify coordination strategies and the tools used to implement those strategies. For example, dependency-oriented analysis might to suggest ways in which AEs can redesign the quoting process to reduce project lead-times. Activity-based analysis, however, can contribute useful detail describing how to redesign a quotation *form* to be used in describing the cost of services to clients over the telephone. Taken together, the two approaches can contribute guidance to information systems development designed to resolve the timing and flexibility problems identified as threats to the custom business. Dependency-focused analysis can contribute to clarity of process purpose, while activity-focused analysis can contribute insight about implementation detail.

The process analysis performed for MAG services as part of this project led to prototypes of process improvements. After completing the analyses described above, the organization developed software based on a commercially available groupware package to experiment with making three changes in the Run Job process.

First, the software provided AEs with cost estimates for any combination of mailing tasks, using an interface that enabled them to build accurately costed job quotations during a telephone conversation. The same software generated quotation letters semi-automatically. Second, the system fed data electronically to instruction forms. These forms were extremely simple in design, and accumulated operational detail only for the tasks specifically required in any one project. Last, the system provided a series of checkpoints so that AEs could electronically monitor job progress, enabling them to report back to customers on a daily basis if necessary. All three of these innovations provided a better way to ensure that the work done is what the customer requested and is correct, that is, to manage the usability portion of the high-level flow dependency discussed above. AEs reported that these design changes had the potential for increasing their capacity for custom work. At the end of our study the company was considering whether to develop a commercial version of the system.

A coordination perspective also provides some insight for goal resolution. To the degree that usability constraints threaten to be incompatible, the process coordinating them may include explicit activities devoted to resolving potential conflicts. In many organizations, for example, order-taking begins to resemble sales negotiation as activities are added to ensure that the order will be usable for both producer and consumer. In engineering-intensive businesses, the RFP (request for proposal) process can be understood in this fashion. In simpler businesses, as well, an important coordination opportunity often arises as new business enters the work flow. At MAG Services, for example, a quoting process controls how orders for customized services are placed.

More specifically, the perspective provides a mechanism for summarizing potentially divergent goals surfaced by MAG's business relationships. For example, it suggests how a customer's purpose might interact with the organization's internal goals. A customer is likely to seek to generate the maximum number of useful sales leads in the shortest available time. MAG has a need for profitable growth. In coordination terms, these goals represent *usability* constraints affecting the flow that MAG coordinates. Each mailing service, this representation implies, must remain usable to both the customer and to the supplier—that is, it must provide sales leads that satisfy some range of customer criteria yet remain profitable to MAG.

11.3.4 Trade-off Matrices

Likewise the models can serve as a basis for articulating the trade-offs available between different versions of a given process. Trade-off matrices contrast process characteristics across different versions of a process. Consider the variations of the 'Run job' activity. One version of the process refers to selling traditional business;

the second refers to selling custom jobs. The dependencies underlying the coordination analyses above apply to both but the strategies employed for coordinating these dependencies differ. The trade-off matrix in table 11.4 suggests some of the ways in which the two types of business compare. The comparison suggests ways in which process performance can be improved by redesigning the ways in which process dependencies are coordinated.

For example, the trade-off matrix suggests that coordinating custom projects is more time-sensitive than initiating noncustom work. This comparison implies that if the company could facilitate AEs' and clients' understanding of the cost implications of custom services, the logistics and productivity of MAG's custom services might be enhanced. Analyzing usability, transfer, and prerequisite dependencies suggests a range of alternatives for improving communication among AEs, customers, and operations staff in all stages of job definition and execution, extending from technology-intensive solutions such as an on-line job definition system that allows new customers to design their own customized service to relationship-intensive solutions such as pairing operating staff with AEs in custom-project teams.

11.4   Discussion

To put our contribution into perspective, we will conclude by briefly comparing our work to other process analysis techniques and evaluating our technique.

11.4.1   Comparison to Other Process Analysis Techniques

Process design and coordination problems have been approached from diverse perspectives, including economics, organization theory, computer science, ecology, and general management theory. We will briefly review alternative approaches (some of this material is adapted from Malone et al. 1993).

Perhaps the simplest form of a process description is a concise verbal account. Such accounts are commonly used and have the advantage that little or no special training is needed to produce or understand them. However, there are two key problems: first, it is difficult to check a verbal description for completeness or consistency; second, verbal descriptions do not easily suggest the space of possible improvements. Therefore most analysts use a more formal representation, as do we. It is interesting to note that soft systems methodology uses "all the verbs in the English language" (Checkland 1981, p. 164) for building conceptual models, but the goal of these models is to "generate radical thought" (p. 170) and deliberately not to be descriptions of the actual system.

A PERT chart provides a detailed representation of a process, specifying the exact activities taken, when they begin and end, sequence dependencies between activities, and even which actors or resources are involved with which activities. PERT charts have one major drawback for the purpose of process improvement: they usually are used to present or plan a single execution of a process and do not represent the range of possible alternatives. However, our representation captures many of these details, such as dependencies between activities and the use of resources.

Managers and analysts interested in improving processes often use some version of a flowchart to represent process characteristics. Flowcharts drop some information of a PERT chart but still indicate the activities to be performed, the order in which they are performed, and may include information on who does each activity or how long an activity takes to perform. However, they are not especially good at suggesting alternative activities that accomplish the same ends, at demonstrating feasible alternative activity sequencing, or at projecting what changes might be required if different actors performed selected activities.

Our representation is most similar to a dataflow diagram, which represents the steps of a process but focuses on the ordering relationships imposed by the fact that data produced by some steps must be used by others (e.g., Yourdon 1989). Many dataflow techniques, such as IDEF0 and SADT, include decomposition as a key aspect. These representations are similar except they do not represent the full range of dependencies nor explicitly note the coordination mechanisms.

To represent processes involving multiple actors, we may want to focus on the interactions among the actors. One approach to modeling interacting processes is suggested by *Petri nets* (Peterson 1977) and various representations derived from them (e.g., Holt 1988; Singh 1992). A Petri net is similar to a finite state machine but allows multiple states to be "marked" simultaneously. Transitions between states may be synchronized, since multiple states may have to be marked at the same time for a particular transition to occur. To the extent that the activities we model have multiple inputs, then our representation can be seen as equivalent to simple Petri nets, although we do not take advantage of that fact.

A second approach to representing multiple actors is to represent the process followed by each individual separately, using any of the techniques described above and explicitly modeling the exchange of information or objects between them. For example, the modeling technique developed by Crowston (1991) represents individual actors as programs written in logic. These actors can perform a variety of actions to achieve their goals, including speech actions to change the states of other actors. We believe that such representations could be used as a basis for simulating processes, thus providing a more detailed approach to examining trade-offs.

11.4.2 Evaluation

While the technique proposed in this chapter embodies a theory, it does not provide a way to test the theory. Indeed, Checkland (1981) argues that methodologies cannot be proved to work (or not to work) in the scientific sense (p. 241). Instead, the evaluation of the technique rests on how well it accomplishes the two goals we set out in the introduction: generativity and ease of use. The technique is a success if analysts can use it and if they find it provides insights into the process and how to change it. These two tests might partially trade off against each other: for example, if the technique provides unique insights, then analysts might be willing to undergo more of a learning process.

As a further test of our technique, one of the authors taught coordination theory and versions of the methodology to four courses and two project teams over three years, totaling approximately 70 master's level students. Learning and applying our methodology occupied six to eight weeks of each course. Approximately half of the students were managers employed in a variety of industries and enrolled in a part-time MBA program. Students were required to redesign a process based on their analysis and to develop an information systems prototype that would support that redesign. Over all, they completed more than 40 process design projects, based on observations and analyses at large and small companies. The result was fairly consistent process innovation that exceeded the expectations of project participants. Our teaching experiences underline the paradigm shift need to think about organizational processes. It has been difficult for participants to make the transition from focusing on inputs (e.g., strategies and resources) and outputs (e.g., organizational results) to focusing on the processes that derive those outputs. Likewise dependency analysis has been the most confusing aspect of methodology, hence our focus on it in this chapter.

11.5 Conclusion

To conclude, we will briefly discuss the implications of our focus on dependencies for the design of analysis tools and the practice of managers and other process analysts.

11.5.1 Suggestions for Design of Tools

The approach presented in this chapter has strong implications for the design of process analysis tools. Many CASE (computer-assisted system engineering) tools can represent a decomposition hierarchy of activities. Some could handle the dependencies linking activities and resources. However, none that we know of explicitly represent the link between coordination mechanisms and the dependencies they manage. For example, to assist analysts building such representations, it would be handy to be able to drag an activity on to a dependency to indicate that the dependency is managed by that activity or to click on a dependency and pop up the list of alternative specializations.

Since dependencies arise from shared use of resources, the representation of an activity could include an indication of the resources they need from which the system could automatically figure out some dependencies. For example, if two activities need a resource of which there is only one known instance, then the system might suggest resource-sharing mechanisms; if there is no known resource, it can suggest resource procurement mechanisms. If the resource is an actor, then a task assignment mechanism is needed. As an example, we are currently using these techniques to compile a Handbook of organizational processes at a variety of levels and in different domains (Malone 1994). Managers or consultants interested in redesigning a process could consult the handbook to identify likely alternatives and to investigate the advantages or disadvantages of each. Coordination theory makes the Handbook feasible by providing a framework for describing more precisely how processes are similar and where they differ.

11.5.2 Implications for Practitioners

Even though many people have documented and studied organizational processes, our approach to this problem is novel in important ways. Most important, in analyzing a given process, we identify the key activities that must be performed for the goal to be achieved, the resources created and consumed by these activities, and the dependencies between them. We define the managing of these dependencies as the coordination activities, and we postulate that there will be a set of generic coordination processes (and their various specializations) that will appear over and over in different processes.

By identifying the various types of dependencies and the generic processes for managing them, we believe that we can create more concise process descriptions. A second benefit, however, is that this approach can help us generate new possibilities for processes. If we know that in general, there are several possible coordination processes for managing a given dependency, then we can automatically generate all of them as possibilities for managing that dependency in any new process we analyze. Some of these possibilities may be new or not obvious, and their generation requires no specific knowledge of the process other than the type of dependencies it involves.

The choice of coordination mechanisms to manage these dependencies results in a variety of possible organizational forms, some already known and some novel. The relative desirability of mechanisms is likely to be affected by the use of new information systems. For example, the use of a computer system may make it easier to find existing solutions to a problem, either in a database or from geographically distributed coworkers. Such a system could reduce both duplicate effort and coordination costs.

IV PROCESS REPOSITORY USES

So far we've seen the basic concepts upon which the Process Handbook is based and a variety of kinds of content in the Handbook. But what good is all this? What can you do with it? In this section we present a number of representative examples of how the concepts, tools, and knowledge base we have developed in the Process Handbook can be used.

The section is divided into three parts, corresponding to the three kinds of uses we have emphasized so far: business process redesign, knowledge management, and software design and generation.

Business Process Redesign

The first part begins chapter 12, by Klein, Herman, Lee, O'Donnell, and Malone, which describes a methodology for inventing new organizational ideas by first analyzing the "deep structure" of the process in question, and then generating many possible alternative "surface structures" for the same deep structure. The chapter shows how using the Process Handbook significantly enhances the power of this methodology. The chapter illustrates these concepts by showing how we used the Process Handbook and this methodology to generate new ideas for how to do hiring in a financial services firm. See Krushwitz and Roth 1999 for a detailed "learning history" of this organizational redesign research project.)

Chapter 13, by Bernstein, Klein, and Malone, describes an automated tool called the "Process Recombinator" that automates part of the methodology described in the previous chapter. The Process Recombinator uses the Process Handbook database to automatically generate new process ideas (new "surface structures") by recombining elements already present in the database. While we don't believe that such tools will completely replace human creativity anytime soon, this chapter suggests intriguing possibilities for how they can enhance it.

Chapter 14, by Klein and Dellarocas, describes a new methodology and an extensive body of Process Handbook knowledge about the kinds of *exceptions* (or "process failures") that can occur in business processes. The methodology provides a systematic way to analyze a process for potential failures and to fix or prevent them from occurring. The chapter applies the methodology in analyzing a real business process crisis involving the unauthorized foreign currency trades that led to the bankruptcy of Barings Bank.

Knowledge Management

The second part of this section focuses on applications that, while they involve some aspect of process redesign, place more emphasis on using the Process Handbook to manage knowledge. This part begins with a brief article, by Carr, about the Process Handbook project that appeared in *Harvard Business Review*. In it are summarized the goals of the project, and a brief description is provided of an early commercial use of the Process Handbook at Dow Corning Corporation.

Chapters 16 and 17 emphasize research—rather than commercial—applications of the Process Handbook for knowledge management. Chapter 16, by Klein, describes how the same concepts of exception management that were described in chapter 14 by Klein and Dellarocas can be applied to problems in large multi-person design projects such as those for airplanes and cars. The chapter shows how a growing repository of knowledge can be developed about possible problems to anticipate in such multi-person design projects and how to avoid these problems.

Chapter 17, by Yoshioka, Herman, Yates, and Orlikowski, describes how the researchers have used the Process Handbook concepts to categorize various communication "genres" within organizations, and also the Process Handbook software tools for documenting and storing their results. This chapter thus illustrates, on a small scale, an important aspect of the vision with which we began this book: how the creation of very precise and explicit taxonomies of organizational actions can help advance organizational theory.

Software Design and Generation

The third part focuses on using the Process Handbook concepts and tools to design and/or customize complex software systems using libraries of preexisting software components. Chapter 18, by Dellarocas, continues the theme of chapters 4 and 10 by Dellarocas, and describes the tools Dellarocas has developed for generating software programs. The chapter includes, for instance, a language for representing the "deep structure" of a software architecture and a "design assistant" for automating parts of the process of generating actual programs from such architectural descriptions.

Chapter 19, by Bernstein, proposes a prototype implementation of a flexible software environment for service organizations (e.g., banks) that is analogous to a CAD/CAM tool for manufacturing organizations. Such a system would allow users to easily reconfigure a flexible set of software building blocks for each different customer or situation. In a sense, then, such a system would allow for the "mass customization" of previously rigid services.

This idea is extended in the next chapter. Chapter 20, also by Bernstein, describes a prototype implementation of a system that allows a great deal of flexibility in using many different kinds of software tools. Here, however, the emphasis is not on tools for providing services to external clients but on tools for supporting cooperative work among groups of people. Interestingly, this system allows users not only to change the way that different software components fit together but also to easily change the amount of support the system provides in the first place: from extensive automated support for highly formalized processes (e.g., an ERP system) to much more limited (but also more flexible) support for completely ad hoc processes (e.g., a simple e-mail system).

IVA *Business Process Redesign*

12 Inventing New Business Processes Using a Process Repository

Mark Klein   Elisa O'Donnell
George A. Herman   Thomas Malone
Jintae Lee

12.1   The Challenge: Coping with Constant Change

It is by now a cliché to talk about how rapidly things are changing in business. Hardly a year goes by without new threats, new opportunities, and new concepts clamoring for managers' attention: globalization, restructuring, e-business, m-commerce, knowledge management, and on and on (Abrahamson 1996; Abrahamson and Fairchild 2000). To some extent, of course, these terms are just buzzwords that represent changes in management fads more than changes in the underlying realities of business. But the seemingly insatiable appetite for new management concepts is driven, in part, by what seems to be an ever-accelerating rate of real change in many aspects of business. Large, successful companies have to innovate continually to remain successful. Small innovative start-ups can become market leaders in a matter of months or years, and they can become bankrupt almost as quickly (Davenport and Perez-Guardado 1999; Davenport 1994, 1995; Glasson 1994).

Of course, many kinds of management capabilities (not to mention a healthy dose of luck!) are needed for success in this environment. But one critical need for innovative companies is the ability to repeatedly generate new ideas about how to meet their business challenges. Such new ideas can, of course, come from many different sources, and some people and organizations seem to be "naturally" better at generating them than others (Boden 1990; Stefik and Smoliar 1995). Wouldn't it be nice, however, if we had a more systematic way of generating such ideas?

In this chapter, we focus on one such systematic approach to generating new business ideas. The key idea of our approach is that a richly structured on-line repository of knowledge about business processes can significantly enhance the creativity of process designers by helping them systematically explore many alternative combinations of process elements. Such an approach could, of course, be used with purely random combinations of process elements. However, by structuring the knowledge repository using a rich network of empirically based process templates, we greatly increase the likelihood that useful alternatives will be generated.

While this approach will certainly not transform all workers into creative business geniuses, we believe it has the potential to increase the ability of almost anyone (or any organization) to reliably generate new and promising possibilities for innovation. We focus here only on the *generation* of these new ideas. The successful *implementation* of the ideas is also, of course, a very important—and very difficult— task, but it is not the focus of this chapter.

The approach we will describe in this chapter is based on two primary elements. First, it relies upon a new theoretical perspective for understanding the *deep structure* of business processes and systematically exploring alternative *surface structures* for realizing these processes. Second, the approach uses a cumulative on-line knowledge repository (which we call a "process handbook") that contains numerous business process patterns and case examples organized according to this new theoretical perspective. Together, these two elements can help people systematically generate novel combinations of existing process components, and provocative analogies with structurally similar, but superficially different, situations. They can also speed the rate of knowledge sharing about innovative ideas (and "best practices") even when no novel combinations are created.

We proceed as follows in the rest of the chapter. In section 12.2 we briefly describe previous work on process generation and innovation. In section 12.3 we describe our approach in detail, including summaries of the key ideas from the Process Handbook project (Malone et al. 1999) and coordination theory (Malone and Crowston 1997) upon which our approach is based. In section 12.4 we illustrate our approach with an extended case study involving the redesign of a hiring process. We conclude in section 12.5 with an evaluation of the work to date and a discussion of future research.

12.2   Background: Previous Approaches to Process Innovation

The most systematic and explicit previous approaches to process innovation come from the literature on business process redesign (Armistead and Rowland 1996; Chen 1999; Davenport and Short 1990; Hammer and Short 1990; Grover et al. 1995; Hammer and Champy 1993; Kettinger et al. 1997b; Kubeck 1995, 1997; Nissen 1998, 1999; Pandya and Nelis 1998). For example, Kettinger et al. (1997b) provide an extensive survey of process redesign practices. Their stage activity framework proposes six stages of business reengineering: 'Envision', 'Initiate', 'Diagnose', 'Redesign', 'Reconstruct', and 'Evaluate' stages. The most relevant for the topic of this chapter is the redesign stage where the new process is defined and selected from among the alternatives.

Kettinger et al. (1997b) categorize the existing tools for this redesign stage as follows:

• Creativity techniques (brainstorming, out-of-the-box thinking, nominal group, visioning, etc.)

• IDEF modeling technology

• Process simulation—variation of process variables such as cycle time, queuing times, inputs/outputs, resources.

• Data modeling—data flow diagramming, flowcharting, case-based information engineering tools.

Only a few of these tools, however, genuinely address the generation of new design. For example, data modeling helps one analyze a given process, but it does not offer much help in redesigning or creating a new process model. Indeed, as Hammer and Champy (1993) point out, reliance on analytical techniques can have just the opposite effect, resulting in "analysis paralysis." Several of the techniques identified by Kettinger et al. (1997b) are explicitly oriented toward search (e.g., brainstorming) while benchmarking (Camp 1995; Committee 1992) helps with the generation of new alternatives by providing the designer with a set of cases that can be used as a template. However, none of these techniques provides any assurance that combinations of ideas are being systematically explored (Lee and Pentland 2000).

Those tools that do support *generation* of new designs are the creativity techniques. These techniques are useful in producing novel ideas, but since they rely only on what happens to be on the minds of the participants, they are unlikely to support *systematic* exploration of the alternatives (Lee and Pentland 2000; Pentland 1995).

Our approach, in contrast, provides a systematic means of designing new processes by finding and customizing cases and patterns selected from a richly structured repository of process knowledge. The advantages of this approach are that (1) it often takes less work to define a process since we are just customizing an existing one rather than designing from scratch, and (2) there is a better chance of producing an innovative high-quality process because it is based on a review of a wide range of practices, including for example those that leverage emerging phenomena such as the Internet. This approach thus offers the potential of designing better processes with less effort.

12.3 Our Approach: Analyzing Deep Structure, Then Generating Alternative Surface Structures

12.3.1 What Is the Deep Structure of a Business Process?

One way of understanding our approach is by an analogy with the concepts of "deep structure" and "surface structure" from linguistics (Chomsky 1965; Winograd 1981). For a linguist, a sentence has both a "surface structure" and a "deep structure." The surface structure of a sentence is the particular sequence of words it contains. The deep structure of the sentence is the underlying meaning of the words. And the same deep structure, or meaning, can often be expressed by a number of different surface structures. For example, the two sentences "John hit the ball" and "The ball was hit by John" have different surface structures but the same deep structure. In fact the rules of grammar can be viewed as rules for generating alternative surface structures for a given deep structure.

By analogy, one could think of a business process (or any collection of activities) as having both a surface structure and a deep structure. The surface structure is the specific sequence of activities that occur in a particular situation. The deep structure is the underlying "meaning" of the process, that is, its underlying goals and constraints.[1] And the deep structure for a process can have many different possible surface structures. That is, there may be many quite different sequences of actions that all achieve the same basic goals and satisfy the same basic constraints. (See Lee and Pentland 2000 for a detailed formal analysis of the "grammars" that can be used to generate many alternative sequences of actions from a single "deep structure" representation of a business process.)

Figure 12.1 shows an example of the surface structure of two different—highly simplified—processes for selling cars. Both processes have the same deep structure: tires are made by one activity and then flow to another activity where the cars are sold. In one surface structure, the cars are made only after an order is received, and then shipped directly to the dealers where the cars are sold. In the other surface structure, the cars are made and stored in inventory until ordered. Then, when the order is received, they are removed from inventory and shipped to the car dealer. Thus, in these two cases, two different *coordination processes* ('Make to order' and 'Make to inventory') are used to manage part of the same underlying flow dependency.

12.3.2 Overview of the Methodology: Systematically Generating New Process Alternatives

The design methodology we propose consists of the following three steps:

1. *Analyze* the deep structure of the process you want to create.

---

1. This sense of "deep structure" is different from the sense in which it was recently used in the organizational literature, namely as hidden part of systems behavior in organization responsible for the regulation of social interactions (Gomez and Jones 2000; Giddens 1986; Gersick 1991; Schein 1980). On the other hand, the work on task or domain ontologies (e.g., Mi and Scacchi 1996; Lee et al. 1998; Guarino 1998; Swartout and Tate) could be viewed as attempts to identify the generic vocabulary needed for describing the deep structure.

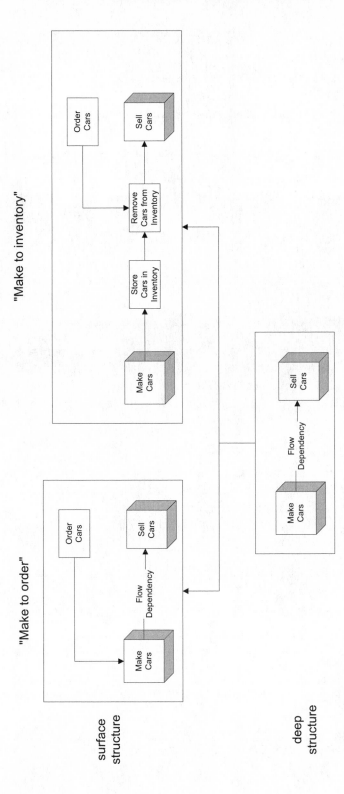

Figure 12.1
Surface structures of two different business processes with the same deep structure. (Activities shown in unshadowed boxes are part of the coordination processes for managing the flow dependency.)

2. *Generate* a set of potentially viable alternative surface structures for this deep structure.

3. *Select* from this set the processes that best match your particular needs.

In order to apply this methodology, we need a conceptual structure that helps us move back and forth between deep structures and surface structures of business processes. It would be possible to use this methodology "manually" without any computer-based tools, but it is also very useful to have tools to help us apply the methodology more efficiently, comprehensively, and systematically. The MIT Process Handbook project provides both a conceptual structure and a set of tools for applying the methodology.

12.3.3   The Process Handbook

The goal of MIT Process Handbook project (Malone et al. 1999) is to produce a repository of process knowledge represented and organized in such a way that users can quickly retrieve and effectively exploit the process knowledge relevant to their current challenges. The Process Handbook has been under development at the MIT Center for Coordination Science for over nine years, including the contributions of a diverse and highly distributed group of over forty university researchers, students and industrial sponsors (see Malone et al. 1999 for more detailed descriptions of the project and the theoretical concepts in the remainder of section 12.3). The current repository has over 5,000 process descriptions ranging from specific examples (e.g., all finalists for the MIT eBusiness Awards for the past three years) to more generic templates (e.g., for supply chain management, product design, and sales). A number of software tools for editing, storing, and viewing this knowledge, in a stand-alone mode and over the Web, have been developed (e.g., see Bernstein et al. 1995; Dellarocas 1996; Bernstein et al. 1999).[2]

The Process Handbook operationalizes the concepts of deep structure and surface structure in terms of *process specialization*. We view the *generalization* of a process as its deep structure and its alternative *specializations* as alternative surface structures. The next section describes these concepts in more detail.

12.3.4   Process Specialization

Practically all process representation techniques (including ours) use the notion of decomposition: that a process can be broken down (or "decomposed") into sub-

---

2. The technology has also been licensed by MIT to Phios Corporation (*www.phios.com*), which has developed commercial products based on the MIT research described here.

activities. Our representation includes, in addition to this, the concept of specialization. While a subactivity represents a *part of* a process; a specialization represents a *type of* (or way of doing) the process (Taivalsaari 1996; van der Alst and Basten 1999; Wyner and Lee 2000).

By this concept, processes can be arranged in a hierarchical network with very generic processes at one extreme and increasingly specialized processes at the other. Figure 12.2 illustrates this approach. Here the generic activity called 'Sell product' is decomposed into subactivities like 'Identify potential customers' and 'Inform potential customers'. The generic activity is also specialized into more focused activities like "Sell by mail order" and "Sell in retail store."

These specialized activities automatically *inherit* the subactivities and other characteristics of their "parent." In some cases, the specialized processes also add to or change the parts they inherit. For instance, in 'Sell by mail order', the subactivities of 'Deliver a product' and 'Receive payment' are inherited without modification, but 'Identify prospects' is replaced by the more specialized activity of 'Obtain mailing lists'. Decomposition and specialization can, of course, be applied to activities at any level.

We have found the "process compass" shown in figure 12.3 to be a useful way of summarizing the two dimensions. The vertical dimension represents the conventional way of analyzing processes: according to their different *parts*. The horizontal dimension is the novel one: analyzing processes according to their different *types*. From any activity in the Process Handbook, you can go in four different directions: (1) *down* to the different parts of the activity (its "subactivities"), (2) *up* to the larger activities of which this one is a part (its "uses"), (3) *right* to the different types of this activity (its "specializations"), and (4) *left* to the different activities of which this one is a type (its "generalizations").

From this point of view, our methodology amounts to starting with a process, moving left to its deep structure, and then moving right again to generate many alternative surface structures. If you think of a generalization as a "parent," then the alternative surface structures we generate are analogous to the siblings, aunts, uncles, and cousins of the process with which we started.

Also, from this point of view, there are not just two levels (a "deep structure" level and a "surface structure" level). Instead, there can be many different levels of increasingly deep structures. We can think of the processes at the far right of the specialization tree as the most "superficial" surface structures and those at the far left as the most "deep" deep structures.

Bundles and Trade-off Tables   We have also found it useful to combine specializations into what we call "bundles" of related alternatives. Generally speaking, bundles

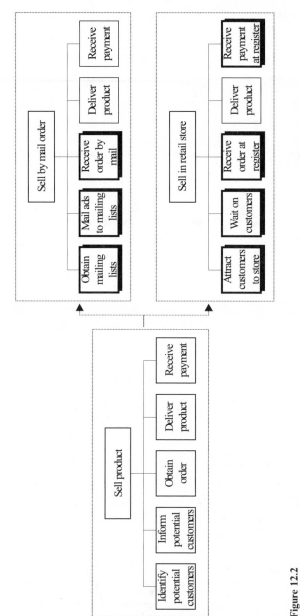

Figure 12.2
Sample representations of three different sales processes. The deep structure of selling is represented by 'Sell product', and two alternative surface structures are represented by its specializations: 'Sell by mail order' and 'Sell in retails store'. Subactivities that are changed in the specializations are shadowed.

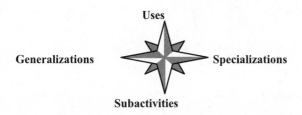

Figure 12.3
"Process compass" illustrating two dimensions for analyzing business processes. The vertical dimension distinguishes different *parts* of a process; the horizontal dimension distinguishes different *types* of a process.

represent alternative answers to the question posed in the bundle. One can thus speak of "who" bundles (which represent different alternatives for who performs an activity), "what" bundles (which represent different alternatives for the resource being manipulated by the activity), and so on. In this sense bundles are similar to the cases in linguistics (Fillmore 1968, 1975; Winograd 1986).

Bundles can have associated trade-off tables that capture the relative pros and cons of the alternative specializations in terms of their ratings on various criteria. A specialization tree so structured can be viewed as a decision tree. If one wants to find a process with given attributes, one traverses down from the root, and at each bundle selects the one or more branches that seem to match what one is looking for. This property will prove important when we use the specialization tree to support process (re-)design.

12.3.5 Core Activities and Dependencies

One very important aspect of the deep structure of a process involves the core activities and the relationships among them. To represent this aspect of process specialization, we draw upon the notion from coordination theory that *coordination* can be viewed as the management of task *dependencies*, and that different types of dependencies can be managed by different *coordination mechanism* (see Malone and Crowston 1994). Dependencies arise from resources (e.g., parts, documents, and signals) that are used by multiple activities. We typically analyze dependencies using three elementary dependency types: flow, sharing, and fit (Crowston 1991; Zlotkin 1995; see figure 12.4). Flow dependencies arise whenever one activity produces a resource that is used by another activity. Sharing dependencies occur whenever multiple activities all use the same scarce resource (e.g., when two people need to use the same machine). Fit dependencies arise when multiple activities collectively produce a single resource (e.g., when several designers create subcomponents for a single system).

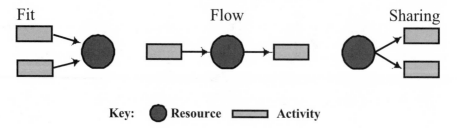

Figure 12.4
Basic types of dependencies among activities

Table 12.1
Examples of dependencies and associated coordination mechanisms

Dependency	Examples of coordination mechanisms for managing dependency
Flow	
Prerequisite ('right time')	Make to order versus make to inventory ('pull' vs. 'push') Place orders using 'economic order quantity', 'just in time' (kanban system), or detailed advanced planning
Accessibility ('right place')	Ship by various transportation modes or make at point of use
Usability ('right thing')	Use standards or ask individual users (e.g., by having customer agree to purchase and/or by using participatory design)
Sharing	'First come–first serve', priority order, budgets, managerial decision, marketlike bidding
Fit	Boeing's total simulations, Microsoft's daily build

The relationships represented by dependencies are managed by processes called coordination mechanisms. As table 12.1 illustrates, there are a number of alternative coordination mechanisms potentially applicable for each kind of dependency (see Malone et al. 1999 for more details).

12.3.6   Advantages of This Approach

The two key concepts of process specialization and dependencies have a number of significant benefits including conciseness and generativity. The specialization hierarchy can substantially reduce the amount of work necessary to represent a new process. By simply identifying a more general process that the new process is intended to specialize, most of the information about the new process can be automatically inherited and only the changes need to be explicitly entered. In addition, instead of having to explicitly list all the coordination activities separately in each different process, we will be able to simply indicate that "the dependency between activities *A* and *B* is managed by an instance of coordination mechanism *X*." These concepts provide a framework within which users can generate process alternatives. Users can find more general instances of the same process (parents) as well as closely related alternatives (siblings and cousins). We can also generate new alternatives by considering alternative coordination mechanisms for managing key dependencies.

12.4   Case Example: Generating Innovative Ideas for the Hiring Process

To illustrate the use of our methodology, we will use examples based on a field study we conducted in collaboration with one of our corporate research sponsors, the AT Kearney consulting firm, and one of their clients, which we call Firm A to preserve the client's anonymity (for more detailed descriptions of this study, see Malone et al. 1999; Kruschwitz and Roth 1999).

Firm A was experiencing increasing problems with their hiring process. They were growing rapidly in a tightening labor market, and they had a culture of independent, competitive business units. Together, these factors led to increases in the time and cost to hire people and to increasingly frequent instances of business units "hoarding" candidates or bidding against each other for the same candidate. In an effort to improve their hiring process, the organization had invested a great deal of time and energy into "as is" process analysis using conventional techniques such as flowcharting. But they also wanted some way to come up with highly innovative ideas about how to improve their process. We next investigate how each of the stages of our methodology can be used in this situation.

12.4.1   Analyzing Deep Structure

The purpose of deep structure analysis is to identify the core activities and key dependencies of the process one wants to (re-)design. In the absence of the Handbook database, one could find a process deep structure by starting with a candidate process (e.g., the process that is currently used, if one is re-designing an existing process) and repeatedly replacing its activities and dependencies by more abstract versions that represent "why" the surface activities are there. Eventually one will end up with a set of core activities that appear essential to the process, connected by a minimally sufficient set of dependencies.

The Handbook database can greatly simplify this procedure by allowing us to find the process(es) in the database that are most similar to the initial target process. The processes to the left of that point then represent increasingly deep structures for the original process, and those to the right represent alternative surface structures.

In Firm A's case an "as is" model of their hiring process had already been developed before we began working with them. Their "as is" model consisted of the four

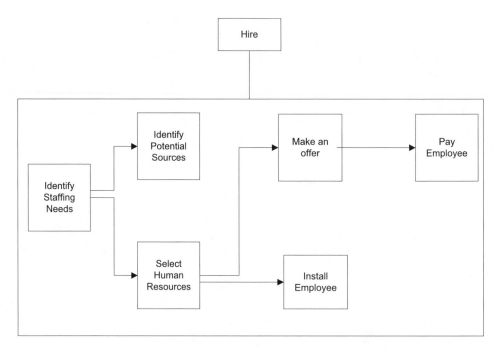

Figure 12.5
Deep structure for 'Hire'. The arrows represent the flow dependency among the components.

steps "identify need," "source and select," "enrollment," and "physical installation." Since our Handbook database already has a generic "hire" process (see figure 12.5), it is straightforward for us to treat Firm A's process as a specialization of this more generic one. One immediate insight from looking at this representation of the deep structure of the hiring process was that the initial "as is" diagrams developed by Firm A had left out the step of 'Pay employee'. When the employees of Firm A saw this representation in the Handbook, they agreed that they should have included this in their initial "as is" analysis.

12.4.2 Generating Alternative Surface Structures

The 'Generate alternatives' step involves generating the set of surface structures that represent potentially viable candidates for achieving a particular deep structure. This is done by identifying the dimensions along which the surface structures can be varied, identifying all the values for each dimension, and then considering some or possibly even all combinations of these values. We thereby define a multidimensional design space in which every point represents a potential surface structure.

Table 12.2
Siblings of the subactivities in the firm A's hire process

Company	Interesting practice
Marriot	Voice response system for candidates which screens and pre-qualifies
AES Corp	Let employees do the hiring
Doubletree	Identifies employee success dimensions and seeks to hire candidates with same traits
BMW	Use of simulations to select new hires (assembly line)
Cessna	Role playing and simulations for executive hires
Best Software	On-line recruitment management software to post jobs and route resumes
Monsanto	Active policy of seeking candidates at conferences

Recall that a process consists of sequenced activities inter-related by dependencies, and that dependencies are managed by coordination mechanisms. There are thus three main dimensions along which alternative surfaces structures can be generated: (1) alternative specializations for a given activity, (2) alternative coordination mechanisms for managing a given dependency, and (3) alternative sequencings for the activities in a process:

Alternative Activity Specializations   Specializations of an activity can be found by generating answers to key questions about the activity such as *who* performs the activity (i.e., the actor), *how* the activity is performed (i.e., the activity decomposition), *where* the activity is performed, and *when* the activity is performed. Using the Handbook, one does not have to imagine all the answers to these questions unaided. Instead, one could browse the specialization tree to the right of the activity to uncover a potentially large number of alternative variations and examples of the activity. One could also look at the alternative specializations for all the parts (and subparts) of the activity that is of interest.

For example, table 12.2 shows a number of examples of "interesting practices" represented in the Handbook as specializations of the 'Select human resources' part of hiring. The employees of Firm A found several of these examples to be quite intriguing stimuli for innovations they might try.

Alternative Coordination Mechanisms   The space of alternative coordination mechanisms for a dependency can be found, as with activity specializations, by generating potential answers to a set of key questions. In this case, however, the key questions include:

• What type of dependency is involved (i.e., flow vs. sharing vs. fit) (Malone et al. 1999).

• When are the activities performed? Options here include the source activity for the dependency must end before the target activity starts, or the source and target activities can overlap in time. These timing options can be formalized using a temporal logic such as that proposed in (Allen 1981; Lee et al. 1998).

• Where do the activities occur?

• What type of resource gives rise to the dependency? The alternatives can be selected from a resource type taxonomy (Fadel et al. 1994; Lenat 1995) and can include such options as divisible or nondivisible, consumable or nonconsumable, and so on.

• How much of the resource is involved?

As with activity specializations, a preexisting knowledge base of coordination mechanisms can greatly simplify the identification of alternatives by providing a set of possibilities. In the Firm A hiring process, for example, there is a dependency between identifying the staffing need (typically done by a manager) and finding candidates that can satisfy that need (done by recruiters). The coordination mechanism typically used is a requisition form sent by the manager to the recruiters on an ad hoc basis, and thus is a kind of 'Make-to-order' process.

An alternative coordination mechanism, accessible as a sibling of 'Make to order' in the Handbook database, is 'Make to forecast'. This process suggests that we create staffing requisitions in response to an overall business plan instead of based on individual manager's requests. Another possibility is suggested by looking at "options markets," which is a specialization of 'Make to forecast'. The notion here is that we can requisition items (in this case employees) when the item is inexpensive, in anticipation of needing the item later when it may be more expensive due to greater general demand.

Alternative Orderings   Another dimension for generating new processes is to re-order the sequence in which the activities occur. The ordering of the activities must, of course, satisfy the "core" prerequisite dependencies inherited from the process deep structure, but aside from this we have complete latitude to change the surface structure dependencies and, therefore, the activity ordering. In the hiring process, for example, the only core dependency is that selection occurs after sourcing. We can re-order the other activities to suggest novel alternatives; we can, for example, place the 'Install employee' step before the 'Enroll' step, which implies that we install the employee (i.e., for a trial period) before deciding to hire him or her.

Keeping Track of the Alternatives Generated   These methods for generating process alternatives can be applied recursively, in the sense that the new activities and

Table 12.3
Multicolumn table for hire process alternatives

Identify staffing needs	Identify potential sources	Select human resources	Make offer	Install employee	Pay employee
Manager Computer-agent People-in-need Standards Committee	Internet Search firm Advertising Self-identification	Aptitude or other success dimensions Interview On-line group screen individual Trial Internship Probation Qualification Certification Education Reference check	Packaging— RPQ Electronic requisition Electronic catalog Blanket order	Standards Customize	Salary Stock options Benefits

dependencies generated can in turn have further subalternatives defined in the same way. We wind up, in any case, with several dimensions of variation (one for each dependency and activity, plus one representing alternative re-orderings of the activities) plus one or more values for each dimension.

We have found that a multicolumn menu represents a convenient metaphor for deriving all the surface structures that can be defined given the alternatives defined by the steps above. An example is given in table 12.3. Each column represents a dimension of variability, and the items in the columns represent choices along that dimension. Process alternatives are then generated by selecting one (or sometimes more) choices from each column. If one does this exhaustively, one can typically generate very many alternatives from all the possible combinations involved.

While these tables can always be constructed manually using knowledge from the Handbook, we have also developed a specialized software tool, called the Process Recombinator that automatically generates such tables and then automatically creates specific combinations based on the user's selections (Bernstein, Klein, and Malone 1999). Figure 12.6 shows a screen shot from this tool showing the selection made for each of the dimensions.

12.4.3 Looking Even "Deeper"

So far we have seen how one can go to the most obvious deep structure representation of a process ("hiring" in this case) and then generate alternative surface

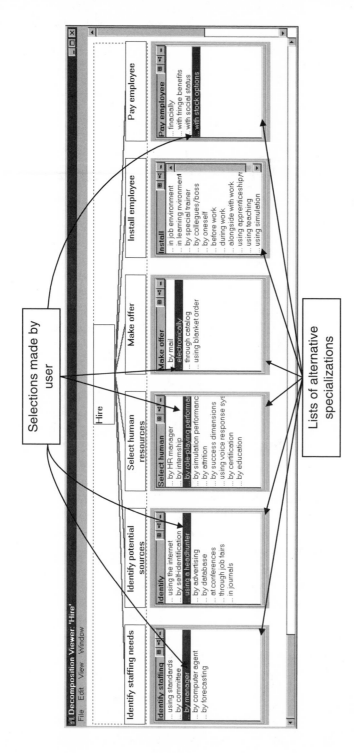

Figure 12.6
Subactivity recombinator user interface

structures. Sometimes the most interesting ideas, however, come from looking at deep structure representations that are even "deeper" than the most obvious ones. In the case of hiring, for example, if we look further left in the specialization tree we see that "hiring" is classified as a specialization of "buying" (figure 12.7).

Based on this observation, we can then get even more potentially interesting ideas by examining some alternative specializations (surface structures) of the generic "buy" process. For example, table 12.4 shows some alternative "interesting practices" for buying represented in the Handbook. These examples suggest, for instance, the possibilities of having different hiring processes depending on the kind of employee (by analogy with Acer's strategy) or using corporatewide hiring standards (à la Motorola).

One can go even farther, for example by looking at specializations of 'Sell', the sibling to 'buy', and the great-uncle to 'Hire' in the specialization tree (table 12.5). These suggest such interesting ideas as letting a company 'Test-drive' a potential employee (à la Cessna/BMW) before making a full-fledged hiring commitment, or data-mining a database of comments from people who applied to work at a company in order to develop a more effective process of "selling" the company to potential employees (à la New Pig).

This process can be carried all the way left in the specialization tree to extremely generic activities: such as 'Create', 'Destroy', 'Modify', 'Preserve', 'Combine', and 'Separate'. If we consider these as means of hiring, we come up with options like:

• *Hire by creation.* Breed employees (as in family-owned businesses or monarchies).

• *Hire by destruction.* Eliminate unusable employees. Hire everyone, and let go any who don't pass muster (as in the Armed services).

We refer to examples like these as "distant analogies"; such analogies represent a particularly powerful property of specialization trees as applied to process design. Generally speaking, the more distant an analogy we consider, the more creative the innovations we are likely to uncover, but the greater the risk that the process idea may prove inapplicable to our problem.

In this case, when we originally did this analysis (several years ago), the idea of buying via the Internet suggested the possibility of hiring via the Internet. Even though this now seems obvious, at the time it was a very novel and interesting idea. Some time later, we generated another—even wilder—idea based on this case example: What if, just as there were on-line auctions to "buy" things, there could be on-line auctions to "hire" people? For several months, we used this in presentations as an example of a wild idea, generated by our methodology, that might someday be useful.

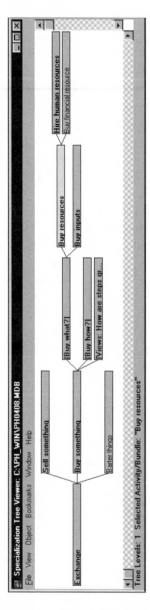

Figure 12.7
Specialization tree generalizations for hiring process

Table 12.4
Selected interesting specializations of the 'Buy' process

Company	Interesting practice
Motorola	Consolidation of suppliers for commodity purchases
	Corporationwide agreements on quality audits, metrics and rating system
	Corporate summaries aggregate track record on all suppliers (on quality, inventory turns, etc), used by line managers
	Partners with selected suppliers to develop products
	Continuous replenishment of inventory
Acer Group	Different sourcing strategy by type of input (computer component)
Trade Wave	Find source and price by logging into Internet and soliciting bids over Web
GE	Trading process network matches buyers in company with suppliers worldwide
Womex	Creates electronic catalog of worldwide manufacturers

Table 12.5
Selected interesting specializations of 'Sell' process

Company	Interesting practice
Chase Manhattan	Customer database—identifies opportunity for cross selling; looks at customer transactions to identify most profitable
Home Depot	Customer intimacy through a central buying database
New Pig	Data mines customer feedback
Cessna/BMW	Lets customer test drive products before buying them

Within less than a year, however, we began to hear about a whole new category of very well-funded Internet startup companies to do exactly this: to provide on-line auctions for employees and contractors! This example therefore provides at least an "existence proof" that our methodology can be used to generate new ideas that have significant practical potential.

12.4.4 Selecting Alternatives

Once a number of alternatives have been generated, one needs to select the ones that appear best suited to one's particular challenges. There are many ways this can be done, but we found that the following approach works well. First, we identify the requirements we are attempting to satisfy by uncovering the key variables and their desired values. In the hiring domain, for example, we found that the key variables included the type of person we want to hire (one with widely available "commodity" skills rather than a senior person with highly unique skills), the quality of the employee hired, the cost and speed of the hiring process, and so on. This analysis thus uncovers the different requirements sets (in this case there are two), each of

Table 12.6
Trade-off table for 'Identify candidates' activity along the 'where' dimension

Identify candidates 'where'	Speed of reaching candidates	Breadth of access	Cost	Quality of candidates
Internet	****	*****	****	***
Search firm	*****	****	*****	*****
Newspaper advertising	**	**	***	***
Self-identification	**	**	***	*****

Note: Greater number of asterisks indicate greater desirability.

which can potentially be achieved using different hiring processes. We then use trade-off tables and other tools to help assess the relative worth of the alternative surface structures implied by the multicolumn tables.

For example, let us consider the case of hiring senior employees. Since we do not want to explore the many potential alternatives blindly, it makes sense to identify the top candidates from each column and then consider at first just the different combinations of those options. We can do this using trade-off tables. The trade-off table for the 'Identify potential sources' activity, for example, is shown in table 12.6. This table suggests that relying on the Search Firm maximizes candidate quality, but using the Internet has advantages in terms of the speed of search and the breadth of access.

If we continue this analysis for all the columns in the table, we come up with two top candidates for surface structures for the senior employee hiring process, one where the applicant approaches the firm and the other where we are finding replacements for an existing position (figure 12.8). We can then produce a trade-off table that compares our two candidate hiring processes with respect to the requirements we identified earlier (figure 12.9).

The entries in the trade-off tables can be generated by combining information from the trade-off tables entered for the component alternatives in the multicolumn tables, by soliciting the judgment of specialists in the process domain (Human Resources experts, in this case), and potentially even by simulating the candidate surface structures using simulation tools. The Handbook includes an evolving interchange format called PIF (the Process Interchange Format) (see chapter 21 in this volume) whose intent is to allow Handbook process descriptions to be exported easily into existing simulation and other process analysis tools. Note, however, that this approach currently produces potentially applicable but not necessarily viable combinations; there may be interactions between choices in the different columns that make a given set

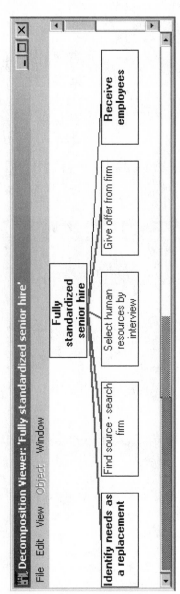

Figure 12.8
Two alternative surface structures for the senior employee hire process

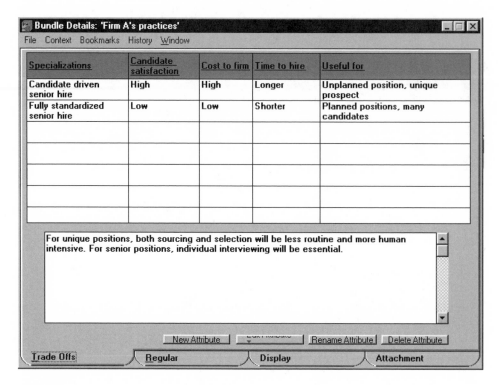

Figure 12.9
Trade-off table for 'Hire' process alternatives

of choices unworkable. The methodology does not automatically prune out invalid combinations for you—this requires human judgment.

12.5   Conclusion

12.5.1   Summary of the Methodology
We can summarize the process design methodology as follows: We (re-)design processes by finding a reasonable starting point in the process specialization tree and then generating/exploring the tree, using a set of key questions, to uncover siblings and more distant analogies for each of the core activities and coordination mechanisms. We can also generate alternative orderings of these activities. These alternatives are then organized as a set of multicolumn tables to make the different potential surface structures explicit as selections from each column. We next use

trade-off tables to guide our selection of individual column choices, as well as eventually our choice among the candidate surface structures for re-designed processes.

Although the process design methodology has been described here as a linear sequence where we abstract out the deep structure completely before generating and then selecting alternatives, these different steps can be interleaved arbitrarily. One can, for example, create a candidate process re-design by replacing an activity with a "sibling" (child of a common parent generalization) or even a "cousin" (child of a common grandparent generalization). This involves, in effect, applying the steps of deep structure analysis, alternatives generation, and selection to a single activity. These steps can also been done to any level of detail; one can generate "high-level" processes or very detailed ones, depending on to what extent the activities and dependencies are refined by adding decompositions and coordination mechanisms.

12.5.2 Evaluation and Future Work

The methodology described above has been used to (re-)design several processes, of which the hiring example described above is one. Our experience is that the methodology, when used in conjunction with the Process Handbook knowledge base, has been very effective in generating a wide range of novel and promising process design alternatives. The power of this approach appears to come from several sources:

• The methodology's recursive application of key questions (who, what, when, where, etc.) fosters the systematic exploration of the space of alternative surface structures.

• The use of "distant analogies" helps uncover farther-flung and potentially powerful re-formulations of the process.

• The process knowledge base allows users to leverage the creativity and expertise of process experts from many different domains. The methodology could be utilized, however, even if we did not have such a knowledge base.

Our process design approach offers, we believe, significant advantages over other process design methodologies. It adds, in effect, some science to what today is mainly an art. As discussed earlier, few of the commonly used process re-design methods address the aspect of generating new alternatives. Those that do suggest simple rules of thumb for streamlining an existing process or recommend locking a design team in a room with a facilitator to brainstorm a new "blank-paper" process. Or they focus on incremental changes despite the usual rhetoric typically associated with business process redesign or reengineering (Jarvenpaa and Stoddard 1995). For example, Harkness, Kettinger, and Segars (1996) found that many process redesign efforts are based on Total Quality Management techniques, which adopt an inherently incremental approach (Mizuno 1988). Other approaches also typically call for an exhaustive analysis of the as is situation (Nissen 1998), which ours does not (although such analysis may well be needed for different purposes such as cost justification).

The Process Handbook and its process design methodology is a work in progress. The generative strength of the methodology is, in particular, a double-edged sword in the sense that it is often easy to uncover an overwhelming number of process alternatives. The procedures are not fully formalized, so human judgment is often needed, for example, to identify core activities and key dependencies, to generate alternatives not represented in the database, to prune out the nonviable surface structure candidates, and eventually select the appropriate processes for one's needs. While we do not expect to obviate the need for human judgment, we do plan to explore how the system can support human users by further reducing the burden of generating and selecting from large design search spaces. For the meantime the general sense of those of us who have used the Handbook is that potentially "too many" options is preferable to "too few."

Other future efforts will include evaluating and refining the process design methodology in other domains (including logistics and manufacturing). Further information on the Handbook and links to several publicly available on-line versions of it are available at the following Web site: *http://ccs.mit.edu/ph*.

Acknowledgments

We would like to thank Jeff Huang and Michael Smith, who participated in the field project described in this chapter. We also thank Martha Broad and John Quimby for their help. Parts of this chapter appeared previously in Malone et al. (1999) and Bernstein et al. (1999). The work was supported, in part, by the National Science Foundation (Grant Nos. IRI-8903034, IRI-9224093, and DMI-9628949) and the Defense Advanced Research Projects Agency (DARPA). It was also supported by the following corporate sponsors: British Telecom, Daimler Benz, Digital Equipment Corporation, Electronic Data Systems (EDS), Fuji Xerox, Matsushita, National Westminster Bank, Statoil, Telia, Union Bank of Switzerland, Unilever, and other sponsors of the MIT Center for Coordination Science and the MIT Initiative on "Inventing the Organizations of the 21st Century." The software described in this paper is the subject of the following patents owned by MIT and licensed to Phios Corporation: US Patent Nos. 5,819,270 and 6,070,163; European Patent No. 0692113.

13 The Process Recombinator: A Tool for Generating New Business Process Ideas

Abraham Bernstein
Mark Klein
Thomas W. Malone

13.1 The Challenge: Designing Innovative Processes

Most management observers today agree that the successful organizations of the twenty-first century will need to be able to develop new business processes more rapidly than they have in the past. In order to take advantage of rapidly changing markets and technologies, companies will need to continually keep developing new processes and new ways of using technology.

But where will the ideas for these new processes come from? Today's business process design tools provide little or no support for generating innovative business process ideas. The available tools are primarily limited to *recording* existing processes in some formal representation (e.g., flowcharts) or to *analyzing* proposed processes (e.g., using quantitative simulations).

Today's business process designers therefore rely almost entirely on their own intuition and experience to generate new process ideas. The typical result of this situation is that relatively few alternatives are generated, and the ideas that do emerge often tend to be quite similar to practices already familiar to the designers (Ulrich and Eppinger 1995, p. 79).

This chapter describes a new approach to this problem, based on the notion that new ideas are most often novel combinations of old ideas. The key idea in our approach is that a richly structured on-line repository of knowledge about business processes can enhance the creativity of process designers by helping them systematically explore many alternative combinations of process elements. The approach can also be used with purely random combinations of process elements. By structuring the knowledge repository as a rich network of empirically based process templates, however, we greatly increase the likelihood that useful alternatives will be generated.

We have termed our tool for implementing this combinatorial innovation process the "Process Recombinator." We built the Process Recombinator as an add-on to the MIT Process Handbook (Malone et al. 1999). The next section provides a brief overview of the Process Handbook and the theoretical concepts upon which it is

An earlier version of this chapter appeared in A. Bernstein, M. Klein, and T. W. Malone (1999), The process recombinator: A tool for generating new business process ideas, *Proceedings of the International Conference on Information Systems*, Charlotte, NC, December 13–15, 1999. © 1999 ACM. Reprinted by permission.

based. Section 13.3 describes the use of the Process Recombinator with examples from a field study. Section 13.4 evaluates the contributions this work has made and concludes with a discussion of possible directions for future research.

13.2 The Process Handbook

The Process Handbook has been under development at the MIT Center for Coordination Science for over ten years, including the contributions of a diverse and highly distributed group of over forty university researchers, students and industrial sponsors (see chapter 1 for more detailed descriptions). The goal of the Handbook is to develop a repository and associated conceptual tools to help users effectively retrieve and exploit the process knowledge relevant to their current challenges. Currently the project focuses on the repository's application to business process re-design, sharing knowledge about business processes, and automatic software generation. The current repository has over 5,000 process descriptions ranging from specific examples (e.g., a Mexican beer factory, an automobile parts manufacturer, and a university purchasing department) to more generic templates (e.g., for logistics, concurrent design, resource allocation and decision techniques). A Windows-based tool for editing the Handbook repository, as well as a Web-based tool for viewing it have been developed (Bernstein et al. 1995). We have applied the Handbook to process re-design in collaboration with a management consulting firm and others. The successful outcomes of these experiences led to the development of the Process Recombinator.

The Process Handbook takes advantage of two simple but powerful theoretical concepts to organize process knowledge: *process specialization*, and the notion of *dependencies and their coordination mechanisms*.

13.2.1 Process Specialization

Practically all process representation techniques (including ours) use the notion of decomposition: that a process can be broken down (or "decomposed") into subactivities. Our representation further includes the concept of specialization. While a subactivity represents a *part of* a process; a specialization represents a *type of* (or way of doing) the process.

Using this concept, processes can be arranged in a hierarchical structure with very generic processes at one extreme and increasingly specialized processes at the other. As in object-oriented programming, the specialized processes inherit properties of their more generic "parents," except where the specialized processes explicitly add, delete or change a property. Unlike traditional object-oriented programming, how-

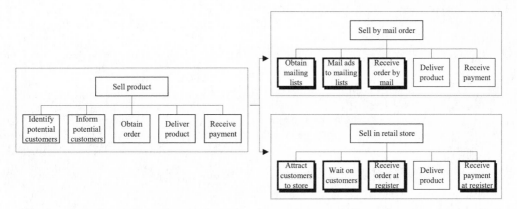

Figure 13.1
Example of inheritance in specialization hierarchy (changed subactivities are shadowed)

ever, our inheritance is organized around a hierarchy of increasingly specialized processes (verbs) not objects (nouns).

The generic activity called 'Sell product', for example, can be *decomposed* into subactivities like 'Identify potential customers' and 'Inform potential customers' (illustrated in figure 13.1). It can also be *specialized* into variations like 'Sell by mail order' and 'Sell in retail store'. These specialized activities inherit many subactivities from their "parent" process, but also typically include changes as well. 'Sell in retail store', for instance, replaces 'Identify potential customers' by the more specialized activity 'Attract customers to store'.

We have found it useful to group specializations into what we call "bundles" of related alternatives. Figure 13.2 gives two examples of such bundles in the specialization hierarchy for the 'Sell product' process. One bundle ('Sell how?') collects alternatives for how the sale is made (direct mail, retail storefront, or electronically), while the other ('Sell what?') concerns what is being sold (beer, automotive components, etc.) Generally speaking, bundles represent different dimensions along which processes can be classified.

Bundles can also have associated trade-off tables that capture the relative pros and cons of the alternative specializations in terms of their ratings on various criteria. Figure 13.3, for example, shows such a trade-off table for the specializations in the 'Sell how?' bundle; specializations are the rows, criteria are the columns, and the cell contents are the values for each criterion and specialization.

Entries in trade-off tables can be generated by academic research, empirical observation, or soliciting the judgment of specialists in the process domain. A specialization

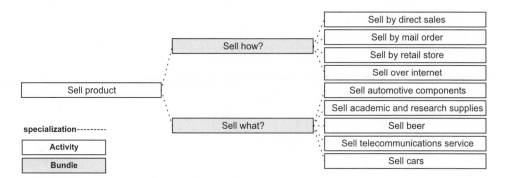

Figure 13.2
Example of bundles in the specialization hierarchy

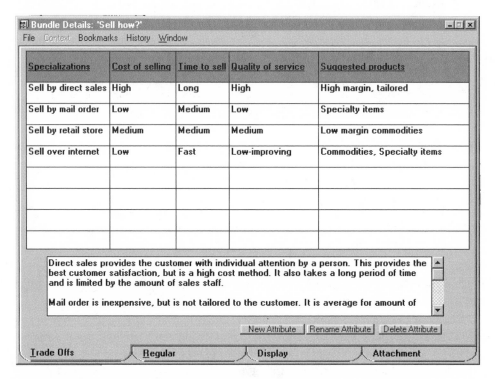

Figure 13.3
Example of a trade-off table (note that these particular values are for illustrative purposes only)

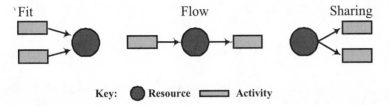

Figure 13.4
Three basic types of dependencies among activities

tree so structured can be viewed as a decision tree. If users want to find a process with given attributes, they can traverse from the root, and at each bundle select the one or more branches that seem to match what they are looking for. This property will prove important below when we use the specialization tree to support process (re-)design.

13.2.2 Dependencies and Coordination Mechanisms

The second key concept we use is the notion from coordination theory that coordination can be viewed as the management of task *dependencies* each managed by their own *coordination mechanism* (see Malone and Crowston 1994). Dependencies arise from resources (e.g., parts, documents, and signals) that are used by multiple activities. We typically analyze dependencies using three elementary dependency types: flow, sharing, and fit (Crowston 1991; Zlotkin 1995); see figure 13.4. Flow dependencies arise whenever one activity produces a resource that is used by another activity. Sharing dependencies occur whenever multiple activities all use the same scarce resource (e.g., when two people need to use the same machine). Fit dependencies arise when multiple activities collectively produce a single resource (e.g., when several designers create subcomponents for a single system).

The relationships represented by dependencies are managed by processes called coordination mechanisms. There is a wide range of coordination mechanisms potentially applicable for each kind of dependency. Managing a flow dependency, for example, usually involves making sure that the right thing (usability) arrives at the right place (accessibility) at the right time (timing). A tire supplier and a car manufacturer, for example, have a flow dependency between them. This flow consists of three parts: First tires have to be transported from the supplier to the manufacturer (i.e., tires have to be made *accessible* to the car manufacturer. Second the tires have to be manufactured before they can be attached to the car (i.e., the tires have to arrive at the *right time*). Finally the tires delivered actually have to match the car

Table 13.1
Examples of dependencies and associated coordination mechanisms

Dependency	Examples of coordination mechanisms for managing dependency
Flow	
Prerequisite ('right time')	Make to order versus make to inventory ('pull' vs. 'push')
	Place orders using 'economic order quantity', 'just in time' (kanban system), or detailed advanced planning
Accessibility ('right place')	Ship by various transportation modes or make at point of use
Usability ('right thing')	Use standards or ask individual users (e.g., by having customer agree to purchase and/or by using participatory design)
Sharing	'First come–first serve', priority order, budgets, managerial decision, marketlike bidding
Fit	Boeing's total simulations, Microsoft's daily build

(i.e., their *usability* has to be ensured). A flow is managed when all of those parts are managed. As table 13.1 shows, two possible coordination mechanisms can be used to manage the prerequisite part, for example, 'make-to-order' (a variant of which is called 'just-in-time' production) and 'make-to-inventory' (where a stockpile of the product is created in anticipation of future demand). These mechanisms can be applied to almost any domain.

An example of a sharing dependency is the management of room usage. An often-used mechanism for ensuring the management of this dependency is 'first come–first served'. As soon as someone signs up for use of the room it is booked. However, most other processes for managing scarce resources could be applied to managing the room's usage.

Microsoft's daily build (see Cusumano and Selby 1995) is an excellent illustration of managing a fit dependency. Given the need of components of the operating system to fit each other, Microsoft chooses to ensure their compatibility by forcing their co-functioning in a daily build, which is then used as a baseline the next day.

13.3   The Process Recombinator

The Process Recombinator is a software tool that uses the Process Handbook to support a process innovation methodology as described above. This methodology consists of three key steps (Herman et al. 1998 contains a detailed explanation of the methodology):

1. *Identify* the core activities and the key dependencies (i.e., the *deep structure*) of the process you want to redesign, using the process specialization hierarchy.

2. Systematically *generate* a set of alternative refinements (i.e., *surface structures*) for the tasks and dependencies in this deep structure model, by "recombining" existing or newly generated alternatives for these process components.

3. *Select* from this set the process(es) that appear to best satisfy your requirements, possibly using information stored in trade-off matrices.

We will describe how these steps are accomplished in the sections below. The capabilities underlying steps 1 and 3 are part of the original set of Process Handbook tools, so we will summarize them quickly and then focus on the Recombinator capabilities of step 2.

To illustrate the capabilities of the Recombinator tool, we will use examples based on a field study we conducted in collaboration with one of our corporate research sponsors, the AT Kearney consulting firm, and one of their clients which we call Firm A to preserve the client's anonymity (for more detailed descriptions of this study, see Malone et al. 1999; Herman et al. 1998; Kruschwitz and Roth 1999).

Firm A was experiencing increasing problems with their hiring process. They were growing rapidly in a tightening labor market, and they had a culture of independent, competitive business units. Together, these factors led to increases in the time and cost to hire people and to increasingly frequent instances of business units "hoarding" candidates or bidding against each other for the same candidate. In an effort to improve their hiring process, the organization had invested a great deal of time and energy into "as is" process analysis using conventional techniques such as flowcharting. But they also wanted some way to come up with highly innovative ideas about how to improve their process.

The Recombinator was completed after the field study. The examples shown here demonstrate how the tool now supports the manual process that was followed in the field study.

13.3.1 Identifying the Process Deep Structure

The first step in our methodology is to identify the *deep structure*, that is, a process model that captures the essence (the core activities and key dependencies) of the process we wish to redesign. This maximizes room for new ideas by abstracting away nonessential features. The Handbook supports this via the specialization hierarchy. Users can either select an existing generic process from the hierarchy or create a new one. Since Firm A wanted to improve their hiring process, we use the "Hire" process as the starting point for our example scenario (see figure 13.5).

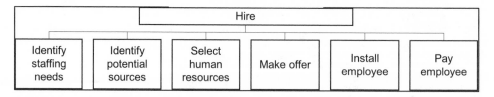

Figure 13.5
The deep structure for 'Hire'

13.3.2 Process Recombination

The next step is to find alternative ways (i.e., different *surface structures*) for implementing the generic activities and coordination mechanisms identified in the deep
structure model. This is achieved by the Process Recombinator, which includes three
parts. The three parts can be used independently; each allows systematic exploration
along a different set of process design dimensions. First, we will look at the *subactivity recombinator*, which generates all possible combinations of the specializations of the subactivities in the process. Next, we will consider the *dependency
recombinator*, which generates different combinations of coordination mechanisms
for the process dependencies. Finally, we will look at the *bundle recombinator*, which
generates different combinations of the alternatives in the dimensions represented as
bundles.

   This order of usage was chosen for illustrative purposes only, however. The three
parts of the Recombinator can be used in different sequences depending on one's
needs.

The Subactivity Recombinator   The subactivity recombinator lets users pick different
specializations for each of the subactivities in a process (see figure 13.6). For example, the "Select human resources" subactivity of the hiring process has specializations
such as (1) 'Select by role-playing' (e.g., a process used by Cessna to screen candidates for executive positions), (2) 'Select based on education' (a screening process
implicitly used by many management consulting firms), and (3) 'Select by attrition' (a
screening process used by universities who admit all applicants and then fail many of
them in the first year). Using the Process Handbook capabilities, users can easily see
more detailed descriptions (and other information) about each of these activities.

   As the figure shows, each subactivity is placed in a separate column, and each
column contains the alternative specializations for that subactivity. Using this display, users select the combination of specializations they want to use in creating a
new process. The system then automatically generates the new process specified. If

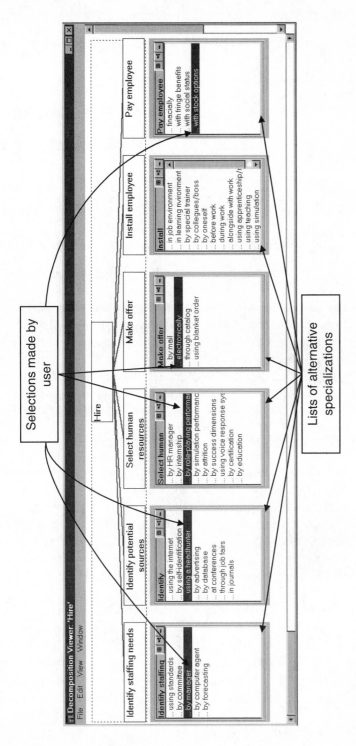

Figure 13.6
Subactivity recombinator user interface

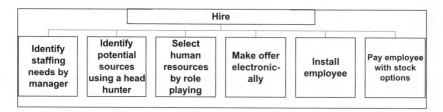

Figure 13.7
Results of using the subactivity recombinator

users make multiple selections in some of the columns, then all combinations are
generated. Figure 13.7 gives an example of the process created for the selections
made in figure 13.16. (Users who want to know more about how the alternatives in a
given column compare can click on the "trade-off" button for the column and see a
trade-off matrix for those alternatives.)

   The power of this approach is that the specialization hierarchy allows the process
designer to draw on relevant ideas and insights from many different kinds of organizations, opening the possibility of useful new combinations never before considered
in a particular setting.

The Dependency Recombinator   The dependency recombinator complements the
subactivity recombinator by allowing one to also consider alternative coordination
mechanisms for process dependencies. Instead of displaying only the subactivities of
a process, it displays both the subactivities and dependencies as a flowchart (figure
13.8).

   Every subactivity and dependency can have an associated list of alternative choices
below it. The lists below dependencies allow users to select the coordination mechanisms used to manage them. In figure 13.8, for example, we can see different alternatives for managing the dependency between "Use headhunter for sourcing" and
"Select human resources ..." There could be a traditional "push-based" coordination, where the headhunter contacts the firm. Alternatively there could be an "open
market" of 'sellers' (headhunters and internal HR departments) and buyers (line-
function departments). The "market with bonus" coordination mechanisms reim-
burses the seller (in our case the headhunter) with a fee depending on the new
employee's performance in the firm. This encourages headhunters to think about
the long-term performance of a candidate. Once the user has selected alternatives for
each subactivity and dependency, the system automatically generates new process
designs in the same way as the subactivity recombinator.

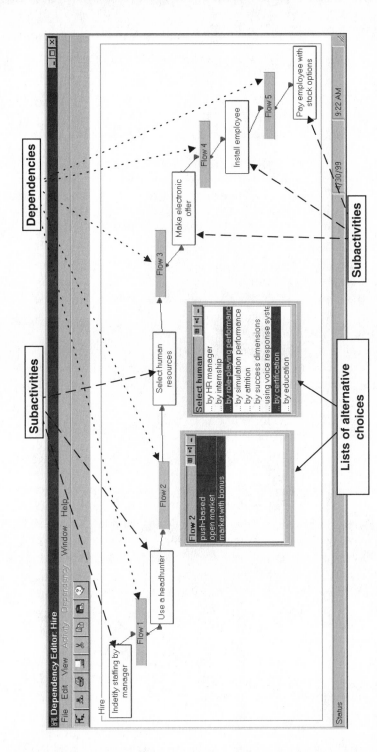

Figure 13.8
Dependency recombinator user interface

In bringing in coordination possibilities from far afield (e.g., as on-line bidding systems for internal recruiting), this approach can generate very innovative process possibilities.

The Bundle Recombinator   The bundle recombinator helps users generate new design alternatives by exploring the multiple possibilities defined by bundles in the specialization hierarchy. Consider, for example, the specialization subtree under 'Install Employee' (figure 13.9).[1]

Recall that the bundles under a given process in the specialization hierarchy group together refinements of that process that differ along a particular dimension such as who does the work and how it is done. Generally, each bundle captures an orthogonal design dimension. The four bundles under 'Install employee' therefore define a four-dimensional space of possible combinations (e.g., figure 13.10 shows the combinations defined by two of these dimensions).

Each cell in this four-dimensional space represents a possible new process specialization formed by making one selection from each bundle dimension. For instance, figure 13.11 shows the combination 'Install by oneself during work within the job environment'. One example idea stimulated by this combination is training novice air traffic control officers by interleaving simulations of unusual situations in the middle of their real work environment (perhaps without the trainees even knowing that these were simulations).

Another interesting combination (stimulated by the combination of two dimensions marked by an asterisk in figure 13.10) is to let new employees "install" themselves by having them decide what they could do best for the firm. In this process new employees look around to find something useful to do for the firm (Kaftan and Barnes 1991 report this type of behavior in some of the hires at SUN Hydraulics).

When users have selected a combination of alternatives (e.g., as in figure 13.11), they press the button shown in the upper left corner of the figure, and the system generates the new process they have specified. The subactivities in the newly created process are derived by "multiple inheritance" from the "parent" processes (Wyner and Lee 1995). The algorithm used for multiple inheritance is as follows: Subactivities that appear in one or both specialization parents are inherited as is. If one parent process has a more specialized form of a subactivity than the other does, then the more specialized version of that subactivity is inherited. If one parent process has deleted a subactivity that appears in another, or if a subactivity is specialized in dif-

---

1. The term "install" may seem mechanistic when applied to employees. The term itself, however, suggests potentially innovative analogies with situations where other kinds of things are "installed."

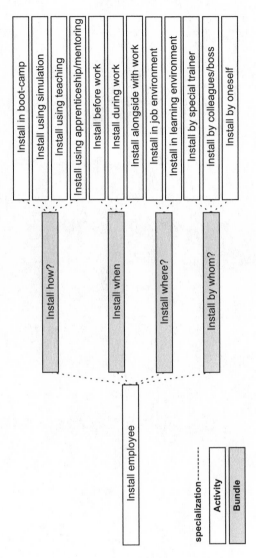

Figure 13.9
Specialization sub-tree for 'Install employee'

		Install when?		
		Install before work	Install during work	Install alongside with work
By whom?	Install by special trainer			
	Install by colleagues/boss			
	Install by oneself		*	

Figure 13.10
Part of the design space for the 'Install employee' process (the cell marked is the example described in the text)

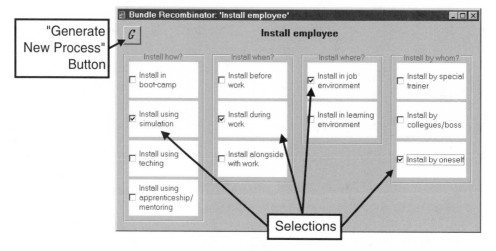

Figure 13.11
Bundle recombinator user interface

ferent ways in the different parent specializations, then the system asks the user what to do. The power of this approach is that it can lead to novel combinations that enable process designers to be more creative in their process designs.

The Roles of the Different Recombinators   As we have seen, the subactivity and dependency recombinators have similar functionality while the bundle recombinator takes an orthogonal approach. All three approaches can be used in a fully integrated way. The subactivity recombinator is useful when we wish to focus on alternatives for the core activities in the process. The dependency recombinator is useful when we wish to also explore different ways of managing the key dependencies in the process.

	Cost of recruiting	Time horizon for recruiter	Complexity of selection
Hire using headhunter (push-based) select by certification	Hi	Short	Low
Hire using head hunter (open-market) select by certification	Medium	Short	Low
Hire using head hunter (market with bonus) select by certification	Medium	Long	Low
Hire using headhunter (push-based) select by role-playing performance	Hi	Short	High
Hire using head hunter (open-market) select by role-playing performance	Medium	Short	High
Hire using head hunter (market with bonus) select by role-playing performance	Medium	Long	High

Figure 13.12
Trade-off matrix for new process re-designs. (All values are for illustration purposes only.)

The bundle recombinator, finally, allows us to create new process specializations suggested by using bundles as design dimensions. The new specializations created by any Recombinator tool can then, of course, be used as alternatives within the other ones. The decision of which Recombinator to use first is dependent on what aspect of a process seems to be most promising for generating novel processes. Exploring the design space of process ideas becomes an iterative process in which the three parts of the Recombinator are used in turn, until a satisfactory set of interesting alternatives is generated.

13.3.3 Comparing the New Process Designs

Once users have used the different components of the Process Recombinator to produce a number of candidate process re-designs, they can use a trade-off matrix to help assess each re-design from the perspective of the criteria that are meaningful to them. The selections made in figure 13.8, for example, would yield the rows shown in the trade-off matrix in figure 13.12.

The Handbook specialization hierarchy can include, for each process, attributes and associated values that describe the process. Attributes that are potentially appropriate for comparing the newly generated process alternatives are thus automatically inherited by the new combinations just as subactivities are. Thus the columns of this trade-off matrix are also automatically generated by the system. In some cases default values for the cells will be inherited as well. It is up to the user, however, to determine whether the values of these attributes are appropriate for each alternative and to change them if necessary. Once this is done, the new processes and associated trade-off values are maintained in the Handbook repository as a source of ideas for future users.

13.4 Contributions of This Work

We view the primary contribution of this work to be the technical demonstration of how a richly structured repository of process examples can be used to automatically generate a wide range of ideas for innovative process designs. We have also, however, informally evaluated the Process Recombinator, and the methodology underlying it, in several real-life contexts.

13.4.1 Informal Evaluation Based on Field Studies

The most substantive example to date has been the field study to re-design the hiring processes for Firm A used as the basis for the examples above (Herman et al. 1998). Though this was not, by any means, a controlled experiment, the participants in this process innovation effort found the methodology and Handbook repository to be very effective in helping them generate a wide range of novel and promising process design alternatives. The Process Recombinator was completed after this field study in order to provide computational support for what we understood to be the key components of the methodology. We have re-enacted portions of these re-design experiences using the Recombinator and have found that it is effective in supporting them.

Since then the Recombinator has been used in another field study to support a large bank's efforts to design new distribution/sales processes for physical financial products like travelers' checks, foreign currency, and precious metals. Before the study, the bank had close to a hundred different processes of this type. After analyzing their processes, they realized that all the processes were captured well as a set of bundles representing such dimensions as type of good, type of trading partner (bank, central bank, person), payment method, payment currency, and internal booking type. Once they had the space so systematized, they were able to use the recombination methodology to identify innovative combinations along these dimensions.

These examples demonstrate well both sources of power of the Recombinator approach: (1) it allows process designers to draw ideas from many different organizations and domains, and (2) it spurs the creative process design through the systematic generation of novel combinations of these "best-practice" ideas. The examples clearly show that a rich repository of appropriately organized process templates, supported by tools like the Recombinator, can have practical use in enhancing the creativity and efficiency of process innovation.

13.4.2 Comparison to Related Process Design Tools

In our view, the Process Recombinator fills an important gap in existing process design technologies. As noted earlier, current techniques (Hammer and Champy 1993; Grover and Kettinger 1995; Harrington 1991; Kettinger, Guha, and Teng 1995; Kettinger and Grover 1995; Davenport 1993) offer little support for identifying new processes (Kettinger, Teng, and Guha 1997). They suggest how organizations can *organize* their process definition efforts (e.g., through brainstorming, visioning, and meeting facilitators) as well as *record* the resulting process designs (e.g., using IDEF or Petri nets) but do not help us actually *generate* new process alternative ideas.

Others have explored the use of re-usable process templates (AT&T Quality Steering Committee 1992; McNair and Leibfried 1992; Schank and Abelson 1977; CIO Magazine 1992; Mi and Scacchi 1993), abstract process models (Sacerdoti 1974; Nau 1987) and systematic process alternative generation (Salancik and Leblebici 1988). Our work is unique, however, in how it systematically uses a large repository of empirically based examples to systematically generate many alternative combinations of process elements.

Also related to our work are systems that automatically generate organizational designs based on descriptions of the organizational tasks and other factors (Baligh, Burton, and Opel 1990; Gasser 1992; Majchrzak and Gasser 1992). Baligh et al., for example, edited "textbook" knowledge about organizational design into an "expert system" that makes recommendations based on rules like "If the environment is stable, then a formal organization is appropriate." Our work differs from these approaches in at least two ways: (1) We are interested not only in providing "conventional" guidance for "traditional" organizations but also in providing tools to help "invent" new organizations. (2) We are not attempting to provide completely automated advice based on simple input parameters (the traditional "expert systems" approach). Instead, we are attempting to provide conceptual frameworks and partly automated tools to help enhance people's abilities to creatively define and systematically explore a large process design space. That is, we want to provide a helpful tool for use by human experts, not an "automated expert" that tells humans what to do.

13.5 Future Work

One of the major limitations of the Recombinator is the availability of a sufficient underlying knowledge base of processes. The size of the underlying knowledge base has a direct influence on the usefulness of the Recombinator. Our experience with the Process Handbook has shown that the current knowledge base of more then

5,000 processes is adequate to generate interesting processes in a variety of domains. We believe that the universality of some of the concepts used (like the notion of the coordination mechanisms or the ubiquity of logistics processes) allow the tool to support some innovation with little prior content in the knowledge base. However, future research about the applicability of the tool in different domains is needed.

In the future we plan to evaluate and refine the Recombinator in other domains (including logistics and manufacturing), and extend it to cover other aspects of our process innovation methodology such as generating new processes by subactivity re-ordering. Another issue we would like to address concerns managing the size of the process design space. The generative strength of our approach is a double-edged sword in the sense that it is often easy to create an overwhelming number of process alternatives. The procedures are not fully formalized, so human judgment is often needed, for example, to select the process design appropriate for one's needs from among the candidates generated by the Recombinator. While we do not expect to obviate the need for human judgment, we do plan to explore how the Recombinator can further reduce the burden of exploring/pruning a large process design space. In the meantime we believe that it will often be preferable to have too many options rather than too few.

Appendix: Implementation Overview

Software Implementation
The Process Handbook software provides a standard set of tools to browse, manipulate, and store process descriptions. Our current system is implemented under the Microsoft Windows operating system using Microsoft's Visual Basic programming language and numerous third-party modules for that environment (i.e., COM/ActiveX-objects). The process descriptions are stored in a relational database (currently Microsoft Access) with an interface layer above the database that represents processes using the concepts described earlier (Ahmed 1998; Bernstein et al. 1995). This interface, implemented as a COM-object, allows programs to retrieve, edit, and add process descriptions. A number of different viewers and editors, including a Web-based browser (see *http://process.mit.edu*), have been implemented as part of the Process Handbook Project (for more information see Malone et al. 1999).

The Process Recombinator is an extension to the Process Handbook software. Using the same development environment we extended the existing tools to provide a user interface for specifying recombinations. Once specified, the Recombinator accesses the Process Handbook database through the same interface layer as the other viewers and editors and generates the new process models directly into the database. Those new models are then available for retrieval and manipulation using all of the tools provided by the Process Handbook software.

Content

The Process Recombinator software accesses the process knowledge base provided by the Process Handbook project. Numerous contributors developed content for the Process Handbook knowledge base, and the content was added to the knowledge base using the tools described above. The current repository has over 5,000 process descriptions ranging from specific examples to more generic templates.

The contents of the Handbook come from both primary sources (e.g., student thesis projects) and secondary sources (e.g., published descriptions of innovative business practices). So far we have focused our data collection on the domain of "supply chain management"—the process by which an organization (or group of organizations) manages the acquisition of inputs, the successive transformations of these inputs into products, and the distribution of these products to customers. For example, the handbook includes results from several MIT master's thesis studies of supply chain processes ranging from a Mexican beer factory to a university purchasing process (Geisler 1995; Leavitt 1995; Lyon 1995; Ruelas Gossi 1995). The entries also include a number of examples drawn from the "Interesting Organizations Database" collected from published sources and student projects as part of an MIT research initiative on "Inventing the Organizations of the 21st Century." Furthermore we have included processes from field studies that the center or its sponsors undertook.

Finally, we have developed a framework of generic process descriptions. To develop such a framework, we reviewed generic business process models from a variety of published sources (e.g., Davenport 1993; Kotler 1997; Ulrich and Eppinger 1995). However, the Process Handbook does not force a single perspective on any of these processes. It can store different views of a process as alternative specializations.

Acknowledgments

We would like to thank George Herman and the other members of MIT Center for Coordination Science, as well as Elisa O'Donnell of A.T. Kearney Consulting, for their invaluable contributions to the ideas underlying this chapter. Section 13.2 was adapted from parts of Malone et al. (1999).

This material is based on work partially supported by the National Science Foundation under Grant No. 9224093. Any opinions, findings, and conclusions or recommendations expressed in this material are those of the author(s) and do not necessarily reflect the views of the National Science Foundation.

14   Designing Robust Business Processes

Mark Klein
Chrysanthos Dellarocas

14.1   Introduction

A critical challenge to creating effective business processes is making sure that they can operate effectively in environments where exceptions (i.e., process failures) can occur. This chapter describes a novel knowledge-based methodology that addresses this challenge, building on an augmentation of the MIT Process Handbook that captures widely applicable expertise about what kinds of exceptions can occur in business processes and how they can be dealt with.

14.2   The Challenge

A critical challenge for organizations of all types is being able to design business processes that can respond effectively when "exceptions" (i.e., process failures) occur (Strong 1992; Suchman 1983; Grudin 1994; Mi and Scacchi 1991; Karbe and Ramsberger 1990; Kreifelts and Woetzel 1987; Chiu et al. 1997). Exceptions can be defined, in general, as any deviation from a process that achieves its goals completely and with maximum efficiency. They include such problems as infrastructure failures (e.g., a manufacturing station breaks down), commitment violations (e.g., a subcontractor is late with a delivery), and "emergent" dysfunctions (e.g., the load on a web server handling orders exceeds its capacity).

Traditionally managers have relied on their experience and understanding of a process in order to handle such exceptions as they occur, but this approach is becoming increasingly unsatisfactory. Modern business processes are becoming more complex, and the pace at which they operate and change is accelerating. These processes are more apt to cross organizational and geographic boundaries, driven by globalization and the ubiquity of telecommunications technology. This effect, along with increasing process automation, is making many details of their operation less accessible to the managers involved. It is thus becoming more difficult to anticipate and avoid, or detect and resolve, exceptions in business processes.

Current business process design methodologies and tools (Davenport 1993; Grover and Kettinger 1995; Hammer and Champy 1993), however, do not address this problem. Process designers are welcome, of course, to include steps designed to handle exceptions within their process models. But they are given no assistance in determining what *kinds* of exceptions can occur, or what the *best practices* are for dealing with them. Some more systematic approach is needed. The remainder of this chapter describes a novel approach for designing robust business processes that utilizes a knowledge base of widely reusable exception handling expertise to help designers quickly and systematically anticipate possible exceptions and select the appropriate process modifications needed to deal with them.

14.3 Our Exception Analysis Methodology

The fundamental insight underlying our methodology is that exceptions represent the *violation of commitments*. The smooth operation of a manufacturing plant, for example, relies implicitly on the commitment that the machinery therein will work reliably. Supply chains rely on commitments, often formalized as contracts, between subcontractors and contractors. A given Web computing infrastructure relies on the commitment that the design was appropriate to the demands that will be placed on it. One can therefore understand the possible exceptions and responses for a business process by enumerating:

• The *commitments* underlying the success of the business process.

• The ways these commitments can be violated (i.e., the *exceptions*).

• The processes by which these exceptions can be anticipated and avoided, and detected and resolved (i.e., the exception *handlers*).

We call this process Role–Commitment–Violation analysis (Klein and Dellarocas 2000).

While this analysis can of course be done from scratch for each new business process, it would be helpful if the results of analyses for other processes could be archived so that designers can take advantage of them when performing new analyses on similar processes. This can save a lot of time, and if the knowledge base is reasonably complete, designers are much more likely to get a full picture of the exceptions and possible handlers for their particular process. We describe, in this chapter, both an exception analysis methodology that is suitable for from-scratch analysis, plus a scheme for capturing the results of previous analyses in a way that facilitates their reuse.

It would be a huge task, however, to try to identify in one knowledge base all the important commitments, exceptions, and handlers for the whole world of possible business processes. The exceptions important in chemical manufacturing (e.g., chemical spills), for example, are largely orthogonal to those that occur in the insurance industry (e.g., claim fraud). There is one subset of exceptions, however, that is critical to business processes cutting across multiple domains: those concerning *coordination* among the tasks in a business process. No matter what kind of work one does, one is faced with the challenge of figuring out who should do what when with what resources in order to achieve private and shared goals in a context of mutual interdependence. We have found that there is a manageably small number of ways that coordination can occur; the same basic ideas (e.g., market mechanisms, just-in-time logistics) tend to get used again and again in a wide range of contexts. Many of the most difficult to detect and resolve exceptions, moreover, take the form of coordination failures, especially failures cutting across organizational boundaries. Coordination-related exceptions thus represent a constrained but important and widely applicable subset of the world of possible business process exceptions. The examples in this chapter will all be drawn from the realm of coordination exceptions.

Identifying Commitments   To identify the commitments involved in a business process, one needs to identify, starting from the penultimate outputs of the process, who (or what) generates those outputs, and what is required in order to do so. Each of these requirements represent commitments that must be honored. One repeats this analysis for the requirements so identified, working backward through the business process, until all the commitments have been identified. There are many different kinds of commitments, ranging from commitments to preserve a given state (e.g., wherein a piece of machinery is operating correctly) to commitments to make some change in state (e.g., pay someone in a timely way for a service they have performed). Every resource flow in a process (which we model in the Handbook as *dependencies*) represents the commitment to get the right amount of the right resource to the right consumer at the right time.

Let us consider a simple example in order to make this concrete. One process commonly used for allocating tasks is the sealed-bid auction. This works as follows: a contractor identifies a task that it cannot or chooses not to do and attempts to find a subcontractor to perform the task. It begins by creating a 'Request for bids' (RFB) that describes the desired work, and then sending it to potential subcontractors. Interested subcontractors respond with bids (specifying such issues as the price and time needed to perform the task) from which the contractor selects a winner. The winning agent, once notified of the award, performs the work (potentially subcontracting out its own subtasks as needed) and submits the results to the contractor (figure 14.1).

This process involves several commitments. The contractor, for example, is responsible for sending the correct RFB to the correct subcontractors in a timely way. The subcontractors, in turn, are responsible for sending accurate bids to the

Contractor Role   **Subcontractor Role**

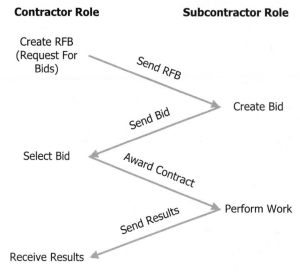

Figure 14.1
The sealed-bid task allocation auction

contractor before the deadline. The contractor should award the work fairly and notify the subcontractors in a timely way. The winning subcontractors should produce the desired results with the promised delivery time, cost, and quality. To achieve these commitments, the contractors and subcontractors will make use of other subprocesses. They may use email, fax machines, or the US postal service, for example, to handle the flow of messages between them. These mechanisms in turn will rely on commitments of their own. If we carry this procedure far enough, we can have a complete picture of the commitments involved in this business process.

Because the range of coordination processes is relatively constrained, it is possible to create a knowledge base of such processes that is fairly complete, and use this to speed the identification of coordination-related commitments in a given business process. The Handbook project has been creating just such a knowledge base (figure 14.2).

The knowledge base consists of generic coordination mechanisms arranged into a taxonomy. A business process designer inspects this taxonomy to find the generic mechanism that most closely matches the part of their business process they are currently analyzing. The commitments that appear in that generic mechanism represent a checklist of commitments that almost certainly appear in the particular business process being analyzed. Using this taxonomy a business process designer could

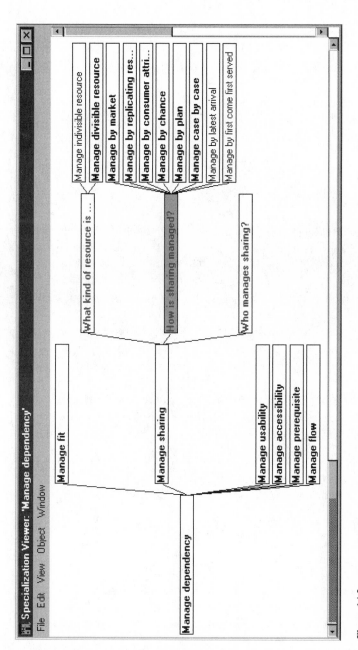

Figure 14.2
Portion of the coordination mechanism taxonomy

quickly determine, for example, that their current process for allocating claims to insurance adjusters is an instance of a 'first-come–first-served' coordination mechanism. They can then look at the commitments in the generic mechanism's description to get a pretty good idea of what coordination commitments must be considered in their own business process.

Identifying Exceptions   The next step is to identify the exceptions that can occur in a process with a given set of commitments. Each kind of commitment has its own characteristic set of ways in which it can be violated. The commitment to maintain a certain response time in a Web server, for example, could be violated because the server broke down, because demand exceeded the limits the server was designed for, and so on.

If one had a complete model of how all of the components in a business process could possibly behave, then it imaginably would be possible to logically, even automatically, deduce all the ways that commitment violations (i.e., exceptions) can occur. As a practical matter, however, one generally derives an understanding of the possible exceptions by experience. As with commitment identification, business process designers could go through this exception identification from scratch for every new process, but this can be made more efficient and complete by maintaining the results of this analysis in a knowledge base. The Handbook includes just such a knowledge base, focused for the reasons noted above on coordination-related exceptions.

The schema is simple. Since coordination can be defined as the management of resource flows across dependencies (Malone and Crowston 1994), the different types of coordination commitments is just another name for the different types of dependencies. There are three main dependency types:

• *Flow*.   A resource flows from a producer to a consumer. Any process that involves transporting messages or physical items can be viewed as a flow.

• *Sharing*.   A resource is produced by a single producer and shared among multiple consumers. A lottery, for example, can be viewed as a way of sharing goods among consumers.

• *Fit*.   Resources from multiple producers are consolidated by a single consumer. The design of a complex artifact like an airplane, for example, includes as an important component the process of 'fitting' together the design for different subsystems into a functioning airplane.

Commitments, including these three main types of dependencies, can be arranged to form a taxonomy like the one maintained in the Handbook knowledge base (figure 14.3). Every commitment in that taxonomy is linked to the exception types to which it can be prone. There are three main classes of exceptions:

• *Infrastructure commitment violations.*   This category includes such problems as communications failures and machinery breakdowns.

• *Agent commitment violations.*   This category includes problems where participants in the business process do not discharge their commitments to each other, such as when a subcontractor is overdue with a task.

• *System commitment violations.*   The designer of a coordination mechanism has the commitment of defining one that works well given the demands that will be placed on it. There are cases, however, where an apparently reasonable coordination mechanism can produce "emergent" dysfunctional behavior even with perfectly reliable infrastructures and participants. One example is "resource poaching," wherein a slew of low-priority but long-duration tasks tie up the subcontractors, thereby freezing out resources needed for the higher-priority tasks that arrive later (Chia et al. 1998). This does not represent an error per se but rather an unexpected consequence of a simple mechanism applied in a complex environment.

Exceptions, like commitments, can be arranged into a taxonomy (figure 14.4). These interlinked taxonomies can be used as follows: for every commitment one identifies in a business process, one finds the closest match in the commitment taxonomy, and then follows the links to the associated exceptions. Imagine, for example, that one's business process includes an auction mechanism with the commitment that the auctioneer accurately announce the winner of each round. This is an instance of a "information contract" dependency (itself a type of "flow") that has such characteristic exceptions as "false information." The power of using the knowledge base in this way is that it may suggest exceptions that one might not have otherwise considered, for example, that the auctioneer may give false information about who won the last auction round.

Identifying Exception Handlers   The final step of the exception analysis process is to identify possible exception handlers for each of the important exceptions identified in the business process being analyzed. There are four main classes of exception handling processes, divided into two pairs. If a exception has not yet occurred, we can use:

• Exception *anticipation* processes.   These uncover situations where a given class of exception is likely to occur. Resource poaching, for example, can be anticipated when there is a flood of long duration tasks requiring scarce, nonpreempting subcontractors to perform them.

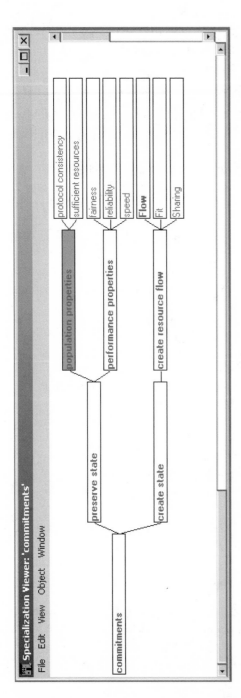

Figure 14.3
Portion of the commitment type taxonomy

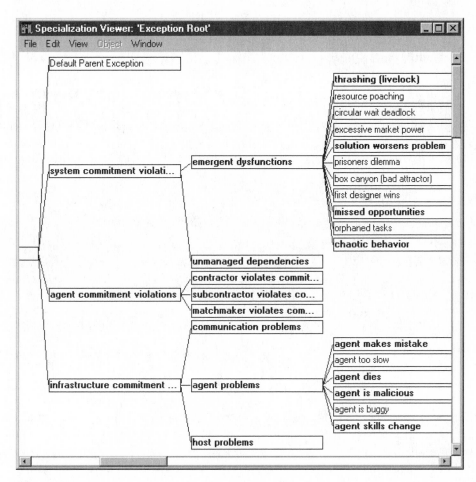

Figure 14.4
Portion of the exception type taxonomy

• Exception *avoidance* processes. These reduce or eliminate the likelihood of a given class of exception. Resource poaching can be avoided, for example, by allowing subcontractors to preempt their current tasks in favor of higher-priority pending tasks.

If the exception has already occurred, we can use:

• Exception *detection* processes. These detect when an exception has actually occurred. Some exceptions, such as bidder collusion, are difficult to anticipate but can be detected post hoc by looking at bid price patterns.

• Exception *resolution* processes.   These resolve an exception once it has happened. One resolution for bidder collusion, for example, is to penalize and/or kick out the colluding bidders and re-start the auction for the good in question.

Like exception *types*, there appears to be no simple way to systematically identify all the potentially useful exception *handlers*. Exception handling techniques have emerged throughout human history, and appear to be limited in scope only by the bounds of human creativity. One can argue that a very significant proportion of human institutional innovations, including the police, law courts, disaster relief agencies, and so on, can all be viewed as representing exception handling mechanisms.

The Handbook contains a growing collection of exception handling techniques linked to the (coordination-related) exceptions to which they are relevant (figure 14.5). These handlers are arranged into a taxonomy such that handlers with similar functions appear close to one another. So, when a designer is looking for an exception handler suitable for a particular exception type, he or she will find that a range of potentially suitable handlers will appear as specializations or siblings of the handlers directly linked to the exception of interest. Note that since handlers are themselves processes, they themselves can have exceptions that require exception handlers.

Summary Our exception analysis methodology can be summarized as follows (figure 14.6). A given *process* is analyzed to determine the *commitments* contained therein. These commitments are then mapped to the ways that they can be violated (i.e., to *exceptions*) and from there to *handlers* potentially suitable for anticipating and avoiding, or detecting and resolving them. The MIT Process Handbook contains a growing knowledge base of generic processes, commitments, exceptions, and handlers relevant to the important realm of coordination-related processes. This knowledge base can be used to increase the speed and completeness of exception analysis in

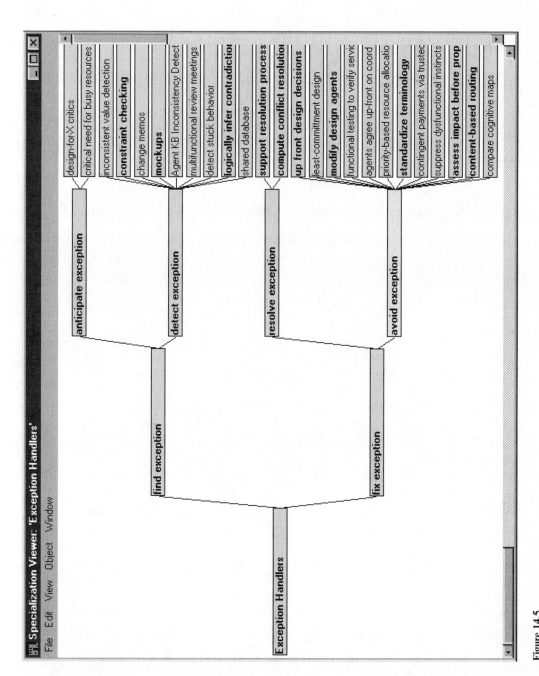

Figure 14.5
Subset of the exception handler taxonomy

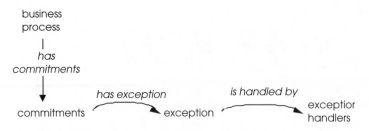

Figure 14.6
Summary of the exception analysis methodology

the coordination domain by archiving this information in a way that makes it applicable to a wide range of business processes.

14.4   An Example: The Barings Bank Failure

We illustrate our exception analysis procedure in the context of a well-known case of a failed business process: the Barings Bank failure.

In February 1994, 233-year old Barings Bank, one of the oldest and most respected investment houses in the United Kingdom, went bankrupt (Fay 1997; Zhang 1995). The entire bank collapsed because of losses of $1.4 billion incurred in a matter of days by a single young trader, Nicholas Leeson. Nicholas Leeson was a futures trader in the Singapore branch of the bank. For a number of reasons, which are still not entirely clear, Leeson began to engage in unauthorized futures trading in the Singapore exchange. Because of inadequate internal controls and other process failures, Leeson was able to maintain his unauthorized and highly risky activity undetected by the bank headquarters in London until the very end. As we will see, the exception analysis methodology outlined above can be used to systematically point out the gaps in the Barings trading process controls that allowed disaster to occur, as well as to suggest ways for closing those gaps.

Our first task is to identify the key commitments in the Barings futures trading process. Figure 14.7 depicts a simplified but accurate model of the process; boxes correspond to process activities, and lines correspond to dependencies between these activities.

When a customer requests a futures trade, the trader asks the bank headquarters for an advance of funds in order to cover the customer's margin account. Once the funds have arrived, the trader performs the trade, waits to receive the corresponding security certificate and finally pays the exchange. In an "ideal" world a trader

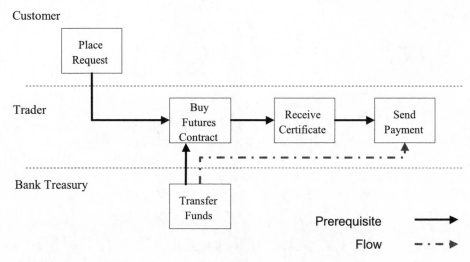

Figure 14.7
Barings futures trading process

only performs trades when authorized to do so by customers, correct certificates are always received, and payment for trades exactly match the funds forwarded to the trader by the bank headquarters. These conditions are implied by the "prerequisite" and "exact flow" dependencies, which represent the key commitments in this business process.

Our next step is to identify the possible exceptions that are associated with each key commitment. By consulting the Handbook knowledge base, one can see that one possible exception for any prerequisite dependency is a prerequisite violation ("B without A"), that is, the possibility of activity B happening without a prior occurrence of activity A. In the context of the Barings trade process such violations would translate into unauthorized trading, unwanted security receipts, and unnecessary payment (figure 14.8). Likewise one possible exception for an "exact flow" dependency is mismatch between the amount produced and the amount consumed. In the context of the Barings process this would translate into a misuse of headquarter funds.

After possible exceptions have been identified, the next step is to find handlers suitable for managing the possible exceptions identified above. It turns out that because the trading process at Barings involves several independent entities (customer, bank, exchange) and requires some initiative from the part of the trader, there

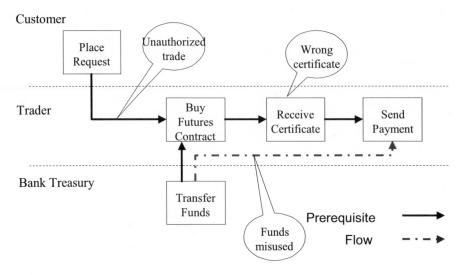

Figure 14.8
Barings futures trading process with associated exceptions

are were no practical mechanisms for avoiding the exceptions. There were, however, several mechanisms for detecting them.

Logging is one (out of several) generic mechanism for detecting prerequisite relationship violations (figure 14.9). Logging involves recording all occurrences of activities A and B in some reliable storage medium and periodically conducting checks for prerequisite violations. In order for logging to be successful, it is in turn required that (1) <u>all</u> occurrences of A and B be reliably logged and (2) the log only be modified by the processes that do the logging.

If we insert a logging process for all dependencies listed in figure 14.10 we get a model of a properly instrumented trading process. At this point we can compare the process derived using our approach with the actual Barings process. It can immediately be seen that although Barings did log some information about trades, it had two crucial gaps relative to the properly instrumented process of figure 14.10 (see figure 14.11).

First, it failed to log and compare the amount of funds forwarded by headquarters to the trader to the amounts actually paid by the trader for customer trades (in other words, the log labeled "Funds" in figures 14.10 was missing from the Barings process). Second, Nick Leeson, in addition to being a trader, was also in charge of the backroom operations in the Singapore branch. This gave him the authorization

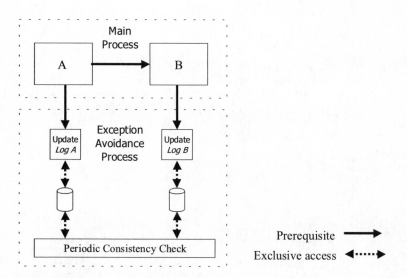

Figure 14.9
Logging is a generic process for detecting prerequisite violations

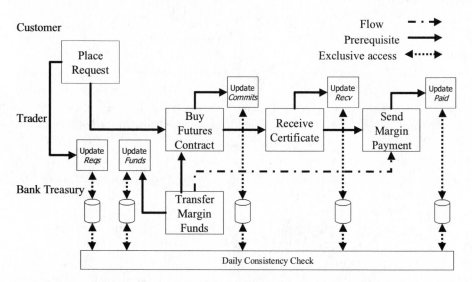

Figure 14.10
Barings process properly instrumented with logging processes

Customer

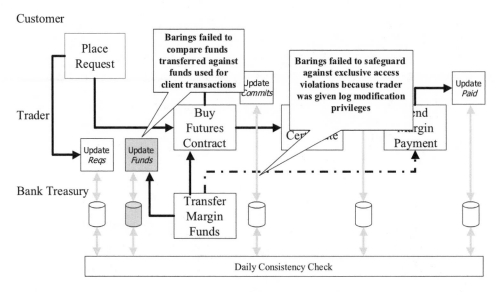

Figure 14.11
Comparison between the ideal and the actual barings process

to modify the trades logs (and thus violated requirement (2) above of the logging process).

Nick Leeson was able to use these two gaps to his advantage as follows: whenever he received a trade request from a customer, he requested an amount of funds far greater than what was required for the customer trade. He then performed the customer trade, as well as some additional unauthorized trades on his behalf. All of these trades were automatically logged into logs "Commits," "Received," and "Paid" (see figure 14.10). Leeson then erased the records of his unauthorized trades from logs "Commits," "Received," and "Paid." Therefore, at the end of each day, the log of "Requests" matched perfectly the other three logs. By not checking for discrepancies between the funds forwarded to Leeson and the total funds recorded at the "Paid" log, headquarters remained unaware of Leeson's activities until it was too late.

It is probably too simplistic to claim that the Barings disaster would have been avoided if the management of Barings had at their disposal knowledge-based exception handling methodologies, such as the ones described in this chapter. Nevertheless, this exercise demonstrates that these methodologies can be used in real-life cases to alert management of potential weaknesses and suggest ways for making vital business processes more robust.

Acknowledgments

This work was supported by NSF grant IIS-9803251 (Computation and Social Systems Program) and by DARPA grant F30602-98-2-0099 (Control of Agent Based Systems Program). We are grateful for many helpful comments from the members of the MIT Center for Coordination Science: John Quimby, George Herman, George Wyner, Abraham Bernstein, and Thomas Malone.

IVB *Knowledge Management*

15 A New Way to Manage Process Knowledge

Nicholas G. Carr

The products of an ambitious MIT study could help you reshape your business. For most of the past decade, a team of researchers at the MIT Sloan School of Management has been quietly laboring on a Herculean task: to document, in meticulous detail, every major business process. The Process Handbook project, as the effort is called, has succeeded in creating an electronic repository of information on more than 5,000 processes and activities, together with a suite of sophisticated software programs for navigating and manipulating the data.

Now MIT is making the process repository and software available to companies everywhere by licensing them to start-up firm Phios Corporation. Phios plans to commercialize the research in two ways. First, it will help individual companies develop their own proprietary versions of the repository, providing an easy way to store, organize, and share diverse information such as process maps, procedure manuals, images, software programs, and Web links. Second, it will put the general process repository on the World Wide Web, giving managers access to a wealth of knowledge on process design.

Thomas W. Malone, professor at the Sloan School and cofounder and chairman of Phios, believes that process management tools are becoming increasingly important. "Electronic commerce, outsourcing, and enterprise software systems are all forcing companies to rethink the way they organize work," he says. "Companies need to be more creative and flexible in managing their processes and that requires a much more systematic approach to capturing and disseminating process knowledge."

One company that's already using the software to manage its process knowledge is Dow Corning. The company found, in the course of installing an SAP system, that it lacked a consistent way to document all its process designs and share that information throughout its organization. It is using the Phios software to create interlinked maps of its key processes, which have proved invaluable in designing and rolling out the new system. The company is also moving ahead with plans to store its process repository on its intranet. Anyone in the company will be able to quickly learn the steps involved in any process, find links to detailed process guidebooks and policy statements, check measures of process performance, and share ideas for improving process designs. (See figure 15.3 for Dow Corning's process repository.)

Much of the power of the Phios process repository lies in its unique two-dimensional structure, which organizes information according to both process parts

An earlier version of this chapter appeared as N. Carr (1999), A new way to manage process knowledge, *Harvard Business Review*, September. © 1999 Harvard Business Review Press. Reprinted by permission.

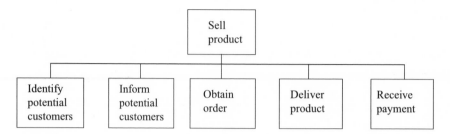

Figure 15.1
Process parts

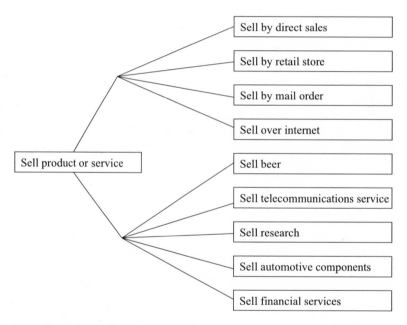

Figure 15.2
Process types

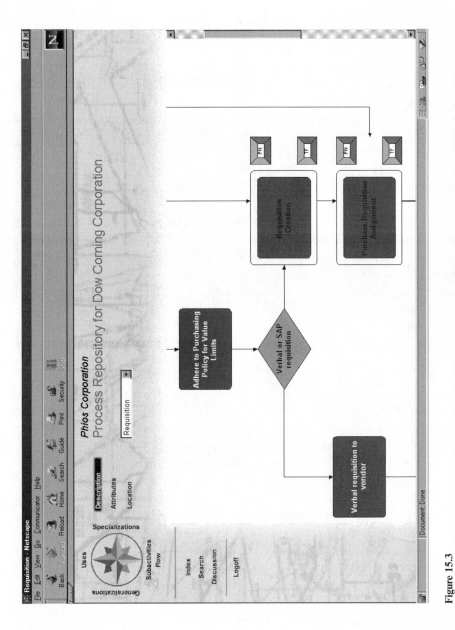

Figure 15.3
Dow Corning's process repository. Dow Corning is putting its process repository on its corporate Intranet. Here, in a sample window, we see a portion of Dow's requisition procedure. Employees can click on any process step for more detailed information on policies and practices. The "process compass" in the upper left corner makes navigating the repository easy.

and process types. A user exploring the general process of selling a product, for example, can move vertically through the database to gain more detailed information about the process's component parts or subactivities (see figure 15.1).

The user can also move horizontally to study more specialized types of the process, such as selling over the Internet or selling financial services (figure 15.2). By making it easy for users to move in both directions through the process repository, Phios's software can spur creative thinking about new ways to do work. (To see how the repository works, visit *www.phios.com/hbr*.)

One large services company, for example, used the repository to generate fresh ideas for restructuring its hiring processes. The company was growing rapidly in a tightening labor market, and it was having trouble bringing qualified new people on board. So it used the repository to explore the hiring processes of other companies, both inside and outside its industry. When it discovered that Marriott used an automated telephone system to screen job applicants, it realized that it could use a similar process for certain entry-level positions. The company also looked at analogues to the hiring process. In the repository's classification scheme, "hiring" is a specialized form of the more general process of "buying." (Hiring, after all, is the purchase of a person's time.) When exploring different buying processes, the company found a description of General Electric's Internet-based purchasing system, which enables buyers to efficiently find and compare different suppliers. The services company realized that a similar electronic clearinghouse might be a productive way of locating and evaluating potential employees. It also considered the possibility of setting up an on-line bidding system for jobs, as electronic auction houses like Onsale have done for products.

The value of well-managed process information will only grow in the future, according to Malone. "As the boundaries between functions and companies crumble, the old organizational chart loses its usefulness as a management tool," he says. "In tomorrow's companies, executives will likely depend on richly detailed process maps to guide their managerial and strategic decision making."

16 Toward a Systematic Repository of Knowledge about Managing Collaborative Design Conflicts

Mark Klein

16.1 The Challenge

Increasingly, complex artifacts such as cars, planes and even software are designed using large-scale and often highly distributed collaborative processes. Conflict (i.e., incompatibilities between design decisions and/or goals) is common in such highly interdependent activities. In one study, for example, half of all interactions between collaborating architectural designers were found to involve detecting and resolving conflicts (Klein and Lu 1991).

Better conflict management practices are needed. Current, mainly manual practices are being overwhelmed by the sheer scale and complexity of modern design artifacts. Consider the Boeing 767-F design project. This project involved the integrated contributions of hundreds of individuals in tens of disciplines and hundreds of teams spread over several continents and a span of years. The design includes millions of components and underwent thousands of changes. Design conflicts were often not detected until long (days to months) after they had occurred, resulting in wasted design time, design rework, and even scrapped tools and parts. Design rework rates of 25 to 30 percent were typical. Since maintaining scheduled commitments was a priority, design rework often had to be done on a short flow-time basis that typically cost much more (estimates ranged as high as 50 times more) and could reduce product quality. Conflict cascades that required as many as 15 iterations to finally produce a consistent design were not uncommon. To give another example, roughly half of the labor budget for the Boeing 777 program (which is measured in the hundreds of millions of dollars) was estimated to be due to changes, errors, and rework, often due to design conflicts. All of this occurred in the context of Boeing's industry-leading adoption of concurrent engineering practices such as multidisciplinary design teams (Klein 1994).

A key barrier to the development and utilization of improved design conflict management practices has been the lack of dissemination of this knowledge in a systematized form. Conflict management is fundamentally a multidisciplinary topic, and information in this area is scattered as a result across multiple disparate communities including computer science, industrial engineering, and management science,

An earlier version of this chapter appeared as M. Klein (2000), Towards a systematic repository of knowledge about managing collaborative design conflicts, *Proceedings of the Sixth International Conference on Artificial Intelligence in Design*, Worcester, MA, June 26–29, 2000. © 2000 Kluwer Academic Publishers. Reprinted by permission.

to mention just a few. Previous efforts to develop taxonomies of conflict knowledge (Matta 1996; Castelfranchi 1996; Ramesh and Sengupta 1994; Feldman 1985) have been small in scope and have left out important classes of information, particularly *meta*-process information, which will be described below. The result is that good ideas developed within one discipline, or even within one industry, do not readily propagate to researchers and practitioners in other settings, and opportunities are lost to carry on a more systematic and cumulative exploration of the range of potentially useful conflict management techniques.

The work described in this chapter addresses these challenges directly by developing a semiformal Web-accessible repository of multidisciplinary collaborative design conflict management expertise organized so as to facilitate key uses:

• Pedagogy. Helping students, researchers and practitioners learn about the state of the art in design conflict management

• Business process redesign. Helping practitioners finding alternative ways of designing their collaborative design processes

• Research. Helping researchers identify gaps in conflict management technology, identify common abstractions, facilitate discussion, and foster development of new ideas

The remainder of this chapter will describe the key ideas and tools making up the conflict repository, evaluate its efficacy with respect to the goals listed above, and describe potential directions for future work.

16.2   Our Approach

Our approach is to capture design conflict management knowledge using a substantively extended version of the tools and techniques developed as part of the MIT Process Handbook project. The Handbook is a process knowledge repository which has been under development at the Center for Coordination Science (CCS) for the past six years (Malone and Crowston 1994; Malone et al. 1998). The growing Handbook database currently includes over 5,000 process descriptions ranging from specific (e.g., for a university purchasing department) to generic (e.g., for resource allocation and multicriteria decision-making). The CCS has developed a Windows-based tool for editing the Handbook repository contents, as well as a Web-based tool for read-only access. The Handbook is under active use and development by a highly distributed group of more than forty scientists, teachers, students, and sponsors for such diverse purposes as adding new process descriptions, teaching classes, and business process re-design.

In the following sections we will present the core concepts underlying the Handbook, describe how these concepts and associated tools were extended to capture conflict management expertise, and give examples of how this can be used to support a range of useful capabilities.

16.2.1   Underlying Process Handbook Concepts

The Handbook takes advantage of four simple but powerful concepts to capture and organize process knowledge: *attributes*, *decomposition*, *dependencies*, and *specialization*.

Process Attributes   Like most process modeling techniques, the Handbook allows processes to be annotated with attributes that capture such information as a textual description, typical performance values (e.g., how long a process takes to execute), and applicability conditions (i.e., constraints on the contexts where the process can be used).

Decomposition   Also like most process modeling techniques, the Handbook uses the notion of *decomposition*: a process is modeled as a collection of activities that can in turn be broken down ("decomposed") into subactivities. A common conflict detection process in industry, for example, is the change memo, wherein a designer that makes a design change describes it in a memo and distributes it to potentially affected designers for their review and comment. The decomposition for this process is shown in figure 16.1.

Dependencies   Another key concept we use is that coordination can be viewed as the management of *dependencies* between activities (Malone and Crowston 1994). Every

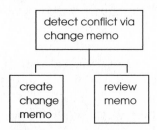

Figure 16.1
Decomposition for the change memo process

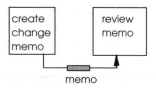

Figure 16.2
Dependencies for the change memo process

dependency can include an associated *coordination mechanism*, which is simply the process that manages the resource flow and thereby coordinates the activities connected by the dependency. The dependency graph for the change memo process, for example, is shown in figure 16.2.

Here the key dependency involves getting the change memo (i.e., the resource created by the originating designer) to the interested parties. In typical industry practice, the memos are handwritten and the coordination mechanism consists of distributing the memos via office mail to all the engineers the originating engineer thought were relevant, as the originating engineer generates them.

The key advantage of representing processes using dependencies and coordination mechanisms is that they allow us to abstract away details about how "core" activities coordinate with each other, and thereby making it easier to explore different ways of doing so. We will see examples of this below.

Specialization The final key concept is that processes can be arranged into a *taxonomy*, with very generic processes at one extreme and increasingly *specialized* processes at the other. Processes are organized based on their function, so that processes with similar purposes appear close to each other. This facilitates finding and comparing alternative ways for performing functions of interest, thereby fostering easy transfer of ideas. Sibling processes that vary along some interesting design dimension can be grouped into "bundles" with trade-off tables that capture the relative pros and cons of these alternatives. Consider, for example, the taxonomy fragment for conflict detection processes in figure 16.3.

The taxonomy shows that there are at least three generic techniques for detecting conflicts (design reviews, change memos, and mockups) and also that mockups can in turn be distinguished into physical and digital versions thereof (a physical mockup involves building a physical scale model of the artifact; a digital mockup utilizes a digital model of the artifact instead). Two bundles distinguish between different kinds of mockup-based conflict detection processes. The [mockup how?] bundle collects the

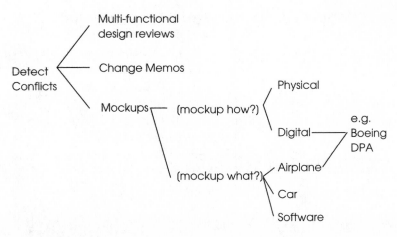

Figure 16.3
Fragment of the process taxonomy for conflict detection

Table 16.1
Trade-off table for the [mockup how?] bundle

Alternative	Detection speed	Up-front cost	Cost of changes
Physical	Slow	Medium	High
Digital	Fast	High	Low

different ways of doing mockups, and includes a trade-off table capturing their relative pros and cons (table 16.1).

Table 16.1 shows that physical mockups have lower up-front cost but detect conflicts relatively slowly, and are expensive to modify as the design changes. Digital mockups have greater up-front costs but are superior on the other counts.

16.2.2   Extending the Handbook to Capture Conflict Knowledge
While the Handbook as described above is well suited for describing conflict management processes by themselves, it does not capture crucial information concerning what *types* of conflicts exist, in what *contexts* (i.e., design processes) they can appear, what *impact* they have, or what conflict management processes are suitable for *handling* them. *The novel contribution of the work described herein involved extending the Handbook so that it can capture this information.* This required two additional elements: the *conflict taxonomy*, and the *conflict management meta-process*. These are described below.

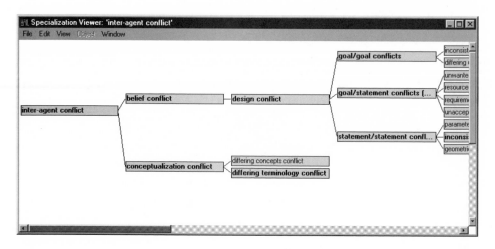

Figure 16.4
Fragment of the conflicts type taxonomy

Conflict Taxonomy The conflict taxonomy is a hierarchy of conflict types, ranging
from general conflict types like "belief conflict" to more specific ones like "resource
budget exceeded" (figure 16.4). There are many types of conflict. A major dividing
point in the taxonomy, for example, concerns whether the conflict involves the way
the designers represent the design (conceptualization conflict) or the content of the
design itself (belief conflict).

Different kinds of collaborative design processes have different characteristic conflict types. This is captured by building on a taxonomy of collaborative design processes (figure 16.5). Every collaborative design process is linked to the conflict types
that characterize it. A processes' characteristic conflicts are inherited by its specializations unless explicitly overridden. Every conflict is annotated with its typical
impact on the associated design process. All collaborative design processes, for
example, are subject to the generic "design conflict," but the severity varies. Concurrent design, for example, generally experiences fewer delays and other costs from
design conflicts than does serial design.

Conflict types are linked, in turn, to the one or more processes suitable for handling them; these processes are themselves arranged into a taxonomy, producing the
overall structure in figure 16.6. The conflict handling process taxonomy (see figure
16.7) is where the bulk of the repository content resides.[1]

---

1. The repository uses the term "exception" because the Process Handbook is currently being applied to
capturing knowledge about coordination failures ("exceptions"), in general, of which conflict is a sybtype.
See Klein and Dellarocas (2000) for more detail on this aspect of our work.

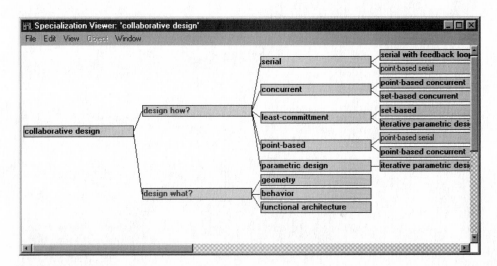

Figure 16.5.
Fragment of the collaborative design process hierarchy

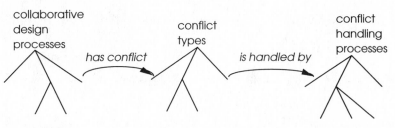

Figure 16.6
Linkages to/from the conflict taxonomy

There are four main classes of conflict handling processes, divided into two pairs. If a conflict has not yet occurred, we can use:

· Conflict *anticipation* processes. These uncover situations where a given class of conflict is likely to occur. An example of such a process is one that looks for design changes that increase the use of a highly limited resource—one can anticipate that the design change may cause a conflict even without calculating the actual resource usage impact.

· Conflict *avoidance* processes. These reduce or eliminate the likelihood of a given class of conflict. Terminological conflicts, for example, can be avoided by leading the designers to standardize their terminology before starting the design.

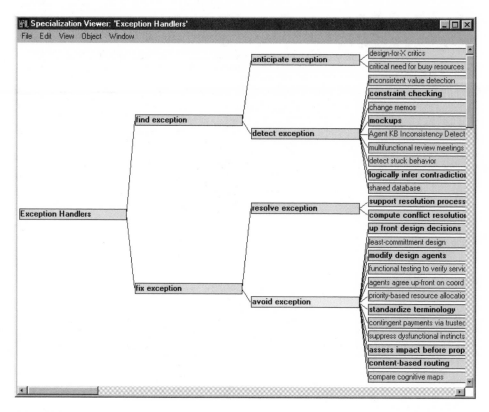

Figure 16.7
Subset of the conflict handling process taxonomy

If the conflict has already occurred, we instead can use:

• Conflict *detection* processes.   These detect when a conflict has actually occurred. Change memos, design mockups, and multifunctional meetings are all, as we have seen, examples of processes used to detect conflict.

• Conflict *resolution* processes.   These resolve a conflict once it has happened. Such processes can include those that structure the conflict resolution interaction between designers (e.g., facilitated negotiation) as well as those that compute a resolution to the conflict outright (e.g., multicriteria optimization)

We have found that the applicability conditions for conflict handler processes fall into two categories:

Table 16.2
Example of conflict handler applicability conditions

Process	Design proceeds by creating new entities and manipulating the parameters associated with these entities. There is a finite known set of entities and parameters.
Agent	Agents can describe their utilities as functions that take the design parameter values as input and produce values expressed in terms of a single mutually understood goodness metric

• Constraints on the *design process*. These describe which class of collaborative design process the conflict handler is suited for.

• Constraints on the *design agent*. These describe capabilities design agents must have in order for the conflict handler to be applicable.

Imagine a conflict resolution process like multicriteria optimization, for example, that involves optimizing a single utility function formed by aggregating the functions of the contending design agents. The applicability conditions for such a procedure would be as shown in table 16.2. This information is useful when trying to determine if a given conflict handler is appropriate for the design context one is currently concerned with.

The Conflict Management Meta-process The conflict taxonomy and associated links described above capture the range of *possible* conflicts and associated conflict handling processes but do not specify *which* handlers should be used *when* for *what* exceptions. This latter information is captured in the augmented Handbook as specializations of the generic *conflict management meta-process* (figure 16.8).

The conflict management meta-process consists of the following subtasks:

• *Identify target conflicts.* This decides which classes of conflicts the process is going to handle, potentially in a time-varying context-sensitive way.

• *Determine conflict finding processes.* This determines which conflict finding (i.e., anticipation or detection) handlers will be used to find the conflicts of these types.

• *Enact conflict finding processes.* This enacts the conflict finding processes identified in the previous step, producing one or more conflict instances.

• *Select conflict instances to fix.* This sorts and prunes the list of conflict instances so uncovered.

• *Determine conflict fixing processes.* This determines which conflict fixing (avoidance or resolution) processes will be used to handle these conflict instances.

• *Enact conflict fixing processes.* This enacts the conflict fixing processes to actually (hopefully) complete the handling of the conflict(s) detected by the system.

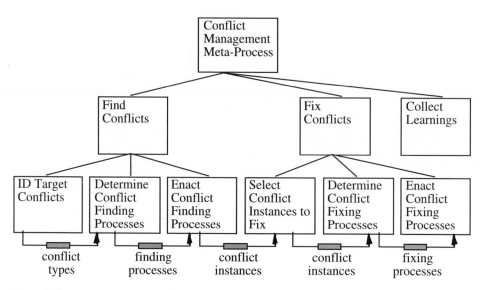

Figure 16.8
Decomposition of the generic conflict management meta-process

• *Collect learnings.* This collects information produced by any of the other steps as input to any learning capability that the conflict management system may have, presumably changing the operation of the other meta-process steps in the future.

This is a *meta*-process because the inputs and outputs of some of the steps are other (conflict handler) processes. The decomposition, patterned originally on that used in diagnostic expert systems (Clancey 1984), has been found adequate to capture all the important classes of meta-process information encountered in the conflict management literature our team has reviewed so far.

To make this process more concrete, let us consider two specializations from the conflict management meta-process taxonomy (figure 16.9). One major distinction in this taxonomy is whether conflict management is done at system development time or at system execution time. Development-time conflict management has been applied extensively in the creation of expert systems whose rules are derived from human experts representing different, often conflicting, areas of expertise. This approach involves finding and resolving all possible conflicts among the knowledge base entries *before* the system is used, typically using some kind of semantic analysis of the knowledge base contents (Bezem 1987; Trice and Davis 1989). Such a conflict management process would have the subtasks listed in table 16.3 when modeled as a specialization of the generic conflict management meta-process.

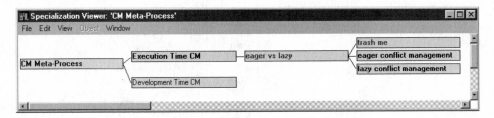

Figure 16.9
Subset of the conflict management meta-process taxonomy

Table 16.3
Conflict management meta-process for development-time conflict management

Subtask	How implemented
Identify target conflicts	Target conflicts are inconsistencies among the potential conclusions of any of the rules in the knowledge base
Determine conflict finding processes	Use hardwired rule consistency checking code
Enact conflict finding processes	Consistency checking code is enacted by the knowledge base developers as desired when the knowledge base is being developed
Select conflict instances to fix	All conflicts are fixed, typically in the order in which they are found
Determine conflict fixing processes	All conflict instances are fixed by the process 'Consult human knowledge base developers'
Enact conflict fixing processes	Process 'Consult human knowledge base developers' is enacted at development time as desired
Collect learnings	N/A

Execution-time conflict management, by contrast, involves detecting and resolving conflicts during the actual design process. The conflict management meta-process for one example of this approach (Klein 1997) is given in table 16.4.

16.2.3 Using the Conflict Repository

As noted above, we have identified three key uses for process repositories:

• Pedagogy.   Helping students, researchers, and practitioners learn about the state of the art in design conflict management

• Business process re-design.   Helping practitioners (re-)design the conflict management aspects of their collaborative design processes

• Research.   Helping researchers identify gaps in conflict management technology, identify common abstractions, facilitate discussion, and develop new ideas

Table 16.4
Conflict management meta-process for execution-time conflict management

Subtask	How implemented
Identify target conflicts	Human designer selects, at any point during the design process, the conflicts he/she is interested in by selecting from a predefined conflict taxonomy
Determine conflict finding processes	Every conflict type has a single predefined (hardwired) conflict detection process
Enact conflict finding processes	Detection processes for the selected conflicts are enacted on-demand—when the human designer requests it
Select conflict instances to fix	Human designer selects which conflicts to fix from the list presented by the system
Determine conflict fixing processes	System uses a diagnostic procedure and a knowledge base of generic conflict handling strategies to generate a sorted list of proposed specific conflict resolutions. The human designer then selects which resolution to use, or may choose to define his/her own resolution
Enact conflict fixing processes	System enacts the selected resolution, if any, on demand
Collect learnings	Completed conflict resolution instances are stored as cases in a database for later use as data to help add to and refine the conflict knowledge base contents

We will now consider how the conflict repository can be used for these purposes.

Pedagogy   The original Process Handbook allows users to browse through the specialization taxonomy for processes in the domain of interest, inspecting their attributes, decompositions, and dependencies and comparing their relative merits using the trade-off tables in bundles. The conflict repository built on the Handbook augments this by providing a richer set of links, as described above. The Web version of the Handbook, designed for pedagogical use, is shown in figure 16.10.

One can traverse the current taxonomy up or down by clicking on the 'generalization' or 'specialization' buttons, or follow crosslinks (in this example, links from the conflict to a conflict handler) by clicking on hotlinked item.

The specialization taxonomies underlying the conflict repository facilitate cross-disciplinary knowledge transfer by revealing commonalities in the goals and approaches of techniques from different domains. They do so by (1) highlighting the extensive overlap in conflict types across different domains and (2) colocating conflict handling processes with similar purposes, regardless of their origin. Should an automobile designer follow the 'is detected by' links from the 'geometric overlap' conflict, for example, he/she will immediately encounter such ideas as 'digital preassembly' (used in the airplane industry) and 'daily mockups' (used in the software industry). Similarly an airplane designer looking at the conflict avoidance processes branch will find such ideas as 'set-based design' (used in the automobile industy).

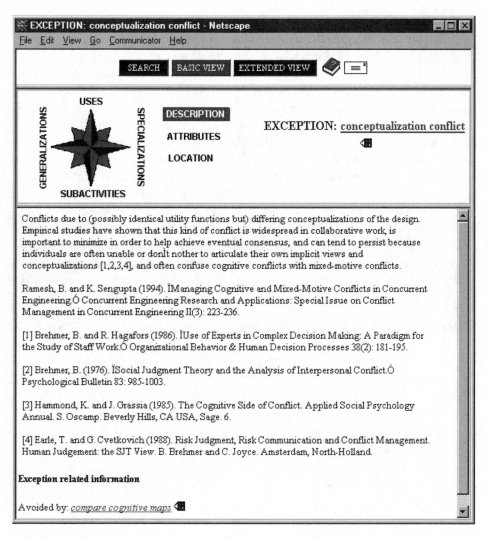

Figure 16.10
Screen snapshot of the Web-accessible version of the conflict repository

Business Process Redesign   The conflict repository supports a simple but powerful methodology for (re-)designing the conflict management procedures used in one's design processes. It involves applying the Handbook's process redesign methodology (Herman et al. 1998) to the conflict management meta-process one is using/starting from. All of the subtasks in this process, as we have seen, have multiple alternative specializations (i.e., ways of realizing that subtask). We can therefore explore many different variations of the process by systematically varying the alternatives we select for each subtask. We can vary, for example, whether 'Enact conflict detection processes' is done immediately after every design change ("eager" conflict detection), on a scheduled basis (as in the 'daily build' process used by Microsoft), or as desired by the designers or design managers ("lazy" conflict detection). We can decide whether 'determine conflict fixing processes' is done using computer tools to suggest resolutions, by providing designers access to the conflict repository, by leaving them on their own, and so on. A tool known as the Process Recombinator (Bernstein et al. 1999), available under the Windows version of the Process Handbook, has been developed to support this systematic exploration of different subtask combinations (figure 16.11).

Facilitating Research   A conflict repository can serve as a valuable resource for fostering more effective, accumulative, and cross-disciplinary research on conflict management, in several important ways. The taxonomic structure of the repository facilitates *finding gaps* in the conflict management knowledge. One can, for example, look for conflict types with no associated resolution strategies, or for sparsely popu-

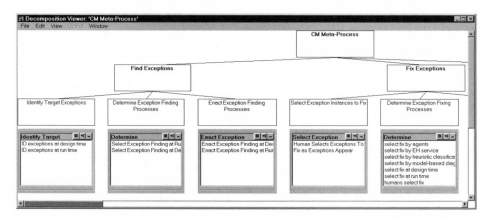

Figure 16.11
Snapshot of the process recombinator

lated regions of the conflict resolution strategy space (e.g., where a trade-off table has no alternatives identified for common values of a key design characteristic). The conflict repository structure can enable *structured discussions* by organizing them around focus topics such as filling in a particular branch of a taxonomy, adding to a trade-off table, or detailing a particular process description. It is our experience that such foci can be more effective than unstructured discussions for capturing process knowledge. The process re-design methodology described above can, finally, be used to help *invent new conflict management techniques.*

Imagine, for example, that one wishes to explore variations to the "change memo" conflict detection process described above. One possibility is to consider different processes for managing the dependency between the "create change memo" and "review memo" steps. This quickly reveals such interesting alternatives as "making" change memos to order (i.e., when the receiving engineers are ready for them), collocating engineers to minimize change memo distribution time, and using content-based routing or filter agents to ensure that engineers get only relevant memos. This can be taken one step further by looking at 'distant analogies' (processes that address different but functionally similar challenges) as a way of suggesting creative alternatives (chapter 12 in this volume).

Consider, for example, the development time conflict management technique mentioned above, wherein rule bases are modified before being merged, based on the results of automated semantic analysis, to prevent them from asserting conflicting conclusions. Pursuing this distant analogy suggests the idea of using semantic conflict analysis to design specialized training curricula for designers involved in large projects, helping them avoid needless conflicts. Not all distant analogies will lead, of course, to useful ideas.

16.3   Evaluation of the Contributions of This Work

The conflict repository described in this chapter makes substantive contributions to previous work in this area. These include greater expressiveness and content coverage, which in turn help make the repository potentially more effective in supporting prototypical uses.

Expressiveness   Previous efforts to create conflict knowledge repositories (Matta 1996; Castelfranchi 1996; Ramesh and Sengupta 1994; Feldman 1985) all include either a conflict type taxonomy or a conflict handler taxonomy, and even both, with links between conflict types and the potentially applicable conflict handlers. None of these efforts, however, capture the linkage between collaborative design processes and their characteristic conflict types, nor do they capture the important information encoded by the conflict management meta-process described in this chapter. Finally, they don't take advantage of process abstraction and bundle/trade-off concepts to enable quick discovery and comparison of alternative processes for similar needs. It is our preliminary judgment that the schema presented above captures all the significant aspects of the conflict management information we have encountered in the literature we have reviewed to date.

Coverage   Previous efforts in this area have produced repositories that are quite small in scale. The taxonomy described in Matta et al. (1998), Feldman (1985), Ramesh and Sengupta (1994), and Castelfranchi (1996) includes no more than about thirty conflict types and handler processes. These efforts in addition focus on individual disciplines. Matta's work, for example, focuses on the concurrent engineering literature, Feldman's on the sociological literature, and Castelfranchi's on multi-agent systems. While one can argue that they provide complete coverage at an abstract level, they necessarily leave out descriptions of a large number of specific, potentially useful conflict management techniques.

   The repository described in this chapter is significantly larger in scope. It includes roughly the same number of conflict types as those described above but a significantly larger number of conflict management processes (about 200 at the time of writing). The contents of the MIT repository have been drawn from several disciplines including distributed artificial intelligence, sociology, and industrial engineering, as represented by roughly fifty publications from such venues as the *Journal of Concurrent Engineering Research and Applications*, the *Journal of Artificial Intelligence in Engineering Design Analysis and Manufacturing*, the *Sloan Management Review*, the *International Conference on Artificial Intelligence in Design*, and the *National Conference on Artificial Intelligence*. Our repository continues to grow, with the support of a continuing three-year grant from the National Science Foundation (Grant No. IIS-9803251).

Better Support for Prototypical Uses   The MIT conflict repository has been evaluated only on a limited internal basis to date, so it is premature to draw definitive conclusions about its utility for students, researchers, and practitioners. It is clear, however, that the Process Handbook provides a level of enabling technology that has not been exploited in previous conflict repository efforts. Previous work has resulted mainly in textual documents (with the notable exception of Matta et al. who made the repository available over the Web), and does not include the kind of search, navigation, business process redesign, and structured discussion tools available as part of the Handbook. Previous experience with these tools suggests that they can be powerful enablers. The Handbook has been successfully used, for example, to teach classes at the Sloan School of Management as well as at Babson College. The Handbook process redesign methodology has been applied in several domains, most recently (in cooperation with the consulting firm AT Kearney) to redesign the hiring processes in a major financial services firm. The participants in this study felt that the approach was effective in generating a much wider range of novel and promising process alternatives than would have been uncovered by traditional methods (chapter 12 in this volume).

16.4 Future Work

The MIT conflict repository is a work in progress. We plan to continue to add to and better structure the repository content, drawing from multiple disciplines. We will explore the use of additional repository structuring schemes and tools, such as the notion of a "guided tour" that provides a suggested sequence for traversing the specialization taxonomies for specific pedagogical purposes. The repository will be submitted to a series of evaluations by different classes of users in order to assess and help improve its utility. The biggest challenge, however, will be evolving the conflict repository into a living self-sustaining community resource. This will require addressing technological issues (e.g., developing a Web-based authoring tool) as well as sociological issues concerning incentives for adding content.

For additional information about this and related work, including access to the MIT conflict repository itself, see *http://ccs.mit.edu/klein/*.

Acknowledgments

This work was supported by the NSF Computation and Social Systems program and by the DARPA Control of Agent Based Systems and Automated Rule-Based Decision Making programs. I am grateful for many helpful comments from Chris Dellarocas (MIT Sloan School of Management), Feniosky Pena-Mora (MIT Department of Civil Engineering), and the members of the MIT Center for Coordination Science: Leon Grekin, John Quimby, George Herman, George Wyner, Abraham Bernstein, and Thomas Malone.

17 Genre Taxonomy: A Knowledge Repository of Communicative Actions

Takeshi Yoshioka
George A. Herman
JoAnne Yates
Wanda Orlikowski

17.1 Introduction

Human communication has always been central to organizational action. It is not too much to say that whether a business is effective or not depends in large part on how well it communicates with its customers. These days many businesses face new communication challenges because they need to move their operations into a new sphere, such as making inroads into foreign markets and creating e-commerce units. As the Internet has spread, it has made communicating with various people easier, and it has facilitated the emergence and use of many types of new communication media within a variety of different business situations. For example, a virtual meeting space is used in daily communication within a software research and development community (Churchill and Bly 1999). Electronic bulletin boards are also used to share information on topics of common interest within communities of practice (Wenger and Snyder 2000) or professional associations such as the American Medical Association (Hagel and Armstrong 1997). Thus thinking strategically about the effectiveness of communication becomes increasingly important for organizations to obtain desired audience responses and achieve stated business goals.

There are many textbooks and guides on managerial communication (e.g., Munter 1997), but they provide only typical knowledge, and do not give us adequate guidance for communicating in a new medium or in a radically new situation. In order to apply knowledge in new conditions, we need an environment where well-categorized, typical examples are documented and available, where we can find similar cases to understand conditions for use and get ideas to apply to new situations or media, and to which we can add emergent examples.

Today knowledge creation, transfer, and transformation are seen as particularly important arenas for communication. The success of an organization often depends on whether or not members of the organization actively create knowledge and how effectively they share that knowledge within the organization through communication. As Senge (1990) claims, dialogue and skillful discussion are critical for

An earlier version of this chapter appeared as T. Yoshioka, G. A. Herman, J. Yates, and W. Orlikowski (2001), Genre taxonomy: A knowledge repository of communicative actions, *ACM Transactions on Information Systems* 19(4): 431–56. © 2001 ACM. Reprinted by permission.

developing "learning organizations." In addition people are said to "make knowledge their own" within a communicative situation, that is, people often learn in the context of ordinary communication (Brown, Collins, and Duiguid 1989). Knowledge management is a buzzword now, and many firms have created their own knowledge repositories to share and reuse knowledge in the organization. However, a typical knowledge repository stores specific domain knowledge such as knowledge related to design and manufacturing in a firm, and the purpose is usually only to share the content of documents and document templates. Thus the knowledge repository provides "know-what" but not "know-how" or "know-why," and typically lacks the shared context for communication that helps with the mastery of new knowledge.

In this chapter we propose a new type of knowledge repository (a genre taxonomy) that represents know-what (the constituent elements of genres of communication) along with know-how and know-why (the typified social context of genre use). A genre, such as a report or a meeting, may be defined as a type of communication recognized and enacted by members of a community or organization (Yates and Orlikowski 1992). Genres may be analyzed in terms of a number of dimensions, particularly those representing the why (purpose), what (content), when (timing), where (location), who (participants), and how (structure and medium) of communication (5W1H). For the last decade or two many new electronic communication media such as electronic mail and the World Wide Web have emerged and evolved, but few people understand what genres to enact within these new media or how to use such media effectively within organizations. We believe that our genre taxonomy prototype, which offers knowledge about genres, as well as their effective use, can help people learn and communicate knowledge about genres, and to adapt or innovate their communication within new electronic media.

In this chapter we will introduce our genre taxonomy and its prototype implementation in the Process Handbook (Malone et al. 1999), a process repository developed by the Center for Coordination Science at MIT. In the next section we introduce and describe the notion of genres of organizational communication. In section 17.3 we describe the genre taxonomy in terms of the 5W1H dimensions and the use and evolution of genres over time. In section 17.4 we use coordination theory (Malone and Crowston 1994) to demonstrate how genres coordinate information in terms of usefulness, location, and timing. In section 17.5 we explain the prototype implementation of the genre taxonomy. In section 17.6 we draw on the genres used within the admissions process at MIT's Sloan School of Management (Orlikowski, Yates, and Fonstad 2001) to describe the relationship between genres and work processes, and illustrate the benefits that may be derived from using the genre taxonomy in practice. We conclude the paper by discussing the implications of the genre taxonomy for researchers and practitioners.

17.2 Genres of Organizational Communication

As a concept, genre has a long tradition in rhetorical and literary analysis (Bakhtin 1986). Recently a number of researchers in cultural, rhetorical, and design studies have begun using it to refer to typified social action (Brown 1994; Bazerman 1988; Berkenkotter and Huckin 1995; Miller 1984). Orlikowski and Yates (1992) have applied the notion of genres to organizational communications such as business letters, memos, face-to-face meetings, reports, and announcements. They define genres as "socially recognized types of communicative action habitually enacted by members of a community to realize particular communicative and collaborative purposes" (Yates and Orlikowski 1992, p. 299). Genres may be identified by their socially recognized purpose and common characteristics of form.

The *purpose* of a genre is not an individual's private motive for communication, but the purpose that senders and recipients of communication within a community socially recognize and invoke in a typical situation, for example, proposing a project, informing and directing in an official announcement, or brainstorming how to resolve a problem. The *form* of a genre refers to the observable aspects of the communication: media, such as pen and paper, face-to-face, and electronic mail; structural features, such as document style and format; and linguistic features, such as informality, humor, and technical language.

Yates and Orlikowski (1992) argue that genres constitute social structures that manifest what Giddens (1984) has called the "duality of structure." That is, structures are enacted by the recurrent social practices that shape and are shaped by them. Understanding this duality of structure helps us to comprehend how and why genres are established, used, and changed over time.

Yates and Orlikowski also examined the genres enacted in such electronic communication media as electronic mailing lists (Orlikowski and Yates 1994), Usenet newsgroups (Yates, Orlikowski, and Okamura 1999), and the Team Rooms of Lotus Notes databases (Yates, Orlikowski, and Rennecker 1997; Yates and Orlikowski 1997; Orlikowski and Yates 1998). Drawing on Bazerman's (1994) notion of genre system—sequences of interrelated communicative actions such as the reviewing process for a scientific journal—Yates and Orlikowski examined the genre systems in use within a US high-technology company using Team Room (Yates, Orlikowski, and Rennecker 1997). They found that a genre system reveals expectations about

purpose, participants, content, form, timing, and location of communicative interactions. For the purposes of this chapter, the key difference between a genre and
genre system is that while each has attributes, a genre system additionally has
relational attributes that indicate relationships among constituent genres, such as
sequence.

17.3 Genre Taxonomy

Our objective in proposing a genre taxonomy is to help people make sense of diverse
types of communicative actions. The genre taxonomy thus has to represent both
widely recognized genres, such as a report, and specific genres, such as a technical
report used in a specific company, so that the context of genre use is highlighted. For
example, comparing the form features evident in a technical report genre used by a
company with those of the more general report genre helps us identify the different
institutions that shaped the specific genre.

The genre taxonomy also has to represent the elements of a genre as embedded in
a social context reflecting the "5W1H" questions (Why, What, Who, When, Where,
and How).[1] In other words, the genre taxonomy represents dimensions of genres in
terms of purpose, content, participants, timing, location, and form (including media
and linguistic devices). We do not intend these six dimensions to be exhaustive or
definitive, but rather offer them as a grounded starting point for classifying characteristics of genres and genre systems based on empirical evidence in organizations.
While other semantic categorization systems have been proposed (e.g., Lehnert 1978;
Pentland and Lee 2001), they are based on formal approaches rather than empirical
data. For our purposes here, we have preferred to base our taxonomic categories on
the dimensions derived from Yates and Orlikowski's empirical work on the use of
genres in organizational practice.[2] We describe each of the six dimensions of genre
below.

17.3.1 *Why*: Purpose of a Genre/Genre System
Berkenkotter and Huckin (1995) use speech act theory (Austin 1975; Searle 1969) as
a deductive analytic framework for describing the textual moves that actors make

---

1. Yates and Orlikowski illustrate that genre systems are a means of structuring six (5W1H) aspects of
communicative actions. We extend their consideration to a genre that also has these aspects. Due to the
imprecision of language, we do not intend the six terms (why, what, etc.) to be taken literally but as
pointing to the underlying genre aspect ('purpose', 'Content', etc.)

2. Future work could include exploring the similarity and differences among the approaches.

when they intend to persuade in a peer review process. Although speech act theory is targeted at a speaker's utterances, they conclude that analysis of the illocutionary acts evident in peer review communication provides empirical evidence that illocutionary acts do get things accomplished in the world, either through direct or indirect means.

We established initial purpose categories in our genre taxonomy based on speech act theory, and modified and added some categories based on the coding schemes that Yates and Orlikowski used in their empirical genre studies (Orlikowski and Yates 1994; Yates, Orlikowski, and Okamura 1999; Yates, Orlikowski, and Rennecker 1997). In addition we referred to Roget's thesaurus (Roget and Chapman 1992) and WordNet (Fellbaum 1998), an on-line lexical database for English developed by the Cognitive Science Laboratory at Princeton University, to clarify notions and write explanations of each category. The purpose categories now consist of eight items: inform, request, express (emotion), decide, propose, respond, record, and other (to allow expansion of a scheme that is inherently open ended).

Some genres, especially generally recognized genres, such as the memo, have multiple purposes, and the genre taxonomy differentiates primary purposes and secondary purposes to help prioritization of genre use in social contexts. For example, the memo genre is used mainly to inform its readers and record information, and it may be used for directing an order or for proposing some course of action.

It is worth noting that a genre system usually has a different purpose than its constituent genres because a genre system itself provides expectations about its socially recognized purposes to coordinate the collaborative activities by means of its constituent genres. We can illustrate this using the ballot genre system (see figure 17.1), which Yates and Orlikowski (1994) identified from studying a group of distributed professionals using electronic mail to negotiate the Common Lisp specifications (hereafter we call this task the Common Lisp project).

The ballot genre system has three interrelated genres: the ballot questionnaire genre issued by the coordinator, the ballot response genre generated by group members, and the ballot result genre, a summary of the replies issued by the coordinator. As the ballot genre system was used to poll opinions and test consensus among the participants, it might belong to the 'decide' purpose. The ballot questionnaire genre might belong to both the 'inform' and 'request' purpose categories, because it was used to inform group members about issues and to request their replies. The ballot response genre might belong to the 'respond' purpose category, and the ballot result genre might belong to the 'inform' and 'record' purpose categories because the coordinator used the genre to notify group members of the results of a ballot and to

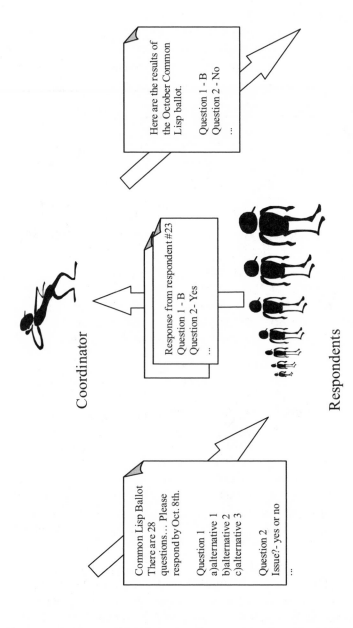

Figure 17.1
Example of correspondences in the ballot genre system in the common lisp project (excerpt)

record them electronically. Thus the ballot genre system as a whole has a purpose different from the purpose of its constituent genres.

17.3.2 *What*: Content of a Genre/Genre System

Genres provide expectations about content of a communication. For example, the recipient of a thank you note expects it to include some words representing the sender's appreciation. Suppose that an organization has a convention of a daily morning meeting and the meeting usually includes the manager's comments about his or her views of the present state of things. The specific face-to-face genre enacted at this organization might include the expectation of managerial comments. The genre taxonomy represents the typical content expected of different types of genres.

As mentioned, sometimes genres are linked to each other so as to constitute a genre system that coordinates communicative actions. For example, the face-to-face meeting genre system may include the meeting announcement genre, the meeting agenda genre, the face-to-face meeting genre, and the minutes genre. Certain genres could be omitted from the genre system (e.g., meeting announcement), or combined (e.g., meeting announcement and agenda), while others are required (e.g., the meeting cannot be excluded).

The genre taxonomy indexes genre systems and also the genre constituents of each genre system. Thus it can be used to discover both what genres a genre system may have and what genre systems are in the taxonomy. Both a genre system and its genre constituents are classified in the genre taxonomy under relevant purpose categories; thus the coordination process in a genre system may be understood through examining the purposes of the genre system and its constituent genres. For example, in the ballot genre system described above, the difference in purpose categories between the ballot genre system and the ballot questionnaire genre suggests that a ballot questionnaire helps to coordinate the decision process by informing recipients about issues and options and requesting responses by a due date.

17.3.3 *Who*: Participants in a Genre/Genre System

A genre is enacted by participants who communicate within a community, whose size may range from very small such as a department, an organization, and a class in a school to very large such as a profession and the citizenry of one or more countries. In the genre taxonomy, each genre is associated with a community to which its participants belong. For example, all genres elicited from the Common Lisp project are associated with the category 'Genres of the Common Lisp project' and all genres used in the on-line Process Handbook (*http://css.mit.edu/pif*) are associated with 'Genres of the on-line Process Handbook.' The collection of genres used in the same community represents that community's genre repertoire, or the set of genres enacted by community members (Orlikowski and Yates 1994).

Different genres within a genre system may also be associated with different senders and receivers. In the ballot genre system, for example, the coordinator issues the ballot questionnaire and the ballot result, while other group members receive these messages and send ballot responses.

17.3.4 *When*: Timing of a Genre/Genre System

Because a genre is invoked in a recurrent situation, its use is associated with particular timing or opportunity (Yates and Orlikowski 1998). Time can be quantitative or qualitative, clock or event based, and so on (Hassard 1996). For example, the thank you note genre is used when a person feels some appreciation for the gift or activity bestowed by another (i.e., event-based timing). Or, the daily morning meeting genre enacted within a specific organization, includes expectations of when it begins and ends (e.g., begins at 8:30 AM and ends at 9:00 AM) (i.e., clock-based timing). The genre taxonomy includes any timing expectations associated with the use of a genre, for instance, that a genre should be used within a certain time period of an event (e.g., thank you notes being sent within a few weeks) or at set time intervals (e.g., the daily morning meeting).

A genre system typically has expectations about the sequence of its constituent elements. Thus the constituent genres of a genre system are related by their relative timing within a genre system. Altering the order of the constituent genres of a genre system creates a different variant of a genre system. For example, if a meeting announcement is sent before an agenda, the decision process used to decide which people will participate may be different than if an agenda is sent out before or along with the meeting announcement.

17.3.5 *Where*: Location of a Genre/Genre System

In a sense a genre reflects the culture shared by participants in a community, since it identifies the recurrent situation or socially defined need from the history and nature of established practices, social relations, and communication media within the community. For example, a kaizen proposal is used in Japanese corporations to facilitate bottom-up quality improvement, a common activity in Japanese manufacturing departments. Thus the genre taxonomy represents the location where a genre is typically enacted such as Japan, or Massachusetts, or northeastern United States. For electronic communication over the Internet, the physical locations of communicative actions are becoming less meaningful because of the shifting borders characteristic of cyberspace. However, because virtual spaces provide expectations of "where" in an

Internet community, the genre taxonomy may also include expectations about virtual space in addition to those for physical space. For example, a study of a Japanese R&D project group by Yates and Orlikowski found that members of different subgroups enacted genres within different "local" newsgroups in the Usenet-based groupware system (Yates, Orlikowski, and Okamura 1999).

A genre system also includes expectations about physical or virtual location. Using the ballot genre system as an example, if the participants are located close to each other, or they have an opportunity to gather at the same place such as an AAAI conference, then a physical or face-to-face balloting system might be easy to implement. In the case of the Common Lisp project, an email approach was used that allowed the coordinator and the various respondents to conduct electronic ballots when participants were geographically dispersed.

17.3.6 *How*: Form of a Genre/Genre System

As we described in the previous section, a genre is typically characterized by a recognizable form. Form refers to observable features that include structural elements, medium, and linguistic features. The genre taxonomy represents these features along with purposes for identifying a genre. For example, the genre taxonomy includes the 'Electronic traditional memo in Japan' genre, identified in the communication of a Japanese R&D group by Yates, Orlikowski, and Okamura, with 'Kanji signature' and 'no embedded message' as structural features, 'Usenet news group adjusted to Japanese environment' as medium, and 'Kanji subject line' and 'no dialect' as linguistic features.

A genre system also has expectations about form, including expectations about media, and about the genres making up the system. For example, the face-to-face meeting genre system typically includes an announcement and an agenda in writing (either paper base or electronic), a face-to-face meeting, and minutes in writing. But form features may vary by local conventions or even by instance. For example, the face-to-face meeting genre system enacted in a certain group may not include the agenda genre and/or minutes genre due to the group's conventions.

17.3.7 Evolution of a Genre/Genre System over Time

From the organizational point of view, a genre is used in a process cycle that consists of enacting a genre and observing genre use.[3] At the same time genre use influences the participants involved in the communication. In enacting a genre, participants

---

3. For analytic purposes we separate 'Enact genre' and 'Observe genre use', though in practice they are intertwined.

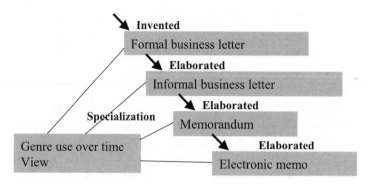

Figure 17.2
Genre evolution example from business letter genre to electronic memo genre

identify (whether reflectively or habitually) a recurrent situation and genre rules from their prior communication experiences in order to select an appropriate genre. They usually reproduce the established genre, but sometimes elaborate, replace, or under-cut it either inadvertently or deliberately in order to adapt to changes in the situation. Recipients identify the genre or genre variant being used based on their identification of a recurrent situation and their own prior experiences. A specific genre such as an email memo typically used in a particular company is a variant from the more general memo, and the genre taxonomy places specific genres in a category named 'Examples of a widely recognized genre' which is a subcategory under this general genre category.

The 'genre use over time' process cycle is a dynamic state of production, repro-duction, and change. A genre can evolve from another genre because participants can elaborate or replace genres during their enactment. For example, in the past, a memo was elaborated from the informal business letter genre and the electronic memo genre was elaborated from the memo genre (see figure 17.2). In each case the genre had been used in an ongoing manner in one form before it was elaborated in another form over time.

17.4   Coordinating Information Using Genres

As described in section 17.2, when the members in a community enact genres and/or genre systems, they draw on expectations of communicative purpose, content, form, participants, timing, and location. In other words, use of genres attempts to facilitate the credible flow of appropriate information to the appropriate place at the appro-

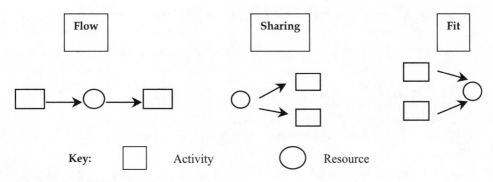

Figure 17.3
Flow, fit, and sharing dependencies

priate time. In this context, appropriateness is that which is socially accepted and credibility is in accordance with socially recognized purpose, participants, communication sequence, and form. As shown in figure 17.1, use of genre coordinates information exchanged in communicative action. In this section we illustrate how genres can be used to coordinate information through coordination theory (Malone and Crowston 1994) and extending the work of Osborn (Osborn 1996) to emphasize genres. We also illustrate coordination mechanisms in which genres address issues of appropriateness related to resource usability, location, and temporality, including divisibility, reusability, accessibility, and timing.

17.4.1   Coordination Theory and the Process Handbook

In coordination theory, coordination is defined as managing dependencies among activities. Malone and Crowston propose three types of elementary dependencies: flow, fit, and sharing (figure 17.3).[4] A *flow* dependency arises whenever an activity produces a resource or resources that are used by another activity. A *fit* dependency occurs whenever multiple activities collectively produce the same resource, and a *sharing* dependency occurs whenever the same resources are used by multiple activities.

Processes called coordination mechanisms manage the relationships represented by dependencies. A flow dependency has coordination mechanisms that ensure the provision of the right resource at the right place and right time. For example, a process to provide resources *just in time* is a coordination mechanism that manages a flow

---

4. Figure 17.3 is borrowed from Malone et al. (1999).

dependency. Another coordination mechanism would be to build a stock of inventory in advance.

The Process Handbook has been under development at the Center for Coordination Science at MIT for over seven years. The goal of the Process Handbook project is to develop a process repository which contains a generic framework for classifying business processes, including selected examples of "best practices," case studies, and other process descriptions, with integrated tools for viewing, retrieving, and authoring process knowledge.

Based on coordination theory, the Process Handbook incorporates two key concepts: process specialization and dependencies.

There are two hierarchies that represent processes in the Process Handbook. One is typical of most process representation tools: a decomposition hierarchy that represents a "has a" relationship network between activities (i.e., X has a Y), in which an activity in Process Handbook is broken down into its subactivities. The other is a specialization hierarchy, an "is a" relationship network between activities (i.e., X is a Y), in which an activity inherits the attributes from its parent activities. This specialization hierarchy is similar to that in object-oriented programming, but it is specialized in terms not of objects (nouns) but processes (verbs).

In figure 17.4 we show the decomposition of 'Sell product' into its component parts or subactivities. The two specializations of 'Sell product' shown are 'Mail order sales' and 'Retail Store sales'. These two specializations inherit the subactivities such as 'Identify prospects' (among other attributes) from the parent activity and then may 'specialize' the subactivity. For example, the way that one identifies prospects in mail order sales is by obtaining mailing lists.

We have a taxonomy of over 5,000 activities in the Process Handbook. Specializations of an activity are often grouped into 'bundles' that are represented by [brackets].

17.4.2   Coordinating Information Flow, Fit, and Sharing with Genres

Genres convey socially recognized information that is associated with the typical communicative interactions occurring within a community. Genres coordinate the *flow* of information from senders to recipients, and legitimate the manner and form in which it is conveyed. For example, in the ballot genre system (figure 17.1), a coordinator uses the ballot questionnaire genre to send information about issues, and to poll opinions and test consensus.

Genres may be used to *fit* information from senders together and coordinate other activities. In the ballot response genre, for example, the responses from participants were sent to the coordinator, who aggregated the data (fit) and posted a ballot result.

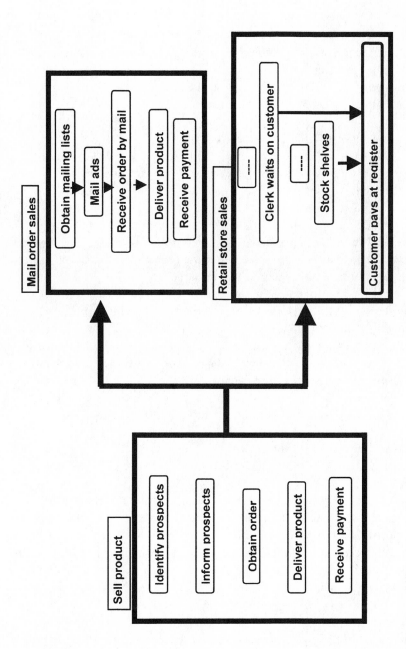

Figure 17.4
Process inheritance and specializations of the activity 'Sell product'

Information carried by certain genres can be *shared* by multiple activities. For example, information in a ballot result could be shared by two or more activities. In the Common LISP project, the coordinator used it to write the manuscript of the Common Lisp manual, and members used it to ask questions about the results or to propose additional solutions using the dialogue genre.

17.4.3 Coordination Aspects Related to Resource Usability

As stated above, a flow dependency occurs when a resource produced by one activity is used by another. Coordination of this dependency depends on certain attributes of the resource: divisibility, concurrency, and reusability. Divisibility means that a resource can be divided without losing its utility. For example, water, money, or chocolate can be divided into smaller units. Concurrency means that multiple users can use the same resource at the same time (e.g., a Web page). Reusability means the same resource can be used multiple times without being consumed. In this section we describe how genres coordinate information as a resource.

The intangible nature of information allows for a wider spectrum of choices for coordination mechanisms. Information is easy to use concurrently or to reuse. Dividing information addresses the level of granularity. In the ballot questionnaire genre, the coordinator could divide a questionnaire into several short questionnaires, or he might bundle all the issues together in a single long questionnaire to ask the participants to contribute solutions to each issue all at once.

In addition information is easy to replicate, especially in electronic form. The coordinator electronically copied ballot responses into the ballot results.

17.4.4 Coordination Aspects Related to Time

We can consider two temporal aspects of coordination mechanisms: timing and the sequencing of activities.

Participants in a genre or genre system have expectations about timing such as a deadline or due date. For example, the ballot questionnaire genre contains information about reply date, so use of the genre coordinates responses from participants, supporting the coordination of the overall ballot genre system. This timing is explicit, but participants may also have implicit timing expectations about genre use. For example, the participants might have expected and accepted the ballot genre system to be invoked when they recognized that there were urgent issues around which they needed to reach consensus.

As constituent genres of a genre system interlock, participants in a community also have common expectations about the sequencing of activities among the constituent genres. The genre system helps the participants act coherently in a socially recognized sequence. For example, the sequence of ballot processes constituting the ballot genre system provided expectations to the Common LISP participants about the sequence of activities involved in a ballot. Even at the first ballot, use of the genre system coordinated participants' activity because they recognized the electronic ballot processes by identifying similarities and differences with their past paper voting activities. All elements of the genre system may not have an exact sequence (e.g., the sequence of responses may vary from ballot to ballot), but certain elements must be in sequence for the whole to be recognizable as a genre system and to successfully coordinate an activity over time.

17.4.5   Coordination Aspects Related to Location

As described in section 17.3.5, genres provide expectations about the location of communicative actions. There are two aspects of coordination mechanisms: space and accessibility.

Using a location coordination mechanism, we can move or collocate produced or consumed resources of activities. Information is easy to move. In the Common Lisp project the coordinator could issue the ballot questionnaire electronically. Information can also be concurrently accessed. The Common Lisp ballot genre system provides a common virtual space to help the participants reach consensus on contentious issues. The ballot response genre also specifies where the responses from the participants should be sent (moved)—that is, to the coordinator's electronic mailbox.

Using an accessibility coordination mechanism, we can control access at the location where resources are assigned. When we use genres in an electronic medium, such as Web pages and e-mail, it is important to consider coordination mechanisms relevant to both openness and trust of information. As genres provide socially recognized expectations about access, the characteristics of the medium may shape the condition of access. For example, in the case of the ballot response genre, which uses a mailing list including all the participants, a participant could expect that the entire content of his or her reply would be accessible to other participants.

17.5   Prototype of the Genre Taxonomy

We implemented a prototype of the genre taxonomy using the Process Handbook developed at MIT (Malone et al. 1999). The prototype of the genre taxonomy currently contains both widely recognized genres and specific genres. Currently the open set of widely recognized genres includes fourteen genres: business letter, memo, expense form, report, face-to-face meeting genre system, personal homepage, and so on. Specific genres include the results of genre analysis from three prior studies undertaken by Yates and Orlikowski: Common Lisp project genres (Orlikowski and Yates 1994), Acorn project genres (Yates, Orlikowski, and Okamura 1999), and Team Room genre systems (Yates, Orlikowski, and Rennecker 1997). Specific genres also include those found in two other cases we analyzed: the on-line Process Handbook genre system, and genres related to the on-line admissions process at the MIT Sloan School of Management (which we refer to as Sloan Admissions). Because the Process Handbook syntax is based on activities that must be named with a verb, a genre in the genre taxonomy is not simply named (as in 'memo') but is named with a verb prefix (as in 'Communicate using memo'). Below we will describe how we implemented the genre taxonomy in the Process Handbook. The genre taxonomy is implemented using the Process Handbook elements of the specialization hierarchy, the decomposition hierarchy, flow, fit, and sharing dependencies and the description field of activities.

17.5.1   Implementation of Information about *Why*: The Purpose of a Genre/Genre System

The genre taxonomy uses a specialization hierarchy and bundles to represent the purpose categories described in section 17.3. Figure 17.5 shows in an outline form the purpose categories currently represented in the genre taxonomy. Each purpose category, such as 'Inform', is under the '[Communicate why?]' bundle.

```
Communicate
        [Communicate why?]
                Inform
                        [Inform using what genre?]
                                Communicate using a report
                                Communicate using memo
                                Communicate using business letter
                                         ...
                Request
                Express
                Decide
                Propose
                Respond
                Record
                Communicate for other purpose
```

Figure 17.5
Excerpt of process categories in the genre taxonomy

If a genre has only one primary purpose, then we use the purpose in its title, such as 'Propose using a proposal'. If it has multiple primary purposes, we use 'communicate' in its title, such as 'Communicate using discussion'.

The description of the genre contains information about its primary and secondary purposes. For example, a memo might primarily be used to inform or record, and secondarily to request, express, and so on.

17.5.2 Implementation of Information about *What*: Content of a Genre/Genre System
The genre taxonomy uses the description field of the activity for representing the content of a genre.

The genre taxonomy uses a decomposition hierarchy to represent a genre system. Figure 17.6 illustrates what genres compose a typical face-to-face meeting genre system. While not all meetings will have all of these components, in this example we can see that the face-to-face meeting genre system typically consists of the meeting announcement genre, the agenda genre, the meeting genre, and the minutes genre.

17.5.3 Implementation of Information about *Who*: Participants in a Genre/Genre System
The "actor" attribute of an activity in the Process Handbook is intended to represent people who take part in a process. Multiple actors can be included in this attribute, so both senders and recipients of a communication can be included. If it is important to segregate senders and recipients for analysis, new attributes can be added to the various activities to reflect this. For example, the coordinator or facilitator sent the ballot questionnaire in the Common Lisp project to the entire Common Lisp community.

The actors in a genre system are the same as those enacting the various genres within the genre system. A genre repertoire consists of those genres and genre systems used by actors within a community or organization. The genre taxonomy uses

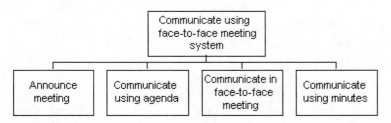

Figure 17.6
Description of the activity 'Communicate using face-to-face meeting system'

the specialization hierarchy and the bundle '[Communicate using genre repertoire—examples]' to show how different communities enact a set or repertoire of genres. For example, the genre repertoire identified in the Common Lisp project (Orlikowski and Yates 1994) consists of four activities: 'Decide using ballot system {Common Lisp Project}', 'Communicate using dialogue {Common Lisp Project}', 'Communicate using memo {Common Lisp Project}', and 'Communicate using CL proposal {Common Lisp Project}.

17.5.4   Implementation of Information about *When*: Timing of a Genre/Genre System

The genre taxonomy uses the description field of the activity to represent the timing and situation of use of a single genre. For example, a thank you note genre is sent at different times in different cultures or for different situations. In the United States, the time within which a thank you note should be sent depends on the number of gifts received. For one or a few gifts, a couple of weeks would be typical. For a large number of gifts such as those received for a wedding, a few months may be typical. In Japan, a thank you note for one or a large number of gifts is typically sent earlier than in the United States, and would be more likely to be sent within a month.

The genre taxonomy uses the Process Handbook's 'dependency diagram' capability to show the sequence of the genre constituents within a genre system. It also represents the dependencies between activities. For example, in the face-to-face meeting system, there are often four elements: announce meeting, communicate using agenda, communicate in face-to-face meeting, and communicate using minutes. The sequence of these activities may vary. For example, if the meeting announcement genre were to also contain the agenda, then the agenda itself must be developed before the announcement is sent.

17.5.5   Implementation of Information about *Where*: Location of a Genre/Genre System

The genre taxonomy uses a special attribute called 'location' to represent the location of a genre. This may be a physical location or a virtual location such as 'cyberspace'. Since a genre system may use multiple locations, the aggregate of the component genres locations make up the overall location for the genre system.

17.5.6   Implementation of Information about *How*: Form of a Genre/Genre System

In the genre taxonomy the description field is used for representing the form of the genres and genre systems. This description field is highly flexible and can include explanatory text, graphic objects, or links to Web sites with more information.

17.5.7 Implementation of Information about the Evolution of a Genre over Time

The specialization hierarchy, the decomposition hierarchy, and flow dependencies are used to depict genre use over time. As mentioned in section 17.3.7, genre use over time involves a process cycle.

Figure 17.7 is a dependency diagram from the Process Handbook where each activity in the cycle is an activity and each relation between processes is represented by a flow dependency. Note that it is usually only possible to identify the initial use of a genre retrospectively, after its establishment as a genre within a community. If no one reinforces the usage of a new 'proto-genre', it will not achieve the socially recognized status of a genre. For example, the ballot questionnaire only became a genre after the Common Lisp members responded to the ballot messages as requested and after further examples were enacted within the group. Moreover, even when the initial use of a genre is retrospectively identified, it may typically be characterized as a variation on a previously existing form (e.g., the ballot request commonly used in face-to-face meetings).

The specialization hierarchy and bundle are used to represent the relations between a general genre and its specific variants enacted in an organization. Figure 17.8 shows an example that uses a specialization hierarchy and a bundle named '[Communicate using genres for official announcement—examples]' to represent the relations between the official announcement genre and its variant genres such as the official announcement genre used in the Acorn project. Detecting the differences among those genres may give us an initial opportunity to consider the context of use of specific genres and employ that to explain why, how, and when the differences emerged.

During the evolution of the electronic memo genre, the informal business letter genre was elaborated from the formal business letter genre, the memo genre was elaborated from the informal business letter genre, and the electronic memo genre was elaborated from the memo genre. To represent this evolution in the Handbook, we use a decomposition hierarchy. Each element of this decomposition is a specialization of 'Genre use over time' activity. In order to represent evolution, 'Enact genre' activity is replaced by various specializations of the activity, such as the activity 'Enact elaboration of genre'. Constituent activities, such as 'Select genre', may also be replaced by a more specialized activity, such as 'Enact genre' activity. This representation using process inheritance is a simple and powerful feature of the Process Handbook. The genre taxonomy can represent the relation between the chronological view and genre use over time effectively, and thus the genre taxonomy enables users an historical review of genres with examples.

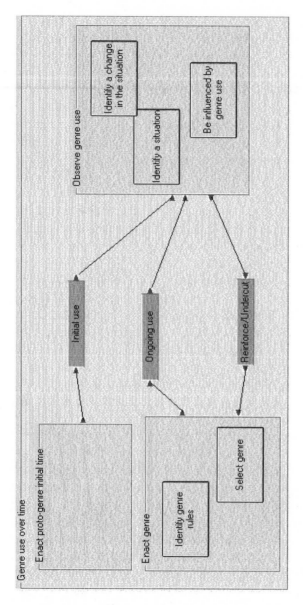

Figure 17.7
Dependency diagram of 'Genre use over time'

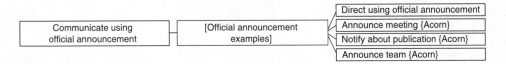

Figure 17.8
Specialization hierarchy example in the genre taxonomy

17.5.8 Representing Aspects of Genre Coordination

In addition to the 5W1H aspects described above, genres can also coordinate information associated with the dependencies described in section 17.4. The genre taxonomy prototype uses the dependency diagram functionality to represent this information. When a dependency diagram includes activities in which the actors use genres for communicative actions, the actors send and/or receive information, which is a resource of the dependency connected to the activity. As discussed in section 17.4.1, a sharing dependency occurs when the same resource is used by multiple activities. When this resource is associated with a genre, the genre plays a role in coordinating the sharing of information for the activities that use the resource. Similarly, when there is a fit dependency among activities with associated genres, the genres play a role in coordinating the fit of information for these activities. Note that when multiple actors perform one activity, a genre associated with this activity may play a role in coordinating the fit of the information provided by the multiple actors. For example, the 'Communicate using the ballot results genre' activity is associated with the 'Respond using the ballot response genre' activity whose actors are the many participants of the Common Lisp project, and the ballot results genre is used to fit together the information carried by the various instantiations of the ballot response genre.

In order to represent aspects of genre coordination related to resource usability, temporality, and location, the genre taxonomy uses a specialization hierarchy and bundles in order to classify the coordination aspects shown in section 17.4. The top activity named 'Coordinating information using genres' is under the activity 'Manage dependency', whose subactivities are other coordination mechanisms in the Process Handbook. Figure 17.9 illustrates a part of the specialization hierarchy under the activity 'Coordinating information using genres'. If the activity using genres can coordinate information in multiple ways, the activity is represented under multiple activities. For example, as shown in figure 17.9, the activity 'Communicate using the ballot questionnaire' is a subactivity of both the activity 'Coordinate divisibility of Info using genres' and the activity 'Coordinate timing of information using genres'.

```
Coordinate information using genres
     [Coordinate information – what aspect?]
               Coordinate usability using genres
                    Coordinate divisibility of information
                         Combine information using ballot
                              Combine using ballot {Common Lisp}
                         Divide info using paper and e-genre
                              …
                    Coordinate concurrency of information
                         …
                    Coordinate reusability of information
                         …
               Coordinate timing using genres
                    …
               Coordinate location using genres
                    …
```

Figure 17.9
Genre coordinating aspects example: An excerpt of the specialization hierarchy of 'Coordinate information using genres'

The specialization hierarchy and bundles of genre coordination mechanisms help us understand how a genre coordinates activities involving information.

17.6   Work Process Analysis Using the Genre Taxonomy

Because communication is a critical activity in and across organizations, there are strong relationships between work processes and communication. We illustrate how we can analyze work processes using the genre taxonomy with an example from the Sloan MBA application process (based on the research done by Orlikowski, Yates, and Fonstad 2001), where an on-line application process has been deployed since 1998. In the following section, we start with a summary of the Sloan Admissions process that involves the online application. We then demonstrate how we analyzed the relationships between work processes and genres and generated ideas for improving the work processes.

17.6.1   Summary of the Sloan Admissions Process

The Sloan School of Management at MIT was the first US business school to accept only on-line applications for MBA students (Orlikowski, Yates, and Fonstad 2001). Late in 1997 the Sloan School's Admissions office decided for various business reasons to require on-line application for the Class of 2001 MBA students who would apply to the school during the spring of 1998. For comparison, we briefly describe the previous admission processes that relied on paper applications and then contrast them with those used for on-line applications.[5]

The Sloan Admissions Process with Paper-Based Applications The previous paper-based Sloan Admissions process was similar to that at other business schools. First, an applicant requested an application package via phone, postal mail, or a fax to the Admissions office. The Admissions office sent the application package (which consisted of two brochures and a paper application form) via postal mail to the applicant. The applicant filled out the form, prepared a cover letter and resume, wrote essays, and requested that others send recommendation letters, GMAT scores, and transcripts from previous schools. After an applicant submitted his or her part of the application to the Sloan School via postal mail and the external sources completed the application with the requested information, the Admissions office sent a notification of completion to the applicant, and gathered the various parts of the application into a single paper file. Then the Sloan School determined whether to admit, reject, or wait list each applicant. The Sloan Admissions office notified each applicant of this result by postal mail. Admitted students were asked to notify the school by a certain date about whether or not they would accept their offer of admission to the school. Applicants who were on a waiting list were also asked to notify the school whether or not they wished to remain on the list. After the Admissions office determined the set of incoming students, they sent information packages to the students, and held events to help them prepare to enter the school.

The Sloan Admissions Process with On-line Applications In changing to on-line applications, the Sloan Admissions office partnered with a firm, GradAdvantage, which had a Web-based on-line application service for MBA and graduate school programs. The Sloan Admissions office also developed a Web site for interested potential applicants, as well as a new site for coordinating subsequent activities with admitted students (the AddMIT Sloan site). Applicants for the Class of 2001 requested brochures via the Sloan Web site or e-mail, as well as via phone, postal mail, or a fax to the Admissions office. In reply, the Admissions office sent two brochures and information about on-line applications via postal mail. Applicants registered biographical information, essays, cover letters, resumes, and other data via the GradAdvantage Web site, and GradAdvantage sent e-mails to applicants with

---

5. These descriptions are necessarily simplified to focus on the basic elements integral to the application process.

tracking numbers. Letters of recommendation and transcripts were sent directly to the Admissions office. The Admissions office downloaded the application data from the GradAdvantage database, and the Admissions office sent notifications to each applicant via e-mail when the application was complete. After the Sloan School determined each applicant's status as in previous years, the Admissions office sent results via e-mail and postal mail. Admitted students received an e-mail first with an informal letter of admission, and then received formal letters of admission via postal mail. Rejected applicants received formal letters via postal mail. Applicants on a waiting list received formal letters, requests to register on the waiting list, as well as FAQs via e-mail. After an admitted student accepted the offer on the AddMIT Sloan site, the Admissions office sent letters acknowledging the acceptance via e-mail. These had been sent via postal mail in the past. The Admissions office had created the AddMIT site for incoming the Class of 2001 students with at least three objectives: "to market the Sloan School to incoming students, manage the matriculation process by facilitating the processing of required forms quickly and accurately, and connect admitted students with one another" (Orlikowski, Yates, and Fonstad 2001).

This site played an important amplifying role when several incoming students, having met in a chat session on the site, created a virtual community of admitted students using Yahoo! The size of the community grew significantly when the Admissions office staff cooperated with incoming students by linking the Yahoo! Club to the AddMIT Sloan site. Incoming students used the virtual community to create social connections and exchange information about preparing for their new life at Sloan. They used a chat room first once a week on average and then three times a week. They also used a message board, on which they posted 1,148 messages in total, and published several electronic newsletters. According to the results of a survey conducted once the students had arrived at Sloan, most admitted students read the message board, two-thirds of them read and/or contributed to newsletters, and almost half joined the chat sessions. Using the virtual community, many incoming students got to know each other in advance of their entrance to Sloan, and shared useful information with their future colleagues.

17.6.2   Relationships among Genres and the Sloan Admissions Work Processes

In this subsection we first illustrate the genres invoked in both the paper-based and the on-line admission processes at the Sloan School. Then, using the genre taxonomy, we demonstrate how to analyze relationships among the genres and the work processes in terms of coordination of information coordination, and display the role of the genre taxonomy in generating ideas for improving the work processes.

Table 17.1
Excerpt of genres relevant to Sloan Admissions process

Widely recognized genre	Traditional Sloan Admissions genre (before Class of 2001)	Sloan Admissions genres for Class of 2001
Brochure	Sloan brochure	Sloan brochure, Sloan e-brochure
Application form	Sloan application form	Sloan e-application form
Form	Sloan data form, Sloan admission form, MIT housing form	Sloan e-data form, Sloan e-admission form, MIT e-housing form
Business letter	Cover letter for application, business letter for informing about Sloan admission, . . .	e-Cover letter for application, business letter for informing about Sloan admission, e-business letter for informing about Sloan admission, . . .
Post card	Sloan postcard for waiting list	Sloan postcard for waiting list
Resume	Resume	e-Resume
Newsletter	N/A	Sloan e-newsletter

Genres Relevant to the Sloan Admissions Process   Using data gathered by Orlikowski, Yates, and Fonstad, we identified both paper-based and on-line genres in the Sloan Admissions process (table 17.1). Genre names with the "e-" prefix refer to genres with electronic form, and genre names without the "e-" prefix denote genres in paper form.

The Sloan Admissions processes involve various people such as the Sloan Admissions office staff and applicants from all over the world. Table 17.1 shows that the genres enacted by Sloan applicants are variants of widely recognized genres such as the brochure genre and the business letter genre.

Genre Coordination Roles in the Sloan Admissions Work Processes   In the following, we take the genres identified from the Sloan Admissions process for the Class of 2001 and demonstrate details of the information coordination, using the genre taxonomy as an analytical lens. Then we explore ideas for how genres could be used for further on-line processes. Note that parenthesized representation, such as '(why)' and '(accessibility)' describe what element of the 5W1H genre framework was addressed, or what kind of characteristics of the genre coordination role was analyzed.

As table 17.1 shows, the Sloan brochure genre is used for advertising the Sloan School, and the Sloan e-brochure genre is used both for advertising the school and for informing applicants about the Sloan application process (why). The content (what) in the Sloan brochure genre contains only general information about the school and the content in the Sloan e-brochure genre includes specific information for Class of 2001 applicants. This example shows that the genre plays a role in coordinating how the information is divided (divisibility). As the Sloan e-brochure genre's medium (how) is a Web page, the genre can inform applicants as well as other people such as those looking for appropriate business schools (who). If the Sloan Admissions office would like to advertise the school so that more people would submit applications, it might be a good idea to put the information in the Sloan paper brochure also on the Sloan Web site (place). Then everyone who can connect to the Internet (concurrency) can access information in the Web page (accessibility).

All genres in the application genre system for the traditional Sloan Admissions were paper-based media (how) sent by postal mail or express delivery. Most applicants sent an application several days prior to the due date because they anticipated time lags for delivery (when), and this lag for an applicant in Asia was much longer than the lag for an applicant in Massachusetts. However, in using the GradAvantage Web site to submit applications, every applicant can submit them on the due date (timing). (Of course, such tight timing requires a robust server. On the first due date for the Class of 2001, the server crashed, requiring an extension of the deadline.) If multiple schools were using the GradAdvantage system for MBA application, an applicant could submit his or her resume and/or essays (if applicable to more than one application) only once (share) and then reuse them for another school. If Grad-Advantage gathered information about applicants' GMAT scores automatically (fit) and provided it to the MBA schools (flow), applicants would only need to take the GMAT, and would not need to contact Educational Testing Services to send their scores to various schools. It is noteworthy that mediators such as Grad-Advantage must consider privacy issues when they plan to flow private information automatically. In the case above, GradAdvantage would need to have the applicant give permission to GradAdvantage to allow them to provide GMAT scores to schools, perhaps by checking a box on the application.

Some constituent genres of the application genre system for the Class of 2001 were used for selecting admitted students. In the Sloan Admissions process for the Class of 2001, the on-line application information was converted into a Sloan Admissions database, and the Sloan Admissions office printed out the information and combined it with the paper-based letters of recommendation and transcripts. If the Sloan Admissions office could request letters of recommendation and transcripts in electronic form (how), the reviewers could choose to share application documents in the database (location) without printing. The Sloan Admissions office could send e-mails to reviewers in which they could provide access to the applications they would need to review in the database (accessibility). To make such a change would require social agreement both from schools with transcripts and from letter writers. Since the latter group consists of an unbounded set of people, it might be difficult to achieve (especially for international students) in the short term. An intermediate step might be to make electronic submissions of recommendation letters optional and to scan in any paper-based recommendation letters.

The Sloan Admissions review has the purpose of choosing suitable students for the school (why). While the details of the review process are necessarily confidential, the genre taxonomy suggests some possible processes based on the review system's purpose—to decide. The process specialization hierarchy suggests two alternative ideas for the current review system: the ballot genre system and the bidding genre system. Both the Sloan admissions review genre and the Common Lisp ballot genre system are under the 'decide' purpose category in the genre taxonomy. That similarity in purpose suggests the substitution of the ballot genre system in which the Sloan Admissions director could be a coordinator who issues ballots for deciding the status of applicants (flow), reviewers could respond to the ballot, and the director could decide using ballot responses (fit). Similarly the 'decide' purpose category includes another potential review process based on the 'Choose classes by bidding (Sloan)' activity. This is the Sloan class bidding genre system that the Sloan students use each semester for choosing classes they wish to take. For admissions, every reviewer could have a number of "bids" and the reviewer could bid on multiple applicants with his or her priority (divisibility), and the Sloan Admissions director would choose admitted students from the bidding results (fit).

As shown in table 17.1, both paper-based and electronic genres identified in the Sloan Admissions process for the Class of 2001 are included in the same widely recognized category. For example, in the business letter genre category we identified genres in both paper form and electronic form (how) for notifying the same Sloan Admissions results (why). As described earlier, the Sloan Admissions office first sent an e-mail (how) to all admitted students for the Class of 2001 informing them about and congratulating them on their admissions (why). Subsequently they sent formal paper-based business letters (how) to all applicants for the Class of 2001 students, including admitted students. The Sloan Admissions staff thought that every admitted student would like to know the result as soon as possible, so they sent an e-mail because it reached admitted students faster than postal mail (timing). However, when one admitted student received the e-mail, she was afraid that it might be a hoax. A partial reason could be that she did not recognize the business letter genre because of the e-mail medium, which is often associated with informality. If the Sloan Admissions staff had previously endorsed this medium and announced that results would be sent by e-mail, applicants might have more easily recognized the admittance e-mail message as invoking a business letter genre and thus as legitimate.

The Sloan postcard genre, while now in electronic form, could be extended through automation. For example, a software agent could send a notification to people who had not registered by a due date. A software agent could also inform those on the waiting list using the electronic business letter genre (flow). In addition people on the waiting list might be given numbers and allowed to see how many people on the list were already admitted via a Web page (concurrency). Those whose waiting number was much bigger than the current number could use this information in their decisions to give up on Sloan and enter another school (sequence).

In order to create social relationships and exchange information, the admitted students created a Sloan Yahoo! Club where they used three electronic media: a message board, a chat facility, and a Web site for electronic newsletters. In an analysis of messages posted to the message board, Orlikowski, Yates, and Fonstad identified use of the dialogue genre where admitted students asked questions and received responses about each other, the Sloan School, and life in the Boston area. The Sloan Admissions staff gathered commonly requested information and created an FAQ for next years' students (fit). The FAQ and the message board might also be used to reduce the time the staff spends answering questions via other media.

The fact that usage of the electronic genres in the Yahoo! Club ended once students arrived at Sloan suggests that the geographic dispersion and desire to share information and get to know each other combined to create support for those genres, but that geographic concentration and change in interests obviated that desire (where).

In summary, analyzing the genres of the Sloan Admissions process through the lens of the genre taxonomy allows us to generate various ideas for improving work processes related to information coordination. It is important to note that these or other ideas might not work as anticipated, since participants may not accept an attempted genre substitution or change, instead drawing on other genres from their past experiences. A community must recognize and enact a genre for it to become a legitimate part of that community's repertoire. Thus we need to analyze genres not only in advance of their implementation but also during use, because a critical component of improving work processes is to understand the continuously changing social context of communication within a community.

17.7   Conclusions

We believe that our proposed genre taxonomy, with its classification of different genres, genre systems, and appropriate contexts of use, can serve as a particularly useful knowledge repository within organizations. It can help managers, consultants, and groupware designers learn communication processes and apply these more effectively to diverse situations. For example, the views of genre use over time and the genre chronology in the genre taxonomy can help people understand how use of a genre both shapes and is shaped by a community's communicative actions over time.

By facilitating the deliberation of how genres can coordinate information, the genre taxonomy offers a source for new ideas that may be useful in the design of new communication processes, the redesign of existing communication processes, and in the resolution of problems related to communicative actions. It may also be possible to anticipate potential changes in a genre by examining any evolutionary histories of similar genres represented by the chronology examples in the genre taxonomy. For example, when an organizational change or technology implementation initiates an evolution of a similar genre, we could anticipate (though never completely accurately) how the genre might evolve. We could also plan to adapt the genre to the change by mimicking or modifying variations of the similar genre as they occurred during its evolution.

The prototype of the genre taxonomy now contains only fifteen generally accepted genres and several kinds of specific genres used in particular organizations. The set of genres is an open set, so no repository can ever be 'finished' or 'complete'. As with all other knowledge repositories, the more knowledge (in this case, genres) stored within it, the more benefits the genre taxonomy can provide. It is obviously necessary to add more genres to the genre taxonomy and to examine the communication practices in more organizations. However, we believe that the prototype highlights the potential of the genre taxonomy to serve as a valuable knowledge repository that could offer benefits to communities attempting to learn to communicate well or to improve their work processes around communication.

Acknowledgment

We thank Nils Fonstad and the Sloan Admissions staff (at the MIT Sloan School of Management) for providing data on the Sloan Admissions process. We would also like to thank Tom Malone, John Quimby, George Wyner, Abraham Bernstein, and other researchers at the MIT Center for Coordination Science for discussions about the genre taxonomy. We acknowledge the research support of Fuji Xerox Co., Ltd. and the Center for Coordination Science at the Massachusetts Institute of Technology.

IVC *Software Design and Generation*

18 A Coordination Perspective on Software System Design

Chrysanthos Dellarocas

18.1 Introduction

In large software systems the identification and proper management of interconnection relationships and constraints among various pieces of a system has become responsible for an increasingly important part of the development effort. In many cases the design, testing, and maintenance of protocols for managing communication, resource sharing, synchronization, and other such interconnection relationships take far more time and effort than the development of the core functional pieces of an application. In this chapter we use the term *dependencies* to refer to interconnection relationships and constraints among components of a software system.

As design moves closer to implementation, current design and programming tools increasingly focus on components, leaving the description of interdependencies among components implicit, and the implementation of protocols for managing them fragmented and distributed in various parts of the system. At the implementation level, software systems are sets of source and executable modules in one or more programming languages. Although modules come under a variety of names (procedures, packages, objects, clusters, etc.), they are all essentially abstractions for components.

Most programming languages directly support a small set of primitive interconnection mechanisms, such as procedure calls, method invocation, and shared variables. Such mechanisms are not sufficient for managing more complex dependencies that are commonplace in today's software systems. Complex dependencies require the introduction of more complex managing protocols, typically comprising several lines of code (e.g., the existence of a shared resource dependency might require a distributed mutual exclusion protocol). By failing to support separate abstractions for representing such complex protocols, current programming languages force programmers to distribute and embed them inside the interacting components (Shaw et al. 1994) (figure 18.1). Furthermore the lack of means for representing dependencies and protocols for managing them has resulted in a corresponding lack of theories and systematic taxonomies of interconnection relationships and ways of managing them.

An earlier version of this chapter appeared as C. Dellarocas (1997), A coordination perspective on software system design, *Proceedings of the Ninth International Conference on Software Engineering and Knowledge Engineering* (SEKE'97), Madrid, June 17–20, 1997, pp. 569–78. © 1997 Knowledge Systems Institute. Reprinted by permission.

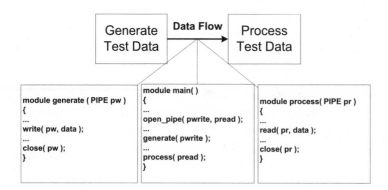

Figure 18.1
Implementation languages often force the distribution of coordination protocols among several code
modules. In this example the implementation code of a pipe protocol for managing a single data flow
dependency has been distributed among three code modules.

This expressive shortcoming of current languages and tools is directly connected to
a number of practical problems in software design:

• *Discontinuity between architectural and implementation models.* There is currently a gap between architectural representations of software systems (sets of activities explicitly connected through rich vocabularies of informal relationships) and
implementation-level descriptions of the same systems (sets of modules implicitly
connected through defines/uses relationships).

• *Difficulties in application maintenance.* By not providing abstractions for localizing information about dependencies, current languages force programmers to distribute the protocols for managing them in a number of different places inside a
program. Therefore, in order to understand or modify a protocol, programmers have
to look at many places in the program.

• *Difficulties in component reuse.* Components written in today's programming
languages inevitably contain some fragments of coordination protocols from their
original development environments. Such fragments act as undocumented assumptions about the structure of the application where such components will be used.
When attempting to reuse such a component in a new environment, such assumptions might not match the interdependency patterns of the target application. In
order to ensure interoperability, the original assumptions then have to be identified,
and subsequently replaced or bridged with the valid assumptions for the target
application. In many cases this requires extensive code modifications or the introduction of additional code around the component.

As a response to these problems, we introduce the principles of our coordination perspective on software system design. Following that, we describe SYNTHESIS, a prototype software development environment that embodies the principles of the coordination perspective. We present our experience with using SYNTHESIS to facilitate software reuse. We discuss related work, describe some future directions of the project, and conclude with a summary of our findings.

18.2 A Coordination Perspective on Software System Design

The practical problems discussed in the previous section are rooted in the failure of most current programming languages and methodologies to recognize the identification and management of dependencies among software components as a design problem in its own right. This shortcoming translates to inadequate support for making interconnection assumptions embedded inside components more explicit, inability to localize information about interconnection protocols, and a lack of theories and systematic taxonomies of software interconnection relationships and ways of managing them.

As a response to this situation, this chapter proposes a new perspective for representing and implementing software systems. Unlike current practice, this perspective emphasizes the explicit representation and management of dependencies among software activities as distinct entities.

The perspective is based on the ideas of coordination theory (Malone and Crowston 1994) and the Process Handbook project (Dellarocas et al. 1994; Malone et al. 1993). In accordance with Malone and Crowston (1994), we define *coordination* as the act of managing dependencies among activities. In this case the activities we are concerned with are software components. We will also use the term *coordination process* or *protocol* to describe the additional code introduced into a software system as a result of managing some dependency. These definitions lead to the principles of our coordination perspective on software system design which can be stated as follows:

• *Explicitly represent software dependencies.* Software systems should be described using representations that clearly separate the core functional pieces of an application from their interdependencies, providing distinct abstractions for each.

• *Build design handbooks of component integration.* The field knowledge on component integration should be organized in systematic taxonomies that provide guidance to designers and facilitate the generation of new knowledge. Such taxonomies will catalog the most common kinds of interconnection relationships encountered in practice. For each relationship, they will contain sets of alternative coordination protocols for managing it. In that way they can form the basis for *design handbooks of component integration*, similar to the well-established handbooks that assist design in more mature engineering disciplines.

The long-term goal of this research is to develop concrete software development tools and methodologies based on the principles stated above, and to demonstrate that such methodologies provide practical benefits in the initial development, maintenance, and reuse of software systems. A crucial part of our efforts revolves around the definition of useful taxonomies of dependencies and coordination protocols and the organization of that knowledge in on-line repositories that can then assist or even automate the integration of the different parts of a system into a coherent whole.

18.3   The SYNTHESIS Application Development Environment

The coordination perspective on software design introduced in the previous section has been reduced to practice by building SYNTHESIS, a prototype application development environment based on its principles. This section is devoted to a brief description of the SYNTHESIS system. A more detailed description can be found in Dellarocas (1996).

The current implementation of SYNTHESIS runs under the Microsoft Windows 3.1 and Windows 95 operating systems. SYNTHESIS itself has been implemented by composing a set of components developed using different environments (Intellicorp's Kappa-PC, Microsoft's Visual Basic, and Shapeware's Visio).

SYNTHESIS consists of three elements:

• SYNOPSIS, a software architecture description language

• An on-line "design handbook" of dependencies and associated coordination protocols

• A design assistant that generates executable applications by successive specializations of their SYNOPSIS description

18.3.1   SYNOPSIS: A Software Architecture Description Language

SYNOPSIS supports graphical descriptions of software application architectures at both the specification and the implementation level. It provides separate language entities for representing software *activities* and *dependencies*. SYNOPSIS language elements are connected together through ports. *Ports* provide a general mechanism for representing abstract component interfaces. All elements of the language can contain

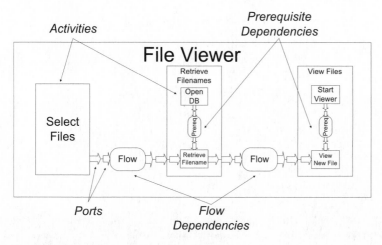

Figure 18.2
Representation of a simple file viewer application using SYNOPSIS

an arbitrary number of attributes. *Attributes* encode additional properties of the element, as well as compatibility criteria that constrain its connection to other elements. For example, figure 18.2 shows the SYNOPSIS description of a simple software system.

SYNOPSIS provides two mechanisms for abstraction: *Decomposition* allows new entities to be defined as patterns of simpler ones. It enables the naming, storage, and reuse of designs at the architectural level. *Specialization* allows new entities to be defined as variations of other existing entities. Specialized entities inherit the decomposition and attributes of their parents and can differentiate themselves by modifying any of those elements. Specialization enables the incremental generation of new designs from existing ones, as well as the organization of related designs in concise hierarchies. Finally, it enables the representation of reusable software architectures at various levels of abstraction (from very generic to very specific).

Activities Activities represent the main functional pieces of an application. They *own* a set of ports, through which they interconnect with the rest of the system. Ports usually represent interfaces through which resources are produced and consumed by various activities. Activities are defined as sets of attributes that describe their core function and their capabilities to interconnect with the rest of the system. Two activity attributes are most important:

• An (optional) *decomposition.* Decompositions are patterns of simpler activities and dependencies that implement the functionality intended by the composite activity.

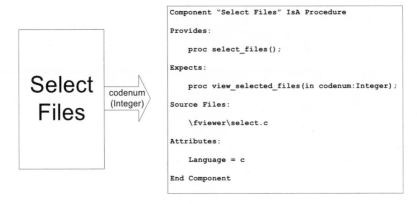

```
Component "Select Files" IsA Procedure

Provides:

    proc select_files();

Expects:

    proc view_selected_files(in codenum:Integer);

Source Files:

    \fviewer\select.c

Attributes:

    Language = c

End Component
```

Figure 18.3
Example of an atomic activity and its associated code-level component description

• An (optional) *component description.* Component descriptions associate SYNOPSIS activities with code-level components that implement their intended functionality. Examples of code-level components include source code modules, executable programs, and network servers, among their number.

SYNOPSIS provides a special notation for describing the properties of software components associated with executable activities. Such properties include the component kind, the provided and expected interfaces of the component, the source and object files needed by the component, and so on (figure 18.3).

Depending on the values of the preceding two attributes, activities are distinguished as follows:

• *Atomic* or *composite.* Atomic activities have no decomposition. Composite activities are associated with a decomposition into patterns of activities and dependencies.

• *Executable* or *generic.* Executable activities are defined at a level precise enough to allow their translation into executable code. Activities are executable either if they are associated with a component description, or if they are composite and every element in their decomposition is executable. Activities that are not executable are called generic. To generate an executable implementation, all generic activities must be replaced by appropriate executable specializations.

Dependencies Dependencies describe interconnection relationships and constraints among activities. Like activities, dependencies are defined as sets of attributes. The most important attributes are:

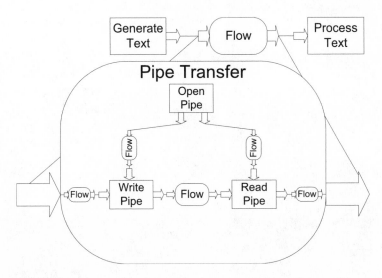

Figure 18.4
SYNOPSIS representation of a data flow dependency and its associated pipe transfer coordination protocol

• An (optional) *decomposition* into patterns of simpler dependencies.   These collectively specify the same relationship as the composite dependency.

• An (optional) *coordination protocol.*   Coordination protocols are patterns of simpler dependencies and activities that describe a mechanism for managing the relationship or constraint implied by the dependency (figure 18.4).

• An (optional) association with a *software connector.*   Connectors are low-level mechanisms for interconnecting software components that are directly supported by programming languages and operating systems. Examples include procedure calls, method invocations, and shared memory.

In a manner similar to activities, dependencies are distinguished into atomic or composite, executable or generic.

Specialization   Object-oriented languages provide the mechanism of inheritance to facilitate the incremental generation of new objects as specializations of existing ones, and also to help organize and relate similar object classes. SYNOPSIS provides an analogous mechanism called *entity specialization*. Specialization applies to all the elements of the language, and allows new entities to be created as special cases of existing ones. Specialized entities *inherit* the decomposition and other attributes of their parents. They can differentiate themselves from their *specialization parents* by

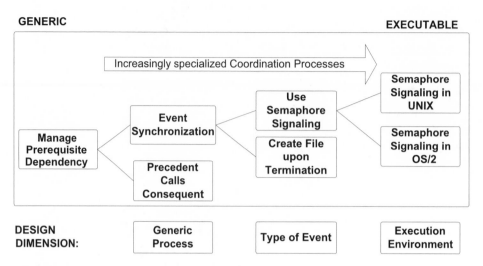

Figure 18.5
Hierarchy of prerequisite dependencies with increasingly specialized associated coordination protocols

modifying their structure and attributes using the operations described below. Entity specialization is based on the mechanism of process specialization that was first introduced by the Process Handbook project (Dellarocas 1994; Malone et al. 1993).

The mechanism of entity specialization enables the creation of specialization hierarchies for activities, dependencies, ports, and coordination protocols. Such hierarchies are analogous to the class hierarchies of object-oriented systems. In specialization hierarchies, generic designs form the roots of specialization trees, consisting of increasingly specialized but related designs. The leafs of specialization trees usually represent design elements that are specific enough to be translated into executable code (figure 18.5).

18.3.2   A Design Handbook of Software Component Interconnection
SYNTHESIS contains our initial version of a handbook of dependencies and coordination protocols commonly encountered in software systems. The prototype handbook is stored on-line as a hierarchy of increasingly specialized SYNOPSIS dependency entities. An entity browser interface (similar to class browsers of object-oriented systems) is available for navigation and selection of handbook entries.

An important decision in making a taxonomy of software interconnection is the choice of the generic dependency types. If we are to treat software interconnection as an orthogonal problem to that of designing the core functional components of an application, dependencies among components should represent relationships that are also orthogonal to the functional domain of an application. Fortunately this requirement is consistent with the nature of most interconnection problems: whether our application is controlling inventory or driving a nuclear submarine, most problems related to connecting its components together are related to a relatively narrow set of concepts, such as resource flows, resource sharing, and timing dependencies. The design of associated coordination protocols involves a similarly narrow set of mechanisms such as shared events, invocation mechanisms, and communication protocols.

The prototype handbook is based on the simple assumption that software component interdependencies are explicitly or implicitly related to patterns of resource production and usage. Beginning from this assumption, we have defined a number of useful dependency families in a way independent of the application context where they might be used. Dependency families represented in the handbook include:

• *Flow dependencies.* Flow dependencies represent relationships between producers and consumers of resources. They are specialized according to the kind of resource, the number of producers, the number of consumers, and so on. Coordination protocols for managing flows decompose into protocols, which ensure accessibility of the resource by the consumers (usually by physically transporting it across a communication medium), usability of the resource (usually by performing appropriate data format conversions), as well as synchronization between producers and consumers.

• *Sharing dependencies.* They encode relationships among consumers who use the same resource. Sharing dependencies are specialized according to the sharing properties of the resource in use (divisibility, consumability, concurrency). Coordination protocols for sharing dependencies ensure proper enforcement of the sharing properties, usually by dividing a resource among competing users or by enforcing mutual exclusion protocols.

• *Timing dependencies.* Timing dependencies express constraints on the relative flow of control among a set of activities. Examples include *prerequisite dependencies* and *mutual exclusion dependencies*. Timing dependencies are used to specify application-specific cooperation patterns among activities that share the same resources. They are also used in the decomposition of coordination protocols for flow and sharing dependencies.

A detailed description of the contents of the prototype handbook can be found in Dellarocas (1996).

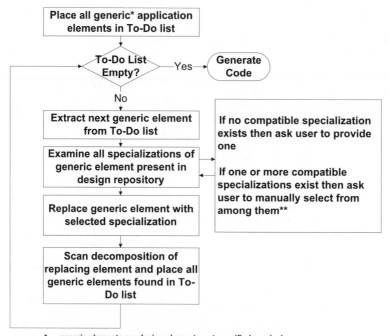

*   generic elements are design elements not specified precisely
      enough for code to be generated from them automatically
**   candidate ranking and selection can optionally be done
      automatically, by means of a user-supplied evaluation function

Figure 18.6
Sketch of an algorithm used by SYNTHESIS to generate executable applications by successive specializations of their SYNOPSIS descriptions

18.3.3   SYNTHESIS Design Assistant

The design methodology supported by SYNTHESIS uses SYNOPSIS descriptions in order to both specify and implement software systems. SYNTHESIS supports a process for generating executable systems by successive specialization of their SYNOPSIS descriptions. The process is summarized in figure 18.6. As can be seen, the existence of on-line design handbooks of activities and dependencies can assist, and often automate, parts of the process.

The design process can be customized in a variety of ways. Designers can manually select each new element to be managed, rather than follow the ordering of the to-do list. They can optionally input an *evaluation function* that helps the system perform an automatic ranking and selection of compatible candidates. Furthermore successive transformations of the original application diagram (stored as composite activ-

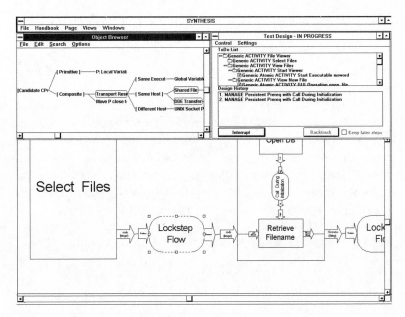

Figure 18.7
Configuration of SYNTHESIS windows during design mode

ities) can optionally be stored as successive specializations in the activity hierarchy. The system can thus keep a *design history*, which allows designers to easily backtrack to a previous stage of the design and choose a different design path. In that manner exploratory design and maintenance of alternative implementations can be facilitated.

Figure 18.7 shows the layout of SYNTHESIS windows during design. The SYNOPSIS *decomposition editor* (in the lower half of the screen) displays the current state of the architectural diagram and updates it automatically whenever a new transformation (replacement of activity or management of dependency) takes place. The *entity browser* (in the upper left part of the screen) is used for displaying and selecting compatible specializations for application design elements. Finally the *design manager* window (in the upper right part of the screen) summarizes the status of the design process and allows users to control its parameters.

18.4 Using SYNTHESIS to Facilitate Component-Based Software Development

The first domain where we tested the practical advantages of our coordination perspective on software system design is the development of new applications by integrating existing software components. This section describes the experience gained by using SYNTHESIS to facilitate the reuse of existing software components in new applications.

One of the important practical difficulties of building new systems by reusing existing parts lies in the amount of effort required in order to bridge mismatches among components. In most cases some additional "glue code" needs to be added to integrate all the independently written software pieces into a coherent application (Garlan et al. 1995). An application development tool based on the principles of our coordination perspective on software design has the potential of helping alleviate the difficulty of component integration by separating the representation of activities and dependencies, localizing information related to coordination protocols, and providing frameworks of common dependencies and coordination protocols.

To test this claim, we have used SYNTHESIS in order to build a set of test applications by reusing independently written pieces of software. Each experiment consisted in:

• Describing a test application as a SYNOPSIS diagram

• Selecting a set of components exhibiting various mismatches to implement activities

• Using SYNTHESIS and its repository of dependencies in order to integrate the selected components into an executable system

• Exploring alternative executable implementations based on the same set of components

The experiments are described in full detail in Dellarocas (1996). Table 18.1 provides a brief summary.

Experiment 1 consisted in building a simple File Viewer application by combining a commercial text editor and pieces of code written in C and Visual Basic. It demonstrated that the system is able to resolve low-level problems of interoperability, such as incompatibilities in programming languages, data types, procedure names, and control flow paradigms. It has also shown how the system can facilitate the exploratory design of alternative component organizations.

Experiment 2 investigated nine different ways of building an indexing system by various combinations of server and UNIX filter components (table 18.2). It provided positive evidence for the ability of the system to resolve *architectural mismatches*, that is, different assumptions about the structure of the application in which they will be used. It also demonstrated that the overall architecture of an application can be specified to a large extent independently of the implementation of any individual component, by appropriate selection of coordination processes.

Table 18.1
Summary of experiments of using SYNTHESIS to facilitate the integration of existing software components in new applications

Experiment	Description	Components	Results
File viewer	A simple system that retrieves and displays the contents of user-selected files	User interface component written in C; filename retrieval component written in Visual Basic; file display component implemented using commercial text editor	SYNTHESIS integrated components suggesting two alternative organizations (client/server, implicit invocation); all necessary coordination code was automatically generated in both cases
Key word in context	A system that produces a listing of all circular shifts of all input lines in alphabetical order (Parnas 1972)	Two alternative implementations for each component (both written in C): as a server and as a UNIX filter	Three different combinations of filter and server implementations were each integrated in 3 different organizations (see table 18.2). SYNTHESIS generated most coordination code; users had to manually write 16 lines of code in 2 cases.
Interactive TEX	A system that integrates the standard components of the TEX document typesetting system in a WYSIWYG ensemble	Standard executable components of TEX system	Target application was completely described in SYNOPSIS. SYNTHESIS was able to generate coordination code automatically
Collaborative editor	A system that extends the functionality of existing single-user editors with group editing capabilities (Knister and Prakash 1990)	Micro-Emacs source code was used to implement single-user editor (Lawrence and Straight 1989)	Same system description was specialized in two different ways to generate micro-Emacs based group editors for Windows and UNIX

Experiment 3 combined the standard components of the T_EX document typesetting system in a WYSIWYG application. It tested the power of SYNOPSIS and our proposed vocabulary of dependencies in expressing nontrivial application architectures.

Finally, experiment 4 attempted to build a collaborative editor by extending the functionality of an existing text editor. It investigated the usefulness of the system in assisting the rapid development of applications for multiple platforms. It demonstrated that different implementations of the same application, suitable for different execution environments, can be generated from the same, partially specialized SYNOPSIS system description, by selecting different coordination processes for managing dependencies.

Table 18.2
Summary of the key word in context experiments

	Components	Architecture	Auto lines[a]	Manual lines[b]
1	Filters	Pipes	34	0
2	Filters	Main program/subroutine	30	0
3	Filters	Implicit invocation	150	0
4	Servers	Pipes	78	16
5	Servers	Main program/subroutine	35	0
6	Servers	Implicit invocation	95	0
7	Mixed	Pipes	66	0
8	Mixed	Main program/subroutine	56	0
9	Mixed	Implicit invocation	131	16

a. Lines of coordination code automatically generated by Synthesis
b. Lines of coordination code manually added by user

Overall, our experiments provided positive evidence for the principal practical claims of the approach. The evidence can be summarized as follows:

• *Support for code-level software reuse.* SYNTHESIS was able to resolve a wide range of interoperability and architectural mismatches and successfully integrate independently developed components into all four test applications, with minimal or no need for user-written coordination software.

• *Support for reuse of software architectures.* SYNTHESIS was able to reuse a configuration-independent SYNOPSIS description of a collaborative editor and the source code of an existing single-user editor, in order to generate collaborative editor executables for two different execution environments (UNIX and Windows).

• *Insight into alternative software architectures.* SYNTHESIS was able to suggest a variety of alternative overall architectures for integrating each test set of code-level components into its corresponding application, thus helping designers explore alternative designs.

18.5   Related Work

The ideas expressed in this work are most closely related to research in coordination theory and architecture description languages. Recent efforts to build open software architectures are an interesting, but contrasting, approach for achieving many of the goals of our coordination perspective on software system design. This section briefly discusses all three research areas.

18.5.1 Coordination Theory

Coordination theory (Malone and Crowston 1994) focuses on the interdisciplinary study of coordination. Research in this area uses and extends ideas about coordination from disciplines such as computer science, organization theory, operations research, economics, linguistics, and psychology. It defines coordination as the process of managing dependencies among activities. Its research agenda includes characterizing different kinds of dependencies and identifying the coordination protocols that can be used to manage them.

The present work can be viewed as an application and extension of coordination theory, in that it views the process of developing applications as one of specifying architectures in which patterns of dependencies among software activities are eventually managed by coordination protocols. The project grew out of the Process Handbook project (Dellarocas et al. 1994; Malone et al. 1993) which applies the ideas of coordination theory to the representation and design of business processes. The goal of the Process Handbook project is to provide a firmer theoretical and empirical foundation for such tasks as enterprise modeling, enterprise integration, and process re-engineering. The project includes (1) collecting examples of how different organizations perform similar processes and (2) representing these examples in an on-line "Process Handbook" that includes the relative advantages of the alternatives.

The Process Handbook relies on a representation of business processes that distinguishes between activities and dependencies and supports entity specialization. It builds repositories of alternative ways of performing specific business functions, represented at various levels of abstraction. SYNOPSIS has borrowed the ideas of separating activities from dependencies and the notion of entity specialization from the Process Handbook. It is especially concerned with (1) refining the process representation, so that it can describe software applications at a level precise enough for code generation to take place, and (2) populating repositories of dependencies and coordination protocols for the specialized domain of software systems.

18.5.2 Architecture Description Languages

Several Architecture Description Languages (ADLs) provide support for representing software systems in terms of their components and their interconnections (Kogut and Clements 1994). Different languages define interconnections in different ways. For example, Rapide (Luckham and Vera 1995) connections are mappings from services required by one component to services provided by another component. Unicon (Shaw et al. 1995) connectors define protocols that are inserted into the system in order to integrate a set of components. In that sense they are similar to the coordination protocols that manage dependencies in SYNTHESIS. Like Unicon, SYNTHESIS views dependencies as relationships among components that might require the introduction of additional coordination code in order to be properly managed. Unlike Unicon, however, SYNTHESIS dependencies are specifications that can then be managed (i.e., implemented) in a number of different ways. The set of dependency types is not fixed. Coordination theory is a framework that assists the discovery of additional dependency types and coordination protocols. Finally, apart from simply supporting dependency representations, the work reported in this chapter proposes the development of taxonomies of abstract dependency relationships and coordination protocols for managing them as a key element in facilitating component-based software development.

18.5.3   Open Software Architectures

Computer hardware has successfully moved away from monolithic, proprietary designs, toward *open architectures* that enable components produced by a variety of vendors to be combined in the same computer system. Open architectures are based on the development of successful bus and interconnection protocol standards. A number of research and commercial projects are currently attempting to create the equivalent of open architectures for software components. Such approaches are based on standardizing some part of the glue required to compose components. The most notable efforts in that direction include object-oriented architecture standards, such as CORBA (Object Management Group 1991), Microsoft's OLE (1994), and Apple's Open Scripting Architecture (1993), and application frameworks such as X-Windows/Motif (OSF 1990; Scheifler et al. 1988) and Microsoft Visual Basic (1993).

Open software architectures and our coordination perspective were both motivated by the complexity of managing component interdependencies. However, the two approaches represent very different philosophies. Open architectures take the stance that designers should not have to deal with software dependencies. In essence they are "hiding interconnection protocols under the carpet" by limiting the kinds of allowed relationships and by providing a standardized infrastructure for managing them. Our coordination perspective, in contrast, is based on the belief that the identification and management of software dependencies should be elevated to a design problem in its own right. Therefore dependencies should not only be explicitly represented as distinct entities, but furthermore, when deciding on a managing protocol, one should consider the full range of possibilities with the help of design handbooks.

Successful software bus approaches can enable independently developed applications to interoperate without the need to write additional coordination code. However, they have a number of drawbacks. First, they can only be used in environments for which versions of the software bus have been developed. For example, OLE can only be used to interconnect components running under Microsoft Windows. Second, they can only be used to interconnect components explicitly written for those architectures. Third, the standardized interaction protocols might not be optimal for all applications.

In contrast, integrating a set of components using SYNTHESIS typically *does* require the generation of additional coordination code, although most of that code is generated semi-automatically. Components in SYNOPSIS architectures need not adhere to any standard and can have arbitrary interfaces. Provided that the right coordination protocol exists in its repository, SYNTHESIS will be able to interconnect them. Furthermore SYNTHESIS is able to suggest several alternative ways of managing an interconnection relationship and thus possibly generate more efficient implementations. Finally, open software architecture protocols can be incorporated into SYNTHESIS repositories as special cases of coordination protocols.

18.6   Future Research

The long-term goal of this research is to demonstrate the practical usefulness of a coordination perspective on software system design and to develop superior software development methodologies based on its principles. To that end, what follows describes some immediate directions for future research suggested by our experience so far:

• *Classify composite dependency patterns.*   Our current taxonomy includes relatively low-level dependency types, such as flows and prerequisites. In a sense our taxonomy defines a vocabulary of software interconnection relationships. A particularly promising path of research seems to be the classification of more complex dependency types as patterns of more elementary dependencies.

• *Develop coordination process design rules.*   It will be interesting to develop design rules that help automate the selection step by ranking candidate processes according to various evaluation criteria such as their response time, their reliability, and their overall fit with the rest of the application. For example, when managing a data flow dependency, one possible design heuristic would be to use direct transfer of control (e.g., remote procedure calls) when the size of the data that flows is small, and to use a separate carrier resource, such as a file when the size of the data is large.

• *Develop guidelines for better reusable components.*   The idea of separating the design of component functionality from the design of interconnection protocols has interesting implications about the way reusable components should be designed in the future. At best, components should contain minimal assumptions about their interconnection patterns with other components embedded in them. More research is needed to translate this abstract requirement to concrete design guidelines.

18.7   Conclusions

This work was motivated by the increasing variety and complexity of interdependencies among components of large software systems. Most current programming languages and tools were observed not to provide adequate support for identifying and representing such dependencies, while the knowledge of managing them has not yet been systematically codified. The initial results of this research provide positive evidence for supporting the claim that software component integration can usefully be treated as a design problem in its own right, orthogonal to the specification and implementation of the core functional pieces of an application.

More specifically, software interconnection dependencies and coordination protocols for managing them can be usefully represented as independent entities, separate from the interdependent components.

Furthermore common dependency types and ways of managing them can be systematically organized in a design handbook. Such a handbook, organized as an on-line repository, can assist, or even automate, the process of transforming architectural descriptions of systems into executable implementations by successive specializations.

Our experience with building SYNTHESIS, a prototype application development environment based on these principles and using it as a tool for facilitating the reuse of existing components in new applications, has demonstrated both the feasibility and the practical usefulness of this approach. With our future research we plan to expand and refine the contents of our design handbook of dependencies and coordination processes as well as investigate the usefulness of our approach in larger-scale software systems.

Acknowledgment

The author would like to acknowledge the support and invaluable help of Thomas W. Malone in supervising the doctoral thesis that forms the basis for the work reported in this chapter.

19 The Product Workbench: An Environment for the Mass-Customization of Production Processes

Abraham Bernstein

19.1 Introduction: IT in an Economy of Perpetual Change

A variety of organizational observers (e.g., Argyris and Schön 1996; Boyton, Victor, and Pine 1993; Laubacher, Malone, and MIT Scenario Working Group 1997) predict new organizational forms that are presumed to be highly flexible, continuously changing their form, their product range, and their structure. Firms will evolve into more flexible forms in which the interrelations between the organizational units are not organized by a hierarchical information flow but much more by a network of communicative links (see Van Alstyne 1997). How can we support the enactment of highly flexible processes in such an organization?

While rapid prototyping environments and CASE tools have been addressing the problems of continuous change they usually produce solutions which are either not scaleable, require highly specialized knowledge or are limited to a single, proprietary enactment environment (e.g., a work flow system or a transaction monitor). This chapter reports on the implementation of a prototype system to support the rapid development of new production processes by end-users, which can then be enacted on a variety of execution platforms. Building on ideas from the product development and innovation literature, it combines concepts from rapid prototyping, component-based programming, object-oriented programming, knowledge-based systems, and human-computer interface design to develop a product workbench for business users.

The chapter is structured as follows: First, we analyze the requirements for a product workbench using foundations from the literature. Second, we describe a prototype implementation, which will be illustrated using a practical scenario from the financial services industry. Finally, we evaluate the proposed solution and discuss future work.

19.2 Analysis of the Requirements and Theoretical Foundations

Boyton, Victor, and Pine (1993) build a framework to explain new production paradigms. In this framework they analyze production as varying on two dimensions: product change and process change. In the mass-production setting, a product and its production process are highly stable. In a research department both product and

An earlier version of this chapter appeared as A. Bernstein (1998), The product workbench: An environment for the mass customization of production processes, *Proceedings of the Workshop for Information Technology and Systems*, Helsinki, Finland.

production process are highly dynamic leading to high costs and low volumes. The question then arises as to whether it is possible to reduce the costs and sell high volumes of customized products. The idea of *mass-customization*, in which the product changes to fit specific demand and the production is organized around "loosely coupled networks of modular, flexible processing units" (ibid., p. 49), seems to allow such a production scheme. One of the scenarios by Laubacher, Malone, and MIT Scenario Working Group (1997) proposes a similar structure for future organizations. A network of loosely coupled specialists (in most cases one person firms), who come together to produce a highly customized product (of batch size one) and then reconfigure to meet the challenges of the next project. To support such an organization, an IT support system will thus have to *enable people to take flexible building blocks of a production process and reassemble them to fit the specific needs of a particular case.*

Unfortunately, end-users are usually not trained to reconfigure and reassemble existing processes, a job that is usually performed by business analysts. We therefore need to "unstick" *the process design knowledge* (von Hippel 1996) and make it accessible to end-users by encoding it in building blocks and consistency rules of a design environment. The result would be a type of integrated *CAD/CAM*[1] *tool for business processes.* This is consistent with von Hippel's (1996) observations in the ASIC's and the computer telephony industry.

The component-based approach contains the problem of how to organize the large number of components in order to make them accessible. Experience in AI has shown that it often makes sense to construct some type of taxonomy of components in which similar components can be found close together, leading to the development of frame inheritance networks and object-type hierarchies (Brachman and Schmolze 1985). Furthermore the usage of template (or prototype) hierarchies, a form of simplified frame inheritance networks, has been observed to be useful in settings with end-user development (MacLean et al. 1990). Thus a *template-oriented component hierarchy*, which can also hold previously completed cases as templates, seems to be advantageous in helping to solve our problem.

19.3   The Implementation

19.3.1   The Basis: Process Handbook
The architectural basis of the implementation is the Process Handbook process knowledge base (see Malone et al. 1997; Bernstein et al. 1995). The goal of the Pro-

---

1. Computer Aided Design/Computer Aided Manufacturing.

cess Handbook project at MIT, which has been under way for over six years, is to develop a process repository and associated tools to allow users to quickly retrieve and effectively exploit the process knowledge relevant to their current challenge. Two of the Process Handbook's features are central to our endeavor: process inheritance and the distinction of processes and their interdependencies. We will therefore explain them before we go on to other parts of the implementation.

Process specialization takes features of frame inheritance networks and transfers them into the process domain. It arranges processes in a hierarchy of 'types of' or 'ways of' doing things that goes from very generic processes at one end to very specialized processes at the other end (see figure 19.1). This specialization hierarchy offers the capabilities we need to store cases, templates, and thus process components. We can use the more generalized processes as templates and specialize them as we develop a new product. Past cases would thus usually be leaves in the specialization hierarchy, which could also be used as templates for new products. At some levels the hierarchy even has special objects (called bundles), whose role it is to facilitate the classification of the specializations of a process by offering a specific dimension by which the processes are compared (see figure 19.2).

The Process Handbook *distinguishes dependencies from their coordination mechanisms* in accord with coordination science (see Malone and Crowston 1994). Dependencies represent the flow of physical resources (e.g., trucks) or informational resources (e.g., signals) between two activities. Alternatively, they can also represent the sharing of such a resource (e.g., a meeting room), the fit thereof (e.g., two artists cooperating in the writing of a song), or some combination of the types presented. Coordination processes are the activities that manage those dependencies. This perspective can be extremely useful for solving our problem of too much unstructured information, because we can hide all the coordination mechanisms from the user of the product workbench, and thus reduce the complexity of the product assembly task. In some specific instances, where the users of the product design workbench are particularly interested in issues of coordination, they will want to highlight coordination problems.

19.3.2   The Scenario

We will introduce the Product Workbench by a scenario that illustrates how an account manager in a bank could use it to construct a new financial product. The account manager in a commercial bank represents the customer's single point of access. Let us assume that a customer wants an account, which automatically adjusts its structure depending on the amount of money in it. If the account has a positive balance, then the sum should be invested in a money market fund. In the case of an overdraft situation, the money should be automatically drawn from the revolving

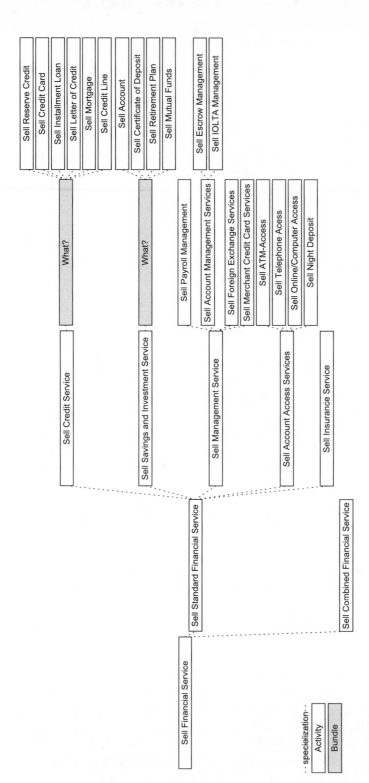

Figure 19.1
Specialization hierarchy for 'Sell financial service' (based on BankBoston 1998)

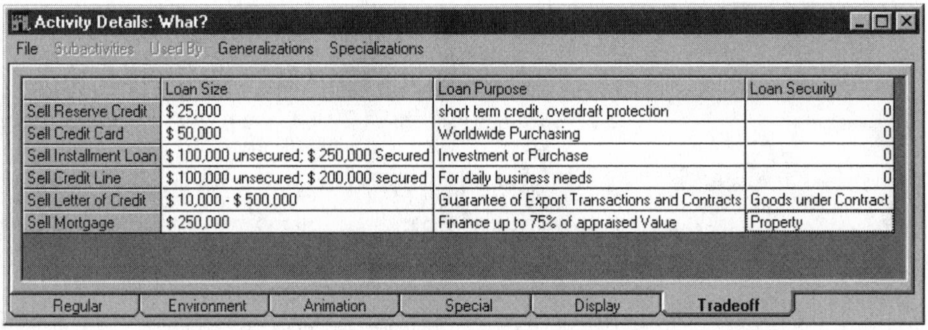

	Loan Size	Loan Purpose	Loan Security
Sell Reserve Credit	$ 25,000	short term credit, overdraft protection	0
Sell Credit Card	$ 50,000	Worldwide Purchasing	0
Sell Installment Loan	$ 100,000 unsecured; $ 250,000 Secured	Investment or Purchase	0
Sell Credit Line	$ 100,000 unsecured; $ 200,000 secured	For daily business needs	0
Sell Letter of Credit	$ 10,000 - $ 500,000	Guarantee of Export Transactions and Contracts	Goods under Contract
Sell Mortgage	$ 250,000	Finance up to 75% of appraised Value	Property

Figure 19.2
Trade-off matrix showing the alternative specializations of 'Sell credit service' compared to 'Loan purpose' and 'Loan security'

loan (or from the money market fund if available). This setting resembles a complex checking account with overdraft protection and an active investment of the funds as opposed to a fixed low interest.

In the classical banking world this request would be a disaster. It would involve the implementation of a number of features in the bank's accounting systems—a time-consuming project. Our account manager, on the other hand, knows that the general building blocks for such a request are in her product workbench. She first starts up her *template/case browser* (see figure 19.3 and figure 19.6, lower left) in order to find an appropriate template for the requested product. The template/case browser offers a three-pane (frame) view. On the left side it displays a hierarchical grouping of the possible choices. When one of those choices is selected, the right side of the browser shows some additional information about the chosen element. At the bottom of the right side is a detailed description of the item and at the top is a comparison matrix, as in figure 19.2, of the possible choices. This browser thus allows the account manager to navigate through the process knowledge base specialization hierarchy stored in the process handbook and make decisions about the appropriateness of processes by (1) offering detailed information about the process and (2) comparing the different specializations. She can choose either a generic process or a product constructed for another customer (a previous case) as a template for the new product. In this example she chooses 'Sell combined financial product' as the template and calls the process 'Sell combined product to Example Inc.'.

The *integrity checker* then takes the chosen process template and tests whether it is in an enactable format (comparable to the first pass of a two-pass compiler). First, it replaces all dependencies with their specified managing process. Second, it

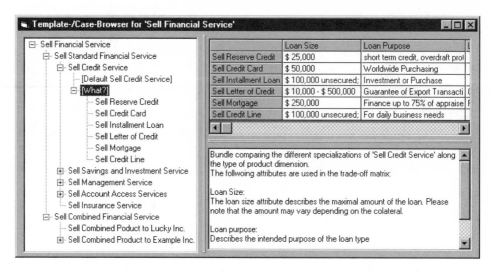

Figure 19.3
Template/case-browser

examines all processes using a depth-first algorithm on the process decomposition tree.[2] When encountering a leaf process, it checks whether all necessary references (e.g., to an executable program) are well defined. Nodes are tested as soon as all their subactivities are examined by scrutinizing the connections between its subprocesses. Finally the integrity checker points out failure of those tests by directing the user to the problems in an appropriate browser (decomposition browser for processes, dependency browser for dependencies) and highlighting the problem areas (see figure 19.5).[3] By examining the problem areas with the case/template browser as described above, the account manager will be able to find well-specified processes for the problematic processes, to further refine the process design and then to reinitiate the integrity checker (see figure 19.4).

In our case the next stage is to examine the problem areas as pointed out by the integrity checker in a decomposition browser. (See figure 19.5, which offers a tree structure that can be used to determine which parts have to be replaced with other components.) Using the template/case browser, she will browse the specialization hierarchy of the nondetermined processes, such as 'Sell credit service', and then

2. Dellarocas (1996) describes in detail a similar algorithm operating on a comparable data-structure.
3. Figure 19.5 shows the result of the integrity checker if it were run after step 1 in figure 19.4.

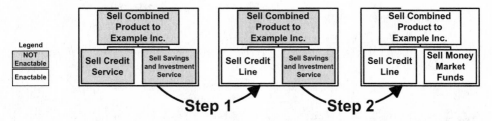

Figure 19.4
Incremental and iterative refinement of the process 'Sell combined product to Example Inc.'

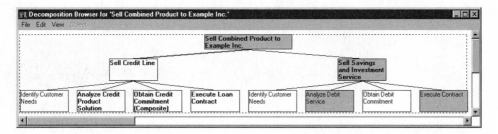

Figure 19.5
Integrity checker pointing out problems in the decomposition browser by coloring the processes 'Analyze debit service' and 'Execute contract' in a darker color. 'Sell savings and investment services' and 'Sell combined product to Example Inc.' are also colored dark because they contain nonenactable subprocesses.

replace each such process with one of its well-defined specializations, such as 'Sell credit line' (see also figure 19.4, step 1). After one more replacement (step 2 in figure 19.4) she can reinitiate the integrity checker. This leads to the incremental refinement of the process by replacing all the underdefined components with well-defined ones.

Finally, when the integrity checker finds no problems in the process description, it passes it to the *code generator*, which traverses the process description and generates the appropriate scripts and programs. To surpass the limitation given by a single-process support system, the product workbench can generate scripts or programs for multiple platforms,[4] which interrelate as defined in the process map. For example, the process could be partly enacted on an ERP and partly on a transaction-processing host, both of which are coordinated by a work flow–management system (WFMS).[5] At last the code generator contacts the involved systems and ensures that

4. New enactment support systems can be added by writing an appropriate code generator.
5. Currently the code generator supports the commercial WFMS Staffware™ and an agent-based research WFMS.

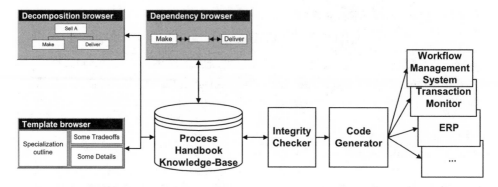

Figure 19.6
Overall product workbench architecture

the scripts and programs are installed and ready for execution. The account manager has accomplished the task of designing a new customized product and could start the process to service her customer.

So far all dependencies have been hidden from the account manager. She will never have to deal with dependencies, provided that the interface of the underdefined process placeholders and the determined replacing components (i.e., well-defined processes) are compatible. When there is a problem with dependencies (e.g., the absence of a coordination mechanism), then the integrity checker will point those out in the *dependency editor*, which offers a flowchart like view of the process and its dependencies (see Ahmed 1998). Using the case/template browser, the account manager can then further refine her product design and by replacing a nondetermined dependency with one of its well-defined specializations. The overall architecture of the Product Workbench, which supports this scenario, is summarized in figure 19.6.

19.4   Discussion

19.4.1   Evaluation of the Solution

The proposed solution fulfills the requirements developed in the analysis section above: it reduces the knowledge-transfer problem by 'unsticking' the process design knowledge and providing high-level process-based operations, understandable to an end-user. Furthermore it offers a repository of available high-level building blocks, which are structured in a nonspecialist accessible fashion (in our implementation a template hierarchy). It thus enables end-users to *take flexible building blocks from the process handbook database and flexibly reassemble them* according to the needs of a particular customer. We therefore think that it supports the rapid incremental development and mass-customization of production processes. We also believe that it could consequently support the enactment of processes in highly flexible organizations.

In some cases a production process may require strictly transactional behavior in one part of its enactment, which can be supported by a transaction monitor. But in another part it may also rely on a loosely coupled succession of activities, which are best supported by a groupware discussion database as a coordination mechanism. Therefore we believe that our system's ability to export to multiple enactment support environments will make it more suitable for the support of mass-customization than work flow–management systems (WFMS), which usually only support their own system as enactment support.

Furthermore our system proposes to close the gap between high-level concepts and low-level program code generation by focusing on business processes and an inheritance framework of components, which offer a better abstraction than traditional CASE tools. Therefore we believe that the system will be usable by end-users and not only by specialists.

The Product Workbench does, however, forgo some of the flexibility of CASE systems and WFMS by using a component-based approach, in which the end-users can only assemble their production processes out of existing components. Developing good and useful product components is a key success factor for such a system. This cannot be accomplished by domain specialists alone, but must involve information systems specialists in order to integrate the components with the back-end systems.[6]

19.4.2 Future Work

There are a variety of open questions in connection with the Product Workbench. The next step is to compose a library of real-world components. This library, and an integration of the Product Workbench into a standard corporate work environment, could be used to explore the practicality of this tool in an actual setting.

A parallel avenue of investigation explores alternate uses of the enactment scripts. One could, for example, use the script to estimate its cost and then price it. This estimate could be improved by connecting the simulation engine to real-world pricing and scheduling information about internal and external resources involved in the

---

6. The system will face the usual challenges of component-based systems like integration problems with the transactional behavior of a collection of components, which may lead to deadlocks. While there are extended transaction mechanisms to deal with complex nested transaction schemes, component developers will have to document all potential side effects (i.e., dependencies to other resources and activities) of their components to ensure the correct application of those mechanisms.

production process. Thus an account manager could quote the price and a planned delivery date (using the scheduling information) for a mass-customized product before the firm would have to invest in the enactment of its production.

19.5   Conclusion

In this chapter we have described a system called the Product Workbench. We believe that its component-based design approach paired with its template-oriented repository of components shows how systems can enable end-users to mass-customize production processes. Furthermore we believe that this approach is likely to be especially suited to supporting the novel organizational structures of the future.

Acknowledgments

We'd like to thank the members of the MIT-Center for Coordination Science, especially Thomas W. Malone for his advice and Zia Ahmed for his fast responses to my implementation requests, for their invaluable contributions to the ideas underlying this chapter.

20 How Can Cooperative Work Tools Support Dynamic Group Processes? Bridging the Specificity Frontier

Abraham Bernstein

20.1 Introduction

Many researchers have commented on the increased pace of change in today's economy. Increasingly groups and organizations have to adapt their processes to rapid changes arising from new technologies, new customer demands, or new competitors. Current process-support systems (e.g., ERP, work flow–management systems), however, are usually focused on supporting fixed organizational processes. Typically they are too rigid to easily support changing processes. They are mainly used for highly specified and highly routinized organizational processes. As an alternative, many organizations use communications support systems or Groupware (like e-mail or Lotus Notes) to support their rapidly changing, nonroutine processes. But these systems typically require users to do a lot of work themselves to keep track of and understand the ongoing processes: what has been done, what needs to be done next, and so forth.

This dichotomy is paralleled by an old debate in the CSCW-literature about the nature of collaborative work (e.g., see Schank and Abelson 1977; Winograd and Flores 1986; Suchman 1987; Winograd 1994; Suchman 1994). Both sides in this ongoing debate present some deeply rooted beliefs about how human actors perceive the world and decide to act.

One side follows the belief that human actors typically follow the cycle of problem analysis, solution search or synthesis, and then the execution of that plan. The goal of a process-oriented collaboration support system in this perspective is to increase the speed and efficiency of each step in the cycle as well as facilitate a seamless integration of the steps. Work flow–management systems (WfMS) and other process support systems like enterprise resource planning systems (ERP) are based on this research stream and have typically focused on the execution of standardized, predefined organizational process (e.g., Hammer et al. 1977; Zisman 1978; Mohan et al. 1995; Jablonski and Bussler 1996).

The other side sees plans as resources for action (Suchman 1987), which are used in conjunction with the environment to articulate and reason about the next action steps (Gasser 1986; Gerson and Star 1986; Suchman 1996). Following this

An earlier version of this chapter appeared as A. Bernstein (2000), How can cooperative work tools support dynamic group processes? Bridging the specificity frontier. *Proceedings of the Conference on Computer Supported Cooperative Work* (CSCW'2000), Philadelphia, ACM Press. © 2000 ACM. Reprinted by permission.

perspective typical WfMSs are too restrictive as they traditionally prescribe the work flow and do not allow users to adapt the process to the local situation. Therefore researchers following this tradition have often advocated using flexible communication support systems (e.g., e-mail and discussion databases) or repositories (e.g., document management/imaging systems) to support organizational processes. Those systems, however, have the disadvantage that an actor typically is on his/her own in deciding what to do next.

To date, none of the approaches has offered a conclusive answer. I concur with others (e.g., Newell and Simon 1972; Keen and Scott Morton 1978; Rock, Ulrich, and Witt 1990) that organizational activities often include a mix of both procedure and ad hoc parts. The research presented in this chapter therefore argues in favor of bridging between both perspectives by developing systems that will support the whole range of dynamic organizational activity: from well-specified and routine (reacting to exceptions as they occur) to highly unspecified and situated.

In this chapter, I will first ground this novel idea in a practical scenario and social science theory. This will help explain the approach as well as facilitate the presentation of the proof of concept prototype system. I will conclude with a brief survey of related work and a discussion of the major lessons learned.

20.2   A Scenario: Heidi's Problem

It is Friday afternoon in Zurich, Switzerland, and Heidi, a local account manager for Zing computers (pseudonym), a worldwide producer of computers, gets a phone call from the Swiss stock exchange. They ask for delivery of a RT2000-server within 48 hours to Zurich, since they need to replace an existing server that got damaged in a fire to recommence trading on Monday morning. Heidi now faces the problem that the traditional order entry/fulfillment system will not be able to accommodate this request, since the truckers in the European Union (EU) are on strike and the major assembly plant for Europe is in Rotterdam. The only other tools available to her are communication support systems like e-mail, telephone or fax, which give her all the flexibility she needs. However, that also puts the burden of contextual sense-making (i.e., understanding the context of the task) on whoever gets her messages/faxes/phone calls.

20.3   The Conceptual Framework

The conceptual framework starts with the commonalties between the situated and the procedural approaches. Both approaches appear to share some minimal assumptions about human actors. First, human actors are boundedly rational and have only limited knowledge about the future. Consequently plans (as well as process maps or work flow descriptions) are often imperfect, for they typically cannot account for all possible circumstances. A process support system will therefore have to allow for run-time changes to the original plan and will have to provide contextual information about the running process to the actor as a basis for reasoning about the possible next steps. Process maps, a representation of plans, can serve as part of such contextual information (Suchman 1987; Weick 1979; Bardram 1997).

Second, as Newell and Simon (1972) point out, our environment includes well-structured and less-well-structured problems. Consequently we have problems with well-defined solution strategies and others, where the solutions strategy is rather unclear (Rock et al. 1990). The transparency of the solution strategy (which can be represented as a process map) may change over time as our understanding of the problem changes. As an elusive problem becomes, for example, better understood its solution strategy may become easier to determine. Or a seemingly simple problem may become highly complex, as new facets of the problem emerge during problem solving, rendering the original solution strategy inapplicable.

20.3.1 The Specificity Frontier

The first consequence of this approach in regard to the enactment of activity is that the specificity of process structure changes over time. Bernstein and Schucan (1998), for example, provide a description of how the money-transfer process gained specificity over time. Before the formalities of banking were established, this process started as a vaguely specified process involving an ad hoc letter sent by a courier. With increasing maturity of the banking industry, the specificity of the process increased significantly. Today a money transfer is a fixed computer-based interbank clearing process with a fixed set of attributes. This illustrates the major pillar of this conceptual framework: organizational processes lie on a continuum from highly specified and routine processes at one extreme to highly unspecified and dynamic processes at the other extreme. I call this continuum the specificity frontier (see figure 20.1). A whole series of points on this frontier are possible, from a highly specific to highly unspecific.

As figure 20.1 depicts the concept of a specificity frontier in some sense bridges the gap between the structured WfMS and the unstructured communication systems. It allows for the coexistence of well-specified and almost procedurally executed processes (traditionally supported by WfMSs), and emergent situated processes (typically supported by communication support systems). It also argues that those two types of processes are at the extremes of a frontier of processes. It proposes that the

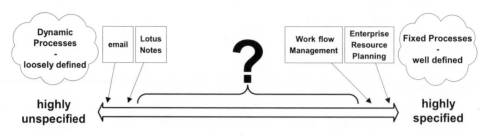

Figure 20.1
Specificity frontier

whole range of processes, from highly specified and routine to highly unspecified and dynamic should be supported.

Heidi's problem, for instance, starts out as having a reasonably well-specified solution strategy (process). When she, however, realizes that the truckers in the EU are on strike, the process suddenly becomes much more problematic: the known description is not applicable anymore. Thus a support system that allows processes to start out as being well defined (and supported by a WfMS-type technology), and lets the structure become flexible (and supported by groupware technology) as soon as she finds out about the strike, would be ideal for her.

Consequently a model of business processes should be able to capture a range of process specificity (from well specified to highly unspecified). A process support system should be able *to interpret process models with varying degrees of specificity*. Furthermore it should *support users when changing the specificity of the processes at run-time*. In achieving those goals, it can close the specificity gap (pictured as a question mark in figure 20.1) between traditional process-support systems and communication support systems, and thus bridge systems following the work flow tradition and the situated action tradition.

20.3.2 Emergent Activity Relies on Structure

The second consequence of those commonalties (i.e., bounded rationality and varying specificity of tasks) is illustrated by Orlikowski (1996), who shows how change can be understood as a series of improvisational embellishments to existing practice. In other words, the actors attempt to solve the problem at hand following their interpretation of the structure and the current context. This illustrates the second pillar of the conceptual framework: that *emergent activity relies on some form of structure and thus some form of specificity*. Emergent activity surfaces "unpredictably from complex social interactions" (Markus and Robey 1988, p. 588). However, we may be able to support it by supplying a fertile environment for new solutions to emerge, "much as does a supersaturated solution in the moment it is disturbed" (Mintzberg and Waters 1985, p. 267). For example, jazz improvisation, a type of emergent activity, depends on the actors "having absorbed a broad base of musical knowledge" (Berliner 1994, p. 492). Analogously, people in an organizational context must have some foundational knowledge about the task at hand. In addition, as Weick (1998) points out "improvisation does not materialize out of thin air" (p. 546). People need something to improvise on. This explains the limited success of communications support systems for business process support: from an improvisational standpoint, human actors using those systems incur the overhead of having to understand the context of the task at hand as a basis for improvisation. In the domain of organizational activity, a process map with a low degree of specificity and information about the enactment context could help actors in their sense-making, provide a basis to improvise on and thus a fertile environment for emergent processes.

Consequently any system that plans to support emergent activity (which is what all activity is to some degree following the situated action approach) *should provide some structure as a contextual basis for situated improvisation*. Process maps (in analogy to geographical maps) can provide such structure.

20.3.3 Other Requirements
Previous research (see Swenson 1993; Abbott and Sarin 1994; Ellis and Nutt 1996; Krammer et al. 2000 among others) has shown that a process support system also should allow for the change, composition, and execution at run-time as well as provide a means of integration into an existing environment (e.g., using an open interface).

20.4 The Specificity Frontier Approach and Prototype System

Now that I have explained the theoretical grounding for the prototype system, I will present the major design ideas I have used. I will discuss the proof-of-concept prototype system that served to clarify, illustrate, and evaluate those design ideas. Since some of the design ideas can be abstract, I will walk through Heidi's problem as a practical example of the day-to-day use of the prototype system as I introduce new concepts.

20.4.1 Key Ideas
The major obstacle in designing a process support system following my conceptual framework is the need for an implementation approach that can handle process

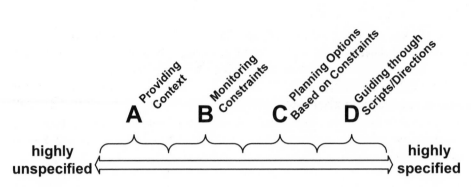

Figure 20.2
Different execution types

specifications at multiple points of the specificity frontier as well as transformations of the specificity of a process during execution. As figure 20.2 shows, I chose to *divide the specificity frontier into subspectra*, each supported by its own interpretation logic. I decided to use four subspectra, since existing process support technology (e-mail/ groupware, constraint monitoring, constraint-based planning, and transaction processing) could be categorized into four groups: providing context for enactment, monitoring constraints about the task, providing/planning options to reach a goal, and guiding through a given script.

The second idea was to develop *run-time transfer mappings between the subspectra*. So processes can be *seamlessly moved to another subspectrum* by increasing or decreasing the specificity of the process definition during run-time.

20.4.2   Specifying and Interpreting Processes Models with Varying Degrees of Specificity

Providing Context   In the least specified of the subspectra (*A*, at the left in figure 20.2), the support system does not have a lot of information about the process. Therefore its major goal is to provide context for the user to be able to decide what to do next. Similar to the Task Manager presented by Kreifelts, Hinrichs, and Woetzel (1993), the system helps the users to *share to-do lists and documents (resources)* that are specific to the task context at hand. The system also integrates with other communication techniques like e-mail, on-line discussions, and on-line synchronous communication support, such as chat, to allow users to communicate with their respective collaborators. The specificity of the task to the user may vary depending on the information contained in the documents. The system's support, however, will remain the same throughout this subspectrum, since the system cannot decode any of the information in the documents.

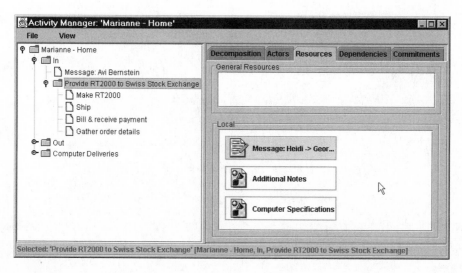

Figure 20.3
Activity manager

This is exactly the type of support Heidi needs to start solving her delivery problem. Since she has to collaborate with Marianne, a European logistics manager in Rotterdam, she should be able to share information about the problem and collect information about the tasks to be done (build the new server, arrange shipment and billing, etc.). As we can see in figure 20.3, the system provides a hierarchical to-do list on the left, and shows the resources associated with the task selected. Whenever Heidi writes a new document in the context of this task (e.g., the highlighted message to George at the right in figure 20.3), it gets automatically added to the resources connected to the task and complements the context.

From an implementation standpoint, the system should provide a shared distributed-accessible, hierarchical to-do list that allows users to attach files (as resources) to each of the to-do items. I chose to implement each to-do item as a software agent that manages collections of other to-do items and of pointers to files in an object-oriented document repository. As we will see, the choice of active software agents, rather than a passive data structure, becomes advantageous when passing the boundary to the next subspectrum.

Monitoring Constraints When the user decides to add some machine-readable constraint to a to-do item, the system provides constraint monitoring services. For instance, adding a deadline to a to-do item could allow the system to prompt the user when the deadline is imminent (similar to a project management system). The

Figure 20.4
Adding constraints

system's support in this subspectrum is comparable to the support a map provides to a hiker. It shows the ravines and the mountains in the area and may therefore help the user to reach his/her goal without long detours by alerting him/her of an obstacle (i.e., a constraint). The more constraints are specified by the user the more helpful the system can be in helping the user to reach his/her goal. Summarizing, the system *helps the user by managing constraints between tasks and resources.*

As Heidi and Marianne quickly discover, there are a series of constraints that they have to keep track of: the deadline for delivery, the type of server, the facts about the strike, and so on. When those constraints get specified, the system can help by reminding the user whenever one of the constraints is about to be invalidated. If they were to become late at arranging the shipment, for example, the system would alert them of the impending problem of a late shipment. So Heidi and Marianne add the most relevant constraints (see figure 20.4) to the 'Provide RT2000' process.

In this subspectrum the system offers the constraint monitoring services in addition to the context provision services. Actors therefore still have the same context information on which to decide what to do next. The boundary between the two subspectra is thus crossed as soon as at least one formalized constraint is defined.

Users form the constraints on attributes of the activities/to-do items or resources in the existing process models. Figure 20.4, for example, shows a constraint defined on the attribute 'Elapsed time' of the 'Provide RT2000' process. I understand that users sometimes experience difficulties using formalized specification languages, such as boolean expressions. In the long run I hope to address this problem by (1) implementing a graphical expression design tool (Spoerri 1993) and (2) providing typical constraints to the user as templates to tailor (this was found to be useful in other situations (MacLean et al. 1990)). Typical constraint types might include: time constraints (e.g., deadlines), budgetary limits (e.g., headcount and funds available), external factors (e.g., no trucking in Europe), specification of resources (e.g., types of processors/prefabricated servers in warehouse), among other things.

Here is where we reap the benefit for using active software agents to represent the to-do items. When the to-do agent detects the definition of a new formally defined constraint it spawns a sentinel agent, an autonomous piece of code, to monitor the constraint. The sentinel agent periodically checks for the validity of the constraints. When it detects the invalidation of the constraint it guards, the sentinel agent raises an exception. Depending on the constraint definition (by the user or template), the system will either handle the exception itself (e.g., using an exception handling routine/engine) or alert the user. Similar to personal schedulers, the users can choose how long before the actual invalidation of the constraints they want to be warned (e.g., 10 minutes before the expiration of the deadline).

Planning Options Based on Constraints   When the user specifies the goal, or postcondition, of an activity in his/her to-do list (via the same mechanism used to define the constraints), the system will try to propose to the user a series of possible approaches to completing his/her work. The system achieves this by taking the constraints on the activities provided by the user in the constraint-preservation subspectrum as well as the goal/postcondition and using them as a problem specification for an Artificial Intelligence planner (see (Weld 1994) for an introduction). The planner will search for a way to achieve the goal while guarding all the constraints using activities that reside in a repository of possible actions (see below). In the best case it may find one or multiple plans. The user can then either choose a plan to follow or can decide that none of the plans is satisfactory. This would typically indicate that there is some constraint about which the system does not know. The user can choose to ignore the proposed solutions and act on his/her own or add the additional constraint (if he/she can formulate it in a machine-readable way) and retry the planner. In some cases the planner may not return a solution. This may either be due to an incomplete repository of possible actions or due to an underspecification of the goal. In this case the user can either choose to add more actions to the repository or just rely on the more limited support functionality of the constraint monitoring subspectrum.

Using the hiking analogy this approach parallels giving a hiker a trail map of the area and having him/her decide what trails he/she would like to take. Since the constraints are specified, the map also contains the ravines and mountains, such that the user might be able to decide that none of the proposed trails are feasible, and choose

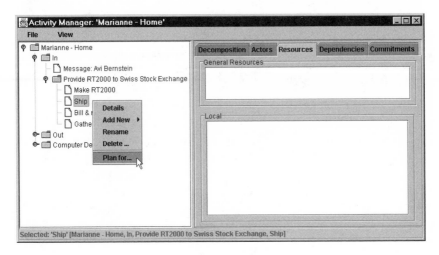

Figure 20.5
Planner

to take his/her own route. Consequently in this subspectrum the system *plans tasks and resources to achieve goals* and lets the user decide which of the possible paths to take.

Marianne realizes that the system might help her to solve the problem of how to ship the server to Zurich in time. She therefore initiates the planner, which uses the constraints defined for monitoring (in the last subspectrum) and the goal specification (i.e., RT2000 delivered to Swiss Stock Exchange) as a problem specification. It proposes three shipping options (see figure 20.5). First, it proposes to airfreight the server from Rotterdam. Second, it proposes to ship the server from the facility in Rotterdam using a train. Last, it suggests airfreighting the server from an American facility in Boston. Marianne did not consider this last option before, since deliveries to Europe typically come from Rotterdam. Given the looming deadline and the EU trucker strike, she decides to explore all three possibilities. She quickly discovers that given the strike, she can't even find a truck to bring the server from the Rotterdam production facility out to the airport. Therefore, the first option, shipping the server by plane from Rotterdam becomes implausible. To investigate the second possibility, using the train, she goes into the repository and looks at the train-shipment process. She realizes that since Switzerland is not part of the EU, the train will have to clear customs at the Swiss border. During a phone call to the Swiss customs authority she learns that Swiss customs at the port of entry (for the train) is closed all day Sunday, which would delay the shipment by an additional 24 hours. Consequently, she chooses the only remaining option: shipping the server from Boston.

This part of the interpreter was implemented as a simple translator to an existing AI-planner (Weld, Anderson, and Smith 1998). The interpreting agent gathers all the constraints relevant for a to-do item, information about the current state of the process (as defined by the state of all the involved agents and datastructures) as well as a goal description (defined as a logical expression derived from the postcondition/goal of the process) and then passes it as a problem definition to the planner. In the scenario, for example, the agents gather the constraints like 'elapsed time < 48 hours' and 'no trucks', the goal description 'having an RT2000-server in Zurich', as well as the definition current state, including the knowledge that the EU truckers are on strike, knowledge about Zing Computer's production facility and information about the current time.

The planner attempts to find a set of actions in the repository that will lead from the current state to the goal and pass the possible results to the interpreter, which translates them back to the process representation used within the system and presents them to the user. The repository contains a collection of possible actions, which are defined by their pre-/postcondition and a description of how the transformation from precondition to postcondition happens in detail.

In Marianne's situation, for example, the repository had to contain descriptions of all kinds of transport mechanisms and their properties. It thus had to have a description of trucking a good, including the property that it typically requires a truck (which are unavailable in our scenario), airplane-shipping (which was incomplete, since it didn't take into account the need for getting the good to the airport), as well as shipping by train.

Obviously the quality of the planner's results is limited by two factors. First, the quality of the constraints entered (including the precision of the goal specification) has a major influence on the ability of the planner to prune its search space. Since the users have entered them, the quality of the specification of those constraints is highly dependent on the abilities of the users. As mentioned above, I hope that the usage of expression design tools as well as the provision of tailorable typical expressions and expression templates provided by process specialists (e.g., residing in the repository) may alleviate this problem. Second, the quality of the plans generated by the planner is dependent on the contents of the repository searched. As with any knowledge-based approach there is a bootstrapping problem in filling the repository with an adequate initial number of possible actions/processes. In most environments, however, a good part of those actions have already been formalized and defined in some system (WfMS, ERP, etc.). Furthermore the repository records past cases as templates for future action. This 'case-based'-like (Kolodner, Simpson, and

Sycara-Cyranski 1985) approach can simplify some of the initial growing phase of the repository by limiting the enormous setup costs.

Providing "Imperative" Scripts/Directions   System support in this last subspectrum can be likened to a traditional WfMS (see Hammer et al. 1977; Zisman 1978; Jablonski and Bussler 1996). Since the process details are algorithmically well defined, the to-do item software agent will direct each step leading to the result. Rather than guarding some constraints, the imperative plan avoids them through direction. Thus the *system directs the execution of tasks using resources to achieve goals.*

The boundary between the constraint-based planning subspectrum and the imperative subspectrum is crossed as soon as one of the results returned by the planner is chosen for enactment that is in an imperative form. The user can delegate the choice between the options to the system by defining a utility function. As an alternative to using the results of the planner, the user can directly browse the repository and compose a process manually (Bernstein 1998), which can also result in an imperative script. The reverse transformation happens when the interpreter executing a task in the imperative subspectrum encounters an exception (which might be raised by a user!), stops its execution, and runs the planner to find a number of alternatives to solve the current problem.

Using the hiker's analogy again this subspectrum can be best compared to giving a hiker a specific set of directions. The directions are useful as long as he/she does not encounter a problem (e.g., an avalanche has cut off an existing path). As soon as a problem is encountered, the hiker has to use a more situated method to finding his/her way to the goal (i.e., he/she has to drop the specificity of the process specification and use the support provided by the system in the other subspectra).

When Marianne chooses to airfreight the server from Boston by choosing to start that process in her Activity Manager (figure 20.6) the system starts the underlying WfMS-like shipment process of a new server from Boston to Zurich using airfreight in the last of the four subspectra. Assuming no new exceptions the system will direct the shipment just like a traditional order fulfillment system.

Division of Labor and Transfer Mappings in the Frontier   It is important to note that this system view relies on a cooperative understanding of the user system collaboration, where the system attempts to provide as much help as it can. *The more specific a task description is, the more the system can support the user* and relieve him/her of some part of the task. The less specific the task is, the more the user will have to do. Consequently the specificity of a process description guides the resulting type of division of labor between the human actor and the system.

Figure 20.6
Starting a WfMS-like script

Another important point is the system's capability to seamlessly integrate between the different spectra. The boundary between the context provision and the monitoring subspectra is automatically crossed when some constraints are formalized in a machine-readable form. The next boundary is traversed when the system can find a series of paths from the current state to the goal (i.e., the planner can find an acceptable plan). Finally the provision of some type of utility function by the user (either implicitly by choosing one of the options or explicitly by defining some sort of sort criteria between the options) helps the system to cross to the scripts subspectrum. From the user's point of view, the transfers between the subspectra happen automatically as soon as the system can find the appropriate information. The user does not need to explicitly tell the system to cross the boundaries between the spectra. He/she does, however, need to enter the information (e.g., the constraint specification) that will prompt the system to cross the boundary.

Providing Structure for Situated Improvisation The second requirement that the conceptual framework puts on process support system is the provision of a context for sense-making and the articulation of next steps. As we have seen, the prototype system provides the user with ample contextual information (past activities in

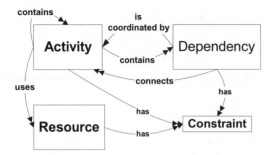

Figure 20.7
Process model parts

process context, documents related to this process, other actors involved, etc.) in order to understand the current state of the process.

In some stages, however, he/she might not exactly know what to do next. The possible options of next actions can, for example, lie beyond his/her experience or an alternative, novel course of action is needed. Malone et al. (chapter 1 in this volume) have described how a repository of re-usable process components as well as past cases can be applied to organizational processes and can be useful in a process-design and innovation setting. I therefore believe that a process repository containing process fragments and past cases can help users to articulate next steps and have included a repository, similar to the one presented in chapter 1, in my prototype.

20.4.3 Implementation Details

Process Models   The prototype system uses a process description, which is comparable to the one used by the MIT Process Handbook (see chapter 1 in this volume, or figure 20.7 for a meta-model). Activities are the central element of the model. Each activity can have an arbitrary number of resources in its context (e.g., for providing the links for the documents related to a task). An activity can also have subactivities (for functional decomposition) and subdependencies. Dependencies represent constraints between activities. In order to ensure the constraint represented by the dependency, it needs to be coordinated by an activity. When two activities share a resource (i.e., a sharing dependency), for example, they can be coordinated using a first-come–first-serve activity. Finally activities, resources, and dependencies can all have an arbitrary number of constraints defined on their attributes and parts. Furthermore all elements can participate in a type of specialization hierarchy. This allows for a construction of an object-oriented-like hierarchy in the process and case

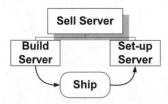

Figure 20.8
Example process

repository. The main difference from conventional object-oriented inheritance is the possibility to 'disinherit' a feature from its parent. So when a person changes an inherited part of an activity, it does not have loose its inheritance relations (see also chapter 1).

20.4.4   System Architecture and Implementation

The overall system consists of five major logical components: a repository, a process-model interpreter, a planner, a user-interface, and an application-programming interface (API), which is used by other programs to interact with the system. The *repository* stores all the process models, process fragments, and past cases. It furthermore contains references to all the resources (e.g., files) that are referenced by processes in the system and has some information about all the actors/users of the system. Distribution of the process data is accomplished through the services of an object request broker (ORB). Each object in the repository is currently stored in a file that transparently gets loaded when needed. Figure 20.8 shows the graphical representation for the 'Sell server' process, as it is stored in the repository. It consists of three parts, the 'Build server' and 'Set up server' processes as well as the 'Ship' dependency. The *interpreter* is implemented using a software agent oriented approach. Each active element of a process model is assigned to an agent. Collaborating with the other agents in the process model the software agent attempts to provide as much support as possible given the process specification. Thus for the 'Sell server' process, a software agent is going to be started for 'Sell server', 'Build Server', 'Set up server', and 'Ship'. All those agents are going to interact using a speech-act-based protocol (Searle 1969) to achieve the goal of the task. If the process specification falls within the context-provision spectrum, the agents ensure that all the resources referenced are accessible. When constraints get defined (i.e., in the constraint-preservation subspectrum), the agents start special sentinel agents, which regularly check the consistency of the constraint. When a postcondition is specified, the agents pass the process definition to the planner (see below). Finally, if the process model contains imperative features, they execute them analogous to a traditional WfMS while still checking on the constraints (to find exceptions). In all cases the agents maintain the relationships to other agents to which they have dependencies. This integration of previously unconnected techniques provides the system its ability to support the enactment of processes that move along the specificity frontier at run-time. Consequently it is the heart of this system's support for dynamic, rapidly changing organizational processes. Using the agent-based approach allowed me to build a dynamic interpreter, where local variation in process specificity and composition is handled by single agents and global changes are handled by the interplay between agents. This greatly reduced the complexity of the interpreter.

As a *planner* I used sensory graph-plan (SGP), a LISP-based research prototype presented by Weld, Anderson, and Smith (1998).

The interpreter agents translate the process model and the repository content to a problem definition in the format understood by SGP. If the planner returns a result, then the interpreter agents translate it back to the internal process specification format.

In our scenario all parts of the process other than the 'Ship' dependency (figure 20.8e are relatively well defined. So, when Marianne initiated the planner (figure 20.5), the interpreter collected all the constraints relevant to the problem (i.e., the constraints on 'Ship' directly, including the fact that it is in relation with both 'Build server' and 'Set up server').

The *user-interface* (see figures 20.3 to 20.6) contains a mixture of a traditional work flow management work list and a task-management user-interface (like the one presented in Kreifelts, Hinrichs, and Woetzel 1993) as well as a process model editor. It provides a direct manipulation interface to all the major functions in the system like a browser for the process fragment/case repository, an activity-manager that provides a look at the activities a user is presumed to complete, a process-editor to change the tasks, and some additional maintenance editors. The *API* provides a bi-directional interface between the prototype system and external tools such as email, discussion databases, and on-line chat programs.

20.5   Evaluation and Lessons Learned

I have chosen three routes to evaluate the validity of the work presented. First, I chose to thoroughly ground my work in existing theory, previous work on requirements for supporting dynamic organizational processes, and some direct exchange with potential users, which provided me with some assurance that the approach would be helpful in a practical setting. Second, I implemented a proof of concept system and used it myself.

I am now developing a number of detailed usage scenarios based on real-world occurrences and am evaluating how those scenarios would play out in different types of support systems: an e-mail/Lotus Notes type of system, a WfMS, and the prototype system presented. At the time of writing, preliminary results support my assumptions about the advantages of a system basing on the specificity frontier, given its guidance in more routine tasks as well as flexibility where needed.

One interesting lesson learned was that the combination of previously unconnected approaches could lead to extremely useful solutions, just as the combination of messaging, database technology, security, and networking approaches led to a versatile tool like Lotus Notes. In my case it led to a system with the capability to support rapidly changing processes. However, I believe that this type of judicious integration could be extremely useful for many problems.

Another insight was that the usage of agent-oriented techniques allowed me to simplify the implementation of my multifaceted prototype system (given its multiple subspectra) by avoiding code tangling, which complicates implementations. As Lopes and Kiczales (1997) points out, code tangling typically happens when different concerns (or implementation issues like synchronization and information exchange) have to be addressed within the same piece of code. Using the agent-based approach, I was able keep the complex parts of the implementation (e.g., the code handling the change in specificity for different types of objects in my system) local to its effects and successfully avoid code tangling. This insight becomes increasingly important for CSCW researchers, as the experimental systems we implement become more complicated and integrated with more technologies (see previous insight).

20.6   Related Work

As explained in the introduction the approach presented here is closely related to systems in the WfMS tradition as well as the Groupware tradition. In the WfMS domain a number of projects have tried to address the issues of adaptiveness and flexibility (Kammer et al. 2000; Norman et al. 1996; Agostini and De Michelis 2000; Ellis and Keddara 2000). However, all of the approaches aim at completely specifying the process before it is started using some formal method (e.g., Petri nets) and adapting them when exceptions occur. They typically do not allow the execution of partially specified or abstractly specified process descriptions. At the other end of the frontier, a number of CSCW projects and Groupware tools have addressed the support for highly flexible processes.

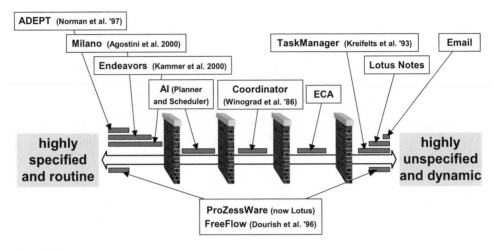

Figure 20.9
Related work

   The biggest problem of all related projects, however, is the impermeability of processes across the specificity frontier. As can be seen in figure 20.9, processes that get started in one category of support system are stuck in that type of support. Thus the support for an emergent process, for example, stays trapped in an ad hoc system, though its process structure may have emerged during a first part of its execution. Even systems basing on event condition–action rules (ECA), which are typically used for constraint preservation or AI-planning systems, do not allow for mobility across the specificity frontier.

   I know of three exceptions: ProZessware (ONEstone 1998), Bramble (Blumenthal 1998), and FreeFlow (Dourish et al. 1996). ProZessware allows embedding Lotus-Notes discussions into well-specified work flows. However, these embedded discussions have to be prespecified, and the actual process structure is fixed. Bramble divides activities into well specified and unstructured. Similar to ProZessware it allows composing semistructured activities from both well-specified and unstructured activities. In addition it provides a rich mechanism for providing process context. Unlike the system presented here, though, it does not seem to allow for run-time transformations of activities from well specified to unstructured, and vice versa. FreeFlow provides a highly unspecified and dynamic and a highly specified and routine mechanism to break the predefined constraints, which specify the work flow. Once a constraint is broken, however, its guidance is lost for the process. Thus the system only allows a one-time reduction of specificity of a process description during run-time. The work presented here is set apart from other projects by proposing a novel well-grounded approach to enabling the mobility of a process instance across the specificity frontier *during run-time*.

20.7   Contributions and Conculsion

The primary contribution of this research project is twofold. First, it suggests a novel approach to addressing the problem of support for dynamic organizational processes. The proposition of using varying specificity as an approach to solving the problem of supporting dynamic organizational processes is novel, nonobvious, promising, and supported by social science theory. Second, the project shows the technical feasibility of this approach. Combining previously separate process-support technologies from well specified and routine, to highly unspecified and dynamic, into a seamlessly integrated system that facilitates the mobility of processes across the specificity frontier during run-time using a common process model is a nontrivial technical achievement. Although the primary focus of this project was not to empirically test the usefulness of the system, it provides some evidence to its plausibility. By developing detailed usage scenarios, based on empirical data, I have shown that a system like the one I have developed could be usable and useful. The preliminary results of the scenario analysis indicate that the variation of process specificity is useful to support dynamic organizational activity. The overhead incurred by actors seems to reduce when attempting to adapt existing (running) processes to changing circumstances compared to traditional approaches. For final proof, however, we will have to wait for a detailed empirical test of the usability and usefulness of such a system in a real-world environment—a substantial research project in its own right.

Acknowledgments

I would like to thank Tom Malone, Mark Klein, and the other members of the MIT-CCS for their invaluable help, support and contribution to the ideas underlying this chapter.

V CONCLUSION

We began this book with a vision—a vision of potentially huge repositories of knowledge about business activities and software processes that could be used for many purposes. These repositories could, for example, be used to advance research in organization theory in the same way that analogous classification systems helped advance research in chemistry and biology. They could be used to help managers, consultants, and business educators find the most current literature and case examples in their areas of interest. They could be used to help software developers significantly reduce the effort needed to create new programs from existing components and to customize programs for use in specific organizations. And they could be used to help invent new ideas about how to organize companies in the first place.

We believe that the work we have done in the Process Handbook project over the past decade demonstrates that this vision need not be just a fantasy. We believe that our work has made significant progress in showing both the feasibility and the desirability of this vision. We have developed a repository of moderate scale with many of the characteristics needed for the vision to be realized, and we have demonstrated the usefulness of this repository in a number of different applications.

But much more work is needed for this vision to become a reality. One area where we believe there is significant opportunity for further research is in developing new user interfaces to help people search and browse through densely (but systematically) interconnected knowledge bases like ours, while still maintaining a sense of "where" they are within the whole network. Another promising direction for many kinds of research is in applying the framework, software tools, and knowledge base to new problems like those described in section IV of this volume.

But perhaps the most important challenge ahead is in developing more business content and keeping it constantly updated. Our repository currently includes a little over 5,000 activities. We believe that before even coming close to reaching the full potential of the vision, this number could easily be multiplied by a factor of at least 100 to 1,000.

We don't believe that a single research group in a single academic institution is well suited to even attempt an effort on the scale that is needed. Instead, we believe that the fulfillment of this vision will require the efforts of many more people in many more academic and commercial organizations. We are not yet sure what organizational structure and what combination of scientific, educational, and economic incentives are appropriate for this effort. But we hope that the publication of this volume will help stimulate discussions about this question.

Most of all, we hope that the vision we have been pursuing for more than a decade will someday become a reality from which we can all benefit.

APPENDIX: ENABLING TECHNOLOGY

Early in the Process Handbook project, we realized that the power of a repository like the Process Handbook would be significantly increased if it were possible to easily and automatically transfer information between the repository and other software applications. In order to do this, however, some common format for exchanging information is needed.

With this goal in mind, we created a working group, including people from a number of other universities and companies, to define such a common format. This appendix describes the results of that group's work. The format defined by the working group is called the Process Interchange Format (PIF) (see *ccs.mit.edu/pif*). This format defines common terminology and representational conventions for many of the concepts that are needed whenever representations of processes are exchanged.

One of the virtues of the approach taken here is that it also exploits the notion of specialization of processes (see chapter 1) to simplify the creation of specialized extensions to the format. These specialized extensions can be shared by subsets of people to communicate detailed information, but the basic "meaning" of the extensions is still interpretable by other users who understand only the basic format.

The work described in this appendix is now being incorporated by the US National Institute of Standards and Technology (NIST) into the definition of their Process Specification Language (PSL) (see *http://ats.nist.gov/psl/*).

The PIF Process Interchange Format and Framework

Jintae Lee
Michael Grunninger
Yan Jin
Thomas W. Malone

Austin Tate
Gregg Yost
Other members of the PIF
Working Group

A.1 Introduction

More and more companies today are attempting to improve their business by engaging in some form of business process redesign (BPR). BPR focuses on a 'process view' of a business and attempts to identify and describe an organization's business processes; evaluate the processes to identify problem areas; select or design new processes, possibly radically different from those currently in place; predict the effects of proposed process changes; define additional processes that will allow the organization to more readily measure its own effectiveness; and enact, manage, and monitor the new processes. The goal is a leaner, more effective organization that has better insight into how it does business and how its business processes affect the organization's health. Successful BPR projects involve the cooperation of many people over extended time periods, including workplace analysts, systems engineers, and workers at all levels of the organization.

Computer applications that support one or more aspects of BPR are becoming increasingly common. Such applications include:

· Modeling tools that help a workplace analyst identify and describe an organization's processes

· Process editors and planning aids to synthesize new processes or to modify existing processes

· Process library browsers that help organizations find new processes that might better meet their needs

· Process animators and simulators that help organizations visualize the effects of existing processes or potential new processes

· Work flow–management tools that help workers follow business processes

· Outcomes analysis tools that help organizations monitor the effectiveness of their processes

An earlier version of this appendix appeared as J. Lee, M. Grunninger, Y. Jin, T. Malone, A. Tate, G. Yost, and other members of the PIF Working Group (1998), The process interchange format and framework. *Knowledge Engineering Review* 13(1). © 1998 Cambridge University Press. Reprinted by permission.

No single application supports all aspects of a BPR engagement, nor is it likely that such an application will ever exist. Furthermore applications that do support more than one aspect rarely do them all well. For example, a work flow tool may also provide some process simulation capabilities, but those additional capabilities are unlikely to be on par with the best dedicated simulation applications. This is to be expected—building an application that supports even one of these aspects well requires a great deal of specialized knowledge and experience.

Ideally, then, a BPR team would be able to pick a set of BPR-support applications that best suits their needs: a process modeling tool from one vendor, a simulator from another, a work flow manager from another, and so forth. Unfortunately, these applications currently have no way to interoperate. Each application typically has its own process representation (often undocumented), and many applications do not provide interfaces that would allow them to be easily integrated with other tools.

Our goal with the PIF project is to support the exchange of process descriptions among different process representations. The PIF project supports sharing process descriptions through a description format called PIF (Process Interchange Format) that provides a bridge across different process representations. Tools interoperate by translating between their native format and PIF.[1]

Any process description format, including PIF, is unlikely to ever completely suit the needs of all applications that make use of business process descriptions. Therefore, in addition to the PIF format, we have defined a framework around PIF that accommodates extensions to the standard PIF description classes. The framework includes a translation scheme called Partially Shared Views that attempts to maximize information sharing among groups that have extended PIF in different ways.

The PIF framework aims to support process translation such that:

• Process descriptions can be automatically translated back and forth between PIF and other process representations with as little loss of meaning as possible. If translation cannot be done fully automatically, the human efforts needed to assist the translation should be minimized.

• If a translator cannot translate part of a PIF process description to its target format, it should:

---

1. A process specification in PIF is utilized in the context in which it is passed to a person, tool, or system in such a way that the task to be performed on it is understood (e.g., analyze the specifications for certain features, perform a simulation using the specification, execute a process that meets the specification, avoid executing any process that meets the specification, etc.). This imperative information about the task to be performed with a PIF process specification is not represented in the specification itself, but should be considered as the context within which the specification is used.

1. Translate as much of the description as possible (e.g., and not simply issue an error message and give up)

2. Represent any untranslatable parts as such and present them in a way that lets a person understand the problem and complete the translation manually if desired

3. Preserve any uninterpretable parts so that the translator can add them back to the process description when it is translated back into PIF

These requirements on the translators are very important. We believe that a completely standardized process description format is premature and unrealistic at this point. Therefore, as mentioned earlier, we have provided ways for groups to extend PIF to better meet their individual needs. As a result we expect that PIF translators will often encounter process descriptions written in PIF variants that they can only partially interpret. Translators must adopt conventions that ensure that items they cannot interpret are available for human inspection and are preserved for later use by other tools that are able to interpret them. Section A.6 describes PIF's Partially Shared Views translation scheme, which we believe will greatly increase the degree to which PIF process descriptions can be shared.

A.2   History and Current Status

The PIF project began in October 1993 as an outgrowth of the Process Handbook project (Malone et al. 1993) at MIT and the desire to share process descriptions among a few groups at MIT, Stanford, the University of Toronto, and Digital Equipment Corporation. The Process Handbook project at the MIT Center for Coordination Science aims to create an electronic handbook of process models, their relations, and their trade-offs. This handbook is designed to help process designers analyze a given process and discover innovative alternatives. The Spark project at Digital Equipment Corporation aims to create a tool for creating, browsing, and searching libraries of business process models. The Virtual Design Team (VDT) project at Stanford University aims to model, simulate, and evaluate process and organization alternatives. The Enterprise Modeling project at the University of Toronto aims to articulate well-defined representations for processes, time, resources, products, quality, and organization. These representations support software tools for modeling various aspects of enterprises in business process re-engineering and enterprise integration.

In one way or another, these groups were all concerned with process modeling and design. Furthermore they stood to benefit from sharing process descriptions across the different representations they used. For example, the Enterprise Modeling group might model an existing enterprise, use the Process Handbook to analyze its trade-offs and explore its alternatives, evaluate the different alternatives via VDT simulation, and then finally translate the chosen alternative back into its own representation for implementation.

Over the past years, through a number of face-to-face, e-mail, and telephone meetings, members from each of the groups have:

· Articulated the requirements for PIF

· Specified the core PIF process description classes

· Specified the PIF syntax

· Elaborated the Partially Shared View mechanism for supporting multiple, partially overlapping class hierarchies

· Created and maintained a database of the issues that arose concerning PIF's design and the rationales for their resolutions

· Implemented several translators, each of which translated example process descriptions (such as a portion of the ISPW-6 Software Change Process) between PIF and a group's own process representation

Based on this work, the PIF Document 1.0 was released in December 1994. Since then, we have received a number of questions and comments on topics that range from individual PIF constructs to how certain process descriptions can be represented in PIF. We have been also assessing the adequacy of the PIF 1.0 by testing it against more complex process descriptions than before. AIAI at the University of Edinburgh also joined the PIF Working Group at this time bringing along their interests in planning, work flow, and enterprise process modeling. The Edinburgh group is also providing a valuable service as a liaison between the PIF group and the Workflow Management Coalition as well as the AI planning community (in particular, the DARPA/ROME Laboratory Planning Initiative) which has been concerned with the activity representation issues for a while.

The revised structure of PIF reflects the lessons extracted from these external and internal input. In particular, two points emerged clearly. One is that the PIF-CORE has to be reduced to the bare minimum to enable translation among those who cannot agree on anything else. The other point is the importance of structuring PIF as a set of modules that build on one another. This way groups with different expressive needs can share a subset of the modules, rather than the whole monolithic set of constructs. As a result the PIF-CORE has been reduced to the minimum that is necessary to translate the simplest process descriptions and yet has built-in constructs for "hanging-off" modules that extend the core in various ways.

A.3   PIF Overview

The PIF ontology has grown out of the efforts of the PIF Working Group to share process descriptions among the group members' various tools. We have used the following guidelines in developing this hierarchy:

• Generality is preferred over computational efficiency when there is a trade-off, for the reason that PIF is an interchange language, not a programming language designed for efficient execution.[2] Therefore the organization of the entity classes is not necessarily well suited to performing any particular task such as work flow–management or process simulation. Instead, our goal has been to define classes that can express a wide variety of processes, and that can be readily translated into other formats that may be more suitable for a particular application.

• The PIF constructs should be able to express the constructs of some existing common process representations such as IDEF (SADT) or Petri nets.

• PIF should start with the minimal set of classes and then expand only as it needs to. The minimal set was decided at the first PIF Workshop (October 1993) by examining those constructs common to some major existing process representations and to the process representations used by members of the PIF Working Group.

• Additions to the standard PIF classes could be proposed by anybody, but the proposal had to be accompanied by concrete examples illustrating the need for the additions. The Working Group decided, through discussions and votes if necessary, whether to accept the proposal. PIF allows groups to define local extensions at will (see section A.6), so new classes or attributes should be added to the standard PIF classes only if they seem to be of sufficiently general usefulness.

A PIF process description consists of a set of frame definitions, which are typically contained in a file. Each frame definition refers to an entity instance and is typed (e.g., ACTIVITY, OBJECT, TIMEPOINT) and they form a class hierarchy (see figure A.1). A frame definition has a particular set of attributes defined for it. Each of the attributes describes some aspect of the entity. For example, a PERFORMS definition has an Actor and an Activity attributes that specifies who is performing which activity. The instance of a frame definition has all the attributes of all of its superclasses, in addition to its own attributes. For example, all the instances

---

2. Although PIF is not an execution language, an execution language can be PIF-compliant. That is, an execution language can be designed to include the PIF constructs and thus not to require a translator to process a set of PIF specifications.

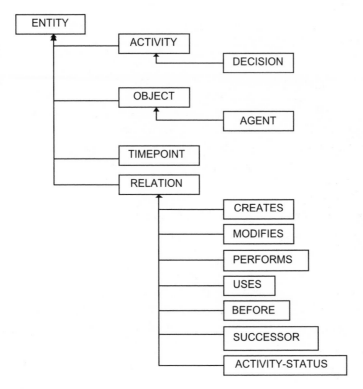

Figure A.1
PIF class hierarchy

of ACTIVITY have the Name attribute, since ENTITY, which is a superclass of ACTIVITY, has the Name attribute.

When an attribute of one frame has a value that refers to another frame, the attribute represents a relationship between the two instances that the two frames refer to. For example, if the Begin attribute of ACTIVITY-1 takes TIMEPOINT-32 as its value, then the Begin attribute represents a relationship between the ACTIVITY-1 and TIMEPOINT-32 instances. The value of a given attribute in a PIF file holds independent of time. Figure A.2 depicts the relationships among the PIF classes. Section A.5 describes all of the current PIF classes.

An attribute in a PIF entity can be filled with the following and only the following PIF expressions: a literal value of a PIF primitive value type or an expression of a composite value type. The PIF primitive value types consist of NUMBER, STRING, and SYMBOL:

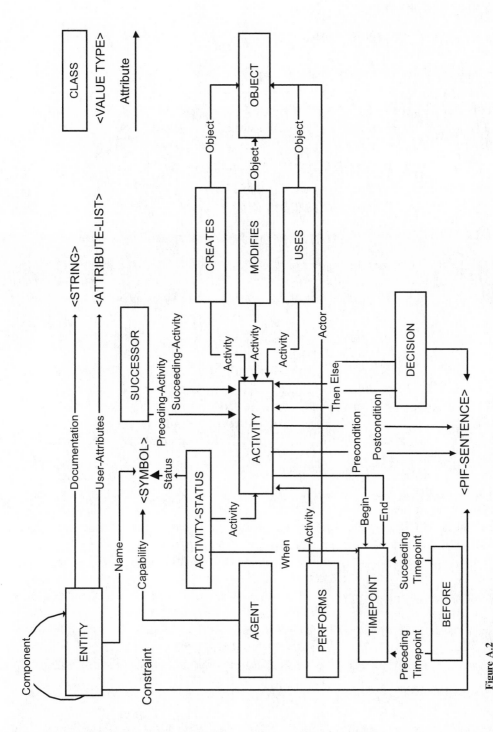

Figure A.2
Relationships among PIF classes

· NUMBER.   A numeric value. The NUMBER type is subdivided into INTEGER and FLOAT types.

· STRING.   A sequence of characters.

· SYMBOL.   Symbols are denoted by character sequences, but have somewhat different properties than strings. PIF symbols are a much-simplified version of symbols in the Lisp programming language (Steele 1990). In PIF, the main difference between strings and symbols is that symbols are not case-sensitive unless specially quoted, but strings are always case-sensitive.

The PIF composite value types consist of LIST and PIF-SENTENCE:

· LIST.   A list.

· PIF-SENTENCE.   A logical expression that evaluates to TRUE or FALSE.

An object variable is of the form, object-name[.slot-name]*, which refers to either the object named or the object which is the value of the named slot (or, if there are more than one slot-names specified, the object which is the value of the named slot of the object which is the value of the next named slot, etc.)

A.4   Rationales

The goal of PIF is to support maximal sharing of process descriptions across heterogeneous process representations. To better serve this goal, PIF consists of not a monolithic set of constructs but a partially ordered set of modules. A module can build on other modules in that the constructs in a module are specializations of the constructs in the other modules. One can adopt some modules but not others depending on one's expressive needs. Hence a module typically contains a set of constructs that are useful for a particular domain or a type of task. More details of this module structure is discussed in section A.6.

The PIF-CORE, on the other hand, consists of the minimal set of constructs necessary to translate simple but nontrivial process descriptions. There is the usual trade-off between simplicity and expressiveness. The PIF-CORE could have been chosen to contain only the constructs necessary for describing the simplest process descriptions such as a precedence network. Such a PIF-CORE then would not be able to translate many process descriptions. On the other hand, the PIF-CORE could have contained constructs sufficient for expressing the information contained in process descriptions of richer complexity. Such a PIF-CORE then would contain many constructs that may not be needed for many simpler descriptions. The PIF-CORE strikes a balance in this trade-off by first collecting process descriptions, starting from the simplest and continuing with more complex until we have reasonably many of them, and then by looking for a set of constructs that can translate the process descriptions in this collection. The following paragraph describes the rationales for each of the constructs in the PIF-CORE. The attributes of each of these constructs are described in section A.5.

In PIF, everything is an ENTITY; that is, every PIF construct is a specialization of ENTITY. There are four types of ENTITY: ACTIVITY, OBJECT, TIMEPOINT, and RELATION. These four types are derived from the definition of process in PIF: a process is a set of ACTIVITIES that stand in certain RELATIONS to one another and to OBJECTS over TIMEPOINTS.

The following discussion provides intuitive rationales for each of these four constructs. Their precise semantics, however, are defined by the relations they have with other constructs (cf. section A.5).

ACTIVITY represents anything that happens over time. DECISION, which represent conditional activities, is the only special type of ACTIVITY that the PIF-CORE recognizes. In particular, the PIF-CORE does not make any distinction among process, procedure, or event. A TIMEPOINT represents a particular point in time, for example "Oct. 2, 2.32 p.m. 1995" or "the time at which the notice is received." An OBJECT is intended to represent all the types of entities involved in a process description beyond the other three primitive ones of ACTIVITY, TIMEPOINT, and RELATION. AGENT is a special type of OBJECT.

RELATION represents relations among the other constructs. The PIF-CORE offers the following relations: BEFORE, SUCCESSOR, CREATES, USES, MODIFIES, and PERFORMS.

BEFORE represents a temporal relation between TIMEPOINTS. SUCCESSOR (Activity-1, Activity-2) is defined to be the relation between ACTIVITIES where BEFORE (Activity-1.End, Activity-2.Begin) holds. It is provided as a shorthand for simple activity precedence relations.

CREATES, USES, and MODIFIES represent relations between ACTIVITY and OBJECT. In these relations the object is assumed to be created, used, and modified at some nondeterminate timepoint(s) in the duration of the activity (i.e., between its Begin and its End timepoint inclusively). Hence the object would have been created, used, or modified by the End timepoint, but no commitment is made as to when the object is actually created, used, or modified. PERFORMS represents a relation between OBJECT (normally an AGENT specialization) and ACTIVITY. In the PERFORMS relation, the actor is assumed to perform the activity at some nondeterminate timepoint(s) in the duration of the activity (possibly for the whole duration, but not necessarily). We understand that there are other possible interpretations of these relations. For example, we might want to specify that a given actor is the only one who performs the activity during the whole activity interval. Such a specification, however, will require a PSV extension of the PIF-CORE (e.g., by introducing a relation such as PERFORMS-EXCLUSIVELY; cf. section A.6).

SUCCESSOR in PIF may not correspond exactly to the notions of successor as used in some work flow or enactment systems because it is common in these systems to bundle into a single relationship a mixture of temporal, causal, and decomposition relationships among activities. PIF provides precise, separate relationships for all three of these activities-to-activity specifications. For example, the temporal relationship is specified with the BEFORE relation, the causal relation with the Precondition and Postcondition attributes of ACTIVITY, and the decomposition relation with the Component attribute. Its intention is to allow the exact meaning to be communicated. Hence one might have to combine some of these constructs to capture exactly the meaning of SUCCESSOR as used in one's own system.

The attribute value of a PIF-CORE object holds independent of time (i.e., no temporal scope is associated with an attribute value in the PIF-CORE). Any property of an object that can change over time should be represented by a RELATION that links the property to a timepoint. An example of one such RELATION in the PIF-CORE is ACTIVITY-STATUS which is used to represent the status (e.g., DELAYED, PENDING) of an ACTIVITY at different times. The ACTIVITY-STATUS is provided in the PIF-CORE because it is the one example of a dynamic property of those objects commonly used in process modeling and work flow systems and modeled in the PIF-CORE. Other properties of those objects included in the PIF-CORE are, for the most part, true for all time. As mentioned before, it is possible to extend the PIF-CORE to express additional temporally scoped properties by introducing additional RELATIONS. It is also possible to add temporally scoped version of the static attributes already in the PIF-CORE. In this case, any such static attributes actually specified in a PIF file holds true for all time.

The attribute value of a PIF object can be one of the PIF value types specified above. The PIF primitive value types consist of NUMBER, STRING, and SYMBOL. The PIF composite value types are LIST and PIF-SENTENCE. LIST is used for conveying structured information that is not to be evaluated by a PIF interpreter, but simply passed along (e.g., as in the User-Attribute attribute of ENTITY). PIF-SENTENCE is used to specify a condition that is either true or false, as required, for example, for the Precondition and the Postcondition attributes of ACTIVITY.

PIF-SENTENCE is a logical expression that may include variables, quantifiers, and the boolean operators for expressing conditions or constraints. A PIF-

SENTENCE is used in the Constraint slot of ENTITY, the Precondition and the Postcondition slots of ACTIVITY, and the If slot of DECISION. A variable in a PIF-SENTENCE takes the following positions in the three dimensions that define the possible usage:

1. The scope of the variable is the frame. That is, variables of the same name within a frame definition are bound to the same object, whereas they are not necessarily so if they occur in different frames.

2. A variable is assumed to be bound by an implicit existential quantifier.

3. The constraints on variables in a frame definition are expressed in the Constraints slot of that frame. These constraints are local to the frame.

These positions are expected to be extended by some PSV modules. Some PSV modules will extend the scope of a variable beyond a single object. Some will introduce explicit existential and universal quantifiers. Yet others will allow global constraints to be stated, possibly by providing an object where such global constraints that hold across all the objects in a PIF file (e.g., 'All purchase order must be approved by the finance supervisor before sent out').

Notable Absence   We have decided not to include ROLE because a role may be defined wherever an attribute is defined. For example, the concept of RESOURCE is a role defined by the Resource attribute of the USE relation. Any object, we view, is a resource if it can be USEd by an ACTIVITY. As a consequence we have decided not to include ROLE or any construct that represents a role, such as RESOURCE. ACTOR is not included in PIF because it is another role concept, one defined by the Actor attribute of the PERFORMS relation. Any object, as long as it can fill the Actor attribute, can be viewed as an ACTOR. Hence we resolved that explicit introduction of the constructs such as ACTOR or RESOURCE is redundant and may lead to potential confusions. We should note, however, that the PIF-CORE provides the construct AGENT, which is not defined by a role an entity plays but by its inherent characteristic, namely its capability (e.g., of making intelligent decisions in various domains).

A.5   Alphabetic Class Reference

ACTIVITY

Parent Classes   ENTITY

Attribute	Value type	Multiple values allowed
Component	ACTIVITY	Yes
Precondition	PIF-SENTENCE	No
Postcondition	PIF-SENTENCE	No
Begin	TIMEPOINT	No
End	TIMEPOINT	No

Attribute Descriptions

· **Component.** The subactivities of the activity. For example, if the activity is 'Develop software', its Component may include 'Design software', 'Write code', and 'Debug software'. The field is inherited from ENTITY, but here it is restricted so that its values must all be ACTIVITY entities.

· **Precondition.** The conditions that have to be satisfied at the Begin timepoint of the activity before it can get executed. For example, a precondition of the activity 'Run software' might state that the executable code must be available. Such conditions are expressed using PIF-SENTENCES.

· **Postcondition.** The conditions that are true at the End timepoint of the activity. For example, a postcondition of the activity 'Run software' might be that a log file has been updated. Such conditions are expressed using PIF-SENTENCES.

· **Begin.**   The TIMEPOINT at which the activity begins.

· **End.**   The TIMEPOINT at which the activity ends.

In the PIF-CORE, the condition in the Precondition is to be true before the Begin timepoint of the ACTIVITY. Similarly, the condition in the Postcondition is to be true after the End timepoint of the ACTIVITY. This requirement may be relaxed later in PSV modules (cf. section A.6) to allow the precondition and the postcondition to be stated relative to other time points.

Many preconditions and postconditions can be expressed in PIF without using the Precondition and Postcondition attributes of ACTIVITY. For example, the USE relation between an activity A and an object O implies that one of A's preconditions is that R is available. In general, the Precondition and Postcondition attributes of ACTIVITY should only be used to express conditions that cannot be expressed any other way in PIF. Doing so will maximize the degree to which a process description can be shared with others.

ACTIVITY-STATUS

Parent Classes RELATION

Attribute	Value type	Multiple values allowed
Activity	ACTIVITY	Yes
Status	SYMBOL	Yes
When	TIMEPOINT	No

Attribute Descriptions

- **Activity.** The activity whose status is being specified.
- **Status.** The status being specified such as DELAYED and PENDING.
- **When.** The timepoint at which the status of the activity is being specified.

AGENT

Parent Classes OBJECT → ENTITY

Attribute	Value type	Multiple values allowed
Capability	SYMBOL	Yes
Component	AGENT	Yes

Attribute Descriptions

- **Capability.** Its possible values are SYMBOLS that represent the kinds of skills the agent is capable of providing. The symbols are supplied by the source language and simply preserved across translations by PIF. A PSV module may introduce a restricted set of symbol values.

An AGENT represents a person, group, or other entity (e.g., a computer program) that participates in a process. An AGENT is distinguished from other ENTITIES by what it is capable of doing or its skills.

BEFORE

Parent Classes   RELATION → ENTITY

Attribute	Value type	Multiple values allowed
Preceding-Timepoint	TIMEPOINT	No
Succeeding-Timepoint	TIMEPOINT	No

Attribute Descriptions

· **Preceding-Timepoint.**   The time point that is before the Succeeding Timepoint

· **Succeeding-Timepoint.**   The time point that is after the Preceding Timepoint.

BEFORE is a relation between TIMEPOINTS not between ACTIVITIES. A shorthand for a common example of the BEFORE relation is available via the SUCCESSOR relation.

CREATES

Parent Classes   RELATION → ENTITY

Attribute	Value type	Multiple values allowed
Activity	ACTIVITY	No
Object	OBJECT	Yes

Attribute Descriptions

· **Activity.**   The activity that creates the object. The object is assumed to be created at some nondeterminate timepoint(s) between its Begin and its End timepoint inclusive.

· **Object.**   The object that the activity creates.

DECISION

Parent Classes   ACTIVITY → ENTITY

Attribute	Value type	Multiple values allowed
If	PIF-SENTENCE	No
Then	ACTIVITY	Yes
Else	ACTIVITY	Yes

Attribute Descriptions

· **If.**   The condition being tested to decide which successor relations to follow. Such conditions are expressed using PIF-SENTENCES.

· **Then.**   The activity to follow if the condition in the If field holds (i.e., if the PIF-SENTENCE in the If field evaluates TRUE).

· **Else.**   The activity to follow if the condition in the If field does not hold (i.e., if the PIF-SENTENCE in the If field evaluates to FALSE).

A DECISION is a special kind of activity that represents conditional branching. If the PIF-SENTENCE in its If attribute is TRUE, the activity specified in its Then attribute follows. If not, the activity in its Else attribute follows.

ENTITY

Parent Classes   None. ENTITY is the root of the PIF class hierarchy.

Attribute	Value type	Multiple values allowed
Name	STRING	No
Documentation	STRING	No
Component	ENTITY	Yes
Constraint	PIF-SENTENCE	No
User-Attribute	LIST	Yes

Attribute Descriptions

· **Name.**   The entity's name.

· **Documentation.**   A description of the entity.

· **Component.**   This attribute is used to specify an homogeneous aggregate of the type itself. For example, in an AGENT object, this attribute can be used to specify that the agent is in fact a group of subagents. In an ACTIVITY object this attribute is used to specify its subactivities that make up the activity. If one needs to specify a group of objects of different types, then one can do so by going up to an object of their common ancestor type and specify them in the Component attribute of this object. When interpreted as a relation, this relation holds between the entity and each value, not between the entity and the set of all the values.

· **Constraint.**   This attribute is used to specify any constraint that should be true of the other attribute values in the current entity (e.g., constraints on the variables).

· **User-Attribute.**   This attribute is used to store additional ad hoc attributes of an entity that are not part of its class definition. For example, a process modeling application might allow users to specify additional attributes for AGENT entities that are not included in AGENT's PIF definition—the user might want to add an attribute recording the AGENT's age, for example. Such additional attributes can be stored in the User-Attribute attribute, which all PIF entities inherit from ENTITY. Another common use is in the Partially Shared Views translation scheme that we propose for interchanging PIF files (see section A.6). Each value of User-Attribute is a list containing an attribute name and its value(s). For example, an OBJECT entity might have (User-Attribute (Color RED GREEN) (Weight 120)).

MODIFIES

Parent Classes   RELATION → ENTITY

Attribute	Value type	Multiple values allowed
Activity	ACTIVITY	No
Object	OBJECT	Yes

Attribute Descriptions

· **Activity.**   The activity that modifies the object. The object is assumed to be modified at some nondeterminate timepoint(s) between its Begin and its End timepoint inclusive.

· **Object.**   The object that the activity modifies.

```
┌──────────────────────────────────────────────────────────────────────┐
│                                                                        │
│  OBJECT                                                                │
│                                                                        │
└──────────────────────────────────────────────────────────────────────┘
```

Parent Classes   ENTITY

Attribute Descriptions   No attribute.

An OBJECT is an entity that can be used, created, modified, or used in other relationships to an activity. This includes people (represented by the AGENT subclass in PIF), physical materials, time, and so forth. The PIF Working Group has discussed adding OBJECT attributes such as Consumable and Sharable, but so far no decision has been made on what attributes are appropriate.

```
┌──────────────────────────────────────────────────────────────────────┐
│                                                                        │
│  PERFORMS                                                              │
│                                                                        │
└──────────────────────────────────────────────────────────────────────┘
```

Parent Classes   RELATION → ENTITY

Attribute	Value type	Multiple values allowed
Actor	OBJECT	Yes
Activity	ACTIVITY	Yes

Attribute Descriptions

· **Actor.**   The object that performs the activity.

· **Activity.**   The activity that is performed. The actor is assumed to perform the activity at some nondeterminate timepoint(s) between its Begin and its End timepoint inclusive.

RELATION

Parent Classes ENTITY

Attribute Descriptions No attribute.

RELATION entities have no attributes of their own. PIF uses it as an abstract parent class for more specific relation classes such as USES and PERFORMS.

SUCCESSOR

Parent Classes RELATION → ENTITY

Attribute	Value type	Multiple values allowed
Preceding-Activity	ACTIVITY	No
Succeeding-Activity	ACTIVITY	Yes

Attribute Descriptions

· **Preceding-Activity.** The preceding activity.

· **Succeeding-Activity.** The succeeding activity.

SUCCESSOR with the Preceding-Activity ACTIVITY-1 and the Succeeding-Activity ACTIVITY-2 is exactly the same as BEFORE with Preceding-Timepoint TP-1 and Succeeding-Timepoint TP-2, where TP-1 is the Begin timepoint of ACTIVITY-2 and TP-2 is the End timepoint of ACTIVITY-1. That is, the SUCCESSOR relation is true if the ACTIVITY-1 ends before the ACTIVITY-2 begins.

TIMEPOINT

Parent Classes ENTITY

Attribute Descriptions   No attribute.

TIMEPOINT represents a point in time. In PIF-CORE, it is used, for example, to specify the Begin and End times of an Activity or the Preceding and Succeeding time points of the BEFORE relation.

USES

Parent Classes   RELATION → ENTITY

Attribute	Value type	Multiple values allowed
Activity	ACTIVITY	No
Object	OBJECT	Yes

Attribute Descriptions

· **Activity.**   The activity that uses the object from its Begin timepoint to its End timepoint. The USES relation is true from the Begin to the End timepoint of the activity. The object is assumed to be used at some nondeterminate timepoint(s) between its Begin and its End timepoint inclusive.

· **Object.**   The object that the activity uses.

A.6   Extending PIF

PIF provides a common language through which different process representations can be translated. Because there will always be representational needs local to individual groups, however, there must also be a way to allow local extensions to the description classes while supporting as much sharing as possible among local extensions. The Partially Shared Views (PSV) scheme has been developed for the purpose (Lee and Malone 1990). PSV integrates different ways of translating between groups using different class hierarchies (e.g., pairwise mapping, translation via external common language, translation via internal common language) so as to exploit the benefits of each when most appropriate.

A PSV module is a declaration of PIF entities that specialize other entities in the PIF-CORE or other PSV modules on which it builds. The class definitions in a

PSV module cannot delete or alter the existing definitions but can only add to them. Examples of PSV modules are given at the end of this section. A group of users may adopt one or more PSV modules as necessary for its task.

A group using a PSV module translates a PIF object X into their native format as follows:

1. If X's class (call it C) is known to the group and the group has developed a method that translates objects of class C into their native format, then apply that translation method. C is known to the group if either C is defined in one of the PSV modules that the group has adopted or the group has set up beforehand a translation rule between C and a type defined in one of the PSV modules adopted.

2. Otherwise, translate X as if it were an object of the nearest parent class of C for which rule 1 applies (its parent class in the most specific PSV module that the group and the sender group both share, i.e., have adopted).

This translation scheme allows groups to share information to some degree even if they do not support identical class hierarchies. For example, suppose that group A supports only the standard PIF AGENT class, and that group B in addition supports an EMPLOYEE subclass. When group A receives a process description in group B's variation on PIF, they can still translate any EMPLOYEE objects in the description as if they were AGENT objects. What happens to any information that is in an EMPLOYEE object that is not in a generic AGENT object? That will vary according to the sophistication of the translator and the expressive power of the target process representation. However, the translator will preserve the additional information so that it can be viewed by users and reproduced if it is later translated back into PIF.

For example, suppose that EMPLOYEE has a "Medical-plan" attribute that is not part of the AGENT object in the PIF-CORE. Then group A's translator would:

· Translate any Medical-plan attributes into a form that the user could view in the target system (even if it only as a textual comment)[3] AND

· When the information is re-translated into PIF in the future (from group A's native format), it is emitted as an EMPLOYEE object with the same value for the Medical-plan attribute (and not simply as an AGENT object with no Medical-plan attribute). MIT researchers are currently investigating this general problem of preserving as

---

3. If the target representation happens to be PIF (albeit group A's variant of it), the uninterpretable attributes would be stored as text in the User-Attribute attribute, which all PIF entities have.

much information as possible through "round trips" from one representation to another and back (Chan 1995).

Translators that can follow these conventions will minimize information loss when processes are translated back and forth between different tools. The details of PSV can be found in (Lee and Malone 1990). In the current version of PIF, each PIF file begins with a declaration of the class hierarchy for the objects described in the file. PSV uses this class hierarchy to translate objects of types that are unknown to a translator. To eliminate the need for PIF translators to do any other inheritance operations, however, all PIF objects should contain all of their attributes and values. For instance, even if the value of a given attribute is inherited without change from a parent, the attribute and value are repeated in the child.

As the number of PSV modules grows large, we need a mechanism for registering and coordinating them so as to prevent any potential conflict such as naming conflict. Although the exact mechanism is yet to be worked out, we are envisioning a scenario like the following: The user who needs to use PIF would first consult the indexed library of PSV modules, which documents briefly the contents of each module and the information about the other modules it presupposes. If an existing set of modules does not serve the user's purpose and a new PSV module has to be created, then the information about the new module and its relation to other modules is sent to a PSV registration server, which then assigns to it a globally unique identifier and updates the indexed library. We foresee many other issues to arise such as whether any proposed PSV module should be accepted, and who decides this, and whether to distinguish an ad hoc module designed for temporary quick translation between two local parties from a well-designed module intended for global use. However, rather than addressing these issues in this chapter, we will address them in a separate document as we gain more experience with PSV modules.

To date, two PSV modules have been specified: Temporal-Relation-1 and IDEF-0 modules. The Temporal-Relation-1 module extends the core PIF by adding all possible temporal relations that can hold between two activities (cf. figure A.3). The IDEF-0 module adds the constructs necessary for translating between IDEF-0 descriptions and PIF. IDEF-0 is a functional decomposition model, but it has historically been used widely as a process model description language. IDEF-0 has been used in various ways with no single well-defined semantics. Hence the IDEF-0 PSV module supports translation between PIF and one particular version of IDEF-0. It introduces two additional relations, USES-AS-RESOURCE and USES-AS-CONTROL, as specializations of the USES relation. They are meant to capture the

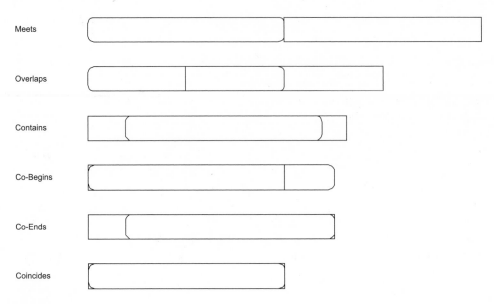

Figure A.3
Possible temporal relations between two activities

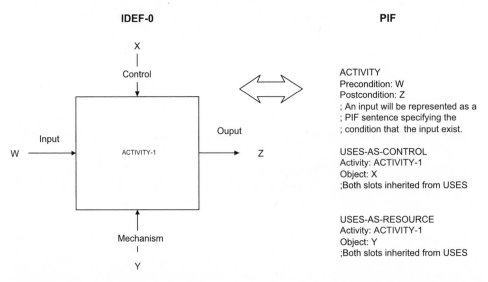

Figure A.4
Mapping between IDEF-0 and PIF constructs

Control and Mechanism input of IDEF-0. The Input and Output relations of IDEF-0 may be translated into PIF by using the Precondition and Postcondition attribute of ACTIVITY. The mapping between IDEF and PIF is shown in figure A.4. These modules have not been officially registered. They are presented here only to provide examples of PSV modules. We are soliciting further inputs before we register them.

A.7 Future Directions

Following the release of PIF version 1.1, PIF developments are expected to take the following course. First, we plan to coordinate further development of PIF with other knowledge sharing projects so as to produce compatibility, if not convergence, among the metamodels produced. We have started exchanging information with the International Workflow Management Coalition (*http://www.aiai.ed.ac.uk/WfMC*), whose goal is to produce interoperability among work flow applications. We have been also talking to the people in the Knowledge Sharing Initiatives (Neches et al. 1991), which has produced KIF (Knowledge Interchange Format) described earlier, tools and protocols for sharing knowledge bases, and Web-based ontology libraries among other things. We plan to intensify these coordination efforts through more structured and active forms such as workshops and regular meetings.

Second, we plan to elaborate on the PIF extension mechanism. We need to discuss and work out the details on such issues as who can propose and accept PSV modules in which domain and how the modules should be named, registered, organized, and accessed. We also need to carefully lay out the space of PSV modules by identifying an initial set of generally useful ones extending the PIF-CORE. Again, this work will require close interactions with the other knowledge sharing groups and experts in various domains. We hope to pursue this objective as a part of pursuing the first objective of coordination with other groups.

In order to use PIF to share process descriptions automatically, we need a PIF-translator for each of the local process representations involved. For example, each of the groups represented in the PIF Working Group built a translator for translating between PIF 1.0 and its own representation. Building PIF-translators is ultimately the responsibility of individual groups who want to use PIF.

Consolidated References

Abbott, A. 1990. A primer on sequence methods. *Organization Science* 1: 375–92.

Abbott, A. 1992. From causes to events: Notes on narrative positivism. *Sociological Methods and Research* 20(4): 428–55.

Abbott, A., and A. Hrycak. 1990. Measuring resemblance in sequence data. *American Journal of Sociology* 96: 144–85.

Abbott, K. R., and S. K. Sarin. 1994. Experiences with workflow management: Issues for the next generation. Presented at Conference on Computer Supported Cooperative Work, Chapel Hill, NC.

Abell, P. 1987. *The Syntax of Social Life: The Theory and Method of Comparative Narratives.* New York: Clarendon Press.

Abelson, R. P. 1981. Psychological status of the scripts concept. *American Psychologist* 36: 715–29.

Abrahamson, E. 1996. Management fashion. *Academy of Management Review* 21: 254–85.

Abrahamson, E., and G. Fairchild. 2000. Who launches management fashions? Gurus, journalists, technicians, or scholars? In C. B. Schoonhoven and E. Romanelli, eds., *The Entrepreneurship Dynamic in Industry Evolution.* Stanford: Stanford University Press.

Adler, R. M. 1995. Emerging standards for component software. *IEEE Computer* (March): 68–77.

Agostini, A., and G. De Michelis. 2000. A light workflow management system using simple process models. *Computer Supported Cooperative Work* 9: 335–63.

Ahmed, Z. 1998. An integrated dependency editor for the Process Handbook. M. Eng. thesis. *Department of Electrical Engineering and Computer Science,* MIT.

Alexander, C. 1964. *Notes on the Synthesis of Form.* Cambridge: Harvard University Press.

Alexander, C. 1979. *The Timeless Way of Building.* New York: Oxford University Press.

Allen, J., J. Hendler, and A. Tate, eds. 1990. *Readings in Planning.* San Mateo, CA: Morgan Kaufmann.

Allen, J. F. 1981. An interval-based representation of temporal knowledge. In P. J. Hayes, ed., *International Joint Conference on Artificial Intelligence,* Los Altos, CA, pp. 221–26.

Allen, J. F. 1984. Towards a general theory of action and time. *Artificial Intelligence* 23: 123–54.

Allen, R., and G. Garlan. 1994. Formalizing architectural connection. In *Proceedings of the 16th International Conference on Software Engineering,* Sorrento, Italy, March 1994, pp. 71–80.

Allen, T. J. 1977. *Managing the Flow of Technology.* Cambridge: MIT Press.

Ahmed, E. 1995. A data abstraction with inheritance in the Process Handbook. M.S. thesis. Department of Electrical Engineering and Computer Science, MIT. May.

Apple Computer. 1993. *Inside Macintosh: Interapplication Communication,* vol. 7. Reading, MA: Addison-Wesley, 1993.

Ashforth, B. E., and Y. Fried. 1988. The mindlessness of organizational behaviors. *Human Relations* 41: 305–29.

Alexander, C. 1979. *The Timeless Way of Building.* New York: Oxford University Press.

Argyris, C., and D. A. Schön. 1996. *Organizational Learning II: Theory, Method, Practice.* Reading, MA: Addison-Wesley.

Armistead, C., and P. Rowland. 1996. *Managing Business Processes: BPR and Beyond.* New York: Wiley.

Arrow, K. J. 1951. *Social Choice and Individual Value,* vol. 12. New York: Wiley.

Arvind, N., and D. E. Culler. 1986. Dataflow architectures. In *Annual Reviews in Computer Science,* vol. 1. Palo Alto, CA: Annual Reviews, Inc.

Arvind, N., R. S. Nikhil, and K. K. Pingali. 1986. I-Structures: Data structures for parallel computing. In *Proceedings of the Graph Reduction Workshop,* Santa Fe, NM, October. New York: Springer-Verlag, pp. 336–69.

Ashforth, B. E., and Y. Fried. 1988. The mindlessness of organizational behaviors. *Human Relations* 41: 305–29.

Attewell, P., and J. Rule. 1984. Computing and organizations: What we know and what we don't know. *Communications of the ACM* 27: 1184–92.

Aumann, R. J. 1976. Agreeing to disagree. *Annals of Statistics* 4: 1236–39.

Austin, J. L. 1962. In J. O. Urmson and M. Sbisa, eds., *How To Do Things with Things with Words*. Cambridge: Harvard University Press.

Avallone, E. A., and T. Baumeister, III, eds. 1996. *Marks' Standard Handbook for Mechanical Engineers*, 10th ed. New York: McGraw-Hill.

Bacharach, S. B. 1989. Organizational theories: Some criteria for evaluation. *Academy of Management Review* 14(4): 496–515.

Bailetti, A. J., J. R. Callahan, and P. DiPietro. 1994. A coordination structure approach to the management of projects. *IEEE Transactions on Engineering Management* 41(4): 394–403.

Bailetti, A. J., J. R. Callahan, and S. McCluskey. 1998. Coordination at different stages of the product design process. *R&D Management* 28(4): 237–47.

Bakeman, R., and J. M. Gottman. 1986. *Observing Interaction: An Introduction to Sequential Analysis*. Cambridge: Cambridge University Press.

Bakhtin, M. M. 1986. *Speech Genres and Other Late Essays*. V. W. McGee, trans.; C. Emerson and M. Holquist, eds. Austin: University of Texas Press.

Baligh, H. H. 1986. Decision rules and transactions, organizations and markets. *Management Science* 32: 1480–91.

Baligh, H. H., and R. M. Burton. 1981. Describing and designing organizational structures and processes. *International Journal of Policy Analysis and Information Systems* 5: 251–66.

Baligh, H. H., R. M. Burton, and B. Obel. 1990. Devising expert systems in organization theory: The Organizational Consultant. In M. Masuch, ed., *Organization, Management, and Expert Systems*. Berlin: Walter de Gruyter, pp. 35–57.

Baligh, H. H., and L. Richartz. 1967. *Vertical Market Structures*. Boston: Allyn and Bacon.

BankBoston. 1998. *Focus on Making Your Business a Success: Business Focus Banking*. Sales catalog. Boston: BankBoston.

Bansler, J. P., and K. Bodker. 1993. A reappraisal of structured analysis: Design in an organizational context. *ACM Transactions on Information Systems* 11(2): 165–93.

Bardram, J. E. 1997. Plans as situated action: An activity theory approach to workflow systems. In *Fifth European Conference on Computer Supported Cooperative Work*. Norwell, MA: Kluwer Academic Publishers.

Barley, S. R. 1986. Technology as an occasion for structuring: Evidence from the observation of CT scanners and the social order of radiology departments. *Administrative Science Quarterly* 31: 78–108.

Barley, S. R. 1990. Images of imaging: Notes on doing longitudinal fieldwork. *Organization Science* 1: 220–47.

Barley, S. R., G. W. Meyer, and D. C. Gash. 1988. Cultures of culture: Academics, practitioners, and the pragmatics of normative control. *Administrative Science Quarterly* 33: 24–60.

Barnard, C. I. 1964. *The Functions of the Executive*. Cambridge: Harvard University.

Bazerman, C. 1988. *Shaping Written Knowledge: The Genre and Activity of the Experimental Article in Science*. Madison: University of Wisconsin Press.

Bazerman, C. 1994. Systems of genres and the enactment of social intentions. In A. Freedman and P. Medway, eds., *Genre and the New Rhetoric*. London: Taylor and Francis, pp. 79–101.

Beard, D., P. Murugappan, A. Humm, D. Banks, A. Nair, and Y.-P. Shan. 1990. A visual calendar for scheduling group meetings. In D. Tatar, ed., *Proceedings of the Third Conference on Computer-Supported Cooperative Work*. Los Angeles: ACM Press, pp. 279–90.

Bell, C. G., and A. Newell. 1971. *Computer Structures: Readings and Examples*. New York: McGraw-Hill.

Benbasat, I., D. K. Goldstein, and M. Mead. 1987. The case research strategy in studies of information systems. *MIS Quarterly* 11(3): 369–86.

Berkenkotter, C., and T. N. Huckin. 1995. *Genre Knowledge in Disciplinary Communication: Cognition/Culture/Power*. Hillsdale, NJ: Lawrence Erlbaum Associates.

Berliner, P. F. 1994. *Thinking in Jazz: The Infinite Art of Improvisation*. Chicago: University of Chicago Press.

Bernstein, A. 1998. The product workbench: An environment for the mass-customization of production-processes. Presented at Workshop on Information Technology and Systems (WITS), Helsinki, Finland.

Bernstein, A., and C. P. Schucan. 1998. Document and process transformation during the product life-cycle. In T. Wakayame, S. Kannapan, C. M. Khoong, S. Navathe, and J. Yates, eds., *Information and Process Integration in Enterprises—Rethinking Documents*. Norwell, MA: Kluwer Academic Publishers.

Bernstein, A., C. Dellarocas, T. W. Malone, and J. Quimby. 1995. Software tools for a Process Handbook. *IEEE Bulletin on Data Engineering* 18(1): 41–47.

Bernstein, A., M. Klein, and T. W. Malone. 1999. The Process Recombinator: A tool for generating new business process ideas. In *Proceedings of the International Conference on Information Systems* (ICIS-99), Charlotte, NC, December 13–15.

Bernstein, P., and N. Goodman. 1981. Concurrency control in distributed database systems. *ACM Computing Surveys* 13(2): 185–221.

Bezem, M. 1987. Consistency of rule-based expert systems. Technical Report CS-R8736. Centre for Mathematics and Computer Science, Amsterdam.

Bhandaru, N., and W. B. Croft. 1990. An architecture for supporting goal-based cooperative work. In S. Gibbs and A. A. Verrijin-Stuart, eds., *Multi-user Interfaces and Applications*. Amsterdam: Elsevier–North Holland, pp. 337–54.

Biggerstaff, T. J., and A. J. Perlis. 1989. *Software Reusability*, vols. 1 and 2. Reading, MA: ACM Press/Addison Wesley.

Birman, K. P., A. Schiper, and P. Stephenson. 1991. Lightweight Causal and Atomic Group Multicast. *ACM Transactions on Computing Systems* 9: 77–113.

Black, J. B., and R. Wilensky. 1979. An evaluation of story grammars. *Cognitive Science* 3: 213–30.

Blumenthal, R. L. 1998. Supporting unstructured activities with a meta-contextual protocol in situation-based workflow. Department of Computer Science. University of Colorado, Boulder.

Boden, M. 1991. *The Creative Mind: Myths and Mechanisms*. London: Widenfeld and Nicholson.

Bond, A. H., and L. Gasser, eds. 1988. *Readings in Distributed Artificial Intelligence*. San Mateo, CA: Morgan Kaufman.

Booch, G. 1991. *Object Oriented Design with Applications*. Redwood City, CA: Benjamin/Cummings.

Borgida, A., J. Mylopoulos, and J. W. Schmidt. 1993. The TaxisDL software description language. In M. Jarke, ed., *Database Application Engineering with DAIDA*, vol. 1. Research Reports ESPRIT. Berlin: Springer-Verlag, pp. 65–84.

Boudreau, M.-C., and D. Robey. 1999. Organizational transition to enterprise resource planning systems: Theoretical choices for process research. In *Proceedings of the 20th International Conference on Information Systems* (ICIS-99). Charlotte, NC, pp. 291–99.

Bourdieu, P. 1977. *Outline of a Theory of Practice*. R. Nice, trans. New York: Cambridge University Press.

Bourdieu, P. 1990. *The Logic of Practice*. R. Nice, trans. Stanford: Stanford University Press.

Boyton, A. C., B. Victor, and B. J. Pine II. 1993. New competitive strategies: Challenges to organizations and information technology. *IBM Systems Journal* 32(1): 60–64.

Brachman, R. J., and H. J. Levesque, eds. 1985. *Readings in Knowledge Representation*. Los Altos, CA: Morgan Kaufmann.

Brachman, R. J., and J. G. Schmolze. 1985. An overview of the KL-ONE knowledge representation system. *Cognitive Science* 9: 171–216.

Bridges, W. 1995. *Job Shift*. Reading MA: Addison-Wesley.

Brint, S. 1992. Hidden meanings: Cultural content and context in Harrison White's structural sociology. *Sociological Theory* 10: 194–208.

Brown, J. S. 1994. Borderline issues: Social and material aspects of design. *Human-Computer Interactions* 9: 3–36.

Brown, J. S., A. Collins, and P. Duguid. 1989. Situated cognition and the culture of learning. *American Educational Research Association* 18: 32–42.

Bruns, W. J., and F. W. McFarlan. 1987. Information technology puts power in control systems. *Harvard Business Review* (September–October): 89–94.

Brynjolfsson, E. 1994. The productivity paradox of information technology. *Communications of the ACM* 36(12): 67–77.

Brynjolfsson, E., and L. Hitt. 1998. Beyond the productivity paradox. *Communications of the ACM* 41(8): 49–55.

Brynjolfsson, E., T. Malone, J. Gurbaxani, and A. Kambil. 1994. Does Information Technology Lead to Smaller Firms? *Management Science*.

Burrell, G., and G. Morgan. 1979. *Sociological Paradigms and Organizational Analysis*. London: Heinemann.

Burton, R. M., and B. Obel. 1980a. A computer simulation test of the M-form hypothesis. *Administrative Science Quarterly* 25: 457–66.

Burton, R. M., and B. Obel. 1980b. The efficiency of the price, budget, and mixed approaches under varying a priori information levels for decentralized planning. *Management Science* 26: 401–17.

Camp, R. C. 1995. *Business Process Benchmarking: Finding and Implementing Best Practices*. Milwaukee, WI: ASQC Quality Press.

Cannella, A. A., Jr., and R. L. Paetzold. 1994. Pfeffer's barriers to the advance of organizational science: A rejoinder. *Academy of Management Review* 19(2): 331–41.

Carley, K., J. Kjaer-Hansen, A. Newell, and M. Prietula. 1992. Plural-Soar: Capabilities and coordination of multiple agents. In M. Masuch and M. Warglien, eds., *Artificial Intelligence in Organization and Management Theory: Models of Distributed Intelligence*. New York: Elsevier Science, pp. 87–118.

Carlson, W. M. 1979. Business information analysis and integration technique (BIAIT)—The new horizon. *Database* (Spring): 3–9.

Carriero, N., and D. Gelernter. 1989. Coordination languages and their significance. Working paper YALEU/DCS/RR-716. Department of Computer Science, Yale University.

Carter, D. E., and B. S. Baker. 1991. *Concurrent Engineering: The Product Development Environment for the 1990's*. Reading, MA: Addison-Wesley.

Castelfranchi, C. 1996. Conflict ontology. In *Proceedings of the Workshop on Conflict Management*, European Conference on Artificial Intelligence (ECAI). Budapest, August.

Chan, F. Y. 1995. The round trip problem: A solution for the Process Handbook. M.S. thesis. Department of Electrical Engineering and Computer Science, MIT. May.

Chandler, A. D., Jr. 1962. *Strategy and Structure: Chapters in the History of the American Industrial Enterprise*. Cambridge: MIT Press.

Chandler, A. D. 1977. Administrative coordination, allocation and monitoring: Concepts and comparisons Working paper 77-21. European Institute for Advanced Studies in Management, Brussels.

Chandrasekaran, B. 1983. Towards a taxonomy of problem solving types. *AI Magazine* 4(1): 9–17.

Chandrasekaran, B., T. R. Johnson, and J. W. Smith. 1992. Task-structure analysis for knowledge modeling. *Communications of the ACM* 35(9): 124–37.

Chapman, D. 1987. Planning for conjunctive goals. *Artificial Intelligence* 32: 333–77.

Checkland, P. 1981. *Systems Thinking, Systems Practice.* New York: Wiley.

Checkland, P., and J. Scholes. 1990. *Soft Systems Methodology in Action.* New York: Wiley.

Chen, M. 1999. BPR methodologies: Methods and tools. In D. J. Elzinga, T. R. Gulledge, C.-Y. Lee, eds., *Business Process Engineering: Advancing the State of the Art.* Norwell, MA: Kluwer Academic, pp. 187–212.

Chia, M. H., D. E. Neiman, and V. R. Lesser. 1998. Poaching and distraction in asynchronous agent activities. In *Proceedings of the Third International Conference on Multi-agent Systems,* July, Paris, France, pp. 88–95.

Child, J., L. Bertholle, and S. Beck. 1981. *Mastering the Art of French Cooking.* New York: Knopf.

Ching, C., C. W. Holsapple, and A. B. Whinston. 1992. Modeling network organizations: A basis for exploring computer support coordination possibilities. Decision and Information Systems, College of Business, Arizona State University.

Chiu, D. K. W., K. Karlapalem, and Q. Li. 1997. Exception handling in ADOME workflow system. Hong Kong University of Science and Technology.

Chomsky, N. 1956. Three models for the description of language. *IRE Transactions on Information Theory* 2: 113–24.

Chomsky, N. 1965. *Aspects of the Theory of Syntax.* Cambridge: MIT Press.

Chomsky, N. 1986. *Knowledge of Language: Its Nature, Origin, and Use.* New York: Praeger.

Churchill, E. F., and S. Bly. 1999. Virtual environments at work: Ongoing use of MUDs in the workplace. In *Proceedings of the International Joint Conference on Work Activities Coordination and Collaboration,* San Francisco: ACM Press, pp. 99–108.

Ciborra, C. U. 1987. Reframing the role of computers in organizations: The transaction costs approach. In *Proceedings of Sixth International Conference on Information Systems,* Indianapolis, December 16–18, 1985.

Cicourel, A. 1964. *Method and Measurement in Sociology.* New York: Free Press.

CIO Magazine. 1992. Back support for benchmarkers. *CIO* (June 1): 16. More detail available at *http://www.apqc.org/apqchome/apqchome.htm.*

CIO Magazine. 1992. Back support for benchmarkers. *CIO* (June 16).

Clancey, W. J. 1983. The epistemology of a rule-based expert system—A framework for explanation. *Artificial Intelligence* 20(3): 215–51.

Coad, P., and E. Yourdon. 1990. *Object-Oriented Analysis.* Englewood Cliffs, NJ: Prentice-Hall.

Cohen, M., and R. A. Regan. 1996. Managing internal consistency in technology intensive design projects. *Competitiveness Review* 6(1): 42.

Cohen, M. D., J. G. March, and J. P. Olsen. 1972. A garbage can model of organizational choice. *Administrative Science Quarterly* 17: 1.

Cohen, P., and H. J. Levesque. 1991. Teamwork. Technote No. 504. SRI International, Menlo Park, CA.

Colby, B. N., S. Kennedy, and L. Milanesi. 1991. Content analysis, cultural grammars, and computers. *Qualitative Sociology* 14: 373–87.

Committee, A. T. Q. S. 1992. *Benchmarking: Focus on World-Class Practices.* Indianapolis: AT&T Bell Laboratories.

Commons, J. R. 1950. *The Economics of Collective Action.* Madison: University of Wisconsin Press.

Conklin, J., and M. L. Begeman. 1988. gIBIS: A hypertext tool for exploratory policy discussion. In *Proceedings of CSCW '88 Conference on Computer-Supported Cooperative Work,* September 26–28. Portland, OR: ACM Press, pp. 140–52.

Cook, V. J. 1988. *Chomsky's Universal Grammar.* Oxford: Blackwell.

Coulter, J. 1989. *Mind in Action*. Cambridge, England: Polity Press.

Crawford, A. B., Jr. 1982. Corporate electronic mail—A communication-intensive application of information technology. *MIS Quarterly* 6(September): 1–13.

Croft, W. B., and L. S. Lefkowitz. 1988. Using a planner to support office work. In R. B. Allen, ed., *Proceedings of the ACM Conference on Office Information Systems*, Palo Alto, CA, pp. 55–62.

Crowston, K. 1991. Towards a coordination cookbook: Recipes for multi-agent action. Ph.D. dissertation. Sloan School of Management, MIT.

Crowston, K. 1994. Organizational processes for coordination. Symposium presentation. In *Academy of Management Conference*. Dallas, TX, August 14–17.

Crowston, K. 1997. A coordination theory approach to organizational process design. *Organization Science* 8(2): 157–75.

Crowston, K. 2000. Processes as theory in information systems research. In *Proceedings of the IFIP TC8 WG8.2 International Working Conference on the Social and Organizational Perspective on Research and Practice in Information Technology*, June 9–11, 2000, Arlborg, Denmark. Norwell, MA: Kluwer Academic Publisher, pp. 149–66.

Crowston, K., and E. Kammerer. 1998. Coordination and collective mind in software requirements development. *IBM Systems Journal* 37(2): 227–45.

Crowston, K., T. W. Malone, and F. Lin. 1987. Cognitive science and organizational design: A case study of computer conferencing. *Human Computer Interaction* 3: 59–85.

Crowston, K., and C. S. Osborn. 1998. A coordination theory approach to process description and redesign. Technical report 204. Center for Coordination Science, MIT.

Crowston, K., S. Sawyer, and R. Wigand. 1999. Investigating the interplay between structure and technology in the real estate industry. Presented before the Organizational Communications and Information Systems Division, Academy of Management Conference. Syracuse University, School of Information Studies.

Crowston, K., and M. E. Treacy. 1986. Assessing the impact of information technology on enterprise level performance. In *Proceedings of the Sixth International Conference on Information Systems*, Indianapolis, IN, ICIS 1986, pp. 299–310.

Crowston, K., and R. Wigand. 1999. Real estate war in cyberspace: An emerging electronic market? *International Journal of Electronic Markets* 9(1–2): 1–8.

Curtis, B. 1989. Modeling coordination from field experiments. In *Proceedings of Conference on Organizational Computing, Coordination and Collaboration: Theories and Technologies for Computer-Supported Work*. Austin, TX.

Curtis, B., M. I. Kellner, and J. Over. 1992. Process Modeling. *Communications of the ACM* 35(9): 75–90.

Cusumano, M. A., and R. S. Selby. 1995. *Microsoft Secrets: How the World's Most Powerful Software Company Creates Technology, Shapes Markets, and Manages People*. New York: Free Press.

Cyert, R. M., and J. G. March. 1963. *A Behavioral Theory of the Firm*. Englewood Cliffs, NJ: Prentice-Hall.

Cytron, R. 1987. Limited processor scheduling of doacross loops. In *Proceedings of the 1987 International Conference on Parallel Processing*, Pennsylvania State University, State College, PA, pp. 226–34.

Daft, R. L., and K. E. Weick. 1984. Toward a model of organizations as interpretation systems. *Academy of Management Review* 9: 284–95.

Dantzig, G. B. 1963. *Linear Programming and Extensions*. Princeton: Princeton University Press.

Danziger, J. N., W. H. Dutton, R. Kling, and K. L. Kraemer. 1982. *Computers and Politics: High Technology in American Local Governments*. New York: Columbia University Press.

Daube, F., and B. Hayes-Roth. 1989. *A Case-Based Mechanical Redesign System*. In *Proceedings of the International Conference on Artificial Intelligence*, IJCAI 1989, pp. 1402–07.

Davenport, T. H. 1993. *Process Innovation: Reengineering Work through Information Technology.* Boston: Harvard Business School Press.

Davenport, T. H., and M. A. Perez-Guardado. 1999. Process ecology: A new metaphor for reengineering-oriented change. In D. J. Elzinga, T. R. Gulledge, C.-Y. Lee, eds., *Business Process Engineering: Advancing the State of the Art.* Norwell, MA: Kluwer Academic, pp. 25–44.

Davenport, T. H., and J. E. Short. 1990. The new industrial engineering: Information technology and business process redesign. *Sloan Management Review* 31(4): 11–27.

Davis, R., and R. G. Smith. 1983. Negotiation as a metaphor for distributed problem solving. *Artificial Intelligence* 20: 63–109.

De Antonellis, V., B. Pernici, and P. Samarati. 1991. F-ORM METHOD: A F-ORM methodology for reusing specifications. In *Proceedings of IFIP TC8/WG8.1 Working Conference on the Object-Oriented Approach in Information Systems*, Quebec City, Canada. Amsterdam: North-Holland, pp. 117–35.

de Certeau, M. 1984. *The Practice of Everyday Life.* Steven Rendall, trans. Berkeley: University of California Press.

de Champeaux, D. 1991. Object-oriented analysis and top-down software development. In *Proceedings of ECOOP '91, European Conference on Object-Oriented Programming.* Geneva, Switzerland. Berlin: Springer-Verlag.

de Champeaux, D., L. Constantine, I. Jacobson, S. Mellor, P. Ward, and E. Yourdon. 1990. Panel: Structured analysis and object oriented analysis. In *Proceedings of Conference on Object-Oriented Programming: Systems, Languages, and Applications/European Conference on Object-Oriented Programming.* Ottawa, Canada: Association for Computing Machinery.

de Remer, F., and Kron, H. 1976. Programming-in-the-large versus programming-in-the-small. *IEEE Transactions on Software Engineering* 2(2): 80–86.

de Sanctis, G., and B. Gallupe. 1987. A foundation for the study of group decision support systems. *Management Science* 33(5): 589–609.

de Saussure, F. [1911] 1969. *Course in General Linguistics.* New York: McGraw-Hill.

Debreu, G. 1959. Theory of value: An axiomatic analysis of economic equilibrium. New York: Wiley.

Decker, K. S., and V. R. Lesser. 1989. *Some initial thoughts on a generic architecture of CDPS network control.* In *Proceedings of the 9th Workshop on Distributed Artificial Intelligence*, Rosario Resort, Eastsound, WA, pp. 73–94.

Deitel, H. M. 1983. *An Introduction to Operating Systems.* Reading, MA: Addison-Wesley.

Dellarocas, C. 1996. A coordination perspective on software architecture: Towards a design handbook for integrating software components. Ph.D. thesis. Department of Electrical Engineering and Computer Science, MIT.

Dellarocas, C. 1997a. Towards a design handbook for integrating software components. In *Proceedings of the 5th International Symposium on Assessment of Software Tools* (SAST'97), Pittsburgh, PA, June 2–5, 1997, pp. 3–13.

Dellarocas, C. 1997b. The Synthesis environment for component-based software development. In *Proceedings of the 8th International Workshop on Software Technology and Engineering Practice* (STEP'97), London, July 14–18. IEEE CS Press.

Dellarocas, C., J. Lee, T. W. Malone, K. Crowston, and B. Pentland. 1994. Using a process handbook to design organizational processes. In *Proceedings of the AAAI '94 Stanford Spring Symposium on Computational Organization Design*, Stanford, CA. Philadelphia: AAAI.

Deneubourg, J. L., and S. Gross. 1989. Collective patterns and decision-making. *Ethology, Ecology and Evolution* 1: 295–311.

Dennis, A. R., F. G. Joey, L. M. Jessup, J. F. Nunamaker, and D. R. Vogel. 1988. Information technology to support electronic meetings. *MIS Quarterly* 12(4): 591–619.

Department of Defense, U.S. 1983. *Reference Manual for the Ada Programming Language.* ANSI/MIL-STD-1815A. January 1983.

Dertouzos, M. L. 1991. Building the information marketplace. *Technology Review* (January): 29–40.

Dijkstra, E. W. 1968. The structure of the T.H.E. operating system. *Communications of the ACM* 11(5): 341–46.

Dourish, P., J. Holmes, A. MacLean, P. Marqvardsen, and A. Zbyslaw. 1996. Freeflow: Mediating between representation and action in workflow systems. Presented at Computer Supported Cooperative Work, Boston.

Drazin, R., and L. E. Sandelands. 1992. Autogenesis: A perspective on the process of organizing. *Organization Science* 3: 230–49.

Drexler, K. E., and M. S. Miller. 1988. Incentive engineering for computational resource management. In B. A. Huberman, ed., *The Ecology of Computation.* Amsterdam: Elsevier, pp. 231–66.

Dubois, M., C. Scheurich, and F. A. Briggs. 1988. Synchronization, coherence, and event ordering in multiprocessors. *IEEE Computer* 21(2): 9–21.

Durfee, E. D., and V. R. Lesser. 1987. Using partial global plans to coordinate distributed problem solvers. In *Proceedings of the 10th International Joint Conference on Artificial Intelligence* (IJCAI-87), pp. 875–83.

Eccles, R. G. 1985. *The Transfer Pricing Problem: A Theory for Practice.* Lexington, MA: Lexington Books.

Elley, Yassir. 1996. A flexible process editor for the Process Handbook. M.S. thesis. Department of Electrical Engineering and Computer Science, MIT.

Ellis, C., and K. Keddara. 2000. ML-DEWS: A workflow change specification model and language. *Computer Supported Cooperative Work* 9: 293–333.

Ellis, C. A., and G. J. Nutt. 1996. Workflow: The process spectrum. Presented at NSF Workshop on Workflow and Process Automation in Information Systems: State-of-the-art and Future Directions, University of Georgia, Athens.

Ellis, C. A., R. Gibbons, and P. Morris. 1979. Office streamlining. In *Proceedings of the International Workshop on Integrated Offices.* Versailles, France: Institut de Recherche d'Informatique de d'Automatique, November 6–9.

Ellis, C. A., S. J. Gibbs, and G. L. Rein. 1990. Design and use of a group editor. In G. Cockton, ed., Engineering for Human-Computer Interaction. Napa Valley, CA: North-Holland/Elsevier, pp. 13–25.

Ellis, C. A., S. J. Gibbs, and G. L. Rein. 1991. Groupware, some issues and experiences. *Communications of the ACM* 34(1): 38–57.

Erman, L. D., F. Hayes-Roth, V. R. Lesser, and D. R. Reddy. 1980. The HEARSAY-II speech understanding system: Integrating knowledge to resolve uncertainty. *ACM Computing Surveys* 12(2): 213–53.

Fabian, J. 1979. Rule and process: Thoughts on ethnography as communication. *Philosophy of the Social Sciences* 9: 1–26.

Fabian, J. 1990. *Power and Performance: Ethnographic Explorations through Proverbial Wisdom and Theatre in Shaba, Zaire.* Madison: University of Wisconsin Press.

Fadel, F. G., M. S. Fox, and M. Gruninger. 1994. A generic enterprise resource ontology. In *Proceedings of the Third Workshop on Enabling Technologies—Infrastructures for Collaborative Enterprises,* West Virginia University.

Farrell, J., and G. Saloner. 1985. Standardization, compatibiity, and innovation. *Rand Journal of Economics* 16(Spring): 70–83.

Fay, S. 1997. *The Collapse of Barings.* New York: Norton.

Feldman, D. C. 1985. A taxonomy of intergroup conflict resolution strategies. *Annual Conference on Developing Human Resources.*

Fellbaum, C. 1998. *WordNet: An electronic lexical database*. Cambridge: MIT Press. Available at *http://www.cogsci.princeton.edu/~wn/w3wn.html*.

Fikes, R. E., and N. J. Nilsson. 1971. STRIPS: A new approach to the application of theorem proving to problem solving. *Artificial Intelligence* 2: 198–208.

Fillmore, C. 1975. *Principles of Case Grammar: the Structure of Language and Meaning*. Tokyo: Sanseido Publishing Company.

Fink, D. G., H. W. Beaty, and W. Beaty, eds. 1999. *Standard Handbook for Electrical Engineers*, 14th ed. New York: McGraw-Hill.

Fish, R., R. Kraut, M. Leland, and M. Cohen. 1988. Quilt: A collaborative tool for cooperative writing. In *Proceedings of the Conference on Office Information Systems*, Palo Alto, CA, March 23–25. ACM Press, pp. 30–37.

Flores, F., M. Graves, B. Hartfield, and T. Winograd. 1988. Computer systems and the design of organizational interaction. *ACM Transactions on Office Information Systems* 6(2): 153–72.

Folger, J. P., D. E. Hewes, and M. S. Poole. 1984. Coding Social Interaction. In B. Dervin and M. J. Voight, eds., *Progress in Communication Science*, vol. 4. Norwood, NJ: Ablex, pp. 115–61.

Fox, M. S. 1981. An organizational view of distributed systems. *IEEE Transactions on Systems, Man and Cybernetics* 11(1): 70–79.

France, R. B. 1992. Semantically extended data flow diagrams: A formal specification tool. *IEEE Transactions on Software Engineering* 18(4): 329–46.

Franks, N. R. 1989. Army ants: A collective intelligence. *American Scientist* 77(March–April): 139–45.

Friedland, P. E. 1979. Knowledge-based Experiment Design in Molecular Genetics. Ph.D. dissertation. Technical report 79-771. Computer Science Department, Stanford University.

Friedland, P. E., and Y. Iwasaki. 1985. The concept and implementation of skeletal plans. *Journal of Automated Reasoning* 1(2): 161–208.

Galbraith, J. R. 1973. *Designing Complex Organizations*. Reading, MA: Addison-Wesley.

Galbraith, J. R. 1977. *Organization Design*. Reading, MA: Addison-Wesley.

Garlan, D., R. Allen, and J. Ockerbloom. 1994. Exploiting style in architectural design environments. In *Proceedings, ACM SIGSOFT '94 Symposium on Foundations of Software Engineering*, December. ACM Press.

Garlan, D., R. Allen, and J. Ockerbloom. 1995. Architectural mismatch or why it's hard to build systems out of existing parts. In *Proceedings, 17th International Conference on Software Engineering*, (ICSE17), Seattle, WA, April.

Garlan, D., G. E. Kaiser, and D. Notkin. 1988. On the criteria to be used in composing tools into systems. Technical report 88-08-09. Department of Computer Science, University of Washington. August.

Gasser, L. 1986. The integration of computing and routine work. *ACM Transactions on Information Systems* 4(3): 205–25.

Gasser, L. 1992. HITOP-A: Coordination, infrastructure and enterprise integration. AAAI-92 Workshop on AI in Enterprise Integration.

Gasser, L., and A. Majchrzak. 1994. ACTION integrates manufacturing strategy, design, and planning. In P. Kidd and W. Karwowski, eds., *Ergonomics of Hybrid Automated Systems IV*. Burke, VA: IOS Press, pp. 133–36.

Gazdar, G., E. Klein, G. Pullum, and I. Sag. 1985. *Generalized Phrase Structure Grammar*. Cambridge: Harvard University Press.

Geisler, M. A. 1995. The evolving health care delivery systems: Applying the Process Handbook methodology to gain a vision of the future. M.S. thesis. Sloan School of Management, MIT. May.

Gersick, C. J. G. 1989. Marking time: Predictable transitions in task groups. *Academy of Management Journal* 32: 274–309.

Gersick, C. J. G. 1991. Revolutionary change theories: A multilevel exploration of the punctuated equilibrium paradigm. *Academy of Management Review* 16: 10–36.

Gerson, E. M., and S. L. Star. 1986. Analyzing due process in the workplace. *ACM Transactions on Information Systems* 4: 257–70.

Gibson, E. J. 1982. The concept of affordances in development: The renaissance of functionalism. In W. A. Collins, ed., *The Concept of Development: The Minnesota Symposium of Child Psychology*, vol. 15. Hillsdale, NJ: Lawrence Erlbaum, pp. 55–81.

Giddens, A. 1984. *The Constitution of Society*. Berkeley: University of California Press.

Gioia, D., and P. Poole. 1984. Scripts in Organizational Behavior. *Academy Management Review* 9: 449–59.

Glaser, B. G., and A. L. Strauss. 1967. *The Discovery of Grounded Theory: Strategies for Qualitative Research*. Chicago: Aldine Publishing.

Glasson, B. C. 1994. Business process re-engineering: Information systems opportunities and challenges. In *Proceedings of the IFIP TC8 Open Conference on Business Process Re-engineering: Information Systems Opportunities and Challenges*, Queensland Gold Coast, Australia, May 8–11. New York: Elsevier, pp. 1–6.

Goffman, E. 1981. *Forms of Talk*. Philadelphia: University of Pennsylvania Press.

Gomez, P.-Y., and B. C. Jones. 2000. Conventions: An interpretation of deep structure in organization. *Organizationa Science* 11(6): 696–708.

Gonzalez, R. C., and M. G. Thomason. 1978. *Syntactic Pattern Recognition: An Introduction*. Reading, MA: Addison-Wesley.

Gottman, J. M., and A. K. Roy. 1990. *Sequential Analysis: A Guide for Behavioral Researchers*. Cambridge: Cambridge University Press.

Grant, R. M. 1996. Toward a knowledge-based theory of the firm. *Strategic Management Journal* 17(Winter): 109–22.

Gray, J. 1978. Notes on data base operating systems. Research report RJ 2188. IBM.

Greif, I., eds. 1988. Computer Supported Cooperative Work. Los Altos, CA: Morgan Kaufmann Publishers.

Greiner, L. 1972. Evolution and revolution as organizations grow. *Harvard Business Review* 50(4): 37–46.

Grice, H. P. 1975. Logic and conversations. In P. Cole and J. L. Morgan, eds., *Syntax and Semantics 3: Speech Acts*. New York: Academic Press, pp. 41–58.

Grover, V., and W. J. Kettinger, eds. 1995. *Business Process Change: Concepts, Methodologies and Technologies*. Harrisburg, PA: Idea Group.

Grudin, J. 1988. Why CSCW applications fail: Problems in the design and evaluation of organizational interfaces. In D. Tatar, ed., *Proceedings of the 2nd Conference on Computer-Supported Cooperative Work* September 26–28. Portland, OR: ACM Press, pp. 85–93.

Grudin, J. 1994. Groupware and social dynamics: Eight challenges for developers. *Communications of the ACM* 37(1): 93–105.

Guarino, N., ed. 1998. Formal ontology in information systems. In *Proceedings of FOIS'98*. Burke, VA: IOS Press.

Gulick, L., and L. Urwick. 1937. Notes on the theory of organization, from *Papers on the Science of Administration*. In J. M. Shafritz and J. S. Ott, eds., *Classics of Organization Theory*. Pacific Grove, CA: Brooks/Cole, pp. 87–97.

Gurbaxani, V., and S. Whang. 1991. The Impact of Information Systems on Organizations and Markets. *Communications of the ACM* 34(1): 59–73.

Hackman, J. R. 1969. Toward understanding the role of tasks in behavioural research 31: 97–128.

Hagel, G. III, and A. G. Armstrong. 1997. *Net Gain: Expanding Markets through Virtual Communities*. Boston: Harvard Business School Press.

Halpern, J. Y. 1987. Using reasoning about knowledge to analyze distributed systems. In *Annual Review of Computer Science*, vol. 2. Palo Alto, CA: Annual Reviews, pp. 37–68.

Halstead, R. H. 1985. Multilisp: A language for concurrent symbolic computation. *ACM Transactions on Programming Languages and Systems* 7(4): 501–38.

Hammer, M. 1990. Reengineering work: Don't automate, obliterate. *Harvard Business Review* 68(4): 104–12.

Hammer, M., and J. Champy. 1993. Reengineering the Corporation. New York: Harper Business.

Hammer, M., W. G. Howe, V. J. Kruskal, and I. Wladawsky. 1977. A very high level language for data processing applications. *Communications of the ACM* 20: 832–40.

Harkness, W. L., W. J. Kettinger, and A. H. Segars. 1996. Sustaining process improvement and innovation in the information systems function: Lessons from the Bose Corporation, *MIS Quarterly* 20(3): 349–68.

Hart, P., and D. Estrin. 1990. Inter-organization computer networks: Indications of shifts in interdependence. In *ACM Transactions on Information Systems*, March 25–27. Cambridge, MA, pp. 370–98.

Harrington, H. J. 1991. *Business Process Improvement: The Breakthrough Strategy for Total Quality, Productivity, and Competetiveness.* New York: McGraw-Hill.

Harrison, D. B., and M. D. Pratt. 1993. A methodology for reengineering business. *Planning Review* 21(2): 6–11.

Heise, D. R. 1989. Modeling Event Structures. *Journal of Mathematical Sociology* 14: 139–69.

Heritage, J. 1984. *Garfinkel and Ethnomethodology.* Cambridge, England: Polity Press.

Herman, G., M. Klein, T. W. Malone, and E. O'Donnell. 1997. A template based methodology for process redesign. Working paper. MIT Center for Coordination Science. October.

Herman, G., T. W. Malone, and P. Weill. 2003. What difference does a business model make? Working paper. MIT Center for Coordination Science.

Hewes, D. E. 1979. The sequential analysis of social interaction. *Quarterly Journal of Speech* 65: 56–73.

Hewes, D. E. 1980. Stochastic modeling of communication processes. In *Multivariate Techniques in Human Communication Research.* New York: Academic Press, pp. 393–427.

Hewitt, C. 1986. Offices are open systems. *ACM Transactions on Office Systems* 4(3): 271–87.

Hines, J., T. Malone, G. Herman, J. Quimby, J. Rice, M. Murphy-Hoye, P. Goncalves, J. Patten, and H. Ishii. 2003. Model construction kits: A new approach to simulation modeling. MIT working paper.

Hirsch, E. D. 1987. *Cultural Literacy: What Every American Needs to Know.* Boston: Houghton Mifflin.

Hoare, C. A. R. 1975. Monitors: An operating systems structuring concept. *Communications of the ACM* 17(10): 549–57. Corrigendum, *CACM* 18(2): 95.

Holmes, M. E., and M. S. Poole. 1991. Longitudinal Analysis. In B. M. Montgomery and S. Duck, eds., *Studying Interpersonal Interaction.* New York: Guilford Press, pp. 286–302.

Holt, A. W. 1980. Coordinator Programs. Technical report. Massachusetts Computer Associates, Inc., Wakefield, MA.

Holt, A. W. 1988. Diplans: A new language for the study and implementation of coordination. *ACM Transactions on Office Information Systems* 6(2): 109–25.

Holt, A. W., H. R. Ramsey, and J. D. Grimes. 1983. Coordination system technology as the basis for a programming environment. *Electrical Communication* 57(4): 307–14.

Horning, J. J., and B. Randell. 1973. Process structuring. *ACM Computing Surveys* 5(1): 5–30.

Huberman, B. A., ed. 1988a. *The Ecology of Computation.* Amsterdam: North-Holland.

Huberman, B. A. 1988b. Open systems: The ecology of computation. PARC working paper P88-00074. Xerox PARC, Palo Alto, CA.

Huberman, B. A., and T. Hogg. 1988. The behaviour of computational ecologies. In B. A. Huberman, ed., *The Ecology of Computation*. Amsterdam: Elsevier, pp. 77–116.

Huhns, M. N., and L. Gasser, eds. 1989. *Distributed Artificial Intelligence*, vol. 3. San Mateo, CA: Morgan Kaufmann.

Hurwicz, L. 1973. The design of resource allocation mechanisms. *American Economic Review Papers and Proceedings* 58(May): 1–30.

Hymes, D. 1972. Models of the interaction of language and social life. In J. J. Gumperz and D. Hymes, eds., *Directions in Sociolinguistics: The Ethnography of Communication*. New York: Holt, Rinehart and Winston, pp. 35–71.

Inmos Ltd. 1984. *Occam Programming Manual*. Englewood Cliffs, NJ: Prentice-Hall.

Jaarvenpaa, S., and D. B. Stoddard. 1998. Business process redesign: Radical and evolutionary change. *Journal of Business Research* 41(1): 15–27.

Jablonski, S., and C. Bussler. 1996. *Workflow Management: Modeling, Concepts, Architecture and Implementation*. Boston: International Thomson Computer Press.

Janis, I. L., and L. Mann. 1977. *Decision-Making*. New York: Free Press.

Jensen, M. C., and W. H. Meckling. 1976. Theory of the firm: Managerial behavior, agency costs and ownership structure. *Journal of Financial Economics* 3: 305–60.

Jepperson, R. L. 1991. Institutions, institutional effects, and institutionalism. In W. W. Powell and P. J. DiMaggio, eds., *The New Institutionalism in Organizational Analysis*. Chicago: University of Chicago Press, pp. 143–63.

Johansen, R. 1988. *Groupware: Computer Support for Business Teams*. New York: Free Press.

Jones, T. C. 1984. Reusability in programming: A survey of the state of the art. *IEEE Transactions on Software Engineering* 10(5): 488–94.

Kaftan, C., and L. Barnes. 1991. Sun Hydraulics Corporation. Case Study. Boston: Harvard Business School.

Kahneman, D., and A. Tversky. 1973. On the psychology of prediction. *Psychological Review* 80: 237–51.

Kammer, P. J., G. A. Bolcer, R. N. Taylor, and M. Bergman. 2000. Techniques for supporting dynamic and adaptive workflow. *Computer Supported Cooperative Work* 9: 269–92.

Kaplan, B. 1991. Models of change and information systems research. In H.-E. Nissen, H. K. Klein, and R. Hirschheim, eds., *Information Systems Research: Contemporary Approaches and Emergent Traditions*. Amsterdam: Elsevier Science, pp. 593–611.

Karbe, B. H., and N. G. Ramsberger. 1990. Influence of exception handling on the support of cooperative office work. In S. Gibbs and A. A. Verrijin-Stuart, eds., *Multi-user Interfaces and Applications*. Amsterdam: Elsevier Science, pp. 355–70.

Karp, D. 1994. Programming lunch from "Table's Ready" to "Here's your check." *New York Times* (August 24): B1.

Keen, P. G. W., and M. S. Scott Morton. 1978. *Decision Support Systems: An Organizational Perspective*. Reading, MA: Addison-Wesley.

Keller, G., and T. Teufel. 1998. SAP R/3 process-oriented implementation: Iterative process prototyping. Reading, MA: Addison-Wesley.

Kettinger, W. J., and V. Grover. 1995. Toward a theory of business process change management. *Journal of Management Information Science* 12(1): 9–30.

Kettinger, W. J., S. Guha, and J. T. C. Teng. 1995. The process reengineering life cycle methodology: A case study. In V. Grover and W. J. Kettinger, eds., *Business Process Change: Concepts, Methodologies and Technologies*. Harrisburg, PA: Idea Group, pp. 211–44.

Kettinger, W. J., J. T. C. Teng, and S. Guha. 1997. Business process change: A study of methodologies, techniques, and tools. *MIS Quarterly* 21(1): 55–80.

Kidder, L. H. 1981. *Research Methods in Social Relations*, 4th ed. New York: Holt, Rinehart and Winston.

Kidder, T. 1981. *The Soul of a New Machine*. Boston: Little, Brown.

Kiesler, S., J. Siegel, and T. W. McGuire. 1984. Social psychological aspects of computer-mediated communication. *American Psychologist* 39: 1123–34.

Kinnear, T. C., and J. R. Taylor. 1991. *Marketing Research: An Applied Approach*. New York: McGraw-Hill.

Klein, K. J., F. Dansereau, and R. J. Hall. 1994. Levels issues in theory development, data collection and analysis. *Academy of Management Review* 19: 195–229.

Klein, K. J., H. Tosi, and A. A. Cannella Jr. 1999. Multilevel theory building: Benefits, barriers and new developments. *Academy of Management Review* 24(2): 243–49.

Klein, M. 1994. Computer-supported conflict management in concurrent engineering: Introduction to special issue. *Concurrent Engineering Research and Applications* 2(3): 145–47.

Klein, M. 1997. An exception handling approach to enhancing consistency, completeness and correctness in collaborative requirements capture. *Concurrent Engineering Research and Applications* 5(1): 37–46.

Klein, M., and C. Dellarocas. 2000. A knowledge-based approach to handling conflicts in workflow systems. *Journal of Computer-Supported Collaborative Work*. Special Issue on Adaptive Workflow Systems 9(3–4).

Klein, M., and C. Dellarocas. 2000. Domain-independent exception handling services that increase robustness in open multi-agent systems. CCS, Massachusetts Institute of Technology.

Klein, M., and S. C.-Y. Lu. 1991. Detecting and resolving conflicts among cooperating human and machine-based design agents. *International Journal For Artificial Intelligence in Engineering* 7: 93–104.

Kling, R. 1980. Social analyses of computing: Theoretical perspectives in recent empirical research. *ACM Computing Surveys* 12(1): 61–110.

Knister, M. J., and A. Prakash. 1990. DistEdit: A distributed toolkit for supporting multiple group editors. In *Proceedings*, CSCW 90, Los Angeles, CA, October 1990, pp. 343–55.

Kogut, P., and P. Clements. 1994. Features of architecture representation languages. Carnegie Mellon University Technical report CMU/SEI. December.

Kohler, W. 1981. A survey of techniques for synchronization and recovery in decentralized computer systems. *ACM Computing Surveys* 13(2): 149–83.

Kolodner, J. L., R. L. Simpson, and K. Sycara-Cyranski. 1985. A process model of case-based reasoning in problem solving. In *Proceedings of the International Joint Conference on Artificial Intelligence*, vol. 1. (IJCAI-85), pp. 284–90.

Kolodner, J. 1993. Case-based reasoning. San Mateo, CA: Morgan Kaufmann.

Kornfeld, W. A. 1982. Combinatorially implosive algorithms. *Communications of the ACM* 25(10): 734–38.

Kornfeld, W. A., and C. Hewitt. 1981. The scientific community metaphor. *IEEE Transactions on Systems, Man and Cybernetics* 11: 24–33.

Kotler, P. 1997. *Marketing Management: Analysis, Planning, Implementation, and Control*. Upper Saddle River, NJ: Prentice Hall.

Kreifelts, T., and G. Woetzel. 1987. Distribution and error handling in an office procedure system. IFIP WF 8.4 Working Conference on Methods and Tools for Office Systems, Pisa, Italy.

Kreifelts, T., E. Hinrichs, and G. Woetzel. 1993. Sharing to-do lists with a distributed task manager. In *Proceedings of the Third European Conference on Computer Supported Cooperative Work* (ECSCW), Milan, Italy.

Krueger, C. W. 1992. Software reuse. *ACM Computing Surveys* 24(2): 131–83.

Kraemer, K., and J. L. King. 1988. Computer-based systems for cooperative work and group decision-making. *ACM Computing Surveys* 20(2): 115–46.

Kramer, J., J. Magee, K. Ng, and M. Sloman. 1993. The system architect's assistant for design and construction of distributed systems. In *Proceedings of 4th IEEE Workshop on Future Trends of Distributed Computing Systems*, September 1993. IEEE Computer Society Press, pp. 284–90.

Kraus, S. 1993. Agents contracting tasks in noncollaborative environments. In Proceedings of the Eleventh National Conference on Artificial Intelligence, Washington, DC.

Krueger, C. 1992. Software reuse. *ACM Computing Surveys* 24(2): 131–83.

Kruschwitz, N., and G. Roth. 1999. Inventing organizations of the 21st century: Producing knowledge through collaboration. 21st century initiative working paper 21CWP031, March. Available at *http://ccs.mit.edu/papers/pdf/wp207and031.pdf*.

Kubeck, L. C. 1995. *Techniques for Business Process Redesign*. New York: Wiley.

Kubeck, L. C. 1997. Techniques for business process redesign. *Interfaces* 27(4): 82.

Kurose, J. F., and R. Simha. 1989. A microeconomic approach to optimal resource allocation in distributed computer systems. *IEEE Transaction on Computers* 38(5): 705–17.

Lai, K. Y., T. Malone, and K.-C. Yu. 1988. Object lens: A spreadsheet for cooperative work. *ACM Transactions on Office Information Systems* 6(4): 332–53.

Lakoff, G. 1987. *Women, Fire and Dangerous Things: What Categories Reveal about the Mind*. Chicago: University of Chicago Press.

Lane, T. G. 1990. A design space and design rules for user interface software architecture. Technical Report CMU/SEI-90-TR-22, ESD-90-TR-223. November.

Laubacher, R. J., T. W. Malone, and MIT-Scenario-Working-Group. 1997. Two Scenarios for 21st Century Organizations: Shifting Networks of Small Firms or All-Encompassing 'Virtual Countries'? 21 Century Initiative working paper. Sloan School of Management, MIT.

Lawrence, D. M., and B. Straight. 1989. *MicroEmacs Full Screen Text Editor Reference Manual, version 3.10*. March.

Lawrence, P., and J. Lorsch. 1967. *Organization and Environment*. Boston: Division of Research, Harvard Business School.

Leavitt, H. J., and T. L. Whisler. 1958. Management in the 1980's. *Harvard Business Review* 36(November–December): 41–48.

Leavitt, W. 1995. Health care delivery systems: Using the MIT CCS Handbook to create organizations for the 21st century. M.S. thesis. Sloan School of Management, MIT. May.

Leblebici, H., G. R. Salancik, A. Copay, and T. King. 1991. Institutional change and the transformation of interorganizational fields: An organizational history of the U.S. radio broadcasting industry. *Administrative Science Quarterly* 36: 333–63.

Lee, A. 1991. Integrating positivist and interpretive approaches to organizational research. *Organization Science* 2(4): 342–65.

Lee, J. 1990. Sibyl: A qualitative decision management system. In P. Winston, ed., *Artificial Intelligence at MIT: Expanding Frontiers*, vol. 1. Cambridge: MIT Press.

Lee, J., and K.-Y. Lai. 1991. What's in design rationale? *Human-Computer Interaction* 6(3–4): 251–80.

Lee, J., and T. W. Malone. 1990. Partially shared views: A scheme for communicating among groups that use different type hierarchies. *ACM Transactions on Information Systems* 8(1): 1–26.

Lee, J., G. Yost, and PIF Working Group. 1994. The PIF Process Interchange Format and Framework. MIT CCS Working report 180. Center for Coordination Science, MIT.

Lee, J., M. Grunninger, Y. Jin, T. Malone, A. Tate, G. Yost, and PIF Working Group. 1996. The PIF Process Interchange Format and Framework Version 1.1. In *Proceedings of Workshop on Ontological Engineering*, ECAI '96. Budapest, Hungary. (Also available as Working paper 194, Center for Coordination Science, MIT, and at *http://ccs.mit.edu/pif*.)

Lefkowitz, L. S., and W. B. Croft. 1990. Interactive planning for knowledge-based task management. Technical report. Collaborative Systems Laboratory, Department of Computer and Information Science, University of Massachusetts, Amherst. May.

Lenat, D. B. 1995. CYC: A large-scale investment in knowledge infrastructure. *Communications of the ACM* 38(11): 33–38.

Levinson, S. C. 1983. *Discourse Analysis.* New York: Cambridge University Press.

Levitt, R. E., G. Cohen, J. C. Kunz, C. I. Nass, T. Christiansen, and Y. Jin. 1994. The virtual design team: Simulating how organizations structure and information processing tools affect team performance. In K. M. Carley and M. J. Prietula, eds., *Computational Organization Theory.* Hillsdale, NJ: Lawrence Erlbaum Associates.

Lewis, H. R., and C. H. Papadimitriou. 1981. *Elements of the Theory of Computation.* Englewood Cliffs, NJ: Prentice-Hall.

Liskov, B., and J. Guttag. 1986. *Abstraction and Specification in Program Development.* Cambridge: MIT Press.

Litwak, E., and L. F. Hylton. 1962. Interorganizational analysis: A hypothesis on coordinating agencies. *Administrative Sciences Quarterly* 6(4): 395–420.

Lopes, C. V., and G. Kiczales. 1997. D: A language framework for distributed programming. Xerox Palo Alto Research Center, Palo Alo, CA, Technical Report SPL97-010, P9710047.

Lotus. 1989. *Lotus Notes Users Guide.* Cambridge, MA: Lotus Development Corp.

Luckham, D. C., and J. Vera. 1995. An event-based architecture definition language. *IEEE Transactions on Software Engineering* 21(9): 717–34.

Lumer, E., and B. A. Huberman. 1990. Dynamics of resource allocation in distributed systems. Technical Report SSL-90-05. Palo Alto, CA: Xerox PARC.

Lyon, W. K. 1995. The Process Handbook supply chain reengineering. M.S. thesis. Sloan School of Management, MIT. May.

MacLean, A., K. Carter, L. Lövstrand, and L. Moran. 1990. User-tailorable systems: Pressing the issues with buttons. In *Human Factors in Computing Systems.* Seattle, WA: ACM-SIGCHI, pp. 175–82.

Madsen, O. L., B. Moller-Pedersen, and K. Nygaard. 1993. *Object-Oriented Programming in the Beta Programming Language.* Reading, MA: Addison-Wesley.

Majchrzak, A., and L. Gasser. 1992. HITOP-A: A tool to facilitate interdisciplinary manufacturing systems design. *International Journal of Human Factors in Manufacturing* 2(3): 255–76.

Maksay, G., and Y. Pigneur. 1991. Reconciling functional decomposition, conceptual modeling, modular design and object orientation for application development. In *IFIP TC8/WG8.1 Working Conference on the Object Oriented Approach in Information Systems*, Quebec City, Canada. Amsterdam: North-Holland.

Malone, T. W. 1987. Modeling coordination in organizations and markets. *Management Science* 33: 1317–32.

Malone, T. W. 1988. What is coordination theory? Working paper 2051-88. Sloan School of Management, MIT.

Malone, T. W. 1990. Organizing information processing systems: Parallels between organizations and computer systems. In W. Zachary, S. Robertson, and J. Black, eds., *Cognition, Computation, and Cooperation.* Norwood, NJ: Ablex, pp. 56–83.

Malone, T. W. 1992. Analogies between human organization and artificial intelligence systems: Two examples and some reflections. In M. Masuch, ed., *Distributed Intelligence: Perspectives of Artificial Intelligence on Organization and Management Theory.* Amsterdam: Elsevier.

Malone, T. W., and K. Crowston. 1990. What is coordination theory and how can it help design cooperative work systems? In D. Tatar, ed., *Proceeding of the Third Conference on Computer-Supported Cooperative Work*, October 7–10. Los Angeles: ACM Press, pp. 357–70.

Malone, T. W., and K. G. Crowston. 1991. Toward an interdisciplinary theory of coordination. Technical report 120. Center for Coordination Science, MIT.

Malone, T. W., and K. Crowston. 1994. The interdisciplinary study of coordination. *ACM Computing Surveys* 26(1): 87–119.

Malone, T. W., K. Crowston, J. Lee, and B. Pentland. 1993. Tools for inventing organizations: Toward a handbook of organizational processes. In *Proceedings of the 2nd IEEE Workshop on Enabling Technologies Infrastructure for Collaborative Enterprises*, April 20–22. Morgantown, WV.

Malone, T. W., K. Crowston, J. Lee, B. Pentland, C. Dellarocas, G. Wynor, and J. Quimby. 1999. Tools for inventing organizations: Toward a handbook of organizational processes. *Management Science* 45(3): 425–43.

Malone, T. W., R. E. Fikes, K. R. Grant, and M. T. Howard. 1988. Enterprise: A market-like task scheduler for distributed computing. In B. Huberman, ed., *The Ecology of Computation*. Amsterdam: North-Holland.

Malone, T. W., K. R. Grant, F. A. Turbak, S. A. Brobst, and M. D. Cohen. 1987. Intelligent information-sharing systems. *Communications of the ACM* 30: 390–402.

Malone, T. W., K.-Y. Lai, and C. Fry. 1992. Experiments with Oval: A radically tailorable tool for cooperative work. In *Proceedings of the ACM Conference on Computer-Supported Cooperative Work* (CSCW '92), October 31–November 4. Toronto, Ontario, pp. 289–97.

Malone, T. W., R. J. Laubacher, and M. S. Scott Morton. (in press). *Inventing the Organizations of the 21st Century*, Cambridge: MIT Press.

Malone, T. W., and J. F. Rockart. 1991. Computers, networks, and the corporation. *Scientific American* 265(3): 128–36.

Malone, T. W., and S. A. Smith. 1988. Modeling the performance of organizational structures. *Operations Research* 36(3): 421–36.

Malone, T. W., J. Yates, and R. I. Benjamin. 1987. Electronic markets and electronic hierarchies. *Communications of the ACM* 30: 484–97.

Mangel, M., and C. W. Clark. 1988. *Dynamic Modeling in Behavioral Ecology*. Princeton: Princeton University Press.

March, J. G., and H. A. Simon. 1958. *Organizations*. New York: Wiley.

March, J. G., and R. I. Sutton. 1997. Organizational performance as a dependent variable. *Organization Science* 8(6): 698–706.

Markus, M. L., and T. Connolly. 1990. Why CSCW applications fail: Problems in the adoption of inter-dependent work tools. In D. Tatar, ed., *Proceedings of the Third Conference on Computer-Supported Cooperative Work*, October 7–10. Los Angeles: ACM Press, pp. 371–80.

Markus, M. L., and D. Robey. 1988. Information technology and organizational change: Causal structure in theory and research. *Management Science* 34(5): 583–98.

Marques, D., G. Dallemagne, G. Klinker, J. McDermott, and D. Tung. 1992. Easy programming: Empowering people to build their own applications. *IEEE Expert* 7(3): 16–29.

Marschak, J., and R. Radner. 1972. *Economic Theory of Teams*. New Haven: Yale University.

Masuch, M., and P. LaPotin. 1989. Beyond garbage cans: An AI model of organizational choice. *Administrative Science Quarterly* 34: 38–67.

Matta, N., C. Ros, and O. Corby. 1998. A generic library to guide decision making in concurrent engineering. In *Proceedings of TMCE-98*, Manchester, UK.

Maull, R., S. Childe, J. Bennett, A. Weaver, and A. Smart. 1995. Different types of manufacturing processes and IDEF0 models describing standard business processes. Working paper WP/GR/J95010-6. School of Computing, University of Plymouth, Plymouth, Devon, UK.

Mayhew, B. H. 1980. Structuralism versus individualism: Part 1, Shadowboxing in the dark. *Social Forces* 59: 336–75.

Maynard, H. B., and K. B. Zandin, eds. 2001. *Maynard's Industrial Engineering Handbook*, 5th ed. New York: McGraw-Hill.

McCann, J. E., and D. L. Ferry. 1979. An approach for assessing and managing inter-unit interdependence. *Academy of Management Review* 4(1): 113–19.

McCann, J. E., and J. R. Galbraith. 1981. Interdepartmental relations. In P. C. Nystrom and W. H. Starbuck, eds., *The Handbook of Organizational Design*, vol. 2. New York: Oxford University Press, pp. 60–84.

McClain, J., L. J. Thomas, and J. Mazola. 1992. *Operations Management*, 3rd ed. Englewood Cliffs, NJ: Prentice-Hall.

McGrath, J. E. 1984. *Groups: Interaction and Performance*. Englewood Cliffs, NJ: Prentice-Hall.

McKelvey, B. 1982. *Organizational Systematics: Taxonomy, Evolution, Classification*. Berkeley: University of California Press.

McNair, C. J., and K. H. J. Leibfried. 1992. *Benchmarking: A Tool for Continuous Improvement*. New York: Harper Business.

Medema, S. G. 1996. Coase, costs and coordination. *Journal of Economic Issues* 30(2): 571–78.

Mettala, E., and M. H. Graham. 1992. The domain-specific software architecture program. Technical report CMU/SEI-92-SR-9. Software Engineering Institute, Carnegie Mellon. June.

Meyer, M., and V. Gupta. 1994. The performance paradox. *Research in Organizational Behavior* 16: 309–69.

Mi, P., and W. Scacchi. 1993. *Articulation: An Integrated Approach to the Diagnosis, Replanning and Rescheduling of Software Process Failures*. In *Proceedings of 8th Knowledge Based Software Engineering Conference*, Chicago, pp. 77–85.

Miao, X., P. B. Luh, and D. L. Kleinman. 1992. A normative-descriptive approach to hierarchical team resource allocation. *IEEE Transactions on Systems, Man and Cybernetics* 22(3): 482–97.

Miclet, L. 1986. *Structural Methods in Pattern Recognition*. J. Howlett, trans. New York: Springer-Verlag.

Microsoft. 1993. *Language Reference, Microsoft Visual Basic Version 3.0*. Redmond, WA: Microsoft Corporation.

Microsoft. 1994. *OLE2 Programmers' Reference*, vols. 1 and 2. Redmond, WA: Microsoft Press.

Milgrom, P. 1981. An axiomatic characterization of common knowledge. *Econometrica* 49(1): 17–26.

Miller, C. R. 1984. Genre as social action. *Quarterly Journal of Speech* 70: 151–67.

Miller, J. G. 1978. *Living Systems*. New York: McGraw-Hill.

Miller, M. S., and K. E. Drexler. 1988. Markets and computation: Agoric open systems. In B. A. Huberman, ed., *The Ecology of Computation*. Amsterdam: North-Holland, pp. 133–76.

Mintzberg, H. 1979. *The Structuring of Organizations*. Englewood Cliffs, NJ: Prentice-Hall.

Mintzberg, H., and J. A. Waters. 1985. Of strategies, deliberate and emergent. *Strategic Management Journal* 6: 257–72.

Mohan, C., G. Alonso, R. Günthör, and M. Kamath. 1995. Exotica: A research perpespective on workflow management systems. *IEEE-Data Engineering* 18: 19–26.

Mohr, L. 1982. *Explaining Organizational Behavior*. San Francisco: Jossey-Bass.

Morgan, G. 1986. *Images of Organization*. Beverly Hills: Sage.

Moses, J. 1990. Organization and ideology. Manuscript. Department of Electrical Engineering and Computer Science, MIT.

Myerson, R. B. 1981. Optimal auction design. *Mathematics of Operations Research* 6: 58–73.

Nadler, D. A., D. N. T. Perkins, and M. Hanlon. 1983. The observation of organizational behavior: A structured naturalistic approach. In S. E. Seashore, E. E. Lawler III, P. Mirvis, and C. Cammann, eds., *Assessing Organizational Change: A Guide to Methods, Measures, and Practices*. New York: Wiley-Interscience, pp. 331–51.

Nau, D. S. 1987. Automated process planning using hierarchical abstraction. *TI Technical Journal* (Winter): 39–46.

Neuwirth, C. M., D. S. Kaufer, R. Chandhok, and J. H. Morris. 1990. Issues in the design of computer-support for co-authoring and commenting. In *Proceedings of the Third Conference on Computer-Supported Cooperative Work* (CSCW 90), October 7–10. Los Angeles: ACM Press, pp. 183–95.

Newmeyer, F. J. 1983. *Grammatical Theory: Its Limits and Its Possibilities*. Chicago: University of Chicago Press.

Newell, A., and H. A. Simon. 1972. *Human Problem Solving*. Englewood Cliffs, NJ: Prentice-Hall.

Nierstrasz, O. 1993. Regular types for active objects. In *Proceedings of Conference on Object-Oriented Programming: Systems, Languages, and Applications*. Washington, DC: Association for Computing Machinery.

Nii, P. 1986. The blackboard model of problem solving. *AI Magazine* (Spring): 38–53.

Nissen, M. 1998. Redesigning reengineering through measurement-driven inferences. *MIS Quarterly* 22(4): 509–34.

Nissen, Mark E. 1999. A configuration-contingent enterprise redesign model. In D. J. Elzinga, T. R. Gulledge, C.-Y. Lee, eds., *Business Process Engineering: Advancing the State of the Art*. Norwell, MA: Kluwer Academic, pp. 145–86.

Nohria, N., and R. G. Eccles, eds. 1992. *Networks and Organizations: Structure, Form, and Action*. Boston: Harvard Business School.

Norman, D. A. 1988. *The Psychology of Everyday Things*. New York: Basic Books.

Norman, T. J., N. R. Jennings, P. Faratin, and E. H. Madami. 1996. Designing and implementing a multi-agent architecture for business process management. Presented at Intelligent Agents III: Agent Theories, Architectures, and Languages, IJCAI'96 Workshop (ATAL), Budapest, Hungary.

NSF. 1991. Coordination Theory and Collaboration Technology Workshop Summary, June 3–5. Washington, DC: National Science Foundation.

NSF-IRIS. 1989. A report by the NSF-IRIS Review Panel for Research on Coordination Theory and Technology. Available from NSF Forms and Publications unit.

Object Management Group. 1991. Common object request broker: Architecture and specification. OMG document 91.12.1.

Olson, G. M., J. D. Herbsleb, and H. H. Rueter. 1994. Characterizing the sequential structure of interactive behaviors through statistical and grammatical techniques, *Human Computer Interaction* 9: 427–72.

ONEstone. 1998. ProZessware for Lotus Domino/Notes. ONEstone Information Technologies GmbH, Paderborn, Germany.

Open Software Foundation. 1990. *OSF/Motif Programmer's Reference. Revision 1.0*. Englewood Cliffs, NJ: Prentice-Hall, 1990.

Orlikowski, W. J. 1992. The duality of technology: Rethinking the concept of technology in organizations. *Organization Science* 3: 398–427.

Orlikowski, W. 1992a. Learning from notes: Organizational issues in Groupware implementation. In *Proceedings of the Conference on Computer-Supported Cooperative Work* (CSCW 92), November. Toronto, Canada: ACM.

Orlikowski, W. 1993. Case tools as organizational change: Investigating incremental and radical changes in systems development. *MIS Quarterly* 20(3): 309–40.

Orlikowski, W. J. 1996. Improvising organizational change over time: A situated change perspective. *Information Systems Research* 7: 63–92.

Orlikowski, W. J., and J. Yates. 1994. Genre repertoire: Examining the structuring of communicative practices in organizations. *Administrative Science Quarterly* 39: 541–74.

Orlikowski, W. J., and J. Yates. 1998. Genre systems as communicative norms for structuring interaction in groupware. *CCS WP205, http://ccs.mit.edu/papers/CCSWP205/.*

Orlikowski, W. J., J. Yates, and N. Fonstad. 2001. Sloan 2001: A virtual odyssey. In L. Chidambaram and I. Zigurs, eds., *Our Virtual World: The Transformation of Work, Play, and Life Via Technology.* Hershey, PA: Idea Group Publishing, pp. 191–218.

Osborn, C. S. 1996. Documents and dependencies: Enabling strategic improvement through coordination redesign. In T. Wakayama, S. Kannapan, C. M. Khoong, S. Navathó, and J. Yates, eds., *Information and Process Integration in Enterprises: Rethinking Documents,* 31–54. Norwell, MA: Kluwer Academic Publishers.

Pandya, V. K., and S. Nelis. 1998. Requirements for process redesign tools. *International Journal of Computer Applications in Technology* 11(6): 409–18.

Parnas, D. L. 1972. On the criteria to be used in decomposing systems into modules. *Communications of the ACM* 15(12): 1053–58.

Pelz, D. C. 1985. Innovation complexity and the sequence of innovating stages. *Knowledge: Creation, Diffusion, Utilization* 6: 261–91.

Pentland, B. T. 1992. Organizing moves software support hot lines. *Administrative Science Quarterly* 37(4): 527–48.

Pentland, B. T. 1995. Grammatical models of organizational processes. *Organization Science* 6(5): 541–56.

Pentland, B. T., C. Osborne, G. Wyner, and F. Luconi. 1994. Useful descriptions of organizational processes: Collecting data for the Process Handbook. Working paper. Center for Coordination Science, MIT.

Perrow, C. 1984. *Normal Accidents: Living with High-Risk Technologies.* New York: Basic Books.

Perry, R. H., D. W. Green, and J. O. Maloney, eds. 1997. *Perry's Chemical Engineers' Handbook,* 7th ed. New York: McGraw-Hill.

Peters, T. 1992. *Liberation Management.* New York: Knopf.

Peterson, D., eds. 1986. *Proceedings of the Conference on Computer-Supported Cooperative Work.* Austin, TX: ACM Press.

Peterson, J. L. 1977. Petri nets. *ACM Computing Surveys* 9(3): 223–52.

Peterson, J. L. 1981. *Petri Net Theory and the Modeling of Systems.* Englewood Cliffs, NJ: Prentice-Hall.

Pfeffer, J. 1978. *Organizational Design.* Arlington Heights, IL: Harlan Davidson.

Pfeffer, J., and G. R. Salancik. 1978. *The External Control of Organizations: A Resource Dependency Perspective.* New York: Harper and Row.

Poole, M. S., and J. Roth. 1989. Decision development in small groups IV: A typology of group decision paths. *Human Communication Research* 15: 323–56.

Poole, M. S., J. P. Folger, and D. E. Hewes. 1987. Analyzing interpersonal interaction. In M. E. Roloff and G. R. Miller, eds., *Interpersonal Processes: New Directions in Communications Research.* Newbury Park, CA: Sage, pp. 220–56.

Price, J. L., and C. W. Mueller. 1986. *Handbook of Organizational Measurement.* Marshfield, MA: Pitman.

Prince, G. 1973. *A Grammar of Stories.* The Hague: Mouton.

Procter, M., and P. Abell. 1985. *Sequence Analysis: Surrey Conference on Sociological Theory and Method.* Aldershot, England: Gower.

Pugh, D. S., D. J. Hickson, and C. R. Hinings. 1968. An empirical taxonomy of work organizations. *Administrative Science Quarterly* 14: 115–26.

Ramesh, B., and K. Sengupta. 1994. Managing cognitive and mixed-motive conflicts in concurrent engineering. *Concurrent Engineering Research and Applications*: Special Issue on Conflict Management in Concurrent Engineering 2(3): 223–36.

Raynal, M. 1986. *Algorithms for Mutual Exclusion*. Cambridge: MIT Press.

Reiter, S. 1986. Informational incentive and performance in the (new)2 welfare economics. In S. Reiter, ed., *Studies in Mathematical Economics*. Mathematical Assocation of America.

Rescher, N. 1977. Dialectics: A controversy-oriented approach to the theory of knowledge. Buffalo, NY: State University of New York Press.

Rich, P. 1992. The organizational taxonomy: Definition and design. *Academy of Management Review* 17: 758–81.

Ripps, D. L. 1991. Task coordination: Specific methods, general principles. *EDN* (March 1): 97–110.

Rittel, H., and W. Kunz. 1970. Issues as elements of information systems. Working paper 131. University of Stuttgart, Institut für Grundlagen der Planung I.A.

Roberts, K. H., and G. Gargano. 1989. Managing a high reliability organization: A case for interdependence. In M. A. V. Glinow and S. Mohrmon, eds., *Managing Complexity in High Technology Industries: Systems and People*. New York: Oxford University Press, pp. 147–59.

Roberts, K. H., S. K. Stout, and J. J. Halpern. 1994. Decision dynamics in two high reliability military organizations. *Management Science* 40(5): 614–24.

Rock Systems. 1994. *Prohost promotional material*.

Rock, R., P. Ulrich, and F. H. Witt. 1990. *Dienstleistungsrationalisierung im Umbruch—Wage in die Kommunikationswirtschaft*, vol. 11. Opladen: Westdeutscher Verlag.

Rockart, J. F., and J. E. Short. 1989. IT and the networked organization: Toward more effective management of interdependence. In M. S. Scott Morton, ed., *Management in the 1990s Research Program Final Report*. Cambridge, MA: Massachusetts Institute of Technology.

Roger, P. M., and R. L. Chapman. 1992. *Roget's International Thesaurus*. New York: Harper Collins.

Rogers, E., and R. Agarwala-Rogers. 1976. *Communication in Organizations*. New York: Free Press.

Rogers, R. V. 1991. Understated implications of object-oriented simulation and modeling. In *Proceedings of IEEE International Conference on Systems, Man, and Cybernetics*. Charlottesville, VA: IEEE. October 13–16, 1991.

Ross, S. 1973. The economic theory of agency. *American Economic Review* 63: 134–39.

Roth, G. 1997. Uniting theory and practice: An illustrative case for bridging knowledge and action. Working paper. MIT Initiative on Inventing the Organizations of the 21st Century.

Rowley, J. 1992. *Organizing Knowlege*, 2nd ed. Brookfield, VT: Ashgate.

Ruelas Gossi, A. 1995. Inventing organizations for the 21st century in Mexico: Supply chain management in a brewery. M.S. thesis. Sloan School of Management, MIT. May.

Rumbaugh, B., W. Premerlani, F. Eddy, and W. Lorensen. 1991. *Object-Oriented Modeling and Design*. Englewood Cliffs, NJ: Prentice-Hall.

Rumelhart, D. E., J. L. McClelland, and PDP Research Group. 1986. *Parallel Distributed Processing: Explorations in the Microstructures of Cognition*. Cambridge: MIT Press.

Ryan, M. 1979. Linguistic models in narratology: From structuralism to generative semantics, *Semiotica* 28(1–2): 127–55.

Sabherwal, R., and D. Robey. 1993. An empirical taxonomy of implementation processes based on sequences of events in information system development. *Organization Science* 4: 548–76.

Sacerdoti, E. D. 1974. Planning in a hierarchy of abstraction spaces. *Artificial Intelligence* 5: 115–35.

Sakamoto, S. 1989. Process design concept: A new approach to IE. *Industrial Engineering* (March): 31.

Salancik, G. R. 1986. An index of subgroup influence in dependency networks. *Administrative Science Quarterly* 31(2): 194–211.

Salancik, G. R., and H. Leblebici. 1988. Variety and form in organizing transactions: A generative grammar of organization. In N. DiTomaso and S. B. Bacharach, eds., *Research in the Sociology of Organizations*. Greenwich, CT: JAI Press, pp. 1–31.

Sanchez, J. C. 1993. The long and thorny way to an organizational taxonomy. *Organization Studies* 14(1): 73–92.

Sandelands, L. E. 1987. Task grammar and attitude. *Motivation and Emotion* 11: 121–43.

Sawyer, S., K. Crowston, and R. Wigand. 1999. ICT in the real estate industry: Agents and social capital. In *Proceedings of Advances in Social Informatics and Information Systems Track, Americas Conference on Information Systems*. Milwaukee, WI.

Schank, R. C. 1982. *Dynamic Memory: A Theory of Reminding and Learning in Computers and People*. New York: Cambridge University Press.

Schank, R. C., and R. P. Abelson. 1977. *Scripts, Plans, Goals and Understanding: An Inquiry into Human Knowledge*. Hillsdale, NJ: Lawrence Erlbaum Associates.

Scheer, A.-W. 1994. *Business Process Reengineering: Reference Models for Industrial Enterprises*, 2nd ed. New York: Springer-Verlag.

Scheifler, R. W., J. Gettys, and R. Newman. 1988. *X Window System. C Library and Protocol Reference*. Digital Press.

Schein, E. H. 1985. *Organization Culture and Leadership*. San Francisco: Jossey-Bass.

Schein, E. 1987. *Clinical Methods in Fieldwork*. Beverly Hills: Sage.

Schein, E. H. 1987. *The Clinical Perspective in Fieldwork*. Beverly Hills: Sage.

Schelling, T. C. 1978. *Micromotives and Macrobehavior*. New York: Norton.

Schelling, T. C. 1960. *Strategy of Conflict*. Cambridge: Harvard University Press.

Schlenoff, C., M. Gruninger, F. Tissot, J. Valois, J. Lubell, and J. Lee. 2000. *The Process Specification Language (PSL): Overview and Version 1.0 Specification*. NISTIR 6459. Gaithersburg, MD: National Institute of Standards and Technology.

Schonberger, R. 1982. *Japanese Manufacturing Techniques*. New York: Free Press.

Schonberger, R. 1986. *World Class Manufacturing*. New York: Free Press.

Schuler, D., and A. Namioka, eds. 1993. *Participatory Design: Principles and Practices*. Hillsdale, NJ: Lawrence Erlbaum Associates.

Schultz, M., and M. J. Hatch. 1996. Living with multiple paradigms: The case of paradigm interplay in organizational culture studies. *Academy of Management Review* 21(2): 529–57.

Searle, J. R. 1969. *Speech Acts: An Essay in the Philosophy of Language*. Cambridge: Cambridge University Press.

Searle, J. R. 1975. A taxonomy of illocutionary acts. In K. Gunderson, ed., *Language, Mind and Knowledge*. Minneapolis: University of Minnesota, pp. 344–69.

Seeley, T. D. 1989. The honey bee colony as a superorganism. *American Scientist* 77(November–December): 546–53.

Sen, S. 1993. *Predicting Tradeoffs in Contract-Based Distributed Scheduling*. Ph.D. dissertation. Department of Computer Science and Engineering, University of Michigan.

Senge, P. 1990. *The Fifth Discipline*. New York: Doubleday/Currency.

Schank, R. C., and R. P. Abelson. 1977. *Scripts, Plans, Goals and Understanding*. Hillsdale, NJ: Lawrence Erlbaum Associates.

Shannon, C. E., and W. Weaver. 1949. *The Mathematical Theory of Communication.* Urbana: University of Illinois Press.

Shapiro, B. P., V. K. Rangan, and J. J. Sviokla. 1992. Staple yourself to an order. *Harvard Business Review* (July–August): 113–22.

Shaw, M. 1994. Procedure calls are the assembly language of software interconnection: Connectors deserve first-class status. Technical report CMU-CS-94-107. Carnegie Mellon University. January.

Shaw, M., R. DeLine, and D. Klein. 1995. Abstractions for software architecture and tools to support them. *IEEE Transactions on Software Engineering* (April): 314–35.

Shaw, M., and D. Garlan. 1996. *Software Architecture: Perspectives on an Emerging Discipline.* Upper Saddle River, NJ: Prentice-Hall.

Shiba, S., A. Graham, D. Walden, T. H. Lee, R. Stata, and Center for Quality Management. 1993. *A New American TQM: Four Practical Revolutions in Management.* Norwalk, CT: Productivity Press.

Shoham, Y. 1993. Agent oriented programming. *Journal of Artificial Intelligence.*

Simon, H. A. 1964. On the concept of organizational goal. *Administrative Sciences Quarterly* 9(1): 1–22.

Simon, H. A. 1976. *Administrative Behavior,* 3rd ed. New York: Free Press.

Simon, H. A. 1981. *Sciences of the Artificial,* 2nd ed. Cambridge: MIT Press.

Simon, H. A. 1991. Organizations and markets. *Journal of Economic Perspectives* 5(2): 25–44.

Simon, H. A. 1992. What is an "explanation" of behavior? *Psychological Science* 3: 150–61.

Singh, B. 1992. Interconnected roles (IR): A coordination model. Technical report CT-084-92. Microelectronics and Computer Technology Corp. (MCC), Austin, TX.

Singh, B., and G. L. Rein. 1992. Role interaction nets (RIN): A process description formalism. Technical Report CT-083-92. MCC, Austin, TX.

Singh, J. V., and C. J. Lumsden. 1990. Theory and research in organizational ecology. *Annual Review of Sociology* 16: 161–95.

Skvoretz, J., and T. J. Fararo. 1980. Languages and grammars of action and interaction: A contribution to the formal theory of action. *Behavioral Science* 25: 9–22.

Smith, A. 1776. *The Wealth of Nations* (1986 ed.). London: Penguin Books.

Smith, G. F. 1988. Towards a heuristic theory of problem structuring. *Management Science* 34(12): 1489–1506.

Smith, R. G., and R. Davis. 1981. Frameworks for cooperation in distributed problem solving. *IEEE Transactions on Systems, Man and Cybernetics* 11(1): 61–70.

Spoerri, A. 1993. InfoCrystal: A visual tool for information retrieval management. Presented at Second International Conference on Information and Knowledge Management, Washington, DC.

Spradley, J. P. 1979. *The Ethnographic Interview.* New York: Holt, Rinehart, Winston.

Stankovic, J. 1985. An applicaiton of Bayesian decision theory to decentralized control of job scheduling. *IEEE Transactions on Computers* 34(2): 117–30.

Stefik, M. 1981. Planning with constraints (MOLGEN: Part 1). *Artificial Intelligence* 16(2): 111–39.

Stefik, M., and D. G. Bobrow. 1986. Object-oriented programming: Themes and variations. *AI Magazine* 6(4): 40–62.

Stefik, M., G. Foster, D. G. Bobrow, K. Kahn, S. Lanning, and L. Suchman. 1987. Beyond the chalkboard: Computer support for collaboration and problem solving in meetings. *Communications of the ACM* 30(1): 32–47.

Stefik, M., and S. Smoliar. 1995. Creative mind; myths and mechanisms; six reviews and a response. *Artificial Intelligence* 79(1): 65–67.

Stoddard, D. 1986. OTISLINE. Case 9-186-304. Harvard Business School.

Stoddard, D., and S. Jarvenpaa. 1995. Business process reengineering: Tactics for managing radical change. *Journal of Management Information Systems* 12(1): 81–108.

Stovsky, M. P., and B. W. Weide. 1988. Building interprocess communication models using STILE. In *Proceedings of the 21st Annual Hawaii International Conference on System Sciences*, vol. 2, pp. 639–47.

Strong, D. M. 1992. Decision support for exception handling and quality control in office operations. *Decision Support Systems* 8(3): 217–27.

Stuart, C. 1985. *An implementation of a multi-agent plan synchronizer.* In *Proceedings of the 9th International Joint Conference on Artificial Intelligence* (IJCAI-85), Los Angeles, CA, pp. 1031–33.

Suchman, L. A. 1983. Office procedures as practical action: Models of work and system design. *ACM Transactions on Office Information Systems* 1(4): 320–28.

Suchman, L. A. 1987. *Plans and Situated Actions: The Problem of Human-Machine Communication.* Cambridge: Cambridge University Press.

Suchman, L. 1994. Do categories have politics? *Computer Supported Cooperative Work* 2: 177–90.

Suchman, L. 1996. Supporting articulation work. In R. Kling, ed., *Computerization and Controversy: Value Conflicts and Social Choices*, 2nd ed. San Diego: Academic Press, pp. 407–23.

Swartout, S., and A. Tate. 1999. Guest editors' introduction: Ontologies. *IEEE Intelligent Systems and Their Applications* 14(1).

Swenson, K. D. 1993. Visual support for reengineering work processes. Presented at Conference on Organizational Computing Systems (COCS).

Taivalsaari, A. 1996. On the notion of inheritance. *ACM Computing Surveys* 28(3): 438–79.

Takagaki, K., and Y. Wand. 1991. An object-oriented information systems model based on ontology. In *Proceedings of IFIP TC8/WG8.1 Working Conference on the Object Oriented Approach in Information Systems*, Quebec City, Canada. Amsterdam: North-Holland.

Tannenbaum, A. S. 1981. *Computer Networks.* Englewood Cliffs, NJ: Prentice-Hall.

Tatar, D., ed. 1988. *Proceedings of the Second Conference on Computer-Supported Cooperative Work.* Portland, OR. New York: ACM Press.

Tatar, D., ed. 1990. *Proceedings of the Third Conference on Computer-Supported Cooperative Work*, Los Angeles. ACM Press.

Tenenberg, J. 1986. Planning with abstraction. In *Proceedings of AAAI-86, 5th National Conference on Artificial Intelligence*, Philadelphia. Los Altos, CA: Morgan Kaufman Publishers.

Thompson, J. D. 1967. *Organizations in Action: Social Science Bases of Administrative Theory.* New York: McGraw-Hill.

Thomsen, K. S. 1987. Inheritance on processes, exemplified on distributed termination detection. *International Journal of Parallel Programming* 16(1): 17–53.

Toffler, A. 1970. *Future Shock.* New York: Bantam Books.

Toulmin, S. 1958. *The Uses of Argument.* Cambridge: Cambridge University Press.

Trice, A., and R. Davis. 1989. Consensus knowledge acquisition. Working paper. Information Technologies Group, Sloan School of Management, MIT.

Tsoukas, H. 1991. The missing link: A transformational view of metaphors in organizational science. *Academy of Management Review* 16: 566–85.

Turoff, M. 1983. Information, value, and the internal marketplace. Manuscript. New Jersey Institute of Technology, Newark.

Tushman, M. L., and P. Anderson. 1986. Technological discontinuities and organizational environments. *Administrative Science Quarterly* 31: 439–65.

Ulrich, K. T., and S. D. Eppinger. 1995. *Product Design and Development.* New York: McGraw-Hill.

Ulrich, D. O., and B. McKelvey. 1990. General organizational classification: An empirical test using the United States and Japanese electronics industries. *Organization Science* 1: 99–118.

Van Alstyne, M. 1997. The state of network organization: A survey in three frameworks. *Journal of Organizational Computing* 7(3): 87–151.

van de Ven, A. H. 1992. Suggestions for studying strategy process: A research note. *Strategic Management Journal* 13: 169–88.

van de Ven, A. H., H. L. Angle, and M. S. Poole, eds. 1989. *Research on the Management of Innovation: The Minnesota Studies.* New York: Ballinger/Harper and Row.

van de Ven, A. H., A. L. Delbecq, and R. Koenig Jr. 1976. Determinants of coordination modes within organizations. *American Sociological Review* 41(April): 322–38.

van de Ven, A. H., and M. S. Poole. 1990. Methods for studying innovation development in the Minnesota innovation research program. *Organization Science* 1: 313–35.

van der Aalst, W. M. P., and T. Basten. 1999. Inheritance of workflows—An approach to tackling problems related to change. Computing science report 99/06 1999. Eindhoven University of Technology, the Netherlands.

Ventola, E. 1987. *The Structure of Social Interaction: A Systematic Approach to the Semiotics of Service Encounters.* London: Frances Pinter.

Victor, B., and R. S. Blackburn. 1987. Interdependence: An alternative conceptualization. *Academy of Management Review* 12(3): 486–98.

von Martial, F. 1989. Multiagent plan relationships. In *Proceedings of the 9th Workshop on Distributed Artificial Intelligence*, Rosario Resort, Eastsound, WA, pp. 59–72.

Von Hippel, E. 1996. Do it yourself versus specialization: Customization of products and services by users of ASICs and CTI. *Management Science*, forthcoming.

Waldspurger, C. A., T. Hogg, B. A. Huberman, J. O. Kephart, and S. Stornetta. 1988. Spawn: A distributed computational ecology. Working paper. Xerox PARC, Palo Alto, CA.

Walsh, J. P. 1995. Managerial and organizational cognition: Notes from a trip down memory lane. *Organization Science* 6(3): 280–321.

Wegner, P. 1987. Dimensions of object-based language design. In *Proceedings of the Conference on Object-Oriented Systems, Languages, and Applications* (OOPSLA '87) Orlando, FL. Now York: ACM Press, pp. 168–82.

Wegner, P., and S. B. Zdonik. 1988. Inheritance as an incremental modification mechanism or what like is and isn't like. In *Proceedings of the European Conference on Object-Oriented Programming*, Oslo. New York: Springer-Verlag.

Weick, K. E. 1979. *The Social Psychology of Organizing*, 2nd ed. New York: Random House.

Weick, K. 1998. Improvisation as a mindset for organizational analysis. *Organization Science* 9: 543–55.

Weick, K., and K. Roberts. 1993. Collective mind in organizations: Heedful interrelating on flight decks. *Administrative Science Quarterly* 38: 357–81.

Weinberg, G. M. 1988. *Rethinking Systems Analysis & Design.* New York: Dorset House Publishing.

Weld, D. S. 1994. An introduction to least commitment planning. *AI Magazine* 15: 27–61.

Weld, D. S., C. R. Anderson, and D. E. Smith. 1998. Extending Graphplan to handle uncertainty and sensing actions. Presented at National Conference on Artificial Intelligence.

Whetten, D. A. 1989. What constitutes a theoretical contribution? *Academy of Management Review* 14(4): 490–95.

White, H. C. 1992. Social grammar for culture: Reply to Steven Brint. *Sociological Theory* 10: 209–13.

Wilensky, R. 1983. *Planning and Understanding: A Computational Approach to Human Reasoning.* Reading, MA: Addison-Wesley.

Wiley, E. O., D. Siegel-Causey, D. R. Brooks, and V. A. Funk. 1991. *The Complete Cladist: A Primer of Phylogenetic Procedures*. Special publication 19. Lawrence, KS: University of Kansas, Museum of Natural History.

Williamson, O. E. 1975. *Markets and Hierarchies*. New York: Free Press.

Williamson, O. 1985. *The Economic Institutions of Capitalism*. New York: Free Press.

Williamson, O. E. 1991. Comparative economic organization: The analysis of discrete structural alternatives. *Administrative Science Quarterly* 36: 269–96.

Winograd, T. 1987. A language/action perspective on the design of cooperative work. *Human Computer Interaction* 3: 3–30.

Winograd, T. 1994. Categories, disciplines, and social coordination. *Computer Supported Cooperative Work* 2: 191–97.

Winograd, T., and F. Flores. 1986. *Understanding Computers and Cognition: A New Foundation for Design*. Norwood, NJ: Ablex.

Woodward, J. 1965. *Industrial Organizations: Theory and Practice*. New York: Oxford University Press.

Wyner, G., and J. Lee. 2001. Defining specialization for process models. Technical report 4159. Sloan School of Management, MIT.

Wyner, G., and J. Lee. 1995. Applying specialization to process models. In *Proceedings of the Conference on Organizational Computing Systems*, Milpitas, CA, August 13–16. New York: ACM Press.

Wyner, G., and G. Zlotkin. 1995. Resource, use and coordination. Presentation at the MIT Center for Coordination Science, April 28, 1995.

Yates, J., and W. J. Orlikowski. 1992. Genres of organizational communication: A structurational approach to studying communication and media. *Academy of Management Review* 17: 299–326.

Yates, J., and W. J. Orlikowski. 1997. Genre systems: Chronos and Kairos in communicative interaction. Paper presented at the 2nd International Symposium on Genre, Vancouver, Canada.

Yates, J., W. J. Orlikowski, and K. Okamura. 1999. Explicit and implicit structuring of genres: Electronic communication in a Japanese R&D organization. *Organization Science* 10: 83–103.

Yates, J., W. J. Orlikowski, and J. Rennecker. 1997. Collaborative genres for collaboration: Genre systems in digital media. In *Proceedings of the Thirtieth Hawaii International Conference on System Sciences*, Hawaii. January, vol. 6.

Yin, R. K. 1989. *Case Study Research: Design and Methods*, rev. ed. Newbury Park, CA: Sage.

Yourdon, E. 1989. *Modern Structured Analysis*. Englewood Cliffs, NJ: Yourdon.

Yu, E. S. K. 1992. Modelling organizations for information systems requirements engineering. In *Proceedings IEEE*.

Yu, E. S. K., and J. Mylopoulos. 1993. An actor dependency model of organizational work—With application to business process reengineering. In *Proceedings of the Conference on Organizational Computing Systems*, Paper presented at the COOCS'93. November 1–4. Milpitas, CA, pp. 258–68.

Zhang, P. G. 1995. *Barings Bankruptcy and Financial Derivatives*. Singapore: World Scientific.

Zisman, M. D. 1978. Office automation: Revolution or evolution? *Sloan Management Review* 19: 1–16.

Zlotkin, G. 1995. Coordinating resource based dependencies. Working paper. Center for Coordination Science, MIT. March.

Zuboff, S. 1988. *In the Age of the Smart Machine*. New York: Basic Books.

Index